Sixth Edition

Criminal Law AND THE Canadian Criminal Code

Sixth Edition

Criminal Law AND THE Canadian Criminal Code

RICHARD BARNHORST
B.A., LL.B., J.S.D.

SHERRIE BARNHORST
B.A., LL.B., LL.M.

McGraw-Hill
Ryerson
Connect. Learn. Succeed.

Criminal Law and the Canadian Criminal Code
Sixth Edition

The Internet addresses listed in the text were accurate at the time of publication. The inclusion of a Web site does not indicate an endorsement by the authors or McGraw-Hill Ryerson, and McGraw-Hill Ryerson does not guarantee the accuracy of the information presented at these sites.

ISBN-13: 978-0-07-032970-6
ISBN-10: 0-07-032970-2

10 WEB 1 9 8 7

Printed and bound in Canada

Care has been taken to trace ownership of copyright material contained in this text; however, the publisher will welcome any information that enables it to rectify any reference or credit for subsequent editions.

Editorial Director: Rhondda McNabb
Sponsoring Editor: Karen Krahn and Marcia Siekowski
Developmental Editor: My Editor Inc.
Marketing Manager: Stacey Metz and Tracy Yan
Senior Editorial Associate: Marina Seguin
Copy Editor: Elspeth McFadden

Production Coordinator: Michelle Saddler
Cover/Interior Design: Sarah Orr, ArtPlus Ltd.
Compositor: ArtPlus Ltd.
Front cover photo: © Michelloiselle/Dreamstime
Supervising Editor: Graeme Powell
Printer: Webcom

Library and Archives Canada Cataloguing in Publication

Barnhorst, Richard, 1947–   Criminal law and the Canadian criminal code / Richard Barnhorst, Sherrie Barnhorst.—6th ed.

Includes bibliographical references and index.
ISBN 978-0-07-032970-6

  1. Criminal law—Canada—Textbooks. 2. Canada. Criminal Code. I. Barnhorst, Sherrie, 1948– II. Title.

KE8809.B38 2013   345.71   C2012-907792-5 KF9220.ZA2B38 2013

BRIEF CONTENTS

CONTENTS

Chapter Three: General Principles for Determining Criminal Liability   34

PART TWO | CRIMINAL CODE OFFENCES   139

Chapter Six: Jurisdiction, Public Order, Terrorism, Firearms, and Other Offences   139

Chapter Seven: Sexual Offences, Pornography, Soliciting, and Bawdy-houses   164

Chapter Eleven: Assaults and Related Offences against the Person   251

Appendices   133

Preface to the Sixth Edition

The sixth edition of *Criminal Law and the Canadian Criminal Code*, like earlier editions, has been written for people who want to understand the principles of criminal law and significant offences in the Criminal Code. This book will be useful to students in college and university programs related to criminal justice, and to police officers, security personnel, probation officers, parole officers, criminologists, law clerks, and others involved in the criminal justice system.

This new edition incorporates changes that have been made to the criminal law since the publication of the fifth edition. All cases and sections of the Criminal Code that are in the fifth edition have been checked and updated. New Code sections include the 2012 amendments to self-defence, defence of others, and defence of property as well as the new provisions on when a "citizen's arrest" can be made.

New cases have been included throughout the book. Some cases overrule previous case law; others rule on areas of law that have not previously been addressed by the courts. Many new cases have been added to provide more current examples of the application of the law. New cases have also been used as the basis for questions for discussion at the end of several chapters. Most court decisions discussed in the book are decisions of the Supreme Court of Canada or provincial courts of appeal. This edition includes more than 25 new and important Supreme Court of Canada decisions. Among the many new provincial court of appeal decisions is *R. v. Bedford*, which struck down key parts of Canada's prostitution law and, at the time of writing, has been appealed to the Supreme Court of Canada.

As in earlier editions, Part One addresses basic concepts and principles of criminal law. The primary approach is to explain the criminal law concepts and principles through an examination of case law in order to demonstrate how they have been applied by courts to actual fact situations. Chapters 1 and 2 provide an introduction to law in general and criminal law in particular. Chapter 3 discusses principles for determining criminal liability, including the physical and mental elements of a crime, attempts to commit an offence, and parties to an offence. Chapter 4 covers defences that may be used by someone who is accused of committing an offence.

Chapter 5 provides an overview of pre-trial criminal procedure, including arrest, release by a police officer, bail hearings, the exclusion of evidence under the Charter of Rights and Freedoms, powers to search, and wiretapping and electronic surveillance.

These areas of criminal procedure are essential to an understanding of criminal law in Canada. They are particularly important for students who need an understanding of the legal limits of police authority and the rights of an individual who has contact with the police. Since the last edition, there have been numerous Supreme Court of Canada decisions on the Charter and criminal procedure; these changes have been included in an expansion of this chapter.

Part Two discusses significant offences contained in the Criminal Code. It is not practical to cover every Criminal Code offence; however, Part Two provides a fair representation of the various types of offences and all of the major offences. Relevant parts of Code sections that set out the offences are reproduced and the required elements of the offences are discussed. As in Part One, a case law approach is used. The discussion of specific cases explains how the offence sections of the Code have been applied to actual fact situations. The discussion also draws on the criminal law concepts and principles discussed in Part One. As a result of suggestions from reviewers as well as developments in the law since the last edition, discussion of several offences has been expanded or added, including the following: terrorism (Chapter 6), child pornography and online luring of a child (Chapter 7), motor vehicle offences (Chapter 10), sexual assault (Chapter 11), and identity theft and computer offences (Chapter 12). Due to the large amount of new material, this edition of the book moves the more significant offences in the former Chapter 14 into Chapter 12 and the less significant offences have been placed in the Instructor's Manual. Less significant offences in other chapters have also been moved to the Instructor's Manual.

For courses that primarily focus on the basic concepts and principles of criminal law, Part Two can be used to provide additional examples of offences and more in-depth discussion of cases that help to illustrate the practical application of the concepts and principles discussed in Part One. This approach of more integration of offences and case law into the discussion of concepts and principles is particularly relevant to the consideration of the Elements of a Crime (Chapter 3) and Defences (Chapter 4). In this edition of the book, Chapters 3 and 4 refer the reader to several specific sections in Part Two that can be used to go into more depth on various aspects of *actus reus, mens rea*, and defences, thereby making it easier to integrate relevant offences and cases from Part Two.

An example of the cross-referencing to Part Two is the discussion of "specific intent" as a type of *mens rea*. After briefly discussing the offences of robbery and break and enter with intent as specific intent offences, Chapter 3, at page 42, states:

These specific intent offences along with relevant case law are discussed in Part Two of the book: robbery (Chapter 12) and break and enter with intent (Chapter 13). Other examples of specific intent offences that are discussed in Part Two include possessing a weapon for a purpose dangerous to the public, under Possession Offences (Chapter 6); murder (Chapter 8); and theft (Chapter 12).

Similarly, Chapter 4, Defences, refers to chapters in Part Two that provide further discussion of certain defences. For example, regarding the defence of consent, Chapter 4, at page 76, states:

Consent and sexual assault and non-sexual assault are discussed in detail in Chapter 11. Consent and the offences of possession, such as possession of stolen property, are discussed in Chapter 13. Consent and sexual offences, such as sexual interference or sexual exploitation, are discussed in Chapter 7.

The Instructor's Manual includes answers to all of the end-of-chapter questions, additional discussion questions, a list of websites related to criminal law and, as mentioned above, supplementary material on less significant offences, from the previous edition of the book.

Additional features of the book are three Appendices, the Glossary, and the Table of Cases. Appendix A discusses drug offences under the Controlled Drugs and Substances Act. Appendix B explains the major features of the Youth Criminal Justice Act, including amendments that came into force in 2012. Appendix C sets out the legal rights under the Canadian Charter of Rights and Freedoms that are particularly relevant to criminal law. The Glossary defines key terms that have been used in the text. The Table of Cases provides an alphabetical listing of cases in the book for easy reference.

Richard Barnhorst, B.A., LL.B., J.S.D.
Sherrie Barnhorst, B.A., LL.B., LL.M.

McGraw-Hill Ryerson wishes to thank the following reviewers for their comments and guidance throughout the development process:

Julian Hermida	Algoma University
Ken Yates	Centennial College
W. Barnwell	Dalhousie University
Mike Durbeniuk	Medicine Hat College
Ralph Ashford	Fleming College
Brian Young	Camosun College
David Osborne	Langara College
Cecelia Reilly	Loyalist College
David MacAllister	Simon Fraser University
Paul MacIsaac	Georgian College
Margaret Hall	Kwantlen Polytechnic University
Richard Jochelson	University of Winnipeg

Abbreviations Used for Case Reports

The following is a list of the case reports used in this text. Some, like Canadian Criminal Cases (C.C.C.), are commercial reports. At times, the text also uses the judgment released by the court instead of a commercial version. For example, [2009] 1 S.C.R. 23 refers to a judgment released by the Supreme Court of Canada. Some recent cases have a different form of citation. Courts across Canada have started to use a uniform and simplified way to cite court decisions. For example, 2012 ONCA 12 gives the year the case was decided (2012), the court, (Ontario Court of Appeal) and a sequential number (12).

All E.R.	All England Reports (English)
Alta. L.R.	Alberta Law Reports
A.J.	Alberta Journal
A.R.	Alberta Reports
B.C.W.L.D.	B.C. Weekly Law Digest
C.C.C.	Canadian Criminal Cases
Cox's C.C.	Cox's Criminal Cases (English)
C.R.	Criminal Reports
Cr. App. R.	Criminal Appeal Reports (English)
C.R.N.S.	Criminal Reports New Series
D.L.R.	Dominion Law Reports
E.R.	England Reports
I.R.	Irish Reports
M.P.R.	Maritime Provincial Reports
M.V.R.	Motor Vehicle Reports
N.S.R.	Nova Scotia Reports
ONCA	Ontario Court of Appeal
ONCJ	Ontario Court of Justice
O.R.	Ontario Reports
Q.B.	Queen's Bench (English)
R.L.	La Revue Légale
Sask. R.	Saskatchewan Reports
S.C.J.	Supreme Court Judgments
S.C.R.	Supreme Court Reports
W.C.B.	Weekly Criminal Bulletin
W.W.R.	Western Weekly Reports

Table of Cases

CHAPTER 1

An Introduction to Law

Key points explained in this chapter are

LO1 the functions of law;

LO2 the differences between public and private law, procedural and substantive law;

LO3 the historical and modern sources of Canadian law, including the Canadian Charter of Rights and Freedoms; and

LO4 how to find case and statute law.

A. THE NATURE OF LAW

Before looking at criminal law, we first consider the nature of the law in more general terms. Let us start with a definition: Law is the body of rules that regulates the conduct of members of society and is recognized and enforced by the government. There are, of course, many rules regulating our conduct that are not part of the law. For example, the rules of a private club regarding the duties of club members are not part of the law. Likewise, the moral values that govern a person's conduct are not part of the law, although moral convictions and legal rules often overlap. These types of rules are not rules of law for two basic reasons: First, they are not officially recognized by the government as laws applying to all members of society; and second, their violation does not involve a penalty or other legal consequence imposed by the government.

LO1 ### 1. Functions of Law

The above definition, although suitable for our purposes, does not indicate the wide range of functions served by the law. The law not only tells us what are our rights, privileges, and obligations, but also determines the structure of our government and assigns duties and powers to its various branches. The law even tells us how and by whom laws are to be made. An example of a law-making law is the Constitution Act, 1982 (formerly the B.N.A. Act, 1867). This statute creates our federal system of government. It divides the authority to make law on various subjects between the federal parliament and provincial legislatures; for example, certain areas of law, such as property and education, are given exclusively to the provinces. Therefore, a federal law on the topic of provincial schooling would be **ultra vires**, or beyond the scope of the federal government's authority. A statute that is *ultra vires* is not enforceable. In the same way, if a province enacts a law that touches an area given to the federal government by the Act, that law is also *ultra vires* and unenforceable.[1]

`LO2` ## 2. Classes of Law

There are two main classes of law: public and private. Public law consists of the rules that govern the relations among various branches of the government, and between the government and private citizens. The main types of public law are constitutional law, criminal law, and administrative law. Private law—or **civil law**—consists of the rules governing the relations between private persons or groups. Types of private law include contract law, which consists of the rules for making legally enforceable agreements; property law, which includes the rules for how to own or pass on property; and **tort law**, which is the law regarding **civil wrongs**.

3. Substantive and Procedural Law

Each class or type of law consists of substantive rules and procedural rules. Substantive rules of law describe our rights and duties; for example, the substantive part of the criminal law prohibits certain forms of conduct from which society has a right to be protected. Procedural law tells us how the substantive law can be enforced—that is, how our rights can be protected and our wrongs redressed. Thus, the rules that must be followed when an arrest is made are part of the law of **criminal procedure**. Whether an accused has a jury trial or not is also a matter of procedure.

`LO3` # B. SOURCES OF CANADIAN LAW

1. Common Law and Civil Law

Systems of law go back many centuries from the time people started living in large communities. One of the earliest sets of laws was the Code of Hammurabi, who was the king of the ancient city of Babylon (present day Iraq). His Code, compiled around 1792 BCE, consisted of 282 laws engraved on a stone stele which was displayed in public. The laws covered such matters as family law, criminal law, and rules for conducting business. Two of the laws which are still remembered are "an eye for an eye" (rule #196) and "a tooth for a tooth" (rule #200).[2] Another ancient system of law was first written around 620 BCE by Draco, a famous law maker from Athens. These laws were so harsh that the term "draconian" is still used today to refer to unusually severe laws. Greek law also included the first form of elected government and laws which were enacted by an assembly of citizens, as well as a court system and jury trials.[3]

Today, there are two major systems of law in the Western world—common law and civil law. Most English-speaking countries have a common law system. Notice that the term "civil law" has two meanings. It may refer to civil or private law, which was discussed earlier; or it may refer to the system of law that is used by many continental European countries. Except for Quebec provincial law, which operates under the civil law system, Canadian law is part of the common law tradition.

The civil law system is the older of the two. Its beginnings are traced back to the law of the Romans, which was influenced by Greek law. In the sixth century, the emperor, Justinian,

---

1 Conversely, if a law is within the authority of the government that made it, it is **intra vires**.
2 The stele on which the Code is written is in the Louvre Museum in Paris. For more information about Hammurabi's Code, see **louvre.fr/en/oeuvre-notices/law-code-hammurabi-king-babylon**.
3 For more information on ancient Greek law, see Adrian Lanni, *Law and Justice in the Courts of Classical* Athens (Cambridge University Press, 2006); Gagarin and Cohen, eds., *The Cambridge Companion to Ancient Greek Law* (Cambridge University Press, 2005).

compiled a code, or book of law, that contained all of the great Roman laws. This code became the law in those parts of Europe under Roman control. After the Roman Empire collapsed, many of Europe's peoples continued to use Justinian's Code, or laws derived from it. In the early nineteenth century, Napoleon established a similar code, which was later adopted by many European countries. The Napoleonic Code also greatly influenced the authors of the Quebec Civil Code.

Between about 55 BCE and 412 CE, the Romans occupied England; naturally, Roman law was used. In the fifth century, various Anglo-Saxon tribes invaded Britain, and the Romans were forced to withdraw. These invasions largely erased the influence of Roman law in England. For many centuries after the Romans left, diverse tribes and groups who had little contact with one another occupied England. Each community had its own law based on its own traditions and customs. There was no body of law that could be called English law.

It was not until William, the Duke of Normandy, conquered England in 1066 that a unified England started to evolve. One of William's first tasks was to establish a central government for the purpose of controlling his new land. Part of the strong central government developed by William and his successors consisted of a royal court system. Under this system, the king's judges travelled through the country holding court in large villages and trading centres. Each judge's route was called a circuit, and court sittings were known as assizes.

These early judges were in the difficult position of not having a set of rules or a code of law to guide them in their decisions. Sometimes, Norman law was used; at other times, local law. Often, neither was appropriate so the judges had to rely on their common sense and base their decisions on what seemed to them principles of justice and fairness. Eventually, the judges began discussing among themselves the cases they had heard and the decisions they had made. Gradually, it became a practice of the judges to follow decisions made in earlier cases if the same or similar facts were involved. In other words, rather than relying solely on their own judgment, judges thought back to previously decided cases. If they found one that matched (or was very similar to) the case presently being heard, they made the same decision as was made in the earlier case. Of course, the facts in one case were often not the same or even very similar to the facts in other cases, so the judges could not always find a case to follow. However, each time a decision was made in a particular situation, it created a **precedent**, or example, to be followed in future cases. The principle that was emerging was that like cases should be treated alike. Even today, we accept this principle as a basic rule of justice.

Once accurate written reports of cases became available to judges in the sixteenth and seventeenth centuries, it became much easier for judges to follow precedent. By the nineteenth century, this practice had become a strict and binding rule called **stare decisis**, which means literally "to stand by." Today, judges in Canada still follow precedent. What this means, generally speaking, is that lower courts must follow the decisions of higher courts, and that courts of equal rank should try to follow one another's decisions, if at all possible. In Canada, the highest court which sets precedent for all of the other Canadian courts is the Supreme Court of Canada.

By the process of making decisions in case after case, guided by the rule of precedent, the early English judges created a body of law that applied to all the people in England. This law was then common to all—hence, the **common law**. Since the common law consists of the decisions of judges in particular cases, it is sometimes called **case law**.

Today, however, Canadian law also includes many statutes; although Canada is called a "common law country," it has both case law and statute law as well as administrative law (discussed below).

2. Statute Law

Another way to make law is to pass a statute or an act that contains all the rules on a particular subject. As mentioned earlier, the Constitution Act, 1982, divides the authority to make **statute law**—also called legislative law—between the federal parliament and the provincial legislatures. In the past, the territories have been governed by federal statutes. In the last few decades, the federal government has established legislative assemblies and executive councils in the territories so that they have province-like powers.[4] Municipalities, which receive their law-making authority from the provinces, make a type of legislative law. Municipal laws are called bylaws.

In Canada, statute law always (with one exception) has priority over case law. This means that if there is a conflict between a court decision and a statute, the statute will overrule the court decision; in fact, judges are obligated to apply statute law where it exists, regardless of what the case law is on the same topic. This principle is called the **supremacy of parliament** rule. The exception to this rule, discussed later in this chapter, relates to cases where the Charter of Rights and Freedoms applies.

Statutes do not always conflict with case law. Sometimes statutes only codify the case law; that is, all the principles of law that are contained in a number of cases are put into one statute. Statutes may clarify an area that is left unclear by case law. There are also statutes that are concerned with modern topics that have never been dealt with by case law. However, there are still large areas of law in the form of case law that have never been the subject of a statute and are still being developed by the courts. For example, much of the law of evidence, which consists of the rules for presenting evidence in court, is still in case law form.

It is important to note that the judges' law-making function does not end once an area is put into statute law. Statutes often need interpreting, and this task becomes the responsibility of the courts. The interpretations given to statutes in turn become part of the law. Why do statutes need interpreting? First, because they usually contain only general rules, there may be questions as to how the general rules apply to specific situations. Second, legislators, like other people, do not always communicate clearly. Even when a statute seems quite straightforward, it may still be possible to read into it more than one meaning. In either situation, the judge becomes the final interpreter and must decide what the legislators intended when they enacted the statute.

Judges have several approaches available when interpreting a phrase (or word) in a statute. They look at the dictionary meaning of the words and at the context within which the words are used in the statute. They look for any interpretive aids in the statute itself, such as a preamble or headings. They may consider the French version of the statute, since the phrase in French may have a clearer meaning. They examine previous decisions to see how other courts have interpreted the phrase. They also try to determine the policy behind the law, to establish what the law is trying to achieve and what its practical applications are. An example of a case where a phrase had to be interpreted by the Supreme Court of Canada is *R. v. Lohnes*.[5] The accused was charged with causing a disturbance under section 175 of the Code:

175. (1) Every one who

    (a) not being in a dwelling-house, causes a disturbance in or near a public place,

        (i) by fighting, screaming, shouting, swearing, singing or using insulting or obscene language, . . . is guilty of an offence . . .

---

4   See the difference between Canadian provinces and territories at **pco-bcp.gc.ca** > Intergovernmental Affairs > Provinces and Territories.
5   *Lohnes v. The Queen* (1992), 69 C.C.C. (3d) 289 (S.C.C.).

The accused's neighbour complained that the accused had shouted obscenities at him, and a charge was laid. The Supreme Court of Canada had to decide whether "causing a disturbance" meant causing emotional upset and annoyance, or whether it meant that the conduct interfered with the public's normal activities. The Court looked at the dictionary meaning of disturbance, which suggests that it is an interference with ordinary use or conduct. Within the context of the statute, the Court found that, by referring to a public place, Parliament seemed to be saying that its objective was to protect the public, not from emotional upset, but from disorder calculated to interfere with normal activities. The Court also noted that s. 175 appears under the heading Disorderly Conduct, which again indicates that Parliament had in mind not emotional upset, but disorder that interferes with the ordinary use of a place. The Court looked at the French version of s. 175, where the word used for disturbance is *tapage*, which connotes a disturbance involving violent noise or confusion disrupting the tranquillity of those in the area. In examining earlier cases, the Court found that the overwhelming majority of decisions stated that the conduct must cause an interference with the public's use of the place. In terms of policy, the Court stated that it would be unjust to expect persons to determine whether their conduct will be disturbing to the emotions of others. Fundamental justice requires that people know in advance whether their conduct is illegal. Also, the Court noted, there is a need to balance the right of persons to have peace with the right of others to express themselves, and this favours a definition of "disturbance" that requires more than emotional upset. The Court's conclusion was that, taking together all of these factors, a disturbance, under s. 175, is conduct that causes more than emotional upset. The accused was acquitted because there was no evidence that there was a disturbance in the use of the premises by the complainant.

3. Administrative Law

As mentioned above, administrative law is a very broad type of public law that concerns government relations with individuals, groups, and legal entities, such as corporations, as well as the relations among various branches of government. Two significant types of administrative law are (a) regulations and (b) decisions by administrative boards and tribunals.

a. Regulations

Statutes, as mentioned above, usually contain general rules. To deal with specific situations, a statute will often have a section giving a person or body such as the Governor in Council (i.e., the Cabinet), Minister, or agency the authority to pass regulations under the act. For example, the Controlled Drug and Substances Act[6] creates drug offences and penalties. Section 55 of the Act gives the Governor in Council the authority to make regulations "for carrying out the purposes and provisions" of the Act. Examples are regulations that set the rules for importing controlled substances (e.g., prescription drugs) into Canada, fees payable for licensing, and the qualifications of persons engaged in the production or selling of a controlled substance. Unlike statutes, regulations are not voted on by the legislature but are made by the government of the day.[7]

b. Decisions by Administrative Boards and Tribunals

Administrative boards and tribunals are created by federal and provincial statutes. For example, the B.C. legislature has enacted the Human Rights Code,[8] which prohibits various forms of

---

6   S.C. 1996, c.19.
7   See **pco-bcp.gc.ca** > Search > Guide to Making Federal Acts and Regulations Part 3—Making Regulations., for more detailed information on how regulations are enacted. See also **adminlawbc.ca** for a video and more detail about administrative law.
8   *R.S.B.C.* 1996, c.210.

discrimination in areas such as employment, rental accommodation, and wages. The statute also sets out the structure of the Human Rights Tribunal and the procedure for filing a complaint with the tribunal. The decisions of administrative bodies, such as the Human Rights Tribunal, form part of administrative case law. Other examples of administrative case law are the decisions of Ontario's Workers' Compensation Board in determining the eligibility of an injured worker for compensation. An example of a federal administrative body is the Canada Employment Insurance Commission, which has a wide mandate that includes setting rates for premiums as well as supporting an appeal system.

C. THE CANADIAN CHARTER OF RIGHTS AND FREEDOMS

1. An Overview

In 1982, when the Constitution was repatriated, an important addition was made to it: the **Canadian Charter of Rights and Freedoms**. The Charter not only consolidated existing personal rights, but also created new rights and freedoms. Although this part of the Constitution applies generally to all areas of public law, it has special relevance to criminal law.

The Bill of Rights, which also sets out rights and freedoms, has been the law since 1960. However, because it is not a part of the Constitution, courts have hesitated to use it to overturn legally enacted legislation. The Constitution Act, 1982, makes it clear that courts are, in certain situations, no longer bound by the principle of supremacy of parliament. Section 52 clearly states that the Charter applies to Parliament, including matters relating to the Yukon and Northwest Territories and to the legislatures and governments of the provinces:

> **52. (1) The Constitution of Canada is the supreme law of Canada, and any law that is inconsistent with the provisions of the Constitution is, to the extent of the inconsistency with the provisions of the constitution, of no force or effect.**

The Charter sets out certain individual rights and freedoms that cannot be infringed upon by the government. Since the government acts through statute law, Section 52 limits the legislative authority of the government. If a court finds that a law violates a right or freedom protected by the Charter, the court may rule that the law is unenforceable. This does not necessarily mean that the entire statute will be ruled unenforceable, but only the part that is inconsistent with the Charter.

There are two important limitations to our rights and freedoms. The first is set out in s. 1 of the Charter:

> **1. The Canadian Charter of Rights and Freedoms guarantees the rights and freedoms set out in it subject only to such reasonable limits prescribed by law as can be demonstrably justified in a free and democratic society.**

In other words, a court may find that, although a statute violates the Charter, it is a **reasonable limitation** of our rights. For example, most provinces today have laws that allow the police to stop cars randomly to check for drunk drivers. These laws have been challenged as a violation of our right to be free from **arbitrary detention**. The Supreme Court of Canada has held that these laws do violate our right to be free from arbitrary detention, but that the laws are justified because they are attempting to control the social evil of drunk driving.[9]

---

9   *R. v. Hufsky* (1988), 40 C.C.C. (3d) 398 (S.C.C.).

Another example relates to the law that prohibits the making and distribution of "obscene material." In *R. v. Butler*,[10] the Supreme Court of Canada held that this is a reasonable limitation on the right of freedom of expression. For such a limitation to be justifiable, (a) the objective of the law (e.g., controlling drunk driving or restricting the distribution of pornography) must be shown to be of sufficient importance to justify overriding a right or freedom, and (b) the law itself must be reasonable and demonstrably justifiable in a free and democratic society.[11]

The second limitation is in s. 33, which allows a legislative body to pass a law that violates certain rights and freedoms if certain procedures are followed:

> **33. (1) Parliament or the legislature of a province may expressly declare in an Act of Parliament or of the legislature, as the case may be, that the Act or a provision thereof shall operate notwithstanding a provision included in section 2 or sections 7 to 15 of this Charter.**

This section is referred to as the **notwithstanding** or **override clause**. To override the Charter, the statute itself must state that the Charter does not apply. The statute will be valid for only five years. After that time, it must be re-enacted. Also, the override clause can only be used for certain rights. Some rights and freedoms are absolutely protected—for example, the right to vote.

TABLE 1-1 | Examples of Rights and Freedoms in the Charter

TYPE OF RIGHT/FREEDOM	EXAMPLES
Fundamental freedoms	Freedom of conscience, religion, thought, belief, opinion, and expression; freedom of peaceful assembly and association.
Democratic rights	The right of Canadian citizens to vote or to run for office.
Mobility rights	The right of Canadian citizens to enter, remain in, and leave Canada, and the right of Canadian citizens and permanent residents to live and work in any province of Canada.
Equality rights	The right to be treated equally before and under the law; the right to the equal protection of the law and benefit of the law without discrimination—in particular, without discrimination based on race, national or ethnic origin, colour, religion, sex, age, or mental or physical disability.
Language rights	The Charter protects the two official languages of Canada: French and English.

2. Legal Rights and the Criminal Law

The Charter has special importance to criminal law. To enforce the law, protect the public, and prosecute offenders, police and others in the criminal justice system are given certain powers

---

10   *R. v. Butler* (1992), 70 C.C.C. (3d) 129 (S.C.C.).
11   The test for determining whether a law is a reasonable limitation is discussed in more detail in Chapter 2.

to interfere with individual liberty. For example, the powers to search and make arrests are significant infringements of personal freedom. The Charter sets out procedural rights and limitations on the authority given to law enforcement personnel. The most important rights for criminal law are the legal rights set out in sections 7 to 14.

Section 7 is a general statement that a person cannot be denied life, liberty, or personal security unless the principles of fundamental justice are followed:

> **7. Everyone has the right to life, liberty and security of the person and the right not to be deprived thereof except in accordance with the principles of fundamental justice.**

Section 7 applies to procedural as well as substantive laws. The Supreme Court of Canada has said that the principles of **fundamental justice** are to be found in the basic tenets of our legal system and that it is up to the courts to develop the limits of these tenets.[12] In other words, the courts will decide on a case-by-case basis whether a tenet of fundamental justice is being violated. For example, in *R. v. Hebert*,[13] the Supreme Court held that the right of the accused, once detained, to remain silent during the investigative stage of an offence is a principle of fundamental justice. This right was violated when the police placed an undercover agent in a cell with the accused, who then made incriminating statements to the agent. In another example, the Supreme Court held that a provincial law that imposed a minimum sentence of seven days' imprisonment for driving with a suspended licence, even though the driver was unaware that his licence was suspended, violated a principle of fundamental justice. It was a violation because the law required the imprisonment of a person who unknowingly and without intent committed an offence for which no defence was available.[14] Another principle of fundamental justice is that people have a right to know in advance what conduct is prohibited. This means that a law that does not give fair notice to people of the conduct being prohibited will be **void for vagueness**.[15]

The Supreme Court has set out a framework for determining whether a rule is a principle of fundamental justice:

1. It must be a legal principle.
2. There must be a consensus that the rule or principle is fundamental to the way in which the legal system ought fairly to operate.
3. It must be identified with sufficient precision to yield a manageable standard against which to measure deprivations of life, liberty, or security of the person.[16]

The Court applied these standards in the case of *R. v. D.B.*,[17] where the issue was whether the presumption that young people are entitled to a diminished moral culpability or blameworthiness because of their age, lack of maturity, heightened vulnerability, and reduced capacity for moral judgment is a principle of fundamental justice. The Court held that it is a principle of fundamental justice for these reasons:

1. Canada has a long history of treating youth differently from adults because of their diminished responsibility. For example, Canada has had a distinct youth criminal justice system since 1908, which has had a stated purpose of treating juvenile delinquents as "misguided and misdirected children."

---

12 Reference Section 94(2) of the Motor Vehicle Act (1985), 23 C.C.C. (3d) 289 (S.C.C.).
13 (1990), 57 C.C.C. (3d) 1 (S.C.C.).
14 Reference s. 94(2) of the Motor Vehicle Act, *supra* note 12.
15 Ref. sections 193 and 195.1(2) of the Criminal Code (1990), 56 C.C.C. (3d) 65 (S.C.C.).
16 See *R. v. Malmo-Levine* (2000), 145 C.C.C (3d) 225 (B.C.C.A.); *R. v. Caine* (2003) 179 C.C.C. (3d) 417 (S.C.C.).
17 [2008] S.C.R. No. 25 (S.C.C.).

2. There is a consensus that this principle is fundamental to the operation of a fair system, since it is widely acknowledged that age plays a role in development of moral judgment and sophistication.

3. The principle of diminished responsibility is not difficult to apply, and in fact has been applied for decades in Canada.

Sections 8 to 14 of the Charter relate to specific situations involving the deprivation of life, liberty, or security of the person. Sections 8 to 10 concern pre-trial procedure and are discussed in Chapter 5. Sections 11, 12, 13, and 14 are related to trial procedure and are discussed in Chapter 2.

Where a court finds that the Charter rights of an accused person have been infringed or denied, s. 24 of the Charter allows the court to order a remedy that the court considers appropriate and just in the circumstances. For example, the court may order that proceedings against a person be stayed or that evidence that has been illegally obtained be excluded. Chapter 5 examines cases where s. 24 has been applied.

04 D. FINDING THE LAW

1. Statute Law

The official government press publishes statutes. Usually, all the statutes (or Acts) passed in one legislative session are contained in one volume. From time to time, all the statutes are revised and consolidated into one set of volumes. Parliament then repeals the former statutes and enacts as law the newly revised ones. Revisions are necessary mainly to correct any errors in the original statutes and to incorporate any subsequent amendments. The last revision of the federal statutes was made in 1985. Thus, a law first passed in 1983 is found in the 1985 revised statutes. Each Act is given a separate chapter number and is listed alphabetically. A statute passed in 1986 is found in the sessional volume for that year. Statutes in the sessional volumes are usually listed in order of enactment. At the back of each sessional volume is a Table of Public Statutes, which lists the Acts by title or subject matter. These tables are very useful for locating statutes and checking for amendments.

The titles of the volumes are often referred to in abbreviated form. Revised statutes are abbreviated "R.S." followed by the initial(s) of the province, or by a "C" for Canada. If a sessional volume is referred to, the "R" is dropped. Next, the year of enactment is given. Thus, "R.S.C. 1985" means "Revised Statutes of Canada enacted in 1985." If a particular statute is mentioned, its chapter number is given after the year. Statutes are divided into sections. If a section is referred to, an "s." followed by the section number is written after the chapter number. For example, Criminal Code R.S.C. 1985, c. C-34, s. 1.

2. Case Law

There are many different series of case reports, including national, regional, and provincial series. Some case reports are official publications; others are printed by private publishing companies. Only the more important cases are contained in these reports. Most likely to be reported are cases that involve appeals, or set precedents, or concern unclear areas of law. Not everything that has occurred in a case is reported. Usually, only the judge's written decision—which often includes a recital of the facts and the reasons for the decision—is reported. If more than one judge has heard the case (an appeal court often has more than one judge sitting), and there is a ***dissenting opinion***, this opinion is included in the report. A dissenting opinion results when the judges who have heard the case fail to reach a unanimous decision. In such a situation, the decision agreed to by a majority of the judges becomes the official decision of the court. The decision of the minority becomes the dissenting opinion. The court's decision is often referred to as the ***"holding"*** in the case. Similarly, a reference may be made to what the judge (or court) "held" in a case.

The case series most frequently referred to in the following pages are Canadian Criminal Cases, abbreviated "C.C.C.," and Criminal Reports, abbreviated "C.R." At the beginning of this book is a table, "Abbreviations Used for Case Report Publications," which provides the names and the accepted abbreviations of all series mentioned.

To locate a case, you must be able to read case citations. Figure 1-1 below shows one form used for citing cases and the meaning of each element of the citation. Although the form of the citation will vary depending on the case series, all citations will give the basic information needed to locate the case.

Notice that the first name given in the case is Rex (King) or Regina (Queen), which indicates that the state or Crown is proceeding against (prosecuting) the accused. If the court's decision is appealed to a higher court, the name of the appellant (the party appealing) is given first, followed by the name of the respondent (the party responding).

| FIGURE 1-1 | Reading a Case Citation |

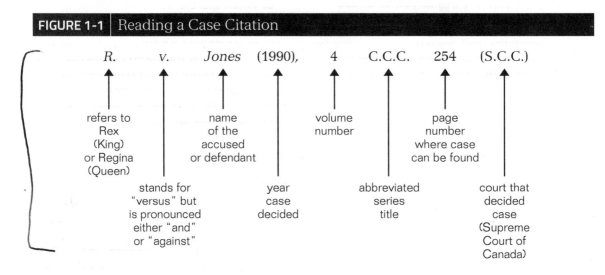

3. Finding the Law Online

Statutes can be found in libraries, of course, but probably the most useful sources of statutes today are found online. The Federal Department of Justice publishes consolidated and sessional federal statutes and amendments at **justice.gc.ca**. This site also contains government statements and information about new or proposed legislation. The status of a Bill—proposed legislation that has not yet become law—can be checked at the Parliament of Canada's website: **parl.gc.ca**.

Another useful source of statute law is the commercially published annotated versions, which include cases that apply and interpret the statute. Commercial versions of the annotated Criminal Code are available as a paper volume or electronically, and are updated throughout the year through supplements that are available electronically.

There are also commercial online services, such as Quicklaw, that give current case law and statute law. Some educational institutions will have subscriptions to these online services available to students.

The Canadian Legal Information Institute is a non-profit organization managed by the Federation of Law Societies of Canada. It is mandated to provide free access to legal information. Access to recent cases and legislation can be obtained at the Institute's website: **canlii.org**.

Decisions of the Supreme Court of Canada are published online at **scc-csc.gc.ca**.

Questions for Review and Discussion

1. Define the term "law."

2. a. Why are the rules of a private club not considered law?
   b. Describe other types of rules that govern our conduct, but are not laws.

3. What are some functions served by the law? Think of specific functions not mentioned in the chapter.

4. a. What are the two main classes of law?
   b. Define each class.

5. a. What is the difference between substantive rule and procedural rules? Make up some examples from a student's life; e.g., are the course requirements for graduating from a program substantive or procedural?
   b. Indicate whether the following are procedural or substantive laws:
   (i) The legal definition of murder
   (ii) The law that states how a search warrant is obtained
   (iii) The law that requires the appeal of a court decision to be made within a certain time limit

6. a. Explain the origins of the common law system.
   b. Why is this system called the common law system?

7. a. Explain the operation of the rule of *stare decisis*.
   b. What is a precedent? Make up an example of a precedent that might affect your life.

8. Explain the two ways judges make laws:
   a. When a statute is involved
   b. When there is no statute involved

9. a. What does the principle of supremacy of parliament mean?
   b. Explain how the Charter of Rights and Freedoms affects the principle of supremacy of parliament.

10. What are the two limitations on our Charter rights and freedoms?

11. Why does the Charter have special relevance to criminal law?

12. Discuss whether the Charter should include an override clause.

13. Discuss whether our rights and freedoms should be subject to reasonable limitations.

14. Write a paragraph explaining what s. 7 of the Charter of Rights and Freedoms means. Include an example of a person being denied fundamental justice.

15. How should the following statutes be abbreviated?
   a. Criminal Law Amendment Act, 1990, Chapter 13, Statutes of Canada.
   b. Canada Evidence Act, Revised Statutes of Canada, 1985, Chapter C-5.

16. What should the citations be for the following cases?

  a. The Crown Attorney prosecuted John Smith. The decision of the court was reported in Canadian Criminal Cases, the fifth volume, on page 305. The trial was held in 1984, in the province of New Brunswick before a provincial court judge.

  b. After being found guilty, Smith appealed the decision of the court to the province's court of appeal. The decision of the appeal court was reported in Volume 12 on page 305 of Canadian Criminal Cases. The appeal was heard in 1986.

  c. In 1988, the Crown prosecuted Sharon Brown in the Court of Queen's Bench in Manitoba. The decision of the court was reported in Volume 7 of Criminal Reports on page 46.

17. a. What is a "holding" in a case?
   b. What is a "dissenting opinion"?

18. Find Hammurabi's Code on the internet. Select a few of the rules to study. Compare and contrast the laws from the Code to laws and values we have today.

19. Research an aspect of ancient Greek law. For example, how were jury trials carried out? How were laws made when Athens had a democracy? Who were considered citizens in ancient Greece?

CHAPTER 2

An Introduction to Criminal Law

Key points explained in this chapter are

LO1   the function of criminal law in our society, particularly the distinction between criminal and civil law;

LO2   the federal authority to make criminal law and how related areas are shared between the provincial and federal governments;

LO3   the structure of the Criminal Code;

LO4   the trial process of criminal offences;

LO5   the Charter rights of an accused at trial; and

LO6   the structure of the court system that deals with criminal offences.

01 A. THE NATURE OF CRIMINAL LAW

1. A Wrong against Society

Under our legal system, crimes are considered wrongs committed against society as a whole. We depend on the government to prevent crime and to provide a safe environment. The primary aims of criminal law are to protect the public and to preserve the peace. Ensuring that the community is safe and secure is a duty carried out by the government through the police, the courts, and the correctional system.

2. The Distinction between Criminal and Civil Wrongs

As mentioned in Chapter 1, civil law governs the interactions among private persons. For example, contract law sets out the rules that must be followed before an agreement between private parties will be enforced by the courts. A breach of a rule of civil law is considered a civil wrong. Many civil wrongs are also criminal wrongs. For example, if Alex is accused of taking Yaman's car without her permission, Alex may have committed both the criminal offence of theft, and the civil offence of trespass to goods. This civil wrong is called a **tort**. Torts can be intentional acts or omissions, but the most common torts today are based on negligence or careless conduct. The famous British case of Donoghue and Stevenson stated the fundamental rule that everyone is under a legal duty to take reasonable care that others will not be injured by their conduct where it is reasonably foreseeable that the conduct would cause harm. Mrs. Donoghue became ill after she drank a bottle of ginger beer, after which a dead snail was found in the bottle. She sued the bottling company for damages. Although the case was eventually settled out of court, the decision of the House of Lords that she did have a right to sue was an important development for today's laws concerning liability for negligence.[1]

The usual remedy a victim of a tort may seek through a civil proceeding is compensation for the loss he or she has suffered. Thus, in the example of Alex and Yaman, if Yaman wishes to seek a civil remedy, she must sue (or proceed against) Alex in a civil court. Yaman, as the person bringing the lawsuit, is called the ***plaintiff***; Alex, as the person being sued, is the ***defendant***. If Yaman is successful against Alex, she is awarded compensation (usually money). If she is not successful, judgment is given in favour of Alex. If Alex is charged with theft, he may be prosecuted (proceeded against) in a criminal court; and if convicted (found guilty), he may be sentenced to a suitable punishment. If Alex is found not guilty, he is ***acquitted*** and the criminal charge dismissed. An example of the overlap of civil law and criminal law involves an incident during an NHL hockey game in 2004. Todd Bertuzzi was charged with assault for an attack on an opposing player during the game. The victim, Steve Moore, was seriously injured, likely ending his hockey career.[2] Bertuzzi pleaded guilty to assault causing bodily harm. He was given a conditional discharge, which included one year of probation. After the criminal proceedings, Steve Moore brought a civil suit claiming damages.[3]

In the early days of the English law, little distinction was drawn between a civil wrong and a criminal wrong. If a person or the person's property was injured, either that person or the person's family sought revenge. Consequently, blood feuds between families were common, although the community might attempt to encourage the victim to accept compensation in the form of money.

At the same time, the idea of the king's peace was becoming established. The king could put certain people or property under his protection. Anyone who injured the persons or property being protected by the king had to pay the king a money fine. Some offences were so serious that a fine was inadequate. In such cases, the offender's "life and limbs" were at the king's mercy. Gradually, the king extended the area of his peace until it encompassed all the territory and persons under his rule. Since any wrong was an offence against the king, breaches of the peace came to be prosecuted by the king's agents in the name of the king.

Today, provincial prosecutors (i.e., ***Crown attorneys***) who are agents of the provincial ***Attorney General***, prosecute most cases under the Criminal Code. Cases prosecuted by federal prosecutors include those involving drugs, organized crime, terrorism, money laundering, crimes against humanity, and Criminal Code offences in the territories.

Two important differences between civil and criminal wrongs should be emphasized. First, where a possibility of a civil action exists, the community has no interest in whether the victim decides to go to court. However, where a crime has occurred, it is usually the Crown attorney's decision whether or not to prosecute, even if the victim would rather not take any steps against the offender. Second, under criminal law, the court has the authority to impose penalties (or sanctions) on convicted offenders, such as fines or imprisonment. However, civil law generally only permits a court to order compensation to the victim for actual losses from the wrongdoer.

---

1   [1932] All E.Rep.1 (House of Lords) To see a video re-enactment of the famous case, go to **justiceeducation.ca/resources/Paisley-Snail**.
2   "Bertuzzi Pleads Guilty to Assault Charge," *Canadian Press*, December 22, 2004.
3   See *Moore v. Bertuzzi*, [2008] O.J. No. 347 (Ont. Ct. J). The Toronto *Star* reported on December 16, 2008, that Moore and Bertuzzi were ordered by the court to enter mediation to try to settle the case without going to court. Moore was seeking 38 million dollars U.S. in damages and lost wages.

Although the role of government through its criminal law authority is to protect society as a whole, in recent years, governments have become more sensitive to the plight of the victims of crime for whom civil remedies may be inadequate or inappropriate. For example, under the Criminal Code, a court must take into account the safety of a victim when setting bail conditions (s. 518(1)(d.2); a court may order a publication ban to protect the identity of a victim of certain offences (s. 486.4); victims are allowed to make "victim impact statements" at the sentencing stage of a trial (s. 722); and part of a sentence may be restitution to the victim (ss. 738–741.2). Also, there are provincial, territorial, and federal support services for victims of crime.[4]

B. CRIMINAL LAW IN CANADA

L02   ## 1. Jurisdiction

The authority to enact criminal legislation is assigned to the federal government under s. 91(27) of the Constitution Act, 1982. This encompasses the authority over criminal offences and procedure. This means that the criminal law concerning what is a crime and how the criminal law is enforced is the same throughout Canada.

Other areas concerned with criminal law—that is, with the police, courts, and correctional facilities—are shared by the federal and provincial governments. For example, the RCMP is a federal police force; however, some provinces have their own police force or have given municipalities the authority to set up municipal police forces. Also, the provinces are authorized by the Constitution to organize courts of criminal jurisdiction, i.e., provincial courts and superior courts; but the federal government appoints and pays the salaries of superior court judges while the province selects and pays the salaries of provincial court judges. As well, under s. 101 of the Constitution, the federal government is authorized to establish the Supreme Court of Canada as a final court of appeal. The federal government runs federal penitentiaries for offenders who receive sentences of two years or more. The provinces are responsible for maintaining prisons and reformatories for federal offenders sentenced to less than two years, as well as for provincial offenders.

Although all crimes are federal offences, the provinces have the constitutional authority under s. 92(15) to create provincial offences for violations of provincial legislation and to impose punishment by fine or imprisonment. Generally speaking, crimes are more serious than provincial offences. Under the common law, true crimes (i.e., today, federal crimes) were considered *malum in se* or morally wrong. Provincial offences are regulatory in nature or *malum prohibitum*, wrong because they are prohibited. Their purpose is to regulate legal conduct for the protection of society in general and not primarily to punish. Provincial offences may seem similar to crimes, particularly because of the types of punishment possible. For example, a person may be imprisoned for violating a provincial law. Also, the court procedure can be similar, and even the same courtrooms may be used, with trials before provincial court judges. However, punishment for provincial offences is generally limited to not more than six months' imprisonment; and many offences are dealt with by paying a fine out of court. Provincial offences include violations of laws covering areas such as landlord–tenant relationships, liquor control, and trespass on private property. There are also regulatory

---

4   See, e.g., **victimsmatter.gc.ca** for more detailed information on victim's rights.

offences under federal law. For example, the Competition Act protects consumers from false advertising (see discussion of regulatory offences in Chapter 3).

Provincial regulatory offences and federal criminal offences overlap in some areas—driving offences, for example. The provinces have the authority to regulate the use of streets and highways; therefore, every province has a statute that creates driving offences, such as speeding and illegal turns. The federal government created the more serious offences of impaired driving and dangerous driving because of the serious harm that motor vehicles may cause. Regulatory offences are sometimes referred to as quasi-criminal offences. The difference between a crime and a regulatory offence can be understood more clearly by looking at two driving offences. A person who fails to stop for a stop sign but causes no injury or harm may be charged with a provincial offence. Although there will be penalties for breaking the law, the person is not considered a criminal by society. The purpose of stop signs is to regulate traffic and promote public safety in use of roads. On the other hand, a person who is convicted of dangerous driving by street racing has committed a crime (s. 249.1), an act that poses a great risk to the safety of members of the public.

2. Sources of Canadian Criminal Law

The main source of both substantive and procedural criminal law in Canada is the *Criminal Code*. This federal statute was first enacted in 1892. It attempted to consolidate the English common law crimes applicable to Canada with the colonial laws. A significant addition was made in 1953 by what is now s. 9, which states that no person can be convicted of an offence at common law, except for criminal contempt of court. This section was necessary to make it clear that a person cannot be convicted of a common law offence that is not in the Code. However, s. 8(3) of the Code preserves all common law defences. Thus, for example, the law regarding the defence of necessity has developed through case law.

Although the focus of this book is on the Criminal Code, there are other federal criminal law statutes. Examples are the Controlled Drugs and Substances Act, S.C. 1996, c.19, which sets out drug offences, and the Youth Criminal Justice Act, S.C 2002, c.1, the law which deals with young people who are charged with offences. These statutes are discussed in Appendices A and B.

C. THE CRIMINAL CODE

LO3   ## 1. Structure

The Code contains both substantive and procedural rules. Substantively, it defines offences and sets out penalties for offences. Procedurally, it states the rules for making arrests, conducting searches, holding trials, and appealing court decisions.

The official Criminal Code is found in Chapter 34 of the 1985 Revised Statutes of Canada. Subsequent sessional volumes must be checked for amendments. Most people use one of the commercial versions of the Criminal Code that are published yearly. These versions incorporate all the amendments to the Code as of the date of publication. Generally, then, only one book is needed for finding the law. Most commercial publishers of the Code also send updates of new Code amendments to purchasers during the year. Of course, for the most up-to-date version of the criminal law, other resources would need to be consulted. The *Canada Gazette*, a weekly government publication, publishes new legislation as soon as it receives Royal Assent. The Criminal Code can also be found online at **justice.gc.ca** > Laws > Criminal Code.

The Code is divided into 28 parts. Each part is divided into numbered sections. Section 2 of the Code is very important, in that it defines certain words used in the Code. For example, the term "highway" is defined to include bridges and tunnels that roads pass over or through. "Dwelling-house" is defined as any whole or part of a building or structure used as a permanent or temporary residence. Section 2 also gives the names of the courts in each province. For example, in Prince Edward Island, the court of appeal is called the Appeal Division of the Supreme Court.

The parts of the Code that are most relevant to this book are these:

- Part I starts with section 4 (or s. 4) and covers general principles. For example, section 9 preserves all common law defences. Section 19 states the principle that ignorance of the law is not an excuse for committing a crime.
- Parts II through XIII define offences and penalties.
- Parts XIV through XXIII deal with procedural rules and procedures for determining criminal liability, including procedures for making an arrest, holding trials of indictable offences, sentencing, and appeals.

As mentioned in Chapter 1, commercial versions of the Code are often annotated. Codes that are annotated list and briefly describe important cases that interpret and apply each section. Annotated codes are useful since the Code, like other statutes, is constantly being interpreted and applied by the courts.

2. Classification of Offences

The Code divides offences into three categories: ***indictable offences***; offences punishable upon summary conviction; and ***hybrid*** or ***dual procedure offences***. Generally speaking, the difference between the first two is that indictable offences are more serious than ***summary conviction offences***. Examples of indictable offences are murder, kidnapping, and robbery. Causing a disturbance in or near a public place and loitering on private property at night are summary conviction offences.

A hybrid, or dual procedure offence, may be tried as either an indictable or a summary conviction offence. Examples of hybrid offences are theft of property valued at $5000 or less, and mischief to property valued at more than $5000. The decision on how to treat a hybrid offence is made by the Crown attorney, usually at the time of the ***arraignment*** (which is when the judge reads the charge to the accused, who is then asked to enter a plea of guilty or not guilty). The Crown bases its decision on such facts as whether the accused has a previous record of law-breaking, and the circumstances surrounding the commission of the offence (e.g., whether violence was involved). Until a decision is made, a hybrid offence is treated like an indictable offence (e.g., for the purposes of a pre-trial bail hearing.) When the case is at the arraignment stage and for some reason the Crown does not make a decision, the case will be tried as a summary conviction offence.

L04 D. TRYING SUMMARY CONVICTION AND INDICTABLE OFFENCES

Summary conviction and indictable offences are treated differently before and during the trial. The penalties that can be imposed are also different. Generally, a summary offence is dealt with in a more "summary" fashion, that is, with less procedure and formality, because it is a less serious offence. An indictable offence refers to the indictment which is preferred (presented) to the court to begin the trial process. The process of a trial can be very complex. The next two sections briefly describe some of the main features and differences between trials of indictable and summary conviction offences.

One similarity for all offences is the practice of plea bargaining. Plea bargaining can take place before or after the accused is formally charged with the offence. Plea bargaining occurs when the accused enters an agreement with the prosecutor to plead guilty in exchange for a less serious charge or a recommendation to the judge for a lighter sentence. This procedure is not governed by statute law but has been developed informally by the police and Crown attorneys. Although sometimes criticized for encouraging innocent people to plead guilty rather than risk a trial, proponents point out that it saves time and money by avoiding a full-blown trial.[5]

1. Summary Conviction Offences Trials

Part XXVII of the Code describes the procedure to be used for the trial of offences punishable upon summary conviction. Section 788 states that before a court proceeding (i.e., the trial) can begin, an information in Form 2 (the forms used in criminal proceedings are found in Part XXVIII of the Criminal Code) must be laid. This means that the informant must swear, under oath, in an affidavit, that he or she has either personal knowledge or **reasonable grounds** for believing that a certain person has committed an offence. The information is then signed by the informant and a justice of the peace. If the accused is not personally present and not represented by counsel or agent, the justice of the peace can issue an **arrest warrant** for the accused, or a **summons** that orders the accused to appear in court on a certain date. The accused does not have to appear personally; instead, an agent or lawyer can appear on his or her behalf.

Although informations are usually laid by police officers, any person may lay an information. A private person can prosecute a summary conviction offence if the Crown does not. A police officer can also be authorized to prosecute cases. However, Crown attorneys prosecute most offences.

Section 786 provides that the proceedings must begin (i.e., the information must be laid) no later than six months after the offence is alleged to have occurred unless the law provides otherwise. This means that there is a six-month limitation period on starting the prosecution of most summary conviction offences. In general, there is no limitation period for indictable offences.

Trials of summary conviction offences are held before "summary conviction courts" as defined in s. 785. Usually, the trials are held before a provincial/territorial court judge or justice of the peace.[6] Jury trials are not held in summary conviction proceedings. Similarly, **preliminary inquiries** are never held. A preliminary inquiry is a hearing that takes place before the trial to determine whether there is enough evidence to commit the accused to trial. This hearing is used only for certain indictable offences and is discussed below.

After the information is laid, and with both the accused (or the accused's agent or **counsel**) and the prosecutor present, the accused is arraigned. Under the arraignment procedure set out in s. 801, the substance of the information must be stated to the accused, who is then asked to enter a plea of guilty or not guilty. If the accused pleads guilty, the court enters a conviction. If the accused pleads not guilty or refuses to plead, the court enters a not guilty plea and proceeds with the trial.

---

5   See, e.g., Kirk Makin, "Top Jurist urges review of coercive plea bargaining system," *The Globe and Mail*, March 7, 2011. See also plea bargaining guidelines prepared for federal prosecutors at **ppsc-sppc.gc.ca/eng/fps-sfp/fpd/ch20.html**, *The Federal Prosecution Service Deskbook, Chapter 20.*
6   Nunavut does not have a territorial court so all trials are held in the Nunavut Court of Justice, before a superior court judge.

The steps in a trial are, in brief, the following: After opening statements by both sides, the prosecutor presents evidence through the testimony of witnesses. Next, the accused may cross-examine the prosecutor's witnesses. At the end of the prosecutor's case, the accused may present a motion to have the charges dismissed on the grounds that the prosecution has not proved its case beyond a reasonable doubt. If the motion is dismissed, the accused can present evidence in defence. The prosecutor may cross-examine the accused's witnesses. Both parties have an opportunity to give summing-up statements to the court. Once the court has heard the evidence and statements presented by the prosecutor and the accused, it decides whether the prosecutor has proved all of the elements of the offence beyond a reasonable doubt. The accused will either be convicted or acquitted. If the accused is acquitted, the information will be dismissed.

Where the accused is convicted, the penalties that may be imposed are limited by s. 787, which provides that, unless the law states otherwise, a person who is convicted of a summary conviction offence is liable to a fine of up to $5000 and/or imprisonment for not more than six months.

2. Trials of Indictable Offences

Trials of indictable offences also usually start with the laying of an information. Similar to summary conviction offences, a private person may lay an information and may, with some limitations, prosecute the case.[7] However, one of the main differences between the two types of offences is that indictable offences may have another step before the trial begins: the preliminary hearing.

a. Origins of the Procedure

Starting in the twelfth century, the English method for bringing suspected criminals to justice was through presenting an indictment by a grand jury. The jury consisted of members of the local community, whose duty it was to report all suspected crimes committed by their neighbours to the king or his agent. This report, which accused certain persons of specific crimes, was called an indictment. Originally, the jurors based their reports on their own personal knowledge. Gradually, as the jury system evolved, the grand jurors became persons without direct knowledge of the crime, who based their report upon the testimony of witnesses to the offence.

A grand jury system was used at one time in some parts of Canada. The Attorney General, or someone authorized by him or her, or by the court, would prefer (i.e., present) a bill of indictment before a grand jury. The jury then heard the testimony of witnesses called by the prosecutor. The accused and his or her counsel were not allowed to be present during the hearing; the proceedings were conducted in complete secrecy. One reason for the secrecy was to protect the reputations of innocent persons falsely accused of crimes.

After hearing the evidence presented by the prosecutor, the jurors decided whether there was enough evidence to send the accused to trial before a judge and jury. If a majority of the jurors decided that there was enough evidence for a trial, the foreman of the jury endorsed the indictment with the words "true bill." If a majority of the jurors decided that there was insufficient evidence for a trial, the indictment was endorsed "no bill."

---

7   See s. 507.1 and discussion at **justice.gc.ca.**

Today, the Attorney General, or his or her agent, prefers the written indictment before the court. This means, in effect, that the Attorney General or his or her agent is performing the functions previously performed by the grand jury.

b. Preliminary Inquiries

Grand juries were abandoned partly because preliminary inquiries serve the same function of disposing of weak cases without the time and expense of a full trial. Preliminary inquiries (or preliminary hearings) take place before the indictment is preferred and just after the accused is arraigned (i.e., charged) with an offence. A preliminary hearing will be held if either the accused or prosecutor requests one. In certain situations, a provincial court judge can require a preliminary hearing (s. 555). Depending on the province, preliminary inquiries are usually held before a provincial court judge or justice of the peace. The main purpose of the hearing is to determine whether there is enough evidence to commit the accused to trial. During the hearing, the prosecutor presents evidence through the testimony of witnesses. The accused has a right to present evidence and to make a statement on his or her own behalf. Both parties can cross-examine each other's witnesses. After considering the evidence, the justice or provincial court judge decides whether to commit to trial or to discharge the accused. If an accused is committed to trial, it does not mean the justice or judge has found him or her guilty. Being committed to trial after a preliminary inquiry simply means that there is "sufficient evidence" to hold a trial. If an accused is ordered to stand trial, an indictment (form 4) will be preferred by the prosecutor. The indictment details the charge, the acts or conduct that support the charge, and the circumstances surrounding it so that the accused is fully informed of the substance of the charge. The court may issue a summons or arrest warrant to order the accused to attend court to answer the charge.

Preliminary inquiries permit the accused to hear the nature, and judge the strength, of the Crown's case. In this way, from the perspective of the accused, preliminary inquiries are preferable to the grand jury system.

The relevant Code sections on preliminary inquiries are sections 535 to 551.

c. Methods of Trial for Indictable Offences

There are three methods of trial for indictable offences: by provincial/territorial court judge, by a superior court judge without a jury, and by a superior court judge and jury. Like summary offences, the process usually starts with the laying of an information (s. 504).

Some offences in the Code are within the absolute jurisdiction of the provincial/territorial court judges. Other offences must be tried by a superior court judge and jury. For most offences, however, the accused can elect the method of trial; that is, he or she may choose a provincial/territorial court judge, a superior court judge alone, or a superior court judge and jury. However, the accused may lose the right of election where the offence being charged is punishable by more than five years' imprisonment. In this situation, the Attorney General under s. 568 may require the accused to be tried by judge and jury. If an indictable offence is tried by a provincial/territorial court judge, there will not be a preliminary hearing. In all other situations, a preliminary hearing will be held if requested by either the accused or the prosecutor. Also, it is not necessary to prefer an indictment if the case is tried in provincial court.

Section 553 lists the indictable offences that are within the absolute jurisdiction of the provincial/territorial court judges; although, strictly speaking, other courts with criminal jurisdiction can try these offences (see sections 468 and 469). These are less serious indictable offences, such as keeping a common gaming house, bookmaking and betting, and hybrid offences, such as theft of property that does not exceed $5000 in value. These offences are tried in the same way as summary conviction offences, in that a formal indictment is not necessary and preliminary inquiries are not held.

Section 469 lists the indictable offences that must be tried in the province's superior court of criminal jurisdiction. This court is the province's highest-ranking trial court with criminal jurisdiction. Section 2 gives the name of the superior criminal court for each province. Generally, it is called the Supreme Court or the Court of Queen's Bench. In Quebec, it is called the Superior Court; in Ontario, it is called the Superior Court of Justice. Generally, all trials of s. 469 offences are by judge and jury. The one exception is that the accused and the Attorney General may jointly consent to the case being tried by a superior criminal court without a jury (s. 473).

The offences contained in s. 469 are considered the most serious offences. They include treason, sedition, piracy, and murder. All other indictable offences in the Code are electable except where (as mentioned above) the Attorney General can require a trial before judge and jury. An accused who elects trial by judge without a jury is tried by a superior court judge as defined for each province in s. 552. All of the provinces have only two levels of trial court—a court of criminal jurisdiction and a superior court of criminal jurisdiction. In general, the judges listed in s. 552 are all Superior or Supreme Court judges.

Part XIX of the Code, which starts with s. 552, describes the procedure to be used where the trial is without a jury and before either a judge or a provincial court judge.

Unlike summary conviction offence proceedings, the accused must be personally present for the trial of an indictable offence (unless the court orders otherwise). In brief, whether or not a preliminary hearing has been held, the trial commences with the preferring of the indictment by the prosecutor. After this is done, the steps in the trial of an indictable offence are the same as the steps in a summary conviction trial. If the trial is before a jury, after the evidence has been presented, the judge sums up the case for the jurors. The judge instructs them on questions of law and may express an opinion regarding the credibility of witnesses or the importance of the evidence. If there is a jury, it will return a verdict of guilty or not guilty. If the trial is before a judge only, the judge makes the finding of guilty or not guilty. Depending on the verdict, the accused is either convicted or acquitted by the court. If the verdict is guilty, the judge determines the sentence for the accused.

The possible penalties for indictable offences are much harsher than those for summary conviction offences. The Code sets out maximum terms of imprisonment for each offence, such as life, 14 years, 10 years, 5 years, or 2 years. In a few situations, the Code sets out a minimum punishment that must be imposed if the accused is convicted. For example, s. 235 states that the minimum sentence for murder is life imprisonment. Usually, however, the judge can choose a sentence up to the maximum term set out in the Code. A first offender, for example, is usually sentenced to far less than the maximum allowed. Section 734 allows the court to impose fines in addition to, or instead of, imprisonment if there is no minimum term of imprisonment required. If the offence is punishable by more than five years' imprisonment, the fine may only be in addition to imprisonment.

FIGURE 2-1 Steps in a Criminal Trial

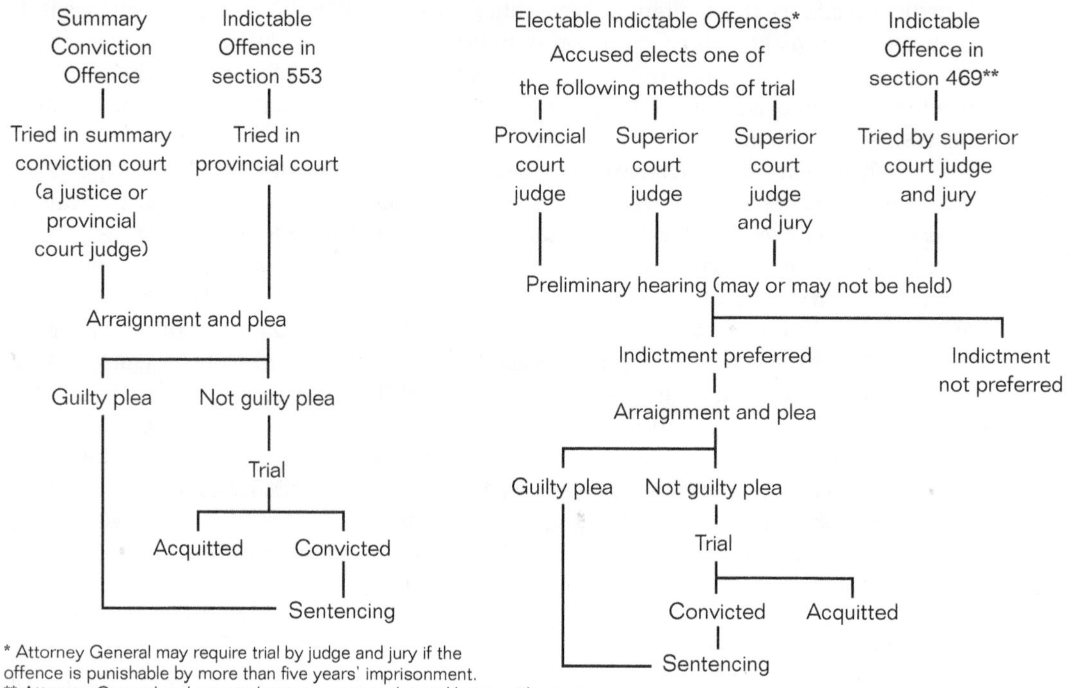

* Attorney General may require trial by judge and jury if the offence is punishable by more than five years' imprisonment.
** Attorney General and accused may consent to the trial being without a jury.

L05 E. THE CHARTER AND THE RIGHTS OF THE ACCUSED AT TRIAL

The Charter of Rights and Freedoms did not create all new rights. Some of the rights, such as the **presumption of innocence**, have a long history in English common law. The Charter has, however, given the courts new authority to examine legislation and to expand and further define the rights and freedoms. Section 11 of the Charter lists the rights and freedoms that apply to criminal trials. The discussion below considers each of the rights and some of the more important court decisions that apply s. 11.

11. Any person charged with an offence has the right

(a) to be informed without unreasonable delay of the specific offence

The purpose of this paragraph is to ensure that the accused person knows reasonably quickly the substance of the allegation so that a full defence can be made to it. It applies not only to criminal but also to quasi-criminal offences, and whenever the accused is subject to true penal consequences (i.e., a fine or imprisonment).[8]

(b) to be tried within a reasonable time

---

8 *Wigglesworth v. The Queen* (1987), 37 C.C.C. (3d) 385 (S.C.C.). See also s. 581 which sets the rules for what must be contained in an indictment to ensure that an accused is fully informed of the specifics of the offence.

The Supreme Court of Canada, in *R. v. Askov*,[9] made a decision that had far-reaching effects on the court system in Canada. In November 1983, the accused were charged with several offences, including conspiracy to commit extortion and assault with a weapon. One of the accused was released on a **recognizance** (an agreement or promise made by an accused to pay a certain amount of money to the court for failing to appear on a particular court date) in December; the others were held until May, when they were released on recognizances. Although there were several court appearances for the accused, for various reasons the trial date was put off until September 1985, almost two years after the charges were laid. The defence counsel asked that the proceedings be stayed because the delay had breached the right of the accused to a trial within a reasonable time. The Supreme Court of Canada agreed and ordered that the proceedings be stayed.[10] The Court found that most of the delay was a result of systemic problems in the particular court district. Courts were overburdened with a backlog of cases. There was, as the trial judge noted, a chronic shortage of courtrooms and judges, with the result that long delays were common. The Court compared this court district to others in Canada and described it as one of the worst. For example, a comparable court district in Montreal had a median delay of 82.5 days compared with this district's median delay of 607 days. The Court concluded, "Justice so delayed is an affront to the individual, to the community, and to the very administration of justice. The lack of institutional facilities cannot in this case be accepted as a basis for justifying the delay."[11]

The Court set some general guidelines for determining whether a delay violates the Charter. It said that six to eight months should be the outside limit in most cases from the time of committal for trial (after the preliminary inquiry) to the trial itself. Factors in deciding whether the delay is reasonable include the following:

- Length of the delay—The longer the delay, the more likely it is unreasonable.
- Reasons for the delay—This includes the inherent time requirement for preparing the case, actions of the Crown, actions of the accused, and delays caused by inadequate resources.
- Waiver—If the accused consents to a delay, it must be a fully informed and freely given consent.
- Prejudice to the accused—This includes the stress and loss of privacy during the delay, as well as factors such as being subject to restrictive bail conditions or possible loss of evidence. There is an inference that a very long delay will unfairly prejudice the accused.

The immediate result of *Askov* was the staying of proceedings in up to 50,000 cases that were awaiting trial. The decision forced provincial governments to take steps to remedy problems caused by lack of resources.

Decisions since *Askov* have clarified and given detail to the decision in this case. In *R. v. Morin*,[12] the accused was charged with impaired driving and her trial date was set for 14.5 months later. On the trial date, her counsel asked that the charge be stayed because of this delay. The counsel's motion was dismissed and she was convicted. On appeal to the Supreme Court of Canada, the Court dismissed her appeal, emphasizing that the *Askov* decision does

---

9   (1990), 59 C.C.C. (3d) 449 (S.C.C.).

10   When proceedings are stayed, the information that commences the proceedings is withdrawn. The Crown can stay proceedings under s. 579 of the Code. Proceedings that are stayed are suspended. The Crown has one year from the time that the proceedings were stayed to recommence the proceedings. After that time, the proceedings are deemed to have never commenced and the court will not allow the Crown to lay a new information. Courts also have the authority to direct a stay of proceedings to prevent an abuse of process where the Crown is acting oppressively. For example, proceedings were stayed in *Askov* because of the abuse of process caused by the lengthy delay in trying the accused.

11   *Askov, supra* note 9 at 490.

12   (1992), 71 C.C.C. (3d) 1 (S.C.C.).

not set out a mathematical formula to be followed when deciding whether a delay is unreasonable; rather, it requires a judicial balancing of the interests protected by s. 11(b) against the causes of the delay. The Court also suggested that comparisons of court districts should be used cautiously, because the length of time that is reasonable is influenced by local conditions and practices. In general, the Court stated that for cases tried in provincial courts, an 8- to 10-month delay from the time the parties are ready for trial to when the trial begins is appropriate. Therefore, a delay of 14.5 months raised the issue of reasonableness. However, the Court decided that when all the factors were considered, the delay was not unreasonable. First, they considered that a case of this kind would take 2 months to prepare. So, the actual delay was 12 months. Given the significant growth in the area where the trial was to be held, a 10-month delay would be reasonable. Since there was no evidence of prejudice to the accused, a 2-month deviation was justified.

The Court also distinguished cases like *Askov*—that is, two-stage trials involving preliminary inquiries—from this case, in which the charge was a summary conviction offence. The Court stated that the *Askov* guideline for institutional delay after committal for trial should remain at six to eight months, while the guideline for cases tried in provincial court should be eight to ten months (the longer period being justified because of the greater caseload carried by provincial courts).

In *R. v. Potvin*,[13] the Supreme Court of Canada clarified that s. 11(b) does not apply to delay in hearing an appeal.

In *R. v. Collins*,[14] the delay was caused by Crown errors rather than by institutional delays. The Supreme Court of Canada ordered that murder charges be stayed where a two-year delay was caused by the Crown's indifference and tardiness in disclosing its case to the defence. The accused had pressed for an earlier trial date and had spent nearly two years in jail waiting for trial.

In *R. v. MacDougall*,[15] the Supreme Court of Canada held that s. 11(b) also applies to delay that occurs between a finding of guilt and sentencing.

In *R. v. Kalanj*,[16] the Supreme Court of Canada held that s. 11(b) does not apply to pre-charge delay.

(c) not to be compelled to be a witness in proceedings against that person in respect of the offence

This paragraph can be considered with s. 13:

> **13. A witness who testifies in any proceedings has the right not to have any incriminating evidence so given used to incriminate that witness in any other proceedings, except in a prosecution for perjury or for the giving of contradictory evidence.**

Section 11(c) of the Charter ensures that an accused person has a **right to remain silent** and the right not to give self-incriminating evidence at his or her trial. Section 13 protects the accused at subsequent proceedings. For example, assume that Henry is convicted at trial and appeals the conviction and that the appeal court orders a new trial. The Crown cannot use Henry's testimony from the first trial to prove his guilt in the second trial.

---

13 (1993), 83 C.C.C. (3d) 97 (S.C.C.).
14 (1995), 99 C.C.C. (3d) 385 (S.C.C.).
15 (1998), 3 S.C.R. 45.
16 (1989), 1 S.C.R. 1594. See also *R. v. Kporwodu* (2005), 195 C.C.C. (3d) 501 (Ont.C.A.).

(d) to be presumed innocent until proven guilty according to law in a fair and public hearing by an independent and impartial tribunal

The presumption of innocence is one of our oldest and most important rights. It means that the accused does not have to prove that he or she is innocent; rather, the Crown has the burden of proving the accused's guilt. It is consistent with the right to remain silent. The fact that a person is charged with an offence does not mean that the person has committed the offence; all it means is that the police or Crown have reasonable grounds for believing that the accused committed the offence. The person is presumed innocent until the Crown proves otherwise in a court of law. The prosecution's burden of proof is to establish the accused's guilt **beyond a reasonable doubt**. This means that if, at the end of the trial, the judge or jury has a **reasonable doubt** as to the guilt of the accused, the accused must be found not guilty. The Supreme Court of Canada has said that proof beyond a reasonable doubt has a specific legal meaning and cannot be understood as an ordinary phrase; juries must be instructed on its meaning. It is "inextricably intertwined with that principle fundamental to all criminal trials, the presumption of innocence."[17] The court stated:

- The burden of proof rests on the prosecution throughout the trial and never shifts to the accused.
- A reasonable doubt is not a doubt based upon sympathy or prejudice.
- A reasonable doubt is based upon reason and common sense.
- It is logically connected to the evidence or absence of evidence.
- It does not involve proof to an absolute certainty; it is not proof beyond any doubt nor is it an imaginary or frivolous doubt.
- More is required than proof that the accused is probably guilty; a jury which concludes only that the accused is probably guilty must acquit.[18]

The Court further stated that these references to the standard of proof should be avoided:

- Describing the term "reasonable doubt" as an ordinary expression which has no special meaning in the criminal law context
- Inviting jurors to apply to the task before them the same standard of proof that they apply to important, or even the most important, decisions in their own lives
- Equating proof "beyond a reasonable doubt" to proof "to a moral certainty"
- Qualifying the word "doubt" with adjectives other than "reasonable," such as "serious," "substantial," or "haunting," which may mislead the jury
- Instructing jurors that they may convict if they are "sure" that the accused is guilty, before providing them with a proper definition as to the meaning of the words "beyond a reasonable doubt"[18a]

It is not necessary for the Crown to disprove every possible defence to the charge; but if the accused does raise a defence that is supported by some evidence, the Crown must disprove the defence beyond a reasonable doubt. Where the Crown must prove that the accused intentionally did an act, the Crown can rely on the presumption that he or she intended the natural consequences of the act. Thus, if Harriet fires a gun at John, a judge or jury may, but not must, presume that she intended to wound him.

---

17   *R.v. Lifchus* (1997), 3 S.C.R. 320.
18   Ibid. at para 36.
18a Ibid. at para 37.

The burden of proof in a criminal trial is much higher than in a civil trial. In a civil trial, the **plaintiff** must prove his or her case on a **balance of probabilities**; that is, prove that it is more likely than not that the plaintiff's claim is true. (The plaintiff is the person claiming an injury.) For example, Anne claims that Boris negligently drove a car and caused damage to her car. She sues Boris for the cost of repairing the car, as well as for any other expenses incurred because of the accident. She must prove that it was more likely than not that Boris drove his car in a negligent manner and caused damage to her car. It is not necessary for her to prove Boris's negligence beyond a reasonable doubt. However, if Boris is charged with dangerous driving, the prosecution must prove beyond a reasonable doubt that Boris committed each element of the offence. The different burdens of proof used in criminal and civil trials can have this result: A person may be acquitted of the criminal charge, because the prosecutor fails to prove the case beyond a reasonable doubt, but found liable by a civil court, because the liability can be proved using the lower burden of proof.

Although the burden of proving that the accused committed the offence is on the prosecutor, some Criminal Code offences contain **reverse onus clauses**. A reverse onus clause shifts part of the burden of proof to the accused. Similar to a reverse onus clause is a **mandatory presumption**, where a fact is presumed to exist unless the accused can prove otherwise.

Since the enactment of the Charter, many of these clauses have been found to be violations of the Charter, and thus unenforceable. For example, in *R. v. Oakes*,[19] the accused was charged under the Narcotic Control Act (replaced by the Controlled Drugs and Substances Act) with possession of narcotics for the purpose of trafficking (i.e., selling). Section 8 of the Act stated that, once the Crown has proved possession, the burden shifts to the accused to prove on a balance of probabilities that he or she did not possess the drugs for the purpose of trafficking. The Supreme Court of Canada held that s. 8 offends s. 11(d) of the Charter because a judge could convict an accused of trafficking even if the judge had a reasonable doubt about whether the drugs were possessed for the purpose of trafficking. In other words, the accused, to avoid conviction, had to disprove on the balance of probabilities the existence of a presumed fact—that he or she had possession for the purpose of trafficking.

Although reverse onus provisions and mandatory presumptions offend the presumption of innocence, it is possible to uphold these provisions as reasonable limitations on a right under s. 1 of the Charter. The Supreme Court in *Oakes* laid out the test for deciding whether a clause is a reasonable limitation. The first criterion the court must consider is whether the objective of the law is of sufficient importance to warrant overriding a right. At a minimum, the objective must relate to concerns that are pressing and substantial in a free and democratic society. For example, in *Oakes*, the objective of the law was to control trafficking in narcotics. Second, the law in question must be reasonable and demonstrably justified. This second criterion involves a proportionality test: To decide whether the law is reasonable and demonstrably justified, the court should ask three questions. First, is the law carefully designed to achieve its objective? That is, is the law rationally connected to the objective and not unfair or arbitrary? Second, does the law impair the right as little as possible? And third, is the effect of the law on the right in proportion to the importance of the objective? In other words, the more serious the impairment of the right, the more important the objective must be.

The Supreme Court in *Oakes* held with regard to the first criterion that the objective of protecting society from the ills associated with drug trafficking is sufficiently important to override a Charter right. However, s. 8 failed the proportionality test in that there is no rational

---

19   *R. v. Oakes* (1986), 24 C.C.C. (3d) 321 (S.C.C.).

connection between possession and the presumed fact of possession for the purpose of trafficking. In other words, it is not rational to presume that because a person has possession of a small amount of a narcotic, he or she intends to traffic in it.

In *R. v. Whyte*,[20] the Supreme Court upheld a law that infringes s. 11(d). The accused was charged with having care and control of a car while impaired. For this offence, an accused can be charged even if he or she is not driving. For example, a person who is impaired and enters the driver's side of a car could be charged. The police do not have to wait for the accused to drive the vehicle before laying a charge. Under s. 258(1) of the Code, it is presumed that a person in the driver's seat of a car is there for the purpose of driving the car. This presumption shifts the burden of proof to the accused to show that his or her purpose for being in the seat was not to set the car in motion.

The Court allowed this infringement of s. 11(d) because protecting the public from drunk driving is a matter of sufficient importance to override a constitutionally protected right. The presumption is a minimal interference, since the accused can avoid a conviction by giving a reason for being in the driver's seat. At the same time, it is impractical to require the Crown to prove an intent to drive.

The Court has said that where a person must produce a certificate or permit to carry on a certain activity legally, it is not a reverse onus clause and is allowable. For example, s. 91 of the Code requires a person to have a permit to possess certain types of firearms. Section 117.11 (then s. 106.7) of the Code states that where there is a question of whether a person has a permit, the onus is on the accused to prove that he or she has the permit. In *R. v. Schwartz*,[21] the Court held that s. 106.7 (now 117.11) does not create a reverse onus provision. The Court said that the section creates a rule of evidence and does not require the accused to prove or disprove an element of the offence. In other words, all the accused must do is present the permit to show that he or she is exempt from the provision under which the charge was laid.

Section 11(d) of the Charter also provides that the accused has a right to a fair and public hearing by an impartial and independent tribunal. This right prevents "secret trials" and ensures fairness. As one court said, "Publicity is the hallmark of justice and trial in open court is the instrument through which publicity is effectively obtained."[22] However, in some circumstances the public can be excluded. For example, under s. 486 of the Code, the judge or justice may exclude the public if he or she is of the opinion that "it is in the interests of public morals, the maintenance of order or the proper administration of justice to exclude all or any members of the public from the courtroom for all or part of the proceedings."

The Supreme Court of Canada has referred to impartiality as "a state of mind or attitude of the court in relation to . . . issues and parties . . . it connotes an absence of bias actual or perceived."[23] One of the reasons for appointing judges to the bench for life is to ensure their independence and impartiality. A judge can only be removed from the bench for a serious breach of duty. This means that judges can make decisions without being influenced by public opinion or by the governments that appointed them.

Note that the Supreme Court of Canada has held that it is not a violation of the presumption of innocence when provincial law provides that an accused can be found guilty of a provincial offence even though the accused does not appear for trial. In *R. v. Richards*,[24] the accused received a ticket for speeding. He was given the time and place of the trial and notice

20   (1988), 42 C.C.C. (3d) 97 (S.C.C.).
21   (1988), 45 C.C.C. (3d) 97 (S.C.C.).
22   *F.P. Publications (Western) Ltd. v. R.* (1980), 51 C.C.C. (2d) 110 (Man.C.A.).
23   *Valente v. The Queen,* (1985), 23 C.C.C. (3d) 193 (S.C.C.).
24   [1996] 3 S.C.R. 525.

of the consequences for failing to appear. He did not appear for trial and was found guilty. The Supreme Court held that where the offence is regulatory and there is no possibility of imprisonment, and the procedure is fair (i.e., that there are sufficient safeguards in place to prevent injustice), it can be inferred that the accused has waived his right to a fair and public hearing and presumption of innocence.

(e) not to be denied reasonable bail without just cause

This right means that a person who is arrested has a right to pre-trial release on reasonable bail unless reasonable grounds exist for not releasing the person. This right flows from the presumption of innocence: Since a person is presumed innocent until proven guilty, it is unjustifiable to detain an accused until a finding is reached, unless there are reasonable grounds to detain the person. Pre-trial release is discussed in Chapter 5.

(f) except in the case of an offence under military law tried before a military tribunal, to the benefit of trial by jury where a maximum punishment for the offence is imprisonment for five years or a more severe punishment

The Supreme Court of Canada has said that s. 11(f) of the Charter confers a benefit on the accused that the accused may choose to waive. However, the waiver must be clear and unequivocal, and the accused must be aware of the consequences of the waiver.[25]

The extent of the jury's responsibility was demonstrated in *R. v. Krieger*.[26] The accused was charged with producing cannabis for his own use. He suffered from a debilitating illness for which cannabis was medically recognized as a palliative. He admitted the facts of the charge but pleaded not guilty and requested a trial by jury. The trial judge directed the jury to return a verdict of guilty, which the jury did. The Supreme Court of Canada held that even though there was overwhelming evidence of guilt, it was a violation of the accused's right to a jury trial for the judge to direct the jury to find the accused guilty. The Court ordered a new trial.

(g) not to be found guilty on account of any act or omission unless, at the time of the act or omission, it constituted an offence under Canadian or international law or was criminal according to the general principles of law recognized by the community of nations

This section sets out the right not to be convicted of a retroactive offence. This section prevents the government from creating a new offence and applying it to previous conduct.

(h) if finally acquitted of the offence, not to be tried for it again and, if finally found guilty and punished for the offence, not to be tried or punished for it again

This section states the protection against double jeopardy, or being tried twice for the same offence.

(i) if found guilty of the offence and if the punishment for the offence has been varied between the time of commission and the time of sentencing, to the benefit of the lesser punishment

This section gives a convicted person the right to the lesser punishment where the penalties have been changed between the time of commission of the offence and the time of sentencing.

---

25 *Turpin and Siddiqui v. The Queen* (1989), 48 C.C.C. (3d) 8 (S.C.C.); *Lee v. The Queen* (1989), 52 C.C.C. (3d) 289 (S.C.C.).
26 (2006), 213 C.C.C (3d) 303 (S.C.C.).

In *R. v. Dunn*,[27] the Supreme Court of Canada held that an accused is entitled to the lesser punishment where the penalty has been lessened between the time of the conviction and the hearing of the appeal.

Section 12 of the Charter deals with sentencing of a convicted person:

12. Everyone has the right not to be subjected to any cruel and unusual treatment or punishment.

The Supreme Court of Canada stated in *R. v. Smith*[28] that the standard used for determining whether a punishment is cruel and unusual is whether it is so excessive as to outrage standards of decency. The guidelines set by the Court are these:

- whether the punishment is necessary to accomplish a valid penal objective,
- whether the punishment is based on valid sentencing principles, and
- whether there are valid alternatives to the punishment.

These guidelines help courts determine whether the punishment is grossly disproportionate in relation to the offence.

In *Smith*, the Supreme Court held that s. 5 of the Narcotic Control Act (now the Controlled Drugs and Substances Act), which imposed a minimum seven-year term of imprisonment for the offence of importing narcotics, violated s. 12 of the Charter. The Court stated that a mandatory seven-year sentence was not justifiable when the quantity of drugs imported could be small and only for personal use.

Section 14 ensures that an accused or witness in any proceeding has a right to an interpreter if needed:

14. A party or witness in any proceeding who does not understand or speak the language in which the proceedings are conducted or who is deaf has the right to the assistance of an interpreter.

In *R. v. Tran*,[29] the Supreme Court of Canada laid out guidelines for when an interpreter needs to be appointed and the standard of interpretation required. The Court noted that the right to an interpreter ensures that the accused hears the case being made and allows the accused to make a full defence. It stated that an interpreter will be appointed by the court where it is clear that the accused does not speak or understand the language being used in court. The standard of interpretation is high but does not need to be perfect; but the translation must be continuous, precise, impartial, competent, and contemporaneous. Finally, the interpretation must be of the proceedings themselves where the accused has a vital interest, not in respect of some collateral matter concerning only administrative or logistic issues.

F. APPEALS

A distinction between appeal courts and trial courts is that appeal courts often have more than one judge hearing the case. The Supreme Court of Canada, for example, usually has nine justices. If the judges do not agree on a decision in a case, they will vote and the majority decision will be the holding in the case. Usually one judge will be asked to write the decision which states the views of the majority while another judge may write a dissenting (or minority) opinion.

---

27   (1995), 95 C.C.C. (3d) 289 (S.C.C.).
28   (1987), 34 C.C.C. (3d) 97 (S.C.C.).
29   (1994), 92 C.C.C. (3d) 218 (S.C.C.).

Sometimes, there may be several written opinions in a complicated case; however, the opinion supported by a majority of the judges is the one that decides the issue in the case.

The procedure for appealing a court decision, where an appeal is possible, depends on a number of factors. The most important factor is whether the offence is indictable or is a summary conviction offence. Part XXI of the Code sets out the procedure for appealing indictable offences; Part XXVII includes the procedure for appealing summary conviction offences. The following is a general discussion of the appeal procedures that apply to both types of offences.

In every trial, there are two main issues that must be determined: the facts of the case, and the law that applies to those facts. Grounds for appeal are based on questions of fact, questions of law, or questions of mixed fact and law. For example, Roberta is charged with murdering Jean by shooting her. Whether Roberta was the person who aimed and fired the gun at Jean is a question of fact. Once the facts of the case are decided, whether the offence of murder was committed is a question of law. That is, assuming that Roberta shot Jean, does this conduct constitute the offence of murder as defined by the Code? When a judge and jury try an accused, the jury's function is to determine the facts of the case, and the judge's function is to determine what law applies to the facts. If the trial is before a judge alone, he or she performs both of these functions (i.e., the judge acts as both the **trier of fact** and the **trier of law**).

Sometimes the accused must obtain permission to appeal. For example, s. 675 of the Code provides that a person convicted of an indictable offence has a right to appeal a question of law but must receive permission to appeal a question of fact or mixed fact and law. The accused may be able to appeal either the conviction or the sentence; that is, the appeal can be based on the decision of the court finding the accused guilty, or only on the punishment imposed by the court. Assume that Owen is convicted of assault under s. 266 (the least serious type of assault) and sentenced to six years' imprisonment. Owen can appeal the sentence on a question of law because s. 266 of the Code provides that the maximum term of imprisonment for this type of assault is five years.

The prosecutor can appeal a dismissal of the information, the **acquittal** of the accused, or the sentence ordered by the court.

An appeal hearing is not a re-trial. Usually an appeal is on "the record" of what happened at the trial. Only rarely can new evidence be submitted, and no witnesses testify. The appeal court will look at a transcript from the trial and hear the arguments of the defence and the prosecution lawyers. The appeal court is looking for trial court errors. If the appeal court agrees that the trial court decision was wrong, it may allow the appeal. If the appeal court finds that the trial court decision was proper, it dismisses the appeal. Where the appeal is allowed, the appeal court may order a new trial, direct an acquittal, enter a verdict of guilty (except where there has been a jury trial), or change the sentence. Sometimes an appeal court decision is appealed to a higher court. The final and highest court of appeal in Canada is the Supreme Court of Canada. In most cases, a person convicted of an indictable offence must have the Supreme Court's permission to appeal a lower court decision. The Court will give permission if it believes that the case concerns an issue of public importance. The Court often gives permission to appeal in cases that deal with interpretations of the Charter. There is an automatic right to appeal in some cases; for example, the Court will hear an appeal if an acquittal has been set aside by a provincial court of appeal where one of the judges dissents on a question of law.

06 G. HIERARCHY OF PERSONS AND COURTS WITH JURISDICTION OVER CRIMINAL MATTERS

One way of picturing the criminal court system is to imagine a staircase. At the top of the stairs is the Supreme Court of Canada, which only hears appeals. At the bottom of the stairs are the justices of the peace. Trial courts occupy the lower stairs. Appeal courts occupy the upper stairs; they only review cases appealed from trial courts. At the middle of the staircase are those courts in which both trials are held and appeals are heard. Generally, as offences become more serious or as they are appealed, they move up the stairs.

Below are some of the main functions of the various levels of judicial authority in criminal matters (see Table 2-1). Each province/territory is responsible for the administration of criminal law within its borders, and also responsible that provincial/territorial variations are common.[30]

TABLE 2-1 | Main Functions of Judicial Authority

Supreme Court of Canada
DUTIES
• Hears appeals from provincial courts of appeal

Courts of Appeal
DUTIES
• The province's highest appeal court
• Hears appeals from the trial court and lower-level appeal court

Supreme or Superior Court
DUTIES
• The province's highest-level trial court
• Trials of the most serious indictable offences are held here, with or without a jury
• Hears some appeals involving summary conviction offences

Provincial or Territorial Court
DUTIES
• Functions of a justice of the peace may be performed here
• All but the most serious indictable offences may be tried here

Justice of the Peace
DUTIES
• Receives informations
• Issues summonses and warrants for search and arrest
• Holds bail and preliminary hearings
• In some jurisdictions, may try summary conviction offences

---

30   See the federal Department of Justice website (**justice.gc.ca**) for a thorough discussion of Canada's court system.

Questions for Review and Discussion

1. Discuss the differences between civil wrongs and criminal wrongs.

2. Make a chart showing how federal and provincial governments share responsibilities for criminal law in Canada.

3. What is the main source of criminal law in Canada? What is the difference between a provincial offence and a criminal offence?

4. **a.** Discuss some of the differences between indictable offences and summary conviction offences.
   b. What is a hybrid offence?

5. What are some of the main differences between the trial of a summary conviction offence and an indictable offence?

6. What is the purpose of a preliminary inquiry? In what situations are preliminary hearings held?

7. Discuss whether plea bargaining should be allowed. Should there be rules regulating the process of plea bargaining?

8. What is the difference between a question of fact and a question of law? Make up some examples of each.

9. What is the difference between the burden of proof in a civil trial and the burden of proof in a criminal trial? Why are the burdens different?

10. Why is it important that trials be held in public? When do you think the public should be excluded?

11. What rights should victims of crime have? Research federal and provincial laws which give victims certain rights. Are these sufficient? Should we be concerned about giving victims too many rights?

12. **a.** What did the case of *R. v. Askov* decide?
    b. What was the immediate effect of this decision on the court system?

c. Do you agree or disagree with this statement of the Supreme Court in *Askov*: "Justice so delayed is an affront to the individual, to the community, and to the very administration of justice." (page 23) Can you think of specific harms that an accused might suffer as a consequence of a long delay?

13. **a.** What does the presumption of innocence mean?
    b. What other Charter rights are consistent with it?

14. **a.** What are reverse onus clauses?
    b. What is the difference between a reverse onus clause and a mandatory presumption?
    c. How have courts dealt with reverse onus clauses and mandatory presumptions?

15. This chapter defines crime as a wrong against society. What is considered a wrong may change over time as community values change (e.g., at one time, a husband could not be charged with sexually assaulting his wife). Also, in a diverse society such as Canada, what is considered a wrong may differ among the various ethnic and cultural groups in Canada. Drug laws, abortion, pornography, and hate crimes are a few current topics of debate concerning what should be a crime in Canada. How should we, as a society, deal with different values in our society? How do we determine community values? These are difficult questions. For a research project, choose a controversial topic concerning an area of criminal law. Write a report giving the pros and cons of making the activity legal or illegal, or organize a debate on the topic.

16. Unlike Canada, in the United States, although there are some federal crimes, criminal law is within the jurisdiction of the states, not the federal government. Thus, what is a crime depends on state law, and what is a crime in one state may not be a crime in another. What are the advantages and disadvantages of the Canadian system in which the federal government has the sole authority over what are criminal offences?

17. As stated in this chapter, the government attempts to ensure public safety through the police, the courts, and the correctional system. Discuss other ways that the government attempts to prevent crime. See the website of the Department of Public Safety, Government of Canada: **publicsafety.gc.ca**. Click on "Crime Prevention" to learn about the work of the National Crime Prevention Centre (NCPC).

CHAPTER 3

General Principles for Determining Criminal Liability

Key points explained in this chapter are

LO1 how conduct, circumstances, and consequences relate to the *actus reus* of a crime;

LO2 the rules for determining causation;

LO3 the different types of *mens rea*;

LO4 the impact of the Charter on the requirements for *mens rea*;

LO5 the principle of concurrence between the *actus reus* and *mens rea* of an offence;

LO6 liability requirements for regulatory offences;

LO7 the rules for determining who can be charged when a crime is committed; and

LO8 criminal liability when a crime is not completed.

This chapter examines the basic elements of a criminal offence, regulatory offences, parties to an offence, and attempts to commit an offence.

LO1 A. THE PHYSICAL ELEMENT OF A CRIME: *ACTUS REUS*

Actus reus is a Latin term that loosely translates as "guilty act" or "wrongful act." Although the term frequently refers to prohibited acts, it is more accurate to say that the *actus reus* is the physical element of a crime and includes all the parts of the crime other than the ***mens rea***, which is the state of mind of the accused. In general, the *actus reus* of a crime consists of a certain type of conduct, the circumstances surrounding the conduct, and a consequence of that conduct.

In order to determine the *actus reus* of a particular offence, it is necessary to consider the definition of the offence. For example, s. 265 defines one way of committing assault:

265. (1) A person commits an assault when

> **(a) without the consent of another person, he applies force intentionally to that other person, directly or indirectly . . .**

In this offence, the *actus reus* consists of (a) applying force to another person, (b) without the other person's consent. These parts of the crime do not refer to what was going on in the mind of the accused; rather, they refer to a physical occurrence (applying force) and a circumstance (without consent). The mental element, or *mens rea*, of the offence consists of the intention to apply force, indicated by the word "intentionally."

Below, these components of the *actus reus* are more closely examined: conduct, circumstances, consequences, and, where there are consequences, causation—whether the conduct of the accused caused the consequences.

1. Conduct

The conduct involved in a crime may be an act, an omission, or a state of being.

a. Act

Most crimes require that some act be committed. In criminal law, an act is a voluntary movement. For example, when Albert throws a punch at Bruce, Albert voluntarily moves his arm. In the same way, when Carol shoots a gun, she is committing an act if she pulls the trigger voluntarily.

b. Omission

An omission is the failure to act when there is a legal duty to act. Section 215(1)(a) refers to such a duty:

> **215. (1) Every one is under a legal duty**
>
> **(a) as a parent, foster parent, guardian or head of a family, to provide necessaries of life for a child under the age of sixteen years . . .**

In brief, a parent has a legal duty to provide food, shelter, and other necessaries for his or her children. If a parent omits or fails to perform this duty, without a reasonable excuse, then he or she has committed an offence. This section is clearly not prohibiting an act; rather, it is creating a duty to act, and a person who omits or fails to perform this duty has committed an offence, unless there is a reasonable excuse for failing to act.

An omission to carry out a legal duty can also result in being criminally liable for an offence committed by another person. Under s. 21(1)(b), a person who is under a legal duty to act and fails to do so can be considered a party to an offence if the failure to act is for the purpose of aiding another person to commit the offence. This section is discussed in this chapter under "Parties to an Offence."

Chapter 9 discusses the duty to provide necessaries of life, as well as other duties and related offences, including the duty of persons undertaking dangerous acts, the duty to complete an act if the failure to do so may be dangerous to life, and the offence of child abandonment by a person who is under a legal duty to care for the child. Chapters 5 and 6 discuss the offence of failing to assist a police officer to make an arrest or to keep the peace.

c. State of Being

Some offences require neither an act nor an omission. Instead, they simply require a state of being or "status." For example, s. 354 prohibits a person from "having in his possession" anything that was obtained by crime:

> **354. (1) Every one commits an offence who has in his possession any property or thing . . . knowing that . . . [it] was obtained by . . .**
>
> **(a) the commission in Canada of an offence punishable by indictment . . .**

For example, if Bill is wearing a stolen watch, then he has it in his possession—simply having it is enough. There need not be some act or omission for the *actus reus* of this offence.

The Criminal Code contains many offences in which the *actus reus* is a state of being. The *actus reus* of "having possession" or "being in possession" in various offences is discussed in other parts of the book. Chapter 13 provides a detailed discussion of the legal meaning of possession, the types of possession, and the offences of possession of breaking-in instruments and possession of property obtained by crime. Additional discussion of possession is in Chapter 6—the offence of possession of a weapon for a purpose dangerous to the public peace; Chapter 7—the meaning of possession in the context of pornographic computer files; and Appendix B—offences involving possession of drugs under the Controlled Drugs and Substances Act.

Other "state of being" offences require being in a place. Section 201, which includes the offence of "being found in" a common bawdy-house, is discussed in detail under "Common Bawdy-houses" in Chapter 7. In addition, Chapter 13 discusses the offence of being unlawfully in a dwelling-house, including whether it is a violation of the Charter to presume that being in the dwelling-house is, in the absence of evidence to the contrary, proof of intent to commit an indictable offence.

Another "state of being" type of *actus reus* is "having care or control" of a motor vehicle, which Chapter 10 discusses in the context of the offences of having care or control of a motor vehicle while impaired and failing to stop a vehicle when involved in an accident.

d. Voluntary Movement

It is a general principle of criminal law that a person's act or omission must be voluntary if he or she is to be held responsible for it. An act was defined above as a voluntary movement. If a movement is involuntary, then under the criminal law, there is no act, and, therefore, no criminal responsibility. Examples of involuntary movements are the bodily movements of a person undergoing an epileptic seizure, and actions committed while sleepwalking. The general point is this: If a person has no control over his or her physical actions, then he or she will not be held criminally responsible.

If the conduct that forms part of the *actus reus* of a crime is not voluntary, then the accused can use the defence of automatism. Automatism and other defences are discussed in Chapter 4.

e. Innocent Agent

A person will not escape criminal responsibility by using the innocent actions of someone else to achieve an unlawful purpose. For example, Allen might try to sell drugs to Brigit by sending his 12-year-old son to deliver the package containing the drugs and to collect the payment. If the son had no idea that he was delivering drugs, he would be innocent of any wrongdoing. However, Allen would be guilty of trafficking even though he was not involved in the actual sale. Under the criminal law, the acts of Allen's son, in this situation, are considered to be the acts of Allen; thus, Allen is held responsible for the *actus reus* of the crime.

2. Circumstances

Usually, conduct is not criminal unless it is committed in certain circumstances that form part of the *actus reus* of a crime. For example, s. 177, trespassing at night includes many circumstances:

> **177. Every one who, without lawful excuse . . . loiters or prowls at night upon the property of another person near a dwelling-house situated on that property is guilty of an offence . . .**

The circumstances that form part of the *actus reus* are these: (a) the loitering or prowling must occur at night; (b) it must occur on another person's property; (c) it must occur near a dwelling-house; (d) the house must be situated on that property; and (e) the loitering must be without lawful excuse. All of these circumstances must be present for the offence to be committed. For example, if the loitering or prowling occurs during the day, or if there is no dwelling-house on the property, then there is no *actus reus*, and thus no offence under s. 177.

Another example is s. 280, abduction:

> **280. (1) Every one who, without lawful authority, takes . . . an unmarried person under the age of sixteen years out of the possession of and against the will of the parent or guardian of that person . . . is guilty of an indictable offence . . .**

The circumstances that must be present for this offence to be committed are these: (a) The taker must not have lawful authority (an example of a taker with lawful authority might be a social worker acting under a court order); (b) the taken person must be unmarried; (c) he or she must be under the age of 16; (d) at the time of the taking, the taken person must have been in the possession of his or her parent or guardian; and (e) the taking must have been against the will of the parent or guardian of the person. If any one of these circumstances is not present, the *actus reus* is not complete, and thus the offence has not been committed.

This offence and other abduction offences are discussed in Chapter 11. Additional examples of offences that involve circumstances as part of the *actus reus* include sexual exploitation, pornography, and soliciting (Chapter 7); assault and sexual assault (Chapter 11); and identity theft (Chapter 12).

3. Consequences

Some crimes require a consequence as part of the *actus reus*. The consequence in a crime is the result of an act or an omission. For example, the consequence or result in homicide is the death of a human being:

> **222. (1) A person commits homicide when, directly or indirectly, by any means, he causes the death of a human being.**

Another example is mischief, in which the "consequence" part of the offence is damage to property:

> **430. (1) Every one commits mischief who wilfully**
>
> **(a) destroys or damages property . . .**

In these examples, the Code section does not mention any particular conduct that must cause the consequence to occur. In other words, a person may cause the death of a human being by shooting or stabbing the person, by planting a bomb in the person's car, or by some other act. Regardless of which act is done, a homicide has been committed if the act caused a person to die. Similarly, a person commits mischief if he or she causes damage to property—for example, by throwing rocks through the windows of a house, by breaking down its front door, or by some other destructive act.

The point is that the definitions of many crimes mention a consequence without mentioning any particular act or omission. In most situations, it is not necessary to distinguish between conduct and consequence. For example, it is usually precise enough to say that Joan killed Maria or that Joan damaged Maria's property. However, the distinction is very helpful when it comes to understanding the concepts of causation, intention, and recklessness, which are discussed later in this chapter.

Another point about consequences is that more serious offences are sometimes distinguished from less serious offences by the consequences of the act or omission. For example, criminal negligence causing bodily harm is punishable by a maximum of ten years' imprisonment, while criminal negligence causing death is punishable by a maximum of life imprisonment.

Offences that require a consequence are discussed in Part Two of the book: homicide (Chapter 8); criminal negligence (Chapter 9); and mischief (Chapter 13). Other examples of offences that include consequences are the following: terrorism (Chapter 6); dangerous driving causing bodily harm (Chapter 10); and assault and sexual assault (Chapter 11). Examples of offences that do not require a consequence are perjury (Chapter 6) and possession offences (Chapter 13).

L02 ## 4. Causation

When the *actus reus* of a crime includes certain consequences, the *actus reus* is established only if the conduct of the accused caused the consequences to occur. The courts have distinguished two types of causation: factual and legal. For example, in a homicide case, factual causation refers to how the victim came to die—the physical way death was caused and the accused's contribution to that death. Courts may use the "but for" rule to determine factual causation; that is, but for the accused's conduct, the death would not have occurred.

Once factual causation is established, legal causation is determined. Legal causation has to do with whether the accused is responsible in law for the consequences.

In *R. v. Horton*,[1] the accused was charged with impaired driving causing death. He was acquitted of the charge but found guilty of impaired driving. The court held that although he was legally impaired, his driving was normal at the time of the accident. The accident occurred because the victim, a pedestrian, had unexpectedly stepped off the curb. Thus, there was factual causation but not legal causation.

Most of the law of causation has been developed by judges, that is, as part of the common law. A series of cases considered the common law rule of causation, that the accused's act must be at least a contributing cause of death outside the *de minimis* (trivial) range. The Supreme Court applied this rule in *R. v. Smithers*,[2] a case which involved two teenage hockey players. Smithers and another boy argued after a hockey game in which Smithers had been subjected to racial taunts. The argument escalated, with Smithers kicking the victim in the chest. The victim vomited and died from suffocation. It was determined that the victim had a rare physical condition that caused him to aspirate his vomit, leading to suffocation. The Supreme Court of Canada held Smithers liable for manslaughter for causing the death, even though the kick would not ordinarily have led to the death of a person. The Court held that the acts of Smithers were a contributing cause outside the *de minimis* range. The Court also recognized that the "thin skull" rule applies in criminal cases; that is, the perpetrator of the crime takes the victim as he or she is. Even if the consequences of the wrongful conduct are greater than expected because of the victim's condition (e.g., a thin skull), the perpetrator is still responsible for the consequences.

The Ontario Court of Appeal applied the *de minimis* test in *R. v. Cribben*.[3] The accused was involved in a robbery. He had punched the deceased hard in the face and kicked him. The co-accused then began to punch and kick the deceased while beating him with a beer bottle. The deceased was left by the side of the road, where he drowned in his own blood. The court

---

1   (2003), 20 C.R. (6th) 161 (Sask.Q.B.).
2   [1978] 1 S.C.R. 506.
3   (1994), 89 C.C.C. (3d) 67 (Ont.C.A.).

held that it did not matter whether it was the co-accused's acts or the accused's acts that caused the death. The judge had correctly instructed the jury that the accused could be found guilty of manslaughter if the assault by the accused contributed outside the *de minimis* range to the death of the victim.

The Supreme Court of Canada held that where the charge is first-degree murder under s. 231(5) (where death is caused in the commission of certain offences, including sexual assault), a higher standard of participation is required for a finding of guilt. In *R. v. Harbottle*,[4] the Crown had to show (a) that the act or series of acts was a substantial and integral cause of death, and (b) that there was no intervening act of another person that resulted in the accused's act no longer being a substantial cause of death. The Court added that, in most cases, the accused must play a very active role in the killing, and that the underlying offence must be part of the same transaction as the murder. In this case, the accused was a party to the brutal sexual assault of a young girl. He had held her down while another man strangled her, causing her death. The Court found that the accused's actions were a substantial and integral cause of the victim's death, and dismissed his appeal of a conviction for first-degree murder.

The Supreme Court in *Harbottle* did not overrule the *de minimis* test in *Smithers*; rather, it said that it is a proper test in a manslaughter charge. However, where the charge is first-degree murder under s. 231(5), a "substantial and high degree of blameworthiness" is required to reflect the seriousness of the crime and severity of the penalty.[5] In other words, there must be an increased degree of participation required before an accused can be convicted of first-degree murder.

The Supreme Court of Canada's decision in *R. v. Nette*,[6] further clarified the common law rule. A 95-year-old widow, who was living alone, was robbed and left "hog-tied" with a garment around her neck and over her head. The medical evidence was that she died from asphyxiation within 24 to 48 hours of the robbery. It also showed that her age, asthma, and heart condition as well as the position she was left in all contributed to her death. The accused was convicted of second-degree murder. The grounds for appeal concerned the proper test of causation for second-degree murder and how that test should be explained to the jury. The Court stated that the standard for causation for all homicide cases, including second-degree murder, is the standard expressed in *Smithers*. The terminology of "substantial cause" in *Harbottle* indicates the increased degree of participation in the killing required to raise the accused's culpability to first-degree murder under s. 231(5).[7]

In other words, only after the accused has been found guilty using the test in *Smithers* does the jury then consider the substantial cause test, which would raise the offence from manslaughter or second-degree murder to first-degree murder. On the issue of instructions to the jury, the court suggested that the test should be expressed in positive terms such as "significant contributing cause" rather than "not a trivial cause or outside *de minimis*." The Court stated that Latin phrases or tests formulated in the negative are not a useful way to communicate the test to a jury.[8] In addition, the Court suggested that because of the similar wording of s. 231(6) (causing death while committing the offence of criminal harassment), the substantial cause test also applies to this section.

---

4   (1993), 84 C.C.C. (3d) 1 (S.C.C.).
5   Ibid. at 13.
6   (2001), 158 C.C.C. (3d) 486 (S.C.C.).
7   Ibid. at para 65.
8   Ibid. at para 71.

As these cases show, to establish causation, the accused's act does not need to be the sole cause of death; there may be concurrent causes of death. As long as the accused's act is a significant contributing cause of death, liability is established.

Another area where problems establishing causation may arise is when intervening events occur. The question is whether the intervening act has broken the chain of causation that connects the acts of the accused to the consequences. Courts have used two strategies when determining liability where there is an intervening act. The first is to ask whether the intervening act was foreseeable by the initial actor. If the answer is yes, then courts have held that the chain of causation is not broken and the initial actor is still liable. The second strategy is to ask whether the intervening act is independent of the initial act. If it is, then it can be argued that the initial actor is not responsible for the consequence.

The issue of when an intervening act breaks the chain of causation was considered by the Supreme Court of Canada in *R. v. Maybin*,[9] in which two brothers were charged with manslaughter. The Maybin brothers were in a busy bar playing pool. The victim touched a pool ball on the table, upsetting the Maybins, who began punching the victim. The victim lost consciousness and collapsed on the table while a large bar fight began. Within seconds, a bouncer appeared and hit the victim in the head after an onlooker indicated that the victim had started the fight. The victim later died in hospital from a brain haemorrhage. The Maybins and the bouncer were charged with manslaughter. Medical evidence was inconclusive as to which blows caused the death. The trial judge acquitted all three on the grounds that factual causation could not be established beyond a reasonable doubt because medical evidence could not determine whether the Maybins' blows or the bouncer's punch was the sole or a significant contributing cause of death. The appeal court overturned the Maybins' acquittals and ordered a new trial; it dismissed the Crown's appeal of the bouncer's acquittal.

On the Maybins' appeal to the Supreme Court of Canada, the issues were these:

1. Did the trial judge err in failing to address whether the Maybins' assaults were, in fact, a cause of death?
2. Could the trial judge have found that the Maybins' assaults remained a significant contributing cause of death despite the intervening act of the bouncer because (a) the intervening act was reasonably foreseeable; or (b) the intervening act was not an intentional, independent act?

On the first issue, the Court found that the Maybins' actions were a factual cause of the victim's death. The Court concluded that, even if the appellants' actions were not the direct and immediate cause, "but for" their actions the victim would not have died. Following *Nette* and *Smithers*, the Court stated that "factual causation is not limited to the direct and immediate cause, nor is it limited to the most significant cause." The Maybins' assaults were either the direct medical cause of death or they rendered the victim vulnerable to the bouncer's assault. Given the uncertainty of the medical evidence, the trial judge had a reasonable doubt about whether the bouncer's blow contributed to the death. As a result, he could not find that the bouncer's actions were a factual cause of death.

On the second question, the Court reaffirmed the rule in *Smithers* and *Nette*, that the legal causation test is whether the actions of the accused were a significant contributing cause of death. Whether the intervening act was reasonably foreseeable or not, and whether the intervening act was or was not an independent act, are analytical tools to determine whether the chain of legal causation has been broken. They do not determine whether the chain has been broken.

---

9   (2012), S.C.C. 24.

The Court went on to state that an intervening act that is reasonably foreseeable will usually not break the chain of causation. The question is the scope of foreseeability. Should the Maybins have foreseen the act of the bouncer or a risk of further bodily harm from anyone? The Court held that the specific harm need not be foreseeable. It is the general nature of the intervening acts and the risk of harm that need to be reasonably foreseeable. The Court found that it was reasonably foreseeable that, in the context of an escalating bar fight, further non-trivial harm would be caused by the interventions of other bar staff or patrons. It was not necessary to foresee that the bouncer would assault the victim, only that someone would assault the victim.

The Court then considered whether the bouncer's intervening act was independent of the actions of the Maybins and severed the causal connection. The Court stated that if the intervening act is a direct response or is directly linked to the accused's actions and does not by its nature overwhelm the original actions, then it is not independent and the accused cannot be said to be morally innocent. The bouncer acted in almost immediate reaction to what the Maybins did. Therefore, it was open to the trial judge to find that the assault by the bouncer was not independent of the Maybins' assaults and that the Maybins' actions remained a significant contributing cause of death. The Court dismissed the appeal.

In addition to court decisions regarding causation, there are specific rules regarding causation in cases of homicide in the Criminal Code. Only if a case does not fall within these rules does a court refer to the common law decisions of judges. These rules are discussed in Chapter 8.

B. THE MENTAL ELEMENT OF A CRIME: *MENS REA*

For a crime to occur, the *actus reus* must be accompanied by *mens rea*, that is, a certain guilty state of mind. The *mens rea* of a crime is the element that makes the crime "blameworthy" or morally wrong. The courts recognize several types of *mens rea*: intention, knowledge, recklessness, wilful blindness, and penal negligence.

1. Intention

In some crimes, it must be shown that the accused person intended or "meant to" cause a certain wrongful consequence. For example, if Alfred hits Bryce without Bryce's consent, then he is guilty of assault—but only if he intended to hit Bryce. If Alfred *accidentally* hits Bryce—for example, while practising his baseball swing—then he did not act intentionally, so no assault was committed.

Many Code sections clearly require intention by using such words as "intentionally," "wilfully," or "means to." For example, under s. 129 a person commits an offence who

> (a) **resists or wilfully obstructs a public officer or peace officer in the execution of his duty or any person lawfully acting in aid of such an officer** . . .

In this offence, a person is guilty only if he or she *intends* or *means* to wrongfully obstruct or interfere with the officer.

It may be difficult to prove what was in a person's mind, that is, whether the person intended a certain consequence. In a Supreme Court of Canada case, it was stated that where intent is required, it is enough to prove that the accused foresaw the consequence as a "substantial certainty."[10]

---

10   *R. v. Chartrand* (1994), 91 C.C.C. (3d) 396 (S.C.C.).

a. Specific Intent

Some offences require a special or ulterior intent. These are called **specific intent offences**. In general, such offences are indicated by the words "with intent" or similar words (e.g., "for the purpose of"). For example, under s. 348 a person commits an offence who

> (a) **breaks and enters a place with intent to commit an indictable offence therein** . . .

In this offence, it must be shown not only that the accused intended to break and enter but also that he or she did so with the specific intent to commit an indictable offence, such as theft. If, for example, it is shown that the person broke into a place in order to obtain shelter from a storm, then the offence has not been committed. On the other hand, it is not necessary to show that the person actually committed an indictable offence. It is enough to show that the person broke and entered with the intent to commit an indictable offence.

Another example of a specific intent offence is a form of robbery found in s. 343(c):

> **343. Every one commits robbery who** . . .

> (c) **assaults any person with intent to steal from him** . . .

To commit this crime, a person must both assault someone and do the assaulting with the intent to steal from the victim. If it is shown that Marla assaulted Blake, but it is not shown that the assault was done with the specific intent to steal, then Marla is guilty of assault, but not robbery. The assault here is a **lesser included offence**, that is, an offence contained within the major offence. A lesser-included offence has some, but not all, of the elements of the major offence.[11]

These specific intent offences along with relevant case law are discussed in Part Two of the book: robbery (Chapter 12) and break and enter with intent (Chapter 13). Other examples of specific intent offences that are discussed in Part Two include possessing a weapon for a purpose dangerous to the public, under Possession Offences (Chapter 6); murder (Chapter 8); and theft (Chapter 12).

Offences, such as assault, that do not require a specific intent are called **general intent offences**. The Supreme Court of Canada explains the distinction between a general intent offence and a specific intent offence in the following way:

> In considering the question of mens rea, a distinction is to be drawn between "intention" as applied to acts done to achieve an immediate end on the one hand and acts done with the specific and ulterior motive and intention of furthering or achieving an illegal object on the other hand. Illegal acts of the former kind are done intentionally in the sense that they are not done by accident or through honest mistakes, but acts of the latter kind are the product of preconception and are deliberate steps taken toward an illegal goal. The former acts may be purely physical products of momentary passion, whereas the latter involve the mental process of forming a specific intent.[12]

A significant difference between specific intent offences and general intent offences is the availability of the defence of intoxication. Generally speaking, intoxication is a defence to specific intent crimes but not to some general intent crimes. The defence of intoxication is discussed in Chapter 4.

---

11   Section 662 of the Code allows an accused to be convicted of an included offence if it is proved and the major offence is not proved.
12   *R. v. George* (1960), 128 C.C.C. 289 (S.C.C.) at 306.

b. Intention and Motive

Intention is different from motive. Motive refers to some reason for committing the crime; it is what explains why the person acted as he or she did. In general, it is not part of the *mens rea* of a crime. A person may commit a crime for a good motive and still be found guilty. For example, in *R. v. Latimer*,[13] a father killed his severely disabled young daughter for the motive of ending what he saw as her intolerable suffering. His motive did not prevent him from being found guilty of second-degree murder.

The important point is that the motive is not usually part of the actual crime. This means that if the *actus reus* and the *mens rea* of a crime are present, the accused is criminally liable, regardless of the motive. One exception may be in the crimes of terrorism where a political or religious motive is an element of the crime.[14] The Ontario Court of Appeal has held that it does not offend the Charter for motive to be an element of the offence.[15]

Motive can be relevant in at least two ways. First, the prosecution can offer a motive as evidence of the intentions of the accused; for example, if Betty stood to inherit $100,000 on Greta's death, then clearly Betty had a motive for killing Greta.

Second, motive can be relevant to sentencing. An accused who has been found guilty of a crime may receive a lighter sentence from the judge if he or she acted with a good motive rather than a bad one. For example, a person who, in an emergency, steals a car to get his sick child to the hospital might receive a lesser sentence than a person who steals a car to resell it.

The *Latimer* case is discussed in more detail in Chapter 4. Another case that highlights the difference between intention and motive is *R. v. Theroux*[16] (Chapter 12).

c. Intention and Voluntariness

It is sometimes difficult to distinguish the intention of the *mens rea* from the voluntary conduct of the *actus reus*. Although *mens rea* is referred to as the mental element of the crime, strictly speaking, the *actus reus* also has a mental element in that the act must be voluntary. In general, voluntariness refers to control over bodily movements, whereas intention refers to the state of mind regarding the consequences or results of those bodily movements. For example, a person may voluntarily shoot a gun but the person may not be intending to kill anyone. The act of shooting is under the person's control and is, therefore, voluntary. But if the person did not intend human death or serious bodily harm as a consequence of the act, then the person did not have the *mens rea* or criminal intent for the offence of murder. As the Supreme Court said, "*Mens rea* . . . refers to the guilty mind, the wrongful intention of the accused. Its function in criminal law is to prevent the conviction of the morally innocent—those who do not understand or intend the consequences of their acts."[16a]

---

13 [2001] 1S.C.R.3. This case is discussed in Chapter 4, Defences Under Necessity
14 See s. 83.01(1)(b)(i)(A) for a definition of terrorist activity.
15 *R. v. Khawaja* (2010), 103 O.R. (3d) 321.
16 (1993), 79 C.C.C. (3d) 449 (S.C.C.).
16a Ibid.

d. Transferred Intent

Under the common law, if a person intends to harm one person and accidentally harms another, the intention or *mens rea* is transferred to the victim. So, for example, Alicia intentionally throws a punch at Phil, misses, and hits Alan instead. She can be charged with assault. The *mens rea* is transferred to the victim who was the subject of the *actus reus*.

Section 229(b) codifies the doctrine of transferred intent with regard to murder. This section is discussed in Chapter 8.

2. Knowledge

In many crimes, it is necessary that the accused have knowledge or awareness of certain circumstances. This is sometimes indicated by the word "knowing" or "knowingly" in the definition of the crime. For example, s. 131 states:

> **131. (1) every one commits perjury who, with intent to mislead, makes before a person who is authorized by law to permit it to be made before him, a false statement under oath . . . knowing that the statement is false.**

If a person gives false evidence at a trial but does not realize that the evidence is false, then the crime of perjury has not been committed. Without knowledge of this circumstance, there is no *mens rea*, and thus no offence is committed.

The general rule is that the word "knowingly" in the definition of an offence applies to all the elements of the *actus reus*. Even when "knowing" or "knowingly" is absent from the definition of the offence, knowledge of relevant circumstances is usually required. For example, in *R. v. McLeod*,[17] the accused was charged with assaulting a police officer, contrary to what is now s. 270(1)(a):

> **270. (1) Every one commits an offence who**
>
> > **(a) assaults a public officer or peace officer engaged in the execution of his duty or a person acting in aid of such an officer . . .**

The accused was a bystander watching a fight between two youths. When a police officer, dressed in plain clothes, tried to stop the fight, the accused, not knowing that he was a police officer, pushed the officer and told him to mind his own business. The court held that the accused was not guilty because he lacked the necessary knowledge to commit the offence. Without the knowledge that the person interfering was a police officer, the accused had no *mens rea*.

3. Recklessness

Recklessness is a third type of *mens rea*. In general, a person is reckless when he or she is extremely or grossly careless. Although the law has not always been clear on this point, it is now settled that recklessness requires **subjective foresight** of harm; that is, that the accused actually foresaw the potential harmful consequence of his or her actions. The Supreme Court of Canada rejected **objective foresight** (i.e., that a reasonable person would have foreseen the harm) and has come down in favour of a subjective standard for recklessness. In *Sansregret v. The Queen*, the Court stated that "recklessness, to form part of the criminal *mens rea*, must have an element of the subjective. It is found in the attitude of one who, aware

---

17   (1954), 111 C.C.C. 106 (B.C.C.A.).

that there is a danger that his conduct could bring about the result prohibited by the criminal law, nevertheless persists, despite the risk."[18]

In other words, a person is reckless when he or she foresees the possibility of a harmful consequence and then takes the risk that the harm will not result. The person must be aware of the danger involved. A person who does not have this subjective awareness or foresight is not reckless. For example, Alice wants to practise her target shooting, so she attaches a target to a tree in a public park. She sees that the tree is in front of a children's play area in which children are playing. She sees the danger but decides to take the risk that she will not harm anyone. Alice's first shot misses the target and wounds one of the children. Alice has clearly been reckless because she foresaw the possibility of injury even though she had no intention of causing injury. She did not intend the harmful consequence, but she foresaw the possibility of it and took the risk.

Under the definition of recklessness, the risk that is taken must be unjustifiable. Some risks are justifiable. For example, the doctor who performs heart surgery foresees the possibility of causing the death of the patient, but the doctor is not being reckless by operating. The risk is reasonable, or justifiable. On the other hand, in the target-shooting example, it is neither reasonable nor justifiable for Alice to take the risk.

In general, where an offence does not specify the type of *mens rea* required, recklessness will be sufficient. Also, where the *mens rea* of the offence is knowledge of certain circumstances, courts have held that recklessness can be sufficient. For example, for the offence of possession of stolen property, a person must have knowledge that the property was obtained through the commission of a crime. Recklessness as to whether the property was obtained through the commission of an offence can satisfy the *mens rea* requirement.

Some Code sections clearly require recklessness by using the words "reckless" or "recklessly." An example is one type of arson:

> **434.1 Every person who intentionally or recklessly causes damage by fire or explosion to property that is owned, in whole or part, by that person is guilty of an indictable offence . . . where the fire or explosion seriously threatens the health, safety or property of another person.**

Arson and other examples of offences for which recklessness is a sufficient *mens rea* are discussed along with relevant case law in Part Two of the book: murder (Chapter 8), criminal harassment (Chapter 11), and arson (Chapter 13).

4. Wilful Blindness

A concept that is closely related to recklessness is **wilful blindness**. The Supreme Court in *Sansregret* defined wilful blindness as "where a person who has become aware of the need for some inquiry declines to make the inquiry because he does not wish to know the truth. He would prefer to remain ignorant."[19]

Wilful blindness was considered in *R. v. Briscoe*.[20] Several men and youths picked up the 13-year-old victim and her friend at a mall saying they would take them to a party. Briscoe drove the car to a golf course and found a secluded spot to park. He opened the car trunk and handed one of the accused a pair of pliers. He stayed near the car while the group walked off on the pretence of finding the party. At one point, he walked over to where the men had taken

18 (1985), 18 C.C.C. (3d) 223 (S.C.C.).
19 Ibid. at 235.
20 [2010] 1 S.C.C. 411 42.

the victim and helped hold the victim after she had been hit in the head. He then observed the victim being assaulted and killed. There was evidence that one of the co-accused, L., had talked earlier in the evening about wanting to find someone to kill. However, Briscoe was unaware of this conversation. In his statement to the police, he testified that he said to the others, "whatever you guys want to do, just do it. Don't do it around me. I don't want to see nothing . . ." He was charged with aiding and abetting the commission of the offences of aggravated sexual assault, first-degree murder, and kidnapping. As discussed below, the offence of aiding and abetting requires that the person know that the principal intended to commit the offence. Briscoe was acquitted. The judge held that although he had the *actus reus* for the crime, he lacked the *mens rea* for the offence because he did not have the required knowledge.

On appeal to the Supreme Court of Canada, the Court found that the trial judge erred by failing to consider whether Briscoe was wilfully blind to the harm the others intended to cause the victim. The Court stated that wilful blindness can be a substitute for knowledge where knowledge is a component of the offence. The Court went on to say: "The doctrine of wilful blindness imputes knowledge to an accused whose suspicion is aroused to the point where he or she sees the need for further inquiries, but deliberately chooses not to make those inquiries."[21] The court dismissed the appeal and ordered a new trial.

Other examples of cases that discuss wilful blindness are in Part Two of the book. Chapter 7 discusses *R. v. Jorgenson*,[22] in which the Supreme Court of Canada held that it is possible to prove wilful blindness where a retailer suspected that material was obscene but refrained from making the necessary inquiries. Chapter 13 discusses two cases that address wilful blindness in relation to s. 354, which requires proof that an accused had knowledge that property in his or her possession was obtained by commission of an indictable offence: *R. v. Vinokurov*[23] and *R. v. Marabella*.[24]

5. Penal Negligence

The debate over subjective versus objective liability was not finally settled with *Sansregret*. The Supreme Court of Canada recognized another type of *mens rea*: **penal negligence**, which is based on an **objective standard**. Penal negligence requires that the Crown establish (a) the *actus reus*—that the conduct was either a **marked departure** from that of a reasonable person or a dangerous and unlawful act, and (b) the *mens rea*—that a reasonable person would have foreseen the risk of harm. The central case that established this principle was *R. v. Creighton*,[25] where the accused was charged with manslaughter for causing death by means of an unlawful act. The accused and the victim were drug users. The accused had injected the victim with cocaine, with the victim's consent. She eventually died from a drug overdose. The unlawful act on which the charge of manslaughter was based was the injection of the cocaine (legally defined as trafficking). Creighton was convicted. His appeal to the Supreme Court of Canada was dismissed. The Court held that the test for *mens rea* of unlawful act manslaughter is, in addition to the *mens rea* required for the underlying offence (injecting the cocaine), objective foreseeability of the risk of bodily harm that is neither trivial nor transitory in the context of a dangerous act. In other words, a reasonable person in Creighton's place would realize that injecting the victim with cocaine is an unlawful and dangerous act that involves a risk of causing

---

21   Ibid. at para 21.
22   (1995), 102 C.C.C. (3d) 97 (S.C.C.).
23   (2001), 156 C.C.C. (3d) 300 (Alta. C.A.).
24   (1957), 177 C.C.C. 78 (Ont. C.A.).
25   (1993), 83 C.C.C. (3d) 346 (S.C.C.).

serious bodily harm. The Court also rejected the argument that the reasonable person standard should include the personality characteristics of the accused. The Court held that "Provided that the capacity to appreciate the risk is present, lack of education, and psychological predispositions serve as no excuse for criminal conduct although they may be important factors to consider in sentencing."[26]

The Supreme Court, in *R. v. Gossett*,[27] which was released with *Creighton*, applied this same test to another case of unlawful act manslaughter. The unlawful act was the careless handling of a firearm under s. 86(2). The issue concerned the *actus reus* for the unlawful act. A police officer had yelled at a fleeing suspect, "Stop or I'll shoot." He then pointed the gun in the direction of the suspect and the gun went off, killing the suspect. The jury acquitted the officer. The Supreme Court ordered a new trial, holding that the proper test to be applied to the accused was whether, in carelessly handling a firearm, his behaviour was a marked departure from the standard of care of a reasonably prudent person. Similarly, in *R. v. Finlay*,[28] a case involving the careless storage of firearms, also under s. 86(2), the Court held that the objective test for penal negligence applies.

In *R. v. Naglik*,[29] the offence charged was a failure to provide necessaries to a child. The Supreme Court held that the responsibility under s. 215, which sets out the duty of parents to provide necessaries for their children, is objective. The question is whether the parent's conduct in not providing necessaries was a marked departure from the conduct of a reasonable parent in the circumstances where it was reasonably foreseeable that the failure to provide necessaries would lead to danger to the life or health of the victim.

In *R. v. Beatty*,[30] the Supreme Court considered the difference between civil negligence and penal negligence. Beatty was charged with three counts of dangerous driving. His pickup truck, for no apparent reason, suddenly crossed the solid centre line on the highway and collided with an oncoming vehicle, killing all three occupants. The issue was whether this act of negligence was sufficient to constitute dangerous driving causing death under s. 249(4). The Court stated:

A mere departure from the standard expected of a reasonably prudent person will meet the threshold for civil negligence, but will not suffice to ground liability for penal negligence. The distinction between a mere departure and a marked departure from the norm is a question of degree. . . .

[T]he trier of fact should be satisfied on the basis of all the evidence, including evidence about the accused's actual state of mind, if any, that the conduct amounted to a marked departure from the standard of care that a reasonable person would observe in the accused's circumstances. Moreover, if an explanation is offered by the accused, then in order to convict, the trier of fact must be satisfied that a reasonable person in similar circumstances ought to have been aware of the risk and of the danger involved in conduct manifested by the accused.[31]

26   Ibid. at 391.
27   (1993), 83 C.C.C. (3d) 494 (S.C.C.).
28   (1993), 83 C.C.C. (3d) 513 (S.C.C.).
29   (1993), 83 C.C.C. (3d) 526 (S.C.C.).
30   [2008] 1 S.C.R. 49.
31   Ibid. at para 7 and 8.

The Court upheld the acquittal, finding that his momentary lapse of attention, although leading no doubt to civil liability, was not sufficient for criminal liability.

The test for penal negligence in *Beatty* is sometimes referred to as the "modified objective test" because it takes account of the state of mind or position of the accused in determining what a reasonable person would do. In other words, the issue is whether a reasonable person in the position of the accused would have been aware of the risks arising from the conduct of the accused. The test is consistent with *Creighton* in not taking account of "personal characteristics" of the accused.

The *Beatty* test was applied in *R. v. Martin*.[32] Martin was charged with dangerous driving causing bodily harm. In convicting Martin, the trial judge found that Martin had the necessary *mens rea* based on the fact that he knew of his inability to be in complete control of the car, which had a standard transmission. Prior to the accident, he had driven the car only a few times and had experienced difficulty in smoothly shifting gears, resulting in the car stalling. The accident happened when Martin shifted gears as he hit wet pavement. The rear wheels spun unintentionally, causing him to lose control of the car, which mounted the curb and hit the victim. The British Columbia Court of Appeal overturned the conviction on the basis that a reasonable, prudent driver in Martin's circumstances would not have recognized a risk of losing control of the car in a manner that would be dangerous to others, and as a result, would have decided to drive the car. The accident was caused by a sudden, unexpected, and unfortunate concurrence of events that Martin had not previously experienced with the car. The difficulty Martin previously had in controlling the car was stalling it. Nothing had occurred when it was in motion to warn him of a possible loss of control in a manner that caused the accident.

These Supreme Court of Canada cases and numerous other examples of penal negligence are discussed in Part Two of the book. The *mens rea* of penal negligence is an important part of the discussion of manslaughter in Chapter 8 as well as the discussion of criminal negligence in Chapter 9 and the discussion of dangerous driving in Chapter 10. Other examples of offences in which the *mens rea* requirement is met by penal negligence include unlawfully causing bodily harm (s. 269) and aggravated assault (s. 270) (Chapter 11).

L04 6. *Mens Rea* and the Charter

Prior to the passage of the Charter, Parliament had the sole authority to determine the level of fault required for a criminal offence. This changed with enactment of the Charter. Section 7 of the Charter of Rights and Freedoms contains the guarantee that a person will not be deprived of life, liberty, or security of the person except in accordance with the principles of fundamental justice. One of the principles of fundamental justice is that there must be evidence of "moral blameworthiness" before a person is held criminally responsible and subject to possible imprisonment. In other words, the criminal law should not punish those who are without fault. The question for the Supreme Court in the penal negligence cases discussed above was this: "What is the minimum requirement of fault (*mens rea*) under the Constitution?" The court stated that for most offences, an objective *mens rea* will be sufficient for criminal liability. However, for a few, subjective *mens rea* is required.

---

32   (2012), B.C.C.A. 194.

a. Offences that Require Subjective Mens Rea

The principles of fundamental justice require that the *mens rea* of an offence reflect the stigma and penalty attached to the offence. Certain crimes are connected with such severe social stigma and penalty that subjective foresight of harm is necessary for the *mens rea*. The Supreme Court has considered these offences as requiring subjective *mens rea*: murder, attempted murder, and war crimes (crimes against humanity).[33] So, for example, the offence of murder requires that the accused either intended to cause a person's death or intended to cause bodily harm that the accused knew was likely to cause death.[34]

Subjective *mens rea*, the Charter, and the offence of murder are discussed in Chapter 8.

b. Offences of Penal Negligence

Those Criminal Code offences that do not have a severe social stigma or penalty attached allow an objective foresight of harm for the *mens rea*. The *actus reus* must be conduct that is a marked departure from that of a reasonable person (or a marked and substantial departure for criminal negligence; see Chapter 9), or it must be a dangerous and unlawful act. As indicated by the cases discussed above, the Supreme Court has been deciding case by case whether the *mens rea* required for an offence is objective or subjective. Note that the Court is setting minimum standards under the Charter. Parliament has the authority to create, and has created, crimes that require a higher level of fault (e.g., theft, fraud, and assault).

05 C. CONCURRENCE OF *MENS REA* AND *ACTUS REUS*

It is a general principle of criminal law that for an offence to occur, both the *mens rea* and the *actus reus* must be present at the same time. In most cases, this principle does not present any problems. For example, in the case of theft, the act of stealing and the intent to steal usually occur at the same time. However, in some cases it is not so clear, and courts have applied a fiction that enables the principle of concurrence to apply. For example, Al picks up a coat in a restaurant thinking that it belongs to him. When he gets home, he realizes that the coat is not his, but he decides to keep it. Here the *actus reus*, the taking of the coat, occurred at the restaurant; the *mens rea*, the intention of depriving the owner, did not arise until later. The question is whether Al should be found not guilty because the *actus reus* and *mens rea* did not occur at the same time. In answering this question, the criminal law relies on the fiction that the act of taking the coat continued until the point at which Al formed the *mens rea* to commit the crime. Thus, Al is guilty of theft.[35]

Another situation where the courts have had to decide whether the *actus reus* and *mens rea* are concurrent is where there is a series of acts and the *mens rea* is present for only part of the time the acts are occurring. In *Meli v. The Queen*,[36] the accused intended to kill the victim, and he beat him until he thought he was dead. He then threw the victim over a cliff. The victim died from exposure and not from the beating. The accused's defence argued that the *mens rea* and *actus reus* were not concurrent; when there was intent, there was no death

---

33   See, for example, *R. v. Vaillancourt* (1987), 39 C.C.C. (3d) 118 (S.C.C.), and *R. v. Finta* (1994), 88 C.C.C. (3d) 417 (S.C.C.). In *Vaillancourt*, it was suggested by Justice Lamer that theft might also require subjective *mens rea*. However this was only *dicta*, i.e., not necessary for the decision and therefore not binding law. See para 28.
34   See, for example, *R. v. Logan and Johnson* (1990), 58 C.C.C. (3d) 391 (S.C.C.).
35   See, for example, *Fagan v. Metropolitan Police Commission*, [1969] 1 Q.B. 439. The accused accidentally drove his car onto a police officer's foot. When he realized what he had done, he refused to move the car. He was convicted of assault based on the fiction that the *actus reus* continued until the intention to assault formed.
36   [1954] 1 All E.R. 373 (P.C.).

(during the beating), and when the death occurred, there was no intent. The appeal court upheld the accused's conviction, stating that the beating and the throwing of the victim over the cliff represented one continuing transaction. At some point, the *mens rea* coincided with the series of wrongful acts that made up the transaction.

This case was cited with approval by the Supreme Court of Canada in *R. v. Cooper*.[37] The accused and his ex-girlfriend had been drinking together. They went for a ride in his car and stopped at a secluded parking lot. The accused testified that they argued. She hit him, at which point, he became angry and grabbed her by the throat. He then said that he recalled nothing until he woke up and found the body beside him. Expert witnesses testified that the deceased probably died after about two minutes of pressure on her throat. The defence argued that the accused was so drunk that he blacked out shortly after he started shaking her; he thus did not have the intent to kill her at the time she died. The Court held that it is not necessary that the *mens rea* continue throughout the commission of the wrongful act, in this case the entire act of strangulation. It rejected the argument that if the intent disappeared before the point when death became likely, then the accused could not be found guilty. The Court stated that if death results from a series of wrongful acts that are part of a single transaction, it is only necessary to establish that the requisite intent coincided at some point with the wrongful acts. When the accused seized the victim by the neck, it was open to the jury to infer either that he intended to cause her death or that he meant to cause her bodily harm that he knew was likely to cause her death.

L06 D. REGULATORY OFFENCES AND STRICT AND ABSOLUTE LIABILITY

A regulatory offence is another category of offence that the Supreme Court has discussed in terms of liability requirements. As mentioned earlier, the general rule is that *mens rea* is an essential element of an offence; however, some offences do not require *mens rea*. These are not true criminal offences in the sense of there being a moral blameworthiness attached to them. They are regulatory in nature; that is, their purpose is to regulate some aspect of human conduct, often to protect vulnerable members of society. In other words, the activity is not illegal, but it is regulated to ensure public safety. Regulatory offences are often created by provincial or federal statutes and municipal bylaws dealing with health, safety, and the general welfare of the public. For example, provincial driving laws regulate speed limits and set other rules of the road. Municipalities set parking rules and fines for those who do not obey the rules. Both provincial and federal governments have passed laws to protect the environment.

Most regulatory offences are **strict liability offences**. After the Crown proves beyond a reasonable doubt the *actus reus* of the offence, the accused will be convicted unless he or she successfully uses the defence of **due diligence**. This defence has two parts: The accused will be found not guilty upon proving on a balance of probabilities that he or she (a) acted as a reasonable person in the circumstances, or (b) had an honest but mistaken belief in facts that, if they had been true, would have rendered the act innocent. In *R. v. Wholesale Travel Group*,[38] the Supreme Court of Canada held that regulatory offences which are based on strict liability do not offend s. 7 of the Charter (the right to life, liberty, and security of the person) as long

---

37 (1993), 78 C.C.C. (3d) 289 (S.C.C.).
38 (1991), 67 C.C.C. (3d) 193 (S.C.C.).

as the due diligence defence is available. This case involved a charge under the Federal Competition Act, which protects consumers from false advertising.

The second type of regulatory offence is one of **absolute liability**. The Crown only has to prove the *actus reus* of the offence to gain a conviction. The accused cannot use the defence of due diligence. This means that a person who acts with no fault at all can be convicted of committing an offence. The Supreme Court of Canada has stated that absolute liability offences are invalid if they violate s. 7 of the Charter.[39] In *R. v. Pontes*,[40] the question was whether the offence was one of strict or absolute liability. The accused was charged under a provincial law with driving while prohibited. The British Columbia Motor Vehicle Act provided that a person convicted of certain serious provincial and Criminal Code driving offences automatically and without notice would be prohibited from driving from the date of sentencing. The penalty for a first conviction for driving while prohibited was a fine and imprisonment for not less than seven days and not more than six months. Another statute, the British Columbia Offences Act, provided that, notwithstanding the provisions of any other act, no person would be liable to imprisonment for committing an absolute liability offence, and no person would be imprisoned for failure to pay a fine. On appeal to the Supreme Court of Canada, the Court held that the effect of the Motor Vehicle Act was to create an absolute liability offence to which the defence of due diligence did not apply. However, because of the Offences Act, which stated that its provisions overrode any other act, no person could be imprisoned for an absolute liability offence; therefore, the offence did not violate s. 7 of the Charter because there was no possibility of imprisonment. The Supreme Court has not yet ruled on whether imprisonment because of failure to pay a fine violates s. 7.

As mentioned, most regulatory offences are strict liability offences. The Supreme Court in *R. v. Sault Ste. Marie*[41] stated that there is a presumption that a regulatory offence will be a strict liability offence unless there is clear legislative intention to create one of absolute liability or one requiring *mens rea* by using words such as knowledge, wilfulness, or recklessness.

E. PARTIES TO AN OFFENCE

In general, parties are persons who are criminally responsible for the commission of the offence. In most situations, all persons who are **parties to an offence** are liable to receive the same punishment. Their involvement may take place either before or during the commission of the offence. Sections 21 and 22 define parties as those who actually commit the crime, or who aid, abet, or counsel the commission of a crime.

1. Aiding and Abetting

21. (1) Every one is a party to an offence who

(a) actually commits it;

(b) does or omits to do anything for the purpose of aiding any person to commit it; or

(c) abets any person in committing it.

39 Ref. Re s. 94(2) of the Motor Vehicle Act (1985), 23 C.C.C. (3d) 289 (S.C.C.).
40 (1995), 100 C.C.C. (3d) 353 (S.C.C.).
41 (1978), 40 C.C.C. (2d) 353 (S.C.C.). See also *Lévis (City) v. Tetreault*, [2006] 1 S.C.R. 420, where the Supreme Court reiterated a rule set out in *R. v. Sault Ste. Marie* that there must be clear legislative intent to create an absolute liability offence.

The person who commits the offence referred to in s. 21(1)(a) is known as the ***principal*** or perpetrator. A person who acts through an innocent agent is considered to actually commit the offence and thus is responsible under s. 21(1)(a).

Although the terms "aiding" and "abetting" are commonly used together, it should be noted that these are distinct offences, so liability may be established on the basis of either one. The *actus reus* of **aiding** is to assist or help. The *actus reus* of **abetting** is to encourage, instigate, promote, or procure the crime to be committed.

In *R. v. Briscoe*,[42] the Supreme Court of Canada stated that the *mens rea* requirement reflected in the word "purpose" under s. 21(1)(b) has two components: intent and knowledge. The aider must intend to assist the principal in committing the crime and must know that the principal intends to commit the crime.

Briscoe does not deal with the *mens rea* for abetting independently of aiding. However, it appears that the *mens rea* for abetting would require that the abettor know that the principal intends to commit the offence and that the abettor encourages or instigates the commission of the offence, intending the principal to commit the offence.

If the conduct of a person has the effect of helping the principal to commit a crime, but the person did not intend to help the principal, then it is not aiding or abetting. In *R. v. Helsdon*,[43] the accused was a reporter who wrote a story naming the victim in a sexual assault. The story was then published in a newspaper in violation of a court-ordered publication ban (s. 486.1). The publisher was charged with violating the ban, and Helsdon was charged as a party under s. 21. Both claimed that they were unaware of the ban. The court held that writing and filing the article satisfied the *actus reus* of s. 21(1)(b) but that the *mens rea* requirement was not met. The court found Helsdon not liable. He had no knowledge of the ban and so could not intend to assist the publisher in violating it.

In *R. v. Hibbert*,[44] the Supreme Court of Canada held that the meaning of the term "for the purpose of" in s. 21(1)(b) refers to intention, not desire. The accused was charged as a party to attempted murder. The principal offender had threatened to shoot him if he did not help him lure the victim into meeting them in the victim's apartment lobby by calling him on the apartment's intercom. The Court stated that, even though the accused did not desire the victim, who was his friend, to come to the lobby, he still intended for him to come to the lobby when he called him on the intercom. The accused could raise the defence of duress (discussed in Chapter 4), but he could not argue that he did not act for the purpose (the intention) of aiding the commission of the offence.

In general, a person who is merely present at the commission of an offence will not be guilty of aiding and abetting. There must be some active assistance or encouragement; not objecting to the offence is not aiding and abetting. In *Dunlop and Sylvester v. The Queen*,[45] the accused were present during a sexual assault involving several men. It was established that they did not know the assault was going to take place and had only brought cases of beer to the place where the assault was occurring. Although they observed the assault, they did not participate. They were not held liable for the crime.

Merely being present at the scene of a crime may lead to criminal responsibility where there is a duty to act. In *R. v. Nixon*,[46] the accused was a police officer in charge of the lock-up at a jail. Police had picked up a man for being drunk in public. He was severely beaten at the

---

42   *Briscoe, supra* note 20.
43   (2007), 216 C.C.C. (3d) 1.
44   (1995), 99 C.C.C. (3d) 193 (S.C.C.).
45   (1979), 47 C.C.C. (2d) 93 (S.C.C.).
46   (1990), 57 C.C.C. (3d) 97 (B.C.C.A.); leave to appeal to S.C.C. refused.

station when he gave a false name. Nixon was present at the beating, but he did not participate. The court held that, under the B.C. Police Act and sections 27 and 28 of the Criminal
Code, the accused had a duty to protect the victim, a duty which he failed to discharge.
Therefore, he was guilty of aggravated assault. In *R. v. Dooley*,[47] the court of appeal approved
the jury instruction of the trial judge that a parent who fails in his or her duty to protect his
or her child from reasonably foreseeable harm can be liable for aiding and abetting the other
parent's abuse of the child.

In some cases, it may be difficult to determine whether there is active assistance or encouragement. In *R. v. Greyeyes*,[48] the accused had assisted an undercover officer in finding a drug
dealer. He was convicted of aiding and abetting the trafficking of a narcotic. On appeal to the
Supreme Court of Canada, the issue was whether he should have been charged with the
much less serious offence of aiding and abetting the possession of a narcotic. The Court
considered these facts: that the undercover police officer had asked for help in buying narcotics;
that Greyeyes found a seller, and with the officer, drove to the seller's apartment; that Greyeyes
acted as the spokesperson, negotiated the price, passed the money on to the seller, and gave the
drugs to the purchaser. The purchaser paid him for his help. The court compared these facts
to a situation where a man's girlfriend threatens to walk through a dangerous neighbourhood
to buy drugs. For her protection, he drives her and waits in the car while she goes into a
house to make the purchase. The Court found that Greyeyes had done more than assist the
purchaser; he had actively assisted the seller; while in the second case, the driver had only
assisted the purchaser. The Court upheld the conviction.

An aider and abettor may be charged with aiding and abetting in the commission of a
particular offence or may simply be charged with the offence.[49] If the offence is one that
requires subjective intent, the person charged with aiding and abetting must have the same
intent as the principal. It is also possible for the party who is not the principal offender to be
found guilty of a lesser included offence; for example, in the case of murder, with manslaughter.
In *R. v. Kirkness*,[50] the accused and the co-accused broke into a house for the purpose of
robbery. During the break-in, the co-accused strangled and suffocated a woman they found
in the house. Both men were charged with first-degree murder. The accused was acquitted
at his trial. The case was appealed, and the appeal court ordered a new trial on the grounds
that the trial judge erred in not leaving to the jury a possible conviction for manslaughter. The
Supreme Court of Canada upheld the accused's acquittal. The Court stated that where a
person is charged with aiding or abetting in the commission of a murder, to be found guilty
of murder, the accused must have the same intent that the principal needs; that is, an intention to cause death, or bodily harm of a kind likely to cause death. Here it was not proved that
the accused knew before entering the house that the other man would kill the victim. There
was no evidence that he was party to the suffocation. In fact, there was evidence that he told
the co-accused not to strangle the victim. The Court confirmed that a conviction for
manslaughter is possible where there is not sufficient proof of intent; however, the accused
was not liable for manslaughter, since there was no evidence that the accused aided or abet-
ted in an unlawful act that would cause bodily harm short of death.

---

47   (2009), 249 C.C.C. (3d) 449 (Ont. C.A.)
48   [1997] 2 S.C.R. 825.
49   *R. v. Harder* (1956), 114 C.C.C. 129 (S.C.C.).
50   (1990), 60 C.C.C. (3d) 97 (S.C.C.).

2. Common Intention

A person is also a party if his or her conduct falls within s. 21(2):

> **21. (2) Where two or more persons form an intention in common to carry out an unlawful purpose and to assist each other therein and any one of them, in carrying out the common purpose, commits an offence, each of them who knew or ought to have known that the commission of the offence would be a probable consequence of carrying out the common purpose is a party to that offence.**

To be convicted under this section, the offence requires that (a) the accused, and at least one other person, form a common intention to carry out an unlawful purpose, and to help each other in doing so; (b) one of them, in carrying out the unlawful purpose, must commit an offence different from the unlawful purpose; and (c) the offence must be one that they knew or ought to have known would probably result from carrying out the common purpose. The difference between s. 21(1) and s. 21(2) was summed up in *R. v. Jackson*:

> *[Section 21] is aimed at those who participate in the actual offence for which liability is imposed. Section 21(2) widens the circle of criminal culpability to include those who do not participate in the alleged crime but who do engage in a different criminal purpose and foresee the commission of the alleged offence by a party . . . as probable consequence [of the criminal purpose].*[51]

The Supreme Court of Canada has considered the words "ought to have known" in s. 21(2), along with the issue of the *mens rea* required for murder. As discussed earlier, in a series of cases, the Court has held that because of the stigma and penalties attached to murder and attempted murder, these offences require a subjective intent; that is, the accused must actually intend to cause death or intend to cause bodily harm that he or she knows will likely cause death. Since the words "ought to have known" are included in s. 21(2), a person who is not the principal could be convicted of murder with a lesser degree of fault than was required for the principal. This was the situation in *R. v. Logan and Johnson*.[52] Logan and Johnson were parties to a robbery of a convenience store. They had entered the store wearing masks and armed with revolvers. One of the other parties shot the clerk, who was severely injured. They were convicted of attempted murder based on s. 21(2); in other words, it was found that they had formed a common intention with the other party to commit an unlawful purpose, the robbery, and they either knew or ought to have known that it was probable the other party would shoot and that a death would result. The Supreme Court ruled that where a party is charged with murder, the section cannot be used to convict the party if he or she did not have the intent required for the offence of murder. To apply the section in this situation would be a denial of fundamental justice under s. 7 of the Charter. More generally, the Court also held that in order to convict a person under s. 21(2) for any offence, the accused must have the necessary intent for the actual offence. Thus, if the offence requires subjective intent, then the accused must have that intent. However, the party who lacks the required intent can be found guilty of any lesser included offence if the intent for the included offence is proved. So, for example, where the charge is murder, and there is not proof that the party had the necessary intent, the party can still be found guilty of manslaughter if the intent for that offence is proved.[53]

---

51   (1991), 68 C.C.C. (3d) 385 (Ont. C.A.), at 421.
52   *Logan and Johnson, supra* note 34.
53   *R. v. Davy* (1993), (indexed as *R. v. Jackson*), 86 C.C.C. (3d) 385 (S.C.C.).

3. Counselling an Offence

To counsel means to advise or recommend. **Counselling an offence** also includes procuring (instigating or persuading), soliciting, and inciting. Two sections of the Code deal with counselling. Section 22 applies where the offence is committed and makes the counsellor a party to the offence.

> **22. (1) Where a person counsels another person to be a party to an offence and that other person is afterwards a party to that offence, the person who counselled is a party to that offence, notwithstanding that the offence was committed in a way different from that which was counselled.**
>
> **(2) Every one who counsels another person to be a party to an offence is a party to every other offence that the other commits in consequence of the counselling that the person who counselled knew or ought to have known was likely to be committed in consequence of the counselling.**

Notice that under s. 22(1) a person who counsels an offence is a party to an offence even if the crime is committed in a way different from what was suggested. So if Parvati encourages Emil to kill Caleb by shooting him and instead Emil kills Caleb by poisoning him, Parvati would still be a party to the offence by counselling the murder.

Notice also that under s. 22(2), a person is a party to any other crime that is committed if the person knew or ought to have known that it is likely to be committed as a result of the counselling. Section 22(2) raises the same issue as s. 21(2) concerning objective and subjective foreseeability and Charter requirements under s. 7. This section has not yet been challenged in court.

Section 464 creates a separate offence of counselling where the offence is not committed:

> **464. Except where otherwise expressly provided by law, the following provisions apply in respect of persons who counsel other persons to commit offences, namely,**
>
> **(a) every one who counsels another person to commit an indictable offence is, if the offence is not committed, guilty of an indictable offence and liable to the same punishment to which a person who attempts to commit that offence is liable; and**
>
> **(b) every one who counsels another person to commit an offence punishable on summary conviction is, if the offence is not committed, guilty of an offence punishable on summary conviction**

The Supreme Court considered the *actus reus* and *mens rea* for this offence in *R. v. Hamilton*.[54] The accused sent out an advertisement on the internet to sell software that would generate "legal" credit card numbers. He obtained the file, which also included instructions for building a bomb and breaking into a house, on the internet. He was charged with four counts of counselling the commission of offences, including fraud. He was acquitted at trial, the judge finding that, although he committed the *actus reus*, he did not have the *mens rea* since he did not intend for the purchasers to commit any offences. On appeal to the Supreme Court, the court rejected the argument that the *mens rea* for counselling requires that the person counselling intend that the offence be committed. The court stated:

---

54   (2005) 198 C.C.C. (3d) 1 (S.C.C.).

. . . *[T]he* actus reus *for counselling [under s. 464] is the deliberate encouragement or active inducement of the commission of a criminal offence and the* mens rea *consists in nothing less than an accompanying intent or conscious disregard of the substantial and unjustified risk inherent in the counselling: that is, it must be shown that the accused either intended that the offence counselled be committed, or knowingly counselled the commission of the offence while aware of the unjustified risk that the offence counselled was in fact likely to be committed as a result of the accused's conduct.*[55]

In other words, intention that the offence be committed is not required. It is enough if the accused is aware of a substantial and unjustified risk that the offence was likely to be committed.

The Supreme Court has said that the words used in counselling must be looked at objectively. In *Mugsera*,[56] the accused made a speech in Rwanda at the time of the fighting between the Hutus and Tutsi, two warring groups. Mugsera was a well-educated Hutu who was involved in politics in Rwanda. During the time of the genocide against the Tutsi, he made a speech that was alleged to incite murder, genocide, and hatred against the Tutsi. The government issued a warrant for his arrest because of the speech. He fled the country and eventually was accepted into Canada as a permanent resident. The Canadian government became aware of his activity in Rwanda and, in particular, this speech, and began the legal process to deport him. Under the Immigration Act, a person can be deported if it is determined that before or after being granted permanent residency, the person committed acts that would be crimes in the person's country of origin or in Canada. The Supreme Court in considering the appeal in his case on the issue of inciting murder noted that the speech must be viewed "objectively" as to whether it "actively promoted, advocated or encouraged the commission of an offence." The court went on to state, "The criminal act will be made out where the statements (1) are likely to incite, and (2) are made with a view to inciting, the commission of the offence." The court found that Mugsera not only intentionally gave the speech but also intended that it result in the commission of murders. On this finding and other grounds, the court upheld the deportation order.

F. ACCESSORY AFTER THE FACT

Section 23 creates the offence of helping someone who has committed an offence. The person who provides such assistance is not a party to the offence but may be convicted of being an **accessory after the fact** (i.e., of helping after the offence has been committed) if his or her actions fall within s. 23:

> **23. (1) An accessory after the fact to an offence is one who, knowing that a person has been a party to the offence, receives, comforts or assists that person for the purpose of enabling that person to escape.**

The *actus reus* of the offence is helping the party to the offence to escape. A person who does not disclose that the offence has been committed in his or her presence, or who does not assist in apprehending the party, is not an accessory. In general, assistance is anything that goes beyond a mere omission to aid in the capture of an offender; the accused must help the party to the offence to escape. In *Young v. R.*,[57] the accused told two murderers that their

---

55 Ibid. at para 29.
56 [2005] 2 S.C.R. 100.
57 (1950), 98 C.C.C. 195 (Que. C.A.).

names were known to the police and that the police had the licence plate number of their car. The court held that this was assistance because it went beyond a mere omission to aid in their capture and actually helped them escape apprehension.

The *mens rea* requires knowledge that the other party has been a party to an offence. In *R. v. Duong*,[58] the court held that wilful blindness is sufficient for *mens rea*. The accused was charged with being an accessory after the fact to a murder. His friend Louis had called him and said that he was "in trouble for a murder." He asked if he could stay at the accused's place because he had nowhere else to go. Duong did not ask him about the murder; he said, "I didn't want to know anything because I knew I would be in trouble for helping him hide." Duong did say that he had seen television and newspaper reports linking Louis to the crime. The prosecution argued that this was a case of wilful blindness. The defence argued that wilful blindness can only be argued if the accused had the means to ascertain the accuracy of his suspicions. The defence stated that since only Louis could have verified his suspicions and there was no evidence to suggest that Louis would have admitted his role in the murder, he should not be held culpable on the basis of wilful blindness. The court rejected this argument and agreed with the prosecution.

In *R. v. Vinette*,[59] the accused did not deny having assisted another person in disposing of a corpse by throwing it to the bottom of a flooded quarry in a weighted trunk. The Court decided that this was enough evidence to indicate that the accused had knowledge that the other party had been a party to the crime of homicide. The accused need only have knowledge of the person's participation, not an awareness of the legal classification of the offence.

The *mens rea* also requires that the assistance be given with the intention of helping the criminal to escape. In *R. v. McVay*,[60] a witness at a murder trial had, at the accused's request, disposed of a pair of jeans that, it was alleged, the accused wore at the time of the offence. The question was whether the witness was an accessory, since by disposing of the jeans he had helped the accused escape. The Ontario Court of Appeal stated that the jury, after weighing the evidence, was required to decide whether the witness knew that the accused had committed a murder at the time he disposed of the jeans. Only if he knew of the murder would he be an accessory after the fact.

Section 592 provides that the accessory may be convicted of the offence, whether or not the principal or any other party to the offence has been indicted or convicted.[61] Section 23.1 sets out a similar rule and has been interpreted by the courts as allowing a person who aids or abets, counsels, or assists to be liable even if the principal is not convicted.

08 G. ATTEMPTS

A person can commit an offence by merely trying to commit an offence. The offence of attempting a crime is defined in s. 24:

> **24. (1) Every one who, having an intent to commit an offence, does or omits to do anything for the purpose of carrying out his intention is guilty of an attempt to commit the offence whether or not it was possible under the circumstances to commit the offence.**

58 (1998), 124 C.C.C. (3d) 392 (Ont. C.A.).
59 (1974), 19 C.C.C. (2d) 1 (S.C.C.).
60 (1982), 66 C.C.C. (2d) 512 (Ont. C.A.).
61 See also *R. v. Shalaan* (1997),115 C.C.C. (3d) 450 (N.S.C.A.); affd. [1998] 1 S.C.R. 88.

There are three essential elements to an attempt: (a) the *mens rea*—the intent to commit an offence; (b) the *actus reus*—some act or omission toward committing the offence; and (c) the non-completion of the offence. The rule is that the act or omission must involve more than mere preparation to commit the crime; it must be immediately, not remotely, connected with the commission of the crime. In other words, a person who is only preparing to commit a crime is not committing the offence of attempting an offence.

At what point a person's conduct goes beyond preparation and becomes an attempt depends on the circumstances of the case. However, the conduct must go forward to the stage where, if there had not been some intervention or interruption, the offence would have been committed. In *R. v. Deutsch*,[62] the accused was charged under s. 212(1)(a) with attempting to procure a woman to have illicit sex with another person. He had advertised for a secretary/sales assistant. During each job interview, he told the applicant that she would be expected to have sex with prospective clients and would earn substantial bonuses for completed contracts. Each applicant ended the interview when she was told what was expected, before being offered the job. The Supreme Court of Canada held that the accused had gone beyond mere preparation and that the attempt was complete. The Court said that there is no general rule for drawing a line between an attempt and mere preparation: "The application of the distinction must be left to common-sense judgment." The Court went on to state that consideration must be given to (a) the nature and quality of the act compared to the nature and quality of the offence, and (b) the relative proximity of the act in terms of time, location, and acts required to complete the offence.

A conviction for an attempt to commit an offence can sometimes result from a lack of concurrence of the *actus reus* and *mens rea*. In *R. v. Williams*,[63] the accused was in a relationship with a woman, the victim, for 18 months, from June 1991 to November 1992. They had unprotected sex for 5 months, until November 15, 1991, when Williams learned that he was HIV positive. He was told to inform all partners but failed to do so. He continued to have unprotected sex for over a year with the victim. The victim subsequently tested positive for HIV. Williams was convicted of aggravated assault under s. 268 ("every one commits an aggravated assault who . . . endangers the life of the complainant"). The court of appeal substituted a conviction of attempted aggravated assault because the act of infecting the victim may have occurred before Williams knew that he was HIV positive and, therefore, knew that he was endangering the life of the victim.[64]

Section 24(1) makes it clear that it is no defence to an attempt charge if it was impossible in the circumstances to commit the offence. In *R. v. Detering*,[65] the accused was charged with fraud. Section 380 makes it fraud if a person

> **. . . by deceit, falsehood or other fraudulent means, whether or not it is a false pretence within the meaning of this Act, defrauds the public or any person, whether ascertained or not, of any property, money or valuable security . . .**

Detering operated a car repair business. A provincial government ministry was investigating car repair businesses suspected of cheating the public. Harris, an inspector from the ministry, brought a car to Detering's garage. The transmission had been slightly damaged so that it could be easily repaired. Detering told her that the transmission needed rebuilding.

---

62   (1986), 27 C.C.C. (3d) 385 (S.C.C.).
63   [2003] 2 S.C.R. 134.
64   Note that although the victim consented to having sex with the accused, her consent was vitiated (made invalid) once Williams failed to inform her of his HIV status.
65   (1982), 70 C.C.C. (2d) 321 (S.C.C.).

Harris had the work done and paid the bill, which stated that the transmission had been rebuilt. When the car was examined, it was found that the transmission had not been rebuilt. Detering was found not guilty of fraud because Harris was not actually deceived. However, the Supreme Court of Canada held that he could still be found guilty of attempted fraud, even though it was impossible for the offence to be committed, since the investigator could not be deceived.

Section 24(2) states that the issue of whether the act of the accused is an attempt or mere preparation is a question of law. This means that it is the judge's function to decide whether the actions of the accused, as found by the jury, amount to an attempt.

Murder is the sole offence where there is a specific offence for an attempt. The offence of attempted murder under s. 239(1) is discussed in Chapter 8.

H. CONSPIRACY

In general, a ***conspiracy*** is an agreement (or "common design") by two or more persons to do an unlawful act or to do a lawful act by unlawful means. It is immaterial whether the unlawful act is committed or not. Even when the conspirators change their minds, or do not get the opportunity to perform the unlawful act, they have committed the offence of conspiracy once they have reached their agreement. So, if Zoya and Irene plan to kidnap Michelle and they are arrested before they can carry out the kidnapping, both of them will be guilty of conspiracy.

Assume that Zoya and Irene made the same agreement as above, but Irene only pretended to agree; that is, Irene agreed but had no intention of carrying out the agreement. This was the situation in *R. v. O'Brien*,[66] where the accused was charged with conspiracy to commit kidnapping. O'Brien asked Tulley to help him kidnap a woman named Pritchard. He offered to pay Tulley for his help. Tulley agreed and received several payments. When O'Brien started pressuring him to actually carry out the kidnapping, Tulley went to the police and to Pritchard's husband and told them the plan. At O'Brien's trial, Tulley testified that he never intended to carry out the kidnapping but was just going along with O'Brien. On appeal, the Supreme Court of Canada ruled that O'Brien could not be convicted of conspiracy because there was no true agreement between Tulley and O'Brien. For the agreement to exist, there would have had to be a common intention to carry out the unlawful plan, and Tulley had only been pretending to have the intention to commit the kidnapping. On the other hand, the Court in *O'Brien* also said that the offence of conspiracy is committed even if one party later withdraws from the plan, since the offence is already complete.

The Supreme Court has said that a husband and wife cannot be found guilty of conspiring together because in law they are considered one. However, if a third party is involved, they can all be convicted.[67]

The main section dealing with conspiracy is s. 465(1): (a) and (b) provide for specific conspiracy offences, conspiracy to commit a murder and conspiracy to unlawfully prosecute a person; (c) makes it an offence to conspire to commit any other indictable offence; and (d) makes it an offence to conspire to commit a summary conviction offence.

It is also the offence of conspiracy to conspire while in Canada to do something outside Canada if it is a crime by the laws of the other place. Similarly, it is conspiracy to agree outside Canada to commit a crime inside Canada. (See sections 465(3) and 465(4).)

---

66   (1954), 110 C.C.C. 1 (S.C.C.).
67   *Kowbel v. The Queen* (1954), 110 C.C.C. 47 (S.C.C.).

Questions for Review and Discussion

1. Define *actus reus* and *mens rea*.

2. What are the components of the *actus reus* of a crime?

3. Explain the common law rules concerning causation.

4. List and define the types of *mens rea* discussed in this chapter.

5. What is the difference between a general intent offence and a specific intent offence? Give an example of each.

6. Why is the difference between general intent offences and specific intent offences important?

7. Explain the difference between intention to commit an offence and the motive for committing an offence. Make up an example illustrating the difference between motive and intention.

8. Explain the difference between a voluntary act and an intentional act.

9. What is the position of the Supreme Court on the *mens rea* for recklessness?

10. What is penal negligence?

11. How are strict liability offences different from other offences?

12. When are absolute liability offences valid?

13. What are the essential elements of aiding and abetting? Give an example of each.

14. What does it mean to counsel an offence? When can counselling itself be an offence?

15. What are the essential elements of being an accessory after the fact?

16. What are the essential elements of attempting an offence?

17. What is the difference between conspiracy and aiding and abetting?

18. Marion asked Sarah to take care of her infant boy for a few days. Marion also asked Sarah to give the infant a teaspoonful of "medicine" every night. In fact, the medicine was poison. Sarah did not think that the infant needed medicine, so she did not give it to him. She put the medicine on a shelf in her living room. Later, Sarah's five-year-old son gave the infant a large dose of the "medicine," and the infant died. Marion was charged with murder. Should she be convicted? What else, if anything, do you need to know?

19. The accused, a 20-year-old man, allowed a 16-year-old girl to drive his car. While he sat beside her, she drove the car over 140 kilometres an hour, and the accused did not do or say anything to stop her. He was charged with aiding and abetting the commission of the offence of dangerous driving. His defence was that he did nothing to encourage the commission of the offence, but was merely a passive observer, and therefore should not be liable for aiding and abetting. Should he be found guilty or not guilty? Make a decision in this case. See *R. v. Kulbacki* (1966), 1 C.C.C. 167 (Man. C.A.).

20. Murray, Josie (Murray's wife), and Rosa agree to steal some money from Adrian's clothing store. They also agree that Adrian will not be harmed and that no weapons will be used. Murray enters the store and gets Adrian's attention by asking him questions about an article of clothing. Then Josie enters the store and walks toward the cash register while Rosa acts as a lookout near the store entrance. Adrian notices Josie reaching into the drawer of the cash register and yells loudly. Rosa panics, pulls a gun, and shoots Adrian, severely wounding him. Murray, Josie, and Rosa run from the store and go to Dan's apartment around the corner. They tell Dan what has happened. Dan agrees to let them use his car; and

Murray, Josie, and Rosa drive to a hiding place. Adrian later dies from the wound he received. Explain the responsibility of Murray, Josie, Rosa, and Dan in this case.

21. A and B exchanged gunfire on a crowded city street. B unintentionally shot V, a shopper who was caught in the crossfire. Is A responsible for V's death? Discuss the causation issue in this case. See *R. v. S.-R. (J.)* (2008), 237 C.C.C. (3d) 305.

22. J discovered that a client and her mother wanted to harm or kill the client's husband. J began recording telephone conversations in which he discussed killing the husband. Eventually, the police became involved and J was charged with counselling murder or unlawfully causing bodily harm. At his trial, J argued that he never intended for the offence to take place and that he was just gathering evidence to take to the husband. Should he be convicted? Explain. See *R. v. Janeteas* (2003), 172 C.C.C. (3d) 97 (Ont. C.A.).

23. The victim met a woman in a bar and offered to take her home. She invited him in when they reached her home. Inside were several other people, including the accused, Soloway. The victim fell asleep on the couch. He woke up when he felt the woman taking his wallet out of his back pocket. He pretended to be asleep to avoid a fight. There was no money in the wallet, and she started to put it back. Soloway then told her to keep the identification papers because they could be sold. With what offence can Soloway be charged? Explain. See *R. v. Soloway* (1975), C.C.C. (2d) 212 (Alta. C.A.).

24. In a case in England, a person was stabbed and taken to hospital. At the hospital, he was given an antibiotic to which he was allergic, and was improperly given intravenous fluids. The direct cause of his death was the improper medical treatment he received; in fact, the original wound had almost completely healed by the time the victim died. The Court held that the accused, who stabbed the victim, was not legally responsible for causing the death of the victim. Would the case have the same outcome if tried in Canada? See *R. v. Jordon* (1956), 40 Cr. App. R. 152 (C.C.A.).

25. Trakas had placed an ad to sell his motorcycle. Chiovitti had come to his house in a pickup truck to see the motorcycle. Trakas agreed to let Chiovitti try the motorcycle, leaving his truck as security. As the motorcycle pulled away, Trakas saw the truck also being driven away by Shilon, who had been hiding in the truck. He jumped into his car to follow the truck and a high speed chase began. Trakas also called the police to inform them of the theft and the location of the truck. Trakas hit and killed a police officer, who was setting up a roadblock to stop the truck. The issue at the preliminary inquiry was whether Shilon should be committed to trial on the charge of criminal negligence causing death. What would you decide? What about Trakas? Should he be held liable for the officer's death? Assume that it was established that Trakas was not speeding at the time he hit the police car. See *R. v. Trakas* (2008), 240 C.C.C. (3d) 401 (Ont. C.A.) and *R. v. Shilon* (2006), 240 C.C.C. (3d) 401.

CHAPTER 4

Defences

Key points explained in this chapter are

LO1 the meaning of mental disorder and the implications of raising it as a defence to a charge;

LO2 the differences between automatism and mental disorder;

LO3 when intoxication by alcohol or drugs can be used as a defence;

LO4 the defences of duress, compulsion, and necessity;

LO5 when force may be used to defend a person or property; and

LO6 when a mistake about the law or the facts can be a defence.

There are many types of defences that an accused can raise. An accused who says, "You have the wrong person; I was at work when the crime occurred," is using an *alibi* defence. A person who raises an alibi defence is saying that he or she was somewhere else when the alleged crime took place, and that it was, therefore, impossible that he or she committed the crime. Some defences are *justifications* for conduct that would otherwise be criminal. For example, a police officer who shoots a fleeing suspect may have a justification for his or her actions. Other defences are excuses; for example, a person who commits a crime because of a threat may raise the defence of duress to excuse his conduct. The difference between a justification and an excuse is that where conduct is justified, it is not wrong in the context in which it occurs. Conduct that is excused is wrong but because certain circumstances exist, the actor is excused from criminal liability. Another type of defence is that an essential element of the offence is missing; for example, the defence of mental disorder is based on the premise that the person was incapable of having the *mens rea* for the offence.

The Criminal Code and the common law contain defences to criminal charges. Section 8(3) of the Code states that all common law defences apply to criminal charges, except as they are changed by Parliament:

> **8. (3) Every rule and principle of the common law that renders any circumstance a justification or excuse for an act or a defence to a charge continues in force and applies in respect of proceedings for an offence under this Act or any other Act of Parliament except in so far as they are altered by or are inconsistent with this Act or any other Act of Parliament.**

This section should be read with s. 9, which abolishes common law criminal offences. In other words, there are no longer any common law crimes (except for contempt of court). However, common law defences are still available unless altered by or inconsistent with an Act of Parliament (i.e., legislation).

The general rule is that an accused does not have to prove his or her defence; it is enough merely to produce some evidence that raises a reasonable doubt in the mind of the jury. Before a judge allows a jury to consider a defence, that defence must have "an air of reality." In other words, an accused person cannot just assert a defence without any evidence. If a judge finds that the defence does meet this minimal threshold, it is then up to the jury to decide whether the defence raises a reasonable doubt as to the accused's guilt.

A. INCAPACITY OF CHILDREN

Section 13 of the Criminal Code states:

> **13. No person shall be convicted of an offence in respect of an act or omission on his part while that person was under the age of twelve years.**

The law presumes that children under the age of 12 do not have the mental capacity to understand the nature and consequences of their acts and to distinguish between right and wrong. Without this mental capacity, there can be no *mens rea* or "guilty mind," and thus there can be no offence.

Children under the age of 12 who commit crimes are handled under provincial legislation, usually in the form of child welfare or protection laws. Children over 12 and under 18 at the time of the alleged offence are held responsible for their criminal acts; however, they are treated differently and separately from adults. The Youth Criminal Justice Act governs the treatment of young people who break the law. An overview of this statute is given in Appendix B.

01 B. MENTAL DISORDER

The defence of mental disorder is that the accused did not have the *mens rea* for the offence. In general, when a person is found not guilty, that person is given a full acquittal and is free to resume his or her life. This is not the situation when the defence of mental disorder is used. As explained in more detail below, a person who successfully uses this defence is not released until a hearing is held to determine whether he or she is a danger to the public.

Section 16 sets out the defence:

> **16. (1) No person is criminally responsible for an act committed or an omission made while suffering from a mental disorder that rendered the person incapable of appreciating the nature and quality of the act or omission or of knowing that it was wrong.**

1. Meaning of Mental Disorder

Section 2 of the Code defines "mental disorder" as a disease of the mind. Whether a specific condition is a disease of the mind is a question of law for the judge to decide. Medical evidence is very relevant in deciding whether the accused suffers from a disease of the mind, but it is not the determining factor, since medical opinion may well differ. The Supreme Court of Canada has stated that part of the consideration is a policy component concerning public safety. For example, one factor to consider is whether the accused suffers from a recurring condition that is a continuing danger to the public. This suggests that the accused's condition should be treated as a mental disorder.[1]

Courts have recognized a number of mental disorders, such as schizophrenia, senile dementia, paranoia, melancholia, and certain types of epilepsy, as diseases of the mind. Excluded, however, are self-induced states caused by alcohol or drugs, and temporary conditions, such as hysteria and concussion. Delirium tremens caused by alcohol abuse is considered a disease of the mind. Once the court decides that the condition is a disease of the mind, it is up to the jury to decide whether the accused suffered from the disease at the time the offence was committed.

In *R. v. Bouchard-Lebrun*,[2] the accused was charged with aggravated assault after he brutally assaulted two people while in a psychotic condition caused by drugs he had taken. It was not in dispute that at the time of the assaults he was incapable of distinguishing right from wrong. He argued that he should be found not criminally responsible on account of mental disorder. The Supreme Court of Canada found that he did not have a mental disorder within the meaning of s. 16. The Supreme Court agreed with the Court of Appeal for Quebec that the symptoms of his psychosis coincided with his intoxication by drugs. The accused did not suffer from a disease of the mind either before committing the assaults or after the effects of the drug-taking had passed. The Supreme Court held that a malfunctioning of the mind that results from self-induced intoxication cannot be considered a disease of the mind because it is not a product of the person's inherent psychological makeup.

2. Appreciating the Nature and Quality of the Act

Appreciating the nature and quality of the act refers to the physical act and its consequences. It means more than knowing what is happening. The Supreme Court considered the meaning of the term "appreciates" in *Cooper v. The Queen*.[3] The accused had killed the victim by choking her to death. The psychiatric evidence was that the accused, because of the state of his mind, would not have been able to (a) form the intent to kill, or even (b) be aware enough to have the capacity to take a life. However, the accused did have the capacity to form the intent to choke the victim. The Court, in considering the meaning of "appreciates," stated:

> [A]ppreciates imports [more than] mere knowledge of the physical quality of the act. The requirement . . . is that of perception, an ability to perceive the consequences, impact and results of the physical act. An accused may be aware of the physical character of his actions (i.e., choking) without necessarily having the capacity to appreciate that, in nature and quality, that act will result in the death of a human being.[4]

3. Knowing that the Act Is Wrong

A person may appreciate the nature and quality of his or her act, but not be capable of knowing that the act is wrong.

The Supreme Court has held that "wrong" means the person knows the act is morally wrong, not just legally wrong. *R. v. Chaulk*[5] involved two teenage boys who had broken into a home. They stabbed and bludgeoned the sole occupant to death. The evidence was that they

---

1   *R. v. Parks* (1992), 75 C.C.C. (3d) 287 (S.C.C.).
2   (2011), SCC 58.
3   (1980), 51 C.C.C. (2d) 129 (S.C.C.). See also *R. v. Rabuse* (1980), 53 C.C.C. (2d) 161 (B.C.C.A.).
4   Ibid. at 147.
5   (1990), 62 C.C.C. (3d) 193 (S.C.C.).

both suffered from paranoid psychosis, and this made them believe that they had the power to rule the world and that killing was a necessary means to that end. Although they knew that killing was against the law, they believed that they were above the law. They were tried in adult court and found guilty. The judge did not allow the jury to consider the defence of insanity, because the accused knew the acts were against the law. (The term "insanity" was used until the law was amended in 1992, when the term "mental disorder" was substituted.) On appeal to the Supreme Court, it was held that the meaning of knowing something is wrong is broader than just knowing it is illegal. The question is whether the accused was unable, because of a disease of the mind, to understand that he ought not to have committed the act and that the act was morally wrong in the circumstances.

A later decision of the Supreme Court emphasizes that the focus is not on whether the accused had a general capacity to know right from wrong but on whether the accused lacked the capacity of an ordinary person to decide rationally whether the particular act was wrong. In *R. v. Oommen*, the Court stated that, although the accused was capable of knowing that killing was wrong, a defence of insanity was possible if his paranoid delusion "at the time of the act deprived him of the capacity for rational perception and hence rational choice about the rightness or wrongness of the act."[6]

4. Presumption of Sanity

> **16. (2) Every person is presumed not to suffer from a mental disorder so as to be exempt from criminal responsibility by virtue of subsection (1), until the contrary is proved on the balance of probabilities.**
>
> **(3) The burden of proof that an accused was suffering from a mental disorder so as to be exempt from criminal responsibility is on the party that raises the issue.**

The effect of the presumption in s. 16(2) is that, unless the issue is raised, an accused is presumed not to be suffering from a mental disorder. This presumption has been challenged under the Charter as violating the right to be presumed innocent. The Supreme Court, in *Chaulk*,[7] held that the presumption of sanity violates the constitutional right to be presumed innocent, but that the violation is justified in a free and democratic society. The Court stated that it would be an "onerous burden" for the Crown to have to disprove insanity in every case. In other words, if it could not be presumed that an accused is sane in every case, the prosecution would have to prove beyond a reasonable doubt that the accused was sane—a heavy burden indeed. The burden of proof where mental disorder is raised is a balance of probabilities. In other words, it must be proved that it was more likely than not that the accused was suffering from a mental disorder when the act was committed.

5. Who Can Raise the Issue of Mental Disorder?

A common law rule stated that the prosecution could raise the issue of mental disorder over the objections of the accused. The trial judge had to give permission for the Crown to do this. Permission would be given only if it were shown that there was substantial evidence of mental disorder and that there was convincing evidence that the accused committed the offence. A Crown might raise mental disorder where, for example, the Crown believed that the accused

---

6   (1994), 91 C.C.C. (3d) 8 (S.C.C.) was cited at 30 C.R. (4th) 195 (S.C.C.).
7   *Chaulk, supra* note 5.

was a danger to the public and that the likely term of imprisonment the accused would receive if found guilty of the offence would not be sufficient to protect the public.

The Supreme Court, in *R. v. Swain*,[8] held that the common law rule that allows the Crown to raise insanity violates the accused's Charter right under s. 7. The Court stated that it is a rule of fundamental justice that the accused is entitled to control his or her defence; that is, to choose which defences to use. Since this was a common law (i.e., judge-made) rule, not a statutory rule, the Supreme Court stated that it could reformulate it so that it did not offend the Charter. To safeguard the accused's right, the rule should be that the Crown can raise insanity only if the accused has already put his or her mental capacity into issue or if the accused has been found otherwise guilty. In the latter case, the trial would have two parts: the first part to determine whether the accused was guilty of the offence, and the second to determine whether the accused was not guilty because of insanity. Since *Swain*, the Code has been amended to incorporate this court decision. Section 672.12 allows the court to order the assessment of the accused's mental condition. Under s. 672.11, the court can order an assessment whenever it has reasonable grounds to believe that such evidence is necessary to determine whether the accused was suffering from a mental disorder so as to be exempt from criminal responsibility. When the assessment is requested by the Crown, the court cannot order the assessment unless (a) the accused has put his or her mental capacity for criminal intent into issue, or (b) the prosecutor satisfies the court that there are reasonable grounds to doubt that the accused is criminally responsible, because of mental disorder.

Section 672.34 preserves the two-part trial required by *Swain* by requiring a finding that the accused committed the act or omission that formed the basis of the offence but is not criminally responsible because of a mental disorder.

6. Disposition on the Finding of Not Criminally Responsible because of Mental Disorder

Until the decision in *Swain*, when an accused was found not guilty by reason of insanity, the court had to order that the accused be kept in "strict custody . . . until the pleasure of the lieutenant governor of the province is known." In other words, the trial judge had no choice regarding the disposition of the case. This practice was called automatic detention. The decision of the Supreme Court of Canada, in *Swain*, rejected the practice of automatic detention. The facts in *Swain* were these: The accused was charged with assaulting his wife and two children. The evidence was that he had swung his children around his head and splashed them with water and then carved an X on his wife's chest. He explained that he was ridding them of devils. While on bail awaiting trial, he received drug therapy for seven weeks as an in-patient. He was then released and lived with his family for 18 months until his trial. The Crown raised the issue of insanity over the accused's objections, and he was found not guilty by reason of insanity. The court ordered his detention.

On appeal, the Supreme Court held that the practice of automatic detention violated Swain's Charter rights under s. 7 and s. 9 (the right to be free from arbitrary detention), and that it was not a justifiable limitation under s.1 of the Charter. There were two reasons: First, there was no requirement that a hearing be held before a detention was ordered to determine whether the accused was a present danger to the community. This was a denial of fundamental justice under s. 7. Second, even if a hearing were required, there were no criteria or standards

---

8   (1991), 63 C.C.C. (3d) 481 (S.C.C.).

set out in the law for a judge to apply in deciding whether the accused should be detained or released. For example, the judge was not directed to consider whether it was likely that the accused would commit a violent crime in the future. The lack of criteria made the detention arbitrary, contrary to s. 9 of the Charter.

The particular facts in *Swain* made this arbitrariness especially obvious. It appeared that he had been successfully treated before his trial and was no longer a danger to the community, yet the trial judge had no choice but to order his detention.

Amendments in 1992 set out the new procedure for dealing with an accused person found not guilty because of mental disorder. The amendments also replaced the term "insanity" with the term "mental disorder." Where a finding of not criminally responsible because of mental disorder is made, the court can either hold a disposition hearing or send the case to a provincial review board, which must review the case within 45 days. If a court holds the hearing and makes an order other than an absolute discharge, the review board must review the case within 90 days.

Section 672.54 states that where a court or review board makes a disposition, it must consider the need to protect the public, the mental condition of the accused, the reintegration of the accused into society, and the other needs of the accused, and make one of the following dispositions: (a) where the accused is not criminally responsible because of mental disorder and is not a significant threat to public safety, order an absolute discharge; (b) order a discharge with conditions; or (c) order the detention of the accused in a hospital with conditions.

7. Capping Dispositions

A criticism of the earlier law was that a person who was found not guilty because of insanity could be detained longer than a person found guilty. As a result, an amendment was passed that a person found not criminally responsible because of a mental disorder could not be detained longer than the maximum period of imprisonment for a person found guilty of the same offence. Another amendment permitted a finding that a person was a dangerous mentally disordered person, which allowed the cap on detention to be increased to life. Although the House and Senate passed these amendments, they were never brought into force and were repealed in 2005.

C. AUTOMATISM

A person whose conduct is involuntary may raise the defence of automatism. Automatism refers to a state in which a person has no conscious control over bodily movements. In other words, the person's behaviour is "automatic." Examples of involuntary, unconscious behaviour are acts done while sleepwalking or during an epileptic seizure. In effect, the accused is saying that there was no *actus reus*.[9]

For automatism to be a defence, the cause of the automatism must be something other than a disease of the mind or voluntary intoxication by alcohol or drugs. If a disease of the mind causes an involuntary, unconscious act, the defence is mental disorder; this is sometimes called "insane" or mental disorder automatism. The defence of automatism is called "non-insane" or non-mental disorder automatism. Similarly, if intoxication causes the involuntary, unconscious act, the defence is usually intoxication, not automatism.

---

9   In *R. v. Luedecke* (2008), 236 C.C.C. (3d) 317, the Ontario Court of Appeal stated that automatism is not a defence "in the true sense" but rather a denial of the *actus reus*.

In *R. v. Stone*,[10] the Supreme Court of Canada set out a two-step approach to claims of automatism. First, the defence must establish a proper evidentiary foundation. The accused must show on a balance of probabilities that he or she acted involuntarily. The assertion of involuntariness must be confirmed by expert psychiatric or psychological evidence. In addition to the psychiatric or psychological evidence, the judge will also consider other evidence that may be available, such as the severity of the triggering impulse, corroborating evidence of bystanders, corroborating medical history of automatism-like dissociative states, whether there is evidence of a motive for the crime, and whether the alleged trigger of the automatism is also the victim of the automatistic violence.

Second, if a proper evidentiary foundation has been established, the trial judge must determine whether the condition alleged by the accused is mental disorder or non-mental disorder automatism. It will only be in rare cases that automatism is not caused by mental disorder. The Court stated that judges should start from the proposition that the condition that the accused claims to have suffered from is a disease of the mind. They must then determine whether the evidence in the particular case takes the condition out of the disease of the mind category.

Automatism caused by a physical injury was a successful defence in *R. v. Bleta*.[11] The accused was charged with murder. Several witnesses testified that they watched a fight between G and the accused that culminated in the accused stabbing G fatally in the neck. Although the stories of the eyewitnesses differed as to the details of the fight, it is clear that blows were exchanged between the two men. The accused either fell down or was knocked down, and struck his head forcibly on the pavement. G started to walk away; the accused, having regained his feet, followed him and pulled out a knife, with which he delivered the fatal blow. Two of the onlookers observed that when the accused got up, he staggered and appeared to be dazed. One police officer also commented on his apparently dazed condition. The accused contended that the blow to his head when it struck the sidewalk deprived him of all voluntary control over his actions. In other words, the accused was saying he was in a state of automatism when he stabbed G.

The trial judge summarized a psychologist's evidence that supported the accused's defence: "The doctor says that the actions of the accused when he stabbed the deceased were purely automatic and without any volition on the part of the accused. He was, in fact, in the condition of a sleepwalker or an epileptic, and since he had been in a fight, he automatically continued it."[12] The jury believed that the accused was in a state of automatism and acquitted him. The Supreme Court of Canada upheld the decision of the trial court.

Automatism may also be used as a defence when the accused's involuntary, unconscious act results from taking a drug without knowing its effect. In *R. v. King*,[13] the accused was charged with impaired driving. His dentist had injected him with a drug. The accused did not know the drug's effects, nor was he made aware of the effects. Shortly after he drove away from the dentist's office, the drug caused the accused to lose consciousness, and he drove into a parked car. His act of driving while impaired was considered an involuntary act, and he was found not guilty. The result would have been different if the accused had known that the drug would produce unconsciousness.

10 [1999] 2 S.C.R. 290.
11 (1965), 1 C.C.C. 1 (S.C.C.).
12 Ibid. at 8.
13 (1962), 133 C.C.C. 1 (S.C.C.).

If the accused is aware of being subject to states of unconsciousness, automatism will not be a successful defence. In *R. v. Shaw*,[14] the accused suffered from a physical disability, which the court concluded was probably epilepsy. Although the accused knew he was subject to attacks that caused unconsciousness, he continued to drive his car. On one occasion, he suffered an attack while driving. He slumped or fell, and this caused the car to accelerate. The car went off the highway and collided with a tree. Two passengers were killed and three others were injured. Because the accused was aware that he could become unconscious while driving, the court held that he could be found criminally responsible for his conduct.

A person who is sleepwalking is considered to be in a state of automatism. In *R. v. Parks*,[15] the accused was charged with murdering his mother-in-law and attempting to murder his father-in-law. The evidence was that he drove 20 kilometres from his home to his in-laws' home and attacked his in-laws in their bed. His defence was that he was sleepwalking at the time. He had recently been under great stress because of a gambling addiction that led him to steal from his employer. The jury accepted psychiatric evidence that Parks was sleepwalking, even though the crime involved very complex behaviour. He was acquitted of both charges. Both the Ontario Court of Appeal and the Supreme Court of Canada rejected appeals by the Crown that the defence should have been insanity, not automatism.

The possibility of automatism being caused by a severe psychological blow was recognized by a court in *R. v. K.*[16] The accused killed his wife and was charged with manslaughter. The trial judge summarized the testimony of the accused:

> *He gave evidence concerning his depression in the months before this tragedy and following the sale of his farm. He described the affection he had for his wife . . . He described his worry over his own depression and the problem that he was facing, whether he was going to leave with his family to go to Vancouver or not. He also described his actions on the day of the tragedy: the telephone call from Mrs. S. saying repeatedly, "your wife is leaving, your wife is leaving," how he went outside looking for the girls [his daughters], met his wife on the street, returning home, going upstairs and then coming down again, and then seeing his wife and putting his arms around his wife, saying to her, "please don't leave." To the accused, in his evidence, the rest is like a dream. He remembers falling and getting up, his wife being on the floor calling for help.*[17]

People who saw the accused after the incident agreed that he appeared to be in shock. His eyes were glazed and he repeatedly answered questions by saying that he did not know what had happened.

A psychiatrist supported the accused's evidence by stating that in the days before the incident, the accused had become extremely depressed about having sold his farm and the possibility of his wife leaving him. The psychiatrist felt that he had entered a state of automatism as a result of the severe psychological blow of learning that his wife was leaving him. This psychological blow produced a state in which "the mind registered little, and from then on the accused did not know what was happening, his mind no longer being in control of his actions."

The judge instructed the jury that if they accepted the above evidence, they should find the accused not guilty. However, if they believed that a disease of the mind caused the state of

---

14   (1938), 30 C.C.C. 159 (Ont. C.A.).
15   *Parks, supra* note 1.
16   (1970), 3 C.C.C. (2d) 84 (Ont. H.Ct.).
17   Ibid. at 85.

automatism, they should find the accused not guilty by reason of insanity. The jury returned a verdict of not guilty.

Note, however, that the ordinary stresses and disappointments of life are not sufficient to be considered psychological blows to induce automatism. In *R. v. Rabey*,[18] a male student learned that a female classmate he had a crush on had written a note making fun of him. He took a rock and attacked her. His defence of automatism failed.

An important difference between the defences of automatism and mental disorder is that an accused who is found not guilty because he or she was in a state of automatism at the time of committing the offence, is immediately released from custody. This is not the situation with the defence of mental disorder.

Automatism is a defence to a charge of committing a strict liability offence. Remember from Chapter 3 that a strict liability offence involves an *actus reus* (physical element) but no *mens rea* (mental element). Since the acts of a person in a state of automatism are not voluntary, no *actus reus* exists.

L03 D. INTOXICATION

Until the Supreme Court of Canada decision in *R. v. Daviault*,[19] intoxication by alcohol or drugs was not a defence to a charge of committing a general intent offence. However, it could be a partial defence to a charge of committing a specific intent offence. That is, if it could be shown that the accused was too intoxicated to form the specific intent required, then the accused would not be guilty of the offence. However, the accused could be found guilty of any included offence if it required only general intent. The decision in *Daviault* and subsequent amendments have changed the situations where this defence can be used. In *Daviault*, the accused was charged with the sexual assault (a general intent offence) of an 85-year-old woman. The accused was a chronic alcoholic; on the day of the assault, he had consumed a large amount of alcohol—so much that it would have caused death or a coma for an ordinary person. Expert evidence was that he may have been in a blackout state in which he lost contact with reality. The trial judge acquitted the accused on the grounds that, because of the accused's intoxication, there was reasonable doubt as to whether the accused had the minimal intent necessary for the assault. The court of appeal held that the trial judge erred in allowing the defence, and substituted a conviction. The Supreme Court of Canada allowed the appeal and ordered a new trial. The Court stated that not allowing the defence of intoxication to general intent offences violates s. 7 of the Charter.

The principles of fundamental justice require that criminal offences have *mens rea*. The intention to become drunk cannot be substituted for the intention to commit an assault. It is also a violation of the presumption of innocence under s. 11(d) of the Charter to convict someone when there is reasonable doubt regarding the existence of *mens rea*. The Court fashioned a new rule to deal with intoxication as a defence. It states that the accused can use the defence of intoxication when it is established that the accused was in a state of intoxication akin to automatism or insanity.[20] Also, as with the defence of mental disorder, the accused has the burden of proving on a balance of probabilities that he or she was in an extreme state of intoxication.

---

18 (1977), 37 C.C.C. (2d) 1 (Ont. C.A.); affirmed (1980), 54 C.C.C. (2d) 461 (S.C.C.).
19 (1994), 93 C.C.C. (3d) 21 (S.C.C.).
20 A previous Supreme Court of Canada case, *R. v. Bernard* (1988), 45 C.C.C. (3d) 11 (S.C.C.), suggested that such a rule might apply in a proper case. It was not until *Daviault* that the Court clearly developed the rule and made it part of the law.

This decision was roundly criticized, especially by women's groups, who felt that allowing drunkenness as a defence—to sexual assault, in particular—would allow men to unfairly escape criminal responsibility. In response, the federal government enacted s. 33.1:

33.1 (1) It is not a defence to an offence referred to in subsection (3) that the accused, by reason of self-induced intoxication, lacked the general intent or the voluntariness required to commit the offence, where the accused departed markedly from the standard of care as described in subsection (2).

(2) For the purposes of this section, a person departs markedly from the standard of reasonable care generally recognized in Canadian society and is thereby criminally at fault where the person, while in a state of self-induced intoxication that renders the person unaware of, or incapable of consciously controlling, their behaviour, voluntarily or involuntarily interferes with or threatens to interfere with the bodily integrity of another person.

(3) This section applies in respect of an offence . . . that includes as an element an assault or threat of interference by a person with the bodily integrity of another person

Section 33.1 places a limit on the self-induced intoxication defence. The defence recognized in *Daviault* will not be available for any of the offences referred to in s. 33.1(3) if the accused departed markedly from the standard of care described in s. 33.1(2). The effect of s. 33.1(2) is to deem a certain level of fault in an accused who departs markedly from the standard of care set out in that subsection. Section 33.1(3) would likely include most of the personal injury offences since even a threat of interference with the complainant's bodily integrity would be sufficient to trigger the limits set down in s. 33.1(3).

Note that this section applies only to crimes of violence. The rule in *Daviault* still applies to general intent offences that do not involve personal violence; for example, mischief (wilfully destroying property). Also, since this law applies to general intent offences, intoxication could still be a defence to a specific intent offence, such as robbery (assault with intent to steal). Presumably, the accused would still be able to raise the defence to the crime of robbery, but could not use it for the included offence of assault.

When the Defence of Intoxication Can Be Used—A Summary

With the decision in *Daviault* and the enactment of s. 33.1, how and whether intoxication is used as a defence will depend on the following factors:

a. General Intent Offences Not Involving Assault or Threat of Violence

The rule in *Daviault* allowing the defence of intoxication applies to general intent crimes that do not involve personal violence. The intoxication must be so extreme that the accused is in a state of unawareness similar to automatism or insanity. Expert evidence will ordinarily be necessary to show that the accused was in such a state.

This defence, however, does not apply in cases in which an element of the offence is intoxication, such as impaired driving.[21] Allowing the defence in these cases would be inconsistent with the purpose of creating the offence.

---

21 *R. v. Penno* (1990), 59 C.C.C. (3d) 344 (S.C.C.).

b. Involuntary Intoxication

Section 33.1(1) does not apply where the Crown fails to prove that the intoxication was self-induced, in the sense that the accused intended to become intoxicated either by voluntarily ingesting a substance knowing, or having reasonable grounds to know, that it might be dangerous, or by recklessly ingesting a substance, such as prescription medication.[22] While section 33.1 violates sections 7 and 11(d) of the Charter, the court held in *Vickberg*,[23] that it was a reasonable limit within the meaning of s. 1, and therefore valid.

c. Specific Intent Offences

If the defence is used for a specific intent offence, such as murder, then evidence of intoxication can be considered to determine whether the accused was so impaired by drugs or alcohol that he or she could not have formed the specific intent necessary for the offence. Recall from Chapter 3 that specific intent crimes require an extra or ulterior intent. The accused does one illegal act for the purpose of achieving another illegal act. *R. v. George*[24] is the classic case on using intoxication as a defence to a specific intent crime. The accused was charged with robbery and the included offence of assault, having violently manhandled an 84-year-old man until the victim agreed to give him his money. The accused raised the defence of intoxication. He was found not guilty of robbery, which requires an assault with intent to steal, but guilty of the included offence of assault. In other words, the Court held that the accused was too drunk to form the specific intent to steal but could form the intent to apply force to another person.

L04 E. DURESS AND COMPULSION

The defence of duress operates as an excuse for criminal conduct. The defence is that the accused had no realistic alternative course of action available where he or she was subjected to an intentional threat from another person. There are two defences of duress. One, referred to as compulsion, is in the Criminal Code; and the other is a common law defence. The two defences apply in different situations.

1. Compulsion under the Code

17. A person who commits an offence under compulsion by threats of immediate death or bodily harm from a person who is present when the offence is committed is excused for committing the offence if the person believes that the threats will be carried out and if the person is not a party to a conspiracy or association whereby the person is subject to compulsion, but this section does not apply where the offence that is committed is high treason or treason, murder, piracy, attempted murder, sexual assault, sexual assault with a weapon, threats to a third party, or causing bodily harm, aggravated sexual assault, forcible abduction, hostage taking, robbery, assault with a weapon or causing bodily harm, aggravated assault, unlawfully causing bodily harm, arson or an offence under sections 280 to 283 (abduction of young persons).

---

22   See *R. v. Vickberg* (1998), 16 C.R. (5th) 164 (B.C.S.C.).
23   Ibid.
24   (1960), 128 C.C.C. 289 (S.C.C.).

Section 17 sets out several requirements for the use of the defence of compulsion:

- The accused committed an offence not listed in s. 17.
- The accused was not a member of a group planning to commit the offence.
- The accused committed the offence because he or she believed the threats of immediate death or immediate bodily harm would be carried out.
- The threats were delivered by a person who was present at the time the accused committed the offence.

The belief that the threat would be carried out is subjective. It is not required that a reasonable person in the circumstances would have believed that the threat would be carried out. As discussed below, the Supreme Court of Canada has struck down the requirements that the threat of death or bodily harm be (a) immediate and (b) made by a person who is present at the time of the offence.

In *R. v. Langlois*,[25] the Quebec Court of Appeal held that s. 17 violates s. 7 of the Charter in that it allows a person who is morally innocent to be convicted of an offence. This is because (a) the defence is not available for all offences, (b) the accused must face threats of immediate death or bodily harm by a person who was present when the crime was committed, and (c) the defence does not apply when the threats are made against a member of the accused's family. In *Langlois*, the accused was a recreation officer at a penitentiary in Quebec who was caught trying to smuggle drugs into the prison. His defence was that threats had been made against the safety of his wife and children. He did not feel that he had time to contact the police or that they would be able to adequately protect his family. A jury acquitted him. The Crown appealed on the grounds that the judge should not have left the defence of duress with the jury. The court of appeal dismissed the appeal, holding that s. 17 violates the Charter, and is, therefore, unenforceable. Without s. 17 operating, the accused was able to use the common law defence of duress.

The Supreme Court of Canada has addressed the s. 17 requirement that the threat of death or bodily harm must be immediate. In *R. v. Carker*,[26] a decision made prior to the Charter, the accused was charged with having unlawfully and wilfully damaged public property—plumbing fixtures in the accused's prison cell. The accused testified that he committed the offence during a disturbance, in the course of which a substantial body of prisoners, shouting in unison from their separate cells, threatened the accused by saying that if he did not break the plumbing fixture in his cell he would be kicked in the head, his arms would be broken, and he would get a knife in the back at the first opportunity. The Court decided that, although there was little doubt that the accused committed the offence under the compulsion of threats of death and grievous bodily harm, these were not threats of "immediate death" or "immediate grievous bodily harm." The persons who were uttering the threats were locked up in separate cells.

In *R. v. Ruzic*, a decision made under the Charter, the Supreme Court of Canada struck down the requirement that the threat be immediate as well as the requirement that the person who made the threat must be present at the time of the offence.[27] The court in *Ruzic* stated

---

25 (1993), 19 C.R. (4th) 87 (Que. C.A.).
26 (1967), 2 C.C.C. 190 (S.C.C.).
27 (2001), 153 C.C.C. (3d) 1 (S.C.C.).

that "a threat will seldom meet the immediacy criterion if the threatener is not physically present at or near the scene. The immediacy and present requirements, taken together, clearly preclude threats of harm. . . . Thus, by the strictness of its conditions, s. 17 breaches s. 7 of the Charter because it allows individuals who acted involuntarily to be declared criminally liable."[28] The Court also found that a threat of death or bodily harm to a third party may meet the requirements of s. 17. In this case, the accused had been told that, if she did not import heroin, her mother, who lived in a foreign country, would be killed.

2. The Common Law Defence of Duress

The Supreme Court, in *R. v. Paquette*,[29] held that the common law defence of duress, which existed before s. 17 was enacted, can be used in situations not covered by s. 17; that is, where the accused is not the principal actor. The accused drove the getaway car from a robbery where an innocent bystander had been killed. He claimed that the principal actors had forced him to do so at gunpoint. Since the charge was murder, Paquette could not use the s. 17 defence. However, the Court held that the common law defence was still available where the accused was not the person who actually committed the offence.

The common law defence of duress does not exclude any offences. An objective test is used to determine whether it is available to the accused: What would a reasonable person have done in the circumstances? Also, it does not require that the threat be of immediate death or bodily harm; that is, the threat could be for the future. Finally, under the common law, the presence of the threatening person is not required when the crime is committed.

In *R. v. Hibbert*,[30] the accused was charged with the attempted murder of his friend, Cohen. Hibbert ran into Bailey in the lobby of an apartment building. Bailey, who was a drug dealer, and who the accused believed was armed with a gun, ordered Hibbert to take him to Cohen's apartment. When Hibbert refused, Bailey forced him into the basement and punched him in the face. Bailey and Hibbert then went to Bailey's car, where two women were waiting. Hibbert sat in the back while Bailey drove. Bailey dropped the women off and ordered Hibbert to sit in the front seat. Bailey drove Hibbert to a phone booth and told him to phone Cohen to ask him to meet him (i.e., Hibbert) in Cohen's lobby. They went to Cohen's building, where Hibbert buzzed Cohen on the intercom. When Cohen arrived in the lobby, Bailey shot him. Bailey was never found, but Hibbert turned himself in to the police the next day. Hibbert was acquitted of murder but convicted of aggravated assault. On appeal to the Supreme Court of Canada, one of the issues was whether, to use the defence of duress, the accused must show that he did not have a "safe avenue of escape." The Court held that a person cannot rely on the defence of duress if he or she had an opportunity to safely remove himself or herself from the situation of duress. Furthermore, whether a safe avenue of escape existed is determined on an objective standard: Would a reasonable person see an avenue of escape? When considering the perceptions of a reasonable person, however, the personal circumstances of the accused are relevant and important and should be taken into account. The Court allowed Hibbert's appeal and sent the case back for retrial.

---

28 Ibid. at 28–29.
29 (1976), 30 C.C.C. (2d) 417 (S.C.C.).
30 (1995), 99 C.C.C. (3d) 193 (S.C.C.).

F. NECESSITY

The defence of necessity is a type of excuse that is related to the defence of duress. In *Hibbert*,[31] the Court explained that the difference between duress and necessity is that, in a case of duress, the danger is caused by intentional threats of bodily harm, while in a case of necessity, the danger is caused by forces of nature or human conduct other than intentional threats of bodily harm. The defence of necessity, which has developed through the common law, is rarely used.

The case that confirmed the existence of this defence is *Perka et al. v. The Queen*.[32] The accused were smuggling drugs by ship from Columbia to Alaska. The drugs were to be dropped in international waters off Alaska. The ship encountered poor weather conditions and developed mechanical problems. For the safety of the crew, the ship entered a Canadian bay to make repairs. The ship then became grounded. The next day, the police investigated and found the drugs. The accused were charged with importing drugs into Canada. Their defence was that they never intended to enter Canada but acted out of necessity to save themselves. The Supreme Court of Canada held that the accused could raise this defence. The Court stated that the defence is limited to these situations: (a) imminent risk exists and the action was taken to avoid a direct and imminent peril; (b) the wrongful action is "morally involuntary," which is "measured on the basis of society's expectation of appropriate and normal response to pressure"; and (c) there is no alternative course of action that does not involve breaking the law (i.e., there is "no legal way out"). In addition, the harm caused by the accused's action must not be greater than the harm that he or she was trying to avoid. If the accused provides sufficient evidence to raise the issue of necessity, the onus is on the Crown to prove beyond a reasonable doubt that the accused's action was voluntary.

The defence of necessity was rejected by the Supreme Court of Canada in *R. v. Latimer*.[33] The accused killed his 12-year-old severely disabled daughter, who had the mental capacity of a four-month-old baby. She suffered several seizures a day and was thought to be in constant pain that could not be reduced by medication. She had undergone numerous surgeries. After learning that the doctors intended to perform additional surgeries, which would cause more pain and which the accused perceived as mutilation, the accused decided that his daughter's life was not worth living. He claimed that he was motivated by wanting to put an end to his daughter's suffering. The Supreme Court found that the elements of the necessity defence, discussed in the *Perka* case, did not apply. The accused did not face any peril and his daughter's ongoing pain did not constitute an emergency. He had a reasonable legal alternative to killing his daughter. He could have continued to try to minimize her pain or he could have permitted an institution to do so. Killing his daughter was not a proportionate response to the harm of his daughter's non–life threatening suffering.

G. CONSENT

When consent is available as a defence, the victim's consent must be a real or valid consent. In order to be real or valid, the consent must be informed and voluntary. If the consent is obtained by fraud, it is not considered real, and, therefore, cannot constitute a defence. For example, if a physician tells a female patient that her treatment requires her to have sexual

---

31 Ibid.
32 (1984), 14 C.C.C. (3d) 385 (S.C.C.).
33 (2001), 150 C.C.C. (3d) 129 (S.C.R.).

intercourse with him, her consent is not valid. Similarly, consent obtained through threats of bodily harm is not valid. The consent would be involuntary.

In limited circumstances, an accused may use as a defence the fact that the victim consented to the accused's act. For example, if the accused engaged in a fight with another individual, and as a result of the fight was charged with assault, he may be able to argue that the other person consented to the fight. If it can be established that both parties consented to the fight, the accused may be entitled to an acquittal.

In *R. v. Paice*,[34] the accused attempted to rely on the victim's consent to answer to a charge of manslaughter. The Court stated that consent involves more than a factual finding that the parties agreed to fight, since a person cannot consent to a fight where the other party intends to inflict serious bodily harm. However, for consent to be vitiated, as the Supreme Court of Canada had previously stated in *R. v. Jobidon*,[35] serious harm must not only be intended, but also must be caused. In other words, "the . . . intention to cause serious bodily harm alone cannot serve to negate the other person's consent, if in fact no bodily harm is caused. The activity, a consensual application of force that causes no bodily harm, would fall within the scope of the consent and not in any way fall within the Code definition of assault."[36] The case was sent back for a retrial because the trial judge had not sufficiently considered the issue of consent.

1. Offences for Which Consent Is Not a Defence

There are several offences for which consent is specifically mentioned as not being a defence. For example, s. 14 states that the victim's consent to be killed is no defence to a murder charge. There are also several sexual offences against children where consent may not be a defence unless certain circumstances exist. These offences include sexual interference (s. 151), invitation to sexual touching (s. 152), sexual exploitation (s. 153), and the offences of sexual assault (sections 271 to 273). These offences are discussed in Chapters 7 and 11.

2. Consent and Sexual Assault

Sections 273.1 and 273.2 of the Code are special provisions regarding consent and the offences of sexual assault. These 1992 amendments to the Code were referred to in the media as the "no means no" provisions. Briefly, s. 273.1 sets out certain situations where "no consent is obtained"; for example, where the accused induces consent by abusing a position of trust, or where the complainant initially agrees to engage in sexual activity and then expresses a lack of agreement to continue. Section 273.2 concerns situations where the accused cannot rely on the defence of mistaken belief in consent; for example, where the accused's mistaken belief arose from self-induced intoxication or wilful blindness.

Consent and sexual assault and non-sexual assault are discussed in detail in Chapter 11. Consent and the offences of possession, such as possession of stolen property, are discussed in Chapter 13. Consent and sexual offences, such as sexual interference or sexual exploitation, are discussed in Chapter 7.

---

34   (2005), 195 C.C.C. (3d) 97 (S.C.C.).
35   (1991), 66 C.C.C. (3d) 454 (S.C.C.). This issue is discussed further in Chapter 11.
36   *Perka, supra* note 32 at 102.

.05 H. THE PERMISSIBLE USE OF FORCE: SELF-DEFENCE, THE DEFENCE OF OTHERS, AND DEFENCE OF PROPERTY

1. Responsibility for Excessive Force

In some situations, a person is justified in using force. Self-defence, defence of others, and the defence of property are justifications for using force against another person. The general rule is that only as much force as necessary in the circumstances can be used. A person who uses an excessive amount of force is held criminally and civilly responsible. In other words, the person could be sued in a civil action or charged with a crime. Section 26 sets out a person's criminal responsibility:

> **26. Every one who is authorized by law to use force is criminally responsible for any excess thereof according to the nature and quality of the act that constitutes the excess.**

So, for example, a person who uses excessive force for self-defence could be charged with assault or even murder depending on the circumstances.

2. Use of Force to Prevent Commission of an Offence

Anyone can use as much force as reasonably necessary to prevent the commission of certain offences. This defence is set out in s. 27:

> **27. Every one is justified in using as much force as is reasonably necessary**
>
> (a) **to prevent the commission of an offence**
>
> (i) **for which, if it were committed, the person who committed it might be arrested without warrant, and**
>
> (ii) **that would be likely to cause immediate and serious injury to the persons or property of anyone, or**
>
> (b) **to prevent anything being done that, on reasonable grounds, he believes would, if it were done, be an offence mentioned in paragraph (a).**

The offences to which paragraph (a) refers are discussed in Chapter 5 under arrest without warrant. However, in general, any offence that is likely to cause serious harm to a person or property falls within this section.

3. Self-defence

In 2012, Parliament amended the provisions of the Criminal Code dealing with self-defence and defence of others (and defence of property, which is discussed below). Section 34 replaces the former sections 34–37, which set out separate defences for persons who used force to protect themselves or someone else from attack, depending on whether they provoked the attack or not and whether they intended to use deadly force:

(a) Where the accused did not provoke the assault—The force used must not have been intended to cause death or grievous bodily harm and was no more force than was necessary.

(b)   Where the accused caused death or grievous bodily harm in repelling the assault—
The accused must have been under reasonable apprehension of death or grievous
bodily harm; and the accused believed, on reasonable grounds, that he or she could
not otherwise protect himself or herself from death or grievous bodily harm.

(c)   Where the accused provoked the assault—The accused must have used the force
under reasonable apprehension of death or grievous bodily harm from the person
whom he or she assaulted; the accused did not, prior to needing to protect himself or
herself from death or grievous bodily harm try to cause death or grievous bodily harm;
and the accused retreated from further conflict before the need to protect himself or
herself from death or grievous bodily harm arose.

(d)   Where the accused was defending a person under his or her protection—The accused
must have used no more force than was necessary to prevent the assault or the
repetition of it.

Although the former sections that applied to these situations varied in their wording, they
all limited the amount of force that could be used to no more force than was necessary.

Section 34 is an attempt to clarify and simplify the law on self-defence by creating one new
self-defence provision. It permits persons who reasonably believe that they or others are at
risk of the threat of force to commit a reasonable act to protect themselves or others.

34. (1) A person is not guilty of an offence if

**(a) they believe on reasonable grounds that force is being used against them
or another person or that a threat of force is being made against them or
another person;**

**(b) the act that constitutes the offence is committed for the purpose of
defending or protecting themselves or the other person from that use
or threat of force; and**

(c) the act committed is reasonable in the circumstances.

Subsection (3) provides that subsection (1) does not apply if the force or threat by another
person is for the purpose of doing something that he or she is authorized to do in the administration or enforcement of the law, unless the accused believes on reasonable grounds that
the other person is acting unlawfully.

Section 34(1) includes protecting another person. This is broader than the former s. 37,
which limited the defence of others to a "person under his protection." The reasonable act
referred to in (c) will usually be an act of force. The use of force must be "reasonable in the
circumstances." This is a different wording from the former limitation that the force must be
"no more than is necessary."

Subsection (2) of s. 34 provides some guidance as to the meaning of "reasonable in the
circumstances" by listing factors for the court to consider:

**(2) In determining whether the act committed is reasonable in the circumstances,
the court shall consider the relevant circumstances of the person, the other
parties and the act, including, but not limited to, the following factors:**

(a) the nature of the force or threat;

(b) the extent to which the use of force was imminent and whether there were other means available to respond to the potential use of force;

(c) the person's role in the incident;

(d) whether any party to the incident used or threatened to use a weapon;

(e) the size, age, gender and physical capabilities of the parties to the incident;

(f) the nature, duration and history of any relationship between the parties to the incident, including any prior use or threat of force and the nature of that force or threat;

(f.1) any history of interaction or communication between the parties to the incident;

(g) the nature and proportionality of the person's response to the use or threat of force; and

(h) whether the act committed was in response to a use or threat of force that the person knew was lawful.

The list of factors in s. 34(2) is not exhaustive. In determining whether the act was reasonable in the circumstances, the court must consider "the relevant circumstances of the person, the other parties and the act," which include, but are not limited to, the listed factors.

The listed factors address issues that were raised in the previous Code sections and case law. For example, (c) refers to the person's role in the incident, which includes whether the person provoked the incident. Factor (g) refers to the nature and proportionality of the person's response to the use or threat of force, which raises the issue of whether the person used more force than was necessary to protect himself or herself or another person. It is likely, therefore, that in determining whether the force was reasonable in the circumstances, courts will find the case law under the former sections 34–37 to be relevant. The following cases were decided before the current s. 34.

a. Unprovoked Assault

In *R. v. Kandola*,[37] the accused was charged with manslaughter after he and the deceased had been involved in a long and escalating argument. The death occurred when the deceased and his friends appeared at the accused's home after telephoning threats to sexually assault all the women in the house. The police were called after the phone call, but no car was dispatched. They were called again when the deceased and his friends arrived at the house. Again, no car was sent to the house. The deceased banged on the door while his friends surrounded the house armed with hockey sticks and possibly a rifle. The police were called for a third time. The tape from this phone call indicated sounds of hysterical fear and bedlam, as the house, which contained 16 people—including four or five women and two children—was clearly under attack. The accused took out a handgun, crawled to a window on the top floor, put his arm out the window, and fired blindly. He did this, he testified, in order to scare off the attackers. One of the bullets killed the deceased. The accused was convicted of manslaughter at his trial. The judge held that the accused had taken an unjustified risk in firing the gun as he did. The appeal court disagreed. The court held that all of the elements for using the defence (under the former s. 34(1)) were present: The accused was unlawfully assaulted; he did not provoke the assault; he

---

37 (1993), 80 C.C.C. (3d) 481 (B.C.C.A.).

was justified in repelling force by force; he had a reasonable doubt whether the appellant intended to cause death or grievous bodily harm; and the force used by the accused—firing a warning shot without aiming at the assailant—was no more than was necessary to enable him to defend himself. Also, the appeal court noted that courts are tolerant in measuring the necessary amount of force needed in genuine cases of self-defence.

b. Death or Grievous Bodily Harm

Under the former s. 34(2), there were three elements required for a person to rely on self-defence if he or she caused grievous bodily harm, or killed another person in repelling an assault:

- There must have been an unlawful assault.
- The accused must have been under a reasonable fear of death or serious bodily harm.
- The accused must have believed on reasonable grounds that there was no other way to save himself or herself.

Regarding the first element, the Supreme Court of Canada, in *R. v. Pétel*,[38] said that the question is not whether the accused was being unlawfully assaulted, but rather, did the accused reasonably believe that she was being unlawfully assaulted? Thus, an honest but reasonable mistake as to the existence of the assault is possible.

Regarding the second element, the issue is whether a person in the situation of the accused would have been under a reasonable fear of death or serious injury. *R. v. Lavallée*[39] involved a woman who had been repeatedly battered by her husband over a four-year period. The question for the Supreme Court was whether a woman in the accused's position and with her experience would have a reasonable apprehension of death or serious physical harm. Although s. 34(2) does not specifically require the accused to have been in "imminent" (immediate) peril when he or she acted in self-defence, courts have "read" this requirement into the defence as a way of ensuring that the self-defence really was necessary. However, later court decisions, discussed below, have ruled that imminent peril is not always necessary for the defence.

Regarding the third element, although the accused's belief that there is no other way to save himself or herself must be based on reasonable grounds, it is not necessary to consider whether an ordinary person would have held the same belief. Rather, the important questions are these: Did the accused actually believe that there was no other way to save himself or herself? And was the belief based on reasonable grounds?

The Supreme Court of Canada has ruled that s. 34(2) applied even though the accused may have provoked the assault, because the words "without having provoked the assault" are not used, as they are in s. 34(1). The Court acknowledged that this is a somewhat illogical result, because s. 35, which specifically deals with provoked assaults, required a person to "retreat" before he or she was justified in using force for self-defence, while s. 34(2) did not have such a requirement. The Court suggested that the law of self-defence needed to be "cleared up" by legislative action.[40]

The Supreme Court, in *R. v. Lavallée*,[41] accepted evidence of "the battered woman syndrome." In this case, experts testified that the accused felt "trapped, vulnerable, worthless" and unable

---

38   (1994), 87 C.C.C. (3d) 97 (S.C.C.).
39   (1990), 55 C.C.C. (3d) 97 (S.C.C.).
40   *R. v. McIntosh* (1995), 95 C.C.C. (3d) 481 (S.C.C.).
41   *Lavallée, supra* note 39.

to leave the relationship despite being repeatedly abused by her husband over a four-year period. On the day of the killing, he found her hiding in a closet. He handed her a gun and dared her to shoot him. He said that if she did not shoot, he would kill her later. When he turned to leave the room, she shot him in the head. The Court held that where the battered woman syndrome applies, the accused does not need to prove imminent peril; a well-founded anticipation of peril is enough. The Supreme Court, in *Pétel*,[42] clarified the place of imminent danger in self-defence cases. The Court stated that, when self-defence is claimed, there is no need for imminent danger. This is only one factor that juries must consider in deciding whether "the accused had a reasonable apprehension of danger and a reasonable belief that she could not extricate herself otherwise than by killing her attacker."[43]

c. Provoked Assault

The former s. 35 specifically dealt with situations where a person provokes an assault on himself or herself by another person (e.g., by insulting the other person or by assaulting him). To justify the use of force under the former s. 35, the accused had to satisfy all of the following criteria:

- The accused must have assaulted someone or in some other way provoked an assault on himself or herself.
- The accused must at no time have intended to cause death or grievous bodily harm.
- After being assaulted, the accused must have been in reasonable danger of death or bodily harm.
- The accused must have believed, on reasonable grounds, that the force used was necessary to prevent death or grievous bodily harm from occurring to himself or herself.
- The accused, before using force, must have exhausted all other ways (such as retreat) of avoiding the use of force.

In *R. v. Bolyantu*,[44] the accused was in a fracas at a tavern and was ejected. He later returned to the tavern, and a second disturbance occurred in the tavern. Bolyantu then left the tavern followed by a mob that was attacking him. At that point, Bolyantu stabbed the victim with a knife. He claimed to be acting in self-defence. At trial, the court rejected the defence on the basis that there was no evidence that the victim had assaulted Bolyantu, and convicted him of assault causing bodily harm. On appeal, the Ontario Court of Appeal found that the trial judge had erred. The court found that there was some circumstantial evidence that the victim was a member of the attacking mob. The trial judge should have told the jury that, under s. 35, Bolyantu was entitled to defend himself if he believed on reasonable grounds that the victim was part of the attacking mob, even though, in fact, he may not have been.

4. Defence of Others

The former s. 37 permitted the use of force in the defence of a person "under his protection." As noted earlier, the current s. 34 is not limited to the defence of a person under the accused's protection. It refers to the defence of "another person."

In *R. v. Wiggs*,[45] the accused was charged with assaulting a boy who, with several other boys, attacked his son. The boys threw his son to the ground, sat on him, and punched and

---

42   *Pétel, supra* note 38.
43   Ibid. at 104.
44   (1975), 29 C.C.C. 174 (Ont. C.A.).
45   (1931), 3 W.W.R. 52 (B.C.C.A.).

kicked him. The father rushed to the defence of his son; in stopping the attack, he struck one of the boys, causing injury to his face. The court found the father not guilty because, in defending his son, he had used no more force than was necessary in the circumstances.

5. Defence of Property

The defence of property involves real property or personal property. **Real property** refers to land and to structures attached to the land. **Personal property** refers to movable things, such as a car, a television set, a chair, and so on. Besides the specific defence of property provision in s. 35, discussed below, recall that s. 27 provides a general defence to anyone who uses force to prevent the commission of an offence "that would be likely to cause immediate and serious injury to the person or property of anyone . . ."

In 2012, Parliament amended the provisions of the Criminal Code dealing with defence of property. Section 35 replaces the former sections 38–42, which set out separate defences for a person who acted to protect his or her personal property, dwelling-house, or other real property. Section 35 is an attempt to clarify and simplify the law on defence of property by creating one new defence of property provision. It eliminates the many distinctions regarding acts a person can take in defence of different types of property. Section 35 permits a person in "peaceable possession" of a property to commit a reasonable act, including the use of force, for the purpose of protecting that property from being taken, damaged, or trespassed upon.

> **35. (1) A person is not guilty of an offence if**
>
> > **(a) they either believe on reasonable grounds that they are in peaceable possession of property or are acting under the authority of, or lawfully assisting, a person whom they believe on reasonable grounds is in peaceable possession of property;**
> >
> > **(b) they believe on reasonable grounds that another person**
> >
> > > **(i) is about to enter, is entering or has entered the property without being entitled by law to do so,**
> > >
> > > **(ii) is about to take the property, is doing so or has just done so, or**
> > >
> > > **(iii) is about to damage or destroy the property, or make it inoperative, or is doing so;**
> >
> > **(c) the act that constitutes the offence is committed for the purpose of**
> >
> > > **(i) preventing the other person from entering the property, or removing that person from the property, or**
> > >
> > > **(ii) preventing the other person from taking, damaging or destroying the property or from making it inoperative, or retaking the property from that person; and**
> >
> > **(d) the act committed is reasonable in the circumstances.**

The elements of this defence can be summarized in this way: (a) The accused reasonably believes that he or she is in peaceable possession of the property; (b) the accused reasonably believes that another person is about to enter, take, or damage the property; (c) the act of the accused is for the purpose of preventing the other person from entering, taking, or damaging the property; and (d) the act of the accused is reasonable in the circumstances.

Subsection (2) provides that the defence does not apply if the accused does not have a claim of right to the property and the other person is entitled by law to possess the property. If the person in peaceable possession has possession under a ***claim of right***, the person must honestly believe, on reasonable grounds, that he or she has a right to possess the property. Thus, a possessor under a claim of right is in a much stronger position than a possessor who does not have some basis for claiming that he or she has a lawful right of possession.

Subsection (3) provides that the defence does not apply if the other person is doing something that they are authorized to do in the administration or enforcement of the law, unless the accused reasonably believes that the other person is acting unlawfully.

It is likely that, in determining whether the defence of property under s. 35 applies, the courts will find the case law under the former sections 38–42 to be relevant. The following cases were decided before the current s. 35.

a. Personal Property

Under the former s. 38(2), a trespasser commited an assault if he or she tried to take movable property from a person in peaceable possession, and if the possessor put his or her hands on the property. In *R. v. Doucette*,[46] C. had failed to make his payments on a television set that he was purchasing under a conditional sales agreement. Three bailiffs, acting for the seller of the television, entered C.'s house to repossess the set. They were not acting under the authority of a court order, and C. told them to leave. While C. was leaning on the television set, the bailiffs grabbed it and began carrying it away. C. followed "in a threatening manner," and the bailiff, Doucette, believing that C. was about to strike him, hit him in the mouth, knocking him to the floor. Doucette was charged with assault. The court found the accused guilty and made the following points:

- It was illegal for the bailiffs to repossess the television set by the use of force.
- As a peaceable possessor of movable property under a claim of right, C. was protected from criminal responsibility for resisting the taking of the property.
- The bailiffs were trespassers, at least from the point at which C. protested against their being in his house.
- Apart from the actual force applied to C., the bailiffs could be charged with committing an assault (under the former s. 38(2)) because they persisted in trying to take the property after C. had leaned on it.

The Supreme Court of Canada considered the defence of personal property in *R. v. Szczerbaniwicz*.[47] In the course of a domestic argument, Ms. S took her husband's mounted diploma off a wall at the landing of a staircase in their home, and threw it on the floor. The husband then pushed Ms. S, causing her to fall backwards; she suffered bruising on her back, legs, and elbow. Mr. S. was charged with assault causing bodily harm. He argued that he was defending his personal property. The court agreed with the trial judge that the actions of the accused could not be justified because he had used more force than was necessary in defending his personal property. The force used must not be disproportionate to the injury or harm that it is intended to prevent. The accused's subjective belief about what force is required is relevant, but the subjective belief must be based on grounds that are objectively reasonable in the circumstances.

---

46   (1960), 129 C.C.C. 102 (Ont. C.A.).
47   [2010] 1 S.C.R. 455 (S.C.C.).

b. Dwelling-house and Real Property

In *R. v. Kephart*,[48] the accused was charged with obstructing a police officer in the execution of his duty. The accused had attempted to prevent a police officer from entering his home. He argued (under the former s. 40) that he was justified in using force to prevent a person from breaking into his dwelling-house. It was established that the officer did not have a lawful right to enter the home; therefore, the accused could use this defence.

As noted above, s. 35 allows a person to use force to remove trespassers not only from his or her home but from any part of his or her real property; for example, a person may forcibly remove a trespasser from the front lawn. The defence of real property also applies to commercial property, for example, shopping malls. In *R. v. Keating*,[49] the owner of a mall grabbed and threatened a boy he found skateboarding in the parking lot of the mall. Signs were posted that prohibited skateboarding. The trial judge found the accused guilty of assault and uttering a death threat. On appeal, the court held that the judge erred in finding that a defence (under former s. 41(1)) was not available to the accused. The court also held that although the complainant was initially an invitee to the mall, once he began skateboarding it was open to the court to find that he was a trespasser, since he had been invited to the mall to shop, not to skateboard.

In *R. v. Montague*,[50] the issue was whether the accused had used more force than was necessary in removing a person from his property. Atkinson came to the door of the accused's home and asked him if he would be interested in a discussion of the Bible. The accused said he was not interested and told him to leave. Atkinson agreed to leave. At this point in the case, there was a conflict in the evidence; however, the accused admitted that he pushed Atkinson to get him to leave. He then followed Atkinson to a point on his property about seven metres from the house and pushed him down into a snowbank. Atkinson got up and ran to the road, with the accused chasing after him. The court concluded that, even if Atkinson was a trespasser, the accused had used more force than was necessary. The court found that Atkinson was actually leaving as requested when the accused proceeded to follow him out. There was nothing to suggest that Atkinson would not have continued leaving if the accused had simply closed the door and stayed in his house. His attack on Atkinson at the snowbank was an assault and was clearly not necessary for the defence of his property.

In *R. v. Gunning*,[51] the accused was convicted of second-degree murder in the fatal shooting of the victim who, uninvited, had entered the home of the accused during a party. The accused denied that he intended to kill the victim. He testified that, after the victim had assaulted him and refused to leave, he had taken out and loaded the shotgun so as to intimidate or scare him into leaving. In the course of the confrontation, the gun discharged, accidentally killing the victim. The Supreme Court of Canada, in ordering a new trial for other reasons, reiterated the four elements of the defence of a house or real property, stating that, in this case, they were intrinsically connected to the underlying offence of careless use of a firearm. For the accused to rely on the defence, "he must have been in possession of the dwelling-house; his possession must have been peaceable; the victim must have been a trespasser; and the force used to eject the trespasser must have been reasonable in all the circumstances."[52] The Court further stated that only the fourth element was an issue in this case—the reasonableness of the force used.

---

48 (1988), 44 C.C.C. (3d) 97 (Alta. C.A.).
49 (1992), 76 C.C.C. (3d) 570 (N.S.C.A.).
50 (1949), 97 C.C.C. 29 (Ont. Co. Ct.).
51 (2005), 196 C.C.C. (3d) 123 (S.C.C.).
52 Ibid. at 132.

The parties agreed that the intentional killing of a trespasser can be justified only where it is a case of self-defence. The accused in this case did not raise self-defence in respect of the shooting. He claimed that he had no *mens rea* because the shooting was an accident. He raised defence of property only in relation to his use of the shotgun to intimidate or scare the victim into leaving.

Under the former s. 41(2), a trespasser who resisted an attempt by the possessor of the property to remove him from that property is guilty of an assault. However, in order to be guilty, the trespasser must perform some overt act of resistance. Passive resistance is not sufficient to justify a conviction. In *R. v. Kellington*,[53] about 25 persons came to the offices of the Social Services Department of the city of Vancouver at about 5 p.m. They were there to get information about the department's policy regarding funerals for indigent persons. The director of the department discussed the policy with them for about 30 minutes. Then disagreements arose between the director and the group, and he asked them to leave the building. They refused, and the police were called to remove them. One member of the group remained seated in a chair until arrested. She was charged with assault under s. 41(2). The court found her not guilty because she had done no overt act to resist her removal from the property.

06 I. MISTAKE OF FACT

A person who commits a prohibited act while believing that certain circumstances exist— circumstances which do not actually exist—may be able to rely on the defence of **mistake of fact**. A mistake of fact is an error as to some circumstance. For example, if Albert takes Nahid's book believing it to be his own, he is acting under a mistake of fact. A mistake of fact will be a defence to a criminal charge if (a) the mistake was an honest one, and (b) no offence would have been committed if the circumstances had been as the accused believed them to be. So, Albert will not be guilty of theft if he had an honest belief that the book belonged to him, since, if the book had belonged to him, no offence would have been committed. Mistake of fact is a defence to most charges under the Code, because a person who is acting under a mistaken belief in the facts does not have the *mens rea* or guilty mind required to commit the offence. Albert did not have the *mens rea* to commit theft (i.e., the intent to deprive the owner).

In *Beaver v. R.*,[54] the accused was charged with illegal possession of a narcotic drug. He had sold heroin to an undercover RCMP officer. His defence was that he honestly believed that he was selling sugar, not heroin, even though he had told the officer he was selling a narcotic. The Supreme Court of Canada found the accused not guilty because "[t]he essence of the crime is the possession of the forbidden substance and in a criminal case there is in law no possession without knowledge of the character of the forbidden substance." In short, to be guilty of illegal possession of a narcotic, the accused must know that he or she has a narcotic. A person who has an honest but mistaken belief that the substance is sugar does not have the knowledge required for possession. The mistaken belief must be honest; it does not have to be reasonable. Whether a reasonable person would have believed that the heroin was sugar is merely one factor to be considered by the jury in determining whether the accused's mistake was an honest mistake.

Consider the following situation: Alice is charged with trafficking in LSD. She says that she intended to sell, and thought that she was selling, a different drug, mescaline.[55] Mistake of

---

53 (1972), 7 C.C.C. (2d) 564 (B.C.S.C.).
54 (1957), 118 C.C.C. 129 (S.C.C.).
55 See, for example, *R. v. Kundeus* (1975), 24 C.C.C. (2d) 276 (S.C.C.).

fact is not a defence here, because, if the facts had been as Alice believed them to be, an offence would still have been committed.

Several sections in the Code limit the defence of mistake of fact for sexual offences involving young people. For example, under s. 150.1, an accused cannot use this defence to a charge of touching a person under 16 years of age for a sexual purpose unless the accused took all reasonable steps to ascertain the age of the young person. These rules are discussed in Chapter 7 under sexual offences. As mentioned earlier, there are also special rules regarding mistaken belief of consent when the charge is sexual assault. These rules are discussed in Chapter 11 with the offences of sexual assault.

J. MISTAKE OF LAW

The general rule that "ignorance of the law is no excuse" is contained in s. 19. In other words, everyone is presumed to know the criminal law. A mistake of fact is an error as to some circumstance or fact. A **mistake of law** is an error as to the legal status of the circumstance or fact. For example, in *Beaver*, the accused was found not guilty of possession of heroin because he honestly believed that the heroin was sugar. This was a mistake of fact. However, if Beaver had known that he had heroin, but honestly believed that it was legal to possess heroin, he would have been making a mistake of law, and thus would have been guilty.

1. Mistake of Civil Law

In some situations, a mistake of civil law may be a defence. A mistake of civil law occurs when a person has an honest belief that he or she has a legal right under the civil law, but in fact does not have the right. In *R. v. Howson*,[56] the accused, the operator of a car-towing service, was charged with theft. Haines had parked his car on private property. There were signs on the property stating that unauthorized cars would be towed away at the owner's expense. After being asked by the owner of the property, the accused removed the car by towing it to a yard enclosed by a high fence and guarded by an attendant. When Haines arrived at the yard, the attendant told him he could not have his car unless he paid $12.00 for the towing and storage. Haines did not get his car back until the next evening, when he paid the towing and storage charges.

The offence of theft is committed if a person deprives a property owner of the property "without colour of right." The term **colour of right** refers to an honest mistake of fact or law that leads a person to believe that he or she has a legal justification for the actions performed. In *Howson*, the accused had no legal right to refuse to release the car, but he honestly believed that he had the legal right to refuse until the money was paid. The court found the accused not guilty because he acted with colour of right. He had made a mistake of law, and thus was acting without the *mens rea* required in the offence of theft. However, the court warned the accused that now that he was aware of his legal position, he could not rely on the same mistake of law as a defence to any similar charges in the future.

Other examples of colour of right are in Part Two of the book. Chapter 12 discusses the meaning of "without colour of right" in the definition of theft. Chapter 13 discusses colour of right as part of the s. 492(2) defence to a charge of mischief, arson, or cruelty to animals.

---

56   (1966), 3 C.C.C. 348 (Ont. C.A.).

2. Officially Induced Error

The defence of **officially induced error** has been recognized by some provincial courts of appeal. Its existence reflects the fact that we live in an extremely complex society and that we need to be able to rely on the advice of government officials regarding the law. The defence may be used for breaches of regulatory laws (not true crimes) where the accused was aware of a possible illegality and sought the advice of the government official in charge of enforcing the law. The Ontario Court of Appeal[57] has said that to use this defence, the accused must show that he or she relied on an erroneous legal opinion and that the reliance was reasonable. Whether the reliance was reasonable will depend on factors such as the efforts the accused made to ascertain the law, the complexity or obscurity of the law, and the position of the official who gave the advice. In *R. v. Bauman and Bauman*,[58] the two accused, a husband and wife, were charged under a municipal bylaw with operating a business in a family dwelling. Before opening the business, the husband purchased a copy of the bylaw and asked a city planner if they could open a business in their home. The planner assured him that they could. The accused were acquitted. Both the trial and appeal courts accepted the defence of officially induced error. In this case, the law was complex, the official had a significant position, and the advice was definitive and reasonable.

There is some indication that the Supreme Court of Canada will, once an appropriate case comes before it, recognize the defence of officially induced error as an excuse to regulatory offences or crimes. In *R. v. Jorgenson*,[59] the accused was the owner of a video store that carried "adult videos." He was charged with selling obscene material under s. 163(2). Although he was acquitted on other grounds, one of the Supreme Court judges who heard the case, Chief Justice Lamer, argued that the defence of officially induced error should be available to Jorgenson because the videos in the case had been approved by the Ontario Film Review Board.[60] Since it was not necessary to consider this defence because the Crown failed to prove the *mens rea* of the offence, the other judges expressly refrained from commenting on the availability of this defence. However, Lamer pointed out that there are an "astounding number" of laws for which a person in Canada can incur criminal liability. Although people are expected to know the law, "it is certainly reasonable for someone to have assumed he knows the law after consulting a representative of the state acting in a capacity which makes him an expert on that particular subject."[61]

K. ENTRAPMENT

In *R. v. Mack*,[62] the Supreme Court of Canada held that the defence of entrapment exists as part of the doctrine of abuse of process. The defence of entrapment may be allowed when someone has been "set up" or trapped into committing a crime by the police or police informants. These situations often arise in drug investigations. In *Mack*, a police informer, over a six-month period, repeatedly asked the accused to sell him drugs. The accused refused to do so until the informer threatened him, at which point he agreed. The accused testified that although he had once been involved with drugs, he had since given up his drug-related lifestyle. The Court held

---

57 *R. v. Cancoil Thermal Corp. and Parkinson* (1986), 27 C.C.C. (3d) 295 (Ont. C.A.).
58 (1994), 32 C.R. (4th) 176 (Ont. C.J. Prov. Div.).
59 (1995), 102 C.C.C. (3d) 97 (S.C.C.).
60 Criminal courts are not bound by the decisions of provincial review boards regarding whether a film is obscene.
61 *Jorgenson, supra* note 59 at 104.
62 (1988), 44 C.C.C. (3d) 513 (S.C.C.).

that the police conduct was unacceptable in this case and that the charges against the accused should be stayed. The Court set out guidelines for deciding whether police conduct amounts to an abuse of process. First, the police cannot provide opportunities for people to commit crimes unless they are acting on reasonable suspicions that the people are already engaged in crime, or unless they are carrying on a bona fide investigation. As one judge said, the police cannot randomly test the virtue of people. Second, even when the police do have reasonable suspicions or are carrying on a bona fide investigation, they cannot go beyond providing opportunities; that is, they cannot actually induce a person to commit a crime.

R. v. Barnes[63] dealt with the issue of what a bona fide investigation is. A police officer approached the accused in a Vancouver shopping mall and asked him if he had any "weed." At first the accused said no. The officer asked several more times. Finally, the accused agreed to sell the officer a small amount of hash. The trial judge allowed the defence of entrapment because the police had been engaged in "random virtue testing." The Supreme Court held that the defence did not apply in this case. The accused had been approached in an area known for drug trafficking, and the police were conducting a bona fide investigation. It did not matter that the police did not have reasonable grounds to suspect that the accused was involved in crime. His physical presence in an area where a particular criminal activity was occurring was enough.

L. PROVOCATION

The defence of provocation can be used to reduce the offence of murder to manslaughter. Section 232(2) states that a wrongful act or insult that is sufficient to deprive an ordinary person of self-control is provocation, if the accused acted on it "on the sudden" and before there was time for his passion to cool. This defence is discussed in Chapter 8.

---

63 (1991), 63 C.C.C. (3d) 1 (S.C.C); aff'g (1990), 54 C.C.C. (3d) 368 (B.C.C.A.).

Questions for Review and Discussion

1. Make a list of different types of defences.
2. Does the accused have to "prove" his or her defence? Explain.
3. Where are defences found?
4. What is the age at which the law presumes children do not have the capacity to commit crimes?
5. What must be established on behalf of the accused if he or she is to be found not criminally responsible because of mental disorder?
6. What is the meaning of the word "wrong" as it is used in the defence of mental disorder?
7. What happens to an accused who is found not criminally responsible because of a mental disorder?
8. **a.** Define the defence of automatism.
   b. What is the difference between insane and non-insane automatism?
9. How is the defence of automatism different from the defence of mental disorder?

10. **a.** What are the rules regarding the defence of intoxication for general intent crimes and for specific intent crimes?
    b. How did the decision in *Daviault* change the law? How did the government respond to this decision?

11. Explain the differences between the Code defence of compulsion and the defence of duress at common law.

12. When can the defence of necessity be used?

13. What did the Supreme Court decide in the case of *R. v. Lavallée*?

14. Discuss situations where consent may not be a defence.

15. What is the general rule concerning the use of force in self-defence, the defence of others, and the defence of property?

16. What does "mistake of fact" mean when it is used as a defence?

17. In what circumstances might mistake of law be a defence to a crime?

18. How is mistake of fact different from mistake of law?

19. **a.** What is the defence of entrapment?
    b. What guidelines must the police follow to avoid this defence being raised?

20. H.'s boat was destroyed in a fire, and he made an insurance claim for his loss. A short while later, a former employee told the police that H. had paid him to destroy the boat. H. was charged with arson, insurance fraud, and perjury. The employee claimed that on a certain date, he and H. had a conversation during which H. asked him to burn the boat. H. testified at his trial that at the time that conversation supposedly took place, he was elsewhere. Is H. raising an alibi defence? Explain. See *R. v. Hill* (1995), 25 O.R. 97 (Ont. C.A.).

21. Henrik owes $500 to Borje, a well-known underworld figure. Borje threatens Henrik by saying, "If you don't pay me by 10 p.m. tonight, you'll be dead tomorrow morning." Henrik knows that Borje is serious and will carry out the threat if necessary. So Henrik breaks into a store, steals $500, and makes the payment to Borje. Henrik is charged with break, enter, and theft. He raises the defence of compulsion. Will his defence be successful? Explain.

22. Sam had been drinking large amounts of alcohol and had taken Valium pills when he broke into his son's school. He broke a lock on the principal's office door, forced open a file drawer, and stole a cash box containing $140. He buried the cash box under a pile of brush. He claimed to have no memory of these events. The police questioned him a few days after the break-in because the police had found his fingerprints at the school. Realizing what he might have done, he searched for the metal box with a metal detector. He found the box and contacted the police. He also arranged to return the box to the principal and to pay for the damage caused by the break-in. Can Sam use the defence of intoxication? Explain. See *R. v. Shea* (1981), 24 C.R. (3d) 189 (P.E.I.S.C.).

23. M. was charged with speeding on the Trans-Canada Highway. She admitted to speeding but claimed that she was doing so because a pickup truck had approached her rapidly from behind. She said that to avoid an accident, she had increased her speed and then changed lanes to let the truck pass. Does she have a defence to the charge? Explain. See *R. v. Morris* (1994), 32 C.R. (4th) 191 (B.C.S.C.).

24. Stone admitted stabbing his wife 47 times but claimed to have done it while in a state of automatism. He testified that his wife berated him throughout a drive to Vancouver to visit his sons from a previous marriage. His wife objected to the visit, which lasted only 15 minutes because his wife threatened to lay on the horn until the police came. On the return drive, his wife asked him if he wanted a divorce. He responded that they might as well get divorced if she was not going to let him see his sons. This answer upset the victim

and she again began to berate Stone. He pulled the truck into an empty lot while his wife continued to yell at him. She said that he was "nothing but a piece of shit," that the police were preparing to arrest him because she had falsely reported to the police that he had been abusing her, and that she was going to get a court order so that he would not be allowed on their property. While kneeling on the seat of the truck, she continued yelling in his face that she felt sick whenever he touched her, that sexual intercourse with him was "lousy," and that she was never going to have sex with him again.

Stone testified that, while sitting in the truck with his head down during the yelling, his wife's voice began to fade off. He recalled wondering why she was treating him and his children in this way. He also remembered thinking about how people in the small town in which he lived would look at him if his wife had him arrested. He then felt a "whoosh" sensation wash over him from his feet to his head. When his eyes focussed again, he was staring straight ahead and felt something in his hand. He was holding the six-inch hunting knife which he kept in the truck. He looked over and saw his wife slumped over on the seat. He knew that she was dead. Should Stone's defence of automatism be successful? Explain. See *R. v. Stone*, [1999] 2 S.C.R. 290.

25. Sections 672.64 and 672.65 on capping dispositions, where a finding of not guilty by reason of mental disorder is made, did not become law. Discuss why you think these sections were never brought into force and whether you think they should be part of the law.

26. Based on an anonymous tip that a man was selling drugs on the twelfth floor of an apartment building, an undercover officer went to the apartment building and took the elevator to the twelfth floor. When the elevator doors opened, Imoro, the accused, approached the officer and said, "Come with me." The officer responded, "You can hook me up?" Imoro answered, "Yeah, man." Imoro led the officer and another man who had been on the elevator with the officer to his apartment. Once inside, Imoro sold some marijuana to the other man. Imoro then asked the officer what he needed. The officer said cocaine. Imoro gave him a bag of powder cocaine, and the officer then gave Imoro $40, which was police "buy money."

The next day, the officer went back to Imoro's apartment. Imoro sold him another $40 worth of cocaine. The police then obtained a search warrant for the apartment. They seized cocaine, marijuana, and the police buy money. Imoro was charged with trafficking in cocaine, and possession of cocaine and marijuana for the purpose of trafficking. Imoro claimed entrapment and brought a motion to exclude the evidence or stay the proceedings. Should the defence of entrapment be successful? See *R. v. Imoro*, [2010] S.C.J. No. 50 (S.C.C.); aff'g [2010] O.J. No. 586 Ont. C.A.

27. Landry was charged with first-degree murder. He admitted that he had planned and committed the physical act of killing the victim, but argued that he should be found not guilty by reason of insanity (now referred to as mental disorder). Landry suffered from a severe psychosis that made him believe that he was God and had a mission to destroy all forces of evil on Earth. He suffered from the further delusion that the victim was Satan and that he had to kill him in order to rid the Earth effectively of all evil forces. Landry knew that murder was a crime and that he would in all likelihood be arrested for this act, but he believed nevertheless that the act was necessary in order to fulfill his divine mission. Did he have an insanity defence? See *R. v. Landry* (1991), 62 C.C.C. (3d) 117 (S.C.C.).

CHAPTER 5

Pre-trial Criminal Procedure

Key points explained in this chapter are

LO1 the various ways of ensuring that an accused appears in court;

LO2 the authority of the police to arrest and detain a person;

LO3 the rights of a person who has been arrested or detained;

LO4 the circumstances in which the police may search a person or property;

LO5 the procedure and limitations related to when the police may intercept a person's private communications; and

LO6 situations when evidence obtained by the police may be excluded from the trial because the police violated the Charter of Rights and Freedoms.

Generally, criminal procedure can be separated into three distinct phases: pre-trial procedure, trial procedure, and post-trial procedure. This chapter considers only the more important aspects of pre-trial procedure, including the powers of arrest and search, pre-trial release, and rights of the accused before and after arrest.

01 A. BRINGING THE ACCUSED BEFORE THE COURT

1. Beginning the Process

Once the police have reasonable grounds for believing that someone has committed a crime and have decided to lay a charge, their next step is to decide how to begin the process that will eventually bring the suspect before a court where criminal liability can be determined. Initially, the police have three choices, not all of which are available in all situations. They can (a) issue an appearance notice, (b) go before a justice to ask for a summons to be issued, or (c) make an arrest, with or without a warrant. Generally speaking, arrests are only made when an appearance notice or summons is inadequate; for example, an arrest would be made if there are reasonable grounds to believe that the accused will not show up in court. As discussed below, even when the accused is arrested, there are many points along the way to trial where he or she may be released and an appearance notice or summons issued.

Part XVI of the Code, starting with s. 493, sets out the procedures for bringing the accused before a justice, who is defined in s. 2 of the Code as a justice of the peace or provincial court judge, and for the pre-trial release of the accused where the accused has been arrested. The forms referred to in this chapter are contained in Part XXVIII of the Code.

2. Appearance Notice (Form 9)

Section 496 provides that where a peace officer does not make an arrest, the officer may issue an appearance notice if the offence is one of the following:

- an indictable offence mentioned in s. 553 (these are the least serious indictable offences),
- a hybrid offence, or
- an offence punishable on summary conviction.

An appearance notice is a written form given to a person, usually at the scene of the crime by the police. It contains the accused's name, the substance of the charge, and the time and place the accused must attend court to answer the charge (s. 501). If the person is being charged with an indictable offence, the appearance notice may state a time and place that the accused is to go for fingerprinting and photographing, as required by the Identification of Criminals Act.[1] The appearance notice also contains the text of s. 145(5) and (6), stating that it is an offence to fail to appear in court, or for the purposes of identification, without lawful excuse. Section 502 is also contained in the appearance notice; it states that a judge may issue a warrant for the arrest of an accused who fails to appear in court or for identification.

The accused is requested, but not required, to sign the form in duplicate and is given a copy, and is then free to go.

Once an appearance notice is issued, an information must be laid before a justice as soon as practicable, or at least before the time stated in the appearance notice for the accused to appear in court. Section 506 provides that the information may be in Form 2. Recall from Chapter 2 that an information is a sworn affidavit that the informant has personal knowledge or reasonable grounds for believing that the named person has committed an offence. If the informant makes out a case against the accused, the appearance notice is confirmed (s. 508).

3. Summons (Form 6)

The police may go before a justice and ask that a summons be issued. A summons is a court order setting out the offence with which the accused is charged and commanding the accused to appear in court on a certain day and time (s. 509). To obtain a summons, the officer must lay an information before the justice of the peace. If the officer makes out a case against the accused and an arrest warrant is not necessary, a summons is issued. A peace officer must deliver the summons personally to the accused. If the accused cannot be found, it must be left at his last or usual residence with someone who appears to be at least 16 years old.

As with an appearance notice, the summons may require the accused to attend a certain place for the purposes of the Identification of Criminals Act; it will contain a notice that failure to appear at court or for identification is an offence and that the judge may issue an arrest warrant (s. 145(4), s. 510).

---

1   R.S.C. 1985, c. I-1.

[LO2] 4. Arrests

An arrest is the detention of a person for the purpose of dealing with the person according to law, including the purpose of bringing an accused person before the court. An arrest can consist of the actual seizure of the accused's body. It is sufficient for the arresting person merely to touch the accused and to announce that the accused is under arrest.

An arrest can also be made by words alone.[2] The arresting person must use words such that the person being arrested is made aware that his or her freedom is being restricted and that he or she is compelled to follow the instructions of the arresting person.

a. Use of Force

Section 25(1) provides that a peace officer may use as much force as is necessary in making an arrest, if the officer acts on reasonable grounds. This section applies not only to the police but also to anyone required or authorized by law to do anything in the administration or enforcement of the law; for example, a private person who is assisting an officer is justified in using reasonable force.

Section 25(3) limits s. 25(1). It restricts the use of force that is intended or is likely to cause death or grievous bodily harm. It states that no one is justified in using such force unless the person believes on reasonable and probable grounds that it is necessary to protect himself or herself, or a person under his or her protection, from death or grievous bodily harm. The subjective belief of the person using the force must be objectively reasonable, which means that the use of force must be judged on both a subjective and an objective basis.[3]

In *R. v. Nasoguluak*,[4] the police received a tip about an intoxicated driver, which led to a high speed chase. After the driver, Nasoguluak, stopped his car, he did not comply with an order to get out of the car. Then a police officer, C, grabbed Nasoguluak and punched him in the head. C testified that this was to prevent Nasoguluak from driving away and striking another officer, who was standing in front of the car. Nasoguluak let go of the steering wheel and reached out to C, who struck him in the head again, pulled him out of the car, and wrestled him onto the ground. C yelled at Nasoguluak to stop resisting and gave him a third hard punch in the head. Nasoguluak was pinned face down on the pavement with C straddling his back. When Nasoguluak refused to offer up his hands to be handcuffed, another officer, D, punched him in the back twice. These blows broke Nasoguluak's ribs, which punctured one of his lungs. A third officer, O, was kneeling on Nasoguluak's thigh throughout the struggle. The Supreme Court of Canada upheld the decision of the Alberta Court of Appeal that the police had violated s. 25(3) by using excessive force. The Supreme Court also concluded that the sentencing judge had appropriately reduced Nasoguluak's sentence for impaired driving as a result of the police misconduct.

Section 25(4) authorizes the use of force that is likely to cause death or grievous bodily harm in order to attempt to prevent a suspect from avoiding arrest by fleeing. However, such force can be used only if the following circumstances exist:

- The peace officer or other person must believe on reasonable grounds that the force is necessary to protect the officer or other persons from imminent or future death or grievous bodily harm.
- The arrest must be lawful.

2   *R. v. Whitfield* (1970), 1 C.C.C. 129 (S.C.C.).
3   *R. v. Nasoguluak*, [2010] 1 S.C.R. 206.
4   Ibid.

- The offence must be one for which a person can be arrested without a warrant.
- The flight must not be preventable by reasonable means in a less violent manner.

Prior to 1994, when this section was amended to its present form, police could use "as much force as necessary" to prevent the escape of a suspect, unless the escape could be prevented by reasonable means in a less violent manner. In effect, the police could use deadly force to prevent the escape of a person for a relatively minor crime. The law did not limit the use of force that was likely to cause death or grievous bodily harm to situations in which the peace officer or person assisting the officer believed on reasonable grounds that such force was necessary to protect the officer or other person from death or grievous bodily harm.

The amendment was made to prevent situations such as in *Priestman v. Colangelo*,[5] where a police officer used the former s. 25(4) to justify his actions. Constables P. and A. were on patrol duty when they received a message on their radio telephone reporting the theft of a car. Almost immediately they saw a motor vehicle that they believed to be—and that later turned out to be—the stolen vehicle. The police car pulled up alongside the stolen car, and P. ordered the driver, S., to stop. Both officers were in uniform, and S. no doubt realized that they were police officers. Instead of stopping, he pulled around the corner and drove away at a high rate of speed. The police car followed and tried three times to pass the stolen car in order to cut it off, but each time S. pulled to the south side of the road and cut off the police car. On the third occasion, the police car was forced over the south curb onto a boulevard and was compelled to slow down in order to avoid colliding with a hydro pole. Following this third attempt, and as the police car went back onto the road, P. fired a warning shot into the air from his .38 calibre revolver. The stolen car increased its speed. When the police car was one-and-a-half to two car lengths from the stolen car, P. aimed at the left rear tire of the stolen car and fired. The bullet hit the bottom of the frame of the rear window, shattered the glass, ricocheted, and struck S. in the back of the neck, causing him to lose consciousness immediately. The stolen car went over the curb on the south side of the road, grazed a hydro pole, crossed a street, and, in coming to a stop, struck the veranda of a house. Before hitting the house, the car ran into and killed two people waiting for a bus.

Constable P. took the position that S.'s escape could not have been prevented by reasonable means in a less violent manner. In other words, P. believed that he was justified in firing his revolver. The court agreed with P., finding that his actions were justified by s. 25(4). He had used no more force than was reasonably necessary to prevent S.'s escape.

Section 25(5) allows a peace officer to use force intended or likely to cause death or grievous bodily harm against an inmate who is escaping from a federal penitentiary. The peace officer must believe on reasonable grounds that the inmates of the penitentiary pose a threat of death or grievous bodily harm to the peace officer or another person, and that the escape cannot be prevented by other reasonable means in a less violent manner.

b. Liability for Excessive Use of Force

If more force than necessary is used to arrest the accused, the arresting person may be sued in a civil court for assault and be required to pay damages. In addition, s. 26 provides that the arresting person can be prosecuted in a criminal court for the offence of assault or one of the more serious criminal offences involving bodily harm. If a court finds that excessive force is used, it may also find that a violation of s. 7 or s. 12 of the Charter has occurred, and may dismiss the charges against the accused. Sections 7 and 12 state:

---

5   *Priestman v. Colangelo* (1959), 124 C.C.C. 1 (S.C.C.).

7. Everyone has the right to life, liberty and security of the person and the right not to be deprived thereof except in accordance with the principles of fundamental justice.

12. Everyone has the right not to be subjected to any cruel and unusual treatment or punishment.

Several cases considering this issue and the Charter have involved the use of tasers by the police when arresting or detaining a person. The death of Robert Dziekanski at the Vancouver Airport after he was tasered by police resulted in the call for the review of the use of tasers by police and government agencies.[6] At this time, the only reported cases are at the trial level and these cases have differing results.

Charges have been stayed because of the unacceptable use of tasers by the police. In *R. v. Walcott*,[7] the police were searching a house suspected of containing a handgun. They found Walcott naked in a room with a woman. The court accepted the evidence that Walcott was tasered after he had been restrained and handcuffed. The court dismissed charges of possession of cocaine against Walcott on the grounds that his Charter rights under sections 7 and 12 had been violated. In *R. v. J.W.*,[8] the court accepted evidence that the youth who was being strip-searched at the police station was compliant during the search and was tasered as a "punishment" by the officer. In stating that there was a "completely unjustified use of force," the court stayed charges of housebreaking against the youth on the grounds that his Charter rights under sections 7 and 12 were violated.

A different result was reached in *R. v. Galloway*.[9] Police officers Galloway and Hope had arrested and handcuffed the accused at her home. She was taken to the police station and placed in a cell. Two female officers entered the cell and attempted to remove her handcuffs. She resisted and a struggle ensued. Galloway and Hope came to the aid of the officers struggling with the accused, and used a taser on her. The trial court dismissed the charges of assault against the officers, holding that the force used was justified. The appeal court agreed that the officers' use of force was reasonable. The officers were coming to the assistance of other officers who were trying to remove the accused's handcuffs for her own safety.

c. The Right to Enter Private Property to Make an Arrest

Whether the arrest is made with or without a warrant, the police have the authority, in some situations, to enter private premises to make an arrest. One situation is where the police are in "hot pursuit" of a suspect. In *R. v. Macooh*,[10] the police observed the accused motorist running a stop sign. When the police attempted to pull the accused over, he accelerated and went through two more stop signs. He then pulled into an apartment parking lot, exited his car, and ran to an apartment. The officer went to the apartment, identified himself, and called to the accused. The accused did not answer. The officer entered the apartment and told the accused he was being arrested. The accused refused to leave, and an altercation broke out. The accused was charged with impaired driving, failing to stop for an officer, failing to submit to a breathalyzer test, and assaulting an officer. The trial judge found that the police did not have the right to enter the apartment, and excluded the evidence gathered after the entry. The

---

6 See **cbc.ca/news/background/tasers** for general information about tasers. Tasers work by discharging an electrical current into a person, causing involuntary muscle spasms and loss of motor control. The purpose is to disable or stun a person; the taser is considered less lethal than a firearm.
7 [2008] O.J. No. 799 (Ont. Ct. J.).
8 (2006), 72 W.C.B. (d) 175 (Alta. Prov. Ct.).
9 (2007), 252 N.S.R. (2d) 319 (N.S.S.C.).
10 (1993), 82 C.C.C. (3d) 480 (S.C.C.).

accused was acquitted. On appeal to the Supreme Court of Canada, the issue was whether the police had a right to enter the apartment. The Court held that under the common law there is a right to enter a private premise to make a warrantless arrest when the officer is in "hot pursuit" of a suspect. To be in hot pursuit or "fresh pursuit," the accused must be followed in a manner that is continuous and conducted with reasonable effort so that the pursuit and capture and the commission of the crime form a single transaction. The Court stated that it is unacceptable that a person about to be arrested should be able to take refuge in his home or the home of another person. Offenders should not be encouraged to seek refuge, since it may create situations of danger. The police authority applies to all offences, provincial or federal, as long as the police have the authority to make the arrest. The Court specifically stated that this decision is limited to cases of hot pursuit.

Other situations where the police can enter a dwelling place to make an arrest are covered in sections 529.1 to 529.5 of the Criminal Code. Section 529.1 provides for judicial authorization of entry into a dwelling-house to make an arrest. Section 529.5 provides that the officer may obtain a "telewarrant" (discussed below) rather than appearing before a justice of the peace to make an application to obtain the warrant to enter.

Section 529.3 provides authority for a warrantless entry where the peace officer has reasonable grounds to believe that the person to be arrested or apprehended is present, and that the conditions for obtaining a warrant exist, but due to exigent circumstances it would be impractical to obtain a warrant. Section 529.3(2) provides that exigent circumstances include circumstances in which the peace officer

(a) **has reasonable grounds to suspect that entry into the dwelling-house is necessary to prevent imminent bodily harm or death to any person; or**

(b) **has reasonable grounds to believe that evidence relating to the commission of an indictable offence is present in the dwelling-house and that entry into the dwelling-house is necessary to prevent the imminent loss or imminent destruction of the evidence.**

This section was enacted in response to the Supreme Court's decision in *R. v. Feeney*,[11] in which the Court considered the effect of s. 8 of the Charter on the issue of the right of the police to enter a dwelling-place to make an arrest. In this case, a man was found dead at his home. Blood was splattered everywhere and Sportsman brand cigarettes were found at the scene. A local resident suggested police speak with Feeney. The officer arrived and knocked at the door of Feeney's house and said, "Police." There was no response, so he entered with his gun drawn. He found Feeney asleep, and when he woke him he noticed blood splattered all over the front of Feeney's shirt and Sportsman brand cigarettes on the table. Feeney was arrested and eventually convicted of second-degree murder. On appeal to the Supreme Court of Canada, the Court held that, as a general rule, a warrant is required to enter a dwelling-house to make an arrest. The Court upheld an individual's privacy interest in a dwelling-house by finding that police violated s. 8 of the Charter by using forcible entry to make a warrantless arrest absent circumstances of "hot pursuit" of a fleeing suspect. The Court noted the increase, under the Charter, of the legal status of the privacy of a dwelling. The Court stated that "the additional burden on the police to obtain a warrant before forcibly entering a private dwelling to arrest, while not justified in a case of hot pursuit is, in general, well worth the

---

11 (1997), 115 C.C.C. (3d) 129 (S.C.C.).

additional protection to the privacy interest in dwelling-houses that it brings."[12] The Court, however, left the door open to Parliament to set out exigent circumstances in which a warrantless entry of a dwelling-house would be allowed.

In sum, whether or not the police have a warrant for arrest, the police can only enter a dwelling-place to make that arrest if (a) the police are in "hot pursuit" of the suspect, (b) they have obtained a warrant under s. 529.1 for entry to the dwelling house, or (c) exigent circumstances under s. 529.3(2) exist.

5. Arrest without Warrant

a. Arrest by Any Person

In England, under the common law, every person had a duty to apprehend persons who broke the "king's peace." The persons who had been arrested would then be turned over to the king's agents for trial. Canadian law continues this practice in the Criminal Code by providing that, in certain situations, a private person can make an arrest. Such an arrest is often referred to as a "citizen's arrest." Section 494 spells out three such situations:

494. (1) Any one may arrest without warrant

(a) **a person whom he finds committing an indictable offence; or**

(b) **a person who, on reasonable grounds, he believes**

(i) **has committed a criminal offence, and**

(ii) **is escaping from and freshly pursued by persons who have lawful authority to arrest that person.**

(2) The owner or a person in lawful possession of property, or a person authorized by the owner or by a person in lawful possession of property, may arrest a person without a warrant if they find them committing a criminal offence on or in relation to that property and

(a) **they make the arrest at that time; or**

(b) **they make the arrest within a reasonable time after the offence is committed and they believe on reasonable grounds that it is not feasible in the circumstances for a peace officer to make the arrest.**

The first situation (subsection (1)(a)) arises when the arresting person finds the accused in the act of committing an indictable offence. Indictable offences include hybrid offences, since a hybrid offence is treated as indictable until the Crown chooses to have it tried as a summary conviction offence. This decision is usually made at the time the accused is arraigned (see Chapter 2).

The second situation (subsection (1)(b)) arises when a person believes on reasonable grounds that the accused has committed any **criminal offence** and is escaping from, and being freshly pursued by, persons having lawful authority to make an arrest. The term "criminal offence" includes summary conviction offences, as well as those that are indictable. It does not include provincial offences.

A person who has "lawful authority" includes not only a peace officer but also any person who is granted the power to make an arrest by the Criminal Code. Thus, a private person who finds someone committing an indictable offence has a lawful authority to arrest the accused.

---

12   Ibid. at 156.

The third situation (subsection (2)) in which a private person may make an arrest arises when an owner of property (either real or personal property), or a person (such as a tenant) lawfully in possession of property, finds an accused committing a criminal offence on or in relation to that property and makes the arrest at that time, or makes the arrest within a reasonable time after the commission of the offence when he or she reasonably believes that it is not feasible in the circumstances for a peace officer to make the arrest. This subsection was passed by Parliament in 2012 as a result of a highly publicized incident in which a grocer arrested a person who he believed had stolen produce from his store a few days before. When the person returned to the store, the grocer seized him so that he could be charged by the police. The grocer was charged with assault. The former subsection (2) permitted a property owner to arrest at the time the offence was committed. The arrest a few days later was considered illegal.

Section 494(3) states that whenever an arrest is made by a person who is not a peace officer, that person must deliver the arrested person to a peace officer "forthwith." One court has said that forthwith does not mean "instantly" but "as soon as reasonably practicable under the circumstances."[13]

Section 30 provides an additional power of **detention** to the private person. Anyone who sees a **breach of the peace** is justified in interfering to prevent the continuation or renewal of the breach, and may detain any person involved in or about to join in the breach. Thus, if a person is in a bar and a brawl starts, the person may grab and hold back anyone who wants to join in, or who has already joined in, until the police arrive.

The criminal law also places a duty, in certain circumstances, on persons to assist the police in making an arrest when requested. Section 129 states that a person commits an offence if the person

(b) **omits, without reasonable excuse, to assist a public officer or peace officer in the execution of his duty in arresting a person or in preserving the peace, after having reasonable notice that he is required to do so . . .**

There are also provincial and federal laws that allow a private person to arrest.[14] In particular, provincial trespass laws may allow a citizen's arrest. This right to arrest for trespassing is used extensively by private security firms that patrol shopping malls, airports, and sports stadiums. An issue that has been considered by the Supreme Court of Canada is whether, and how much, force can be used by a private person who is authorized to make an arrest.

In *R. v. Asante-Mensan*,[15] the accused was charged with escaping lawful custody and assault with intent to resist a lawful arrest. He was a taxi driver who had been picking up fares at the airport without a permit. He had been warned several times to stop "scooping" fares. A notice was issued under the Ontario Trespass to Property Act (TPA) prohibiting him from entering the airport property for any reason. He ignored the notice and continued to "scoop" fares. The airport authorities decided to exercise their authority to make a citizen's arrest under the provincial TPA, which allowed them to arrest any person that they believed on reasonable and probable grounds to be trespassing. It also required them to promptly call for police assistance and give the arrested person to the police.

An airport inspector approached the accused, touched his shoulder, and informed him that he was under arrest for trespassing. The accused attempted to flee in his car, but the inspector blocked his way. The accused then shoved his car door into the inspector causing

---

13   *R. v. Cunningham and Ritchie* (1979), 49 C.C.C. (2d) 390 (Man. Co. Ct.).
14   Over twenty federal laws authorize some form of citizen's arrest.
15   [2003] 2 S.C.R. 3.

the inspector to back away, and, ignoring the inspector's protests, he drove away. The incident resulted in charges of assault with intent to resist arrest, and escaping lawful custody. The trial court dismissed the resisting arrest charge on the grounds that, although the accused was guilty of escaping lawful custody, the inspector had no authority under the TPA to use force in making the arrest. The court of appeal disagreed with the trial judge. It held that the use of reasonable force was incidental to the statutory authority to make the arrest, and set aside the acquittal and entered a conviction. The Supreme Court of Canada agreed with the court of appeal. The Court stated that the power of arrest given by the legislation should be interpreted in accordance with the common law power to arrest, which allows the use of reasonable force, and that in this case no more force than was necessary and reasonable was used, given the circumstances. It noted that "reasonable force in the context of the TPA may have to have regard to not only what is necessary to accomplish the arrest, but also to whether a forcible arrest was in all the circumstances a reasonable course of action in the first place." In other words, the use of force may not always be justified. Many cases of trespass are trivial, the Court noted, and are best handled short of arrest. In this case, the airport authority was justifiably frustrated with the accused's behaviour, and all other attempts to secure the accused's compliance had failed.

The Court also noted that not all provinces allow occupiers to arrest under their trespass laws, keeping the potential use of force in the hands of the police. Finally, the Court stated that individuals who have been wrongly arrested or against whom unreasonable force has been used have successfully pursued prosecutions for assault or claims for civil damages.

b. Arrest by Peace Officer

Peace officers have the same authority to arrest under s. 494(1) as any other person. In addition, they have been given other powers by the Criminal Code.

Section 495 of the Code defines the situations where a peace officer may make an arrest without a warrant. Subsection (1) lists the general rules for making an arrest without a warrant. These general rules are limited by the exceptions in subsection (2). In other words, to decide whether an officer can make an arrest without a warrant, it is necessary to first look at the general rules in subs. (1) and then check the limitations in subs. (2). This two-step scheme is a result of the bail reform legislation that was passed in the 1970s. The philosophy of the legislation is that people should be held before trial only if there is a clear reason for holding them. The law had been criticized on the basis that too many people were being arrested, and/or detained while awaiting trial. Thus, one purpose of the legislation is to limit the authority of the police to make arrests when other methods, such as appearance notices and summonses, would do just as well for ensuring attendance at trial.

Section 495(1) provides:

495. (1) A peace officer may arrest without warrant

    (a) a person who has committed an indictable offence or who, on reasonable grounds, he believes has committed or is about to commit an indictable offence,

    (b) a person whom he finds committing a criminal offence, or

    (c) a person in respect of whom he has reasonable grounds to believe that a warrant of arrest or committal . . . is in force within the territorial jurisdiction in which the person is found.

The term "peace officer" is defined in s. 2 of the Code. In addition to police officers, it includes a mayor, a warden, a sheriff, a prison guard, certain customs officials, a pilot in command of an aircraft while the aircraft is in flight, and certain military personnel. Note that private security officers employed by department stores or businesses are not peace officers. These people have only the same power of arrest that other ordinary persons possess, as discussed earlier.

Section 495(1) sets out five situations where a peace officer may make an arrest without a warrant:

1. Where the arresting officer knows that the person has committed an indictable offence.
2. Where the arresting officer believes on reasonable grounds that the accused has committed an indictable offence. This situation demands that a "reasonable grounds" test be used to determine whether an arrest can be made. It is not necessary that an indictable offence has actually been committed. It is enough if the arresting officer personally believes that there are reasonable grounds to make the arrest (i.e., to believe that an indictable offence has been committed). However, it must be objectively established that the reasonable grounds existed.

   Generally, "reasonable grounds" are grounds that would lead any ordinary, prudent, and cautious person to have a strong and honest belief that the person to be arrested has committed the offence. If the accused is later acquitted of the charge, the arrest may still be lawful. The important questions are these: whether a reasonable person standing in the shoes of the peace officer would have believed that reasonable grounds existed for making the arrest; and whether the officer personally believed that the reasonable grounds existed.

   In *Koechlin v. Waugh and Hamilton*,[16] the neighbourhood in which the accused was arrested had been subject to a number of break-ins a few nights earlier. The accused and a friend were stopped by the police at approximately 11 p.m. The accused was observed to be wearing shoes that matched the shoes worn by the suspect. The accused explained that he was returning home from a show. The police decided to arrest him on the suspicion of having committed the break-ins. The court held that these facts did not amount to reasonable and probable grounds for believing that the accused committed the break-ins.

3. Where the arresting officer has reasonable grounds to believe that an indictable offence is about to be committed. This situation also involves a reasonable grounds test. If a police officer has an honest belief based on reasonable grounds that an individual is about to commit an indictable offence, then he or she may make the arrest, even though that person has not yet made an attempt to commit the offence. Under s. 503(4), where a person about to commit an offence has been arrested, the police must release the person unconditionally as soon as practicable after they are satisfied that detaining the person is no longer necessary to prevent the commission of an indictable offence.

4. Where the arresting officer finds the accused committing any criminal offence. The Supreme Court of Canada has held that this situation applies where the officer finds the accused "apparently" committing an offence. This interpretation protects the officer from being sued for false imprisonment if the accused is later found not guilty of the offence.[17] "Any criminal offence" includes summary conviction offences as well as those that are indictable. It does not include provincial offences. Arrest powers for provincial offences are contained in provincial statutes.

---

16   (1957), 118 C.C.C. 24 (Ont. C.A.).
17   *R. v. Biron* (1975), 23 C.C.C. (2d) 513 (S.C.C.).

Note that the only powers a peace officer has to arrest for a summary conviction offence without a warrant are those granted by situation 4 and by the right that everybody has under s. 494 (i.e., to arrest anyone where there are reasonable grounds to believe that the person has committed a criminal offence and is being freshly pursued by persons with lawful authority to make an arrest).

5. Where the arresting officer believes on reasonable grounds that the accused is the subject of a warrant. The warrant must be in force in the territorial jurisdiction in which the accused is found at the time of arrest. In other words, if it is in force in only one county or district of a province, then it cannot be used to arrest an accused who is found in a different county or district.

c. Limitations on Power to Arrest without a Warrant

A peace officer's right to arrest without a warrant is limited by s. 495(2), which states that, unless certain circumstances exist, an arrest cannot be made without a warrant for indictable offences listed in s. 553 (these are primarily offences involving gambling, keeping a common bawdy house, and fraud in relation to fares), for hybrid offences, or for summary conviction offences. A peace officer cannot make an arrest without a warrant unless he or she considers, on reasonable grounds, that it is in the public interest to do so. "In the public interest" is a general term that means that the safety and well-being of the public are to be given priority.

An example of when an arrest could be made under s. 495(2) is if a person refuses to give his or her name to an officer who has reasonable grounds to believe an offence has been committed by that person. In such a situation, an arrest is in the public interest.

In determining whether the public interest is served by an arrest, the peace officer must consider all the circumstances of the offence, including the following:

- the need to establish the identity of the person,
- the need to protect and/or keep evidence, and
- the need to prevent the continuation or repetition of the offence or the commission of another offence.

The arresting officer must also decide whether there are any good reasons for believing that the accused, if not arrested, will fail to show up on the court appearance date.

A peace officer who decides that an arrest is not needed may issue the accused with an appearance notice or obtain a summons. Recall that an officer who issues an appearance notice must also lay an information before a justice.

d. Summary of Power to Arrest without Warrant

The following briefly summarizes a peace officer's powers to arrest without a warrant:

- The officer must be presented with one of the five situations outlined in s. 495(1), or in that part of s. 494 that entitles any person to make an arrest.
- The officer who is presented with such a situation must then consider whether the offence in question falls within the three categories of offences in s. 495(2). If it does not, an arrest can be made.
- If the offence does fall within one of the three categories, then the officer must decide whether an arrest should be made, on the basis of the public interest. If an arrest should not be made, the officer can give an appearance notice to the accused or go before a justice to have a summons issued.

e. Additional Powers to Arrest without Warrant

The Criminal Code provides three additional powers of arrest without a warrant.

First, Section 31(1) allows arrest of a person who breaches, or is about to breach, the peace:

31. (1) Every peace officer who witnesses a breach of the peace and every one who lawfully assists the peace officer is justified in arresting any person whom he finds committing the breach of the peace or who, on reasonable grounds, he believes is about to join in or renew the breach of the peace.

Breach of the peace is not defined in the Code. Generally, situations that may amount to a breach of peace involve threats of violence, such as when a group of people are loitering and becoming unruly. The British Columbia Court of Appeal said that this section applies only to breaches of the peace that have actually happened.[18] It also stated, however, that under the common law a peace officer can arrest without warrant where the officer honestly and on reasonable grounds believes that a breach of the peace is about to occur. Since there is no offence of committing a breach of the peace, this is a similar situation to where an officer arrests a person about to commit an offence; that is, the person cannot be charged with an offence. However, it is possible for the arrested person to be taken before a justice and required to enter a peace bond at common law. This procedure is discussed in more detail in Chapter 11.

Second, s. 199(2) allows a peace officer to take into custody any person whom he or she finds in a gaming house.

Third, under s. 524(2)(a), an officer can arrest where he or she believes on reasonable grounds that (a) an accused has contravened or is about to contravene any summons, appearance notice, promise to appear, undertaking, or recognizance that was given or entered into, or (b) an accused has committed an indictable offence after any summons, appearance notice, or similar has been issued or given.

6. Pre-trial Release When Arrest Is without a Warrant

The general principle of the law is that a person should not be held before trial unless there is a reason. If the offence is not one listed in s. 469—which includes the most serious offences (e.g., murder)—the Code sets out several points where the reasons for the arrest are reviewed and the person who has been detained can be released.

If the accused has been arrested without a warrant and the offence for which he or she has been arrested is one of the following: (a) an indictable offence listed in s. 553, (b) a hybrid offence, or (c) a summary conviction offence, s. 497 provides that the peace officer must release the accused as soon as is practicable once there is no longer a reason for the arrest, and either obtain a summons or issue an appearance notice. So, for example, where a police officer arrests an accused in order to confirm the accused's identity, once the person's identity is confirmed, if no other reason for holding the accused exists, the accused must be released.

If the accused is not released, then under s. 498 the officer in charge of the lockup must review the arrest. The "officer in charge" is the person responsible for the place where the accused has been taken. The officer in charge has the same obligation as the arresting officer to release the accused if the offence is one of those listed earlier and there is no longer a reason for the arrest. The officer in charge has an additional duty to release a person if the offence is one punishable by imprisonment for five years or less, and if the reason for the arrest no longer exists. If the officer in charge releases the accused, that officer can have a summons

---

18   *Hayes v. Thompson et al.* (1985), 18 C.C.C. (3d) 254 (B.C.C.A.).

issued or have the accused give a promise to appear (Form 10), or have the accused enter a recognizance not exceeding $500. A recognizance is an agreement made by the accused that he or she will pay a certain amount of money on failing to appear in court as required (Form 11). If the accused is not ordinarily resident in the province or lives more than 200 kilometres from the place of custody, but the offence occurred in the province in which he or she is being held, the officer in charge must release the person on a recognizance not exceeding $500. The officer can also require the person to deposit money or other valuable security up to the value of $500. If the offence is alleged to have been committed in Canada, but outside the province in which the person is being held, the officer in charge cannot release the person.

7. Arrest with a Warrant (Form 7)

When the police lay an information alleging that a named person has committed an offence and the accused has not been arrested or issued with an appearance notice, and has not given a promise to appear or entered a recognizance, the justice will issue either a summons or a warrant for arrest. A warrant for arrest is a document issued by a justice that commands the police to arrest a named person and to bring the person before the court. A justice may issue a warrant pursuant to s. 507 for the arrest of a person where there are reasonable grounds to believe that the person has committed a criminal offence. Before issuing the warrant, the justice must also believe that an arrest is in the public interest. A justice must issue a summons unless there are reasonable grounds for believing that it is necessary, for the public interest, to issue an arrest warrant. An arrest warrant may also be issued if the accused disobeys an appearance notice or a summons.

Under s. 29(1), anyone who executes a warrant has a duty to have the warrant in hand, where this is feasible, and to produce it for the inspection of the accused if requested.

8. Pre-trial Release When Arrested with a Warrant

Unless the offence is one listed in s. 469, a justice may endorse the arrest warrant so that it authorizes the release of the accused by the officer in charge. If the justice endorses the warrant, the officer in charge can release the accused on a promise to appear, or on entering a recognizance for an amount not exceeding $500 (s. 499). If the person being released is not a resident of the province or does not ordinarily reside within 200 kilometres of where he or she is being held in custody, the officer in charge must require the accused to enter a recognizance not exceeding $500.

In addition, the officer in charge can require the person who is being released on a recognizance or promise to appear to enter an undertaking in Form 11.1. Thereby, the person undertakes to do one or more of the following:

- report at a certain time to a named police officer or other person,
- remain within a certain territorial jurisdiction,
- notify the police or other designated person of any change of address or employment,
- abstain from communicating with a witness or other person or going to a place except in accordance with certain conditions, or
- deposit his or her passport.

9. Pre-trial Release with or without an Arrest Warrant

Under s. 503(2), an officer in charge can release any person charged with any offence except for those listed in s. 469, whether the person is arrested with or without a warrant. This release power is discretionary, unlike the other situations discussed earlier, where the officer must release the accused if the reasons for making the arrest no longer exist. The officer can release the accused on the person giving a promise to appear or entering a recognizance not exceeding $500, with or without further undertakings.

10. Pre-trial Release by Justice or Superior Court Judge

An accused in custody must be taken before a justice within 24 hours or as soon as possible (s. 503, s. 515). Unless the accused pleads guilty or is charged with an offence under s. 469, the justice will determine whether the accused will be kept in custody or released. As a general rule, there is a presumption that an accused brought before a justice should be released without conditions. The justice is required to order the release of the accused without conditions, unless detention or another order under s. 515 is justified. If the justice does not order the release of the accused person without conditions, he or she must, unless the prosecutor shows cause why detention is justified, order the release of the accused, subject to one of the following:

- an undertaking with conditions,
- a recognizance with or without sureties[19] in such amount and with such conditions as the justice directs, or
- a recognizance without sureties in such amount and with such conditions as the justice directs and the deposit of a sum of money or other valuable security.

Conditions may be attached to an undertaking (Form 12) or a recognizance (Form 32), including these:

- report at specified times to a peace officer or other person designated in the order,
- remain within a specified territorial jurisdiction,
- abstain from communicating with any person or going to any place specified in the order, and/or
- comply with "other reasonable conditions" specified in the order.

Section 515(10) allows the detention of the accused in custody where the detention is necessary for one or more of the following reasons:

(a) To ensure that the accused attends court—Some of the factors courts rely on in making predictions about whether an accused person will attend court, include these: the nature of the offence and the potential penalty, the strength of the evidence against the accused, the accused's record regarding complying with previous court orders, and the ties the accused has to the community.

(b) To protect the public—In determining whether detention is necessary for the protection of the public, the justice must have regard to all the circumstances, including any substantial likelihood that the accused will, if released, commit a criminal offence or interfere with the administration of justice. Examples of factors that courts use to make this determination include the current offence, prior record, a new charge while on release, and history of compliance with previous orders. These factors reflect a reliance on previous behaviour.

(c) To maintain confidence in the administration of justice—In determining whether detention is necessary to maintain confidence in the administration of justice, the court must have regard to all the circumstances, including the strength of the prosecution's

---

19 A surety is a person who agrees to pay the money set out in the recognizance if the accused does not appear for his or her court date. In effect, the surety is responsible for ensuring that the accused appears for his or her court date.

case; the gravity of the offence; the circumstances of the offence, including whether a firearm was used; and whether the accused is liable, on conviction, for a lengthy term of imprisonment. In *R. v. Hall*,[20] a slim majority of the Supreme Court of Canada upheld the constitutionality of the current wording of (c). The Court noted that the use of (c) may be infrequent, but "it is essential that a means of denying bail be available because public confidence is essential to the proper functioning of the bail system and the justice system as a whole." Four of the nine judges dissented, arguing that (c) is too vague to be the basis of denying a person of liberty and that it does not provide a ground for detention that is not already covered by the more specific grounds in (a) and (b).

For most offences, it is up to the Crown to "show cause" why the accused should not be released. For example, the Crown might establish that the accused has failed on previous occasions to appear for court and that, therefore, detention is necessary to ensure attendance. In some situations, the onus shifts to the accused to show why he or she should be released. These "reverse onus" situations include the following:

- where a person is charged with an offence listed in s. 469, which includes the most serious offences, such as murder and treason (the hearing must be held before a superior court judge of the province);
- where a person is charged with committing an indictable offence while on pre-trial release for another indictable offence;
- where a person fails to comply with a condition of his or her undertaking or recognizance; and
- where a person fails to attend court in accordance with an appearance notice or promise to appear.

11. Civil and Criminal Responsibility of Arresting Person

Section 28 of the Criminal Code states that where a person who is authorized to execute an arrest warrant believes, in good faith and on reasonable grounds, that the individual arrested is the person named in the warrant, the arresting person is protected from criminal responsibility.

When a police officer or private citizen makes an arrest without a warrant, the arresting individual must have an honest belief based on reasonable grounds that the accused has either committed the offence for which he or she is arrested, or is about to commit an offence. If the accused proves that the arresting person's belief was not based on reasonable grounds, he or she may sue for damages for false imprisonment (sections 495(3), 497(3), and 498(3)).

LO3   12. Rights upon Arrest or Detention

a. Right to Remain Silent

Chapter 1 described the right to remain silent during the trial process as a principle of fundamental justice under s. 7 of the Charter. This right also applies at the pre-trial stage. This means that the accused has the right not to answer police questions.

Usually, the police inform the accused that he or she does not have to answer questions; however, it is generally thought that there is no obligation to inform the accused of this right.[21] The right to remain silent is based on the principle of the presumption of innocence and on the right not to incriminate oneself.

---

20   *R. v. Hall* (2002), 3 S.C.R. 309 (S.C.C.).
21   See, for example, *R. v. Van Den Meerssche* (1989), 53 C.C.C. (3d) 449 (B.C.C.A.); but in *R. v. Campbell* (1989), 7 W.C.B. (2d) 301 (P.E.I.S.C. Gen. Div.), the court held otherwise.

Once an accused person indicates that he or she does not want to make a statement, the police cannot use deception or trickery to override the person's decision. In *R. v. Hebert*,[22] the accused was arrested and charged with robbery. After talking with his lawyer, he stated that he did not wish to make a statement. The police placed an undercover agent in his cell. The accused made incriminating statements to the officer. The trial judge excluded the statements and acquitted the accused. On appeal to the Supreme Court of Canada, the issue was whether the accused's right to remain silent had been violated because the statements were allowed as evidence. The Court held that the right to remain silent in s. 7 includes the right to choose whether to make a statement to the authorities. The question was whether the conduct of the authorities had effectively and unfairly deprived the accused of his right to choose. The Court found that the police had improperly elicited information that they could not otherwise have obtained. The Court stated that the right applies after detention, so evidence gathered from undercover operations before detention is not protected. Also, the right to silence does not cover voluntary statements made to cellmates.

In *R. v. Broyles*,[23] a case decided shortly after *Hebert*, the accused was charged with murdering his grandmother. While the accused was in custody, the police arranged for him to be visited by a friend who was wearing a recording device. During their conversation, the friend asked the accused about the killing. He also made negative comments about Broyles' lawyer and suggested that he change counsel. The accused eventually made an incriminating statement. The accused was convicted at his trial. In deciding whether to allow the statement, the Supreme Court of Canada first considered whether the friend was acting as an agent of the state. The test to be applied was whether the conversation between the accused and the friend would have taken place in the way that it had but for the intervention of the police. Here there was no doubt that the friend was acting as an agent of the state, since the police had set up the meeting. However, the Court went on to say that obtaining evidence in this way violates s. 7 of the Charter only if the agent elicits the statement. Evidence is elicited if there is a causal link between the conduct of the agent and the making of the statement. The Court looked at the nature of the conversation (e.g., whether the conversation was in fact an interrogation), and at the nature of the relationship (e.g., whether it was based on trust). Here, the agent undermined the accused's confidence in his lawyer (who had told him to remain silent), exploited his relationship as a friend, and actively asked questions about the killing. Therefore, he had elicited the damaging statement. The Court considered that a serious violation of the accused's s. 7 rights had taken place and ordered a new trial, with the damaging statement to be excluded.

In *R. v. Singh*,[24] Singh argued that police officers should be required to inform the detainee of his or her right to silence and, absent a signed waiver, to refrain from questioning any detainee who states that he or she does not wish to speak to the police. The Supreme Court of Canada disagreed and upheld the principles it set out in the Hebert case. The police may use legitimate means of persuasion after the detainee asserts the right to silence, but the police are not allowed to ignore the detainee's freedom to choose whether to speak or not. However, the Court stated, "Under both common law and Charter rules, persistence in continuing the interview, despite repeated assertions by the detainee that he wishes to remain silent, may well raise a strong argument that any subsequently obtained statement was not the product of a free will to speak to the authorities."

---

22   (1990), 57 C.C.C. (3d) 1 (S.C.C.).
23   (1991), 68 C.C.C. (3d) 308 (S.C.C.).
24   [2007] 3 S.C.R. 405.

There are exceptions to the right to remain silent. In *R. v. Moore*,[25] the accused had run a red light on his bicycle. An officer saw him and attempted to give him a ticket for a provincial offence. Moore refused to stop or to give his name to the officer. Since he refused to identify himself, Moore was finally charged with the Criminal Code offence of obstructing a police officer in the performance of his duty. The provincial Summary Convictions Act stated that s. 495(2) of the Criminal Code applied to situations like this, so the officer could not arrest Moore unless, among other reasons, it was necessary to establish his identity. The Supreme Court of Canada held that Moore had obstructed the officer, who was performing his duty when asking Moore his name, so Moore could be charged with the offence. This decision is limited to situations where the officer actually observes the accused committing an offence, and where there is no power to arrest unless and until the officer tries to identify the accused so that the accused can be charged with the offence.

The Court distinguished *Moore* from another case, where a person was acting in what the police regarded as a suspicious manner. The accused refused to identify himself, saying that the police would have to arrest him. In this case, the Court held that the accused did not need to identify himself. The difference was that the police did not observe the accused committing an offence.

Moore was decided before the Charter, so it is not known how the Supreme Court would rule today. However, a decision of the Saskatchewan Queen's Bench in 1990 followed *Moore*. In *R. v. Hudson*,[26] the accused allowed his dogs to run loose, which violated a city bylaw. He was observed by a police constable. When asked to identify himself, he refused, saying that he would get a ticket if he did. The court held that he had obstructed a police officer in the performance of his duties. The court stated that even if requiring people found committing offences to identify themselves violated the Charter, it was a reasonable limit under s. 1.

Another exception is found under provincial law (such as Ontario's) that requires motorists to produce a driver's licence, vehicle registration, and proof of insurance when requested by an officer.

b. Statement Must Be Voluntary

Any statement that the accused does make to the police must be voluntary if it is to be admitted at trial. The courts have developed rules regarding voluntary statements. In *R. v. Oickle*,[27] the Supreme Court of Canada summarized the law by identifying four factors that may raise a reasonable doubt about the voluntariness of a statement:

(1) Threats or Promises

Statements are inadmissible if they are the result of "fear of prejudice or hope of advantage" held out by a person in authority, such as a police officer.[28] For example, if a person is promised a more lenient sentence, or is threatened with a greater punishment if a statement is not given, the statement is not voluntary. In *R. v. Zappone*,[29] the accused was involved in a traffic accident in which one person was killed. The accused asked the arresting officer if she would be charged with manslaughter. The officer told her that he was charging her with an offence under the provincial Highway Act and that she would receive a ticket and that the maximum fine was $2000 under the Act. The accused then gave a statement to the officer suggesting that she had

25   (1979), 43 C.C.C. (2d) 83 (S.C.C.).
26   (1990), 83 Sask. R. 177 (Sask. Q.B.); aff'd (1990), 87 Sask. R. 288 (Sask. C.A.).
27   (2000), 147 C.C.C. (3d) 321 (S.C.C.).
28   *Ibrahim v. The King*, [1914] A.C. 599.
29   (1991), 80 Alta. L.R. (2d) 424 (Alta. C.A.).

failed to stop for a stop sign. The accused was charged with the provincial offence but also with dangerous driving causing death, an indictable offence under the Code. At her trial, she testified that she had given a statement to the officer because the officer had led her to believe that she would be charged with the less serious offence if she cooperated.

The court of appeal held that the officer had offered her an inducement; in this instance, a lesser charge. Therefore, her statement should not have been admitted. The court ordered her acquittal.

(2) Oppression

If the police create intolerable conditions, the suspect may make a confession to escape the conditions. Oppressive conditions can also overpower the suspect's will and cause the suspect to doubt his or her own memory, believe the accusations made by the police, and make a confession. Factors that can create an oppressive atmosphere include depriving the suspect of food, clothing, water, sleep, or medical attention; denying access to counsel; and excessively aggressive, intimidating questioning for a prolonged period of time.

In *R. v. Hoilett*,[30] the court held that a statement was involuntary due to oppressive conditions. The accused was arrested while under the influence of crack cocaine and alcohol. After being held in a cell for two hours, his clothes were removed for forensic testing and he was left naked in a cold cell. The only place to sit in the cell was a metal bunk, which was so cold he had to stand up. After another one and one-half hours, the police gave him some light clothes, but no underwear, and shoes that did not fit him. Shortly thereafter, at about 3:00 a.m., he was awakened to be interrogated. During the interrogation, he fell asleep at least five times. The police refused his requests for warmer clothes and a tissue to wipe his nose. He admitted that he knew that he did not have to talk, and that the police had not made explicit threats or promises; but he hoped that, if he talked, the police would give him some warm clothes and stop the interrogation.[31]

(3) Operating Mind

The Supreme Court of Canada, in *R. v. Whittle*,[32] considered the mental capacity necessary for a statement to be deemed voluntary. Whittle had been panhandling on the street when he was stopped and questioned by the police. A computer check turned up three committal warrants against the accused for unpaid fines for provincial offence convictions. He was cautioned and arrested. The officer observed that the accused appeared to be mentally unstable. The accused confirmed that he suffered from schizophrenia. Once in custody, the accused began to talk about some "heavy matters" he had been involved in. He eventually confessed to committing robberies and to murdering a man with an axe. He was cautioned again and then charged with the offences. A lawyer was contacted for him. The lawyer told him "to keep his mouth shut." However, the accused continued to talk to the police, stating that he had voices in his head and that he needed to talk to the police to stop the voices. The incriminating statements were excluded at his trial, and he was acquitted. On appeal to the Supreme Court, the Court held that the test for mental capacity to give a voluntary statement is not the same as the test for the defence of mental disorder, but is the same as the test for fitness to stand trial. The Court noted that many people who are found not guilty by reason of mental disorder are fit to stand trial. The key issue is whether the accused has an "operating mind." The test is whether the accused

---

30 (1999), 136 C.C.C. (3d) 449.
31 Also see *R. v. Horvath* (1980), 44 C.C.C. (2d), in which an intensive interrogation left the accused in a state of "complete emotional disintegration."
32 (1994), 92 C.C.C. (3d) 11 (S.C.C.).

possesses a limited degree of cognitive ability so that he understands what he is saying and what is said to him. Similarly, the question is whether he can communicate with counsel and understand the function of counsel. The accused did understand what he was saying and was fit to instruct counsel; but because of the voices that were telling him to unburden himself, he did not care about the consequences. Therefore, his statements were voluntary and admissible.

(4) Police Trickery

The police use of trickery to obtain a confession was addressed in *R. v. Rothman*.[33] The Supreme Court of Canada admitted a suspect's statement to an undercover police officer who had been placed in a cell with the suspect. The issue was not whether the statement was reliable, but whether the police did anything that could have induced the accused to make a statement that was or might be untrue. The Court stated that the police, in dealing with shrewd and sophisticated criminals, must sometimes necessarily use tricks or other forms of deceit; however, they should not be allowed to engage in conduct that shocks the community. As examples of what might "shock the community," the Court suggested a police officer pretending to be a chaplain or a Legal Aid lawyer, or injecting truth serum into a diabetic under the pretence that it was insulin.

c. Fingerprinting and Photographing

A person under arrest for an indictable offence (including a hybrid offence) is required to submit to being photographed and fingerprinted. Mandatory fingerprinting has been challenged under the Charter; however, the Supreme Court of Canada has held that it is not a violation of the right against self-incrimination.[34] This requirement is dictated by the Identification of Criminals Act. Note that if an accused is under arrest for a summary conviction offence, the police have no right to require photographing or fingerprinting. Also, under s. 502, a person may be given a date and time to appear for fingerprinting and photographing along with the appearance notice, promise to appear, recognizance, or summons.

d. Arbitrary Detention and Investigative Detention

Section 9 of the Charter provides:

> **9. Everyone has the right not to be arbitrarily detained or imprisoned.**

In *R. v. Hufsky*,[35] the Supreme Court of Canada considered the meaning of "arbitrary." The issue in this case was whether random spot checks of motorists by the police for the purpose of checking driver's licence, insurance, and sobriety are arbitrary detentions. The Court said that such spot checks are detentions, and that they are arbitrary because the police can stop any motorist without any criteria. However, even though the legislation allowing for random spot checks violates s. 9 of the Charter, the legislation is justified under s. 1 as a reasonable limitation, in that the police must be able to prevent and stop impaired drivers.

In a later decision in a similar case, the Court held that routine stops of vehicles can be justified on the basis of the pressing and substantial concern for safety on the highway.[36] The stop must be for legal reasons—for example, like those in *Hufsky*—or to check for mechanical safety of the vehicle. Once stopped, the occupant can only be questioned regarding driving offences. More intrusive procedures can be taken only if there are reasonable and probable grounds to suspect that an offence has occurred.

33 [1981] 1 S.C.R. 640 (S.C.C.).
34 *R. v. Beare; R. v. Higgins* (1988), 45 C.C.C. (3d) 57 (S.C.C.).
35 (1988), 40 C.C.C. (3d) 398 (S.C.C.).
36 *R. v. Ladouceur* (1990), 56 C.C.C. (3d) 22 (S.C.C.).

These "check stop" cases have established the right of the police to arbitrarily detain persons for the purpose of enforcing laws related to driving. A case that looked at the issue more broadly is *R. v. Simpson*,[37] a decision of the Ontario Court of Appeal. A police officer stopped a car because he had seen it at a suspected crack house. The officer pulled the car over to see "what story" the occupants would give and to see if they would trip themselves up and give him grounds to make an arrest. While questioning the occupants, the officer noticed a bulge in the accused's pocket. He asked the accused (who was a passenger in the car) to remove the object. As the accused was doing so, the officer grabbed the accused's hand and removed a bag containing cocaine. The accused was charged with possession for the purpose of trafficking. The trial judge held that the officer had a right to stop the car and seize the drugs and convicted the accused. The accused appealed on the grounds that his rights under s. 9 of the Charter had been violated.

The court, in considering whether the detention was arbitrary, noted that the officer had no authority under any federal or provincial statute to stop the car; for example, the officer was not stopping the car under a Highway Traffic Act law to check for impaired driving. Therefore, the "check stop" cases did not apply here. The court then considered whether there was a general common law right to detain persons. The court held that, under the common law, a police officer may detain persons for "investigatory purposes" where the officer has an "articulable cause"; that is, the officer has a reasonable suspicion that the detainee is involved in the criminal activity being investigated. Having an articulable cause may or may not be enough to justify the detention, however; other circumstances must exist that make the detention at that time and place reasonable. For example, Constable Jones is justified in detaining on a public street a man whom she suspects is fleeing from the scene of a violent crime he has just committed. In contrast, the detention of a person in the same circumstances based on a suspicion that the person committed a property offence in the far distant past is not justifiable, even though the articulable cause exists.

The *Simpson* case clearly recognized the right of the police to detain where there are not sufficient grounds to arrest; that is, where they have only a reasonable suspicion that the person is involved in a crime. This is referred to as investigative detention. In this case, however, the judges found that the officer did not have an articulable cause for detaining the accused.

The officer's information about the "crack house" was of an unknown age and was from an officer who heard it from someone else. He had no reason to think that the information was reliable. He knew nothing about the occupants of the car, and they had done nothing to suggest that they were involved in criminal activity. Where the sole factor was attendance at a house where criminal activity may have been going on based on information of unknown age and reliability, no articulable cause exists. "Were it otherwise, the police would have a general warrant to stop anyone who happened to attend at any place which the police had reason to believe could be the site of ongoing criminal activity."[38] Therefore, the search was unlawful and the evidence excluded. The court ordered an acquittal.

In a case decided after *Simpson*, the Supreme Court of Canada considered the grounds for investigative detention. In *R. v. Mann*,[39] the accused was walking down the street when he was detained because his description matched that of a suspect in a break-in at a nearby address. The Court reiterated that there is a common law rule governing police powers of investigative detention. The Court stated:

---

37   (1993), 79 C.C.C. (3d) 482 (Ont. C.A.).
38   Ibid. at 504.
39   (2004), 185 C.C.C. (3d) 308 (S.C.C.) at 319. See also *R. v. Bilodeau* (2004), 192 C.C.C. (3d) 110 (Que. C.A.).

The detention must be viewed as reasonably necessary on an objective view of the totality of the circumstances, informing the officer's suspicion that there is a clear nexus between the individual to be detained and a recent or on-going criminal offence. Reasonable grounds figure at the front-end of such an assessment, underlying the officer's reasonable suspicion that the particular individual is implicated in the criminal activity under investigation. The overall reasonableness of the decision to detain, however, must further be assessed against all of the circumstances, most notably the extent to which the interference with individual liberty is necessary to perform the officer's duty, the liberty interfered with, and the nature and extent of that interference . . .[40]

The Supreme Court preferred the phrase "reasonable grounds to detain," rather than the phrase "articulable cause" used in *Simpson*, as the grounds for the detention. The Court included that the detention must be as brief as possible, that at a minimum the person must be told the reason for the detention, and that there is no obligation for the person to answer questions. The Court concluded that in this case the police had reasonable grounds to detain Mann.

In *R. v. Clayton*,[41] the police received a 911 call that ten black males with guns were in a parking lot of a club. The caller also identified four cars in the parking lot. Within two minutes of being notified of the call, two officers arrived at the parking lot. Almost immediately, a car in the lot drove towards the exit. The officers blocked the exit, stopped the car, and observed that the two occupants were black males. The car was not one of the cars identified by the 911 caller. The Ontario Court of Appeal concluded that the investigative detention was unlawful because there was no imminent danger and because the police did not tailor their intervention to stop only the four vehicles identified in the 911 call. The Supreme Court of Canada disagreed, stating that requiring the police to stop only those vehicles described in the 911 call would impose an unrealistic burden on the police in this case, and one inconsistent with their duty to respond in a timely manner. The investigative detention was reasonably necessary to respond to the seriousness of the offence and the threat to the police's and the public's safety inherent in the presence of prohibited weapons in a public place.

e. Section 10 Charter Rights

Section 10 of the Charter contains two specific rights upon arrest or detention.[42]

(a) to be informed promptly of the reasons therefore . . .

A person who has been arrested or detained has a right to know why he or she has been arrested or detained. Also, recall that if a warrant is used, under s. 29(2)(a) the officer needs to have the warrant, if feasible, and the accused has a right to examine it.[43]

(b) to retain and instruct counsel without delay and to be informed of that right . . .

---

40 Ibid. at 323–324. See also *R. v. Clayton* (2007), 220 C.C.C. (3d) 449 (S.C.C.).
41 *Clayton*, ibid.
42 Section 10 also includes the right to "have the validity of the detention determined by way of *habeas corpus* and to be released if the detention is not lawful." The right of *habeas corpus* is one of our oldest rights. It means that a person has a right to a hearing to determine whether the detention is legal and, if it is not, to be released. Although an important right, it is not generally used at the pre-trial stage. It tends to be used to test detention issues that arise once a person is in an institution; for example, where an inmate challenges being placed in solitary confinement or in a special handling unit. It allows a court to examine whether the decision for detention was made fairly, and whether the decision maker had the authority to order the detention. See *Charkaoui v. Canada* (2007), 216 C.C.C. (3d) 418 (S.C.C.), which held that the guarantee against arbitrary detention in s. 9 of the Charter encompasses the right to a prompt review of detention under s. 10(c) of the Charter. As a result of this decision, the Immigration and Refugee Protection Act was amended to provide for the appointment of special advocates and regular detention reviews. The amendments came into force on February 22, 2008.
43 See *R. v. Nguyen* (2008), O.J. No. 219 (Ont. C.A.). This is a case of failure to comply with the informational requirement of s. 10(a).

The right to counsel does not arise until a person has been arrested or detained. As noted earlier, "detention" is a broader term than "arrest"; all arrests involve detentions, but not all detentions involve arrests. Because of the importance of the s. 10(b) right, there have been many cases considering the meaning of detention under this section.[44]

(1) Meaning of Detention

There are three ways a person can be detained: by physical restraint; by psychological means (i.e., where a person is made to believe that he or she has no choice but to remain, even though no threat has been made); and by giving a demand or direction (i.e., where there will be legal consequences if the person refuses the demand or direction). An example of the last type of detention is found in *R. v. Therens*.[45] The accused had a car accident. When the police arrived, they asked him to take a breathalyzer test. The police did not inform him of his right to counsel. In deciding whether he had been denied his right to counsel, the issue for the Court was whether the accused had, in fact, been detained. The Court stated that a person is detained when he or she submits or acquiesces to the deprivation of liberty in the reasonable belief that the choice to do otherwise does not exist. Since refusing to take the test is an offence, the accused did not have a reasonable choice not to take the breathalyzer. Therefore, the Court found that he had been detained.

The Supreme Court of Canada considered the meaning of psychological detention in *R. v. Grant*.[46] Two undercover police officers, driving in an unmarked car, were monitoring an area with four schools and a history of student assaults, robberies, and drug offences. Grant, an 18-year-old male who was walking down a sidewalk, aroused the suspicions of the officers because of the way he fidgeted with his coat and pants and stared at them. The officers suggested to a third officer, who was in uniform and driving a marked police car, that he "have a chat" with Grant. The uniformed officer approached Grant, stood directly in front of him, and asked for his name and address. Grant behaved nervously and adjusted his jacket, which prompted the officer to ask him to keep his hands in front of him. Then the two undercover officers approached, flashed their police badges and stood behind the uniformed officer, obstructing the way forward. Upon being asked whether he had anything that he should not have, Grant answered that he had a small amount of marijuana and a firearm. The officers then arrested and searched him, finding the marijuana and a loaded revolver. The police acknowledged in court that they did not have a legal basis to detain Grant. The issue was whether Grant had been unlawfully psychologically detained. The Supreme Court stated that a person is psychologically detained if he or she has a reasonable belief that he or she is not free to go. The Court identified several factors that should be considered in the determination of whether a person has been psychologically detained:

- the circumstances giving rise to the encounter as they would be reasonably perceived by the person;
- whether the police were providing general assistance, maintaining general order, making general inquiries regarding a particular occurrence, or singling out the person for a focused investigation;
- the nature of the police conduct, including the language used, the use of physical contact, the place where the interaction occurred, the presence of others, and the duration of the encounter; and

---

44 See *R. v. Harris* (2008), 225 C.C.C. (3d) 193 (Ont. C.A.), where the Ontario Court of Appeal held that police are not required to inform a detained person of his right to counsel during a brief lawful Highway Traffic Act check stop, or before asking him for identification.

45 (1985), 18 C.C.C. (3d) 481 (S.C.C.).

46 (2009), 245 C.C.C. (3d) 1 (S.C.C.).

- the particular characteristics or circumstances of the person, including age, physical stature, minority status, and level of sophistication.

The Supreme Court found that Grant had been psychologically detained. A reasonable person in Grant's position (18 years old, alone, faced by three physically larger police officers in adversarial positions) would conclude that his or her right to choose how to act had been removed by the police, given their conduct. The Court concluded that Grant was detained when the uniformed officer told him to keep his hands in front of him, the other two officers moved into position behind the uniformed officer, and the uniformed officer began a pointed line of questioning.

Another case involving psychological detention is *R. v. Hawkins*.[47] The accused was charged with sexually assaulting a 13-year-old girl who was the daughter of his girlfriend. The victim reported the assault to her school guidance counsellor, who contacted the police. An officer called Hawkins and requested an interview about the complaint. He stated that the interview could be held at the station or at Hawkins' home or place of business. Hawkins agreed to be interviewed at the station. At the station, he was given a standard police caution but not advised of his right to counsel since the officer did not believe that Hawkins was detained. Hawkins gave a statement to the police in which he admitted entering the girl's bedroom and tickling her sometimes. He said that if he had ever touched her breast, he "never meant anything by it. It was all done in fun." At the end of the interview, the officer said that he did not know if charges would be laid, because he had to wait for legal advice. The charges were laid, and Hawkins was convicted. The issue for the court of appeal was whether he had been psychologically detained and, therefore, denied his right to counsel. The court held that Hawkins had been detained and stated that psychological detention can arise even if there are no feelings of compulsion by the person. Detention arises when the officer begins to question the person with a view to charging the person. Here the purpose of the interview was to investigate the accused's involvement in an alleged crime. There was a dissenting opinion in this case, with one judge stating that there was no detention. His opinion was that it is not a detention where an officer requests a statement without any sense of compulsion on the part of the accused. On appeal to the Supreme Court of Canada, the Court, without giving reasons, stated that there was no detention. Presumably, the Court, agreeing with the dissenting opinion, found the lack of compulsion a factor in not finding a detention.

Another type of case in which the meaning of detention has been considered involves people being questioned by customs officials at border crossings. In *R. v. Simmons*,[48] the Supreme Court of Canada said that the routine questions that are asked at border crossings are not a detention, nor are baggage checks or a pat or frisk of outer clothing. However, it is a detention if a person is given a strip or skin search in a private room or is taken to a hospital for a search of body cavities.

(2) Right to Counsel

The right to counsel under s. 10 of the Charter applies once the person has been arrested or detained. In *R. v. Suberu*,[49] a police officer, R, was advised that two males were suspected of attempting to use a stolen credit card at a store. Upon entering the store, R saw another officer

47   (1993), 79 C.C.C. (3d) 576 (S.C.C.); rev'g (1992), 72 C.C.C. (3d) 524 (Nfld. C.A.).
48   (1988), 45 C.C.C. (3d) 296 (S.C.C.).
49   (2009), 245 C.C.C. (3d) 112 (S.C.C.).

talking to an employee and a male customer. Suberu walked past R and said, "He did this, not me, so I guess I can go." R followed Suberu outside and said, "Wait a minute. I need to talk to you before you go anywhere," while Suberu was getting into the driver's seat of a minivan. After a brief exchange, R received by radio the description and licence plate number of the van driven by the men who had used a stolen credit card at another store earlier that day. The description and the licence plate number matched that of the van in which Suberu was sitting. R also saw shopping bags between and behind the front seats. R then arrested S for fraud and advised him of the reason for his arrest and his right to counsel. Suberu applied under s. 24(2) of the Charter for an order to exclude his statements and physical evidence seized at the time of his arrest. He argued that he was detained as soon as he was told to "wait" and was questioned by R, and that R's failure to inform him of his right to counsel at that time constituted a Charter breach.

The Supreme Court of Canada held that Suberu's right to counsel had not been violated. The Court noted that the line between general questioning and focused interrogation amounting to detention may be difficult to draw in particular cases. In this case, the Court concluded that although Suberu was momentarily "delayed" when the police asked to speak to him, he was not subjected to physical or psychological restraint amounting to detention within the meaning of the Charter. A reasonable person in the circumstances would have concluded that the initial encounter was preliminary investigative questioning falling short of detention. Therefore, Suberu's right to counsel was not engaged. The Court also stated that the phrase "without delay" in s. 10(b) must be interpreted as "immediately." The immediacy of this obligation is only subject to concerns for officer or public safety, or to reasonable limitations that are prescribed by law and justified under s. 1 of the Charter.

The right to counsel has two parts: the right to be informed of the right to counsel and the right to consult counsel.

• Right to Be Informed

Court decisions have expanded the right to be informed to more than being told simply, "You have a right to a lawyer." The Supreme Court of Canada[50] has held that the police must tell the accused of the existence and availability of Legal Aid and **duty counsel** (duty counsel is a Legal Aid lawyer who is available to advise accused persons, usually before the first court appearance). The police must also inform the accused of whatever system for free, preliminary legal advice may exist and of how such advice can be accessed (e.g., by calling a 1-800 telephone number).[51] However, there is no obligation on the government to provide free preliminary advice or 24-hour-a-day legal advice[52] and there is no breach of s. 10(b) by not providing an accused with the local telephone number when the accused is detained during regular business hours.[53]

The accused also has the right to be informed about the above at a time he or she is capable of understanding,[54] and in language he or she can understand.[55]

In *R. v. Evans*,[56] the accused, who was mentally handicapped, was charged with first-degree murder. He was arrested for possession of marijuana and told that he had a right to a lawyer. When he was asked if he understood his rights, he said "no." As the police questioned him, they came to believe that he was the prime suspect in two murders. The focus of

50   *R. v. Brydges* (1990), 53 C.C.C. (3d) 330 (S.C.C.).
51   *R. v. Bartle* (1994), 92 C.C.C. (3d) 289 (S.C.C.).
52   *R. v. Matheson* (1994), 92 C.C.C. (3d) 434 (S.C.C.).
53   *R. v. Latimer* (1997), 92 C.C.C. (3d) 193 (S.C.C.) at 207.
54   *R. v. Vanstaceghem* (1987), 36 C.C.C. (3d) 142 (Ont. C.A.).
55   *R. v. Clarkson* (1986), 25 C.C.C. (3d) 207 (S.C.C.).
56   (1991), 63 C.C.C. (3d) 289 (S.C.C.).

the interview then changed. However, the police did not restate to him his right to a lawyer. Nor did they formally tell the accused that he was being detained for the murders, although the accused made several statements that indicated that he knew he was suspected of committing the murders. The police then lied to the accused, saying that his fingerprints had been found at the murder scene. At this point, he confessed. The Supreme Court of Canada held that his rights had been seriously violated. First, when the accused was advised of his right to counsel and he stated that he did not understand, the police were obligated to take steps to help him understand, particularly since they were aware of his limited mental capacity. Second, the police failed to restate his right to counsel when the investigation shifted to the murders. The police must restate the right whenever there is a fundamental change in the investigation involving a different, unrelated offence or a significantly more serious offence.

• Right to Consult a Lawyer

The Supreme Court of Canada, in *R. v. Sinclair*,[57] decided that the right to consult counsel under s. 10(b) of the Charter does not include a right to have a lawyer present during a police interrogation. After being arrested for murder, Sinclair was advised of his right to counsel, and twice spoke by telephone with a lawyer of his choice. He was later interviewed by a police officer for five hours. Sinclair stated several times during the interview that he had nothing to say until he spoke to his lawyer again. The officer confirmed that Sinclair had the right to choose whether to talk or not; however, he refused to allow Sinclair to consult with his lawyer again. He also told Sinclair that he did not have the right to have his lawyer present during questioning. The officer continued the interview, during which Sinclair implicated himself in the murder. Sinclair appealed to the Supreme Court of Canada that his incriminating statements should not have been admitted into evidence because his right to counsel had been violated. The Court dismissed the appeal.

In a 5–4 decision, the Court stated that the purpose of s. 10(b) is to support detainees' right to choose whether to cooperate with the police investigation or not, by giving them access to legal advice on the situation they are facing. In most cases, an initial warning, coupled with a reasonable opportunity to consult counsel, satisfies s. 10(b); s. 10(b) does not require that counsel be present during the police interrogation. However, the police must give the detainee an additional opportunity to receive advice from counsel where developments in the course of the investigation make this necessary to serve the purpose underlying s. 10(b). Changed circumstances can suggest that re-consultation is necessary in order for the detainee to have the information relevant to choosing whether to cooperate with the police investigation or not. Examples of such a change in circumstances would be where the police want the detainee to submit to a polygraph test or where developments in the investigation suggest that the detainee may be confused about his or her choices and right to remain silent.

The Court concluded that in this case there had not been a change in circumstances requiring Sinclair to be given the opportunity to consult again with counsel. One of the four dissenting judges stated that the majority's decision would prevent lawyers from functioning effectively for their clients because they would not be aware of the unfolding situation in an interrogation room. Until aware of that situation, the lawyer may not be able to give any meaningful assistance beyond what could be accomplished by a recorded message: "You have reached counsel. Keep your mouth shut. Press one to repeat this message."

---

57   (2010), 259 C.C.C. (3d) 443 (S.C.C.).

Although a detainee may request to consult with a particular lawyer, if he or she agrees to speak to duty counsel instead, the right to counsel under s. 10(b) is satisfied. In *R. v. McCrimmon*,[58] after being informed of his right to counsel, McCrimmon stated that he wished to speak to a particular lawyer. When the police failed to reach the lawyer he requested, McCrimmon agreed to the police contacting Legal Aid and he spoke to duty counsel briefly. During the police interrogation that followed, McCrimmon made incriminating statements. The Supreme Court of Canada dismissed his appeal to have his statements ruled inadmissible on the ground that the police breached his rights by failing to hold off the interview until he had an opportunity to consult with counsel of his choice. The Court stated that while McCrimmon expressed his preference for consulting with a particular lawyer, the police rightly inquired whether he wanted to contact duty counsel instead when that lawyer was not immediately available. McCrimmon agreed, exercised his right to counsel, and stated to the police that he was satisfied with the consultation.

Once a person indicates a desire to speak to a lawyer, the police cannot question that person further until he or she has a reasonable opportunity to consult a lawyer. What a reasonable opportunity is depends on the circumstances; for example, in jurisdictions where duty counsel is not available, the accused has a longer period to obtain the advice of counsel. The reasonable opportunity might extend to when the Legal Aid office opens or a lawyer is found who will give free advice.[59] The Supreme Court of Canada said, in *R. v. Burlingham*,[60] that reasonable opportunity includes the means to call a lawyer, and privacy when talking to a lawyer. The accused was charged with first-degree murder. During his interrogation by the police, the accused had spoken to a lawyer, who advised him to say nothing to the police. The police continued questioning him, however, despite his protests that he wanted to follow his lawyer's advice. The police also spoke badly about his lawyer, suggesting that the lawyer did not have his interests at heart whereas the police did. The police also said that if he cooperated, the charge would be second-degree murder instead of first-degree murder, but the deal would only be available for a short time. The questioning took place on a Saturday, and the police knew that the lawyer would not be available until Monday. The Supreme Court held that the accused's right to counsel was violated in three ways. First, the police continued questioning him after he said he would say nothing until he talked to his lawyer, as s. 10(b) requires the police to stop questioning once the accused asserts the right to speak to a lawyer. Second, s. 10(b) prohibits the police from belittling an accused's lawyer for the purpose of undermining their relationship. And third, by unduly pressuring the accused to accept the deal without consulting his lawyer, the police again violated s. 10(b).

R. v. Willier[61] addressed another aspect of the right to counsel under s. 10(b): the right to counsel of choice. After Willier's arrest for murder, the police informed him of his right to counsel and facilitated a telephone conversation with Legal Aid. On the next day, he attempted to call a specific lawyer and left a message on his answering machine. When asked if he wished to speak with another lawyer, Willier said he wanted to wait to hear back from his chosen counsel; however, when the police informed him that his preferred lawyer was unlikely to call back quickly because it was Sunday and reminded him of the immediate availability of free Legal Aid, Willier chose to speak with duty counsel a second time. Before beginning an interrogation, the police gave him an open-ended invitation to contact counsel

58   (2010), 259 C.C.C. (3d) 515 (S.C.C.).
59   *R. v. Prosper* (1994), 92 C.C.C. (3d) 353 (S.C.C.).
60   (1995), 97 C.C.C. (3d) 385 (S.C.C.).
61   (2010), 259 (C.C.C. (3d) 536 (S.C.C.).

at any point during the exchange. Willier expressed satisfaction with the advice he had received from Legal Aid and did not attempt to contact counsel again before providing an incriminating statement to the police.

Willier argued that his statements should have been excluded because, before he spoke to duty counsel, the police were required under s. 10(b) to inform him of his right to a reasonable opportunity to contact counsel of his choice and of their duty to refrain from questioning him until he had been afforded that opportunity. The Supreme Court of Canada disagreed, holding that the police did not interfere with Willier's right to a reasonable opportunity to consult with counsel of choice by reminding him of the immediate availability of Legal Aid. When Willier stated his preference to wait, the police reasonably informed him that it was unlikely that the lawyer would be quick to return his call and reminded him of the immediate availability of duty counsel. His choice to call duty counsel was not the product of coercion. The police had a duty to ensure that he was aware of the availability of Legal Aid.

In *R. v. Black*,[62] the accused was arrested for attempted murder. She called her lawyer from the police station and had a brief conversation. Two hours later, the police told her that the victim had died and that the charge was being upgraded to first-degree murder. She again asked to speak to her lawyer, but attempts to reach him were not successful. At this time, she was intoxicated, upset, and physically injured. The police knew that she had limited intelligence and only a grade four education. She asked the police if she would be held over the weekend and they told her she would be. At that point, a police officer asked her where the knife was. She told him it was in the kitchen drawer. He then asked her to tell him the whole story. She responded by giving a long statement to the officer. The Supreme Court of Canada held that she had been denied her right to counsel. The right to counsel can only be exercised meaningfully if the accused is aware of the jeopardy she is in. When she first spoke to her lawyer, the charge was attempted murder, a significantly different offence from first-degree murder. In other words, after the charge became murder, and before questioning the accused, the police should have waited until she had an opportunity to speak to her lawyer again.

An accused person can waive the right to consult a lawyer. However, the waiver must be voluntary and with full knowledge of the right being waived. The Supreme Court considered the issue of whether a waiver was valid in *R. v. Smith*.[63] The accused was charged with first-degree murder. He had been drinking with some friends when an argument began. He eventually left his friends but returned with a 12-gauge shotgun. He shot the victim in the face and body from a distance of 30 metres. The victim died immediately. Smith called the police the next morning to surrender. During the arrest, the police had him walk out of his sister's house while three officers trained guns on him; they then ordered him to fall to his knees before they handcuffed him. He was told that he was being arrested for the shooting incident and that he had a right to counsel. The police asked him if he understood what that meant. He said that he didn't want a lawyer and then made a statement to the police. After he made the statement, he was told that the victim had died. The Court held that it is not necessary for the accused to know the exact charge or all of the facts of the case before validly waiving the right to counsel. Here, the accused must have known that he was in serious jeopardy when he chose not to call a lawyer. He saw the shotgun blast, and the fact that three officers had been sent to arrest him indicated the gravity the situation. Although the Crown conceded that the accused's s. 10(a) right had been violated, the Court held that the violation was not serious, since the accused probably knew that the victim had died. The Court held that the waiver was valid.

---

62 (1989), 50 C.C.C. (3d) 1 (S.C.C.).
63 (1991), 63 C.C.C. (3d) 313 (S.C.C.).

LO4 B. POWERS TO SEARCH

1. General Powers and the Charter

Section 8 of the Charter states:

8. Everyone has the right to be secure against unreasonable search or seizure.

The Supreme Court of Canada has said that this section is intended to prevent unreasonable searches and seizures before they occur.[64] This means that, generally, searches require a prior authorization (i.e., a search warrant). If the police do search without a warrant, the Crown will have the burden of showing that the search was reasonable. The Supreme Court has said that a search is reasonable if it is authorized by law, if the law itself is reasonable, and if the search is carried out in a reasonable manner.[65]

As a general rule, then, the police cannot search a place without first obtaining a search warrant. There are a few exceptions to this rule. Some warrantless searches are authorized by the Criminal Code and under the common law. Others are authorized by such federal acts as the Controlled Drugs and Substances Act (CDSA) and the Customs Act. The authority to search under the CDSA is discussed in Appendix A. Note that the authority given to the police under these statutes is somewhat broader than the general authority given under the Criminal Code. Also, certain provincial statutes grant search powers to the police. Finally, a warrantless search is legal if the person consents to the search.

A reasonable amount of force may be used in making the search. However, if the searching officers use an excess of force, they may be liable in a civil action for damages, or charged with the offence of assault. Sections 25 and 26 protect any person who is legally authorized to conduct a search from criminal or civil liability if the person acted on reasonable grounds.

2. Search with a Warrant (Form 5)

Section 487 authorizes a justice to issue a search warrant:

487. (1) A justice who is satisfied by information on oath in Form 1 that there are reasonable grounds to believe that there is in a building, receptacle or place

    (a) anything on or in respect of which any offence . . . has been or is suspected to have been committed,

    (b) anything that there are reasonable grounds to believe will afford evidence with respect to the commission of an offence, or will reveal the whereabouts of a person who is believed to have committed an offence . . .

    (c) anything that there are reasonable grounds to believe is intended to be used for the purpose of committing any offence against the person for which a person may be arrested without warrant, or

    (c.1) any offence-related property may at any time issue a warrant authorizing a peace officer. . .

    (d) to search the building, receptacle or place for any such thing and to seize it, and

64 *Hunter v. Southam Inc.* (1984), 14 C.C.C. (3d) 97 (S.C.C.).
65 *R. v. Collins* (1987), 33 C.C.C. (3d) 1 (S.C.C.).

(e) . . . bring the thing seized before, or make a report in respect thereof to, the justice . . .

The courts have consistently held that a search warrant should not be lightly granted. A search warrant cannot authorize what in reality would amount to a "fishing expedition" for evidence. When requesting that a search warrant be issued, the police must convince the justice in writing and under oath that there are reasonable grounds for believing that the conditions set forth in s. 487 are satisfied. The evidence that is being sought needs to be described with enough particularity that the searchers can identify the thing to be seized.[66]

The Supreme Court of Canada considered the standard of proof necessary to establish reasonable grounds for conducting a search in *R. v. Debot*.[67] Although this case involved a warrantless search that was authorized under the Food and Drugs Act (now part of the CDSA), the principles stated by the Court for establishing reasonable grounds also apply when obtaining a search warrant. The police searched the accused based on information from an informer that the accused would be completing a drug transaction. Drugs were found on him, and he was charged with possession. At the accused's trial, the judge held that the search was unreasonable and excluded the evidence of the drugs. On appeal, the Supreme Court of Canada said that the standard of proof is a finding of reasonable probability or reasonable belief. To determine if this standard has been met, courts must consider all the circumstances, including these:

- Was the information predicting an offence compelling?
- When information is based on an informer's tip, was the informer credible?
- Was the information corroborated by a police investigation before it was decided to conduct the search?

In *Debot*, the information about the offence was specific: The time and location were named, as well as the parties to the transaction. The following circumstances were also noted:

- The informer gave the basis for the allegations.
- The police could take into account the accused's past record of drug offences.
- The informer was known to the police as being reliable.
- Police information had confirmed that the accused and the informer had been seen together.
- Police surveillance confirmed the arrival of the accused's vehicle at the location of the transaction.

Therefore, the police had reasonable grounds to search Debot. The Court noted that if the informer had not been known as reliable, or if fewer details of the transaction had been given, greater police corroboration that the offence had occurred would have been required.

In *R. v. Berger*,[68] the Saskatchewan Court of Appeal held that a warrant based on information from unnamed confidential sources, where there was no evidence to support the truth of the sources' information, no information about how the sources obtained their information, and no independent evidence to support the sources' information, was not a sufficient basis for issuing a warrant.

The search warrant must be based on information that provides reasonable grounds to believe that the alleged offence has been committed and that evidence of that offence will be found at the place to be searched. In addition, the person seeking the warrant must make a

---

66 *Purdy v. R.* (1972), 8 C.C.C. (2d) 52 (N.B.C.A.).
67 (1989), 52 C.C.C. (3d) 193 (S.C.C.).
68 (1989), 48 C.C.C. (3d) 185 (Sask. C.A.).

full and frank disclosure of material facts.[69] In *R. v. Morelli*,[70] a computer technician, while repairing Morelli's computer in Morelli's house, noticed several links to child pornography. Based on the technician's statement, the police prepared an information to obtain a search warrant (ITO), alleging that Morelli was in possession of child pornography, contrary to s. 163.1(4) of the Criminal Code. After obtaining a warrant to search the computer, the police found pornographic images of children on the computer and the accused was charged with, and convicted of, possession of child pornography.

The Supreme Court of Canada held that the search and seizure of the accused's computer infringed his right under s. 8 of the Charter because it was not based on reasonable grounds to believe that Morelli had committed the alleged offence. The Court found that the ITO contained false statements and gave an incomplete and misleading account of the facts, in violation of the informant's duty to make full and frank disclosure of all material information. The ITO used an unsupported stereotype of an ill-defined "type of offender" and imputed that stereotype to the accused. In addition, it presented a distorted portrait of the accused and of his surroundings and conduct in his own home. Stripped of its defects and deficiencies, all that remained in the ITO were references to two Internet links, seen four months earlier in the "Favorites" menu of a Web browser. An ITO to support a warrant to search for evidence of *possession* of child pornography, rather than the different offence of *accessing* child pornography, must provide reasonable grounds to believe that the alleged offender possesses digital files of an illegal image. Unlike traditional photographs, the digital information encoding the image—the image file—can be possessed even if no image is visible. Likewise, even if the image is displayed on a person's computer monitor, the underlying information might remain firmly outside that person's possession, located on a server thousands of kilometres away, over which that person has no control. The Court held that the illegally obtained evidence must be excluded, quashed the conviction, and acquitted Morelli. (This case is discussed in more detail under Child Pornography in Chapter 7.)

The place of search must be specified in the warrant. "Building, place or receptacle" is given a very wide meaning. It includes, for example, boats, cars, backyards, safety deposit boxes, furniture, household plumbing, dwelling-houses, business offices, and summer cottages. As well, the owner or occupier of the property must be identified, along with the name of the accused. In addition, the warrant must describe the offence for which the evidence is being sought.

Police searchers may seize, in addition to the things mentioned in the warrant, anything that they believe on reasonable grounds has been obtained or used in the commission of an offence (s. 489). However, they can only search in areas where the things listed in the search warrant might be located. Also, the police must have reasonable grounds, and cannot seize property on the mere suspicion that the goods have been used or obtained through the commission of an offence. In *R. v. Askov*,[71] the police had a warrant to search the accused's home for weapons. While searching the home, they also seized property that they suspected was stolen. The property was taken to the police station for investigation to determine whether it was indeed stolen. The court stated that the police action was a deliberate and flagrant disregard of the accused's right under the Charter to be free from unreasonable seizure. The police had no reasonable or probable grounds to believe that the goods were stolen.

69   *R. v. Araujo*, [2000] S.C.R. 992 (S.C.C.).
70   [2010] 1 S.C.R. 253 (S.C.C.); also see *R. v. Campbell*, [2011] SCC 32.
71   (1987), 60 C.R. (3d) 261 (Ont. Dist. Ct.).

Section 488 states that the warrant must be executed by day unless it specifically authorizes the officers to use it at night. "Day" is defined in s. 2 as "the period between six o'clock in the forenoon and nine o'clock in the afternoon of the same day." The same section defines "night" as "the period between nine o'clock in the afternoon and six o'clock in the forenoon of the following day."

There are other sections in the Criminal Code that grant the right of search to the police if certain specific offences are involved. For example, s. 164 authorizes a police officer to apply for a warrant to seize obscene publications. Section 199 allows a police officer to apply for a search warrant for any premises if he or she believes on reasonable grounds that a gaming house (s. 201), bookmaking place (sections 202 and 203), lottery (sections 206 and 207), or common bawdy house (s. 210) exists. Under s. 462.32, a warrant can be issued to seize "proceeds of crime." Such a warrant must be applied for by the Attorney General.

When executing the warrant, the police have the same duties as discussed earlier when entering private premises to make an arrest. That is, the police must give notice of their presence, authority, and purpose. Section 29, which requires the person to have the warrant on his or her person, where feasible, and to produce it, when requested to do so, applies to search warrants as well as to arrest warrants. If entry is refused, the police are entitled to use force. They do not have to announce themselves if, for example, evidence will be destroyed. However, as the Supreme Court of Canada said in *R. v. Genest*,[72] a case that concerned an illegal search:

> *The greater the departure from the standards of behaviour required by the common law and the Charter, the heavier the onus on the police to show why they thought it necessary to use force in the process of an arrest or a search. The evidence to justify such behaviour must be apparent in the record, and must have been available to the police when they chose their course of conduct. The Crown cannot rely on* ex post facto *justifications.*[73]

3. Searches of the Human Body

In general, a search warrant cannot be obtained to search a human body. In *Laporte v. Laganière*,[74] the police sought a warrant to search in the body of the accused for a bullet that was alleged to have been fired from a police revolver. To conduct the search, a major operation would have been necessary, because the bullet was deeply embedded in the accused's shoulder. The Quebec court held that, for the purposes of s. 487, the body is not a "place or receptacle."

A significant exception is s. 487.05, which allows police to obtain a warrant to collect bodily substances for DNA testing from persons who are suspected of committing certain serious crimes. There are three types of samples that can be taken: hair, blood, and skin cells from a mouth swab. The application for a warrant must be made to a provincial court judge. Section 487.05 states:

487.05 (1) A provincial court judge who . . . is satisfied by information on oath that there are reasonable grounds to believe

(a) **that a designated offence has been committed,**

(b) **that a bodily substance has been found**

---

72   (1989), 45 C.C.C. (3d) 385 (S.C.C.).
73   Ibid. at 408.
74   (1972), 8 C.C.C. (2d) 343 (Que. Q.B.).

>   (i) at the place where the offence was committed,
>
>   (ii) on or within the body of the victim of the offence,
>
>   (iii) on anything worn or carried by the victim at the time when the offence was committed, or
>
>   (iv) on or within the body of any person or thing or at any place associated with the commission of the offence,
>
> (c) that a person was a party to the offence, and
>
> (d) that forensic DNA analysis of a bodily substance from the person will provide evidence about whether the bodily substance referred to in paragraph (b) was from that person
>
> **and who is satisfied that it is in the best interests of the administration of justice to do so may issue a warrant in Form 5 authorizing a peace officer to obtain . . . a bodily substance from that person . . .**

The peace officer who is executing the warrant must inform the person of the nature of the procedure, its purposes, the possibility of the results being used as evidence, and the authority of the peace officer to use reasonable force to execute the warrant (s. 487.07).

Under s. 487.09, the bodily substance and test results must be destroyed (a) if the results establish the bodily substances were not from the person; (b) if the person is acquitted of the offence or any related offence (except for a finding of not criminally responsible because of a mental disorder); or (c) if, one year after the person is discharged from a preliminary inquiry, the charges are dismissed or withdrawn or proceedings are stayed, unless within the year the person is charged with the same offence or another arising out of the same transaction. However, a provincial court judge can order that the substance and results not be destroyed for a designated period if the judge is satisfied that the substance or results might reasonably be required in an investigation or prosecution of the person for another designated offence or of another person for the offence.

The designated offences include crimes of personal violence such as assault, murder, sexual assault, kidnapping, and robbery, as well as breaking and entering and arson.

Note that this law deals only with collecting the evidence. It is up to the courts to determine under what circumstances the evidence will be admissible.

4. Telewarrants

In most situations, to obtain a search warrant, the police officer must appear before a justice and lay an information. The Code allows the police in certain circumstances to obtain warrants over the phone or through other methods of telecommunication. Such warrants are called telewarrants. Section 487.1 states:

> **487.1 (1) Where a peace officer believes that an indictable offence has been committed and that it would be impracticable to appear personally before a justice . . . the peace officer may submit an information on oath by telephone or other means of telecommunication to a justice . . .**

The justice will record the information verbatim and must, as soon as practicable, file it with the court.

The information must include the following:

- a statement of the circumstances that make it impracticable for the officer to appear personally before a judge;
- a statement of the offence alleged, the place to be searched, and the items likely to be seized; and
- a statement as to the officer's grounds for believing that the items will be found in the place to be searched.

Once the search warrant has been issued, the officer must file a written report stating when the warrant was executed and what was seized.

The Code also allows a justice to receive an information by a telecommunication that produces a written document (e.g., a fax). When the justice receives the written communication, he or she must file it with the clerk of the court as soon as practicable.

A telewarrant must be executed by day, unless the justice authorizes execution of it by night.

5. Searches without a Warrant

a. Investigative Detention

As discussed above, a person can be detained for investigative purposes. In such a situation, the police have the authority under the common law to conduct a pat-down search to ensure the safety of themselves or others.[75]

b. For Certain Offences

The Code allows the police, in certain limited circumstances, to conduct a search without a search warrant for specific offences. For example, s. 117.02 of the Code concerns situations where guns or other weapons are involved.[76] If a peace officer believes on reasonable grounds (a) that a gun or weapon was used in an offence or (b) that an offence is being or has been committed that involves a gun or weapon and (c) any evidence of the offence is likely to be found on a person, in a vehicle, or in any place other than a dwelling-house, the peace officer may search the person, vehicle, or place without a warrant and the officer may seize anything that he or she reasonably believes is related to the offence. However, the officer may do so only if the conditions for obtaining a warrant exist but, due to exigent circumstances, it would not be practicable to obtain a warrant.

c. Incident to Lawful Arrest

Apart from the provisions in the Criminal Code and other federal acts, such as the Customs Act, Controlled Drugs and Substances Act, and the common law, the right to search the person exists only as an incident to arrest. This power is not conferred by the Criminal Code; rather, it comes from the common law, which is preserved in such matters by s. 8 of the Code. After the police have arrested an accused, they are entitled to conduct a search of the accused's person and to seize anything in his or her possession or immediate surroundings for the purpose of securing evidence, preventing escape, and guaranteeing the safety of the accused and the officer.[77]

In *Cloutier v. Langlois*, the Supreme Court of Canada considered the application of the authority to search incident to arrest. Cloutier had been stopped by the police for making an

75 *Mann, supra* note 39.
76 Section 117.02 refers not only to guns and weapons but also to imitation firearms, prohibited devices, ammunition, and explosive substances.
77 *Cloutier v. Langlois* (1990), 53 C.C.C. (3d) 257 (S.C.C.).

illegal right-hand turn with his car. A police check showed that he had several unpaid traffic fines. He became highly agitated and verbally abusive. The police had him put his hands on the car roof and spread his legs. They then frisked him (lightly patted him down). He sued the officers for assault. The Court held that reasonable grounds were not necessary for the search: "[A] frisk search incidental to a lawful arrest reconciles the public's interest in the effective and safe enforcement of the law on one hand, and on the other its interest in ensuring the freedom and dignity of individuals."[78]

The Court set out these limits on the common law right to search incident to arrest:

- The police have a discretion as to whether a search is necessary for the effective and safe application of the law.
- The search must be for a valid objective of criminal justice (e.g., to check for weapons or prevent escape).
- The search cannot be used to intimidate, ridicule, or pressure the accused to gain admissions.
- The search must not be conducted in an abusive way.

The Court concluded that the search was justified. Although, in retrospect, the police did not have any real reason to fear physical violence, there was ample evidence that at the time they believed the search was necessary for their safety. The Supreme Court has also held that, before conducting a frisk search, the police must inform the accused of the right to counsel. However, the police do not have to wait until the accused calls a lawyer before conducting the search.[79]

Another Supreme Court of Canada case reached a different result. In *R. v. Greffe*,[80] the police had information that the accused would be bringing drugs into Canada from Amsterdam. The accused was detained at the airport by Customs authorities. His luggage was searched. Nothing was found. He was then taken to a room for a strip search. At this point, he had not been told of his right to counsel. He was then turned over to the RCMP, who told him that he was being arrested for outstanding traffic warrants, that he had a right to consult counsel, and that he was being taken to a hospital for a rectal search. He was then taken to a hospital for a rectal exam. Two plastic bags containing heroin were recovered from his body.

The Court held that there were two serious violations of Charter rights in this case. First, although the Customs Act authorizes this type of search without an arrest if there are reasonable grounds for the search, the accused was not informed of his right to counsel when he was detained for the strip search at the airport. Second, the intrusive body search that took place at the hospital on the basis of an arrest for traffic violations was a violation of the accused's right to be secure against unreasonable search and seizure. In other words, a rectal search cannot be justified on the basis of an arrest for outstanding traffic warrants. Also, even though the accused was informed of his right to counsel before the rectal search, the notification was "tainted" because he did not know the true reasons for his arrest. The Court also found that the police had not acted "in good faith." In other words, the violation of the accused's rights was not unintentional. The Court concluded that the evidence of the heroin had to be excluded because of the cumulative effect of the denial of the accused's rights: "Therefore, and not without great hesitation given the manifest culpability of the appellant, of a crime I consider heinous, I conclude that the integrity of our criminal justice system and the respect owed to our Charter are more important than the conviction of this offender."[81]

---

78 Ibid. at 255.
79 *Debot, supra* note 67.
80 (1990), 55 C.C.C. (3d) 161 (S.C.C.).
81 Ibid. at 194.

d. Where Exigent Circumstances Exist

Section 487.11 permits the search of a place or premises without a warrant if the conditions exist for obtaining a warrant under s. 487(1) or s. 492.1(1) (which allows the use of tracking devices), but by reason of exigent circumstances it would be impractical to obtain a warrant. Exigent circumstances would include the danger of immediate loss or destruction of evidence or immediate threat to the safety of others.

6. Searches and the Expectation of Privacy

The courts have held that s. 8 protects a person's reasonable expectation of privacy. Before a s. 8 violation can be claimed, the accused must establish that he or she had a reasonable expectation of privacy in the thing searched or seized. There have been several Supreme Court decisions considering what a person's private space is.

In *R. v. Buhay*,[82] the space was a rented locker at a bus station. Two security guards who worked at the bus station smelled marijuana near the locker, so they had an employee of the bus line open it. They discovered marijuana inside. The security guards put the marijuana back in the locker and called police. When the police arrived, the locker was opened again and the marijuana seized. The accused was charged with possession of marijuana for the purposes of trafficking. At trial, one officer testified he did not think of obtaining a warrant and the other officer testified he thought of it, but he did not think he had sufficient grounds to obtain the warrant. He also testified that he believed that the accused did not have a reasonable expectation of privacy in the locker. In finding that the accused did have a reasonable expectation of privacy in the locker, and that the warrantless search was unreasonable, the trial judge excluded the evidence under s. 24(2), and the accused was acquitted. On appeal to the Supreme Court of Canada, the Court agreed that the accused should be acquitted, stating that the accused had a reasonable expectation of privacy in the locker unless the contents posed a risk to security. The Court considered that he had rented the locker for a 24-hour period, which had not expired. He had control and possession of the locker's contents through possession of a key, and there were no signs near the lockers saying that the lockers might be opened and searched. The Crown failed to rebut the presumption that the warrantless search was unreasonable; that is, there were no exigent circumstances justifying the warrantless search. The police should have obtained a warrant to search the locker.

In *R. v. Patrick*,[83] the issue was whether the accused had a reasonable expectation of privacy in the contents of garbage bags that he had placed at the edge of his property. The police suspected that Patrick was operating an ecstasy lab in his home. They seized bags of garbage that he had placed for collection at the rear of his property adjacent to a public alleyway. The police did not have to step onto Patrick's property to reach the bags but they did have to reach through the airspace over his property line. The police used evidence taken from the garbage bags to obtain a warrant to search his house. They seized more evidence during the search. Patrick argued that the taking of his garbage bags by the police was a breach of s. 8 of the Charter. The Supreme Court of Canada found that the police did not breach Patrick's right to be free from unreasonable search and seizure. He abandoned his privacy interest when he placed his garbage for collection at the rear of his property where it was accessible to any passing member of the public. He did everything required of him to have the bags removed by the municipal garbage collection system.

---

82 (2003), 174 C.C.C. (3d) 97 (S.C.C.).
83 (2009), 242 C.C.C. (3d) 158 (S.C.C.).

In *R. v. Nolet*,[84] a police officer, acting under the authority of Saskatchewan's Highway and Transportation Act (H&TA), made a random stop of Nolet's truck. After finding violations of the Act, including defective trucking documents, the officer conducted a search of the truck's cab, which included a sleeping compartment behind the driver's seat, where he found a small duffle bag. When he touched it, it appeared to contain paper. After opening the bag, he found $115,000 bundled in small denominations. As this was typical of drug transactions, he placed Nolet under arrest for possession of the proceeds of crime. The police then searched the truck's trailer and found 392 pounds of marijuana. The Supreme Court of Canada held that the search did not violate s. 8 of the Charter. At the time the officer began to search the truck cab, it was within his statutory authority to search for further evidence related to H&TA offences. Although a trucker has a reasonable expectation of some privacy in the sleeping compartment, the level of expectation is low. Commercial trucking is a highly regulated industry and commercial drivers are well aware of the police authority to conduct random stops and to search a vehicle for evidence of infractions. Nolet argued that the officer's search of the duffle bag was primarily due to the officer's interest in criminal activity and, as such, fell outside any valid regulatory purpose under the H&TA. The Court said that it was sufficient that the search was at least in part related to H&TA offences. The officer pushed down on the bag and felt and heard what seemed like paper, suggesting the existence of items connected to the H&TA inquiry. The Court found that it was not unreasonable for the officer to open the bag, given the very limited privacy interest of the accused.

In *R. v. A.M.*,[85] the issue concerned the right to privacy of a student's backpack. The principal had invited the police to school to search for drugs. During the search, students were confined to their classrooms. A police dog led the police to a backpack in the gym that contained marijuana and psilocybin. The student owner of the backpack was charged with possession for the purposes of trafficking. The Supreme Court held that a backpack is like a purse or briefcase—the depository of much that is personal—and that there is a reasonable expectation of privacy in its contents. The Court concluded that the dog-sniff search was unreasonably undertaken because there was no proper justification. The Court upheld the lower courts' decisions in dismissing the charges.

In *R. v. Kang-Brown*,[86] an officer was patrolling a bus station when he observed a man acting strangely. He started talking to him and called over his dog. The dog indicated that there were drugs in the man's bag. He was searched and found to be in possession of cocaine and heroin. He was charged with possession and trafficking. He was convicted at trial, with the trial judge holding that there was no arbitrary or unlawful search, since the odours from the bag emanated freely in a public space, and that the accused did not have a reasonable expectation of privacy. The Supreme Court of Canada disagreed and held that the police have the right to use drug-sniffing dogs only where they have a reasonable suspicion to believe contraband is present.

A different result was reached in *R. v. Tessling*.[87] The police received information from an unproven source that the accused was producing and trafficking in marijuana in his home. The police contacted the power company and conducted surveillance of the home, but nothing out of the ordinary was revealed. They then used a thermal imaging device to take a "heat" picture of the accused's home from an overhead aircraft. The camera, utilizing "Forward Looking

84   [2010] 1 S.C.R. 851 (S.C.C.).
85   (2008), 230 C.C.C. (3d) 377 (S.C.C.).
86   [2008] S.C.R. 18.
87   (2004), 189 C.C.C. (3d) 129 (S.C.C.); see also *R. v. Plant* (1993) discussed on p. 130.

Infra-Red" ("FLIR") technology, recorded not patterns of light, but the relative distribution of heat over the surface of the building. The police did not obtain a search warrant prior to the over-flight. The FLIR image, taken together with other evidence, caused the police to infer the existence in the accused's home of a marijuana-growing operation ("grow op"). A warrant was obtained based on the informant's statements and on the FLIR camera images. The accused was charged with possession of marijuana for the purpose of trafficking, and other drug and weapons offences. The evidence was admitted and the accused was convicted. The Ontario Court of Appeal held that the use of the FLIR technology intruded on the accused's privacy interest, and, therefore, amounted to a search. As the police did not have a warrant at that time, the appeal was allowed and an acquittal entered. However, in restoring the accused's conviction, the Supreme Court of Canada stated:

> *I do not regard the use of current FLIR technology as the functional equivalent of placing the police inside the home. Nor is it helpful in the Canadian context to compare the state of technology in 2004 with that which existed at Confederation in 1867, or in 1982 when s. 8 of the Charter was adopted. Having regard to its purpose, I do not accept that s. 8 is triggered by a FLIR image that discloses that heat sources of some unknown description are present inside the structure, or that the heat distribution is uneven. Certainly FLIR imaging generates information about the home but s. 8 protects people, not places. The information generated by FLIR imaging about the respondent does not touch on "a biographical core of personal information", nor does it "tend to reveal intimate details of [his] lifestyle." It shows that some of the activities in the house generate heat. That is not enough to get the respondent over the constitutional threshold.*[88]

05 C. WIRETAPPING AND ELECTRONIC SURVEILLANCE

A police officer may intercept private communications in several situations. The meaning of "intercept" includes listening, recording, or acquiring a communication (see s. 183). A private communication is defined as "any oral communication or any telecommunication . . . that is made under circumstances in which it is reasonable for the originator to expect that it will not be intercepted by any person other than the person intended by the originator to receive it." The key point is whether it is reasonable to expect the communication to be private. In *Goldman v. The Queen*,[89] the accused had called a police station and made threatening remarks to an officer. The remarks were recorded. The Supreme Court of Canada held that, in this situation, it was not reasonable to expect that the remarks would not be overheard or recorded by another person. In most, but not all, situations, interceptions must be authorized by a judge.

1. Authorized Interceptions

There are two situations where authorization can be obtained for interceptions.

a. Section 185

This section sets out the procedure for applying for authorization to intercept private communications. The application must be made in writing before a superior court judge (or a judge as defined in s. 152). It must be signed by the Attorney General of the province, the Solicitor

---

88   Ibid. at 151.
89   (1979), 51 C.C.C. (2d) 1 (S.C.C.).

General of Canada, or an agent specially designated by one of them. The application must be accompanied by an affidavit, which must state:

(c) **the facts relied upon to justify the belief that the authorization should be given together with the particulars of the offence,**

(d) **the type of private communication proposed to be intercepted,**

(e) **the names, addresses and occupations, if known, of all persons, the interception of whose private communications there are reasonable grounds to believe may assist the investigation of the offence, a general description of the nature and location of the place, if known, at which private communications are proposed to be intercepted and a general description of the manner of interception proposed to be used,**

(f) **the number of instances, if any, on which an application has been made under this section in relation to the offence and a person named in the affidavit . . . and on which the application was withdrawn or no authorization was given, the date on which each application was made and the name of the judge to whom each application was made,**

(g) **the period for which the authorization is requested, and**

(h) **whether other investigative procedures have been tried and have failed or why it appears that they are unlikely to succeed or that the urgency of the matter is such that it would be impractical to carry out the investigation of the offence using only other investigative procedures.**

Section 186 requires that before authorizing an interception, the judge must be satisfied that (a) it would be in the best interests of the administration of justice to do so; and (b) other investigative procedures have been tried and have failed, are unlikely to succeed, or would be impractical due to the urgency of the matter.

Authorization for an interception under s. 186 is allowed only for the offences listed in s. 183. The list is long and includes treason, weapons offences, various fraud offences, offences involving personal violence, drug offences, and any other offence for which an offender may be imprisoned for five years or more.

b. Section 184(2)(a)

This section provides that it is not an offence to intercept a communication if one of the parties to the conversation consents. At one time, the police used this exception to intercept conversations between police informers and suspects without authorization. The Supreme Court of Canada held, however, that the right to be secure against unreasonable searches and seizures applies to interceptions of private communications. This means that where the state (i.e., the police) is recording the conversation, s. 8 of the Charter requires that the police get judicial authorization for the interception.[90] The Court's decision is reflected in s. 184.2, which sets out a procedure for obtaining authorization from a judge where one party consents to the interception. The authorization can be applied for any offence.

---

90   *R. v. Duarte* (1990), 53 C.C.C. (2d) 1 (S.C.C.).

c. Wiretaps in Exigent Circumstances

Section 184.4 permits a peace officer to intercept certain private communications, without prior judicial authorization, if the officer believes on reasonable grounds that the interception is immediately necessary to prevent an unlawful act that would cause serious harm, provided judicial authorization could not be obtained with reasonable diligence. In *R. v. Tse*,[91] the police used s. 184.4 to carry out unauthorized warrantless interceptions of private communications when the daughter of an alleged kidnapping victim began receiving calls from her father stating that he was being held for ransom. Approximately 24 hours later, the police obtained a judicial authorization for continued interceptions, pursuant to s. 186 of the Code. The trial judge found that s. 184.4 contravened the right to be free from unreasonable search or seizure under s. 8 of the Charter and that it was not a reasonable limit under s. 1.

On appeal to the Supreme Court of Canada, the Court found that the conditions in s. 184.4 to ensure that it is used only in exigent circumstances strike an appropriate balance between an individual's reasonable expectation of privacy and society's interest in preventing serious harm. To that extent, s. 184.4 is constitutional. However, the Court also found that s. 184.4 contains no accountability measures to permit oversight of the police use of the power and, therefore, is unconstitutional. The Court stated that s. 184.4 "does not require that 'after the fact' notice be given to persons whose private communications have been intercepted. Unless a criminal prosecution results, the targets of the wiretapping may never learn of the interceptions and will be unable to challenge police use of this power." The Court concluded that s. 184.4 fails to meet the minimum constitutional standards of s. 8 of the Charter. The Court gave Parliament 12 months to redraft the provision to make it compliant with the Charter.

2. Unauthorized Interceptions

In certain other circumstances, an interception can be done without court authorization. Under s. 184.1, an agent of the state (e.g., a peace officer) can intercept a private communication with the consent of one of the parties to the communication if the agent reasonably believes that there is a risk of bodily harm to the person who consented to the interception, and if the purpose of the interception is to prevent the bodily harm. So, for example, if a woman is being harassed or threatened over the telephone, this section can be used to allow the police to intercept the call. Section 184.4 also allows interception without authorization where a peace officer, on reasonable grounds, believes the following:

- that the urgency of the situation is such that authorization could not with reasonable diligence be obtained,
- that the interception is immediately necessary to prevent an unlawful act that would cause serious harm to any person, and
- that either the originator of the communication or the person intended by the originator to receive the communication is the person who is likely to perform the unlawful act or is the intended victim.

Unless the interception is authorized, or falls under the exceptions where authorization is not required, or is required to maintain service or to manage radio frequencies, it is an offence under s. 184 of the Code.

---

91   [2012] SCC 16.

3. Warrants under Section 487.01

The Code allows the police to obtain warrants for gathering information in ways that are not covered by s. 487 warrants or warrants under any other federal law. Section 487.01 allows an officer to apply to a judge to obtain a warrant to use "any device or investigative technique or procedure or to do any thing described in the warrant that would, if not authorized, constitute an unreasonable search or seizure." This section has been used, for example, to authorize video surveillance. Before issuing the warrant, the judge must be satisfied by information under oath that there are reasonable grounds for believing that an offence has been or will be committed, and that information concerning this offence will be obtained through the use of the technique, procedure, or device, or for the doing of the thing. The judge must also be satisfied that it is in the best interests of the administration of justice to issue the warrant, and that there is no other provision in the Code or in any other Act of Parliament that would provide for a warrant for the technique, procedure, or device, or for the doing of the thing. Subsection (2) limits the scope of the search warrants:

(2) Nothing in subsection (1) shall be construed as to permit interference with the bodily integrity of any person.

Where the warrant authorizes videotaping or the use of similar devices in circumstances where a person has a reasonable expectation of privacy, the warrant must contain such conditions as the judge considers advisable to ensure that the person's privacy is respected as much as possible.

Section 492.1(4) allows the police to obtain a warrant to install a "tracking device [defined as] any device that, when installed in or on any thing, may be used to help ascertain the . . . location of any thing or person."

Section 492.2(1) allows a judge to issue a warrant to install a "number recorder [defined as] any device that can be used to record or identify the telephone number or location of the telephone from which a telephone call originates, or at which it is received or is intended to be received."

The Supreme Court considered whether the unauthorized use of computerized electricity records was an unreasonable search or seizure. In *R. v. Plant*,[92] the police suspected that marijuana was being grown in a particular house. They were able to gain access, through the police station's computer terminal, to the City of Calgary's utility company mainframe computer, and to determine that the dwelling's electrical consumption was four times more than that of similar dwellings. This information formed part of the grounds for obtaining a search warrant. Among other issues, the Supreme Court considered whether accessing the city's utilities computer was a violation of s. 8 of the Charter. The Court first noted that the s. 8 guarantee against unreasonable searches protects a right of privacy. Section 8 can be used to protect "a biological core of personal information" that individuals in a free and democratic society would wish to shield from the state. However, in this case, the Court found that the computer records could not be said to reveal intimate details of the accused's life. As well, there was no relationship of confidence between the utility company and the accused. Furthermore, because of the place and manner in which the information was retrieved, the accused had no reasonable expectation of privacy. Also, the seriousness of the offence supported the use of the evidence. In sum, using the utility records was not a violation of s. 8.

---

92   (1993), 84 C.C.C. (3d) 203 (S.C.C.).

TABLE 5-1	Pre-trial Forms

1. Warrants	• Warrants may be issued if, based on information submitted by the police, there are reasonable grounds to believe that the warrant is justified.
Search Warrant — Form 5 (s. 487)	• Issued by a justice • Authorizes the police to enter specified premises and to search for things described in the warrant and related to a specified offence
Warrant to Take Bodily Substances — Form 5.02 (s. 487.05)	• Issued by a provincial court judge • Authorizes the police to take from specified person samples of bodily substances that are reasonably required for forensic DNA analysis
Telewarrant to Search — Form 5.1 (s. 487.1)	• Issued by a justice • Obtained by telephone or other means of telecommunication where there are reasonable grounds for dispensing with an information presented personally and in writing
Arrest Warrant — Form 7 (ss. 475, 493, 597, 800, and 803)	• Issued by a justice • Authorizes police to arrest a specified accused who has been charged with a specified offence
2. Summons — Form 6 (ss. 493, 508, and 512)	• Issued by a justice • Requires accused to attend court in relation to an alleged offence
3. Appearance Notice — Form 9 (s. 493)	• Issued by police • Requires accused to attend court at a specified time in relation to a specific offence • May also require accused to appear at a police station at a specified time for the purposes of the Identification of Criminals Act
4. Release Forms Promise to Appear — Form 10 (s. 493)	• Promise made to the police • In order to be released from custody, accused promises to appear in court at a specified time in relation to a specific offence • Accused may also promise to appear at a police station at a specified time for the purposes of the Identification of Criminals Act

Recognizance — Form 11 (s. 493)	• Agreement entered into before a police officer • In order to be released from custody, accused agrees to pay an amount not greater than $500 if he or she fails to attend court at a specified time in relation to a specific offence. Police may require a deposit not greater than $500 if accused does not ordinarily reside in the province or within 200 km of the place of custody • Accused may also acknowledge that he or she is required to appear at a police station for the purposes of the Identification of Criminals Act
Undertaking to Peace Officer — Form 11.1 (ss. 493, 499, and 503)	• Promise made to the police • In order to be released from police custody by way of a promise to appear or a recognizance, accused promises to comply with one or more conditions specified by police (e.g., remain within the province)
Undertaking to Justice — Form 12 (s. 493)	• Promise made to a justice • In order to be released from custody, accused promises to comply with one or more conditions specified by the justice (e.g., remain within the province)
Recognizance — Form 32 (s. 493)	• Agreement entered into before a justice • In order to be released from custody, accused and sureties, if any, agree to pay an amount of money if the accused fails to attend court at a specified time or fails to comply with any other condition included in the recognizance

L06 D. EXCLUSION OF EVIDENCE UNDER THE CHARTER

Where a person's rights under the Charter are violated, the person may attempt to have any evidence that was obtained as a result of the violation excluded from the trial.

Section 24 provides:

> **(2) Where . . . a court concludes that evidence was obtained in a manner that infringed or denied any rights or freedoms guaranteed by this Charter, the evidence shall be excluded if it is established that, having regard to all the circumstances, the admission of it in the proceedings would bring the administration of justice into disrepute.**

1. Factors in Determining Whether Evidence Should Be Excluded

In *R. v. Grant*,[93] the Supreme Court of Canada clarified the criteria for determining when admission of evidence obtained by a Charter breach "would bring the administration of justice into disrepute." Section 24(2) does not focus on immediate reaction to the individual case. Rather, it

---

93 (2009), 245 C.C.C. (3d) 1 (S.C.C.).

focuses on whether the overall reputation of the justice system, viewed in the long term, will be adversely affected by admission of the evidence. The test is whether a reasonable person, informed of all relevant circumstances and the values underlying the Charter, would conclude that the admission of the evidence would bring the administration of justice into disrepute. Section 24(2) is not aimed at punishing the police or providing compensation to the accused, but rather at systemic concerns.

In determining whether evidence should be excluded under s. 24(2), the Supreme Court stated that a court must assess and balance the effect of admitting the evidence on society's confidence in the justice system, having regard to three factors:

a. The Seriousness of the Charter-infringing State Conduct

The court must assess whether the admission of the evidence would bring the administration of justice into disrepute by sending a message to the public that the courts effectively condone state violations of the law. The more severe or deliberate the state conduct is that led to the Charter violation, the greater the need for the courts to dissociate themselves from that conduct, by excluding evidence linked to that conduct.

State conduct resulting in Charter violations varies in seriousness. Admission of evidence obtained through inadvertent or minor violations of the Charter may minimally undermine public confidence in the rule of law. Admitting evidence obtained through a wilful or reckless disregard of Charter rights will have a negative effect on the public confidence in the rule of law, and risk bringing the administration of justice into disrepute.

Extenuating circumstances, such as the need to prevent the disappearance of evidence, may reduce the seriousness of police conduct that results in a Charter breach. "Good faith" on the part of the police will also reduce the need for the court to dissociate itself from the police conduct. However, the Supreme Court was clear that ignorance of Charter standards must not be rewarded or encouraged and negligence or wilful blindness cannot be equated with good faith.

Deliberate police conduct in violation of the Charter tends to support exclusion of the evidence. The Supreme Court also noted that it is important to keep in mind that for every Charter breach that comes before the courts, many others may go unidentified because they did not turn up relevant evidence leading to a criminal charge.

b. The Impact of the Breach on the Charter-protected Interests of the Accused

The court must evaluate the extent to which the breach actually undermined the interests protected by the right infringed. The more serious the impact on the accused's protected interests is, the greater the risk that admission of the evidence may signal to the public that Charter rights are of little actual value, leading to public cynicism and bringing the administration of justice into disrepute.

The interests protected in the case of a statement to the police obtained in violation of the Charter include the s. 7 right to silence, or to choose whether or not to speak to police, which stem from the principle against self-incrimination. An unreasonable search contrary to s. 8 of the Charter may have an impact on the protected interests of privacy and human dignity. An unreasonable search that intrudes on an area in which the individual reasonably has a high expectation of privacy, or that demeans his or her dignity, is more serious than one that does not.

c. Society's Interest in the Adjudication of the Case on Its Merits

The court must determine whether the truth-seeking function of the criminal trial process would be better served by admission of the evidence or by its exclusion. Society has an interest in ensuring that those who violate the law are brought to trial and dealt with according to the law.

Factors such as the reliability of the evidence and its importance to the prosecution's case should be considered. If a breach of the Charter, such as compelling a suspect to talk, undermines the reliability of the evidence, it is more likely that the evidence should be excluded. The admission of unreliable evidence serves neither the accused's interest in a fair trial nor the public interest in uncovering the truth. On the other hand, exclusion of reliable evidence may undermine the truth-seeking function of the justice system and make the trial unfair, thus bringing the administration of justice into disrepute.

The importance of the evidence to the prosecution's case is linked to reliability of the evidence. The admission of evidence of questionable reliability is more likely to bring the administration of justice into disrepute if it forms the entire case against the accused. On the other hand, the exclusion of highly reliable evidence may have a more negative impact on the reputation of the administration of justice if it effectively destroys the prosecution's case.

Having considered these factors, the judge must then determine whether, on balance, the admission of the evidence obtained by Charter breach would bring the administration of justice into disrepute.

2. Applying the Factors

In *Grant*, discussed earlier (see pages 132–133), the Supreme Court found that the police violated s. 9 of the Charter by arbitrarily detaining Grant and s. 10(b) by denying him his right to counsel. The Court then addressed the issue of whether the gun found on Grant by the police as a result of the violations of the Charter should be excluded from the evidence at his trial. In considering the first factor, the seriousness of the improper police conduct that led to the discovery of the gun, the Court found that the police conduct was not abusive. The point at which an encounter becomes a detention is not always clear. Having been under a mistaken view that they had not detained the appellant, the officers' failure to advise him of his right to counsel was erroneous but understandable. Given that the police conduct in committing the Charter breach was neither deliberate nor egregious, the Court concluded that the effect of admitting the evidence would not greatly undermine public confidence in the rule of law.

Regarding the second factor, the arbitrary detention curtailed Grant's liberty interest. The interaction with the police became a coercive situation that deprived Grant of his freedom to make an informed choice about how to respond to the police. The violation of his right to counsel led to Grant's incriminating statements. The fact that the evidence of the gun would not have been discovered without the breach of his Charter rights aggravated the impact of the breach on Grant's interest. The Court concluded that the impact of the violation of Grant's rights under sections 9 and 10(b) of the Charter was significant.

In considering the third factor, the Court found that the gun was highly reliable evidence and essential to a determination on the merits. The Court also found that the seriousness of the offence was not of much assistance in this case in deciding on the third factor.

The Court balanced these three factors in determining whether admitting the gun would put the administration of justice into disrepute. After noting that it was a "close case," the Court held that the lower courts were not wrong in concluding that the admission of the gun into evidence would not bring the administration of justice into disrepute. The significant impact of the breach on Grant's Charter-protected rights weighed strongly in favour of excluding the gun, while the public interest in the adjudication of the case on its merits weighed strongly in favour of its admission. However, the balance was tipped in favour of admission by the fact that the police officers were operating in circumstances of considerable legal uncertainty about the point at which their encounter with Grant became a detention.

In *R. v. Harrison*,[94] the Supreme Court of Canada applied the *Grant* factors and reached a different conclusion, based on the facts of the case. A police officer noticed that Harrison's car had no front licence plate. After turning on his roof lights to pull over the car, the officer realized that, because it was registered in Alberta, the car did not require a front licence plate. The officer was informed by radio dispatch that the car had been rented in Vancouver. Even though he had no grounds to believe that any offence was being committed, the officer testified at trial that abandoning the detention might have affected the integrity of the police in the eyes of observers. He arrested Harrison after discovering that his driver's licence had been suspended. The officer then searched the car and found 35 kg of cocaine. On appeal to the Supreme Court of Canada, the issue was whether the cocaine should be admitted into evidence. The Court found that the balancing of the *Grant* factors favoured exclusion of the evidence. The conduct of the police that led to the Charter breaches represented a blatant disregard for Charter rights, further aggravated by the officer's misleading testimony at trial. The deprivation of liberty and privacy represented by the unconstitutional detention and search was a significant, although not egregious, intrusion on Harrison's Charter-protected interests. On the other hand, the drugs were highly reliable evidence tendered on a very serious charge. However, the seriousness of the offence and the reliability of the evidence did not in this case outweigh the factors pointing to exclusion.

In *R. v. Cote*,[95] the accused was charged with the murder of her husband. After receiving a report from a doctor at a hospital that the husband was suffering from head injuries and had a metal object in his skull, the police went to Cote's home at about midnight. The police explained that they were there to find out what happened and to make sure the premises were safe, but they did not tell Cote that they believed that her husband was suffering from a gunshot wound. The police inspected the interior of the house and the property around it. The police questioned Cote about the presence of firearms in the house. She confirmed the presence of two firearms but could only locate one, to which she led the police. The police later obtained warrants, returned to the house and found a rifle of the same calibre as the bullet recovered from the husband's skull. The police took Cote to the police station at 3 a.m. and interrogated her until 8 p.m., when she was informed that her husband was dead and she was charged with murder. At trial, Cote applied for the exclusion of the evidence against her.

The trial judge concluded that the police embarked on a systematic violation of Cote's rights from the time they first entered onto her property until the end of her interrogation. The trial judge held that the police's entry on her property, and the search of her house and property, constituted unreasonable searches and seizures contrary to s. 8 of the Charter. He held that the police detained her without telling her why, in violation of s. 10(a) of the Charter, and that the police violated her right to obtain the assistance of a lawyer and to be advised of that right, in violation of s. 10(b) of the Charter. He also held that the police violated her right to silence as protected by s. 7 of the Charter and obtained a statement that was not voluntary. The trial judge also found that the police had misled a judicial officer to obtain the warrants. The trial judge excluded all of the evidence. The Court of Appeal for Quebec agreed that

---

94 (2009), 2 S.C.R. 494 (S.C.C.).
95 2011 SCC 46.

Cote's statements to the police should be excluded but held that the judge erred by excluding the physical evidence and ordered a new trial.

The Supreme Court of Canada held that the Court of Appeal had erred by placing undue weight on the "discoverability" of the physical evidence in its s. 24(2) analysis. Its main basis for ordering a new trial was that the physical evidence could have been obtained legally by warrant without Cote's participation. The Supreme Court stated that discoverability is a relevant factor in a s. 24(2) analysis but it is not determinative. The Court agreed with the s. 24(2) analysis of the trial judge. The police officers' misconduct was very serious and the absence of prior judicial authorization for the search of Cote's property was a significant infringement on her right to privacy. The Court agreed with the trial judge that the courts must not tolerate the disturbing police behaviour of showing systematic disregard for the law and the Constitution.

Questions for Review and Discussion

1. Explain the difference between a summons and an appearance notice.
2. When can an appearance notice be used?
3. When can force be used in making an arrest?
4. Summarize the situations in which a police officer can make an arrest without a warrant.
5. Explain the authority of private security guards to make arrests.
6. Outline the pre-trial release procedures that must be followed.
7. What can happen to a police officer who makes an illegal arrest?
8. Briefly list the rights of a person on being arrested.
9. How have the courts defined detention?
10. When is a detention arbitrary?
11. Explain how the Supreme Court of Canada has interpreted the accused's right to retain and consult counsel.
12. What is the usual procedure the police must follow to obtain a search warrant?
13. What can the police seize with a warrant?
14. What is a telewarrant?
15. In what circumstances can the police search without a warrant?
16. What must a judge be satisfied about before authorizing the interception of a private communication?
17. Explain under what authority and when a court might exclude evidence in a criminal trial.
18. The RCMP were investigating a serious assault on three Americans who had been driving to their homes in Michigan. As they approached the international bridge in Windsor, the Americans were cut off by another vehicle and forced to stop. The Americans were punched and attacked with a knife. The assailants then sped away. The victims identified the car of the assailants as a 1973 or 1975 blue Thunderbird. They picked a photograph from police files of a man who looked like one of the attackers. However, it turned out that this man was not in Ontario at the time of the assault.

    One of the officers, Larkin, reviewed police files looking for owners of Thunderbirds. He found that a man named Storrey had been stopped numerous times driving a 1973 blue Thunderbird. Larkin discovered that Storrey's police photograph closely resembled the photograph of the man identified by the victims. Also, Storrey had a record of violent crime.

    Did the police have authority to arrest Storrey? Explain. See *Storrey v. The Queen* (1990), 53 C.C.C. (3d) 316 (S.C.C.).

19. **a.** If a police officer finds a person committing an offence under s. 553, what must that officer first consider before he or she can lawfully make an arrest?

    b. What might the officer do, if he or she doesn't arrest the person, to compel the person's appearance in court?

20. Sam is walking down the street. Behind him he hears a woman shout, "My purse! He's stolen my purse!" Sam turns around. He sees the woman who has had her purse stolen. She is standing still, staring at her empty hands. He can also see the head and shoulders of a man who appears to be running through the crowd on the sidewalk. A lot of people are staring at him but nobody is chasing him.

    a. Explain the authority of a private person to make an arrest.

    b. Should Sam chase the man who is running and make an arrest?

21. Constable Dust has been issued a search warrant in accordance with s. 487 of the Criminal Code, empowering him to search Gerry's house. When he arrives at the house, he insists that the warrant also entitles him to search Gerry. Is he right?

22. Constable Armstrong arrests Blaine in a department store for theft. She asks Blaine where his car is and is informed that the car is outside in the parking lot. Constable Armstrong proceeds to the parking lot. She finds Tom and John sitting in the car. She orders them out and then searches them both. Was she legally entitled to search Tom and John?

23. At the beginning of a visit to the supermarket, L. picked up a carton of cigarettes. He subsequently made a trip to his car and returned. When he checked out, the cigarettes were not among his purchases. The manager of the store called Constable P., and told him that several employees had seen L. pick up the carton of cigarettes and that it had been neither returned nor paid for. The constable came to the store and stopped L.'s car as it was leaving the parking lot. The constable told L., "There appears to be a mix-up in your order. The store believes that you have something for which you have not paid." Constable P. then asked L. to move his car to where the police car was parked. The officer asked L. if he could search the vehicle. L. replied, "Go ahead. I'd like to get this cleared up." The constable proceeded to search the main area of the car, the glove compartment, the trunk, and the back seat.

    The police officer was polite and almost apologetic for the inconvenience he was causing. L. was cooperative, polite, calm, and not visibly upset. L. made no attempt to leave and made no request to be allowed to leave. However, L. said that he felt he had no alternative but to submit to the search, and that he unlocked the trunk of the car at the request of Constable P. because he felt he would be arrested if he refused to do so.

    Was L., in fact, arrested? Explain. See *Lebrun v. High-Low Foods Ltd.* (1970), 70 D.L.R. (2d) 433 (B.C.S.C.).

24. C. attended an Eaton's store to obtain a cash refund. He and the clerk had a disagreement, and the clerk called security. The security officer told C. to leave the store. He was taken by the elbow and walked to the exit doors. As he approached the exit, he pushed away the guard's hand for the purpose of leaving the store unassisted. In response, the guard swung him around and put him in a headlock. C. was then dragged to the security office where he was handcuffed to a chair. Over two hours elapsed before the police were called. C. sued the guard and the store for false imprisonment. Should C.'s case succeed? See *Chopra v. Eaton (T.) Co.* (1999) 240 A.R. 201 (Alta. Q.B.).

25. Design a set of rules for the reasonable use of tasers. Consider who should be

authorized to use them as well as in what situations.

26. Are the decisions in *R. v. A.M.*, *R. v. Kang-Brown*, and *R. v. Tessling* (see page 126) consistent? Discuss.

27. The police suspected that G had a marijuana grow operation in his home. They asked the utility company to install a digital recording ammeter ("DRA"), which would measure electrical power flowing into the home. The DRA graph showed a pattern consistent with a marijuana grow operation. On the basis of police observations and the information provided to them, including the DRA graph, the police obtained a search warrant. As a result of the search, the police seized over 165 kilograms of marijuana and numerous items relating to a marijuana grow operation. G applied to exclude the evidence disclosed by the search on the basis that no warrant had been obtained prior to the installation of the DRA. Should the evidence be excluded? See *R. v. Gomboc*, [2010] S.C.J. No. 55 (S.C.C.).

Jurisdiction, Public Order, Terrorism, Firearms, and Other Offences

PARTS I, II, III, AND IV OF THE CODE

Key points explained in this chapter are

LO1 the acts that constitute treason, sedition, and unlawful assembly;

LO2 the meaning of terrorist activity, terrorist group, and terrorism offences;

LO3 the restrictions on the use and possession of firearms and other weapons; and

LO4 the differences between obstructing a peace officer and obstructing justice.

In general, Canadian criminal law deals with crimes that are committed in Canada. Section 6(2) provides:

> **(2) Subject to this Act or any other Act of Parliament, no person shall be convicted or discharged . . . of an offence committed outside Canada.**

Section 7 creates some of the exceptions by stating that if certain acts are committed outside Canada, they will be deemed to have been committed in Canada if certain circumstances exist. For example, acts or omissions that are indictable offences if committed in Canada and that are committed on a Canadian aircraft, or on any aircraft if the flight is terminated in Canada, are deemed to have been committed in Canada. Other exceptions created by s. 7 concern international law.

A. OFFENCES AGAINST PUBLIC ORDER

The offences in Part II of the Code have to do with harm to the government or to the government's authority. This part of the chapter discusses several of the offences: treason, sedition, unlawful assemblies, and explosive substances. Breach of the peace, which is not in Part II of the Code, is discussed in Chapter 5.

1. Treason

Treason is a rarely charged offence under s. 46. Its general purpose is to prohibit acts that threaten the security of Canada. There are two types of treason: high treason under s. 46(1) and treason under s. 46(2).

High treason includes killing or attempting to kill the Queen, levying war against Canada, and assisting an enemy at war with Canada. High treason is a very serious indictable offence, as is indicated by the penalty for its commission: a minimum term of life imprisonment.

Treason, an indictable offence, includes using force or violence to overthrow the government and providing to an agent of another country military or scientific information that might threaten the safety of Canada. Treason also includes conspiring with another person to commit high treason or treason, forming the intention to commit high treason or treason, and demonstrating that intention by some overt act. In *R. v. Bleiler*,[1] the accused wrote letters to the German Emperor during World War I advising him to purchase a certain device or invention that would be of assistance to the German army. Writing those letters was held to be an overt act that demonstrated an intention to commit treason.

One of the few cases of treason is *Lampel v. Berger*,[2] which involved the meaning of the phrase "assisting an enemy at war with Canada" (s. 46(1)(c)). During World War I, Berger agreed to sell to Lampel a piece of property in Sarnia, Ontario. Berger was a Hungarian citizen living in the United States. At the time of this contract, Hungary was at war with Canada, and the United States was a neutral country. Therefore, Berger was an alien enemy subject living in neutral territory. Before paying for the property, Lampel (a Canadian citizen) learned that Berger regularly sent money to his wife and children in Hungary. Lampel was in doubt as to whether he could lawfully pay the purchase money to Berger, since this might be construed as assisting an enemy at war with Canada. So he started a civil action to have a court determine the matter. The first issue was whether the contract regarding the property was valid. The court held that it was unlawful for a resident of Canada to trade with "the enemy." However, for the purposes of contract law, Berger was not considered an enemy because he was not residing or carrying on business in an enemy country. Therefore, the contract was valid. The second issue was whether Lampel could pay the purchase money to Berger, knowing that Berger would send some of the money to Hungary. The court said that money sent to Hungary would become part of the financial resources of that enemy country and thus would aid the enemy by contributing to its capacity to prolong the war. Lampel knew of Berger's intention to send the money to Hungary; and if he enabled Berger to carry out his intention by paying to him the purchase money, he would be assisting an enemy at war with Canada, contrary to the Criminal Code. The court concluded that it was its duty to intervene by impounding the money and keeping it in court, to the credit of Berger, until after the war.

2. Sedition

In general, the offences of sedition involve advocating the overthrow of the government by the use of force. Section 61 contains three separate crimes of sedition: speaking a seditious libel; publishing such a libel; and being part of a seditious conspiracy. For each offence, a seditious intention must be involved; that is, spoken words or a published libel (e.g., written words) are seditious only if they express a seditious intention. Similarly, a seditious conspiracy is an agreement between two or more persons to carry out a seditious intention. The Criminal Code does not provide an exhaustive definition of seditious intention. However, under s. 59(4), a person is presumed to have a seditious intention if he or she (a) teaches or advocates, or (b) publishes or circulates any writing that advocates the use of force to bring about governmental change in Canada.

---

1   (1917), 28 C.C.C. 9 (Alta. C.A.).
2   (1917), 38 D.L.R. 47 (Alta. C.A.).

In *R. v. Boucher*[3] the Supreme Court of Canada was split on whether a seditious intention always requires an intention to incite violence or public disorder. Four of the judges found that it did, while four other judges found that an exception to this requirement is when the sedition is intended to bring the administration of justice into hatred or contempt. This case concerned a member of the Jehovah's Witnesses who was charged with seditious libel for publishing a pamphlet that alleged that the courts and the police were persecuting members of the religion.

Since this offence is rarely charged, the scope of the offence is not clear, as the decision in *Boucher* indicates. Some legal authorities believe that the offence could be found to violate the Charter because of vagueness.[4]

3. Unlawful Assemblies and Riots

a. Unlawful Assemblies

It is a summary conviction offence for a group of three or more persons who have assembled for a common purpose to conduct themselves in such a way that their neighbours have reasonable fears that the peace will be disturbed.

Section 63(1) defines the term "unlawful assembly":

> **63. (1) An unlawful assembly is an assembly of three or more persons who, with intent to carry out any common purpose, assemble in such a manner or so conduct themselves when they are assembled as to cause persons in the neighbourhood of the assembly to fear, on reasonable grounds, that they**
>
> > **(a) will disturb the peace tumultuously; or**
> >
> > **(b) will by that assembly needlessly and without reasonable cause provoke other persons to disturb the peace tumultuously . . .**

There are three elements of an unlawful assembly: (1) there is an assembly of three or more persons; (2) those persons have the intent to carry out a common purpose; and (3) their conduct (or manner of assembling) causes the persons in the neighbourhood to fear that there will be a disturbance of the peace. The disturbance of the peace can be by the members of the assembly or by others who are needlessly or without reasonable cause provoked to disturb the peace.

Under s. 63(2), an assembly that starts out lawful can become unlawful if the conduct of the group creates fear of a disturbance. Also, there may be an unlawful assembly even though the common purpose of the persons involved is lawful. The important point is the manner in which the purpose is, or is likely to be, carried out. If the manner causes persons in the neighbourhood to fear that there will be a disturbance, an offence is committed regardless of the lawfulness of the common purpose. Of course, the fear must be based on reasonable grounds. For example, in *R. v. Kalyn*,[5] the accused set up a stereo system in front of his cottage and organized a party. The party got out of control, and eventually there was a confrontation with the police. The court held that the common intention was to have a party, and that this was not unlawful; therefore, the assembly was at first lawful. However, the assembly became unlawful when the crowd became unruly and violent. The court also held that the conduct of a few members of the assembly could make the assembly unlawful and that all the members would be liable for the offence.

---

3   (1951), 99 C.C.C. 1 (S.C.C.) at p. 106.
4   See Alan W. Mewett and Morris Manning, *Mewett & Manning on Criminal Law*, 3rd ed. (Toronto: Butterworths, Canada, 1994), p. 604.
5   (1980), 52 C.C.C. (2d) 378 (Sask. C.A.).

This decision was considered in *R. v. Brien*.[6] The defence counsel argued that the offence of unlawful assembly was one of absolute liability and therefore unconstitutional. Their argument was that it was possible for persons in the neighbourhood to reasonably, but mistakenly, fear that the assembly would disturb the peace, and that the persons assembled might be unaware of these reasonable fears. In other words, the offence does not require *mens rea*, or an awareness that the assembly has become unlawful, on the part of the persons assembled. The court disagreed, stating that the reasonable grounds referred to in s. 63 would be apparent to persons in the neighbourhood as well as to anyone in the assembly. Therefore, the *mens rea* required is objective foreseeability that the assembly would become unlawful.

b. Riots

A riot occurs when the unlawful assembly actually begins to disturb the peace.

> **64. A riot is an unlawful assembly that has begun to disturb the peace tumultuously.**

The term "tumultuous" is not defined in the Code, but in *R. v. Lockhart et al.*,[7] the Nova Scotia Court of Appeal said that "the word must connote in a general sense some element of violence or force which may be exhibited by menaces or threats." In this case, Keddy was arrested for disturbing the peace. A short while later, a group of 20 or 30 people arrived at the police station demanding his release. One person in the crowd threatened to break Keddy out if he was not released. Another person offered to fight the police. The court held that a riot had taken place when the threats were made. The threats, swearing, and yelling created an atmosphere of violence that was "tumultuous."

R. v. Brien concerned a charge of taking part in a riot. The court held that taking part in a riot is different from being part of an unlawful assembly because s. 65 requires that the person actually take part in the rioting; that is, he or she must take part in causing the disturbance. A person who is part of the unlawful assembly that has begun to disturb the peace is not necessarily part of the rioting. In addition, the person must either intend to take part in the riot or be so reckless as to have acted as if he or she intended to take part in the riot.

In *R. v. Bernt*,[8] the accused was charged with taking part in a riot that became known as the "Stanley Cup Riots" that took place in Vancouver. The accused was a member of a crowd of fans shouting at police and throwing a variety of items. At one point, the accused brandished a screwdriver and threw a long stick at police. In upholding the accused's conviction and applying *Lockhart*,[9] the court held that "the word 'tumultuously' must be read with the word 'riot'. . ."[10]

Under s. 67, where a riot of at least 12 persons is taking place, a justice, a mayor, a sheriff, or the head of a prison can, after commanding silence, order those assembled to disperse and depart and inform them that if they fail to do so they can be charged with an offence. This proclamation is often referred to as "reading the riot act".

It is an indictable offence under s. 68 to oppose, hinder, or assault anyone making or beginning to make the proclamation. It is also an offence under this section not to disperse within 30 minutes after the proclamation has been made, or within 30 minutes of when the proclamation would have been made if the person trying to make it had not been opposed, hindered, or assaulted.

---

6   (1993), 86 C.C.C. (3d) 550 (N.T.S.C.).
7   (1976), 15 N.S.R. (2d) 512 (C.A.).
8   (1997), 120 C.C.C. (3d) 344 (B.C.C.A.).
9   *Lockhart, supra* note 7.
10 *Bernt, supra* note 8 at 349–350.

4. Explosive Substances

Section 79 states that any person who has explosives in his or her possession is under a duty to use reasonable care to prevent harm to property or persons:

> **79. Every one who has an explosive substance in his possession or under his care or control is under a legal duty to use reasonable care to prevent bodily harm or death to persons or damage to property by that explosive substance.**

Section 2 defines "explosive substance" as including a bomb, grenade, dynamite, or any other incendiary substance or device. The term also includes anything intended to be used to make an explosive substance, as well as anything used or intended to be used to cause an explosion with an explosive substance.

Section 80 makes it an indictable offence to fail, without lawful excuse, to perform the duty regarding explosives. If an explosion resulted from the breach of the duty and a person was killed, or was likely to have been killed, the punishment is life imprisonment. If the explosion caused, or was likely to have caused, bodily harm or property damage, the punishment is imprisonment for 14 years. It is not necessary that harm or damage actually took place—only that death, harm, or damage was likely. On the other hand, when a person fails to perform the duty but no explosion takes place, no offence under this section has occurred.

Under s. 81, it is an indictable offence (a) to do anything with the intent to cause an explosion that is likely to cause serious bodily harm, death, or serious property damage; (b) to cause an explosion with the intent to do bodily harm; (c) to throw or place an explosive anywhere with the intent to damage property without lawful excuse; and (d) to make or possess an explosive with the intent to endanger life or cause serious property damage. These and other offences in s. 81 require proof of the specific intents mentioned, unlike s. 80 offences, which simply require proof of a failure to exercise reasonable care. Offences under s. 81 have been part of the charges in terrorism cases, discussed below.

A separate offence of making, or having in possession or under care and control, an explosive without lawful excuse is contained in s. 82. The section puts the onus on the accused to show the "lawful excuse." This section is open to challenge under the Charter because it sets up a reverse onus clause. (See Chapter 2 for a discussion of these clauses.)

.02 B. TERRORISM

In 2001, Parliament passed a long and detailed set of amendments to the Criminal Code to address terrorism (sections 83.01–83.33). Key provisions can be summarized as follows:

1. Terrorist Activity

Terrorist activity, which is defined in s. 83.01(1) of the Code, can be summarized as follows:

(a) an act or omission that is committed either in or outside Canada that, if committed in Canada, is an offence under one of the United Nations anti-terrorism conventions and protocols; or

(b) an act or omission, in or outside Canada,

   (i) that is committed

      (A) for a political, religious, or ideological purpose and

(B) with the intention of intimidating the public concerning its security or compelling a person, a government, or an international organization to do or refrain from doing any act, and

(ii) that intentionally

(A) causes death or serious bodily harm,

(B) endangers a person's life,

(C) causes serious risk to the public health or safety,

(D) causes substantial property damage that is likely to result in serious bodily harm or a serious risk to public health or safety, or

(E) causes serious interference with an essential service, facility, or system other than as a result of advocacy or protest that is not intended to result in serious bodily harm or a serious risk to public health or safety.

Terrorist activity does not include an act or omission that occurs during an armed conflict and is in accordance with international law or the activities of the military forces of a state in the exercise of their official duties if the activities are governed by international law.

The definition of terrorist activity has been found not to violate s. 7 of the Charter by being vague and overly broad, despite the use of broad terms such as "security" and "economic security."[11]

The definition of terrorist activity has both a conduct component and a mental component. The conduct component includes an act or omission referred to in (a) above, or an act or omission referred to in (b) that causes one of the consequences listed in (b)(ii)(A)–(E)). It also includes a conspiracy, attempt, or threat to commit such an act or omission, or being an accessory after the fact, or counselling related to such an act or omission.

The mental component has three parts. The act or omission must be done (1) with the intention of bringing about one of the consequences described in (b)(ii)(A)–(E); (2) with the further intention of intimidating the public concerning its security or compelling a person, a government, or an international organization to do or refrain from doing any act; and (3) for a political, religious, or ideological purpose, objective, or cause.

2. Terrorist Groups

A terrorist group means (a) an entity that has as one of its purposes or activities facilitating or carrying out any terrorist activity or (b) an entity that has been listed by the Cabinet of the federal government as a terrorist group under s. 83.05. An entity may be placed on the list if the Cabinet is satisfied that there are reasonable grounds to believe that the entity (a) has knowingly carried out, attempted to carry out, participated in, or facilitated terrorist activity or (b) is knowingly acting on behalf of, at the direction of, or in association with an entity doing any of the things referred to in (a). The entity listed as a terrorist group may apply for judicial review of the Cabinet's decision.

3. Offences

The amendments made in 2001 make it a criminal offence to do the following:

- knowingly collect or provide funds to carry out terrorist crimes;
- knowingly participate in, contribute to, or facilitate the activities of a terrorist group;

---

11   *R. v. Khawaja* (2006), 214 C.C.C. (3d) 399 (Ont. S.C.J.).

- commit an indictable offence for the benefit of, at the direction of, or in association with a terrorist group;
- instruct anyone to carry out a terrorist activity on behalf of a terrorist group; or
- knowingly harbour or conceal a terrorist.

4. Investigative Hearing and Recognizance

New investigative measures were introduced by the amendments—an investigative hearing and a recognizance with conditions. Under the investigative hearing provisions, individuals with information relevant to an ongoing investigation of a terrorist crime could be required to appear before a judge to provide that information. The consent of the Attorney General was required before this measure could be used.

The authority to impose a recognizance with conditions is sometimes referred to as "preventative arrest." The amendments allowed a peace officer to arrest and bring a person before a judge to impose supervisory conditions on the person if there were reasonable grounds to suspect that the person was about to be engaged in terrorist activity. An example of an imposed condition would be having no contact or communication with certain persons. If the person failed or refused to enter into the recognizance, the judge could commit the person to prison for up to twelve months. The consent of the Attorney General was required before this measure could be used.

The provisions dealing with investigative hearings and recognizance with conditions expired on March 1, 2007, because they were not extended by a resolution passed by both Houses of Parliament.[12]

The first convictions under the anti-terrorism provisions were in relation to a group of eighteen young men who became known as the "Toronto 18." The cases involved two plots. The "bomb plot" was a scheme to build and detonate three large truck bombs. The bombs were to be directed at the Toronto Stock Exchange, the offices of the Canadian Security Intelligence Service in downtown Toronto, and a military base close to Highway 401. The "camp plot" involved a terrorist training camp that was held in Orillia, Ontario, in 2005. The main objective of the group was to change Canada's foreign policy regarding Afghanistan. All of the accused were charged under s. 83.18(1) with participating in an activity of a terrorist group for the purpose of enhancing the ability of the terrorist group to facilitate or carry out a terrorist activity. Those involved in the bomb plot were charged under s. 83.2 with committing an indictable offence for the benefit of, at the direction of, or in association with a terrorist group.[13] The indictable offence was doing anything with intent to cause an explosion of an explosive substance that was likely to cause serious bodily harm or death to persons or likely to cause serious damage to property, contrary to s. 81(1)(a). Charges against seven of the eighteen accused were eventually dropped, but eleven were convicted. Most of them received sentences between seven years in prison and life in prison.

In *R. v. Khawaja*,[14] the accused was charged under s. 83.2 with committing an indictable offence for the benefit of, at the direction of, or in association with a terrorist group. The alleged terrorist group was in England led by Omar Khyam ("the Khyam group") and was allegedly engaged in terrorist activity. The indictable offences were (1) developing a device to

---

12 A bill to re-enact investigative hearings and recognizances with conditions was introduced in Parliament by the Government in 2011. It also included new offences of leaving or attempting to leave Canada to commit acts of terrorism. As of June 5, 2012, Bill S-7, the Combatting Terrorism Act, had completed first reading in the House of Commons.
13 See, for example, *R. v. Abdelhaleem*, [2001] O.J. No. 5693 (Ont. S.C.J.).
14 2010 ONCA 862 (Ont. C.A.); leave to appeal to the Supreme Court of Canada granted, Supreme Court of Canada Bulletin, June 30, 2011.

activate a detonator, with intent to cause an explosion of an explosive substance likely to cause serious bodily harm or death to persons or serious damage to property, contrary to s. 81(1)(a), and (2) making or possessing an explosive substance with intent to enable another person to endanger life or cause serious damage to property. The trial judge concluded that the Crown had proved the commission of the underlying indictable offences but had failed to prove that Khawaja had intended to facilitate or otherwise assist in the Khyam group's specific bomb plot. Therefore, Khawaja was convicted of the underlying indictable offences but not the terrorism offence under s. 83.2.

Khawaja was also convicted of five terrorism offences. Three of the offences required proof that his conduct was for the purpose of enhancing the ability of a "terrorist group" to facilitate or carry out terrorist activity:

- knowingly participating in or contributing to the activity of a terrorist group by receiving training (s. 83.18(1));
- knowingly instructing a person to carry out financial activity for the benefit of a terrorist group (s. 83.21(1)); and
- participating in dialogue, meetings, or exchanges of information relating to the development of an explosive device intended to endanger life or cause serious damage to property (s. 83.18).

Two of the offences required proof that he knew that his conduct would facilitate terrorist activity:

- providing or making available property or financial services (s. 83.03(a)), and
- facilitating a terrorist activity (s. 83.19).

5. Motive Clause

Khawaja challenged the constitutionality of the "motive clause" in the definition of terrorist activity (s. 83.01(1)(b)(i)(A)). The motive clause requires that the relevant act or omission was committed "for a political, religious or ideological purpose, objective or cause." Khawaja argued that the clause infringes s. 2 of the Charter, which protects freedom of thought, belief, opinion, and expression.

The Ontario Court of Appeal held that the motive clause does not infringe s. 2 of the Charter:

[N]one of the activity that falls within the definition of "terrorist activity" is protected under s. 2(b) for one of two reasons. First, some, if not all, of the conduct involves the use of violence to convey a meaning. Second, to the extent that the activity does not involve the conveying of meaning through violence, it does involve the conveying of meaning in a manner that is contrary to and destructive of the principles underlying the right to freedom of expression. As the purpose of the legislation is not to limit expression, the fact that it has that effect, but only with respect to a form of expression that is destructive of the principles underlying freedom of expression, does not constitute an infringement of s. 2(b).

The court also rejected the trial judge's view that the motive clause is unconstitutional because it has a "chilling effect" on the rights protected by s. 2 of the Charter. The trial judge found a violation of s. 2 based on his conclusion that the motive clause would inhibit persons who wished to engage in activity that is not "terrorist activity" from expressing certain beliefs and opinions that might be shared by those who were engaged in terrorist activity. The court found that the problem with the trial judge's view was that it was based entirely on speculation, both as to the existence of the "chilling effect" and the cause or source of that "chilling effect," if one existed. In addition, the court noted that s. 83.01(1.1) is inconsistent with finding a "chilling effect." That provision declares that one need not fear expressing any political, religious, or ideological belief as long as one does not engage in conduct that falls within the meaning of terrorist activity.

6. Armed Conflict Exception

Khawaja also argued that the "armed conflict exception" to the definition of terrorist activity set out in s. 83.01(1)(b)(ii) was a complete answer to all of the charges. Khawaja claimed that his activities were designed solely to further his desired participation in and support of "armed conflict" in Afghanistan and that the Crown had the burden of establishing that the armed conflict exception did not apply because the actions did not comply with international law applicable to the war in Afghanistan. The court found that the exception did not apply in this case because there was no evidence to suggest that Khawaja's activities (1) were undertaken while an armed conflict was in progress, and (2) were in accordance with the rules of war established by international law applicable to that armed conflict. The court stated that the exception is concerned with armed conflict in the context of the rules of war established by international law. It is designed to exclude activities sanctioned by international law from the reach of terrorist activity as defined in the Criminal Code. It reflects the principle that combatants in an armed conflict, who act in accordance with international law, do not commit any offence.

03 C. FIREARMS AND WEAPONS

Canada's gun control legislation, the Firearms Act, was enacted in 1995 after much heated debate over the central core of the law, which requires gun owners to be licensed and to register their firearms in a central registry. As amended in 2012, the law no longer requires the registration of firearms that are neither restricted nor prohibited, such as hunting rifles and shotguns. Although mainly concerned with guns, the Act also regulates other weapons and devices such as knives, crossbows, and ammunition. The Act also includes penalties for gun-related offences and the categories of restricted and prohibited weapons and devices.

Under the Firearms Act, everyone, with a few exceptions, must have a licence to possess a firearm. Persons such as police officers and members of the Canadian Forces do not need licences. Gun owners had until 2001 to obtain a licence and until 2003 to register their firearms. There are also transitional provisions to recognize firearms acquisition certificates (FACs) as licences. FACs were required before the Firearms Act was passed to purchase guns.

Generally speaking, to be licensed to possess a firearm or other device, a person must be at least 18 and pass a firearms safety test. There are exceptions to these rules. For example, Jacques, even though under 18, may be licensed if he hunts and traps to sustain himself and/or his family. When a person applies for a licence, the chief firearms officer will determine whether the person is eligible. Section 5 establishes that a person is not eligible if "it is desirable, in the interests of the safety of that or any other person, that the person not possess a firearm, a cross-bow, a prohibited weapon, a restricted weapon, a prohibited device, ammunition or prohibited ammunition." In determining whether a person is eligible, the officer will consider such circumstances as whether the person has been convicted of an offence involving violence against other persons or of a weapons offence in the last five years, has been treated for a mental illness associated with violence, or has a history of violent behaviour.

A person can be licensed to have a restricted firearm for special purposes, such as target shooting, or if a restricted firearm is required for his or her lawful occupation (e.g., a Brinks guard). A licence to possess a prohibited firearm will only be issued to the person who owned the firearm before it was declared prohibited. Allowing persons to keep firearms that are now prohibited was an amendment to the bill in response to criticism that it would not be fair to make people give up the guns they already have. For the sake of further controlling prohibited firearms, a person can only transfer or sell the prohibited firearm to a person who already is licensed to possess a prohibited firearm.

Before the enactment of the Firearms Act, Part III of the Criminal Code contained the regulatory provisions related to gun control (such as the procedure for obtaining permits for transporting restricted weapons). The Firearms Act takes over this regulatory function, leaving in the Code most of the offences and penalties related to firearms and weapons.

The following discusses Part III of the Criminal Code as it has been changed by the Firearms Act. Cases under the previous Part III that are still relevant are included.

1. Definitions

The offence provisions on the use, possession, or trafficking of firearms and weapons refer to key terms that are defined in the Criminal Code. Section 2 defines "firearm" and "weapon."

Firearm means "any barreled weapon from which any shot, bullet, or other projectile can be discharged and that is capable of causing serious bodily injury or death to a person, and includes any frame or receiver of such a barrelled weapon and anything that can be adapted for use as a firearm." However, s. 84 states that certain types of weapons are not considered firearms in certain situations. These include antique firearms, devices used for such purposes as signalling distress or firing blanks, and devices used for slaughtering or tranquillizing animals.

In *R. v. Covin and Covin*,[15] the Supreme Court of Canada considered the last part of the definition of firearm (i.e., "anything that can be adapted for use as a firearm"). The Court noted that most pieces of wood, pipe, and metal could, given time and expertise, be adaptable for use as firearms. The Court held that the exact meaning of this part of the definition depends on the offence for which it is being used. The accused were charged with robbery and with using a firearm while committing an indictable offence. Their conviction for robbery was not appealed. However, their conviction for the second offence was appealed on the grounds that the weapon they used was not a "firearm." The gun they had used in the robbery was a damaged airgun with several missing pieces, some of which were necessary for the gun's operation.

The Court looked at the purpose of the offence and stated that it is to protect the victim of an offence (e.g., robbery) from serious injury or death by discouraging the use of firearms during the commission of offences. The Court concluded:

> *Therefore, whatever is used at the scene of the crime must . . . be proven by the Crown as capable, either at the outset or through adaptation or assembly, of being loaded, fired and thereby having the potential of causing serious bodily harm during the commission of the offence, or during the flight after the commission of the main offence . . . .*[16]

In this case, it would have taken an experienced person 10 to 15 minutes to replace the missing parts. The Court concluded that there were not the necessary "ingredients" to make the gun operable.

---

15   (1983), 8 C.C.C. (3d) 240 (S.C.C.).
16   Ibid. at 243.

"Weapon" means anything used or intended to be used (a) to cause death or injury to persons, or (b) for the purpose of threatening or intimidating any person; it includes a firearm.

Almost any object can be a weapon. Two provincial courts of appeal have held that it is the subjective intent of the user, not the objective intent of the manufacturer, that determines whether a thing is a weapon.[17] For example, a rifle is designed to be used as a weapon. A beer bottle is not designed to be used as a weapon; it is designed to be used as a container for beer. However, a beer bottle could be a weapon if a person used it or intended to use it to assault another person.

Section 84 defines the "prohibited" and "restricted" classes of firearms and weapons. "Prohibited firearms" include these:

- handguns with a barrel length of 105 mm or less and handguns that can discharge .25 or .32 calibre ammunition, except for a few handguns that are used in sporting competitions under the rules of the International Shooting Union;
- rifles and shotguns that have been altered by sawing or other means so that their barrel length is less than 457 mm or their overall length is less than 660 mm;
- automatic firearms, including those that have been altered to fire only one projectile when the trigger is squeezed; and
- firearms prohibited by regulation under the Criminal Code.

"Restricted firearms" include these:

- handguns that are not prohibited firearms;
- non-prohibited, semi-automatic, centre-fire firearms (e.g., rifles and shotguns) with a barrel shorter than 470 mm;
- firearms (e.g., rifles and shotguns) that can be fired when they are reduced to less than 660 mm in length by folding, telescoping or other means; and
- firearms restricted by regulation under the Criminal Code.

"Prohibited weapon" means one of the following:

- a knife that has a blade that opens automatically by gravity or centrifugal force or by hand pressure applied to a button, spring, or other device, or
- a weapon other than a firearm prohibited by regulation under the Criminal Code.

"Restricted weapon" means a weapon other than a firearm that is restricted by regulation under the Criminal Code.

The New Brunswick Court of Appeal considered the meaning of (a), "a knife that has a blade that opens automatically by gravity or centrifugal force." The court stated that a knife can fall within this definition even if it was not designed to open as such if, because of wear or alteration, it can be opened through gravity or centrifugal force.[18] In *R. v. Vaughn*,[19] the Supreme Court of Canada held that even though an additional manual operation that required some skill had to be performed before the knife would open automatically by centrifugal force, the knife fell within the definition of a prohibited weapon.

2. Use Offences

Section 85 makes it an indictable offence to use a firearm or an imitation firearm while committing or attempting to commit an indictable offence or while in flight after committing

---

17   *R. v. Murray* (1991), 65 C.C.C. (3d) 507 (Ont. C.A.); *R. v. Roberts* (1990), 60 C.C.C. (3d) 509 (N.S.C.A.).
18   *R. v. Richard and Walker* (1981), 63 C.C.C. (2d) 333 (N.B.C.A.).
19   (1991), 69 C.C.C. (3d) 576 (S.C.C.).

or attempting to commit an indictable offence. Mandatory minimum sentences are to be imposed for the offence. Several serious indictable offences are excluded from this offence because the Criminal Code provides for more severe mandatory minimum sentences for using a firearm during the commission of these offences, which include criminal negligence causing death, manslaughter, attempted murder, aggravated sexual assault, and robbery.

In *R. v. Scott*,[20] the British Columbia Court of Appeal considered what the Crown must prove if the accused is charged under s. 85(2) with using an imitation firearm. At trial, the accused was acquitted because the Crown failed to prove that the firearm was an imitation firearm. The Crown was unable to show that the firearm was incapable of discharging a shot, bullet, or other projectile. In allowing the Crown's appeal, the court held that an imitation firearm includes a real firearm. The court found that Parliament intended that an object which resembles a firearm, and is used to facilitate a robbery, satisfies the requirements of s. 85(2). Requiring the Crown to prove that a firearm is not a real firearm defeats the intention of Parliament.

In *R. v. Steele*,[21] the Supreme Court of Canada addressed the meaning of "use" in s. 85(1). The accused and three accomplices forcibly entered a home at night expecting to find a marijuana grow operation. Instead, they awakened the three residents. The residents heard the intruders say, "We have a gun," or "Get the gun." The residents observed an item about the size of a gun in one intruder's hand, and another intruder pulled a dark metal object out from under his jacket. The intruders fled shortly thereafter. Police later intercepted a vehicle matching the description of the getaway car. Four individuals, including the accused, were inside. Several weapons, including a loaded handgun, were found in the car. The accused was charged and convicted of several offences, including using a firearm while committing or attempting to commit the indictable offence of break and enter. In upholding the conviction, the Supreme Court stated:

> [A]n offender "uses" a firearm, within the meaning of s. 85(1), where, to facilitate the commission of an offence or for purposes of escape, the offender reveals by words or conduct the actual presence or immediate availability of a firearm. The weapon must then be in the physical possession of the offender or readily at hand. . . [T]his test does not bring within s .85(1) of the Criminal Code any threat—including an idle threat— that refers to a firearm. Use, at least in this regard, is a matter of fact, not fiction. Section 85(1) does not capture the threatened use of a non-existent firearm. However effective and objectionable, it is the threat in that case that is "used", and not a firearm. Moreover, had Parliament intended to capture idle threats under s. 85(1), it would have said so expressly, as it did in ss. 267 and 272 of the Criminal Code.[22]

Section 86(1) makes it a hybrid offence for anyone without lawful excuse to use, carry, handle, ship, transport, or store a firearm, a prohibited or restricted weapon, a prohibited device, or ammunition in a careless manner or without reasonable precautions for the safety of others.

Two Supreme Court of Canada decisions considered the *mens rea* required for this offence. Both cases involved careless use of firearms. In *R. v. Gossett*,[23] a police officer arrested a man suspected of being in illegal possession of 150 packs of cigarettes. At the police station, the suspect attempted to flee. The officer yelled at him, "Stop or I'll shoot." He then pointed the gun at the suspect with his finger on the trigger. The gun went off killing the suspect. The officer was charged with manslaughter. The unlawful act was the careless handling of a firearm. In *R. v. Finlay*,[24] the accused was charged with the careless storage of

---

20   (2000), 145 C.C.C. (3d) 52 (B.C.C.A.).
21   (2007), 221 C.C.C. (3d) 14 (S.C.C.).
22   Ibid. at 23.
23   (1993), 83 C.C.C. (3d) 494 (S.C.C.).
24   (1993), 83 C.C.C. (3d) 513 (S.C.C.).

firearms and ammunition. In both cases, the Court held that the proper test to be applied for liability is objective: Was the behaviour of the accused a marked departure from the behaviour of a reasonable person? Would a reasonable person be aware of the risk?

It is also an offence under s. 86(2) to contravene regulations under the Firearms Act respecting the storage, handling, transportation, shipping, displaying, advertising, and mail-order sales of firearms and restricted weapons.

In *R. v. Carlos*,[25] the Supreme Court of Canada addressed the *actus reus* for the offences in s. 86(1) and (2), specifically the meaning of "storing" a firearm. Carlos was cleaning and examining his guns in his house when he learned that the police were coming to his house. He quickly placed two handguns in a safe and placed a .357 Magnum behind a stereo cabinet. The police found the three guns loaded and without trigger locks. The Supreme Court held that the *actus reus* of storage within the meaning of s. 86 had not been made out. There is no requirement that an accused plan a long-term or permanent storage. There are situations in which a short interruption in the use or handling of firearms would still constitute use or handling rather than storage. However, Carlos put away and hid the firearms in a manner that is properly characterized as storing them, even though the storage was temporary, rather than as continuing his use and handling of them. The court found that the storage of the .357 Magnum was careless, contrary to s. 86(1), and that the storage of the two handguns in the safe violated the regulations under the Firearms Act.

3. Possession Offences

Under s. 88, it is an indictable offence to possess a weapon or an imitation of a weapon for a purpose dangerous to the public peace or for the purpose of committing an offence. In *R. v. Cassidy*,[26] the Supreme Court of Canada stated that the offence requires proof of possession of a weapon and proof that the accused's purpose in possessing the weapon was dangerous to the public peace. In general, the purpose will have been formed prior to taking possession of the weapon and will continue as the person takes possession of it.

The fact that a person is carrying a weapon for a defensive purpose does not necessarily mean that the weapon is not possessed for a purpose dangerous to the public. In *R. v. Nelson*,[27] the accused feared being attacked by two men, the Bougie brothers, with whom he had had some previous trouble. Before going to a club where he expected that they would be, he armed himself with a homemade knife with a double-edged, 18-inch blade. After drinking some beer at the club, the accused got into a fight with one of the Bougies; and the two of them were required to leave the club. Outside the club, the Bougie brothers confronted the accused, who began swinging his knife at them, injuring both of them. The accused was convicted of carrying a weapon for a purpose dangerous to the public peace. The court noted that even though the weapon was intended for defence, other factors, such as the nature of the weapon, how it was acquired, the manner of its use, the time, the place, and relevant statements or actions of the accused, had to be considered. The court concluded:

> [T]he character of the weapon and the reasons for its acquisition as well as the clear intention of the [accused] to make use of what was, under the circumstances, a clearly illegal method of defence make it clear that the weapon was being carried for a purpose dangerous to the public peace.[28]

---

25   [2002] 2 S.C.R. 411, 163 C.C.C. (3d) 449 (S.C.C.).
26   (1989), 50 C.C.C. (3d) 193.
27   (1972), 8 C.C.C. (2d) 29 (Ont. C.A.).
28   Ibid. at 35.

In *R. v. Kerr*,[29] the accused was an inmate in a maximum-security prison, and the victim was a member of a gang that exerted control over other inmates. The accused worked in the servery of the prison; and when the victim demanded coffee, the accused refused to serve him. The victim threatened the accused, saying that the accused would be found with his head smashed in. The accused armed himself with a homemade metal knife and an ice pick. When the victim and some other gang members came into the dining area, the victim brandished a knife, and the victim and the accused began to fight, stabbing each other several times. The victim died as a result of his injuries, and the accused was charged with second-degree murder and possession of a weapon for a purpose dangerous to the public peace. He was acquitted on both counts at trial. The court of appeal substituted a conviction on the s. 88 charge. In restoring the acquittal, the Supreme Court of Canada stated that, to succeed on a charge under s. 88, the Crown must prove possession of a weapon, and that the purpose of that possession is dangerous to the public peace. The accused did not possess the weapon for a purpose dangerous to the public peace, but for the purpose of defending himself against specific individuals. When an accused is found to have had a weapon for a defensive purpose, a key issue is whether the attack that the accused purported to thwart was avoidable. If the attack was avoidable, possession of the weapon would be possession for a purpose dangerous to the public peace.[30] In citing *Nelson*,[31] the Court indicated "that no single factor, including acquisition and possession of a weapon only for the purpose of self-defence, is determinative of the issue of guilt or innocence on a charge of possession of a weapon for a purpose dangerous to the public peace . . ."[32]

The Court continued:

> *The correct approach—a hybrid subjective-objective test—was adopted by the Ontario Court of Appeal in Nelson. By this approach, the trier of fact must first determine what was the accused person's purpose; this is a subjective determination. The trier of fact must then determine whether that purpose was in all the circumstances dangerous to the public peace; this is an objective determination. . . . The conclusion that s. 88 requires application of a hybrid subjective-objective test is further reinforced through consideration of those other specific intent crimes in the Criminal Code, all of which clearly require by the terms of the particular provision an ulterior intention to achieve a specific consequence.*[33]

In *R. v. Proverbs*,[34] the Ontario Court of Appeal considered the meaning of the phrase "having possession for a purpose dangerous to the public peace." It stated that the purpose must be determined as at the instant of time that preceded the use of the weapon. The police had a warrant to search Proverbs' apartment. When they arrived at the apartment, they knocked on the door and announced that they were the police. There was no response, but they believed that someone was inside. They eventually had the caretaker open the door. They found the accused crouched over a loaded shotgun. He claimed that he had only heard the knocking and thought someone was breaking in, and that he did not know the visitors were police. He was convicted of an offence under the former s. 87. On appeal, on the issue of whether the trial judge properly instructed the jury, the court stated:

> *If the jury were satisfied that prior to the entry of the police into his premises, Proverbs did not have the weapon for a purpose dangerous to the public peace, and he only loaded it on*

29 (2004), 185 C.C.C. (3d) 1 (S.C.C.).
30 Ibid. at 20–23.
31 *Nelson, supra* note 27.
32 *Kerr, supra* note 29 at 8.
33 *Kerr, supra* note 29 at 12–15.
34 (1983), 9 C.C.C. (3d) 249 (Ont. C.A.).

the sudden . . . unaware that it was the police seeking entry, because he was in fear of harm to himself and only intended to use it if necessary to defend himself . . . then the Crown would not have proved [the elements of the offence] . . .[35]

The court ordered a new trial.

It is a summary conviction offence under s. 89 to, without lawful excuse, have possession of a weapon while attending or on the way to attend a public meeting.

Section 90 makes it a hybrid offence to carry a concealed weapon, a prohibited device, or any prohibited ammunition unless authorized to do so under the Firearms Act. In *R. v. Felawka*,[36] the Supreme Court of Canada held that to prove the weapon was concealed, the Crown must establish that the accused took steps to hide an object that he knew to be a weapon so that it would not be observed or come to the attention of others.

Sections 91 to 95 create various offences for possessing a firearm or weapon without a licence or without registering the firearm or weapon. Section 95(1) refers to "a loaded prohibited firearm or restricted firearm." In *R. v. Williams*,[37] the accused was charged specifically with possessing a prohibited firearm under s. 95(1). When Williams got out of a motor vehicle that had been stopped by the police, he was carrying a loaded handgun—a Krieghoff Suhl 9 millimetre Luger, which is a prohibited firearm. Williams argued that he did not have the required *mens rea* for the offence because he was unaware that the barrel was shorter than 105 millimetres, which is the demarcation point between a prohibited firearm and a restricted firearm under s. 84(1), and, therefore, he did not know that the firearm was prohibited. The Ontario Court of Appeal rejected his argument. The court stated that s. 95(1) creates only one offence, the possession of a loaded firearm. It does not matter whether the firearm is "prohibited" or "restricted." The *mens rea* under s. 95(1) is satisfied where the offender knew that he or she was in possession of a loaded firearm. Knowledge of the length of the handgun's barrel is not part of the *mens rea* required for the offence. There was no doubt that Williams knew he was in possession of a loaded handgun.

4. Trafficking Offences

Sections 99 to 101 create "trafficking" offences for the unauthorized transfer of firearms and weapons. Section 100(1) deals with possession for the purpose of weapons trafficking:

> **100. (1) Every person commits an offence who possesses a firearm, a prohibited weapon, a restricted weapon, a prohibited device, any ammunition or any prohibited ammunition for the purpose of**
>
> > **(a) transferring it, whether or not for consideration, or**
> >
> > **(b) offering to transfer it,**
>
> **knowing that the person is not authorized to transfer it under the Firearms Act or any other Act of Parliament or any regulations made under any Act of Parliament.**

In *R. v. Grant*,[38] the Supreme Court of Canada addressed the meaning of "transfer." As discussed in Chapter 5, this case involved a young man who was stopped by police on the sidewalk. After finding a firearm in Grant's possession, the police charged him under s. 100(1).

---

35   Ibid. at 261.
36   (1993), 85 C.C.C. (3d) 248 (S.C.C.).
37   (2009), 244 C.C.C. (3d) 138 (Ont. C.A.)
38   (2009), 245 C.C.C. (3d) 1 (S.C.C.).

Grant admitted that he was "dropping off" the gun somewhere "up the road." The Ontario Court of Appeal found that Grant was moving the gun from one place to another, and this met the meaning of transfer as used in s. 100(1). Applying a dictionary definition, the Ontario Court of Appeal interpreted transfer as not requiring transfer of a firearm to another person but rather as including carrying or moving a firearm from one place to another. The Supreme Court disagreed, finding that Parliament did not intend to criminalize simple movement of firearms by this provision, but rather to criminalize transport for purposes that implicate another person. Transfer of a firearm involves a transaction in which the firearm changes hands. The court said that the same definition also applies to "transfer" under s. 99, which deals with the offence of weapons trafficking.

Section 101 makes it an offence to transfer a weapon or ammunition to any persons unless the transfer is authorized under the Firearms Act or other Act of Parliament. In *R. v. Hault*,[39] the owner of a gun shop sold ammunition to an undercover police officer three times. Although the owner knew that a purchaser had to show a firearm licence before the ammunition could be sold, he did not ask to see a licence. He also did not ask the officer his last name. He was charged under s. 101 and convicted. The court held that the owner had the necessary *mens rea* to commit the offence because he was reckless and wilfully blind. Despite being aware of the requirements under the law, he failed to make the necessary inquiries to determine that the purchaser had a firearm licence.

L04 D. BRIBERY, OBSTRUCTING A POLICE OFFICER, PERJURY, AND OBSTRUCTING JUSTICE

1. Bribery

In general terms, bribery is the accepting or offering of an undue reward or "payoff," in relation to influencing the conduct of public officials. There are several Code sections involving bribery. These sections mention various types of rewards, public officials, and behaviours.

An example of a Code section involving bribery is s. 119, which makes it an indictable offence if a person

(a) **being the holder of a judicial office, or being a member of Parliament or of the legislature of a province, directly or indirectly, corruptly accepts, obtains, or agrees to accept or attempts to obtain, for themselves or another person, any money, valuable consideration, office, place or employment in respect of anything done or omitted or to be done or omitted by them in their official capacity, or**

(b) **directly or indirectly, corruptly gives or offers to a person mentioned in paragraph (a), or to anyone for the benefit of that person, any money, valuable consideration, office, place or employment in respect of anything done or omitted or to be done or omitted by that person in their official capacity.**

In this bribery offence, it is clear that the public official could be a judge, a member of Parliament, or a member of a provincial legislature. The reward could be money, a job, or

---

39 (2004), 201 C.C.C. (3d) 375 (Alta. Q.B.).

practically anything of value. The behaviour involved could be any act or omission by the official in carrying out his or her public duties.

Bribery involves two parties: the public official and any other person. Offences may be committed by one or both of them. Paragraph (a) refers to three separate offences that may be committed by the public official: actually accepting a bribe, simply agreeing to accept a bribe, and soliciting or trying to obtain a bribe. Paragraph (b) refers to two offences that may be committed by the other person: actually giving a bribe to the official, and simply offering a bribe to the official.

When a person offers a bribe to an official, it is no defence that the official refused it. In other words, the offence is complete when the offer is made.

It is also necessary that the offering, giving, or accepting be done "corruptly." The word "corruptly" has been interpreted as meaning with the intention to accomplish the purpose forbidden by the Code.[40] Thus, under s. 119 it must be shown that the offering, accepting, and so on, was done with the intention of having the official do or omit to do some act in his or her official capacity.

In *R. v. Bruneau*,[41] the accused was charged with agreeing to accept $10,000 for the use of his influence in his official capacity as a member of Parliament. Bruneau had agreed to accept the money from B., one of his constituents, in return for using his influence to have the federal government buy B.'s property as the site for a post office. The usual practice, which was followed in this case, was that after a number of possible sites were examined by federal officials, the local MP was consulted for a recommendation. B.'s property was purchased, and Bruneau accepted $10,000 from B. Bruneau's lawyer argued that Bruneau had not been acting "in his official capacity" because that phrase refers to an MP's power to take part in legislation and matters directly related to it in the House of Commons. The court rejected this argument and found Bruneau guilty. The court felt that since the accused had been consulted because of his membership in Parliament, any action taken by him was "in his official capacity."

2. Breach of Trust by Public Officer

Section 122 makes it an indictable offence for an official who, in connection with the duties of his office, commits fraud or breach of trust, regardless of whether the fraud or breach of trust would be an offence if it were committed in relation to a private person.

In *R. v. Boulanger*,[42] the Supreme Court of Canada clarified the *mens rea* and *actus reus* of the offence of breach of trust by a public official. Boulanger was the director of public security of a municipality. Following a car accident in which his daughter was involved, he asked the police officer in charge of the case to prepare a second, more complete accident report. The supplementary report led to the conclusion that his daughter was not at fault, with the result that the appellant did not have to pay the insurance deductible of $250. Boulanger was clearly an official who was acting in connection with the duties of his office. Regarding *mens rea*, the question was whether he had an intention to use his public office for a purpose other than the public good, for example, for a dishonest, partial, corrupt, or oppressive purpose. The Court found that, although Boulanger knew that he would benefit from the police report, this alone did not establish a culpable state of mind. The Court concluded that Boulanger's private purpose did not seek to undermine the public good. Regarding *actus reus*, the issue was

---

40   *R. v. Gross* (1946), 86 C.C.C. 68 (Ont. C.A.).
41   (1964), 1 C.C.C. 97 (Ont. C.A.).
42   [2006] 2 S.C.R. 49 (S.C.C.).

whether his conduct represented a serious and marked departure from the standards expected of an individual in his position of public trust. The Court found that Boulanger's conduct was not a serious and marked departure, but rather simply an error in judgment.

3. Obstructing a Peace Officer

Section 129 makes it an offence if a person

(a) **resists or wilfully obstructs a public officer or peace officer in the execution of his duty or any person lawfully acting in aid of such an officer,**

(b) **omits, without reasonable excuse, to assist a public officer or peace officer in the execution of his duty in arresting a person or in preserving the peace, after having reasonable notice that he is required to do so, or**

(c) **resists or wilfully obstructs any person in the lawful execution of a process against lands or goods or in making a lawful distress or seizure.**

The essential elements of a charge under s. 129(a) are that the accused obstructed, that the obstruction was wilful, that the person obstructed was a public officer or peace officer, and that the officer was in the lawful execution of his or her duty. In general, "peace officer" and "public officer" refer to persons who have the duty of enforcing the law. A "peace officer" is defined in s. 2 and was discussed in Chapter 5. In most situations, it refers to a police officer.

a. Obstruction

The ordinary meaning of the term "obstruct" is to hinder, block, or stop up.[43] The obstruction may involve physical force, such as assaulting a police officer.[44] The obstruction may occur without the use of physical force, where the accused does an act that leads the officer to believe that there will be violence if the officer proceeds.[45] However, it is not obstruction to not do anything. In *R. v. Lavin*,[46] a police officer observed the accused driving a car with an illegal radar detector. When the accused saw the officer, he put the detector in his pocket. The officer then stopped the accused, told him he had seen the detector, and asked him to hand it over. The accused refused to do so and was charged with obstruction. The Court of Appeal held that a person cannot be found guilty of obstruction for not doing something unless there is a duty to act. In this case, the court could not find any duty prior to arrest for the accused to hand over the device. The court distinguished this case from others where (a) the accused was found guilty after he denied possession of a detector, and (b) the accused hid a weapon and then lied about its existence. In *Lavin*, the accused was not charged because he hid the detector or lied about it but because he refused to hand it over.

It is obstruction to mislead the police. For example, in *R. v. Johnson*,[47] the driver of a car was stopped for speeding. He gave the officer a false name and was given a ticket under that name. The Saskatchewan Court of Appeal held that the accused's intent was to mislead the officer and thereby obstruct the officer in the execution of his duty. This case referred to *R. v. Moore*,[48] which was discussed in Chapter 5. In that case, the Supreme Court of Canada said that the accused had obstructed an officer in the execution of his duty by not providing his name where the officer had no authority to make an arrest except for the purpose of establishing the person's identity. On the

43   *R. v. Matheson* (1913), 21 C.C.C. 312 (N.B.C.A.).
44   *R. v. Bain* (1955), 111 C.C.C. 281 (Man. C.A.).
45   *Matheson, supra* note 43.
46   (1992), 76 C.C.C. (3d) 279 (Que. C.A.).
47   (1985), 41 Sask. R. 205 (Q.B.).
48   (1979), 43 C.C.C. (2d) 83 (S.C.C.).

other hand, the Alberta Court of Appeal held that an accused was not guilty of obstruction where she refused to give her name where the officer had no evidence that the accused had committed an offence.[49] In *R. v. B*,[50] the police were looking for a runaway youth. They spoke to the accused, who gave them false information about her whereabouts. He was convicted of obstruction.

b. Wilfully

The term "wilfully," as used in this section, means deliberately or intentionally. It refers to a deliberate purpose to accomplish something forbidden—a determination to carry out one's own will in defiance of the law.[51]

c. Execution of Duty

The officer must be in the lawful execution of duty when obstructed. This means that the officer must be carrying out some duty or obligation imposed by law. If the officer is not carrying out such a duty, then there is no offence committed under s. 129 if the person resists or obstructs the officer.

The courts have recognized that the police have a common law duty to preserve the peace, prevent crime, and protect lives and property.[52] Where there is a charge of obstruction and a question of whether the police were in the execution of their duty, courts have said that it must first be determined whether the specific conduct of the police fell within the scope of a general duty. In *R. v. Westlie*,[53] two plain-clothes police officers were working in the skid row area of Vancouver. The accused knew that they were police officers and starting shouting, "Undercover pigs! Undercover fuzz! Watch out for the pigs!" Many people in the area were attracted by the shouting. One of the officers told the accused that he was on duty in the area and warned him to stop. At that point, the accused began stopping people on the street, pointing at the two officers, and referring to them as "undercover pigs." The accused was charged with wilfully obstructing a peace officer in the execution of his duty.

There were three main issues in the case: At the time of the incident, were the police officers in the execution of their duty? Was there obstruction of the police officers? And was the obstruction wilful? The court held that the officers were in the execution of their general duty, which was to take all steps necessary to ensure that the public peace was kept, to prevent and detect crime, to bring offenders to justice, and to protect property from criminal damage. The accused did all he could to identify them to the public and thus frustrate them in the execution of their duty. This amounted to obstruction. There was no question that the conduct of the accused was intentional and deliberate. The accused was trying to warn law violators in the area that the two men were police officers and that they should stop breaking the law until the officers had left the area. The accused was convicted.

In *Knowlton v. R*,[54] Premier Alexei Kosygin of the Soviet Union was to visit Edmonton as part of his official visit to Canada. He was going to make a short stop at a hotel. A few days before the visit, Kosygin had been assaulted in Ottawa by a man who grabbed him and tried to drag him to the ground. To prevent another such incident, 26 police officers cordoned off an area in front of the hotel. The accused wanted to enter the cordoned-off area to take pictures. A police officer told him that he could not enter the area and warned him that if he

49 *R. v. Guthrie* (1982), 69 C.C.C. (2d) 216 (Alta. C.A.).
50 (1985), 41 Alta. L.R. (2d) 341 (Prov. Ct. Youth Div.).
51 *R. v. Griffin* (1935), 63 C.C.C. 286 (N.B.C.A.).
52 *R. v. Dedman* (1985), 20 C.C.C. (3d) 97 (S.C.C.).
53 (1971), 2 C.C.C. (2d) 315 (B.C.C.A.).
54 (1973), 10 C.C.C. (2d) 377 (S.C.C.).

did, he would be arrested. The accused ignored the warning. He began to enter the restricted area, pushing his way through two constables. He was charged with wilfully obstructing a peace officer in the execution of his duty. The incident took place at about the time Kosygin was scheduled to arrive. The Supreme Court of Canada said that the police had interfered with Knowlton's right to move freely on a public street. Such an interference could only be justified if the police were carrying out some duty imposed on them by law. The Court held that the police acted in the execution of their general duty to preserve peace, order, and public safety. They had a duty to prevent another criminal assault on Kosygin, and the accused obstructed them in carrying out that duty.

In *R. v. Plummer*,[55] the accused was charged with assaulting a police officer in the execution of his duty and assault with intent to resist arrest. The accused was a taxi driver who was stopped by police for not wearing his seatbelt. At trial, the accused was convicted of assault with intent to resist arrest. The Ontario Court of Appeal held that the police officer did not have the authority to arrest the accused under the Highway Traffic Act and dismissed the charges, stating:

> In attempting to arrest the appellant without legal authority, the officer unlawfully assaulted him. This appellant was therefore not guilty of the included offence of assault. S. 34(1) of the Criminal Code gave him the right to resist unlawful assault by the officer provided the force used was not intended to cause death or grievous bodily harm and was no more than necessary to defend himself.[56]

One type of case where a conflict arises between the police officer's general duty and an individual's rights is a situation when the police trespass on private property while executing their duty and the occupier resists. As noted in Chapter 5, the police can trespass on private property to make an arrest or when in hot pursuit of a suspect.[57] There are a few other situations where they may be authorized to enter private property. A case that discussed some of these situations is *R. v. Custer*.[58] The police received a report of a stabbing and went to investigate. When they arrived at the house where the stabbing was reported to have taken place, the man who answered the door stated that his wife had been stabbed but that she was all right. The accused told the officers to leave, but they insisted on entering the house to investigate the stabbing. A fight ensued, and the accused was charged with obstruction. The court held that although the police were exercising their general duty under statute to investigate crime, entering the house was not justified under that duty. The police cannot enter a private home against the owner's will to investigate a possible offence with a view to apprehending the offender. However, under the common law, the police have the right to enter private property to prevent death or serious injury. The police would have been justified in entering the home if they had had reasonable grounds to believe that an emergency situation existed involving the preservation of life or the prevention of serious injury.[59]

Another case that considered whether the police were justified in trespassing is *R. v. Thomas*.[60] The police were called to investigate complaints of a noisy party. When the police arrived at the house, they were taken by one of the guests to the accused's bedroom.

---

55   (2006), 214 C.C.C. (3d) 84 (Ont. C.A.).
56   Ibid. at 102–103.
57   See Chapter 5, page 95.
58   (1984), 12 C.C.C. (3d) 372 (Sask. C.A.).
59   The accused was acquitted, however, because this argument was not made at the trial and therefore could not be considered at the appeal.
60   (1991), 67 C.C.C. (3d) 81 (Nfld. C.A.).

After being asked some questions, the accused ordered the police to leave the house. A fight erupted between the police, a guest, and the accused. The accused was found not guilty on the grounds that the guest did not have the authority to invite the police in, and even if there was an implied permission to enter the house, once the police were asked to leave, they became trespassers. Therefore, the accused could not be charged with obstruction.

Where the police make a warrantless arrest under s. 495(b), and where the accused is later found not guilty of the offence, a charge for resisting arrest can still stand. In *R. v. Biron*,[61] the accused was charged with causing a disturbance and resisting arrest. He was acquitted of the disturbance charge. He then argued that since he had not committed an offence, the arrest was unlawful and the obstruction charge should be dismissed. The Supreme Court of Canada disagreed, holding that for an arrest to be lawful, the officer need only find a person apparently committing an offence.

There will be a different result where the police misapply the law. In *R. v. Potvin*,[62] the accused was charged with resisting a peace officer. The accused and a friend had gone to a park in Montreal. The accused had placed his kayak on a lake in the park when a police officer told him that boating was not permitted on the lake and warned him that he would be arrested if he did go boating. The accused went for a boat ride and was arrested. He resisted the arrest, and two police officers had to push him into a patrol car. The Crown argued that the accused had violated a city bylaw that prohibited throwing anything in city lakes and playing unauthorized games. The Crown also argued that the arrest was lawful. The court disagreed, saying that the accused had the right to resist the arrest because he had not violated the bylaw and, even if he had, it was not an offence that allows an arrest without a warrant. The police officers were acting without authority and thus were not in the execution of their duty. Therefore, the accused had a lawful excuse for resisting the arrest.

The police will not be acting in the execution of duty where the law is not in force. In *R. v. Sharma*,[63] the accused was a street vendor. He was given a ticket for not having a street vending licence and told to move on. When the officer returned, the accused was still selling goods on the street. He was charged with obstruction for failing to obey the officer's instructions. The Supreme Court of Canada held that the bylaw the accused was charged with violating was *ultra vires*. Since the bylaw was invalid, Sharma could not be convicted of obstruction for disobeying the officer's order to comply with it.

d. Failure to Assist

Section 129(b) makes it an offence to fail to help a peace officer to arrest a person or to keep the peace, unless there is a reasonable excuse for not helping. In *R. v. Foster*,[64] a police officer observed a car being driven in a dangerous manner. He stopped the vehicle. The driver got out and started running away. The officer caught up with him in a place where several people were camping. The driver struggled with the officer. The officer asked Foster, who was watching, to help him get the man back to his police car. Foster told the man to go with the officer. The officer again requested his help. Foster said, "No way," and walked away. It turned out that the driver was Foster's son. The court held that the fact that the driver was Foster's son was no excuse for Foster not to help the police officer.

---

61   (1975), 23 C.C.C. (2d) 513 (S.C.C.); see discussion of this in Chapter 5 at 100.
62   (1973), 15 C.C.C. (2d) 85 (Que. C.A.).
63   (1993), 79 C.C.C. (3d) 142 (S.C.C.).
64   (1981), 65 C.C.C. (2d) 388 (Alta. C.A.).

4. Perjury

Perjury involves knowingly making a false statement under oath. Section 131(1)[65] states that a person commits perjury who

> **. . . with intent to mislead, makes before a person who is authorized by law to permit it to be made before him, a false statement under oath or solemn affirmation, by affidavit, solemn declaration or deposition or orally, knowing that the statement is false.**

The offence of perjury can be committed at a judicial proceeding, which is defined in s. 118 as including proceedings before a court, the House of Commons, the Senate, or any other body or person authorized to make an inquiry and to take evidence under oath. Perjury can also be committed during extra-judicial proceedings.

For a witness to be convicted of perjury, the following must be proved beyond a reasonable doubt: that evidence given by the witness was false; that the witness knew when giving the evidence that it was false; and that the false evidence was given with the intent to mislead. In *Calder v. R.*,[66] the accused was a witness in a divorce case. He made a false statement at the trial regarding the length of time a woman had been living in a trailer on his business premises. At the perjury trial, he claimed that his evidence was an honest statement of what he remembered. The Supreme Court held that he was not guilty of perjury because, even though he had made a false statement, there was no proof that he knew the evidence was false or that he intended to mislead the court.

In *R. v. Regnier*,[67] the Ontario Court of Appeal held that to constitute perjury, it is not necessary that the false statement mislead the court. It is enough that the witness knew the statement was false and that the intent was to mislead.

In *R. v. Hayford*,[68] the Saskatchewan Court of Appeal held that if a witness makes a statement that is true in one sense and false in another, the Crown must prove that the statement was false in the sense that the witness used it. The accused had been a witness at a preliminary hearing on a charge of assault. He stated at the hearing that he had not agreed to sell to R. certain furniture. A month before, he had told a police officer that he had made an agreement with R. to sell the furniture. It was decided at the assault trial that the agreement was void. At the perjury trial, the court said that there was an agreement in the sense that the accused and R. had gone through the form of an agreement. However, there was no agreement in the sense that it was not legally binding. The Crown failed to prove in which sense the accused had stated that there was no agreement. Thus, the accused could not be convicted of perjury.

5. Obstructing the Course of Justice

Under s. 139(2), a person who wilfully attempts to obstruct, pervert, or defeat the course of justice is guilty of an indictable offence. The phrase "course of justice" has been given a broad meaning and is not limited to proceedings that follow the laying of a charge. In *R. v. Morin*,[69] the Quebec Court of Appeal held that "course of justice" should be given the same meaning as "administration of justice," which has been interpreted by the Supreme Court of Canada as a

---

65   See s. 131(2) regarding statements given in Canada which are for use in proceedings in another country.
66   (1960), 129 C.C.C. 220 (S.C.C.).
67   (1955), 112 C.C.C. 79 (Ont. C.A.).
68   (1921), 35 C.C.C. 293 (Sask. C.A.).
69   (1968), 5 C.R.N.S. 297 (Que. C.A.).

very wide term covering the detection, prosecution, and punishment of offenders.[70] Morin was convicted of attempting to obstruct the course of justice by offering a bribe to a peace officer. While being driven to the police station, he had offered money to the officers in the hope of avoiding arrest. Note that Morin could have been charged with offering a bribe to a peace officer, contrary to s. 109, instead of attempting to obstruct justice.

In *R. v. Zeck*,[71] a police officer observed the accused destroying parking tickets that he had placed on cars. The Ontario Court of Appeal held that Zeck was properly convicted of obstructing the course of justice. The offence applies to wilful attempts to obstruct the enforcement by the police of a municipal parking bylaw.

In *R. v. Balaram*,[72] the accused sent a threatening letter to a judge and made two threatening phone calls. The accused was unhappy about a sentence he had received from the judge. He was convicted of obstruction for making the threats, even though there was little chance that he could follow through on them.

If something is said or done that obstructs justice, but the person did not have the *mens rea* to obstruct justice, then no offence is committed. In *R. v. Savinkoff*,[73] the accused was charged with attempting to obstruct justice after he had tried to induce two men to give false evidence at their trial. The Crown failed to prove that the accused knew that the evidence was false. Without this guilty knowledge, the accused had no *mens rea*.

In *R. v. Beaudry*,[74] a police officer was charged with obstructing justice under s. 139(2) for deliberately failing to gather evidence needed to lay criminal charges against a fellow police officer whom he had reasonable grounds to believe had been operating a motor vehicle while intoxicated. Beaudry argued that his decision was a proper exercise of police discretion. The Crown argued that the decision was founded not on police discretion, but on preferential treatment of a fellow police officer. The Supreme Court of Canada stated that a person cannot be convicted under s. 139(2) solely because he or she exercised discretion improperly. The Court set out the following approach to police discretion and obstruction of justice.

First, it must be determined whether the conduct can be regarded as a proper exercise of police discretion. The exercise of the discretion must be justified on the basis of objective factors. It must be determined what a police officer acting reasonably would do in the same situation. Second, if it was not a proper exercise of police discretion, it must be determined whether the offence of obstructing justice has been committed. The offence requires that the act tended to defeat or obstruct the course of justice and that the accused intended to act in a way tending to defeat or obstruct the course of justice. A simple error of judgment will not be enough. An accused who acted in good faith, but whose conduct cannot be characterized as a legitimate exercise of the discretion, has not committed the criminal offence of obstructing justice.

In *R. v. Barros*,[75] the accused was a former police officer who was working as a private investigator. He was hired by the lawyer for Qureshi who had been charged with various drug offences. Barros discovered the identity of a police informant who had provided information leading to the drug charges. He set up a meeting with police officers to explain that if the charges were not dropped, Barros would be forced to report the informer's identity to Qureshi's lawyer and whatever the lawyer did with that information would be up to him. Barros pointed out to the police officers that his police experience was that in these circumstances, the

---

70 *R. v. Kalick* (1920), 35 C.C.C. 159 (S.C.C.).
71 (1980), 53 C.C.C. (2d) 551 (Ont. C.A.).
72 [1991] OJ No 3442; (1991), 13 W.C.B. (2d) 346.
73 (1963), 3 C.C.C. 163 (B.C.C.A.).
74 (2007), 216 C.C.C. (3d) 353 (S.C.C.).
75 2011 SCC 51; [2011] 3 S.C.R. 368. Another aspect of this case—extortion charges—is discussed in Chapter 12.

charges would be stayed. He also noted that Qureshi's lawyer had used such information in the past to obtain a stay of charges. One of the officers testified that he understood Barros to be asking him to drop the charges against Qureshi if he didn't want the identity of the informer to be revealed. Barros was charged with obstruction of justice. The trial judge directed a verdict of acquittal. She found that identifying a police informant does not in itself constitute an obstruction of justice; at the most, it might constitute preparation for an attempt to obstruct justice if the information concerning the police informant is used in a way which tends to obstruct the administration of justice.

The Supreme Court of Canada held that the judge erred in directing an acquittal. In characterizing the conduct of Barros as mere "preparation," the judge failed to take into account the entire chain of events. There was evidence which, if believed, went far beyond the preparation stage. The court stated that the gist of the charge was not just that Barros sought the name of the police informant, but that he did so "for the purpose of interfering with criminal proceedings," that is to have the charges against Qureshi dropped. This, if established, was not information gathering for a lawful purpose. There was evidence that, if believed, would establish an intent to obstruct unlawfully the trial of the charges against Qureshi. The Supreme Court ordered a new trial.

Questions for Review and Discussion

1. Does an offence have to be committed in Canada for a person to be tried in Canada? Explain.

2. Explain the difference between treason and sedition.

3. **a.** What are the essential elements of an unlawful assembly?
   b. How is a riot different from an unlawful assembly?

4. What is a lawful excuse for being in possession of an explosive substance? Would this lawful excuse protect the possessor from criminal liability for an injury caused by the explosion of the explosive substance? Explain.

5. What is the main object of the Firearms Act?

6. What is the *mens rea* requirement for the offence of carelessly using a firearm?

7. What did the Supreme Court of Canada decide in *R. v. Covin* and *Covin*?

8. What is the offence of bribery? Give an example.

9. How have the courts defined the term "administration of justice" in the offence of bribery?

10. Give an example of a police officer not acting in the execution of duty.

11. What are the essential elements of the offence of perjury?

12. Mrs. C. called the police to report damage to her car. The police came to her house to talk to her about the incident. Mrs. C. suggested that her son D. might know something about the damage. When the officer started questioning D., he became upset and ordered them out of the house. He then ran and got a gun. The police left the house. D. was charged with possession of a weapon for a purpose dangerous to the public. Should he be convicted? Explain. See *R. v. Cassidy* (1989), 50 C.C.C. (3d) 193 (S.C.C.).

13. Frank sent a letter to his brother in prison asking that he intimidate a witness at his upcoming trial. The letter was intercepted by the prison authorities and never received by the brother. Has Frank committed an offence? Explain. See *R. v. Graham* (1985), 20 C.C.C. (3d) 210 (Ont. C.A.).

14. R. was a lawyer representing clients who were charged with theft. It was alleged that R. offered to pay a certain amount of money to the investigating police officer if the charges were withdrawn. What can R. be charged with, and what must be proved to convict R.? See *Rousseau v. The Queen* (1985), 21 C.C.C. (3d) 1 (S.C.C.).

15. K.'s friend was charged with shoplifting. K. approached the owner of the store and offered to make a $20,000 donation to a charity on behalf of the store if they would withdraw the charge. He also suggested that the donation could be used as a promotion. K. had spoken to a lawyer before talking to the manager, and was told that his offer would not be a bribe as long as there was no benefit going to the store. K. did not tell the lawyer about making the donation on behalf of the store, or about the promotion. What can K. be charged with? Should he be convicted? Explain. See *R. v. Kotch* (1990), 61 C.C.C. (3d) 132 (Alta. C.A.).

16. Hebert gave false evidence at a preliminary inquiry and was charged with perjury and obstructing justice. He admitted that he had lied but stated that he did not intend to mislead the court. Relying on s. 17 of the Criminal Code (compulsion), he claimed that he had lied because he had been threatened with death. Should he be acquitted? See *R. v. Hebert* (1989), 49 C.C.C. (3d) 59 (S.C.C.).

17. Acting under the authority of the provincial Highway Traffic Act, a police officer ordered Waugh to stop his car because the car appeared to be in poor condition and did not have a front licence plate. Waugh was unable to produce a driver's licence, a valid vehicle permit, or proof of valid insurance. Based on his reasonable belief that the car was uninsured, the officer advised Waugh that the car would be impounded and towed away. Waugh refused to get out of the car. He locked himself inside the car and asked that a police supervisor be called. While waiting for the supervisor, the officer served Waugh with several provincial offence notices. Shortly thereafter, Waugh drove away. While being pursued by the police, he turned off the road and parked the car in a private laneway. Because the car was parked on private property and not on a highway, the police were unable to tow it away. Waugh was then charged with obstructing a peace officer in the execution of his duty. Waugh claimed that once he had received the provincial offence notices, he thought that he was free to drive off. The provincial Highway Traffic Act and Compulsory Automobile Insurance Act do not expressly give the police the authority to impound a vehicle that is uninsured. The prosecutor argued that the authority to impound the vehicle was based on the police officer's common law duties. Waugh argued that the police officer was not engaged in the execution of his duties. Should he be convicted? See *R. v. Waugh* (2010), 251 C.C.C. (3d) 139 (Ont. C.A.); leave to appeal dismissed by the Supreme Court of Canada (2010), S.C.C.A. No. 127 (S.C.C.).

CHAPTER 7

Sexual Offences, Pornography, Soliciting, and Bawdy-houses

PART V OF THE CODE

Key points explained in this chapter are

LO1 a range of sexual offences other than sexual assault, including sexual offences against minors;

LO2 when consent or a mistake as to the age of the complainant can be a defence to a sexual offence charge;

LO3 what constitutes pornography, obscenity, and undue exploitation of sex;

LO4 when images of children can be considered child pornography;

LO5 the legal meaning of prostitution;

LO6 offences related to prostitution, such as procuring and soliciting; and

LO7 when a place will be considered to be illegally used for "acts of indecency."

At one time, Part V of the Criminal Code contained the offence of rape and various offences involving intercourse with female minors. Most of these offences have been repealed. "Rape" is now defined as a type of assault and is contained in Part VII of the Code, which deals with offences against the person. Part V now deals mainly with public morality offences, offences involving disorderly conduct, and sexual offences against children.

LO1 A. SEXUAL OFFENCES

With a few exceptions, which are noted below, the Part V sexual offences relate to sexual activity with minors— persons under the age of 18. The offences vary as to the specific age of the minor. Some of the offences pertain to sexual activity with any person under the age of 18 while others are limited to persons under 16 or under 14. In general, "child" and "young person" are not used in these sections. However, "child" is used in the section on child pornography (s. 163.1) and refers to a person under the age of 18. "Young person" is defined for the purpose of the offence of sexual exploitation (s. 153) as a person 16 to18 years old.

1. Sexual Interference

Section 151 provides that a person commits the offence of sexual interference if the person

> **for a sexual purpose, touches, directly or indirectly, with a part of the body or with an object, any part of the body of a person under the age of sixteen years. . .**

2. Invitation to Sexual Touching

Section 152 provides that a person commits the offence of inviting sexual touching if the person

for a sexual purpose, invites, counsels or incites a person under the age of sixteen years to touch, directly or indirectly, with a part of the body or with an object, the body of any person...

Sections 151 and 152 are distinct offences. Section 151 makes it an offence to touch, directly or indirectly, for a sexual purpose, a child under 16. Section 152 makes it an offence to encourage a child under 16 to touch, directly or indirectly, for a sexual purpose, the body of any person. For an offence under s. 152, there may or may not be a sexual touching by the child. The offence only requires an invitation to touch. The person to be touched can be either the accused or a third person. The term "sexual purpose" is not defined, but presumably it refers to any contact for the purpose of sexual gratification.[1]

In *R. v. Sears*,[2] the Manitoba Court of Appeal considered a case where a 12-year-old girl offered to perform a sexual act in return for money. The accused agreed to it, and the child performed an act of fellatio on him. He was charged with sexual assault and sexual interference. He was acquitted of assault but convicted of sexual interference. On appeal, he argued that since he did not initiate the act and was a passive participant, an offence under s. 151 was not committed. The court disagreed, stating that a person who intends sexual interaction of any kind with a child and who, with that intent, makes contact with the body of the child, "touches" the child—regardless of who initiated the contact and who is the active participant.

The Alberta Court of Appeal found in *R. v. B.(T.L.)* that the fact that the accused experienced no sexual gratification from an act of sexual interference with a child was not a mitigating factor at sentencing.[3]

The meaning of "touches" was considered in *R. v. Fong*.[4] The accused was charged under s. 152 when he invited a seven-year-old girl to hold a tissue onto which he had ejaculated. He argued that there had been no physical contact, either directly or indirectly, since the semen was no longer part of his body once it left his body. The court did not accept this argument. It held that the objective of s. 152 is to prevent the sexual exploitation of children and that the section must be interpreted in a way that is consistent with its purpose. The court stated, "in the terms of s. 152, the appellant invited the child complainant to indirectly touch his body—through his semen—with the use of an object, the tissue."[5]

The meaning of "incite" in s. 152 was addressed in *R. v. Rhynes*.[6] In separate incidents, two females under the age of 14, J.L.B. and J.J., performed oral sex on the accused, an 18-year-old male. In the first incident, J.L.B. was riding in a car with the accused. She attempted to kiss the accused and he resisted. She continued trying to kiss him, and eventually removed his pants and performed oral sex. In a second incident, J.J. was picked up by the accused, they went to the home of another person, and there she performed oral sex on the accused. In a third incident, the accused invited J.J. to meet him at an abandoned restaurant where she again performed oral sex on him. In overturning his convictions, the Prince Edward Island Court of Appeal stated that "incite" requires some positive conduct by the accused, not passive acquiescence, to cause the complainant to engage in sexual touching. Failure to resist is not

1   See, for example, *R. v. Sears* (1990), 58 C.C.C. (3d) 62 (Man. C.A.).
2   Ibid.
3   (2007), 218 C.C.C. (3d) 11 at 21 (Alta. C.A.); leave to appeal refused (July 12, 2007), Doc. 31857 (S.C.C.).
4   (1994), 92 C.C.C. (3d) 171 (Alta. C.A.).
5   Ibid. at 175.
6   (2004), 186 C.C.C. (3d) 29 (P.E.I.C.A.).

synonymous with "incitement," which requires an act of persuasion or spurring on. The court found that the evidence did not support a conclusion that the accused had incited sexual touching in any of the three incidents.

3. Sexual Exploitation

153. (1) Every person commits an offence who is in position of trust or authority towards a young person, who is a person with whom the young person is in a relationship of dependency or who is in a relationship with a young person that is exploitative of the young person, and who

> **(a) for a sexual purpose, touches, directly or indirectly, with a part of the body or with an object, any part of the body of the young person, or**
>
> **(b) for a sexual purpose, invites, counsels or incites a young person to touch, directly or indirectly, with a part of the body or with an object, the body of any person, including the body of the person who so invites, counsels, or incites and the body of the young person.**

(1.2) A judge may infer that a person is in a relationship with a young person that is exploitative of the young person from the nature and circumstances of the relationship; including

> **(a) the age of the young person;**
>
> **(b) the age difference between the person and the young person;**
>
> **(c) the evolution of the relationship; and**
>
> **(d) the degree of control or influence by the person over the young person.**

(2) In this section, "young person" means a person sixteen years of age or more but under the age of eighteen years.

Notice that s. 153 combines elements of the offences of sexual interference and invitation to sexual touching where the complainant is 16 to 18 years old and the accused is in a position of trust or authority, and the complainant is in a relationship of dependency or one that is exploitative of the young person. The Code does not define "position of trust or authority" and "relationship of dependency." Presumably these terms refer to persons such as parents, teachers, babysitters, and employers. However, court decisions have generally held that the question of whether a special relationship exists depends on the facts of each given case. Such a relationship cannot be presumed just because the accused and the complainant are parent and child, or employer and employee, for instance.[7] Section 153(1) was amended in 2005 to include a relationship that is "exploitative of the young person."

a. Relationship of Dependency

In *R. v. Galbraith*,[8] the meaning of "relationship of dependency" was considered. The accused was a 27-year-old male who had been living with and supporting a 14-year-old girl. (At the time of

---

7   For example, see *R. v. J.(R.H.)* (1993), 86 C.C.C. (3d) 354 (B.C.C.A.); leave to appeal to S.C.C. refused 87 C.C.C. (3d) vi. In this case, the relationship between a man and his 17-year-old stepdaughter did not automatically give rise to one of authority, trust, or dependency. See also *R. v. Casknette* (1993), 80 C.C.C. (3d) 439 (B.C.C.A.) for the same result, where the relationship was between an employer and a teenage boy. However, on May 30, 1996, the Supreme Court of Canada, in *R. v. Audet* (1996), 106 C.C.C. (3d) 481 (S.C.C.), held that teachers will almost always be found to be in a position of trust and authority.

8   (1994), 90 C.C.C. (3d) 76 (Ont. C.A.); leave to appeal to S.C.C. refused 92 C.C.C. (3d) vi.

this case, "young person" was defined as a person between the ages of 14 and 17.) He was convicted of sexual exploitation. The appeal court held that the trial judge erred in interpreting "relationship of dependency" as meaning one where a person relies on another for economic support. The court pointed out that a sexual relationship with a person between 14 and 18 is an offence only if there is a relationship of trust, authority, or dependency. The judge held that the term "relationship of dependency" must be given a meaning similar to relationships of trust or authority. All of these relationships under s. 153 refer to ones in which there is a reliance by a young person on a figure who has assumed a position of power, such as one based on trust or authority, over the young person. Sexual relations are prohibited in these situations because the nature of the relationship makes the young person particularly vulnerable to the influence of the other person. The circumstances of this case did not establish a relationship of dependency. The relationship was described as boyfriend/girlfriend. There was no evidence that the relationship was exploitative, or that there was an obvious power imbalance. The accused did not force her to work. He did not take her away from her friends, home, school, or parents. She had the option of living with her mother but chose not to because she did not like the house rules. There was no evidence that the rules at her mother's house were onerous or inappropriate. She had been living with friends before living with the accused and was living with friends at the time of the trial. The Crown conceded that she liked the appellant and that he was good to her.

b. Position of Trust

Contrast the *Galbraith* case with *R. v. Edwards*,[9] where the accused was also a 27-year-old male and the victim a 14-year-old girl. (At the time of this case, "young person" was defined as a person between the ages of 14 and 17.) The accused was charged with sexual exploitation and convicted at trial. He was a dance instructor employed by the local parks and recreation department, which sponsored a dance program in a local high school. The victim was a 14-year-old girl who testified she consented to the sexual relationship (the accused had intercourse with the victim over the course of four or five months). In dismissing the appeal, the court reiterated that consent did not negate the seduction by the accused.[10] Applying *Audet*,[11] the court stated:

> In discussing this element of the offence, the trial judge referred to aspects of the evidence that were relevant to the existence of a position of trust, particularly that Mr. Edwards was an instructor of the young person, that he was significantly older than she was, that Mr. Edwards was employed by Burnaby Parks and Recreation, that the venue of the class was a secondary school, that he appeared to single her out in class and invited her to confide in him concerning problems she may have, and that the relationship developed while he was in the position of her dance instructor. . . In my view, the facts found by the trial judge are capable of demonstrating a position of trust. Of particular significance is the sponsor of the instruction, a branch of local government; the venue of the class, a school; the mix of dance students, teenagers; and Mr. Edwards' role, that of a significantly older person paid by Burnaby Parks and Recreation to instruct the teenage attendees.[12]

---

9   (2003), 172 C.C.C. (3d) 313 (B.C.C.A.).
10   Ibid. at 317.
11   *Audet, supra* note 7.
12   *Edwards, supra* note 9 at 319. See also *R. v. LeBlanc* (2000), 147 C.C.C. (3d) 1 (N.S.C.A.), which discusses consent and positions of trust or authority.

c. Exploitative Relationship

In *R. v. Anderson*,[13] the court addressed the meaning of exploitative relationship. The accused was a female university student between the ages of 22 and 23 who was charged under s. 153(1). It was alleged that, while in an exploitative relationship with a 15-year old complainant, she and the 15-year-old engaged in sexual relations. Anderson had been an assistant coach on the complainant's soccer team, but the charges did not relate to the time when Anderson was a coach. The court stated that an exploitative relationship under s. 153(1) exists where

(a) the accused is not in a position of trust or authority and the relationship is not one of dependency;

(b) there is a power imbalance between the accused and the young person; and

(c) the power imbalance results in the young person being vulnerable to the actions of the accused, who is taking advantage of the young person for his or her own benefit.

The court found that there was not an exploitative relationship. The court considered the nature and circumstances of the relationship, including the factors listed in s. 153(1.2). The age difference of seven years was not a basis on which it could be inferred that there was a power imbalance that would render the complainant incapable of providing her consent. There was no evidence that Anderson used the player–coach relationship as a launching pad to manipulate the complainant in the future, thereby contributing to bringing the complainant under her control. Anderson tried to stop all contact with the complainant, despite the complainant's best efforts to keep the relationship intact. After six months during which they had no contact, the relationship resumed only after the complainant made contact with Anderson and confided that she had questions as to her sexual identity. The court found that the relationship was wanted by both of them. It was not a relationship fostered by the manipulative actions of Anderson for her own benefit but rather one which arose from the complainant's need to be with and confide in a young woman almost seven years older.

LO2   ## 4. Consent and Mistake of Age as Defences

> **150.1 (1) Subject to subsection (2) to (2.2), when an accused is charged with an offence under section 151 or 152 or subsection 153(1). . . or is charged with an offence under 271, 272 or 273** *(sexual assaults—see Chapter 11)* **in respect of a complainant under the age of 16 years, it is not a defence that the complainant consented to the activity that forms the subject-matter of the charge.**

Under s. 150.1(1), the general rule is that consent is not a defence to the offences of sexual interference (s. 151), invitation to sexual touching (s. 152), and sexual exploitation (s. 153(1)). There are exceptions to this general rule. Consent can be a defence to a charge of sexual interference or invitation to sexual touching, depending on the ages of the complainant and the accused and their relationship:

- if the complainant is at least 12 but under 14 and the accused is less than 2 years older and is not in a position of trust or authority toward the complainant, and their relationship is not one in which the complainant is dependent or is exploited (s. 150.1(2));

---

13   (2009), 241 C.C.C. (3d) 432 (P.E.I.C.A.).

- if the complainant is at least 14 but under 16 and the accused is less than 5 years older and is not in a position of trust or authority toward the complainant and their relationship is not one in which the complainant is dependent or is exploited, or they are married (s. 150.1(2.1)); and
- if the accused is 5 or more years older than the complainant and (a) they are common-law partners or they have been cohabiting in a conjugal relationship for less than a year and have or are expecting to have a child, and (b) the accused is not in a position of trust or authority toward the complainant and their relationship is not one in which the complainant is dependent or is exploited (s. 150.1(2.2)).

In addition, s. 150.1(3) provides that a person who is 12 or 13 years old cannot be tried for sexual interference or invitation to sexual touching unless the person is in a position of trust or authority toward the complainant or their relationship is one in which the complainant is dependent or is exploited.

These various exceptions mean that no offence takes place where the victim and the accused are in more or less equal positions.

The general rule in s. 150.1(1) has been challenged under the Charter as violating sections 7 and 15 of the Charter by limiting the defence of consent. Most court decisions have found that it is not a violation of the Charter, or that it is a reasonable limitation.[14]

Section 150.1(4) provides for the defence of mistake of age:

(4) It is not a defence to a charge under section 151 or 152,. . . or 173(2) . . . that the accused believed that the complainant was sixteen years of age or more at the time the offence is alleged to have been committed unless the accused took all reasonable steps to ascertain the age of the complainant.

Section 150.1(4) allows an honest mistake if it was reasonable. However, the accused must show what steps he or she took to determine the age of the victim and show that these steps were all that could be reasonably required in the circumstances.[15]

A similar defence that applies to sexual exploitation (s. 153(1)) is set out in s. 150.1(5), where the accused mistakenly believes that the complainant is 18 or over. Subsection (6) states that an accused cannot raise a mistaken belief in the age of the complainant in order to use the defence under subsection (2) or (2.1) unless the accused took all reasonable steps to ascertain the age of the complainant.

B. CORRUPTION OF MORALS

1. Pornography

The Criminal Code creates certain offences concerning obscene materials (i.e., pornography). The main section is s. 163:

163. (1) Every one commits an offence who

(a) makes, prints, publishes, distributes, circulates, or has in his possession for the purpose of publication, distribution or circulation any obscene written matter, picture, model, phonograph record or other thing whatever; . . .

---

14   See, for example, *R. v. M.(R.S.)* (1991), 69 C.C.C. (3d) 223 (P.E.I.C.A.); *R. v. Gallant* (1986), 29 C.C.C. (3d) 291 (B.C.C.A.).
15   *R. v. Osborne* (1992), 17 C.R. (4th) 350 (Nfld. C.A.).

(2) Every one commits an offence who knowingly, without lawful justification or excuse,

  (a) sells, exposes to public view or has in his possession for such a purpose any obscene written matter, picture, model, phonograph record or other thing whatever; . . .

Subsection (1)(a) is directed toward publishers and distributors of obscene material. However, the Supreme Court of Canada has said that this section includes private individuals who make obscene material even if the material is not meant for publication.[16] Courts have held that a person who shows an obscene film in a private home is not "circulating," but a person in the business of renting videos is "circulating or distributing."[17]

Subsection (2)(a) is directed toward sellers of obscene material (such as the operator of a bookstore) and toward those who expose obscene material (such as the manager of an art gallery).

An important difference between s. 163(1) and s. 163(2) is that under s. 163(2) the Crown must prove that the accused acted knowingly—that is, that the accused knew of the nature of the material. Under s. 163(1), the Crown does not have to prove knowledge.

The requirement of "knowingly" under s. 163(2) was considered by the Supreme Court of Canada in *R. v. Jorgenson*.[18] The accused, who owned a video store, was convicted of "knowingly" selling obscene videotapes. On appeal to the Supreme Court of Canada, the issue was whether the Crown had to prove that the accused had actual knowledge that the videos sold contained specific scenes that were obscene, or was aware of the qualities that made the video obscene overall. The Court held that the word "knowingly" means that the Crown must prove actual knowledge. The Court acquitted the accused because the Crown only proved that the accused had a general knowledge that the films dealt with the exploitation of sex. The Court noted that a person is not protected from charges because he or she did not know that the material was obscene or was unaware that there are laws against selling obscene materials. For the accused to be convicted, it only has to be proved that he or she knew of the qualities or specific scenes that make the material obscene. The Court also noted that it may not be necessary to prove that the accused actually watched the video. The *mens rea* could be proved, for example, by showing that the accused was warned of the material or failed to comply with requirements to excise portions of a film. It would also be possible to prove wilful blindness if the retailer suspected material was obscene but refrained from making the necessary inquiries.

a. The Meaning of Obscenity

A major issue in defining obscenity is how to strike the proper balance between protecting freedom of expression and limiting a type of expression that violates societal values.

The basic definition of obscenity is in s. 163(8):

(8) For the purposes of this Act, any publication a dominant characteristic of which is the undue exploitation of sex, or of sex and any one or more of the following subjects, namely crime, horror, cruelty and violence, shall be deemed to be obscene.

This definition is not limited to print publications but has been applied to films, videos, and sexual devices and articles.[19]

---

16 *Hawkshaw v. The Queen* (1986), 26 C.C.C. (3d) 129 (S.C.C.).
17 *R. v. Rioux*, [1970] 3 C.C.C. 149 (S.C.C.); *R. v. Red Hot Video* (1985), 18 C.C.C. (3d) 1 (B.C.C.A.).
18 (1995), 102 C.C.C. (3d) 97 (S.C.C.).
19 *Rioux, supra* note 17.

b. What Is "Undue Exploitation of Sex"?

The Supreme Court of Canada considered the meaning of "undue exploitation of sex" in *R. v. Butler*.[20] The accused was the operator of a video store that carried "hard porn" videos. In this landmark decision, the Court pulled together the various tests that lower courts had developed.

Community Standards of Tolerance Test

The Court noted that the community's standard of tolerance has become the most important factor in deciding whether material is obscene. The Court quoted a previous judgment that stated that the community standards must be Canadian and in keeping with the times.[21] In a case it had examined earlier, *Towne Cinema Theatres Ltd. v. R.*,[22] the Court had stated that, in determining community standards, the test is not what the average Canadian would want to see, but what the average Canadian would tolerate others seeing.

Degradation and Dehumanization Test

The Court noted that many decisions have recognized that material which may be said to exploit sex in a "degrading or dehumanizing" manner will necessarily fail the community standards test, not because it offends against morals but because it is perceived by public opinion to be harmful to society, particularly to women.

Internal Necessities Test

The third test considered is the "internal necessities test" or artistic defence. The Court stated, "Even material which by itself offends community standards will not be considered 'undue' if it is required for the serious treatment of a theme."[23] The question here is whether the exploitation of sex is justifiable in light of the work's plot or theme; in considering this, it is necessary to consider the work as a whole.

Applying the Tests

The Court, having established these tests, put them together in a working relationship. First, the Court divided pornography into three categories:

* explicit sex with violence,
* explicit sex without violence but that subjects people to degrading or dehumanizing treatment, and
* sex without violence that is neither degrading nor dehumanizing.

Next, the Court combined the first two tests, stating this:

[T]he courts must determine as best they can what the community would tolerate others being exposed to on the basis of the degree of harm that might flow from such exposure. Harm in this context means that it predisposes persons to act in an antisocial manner as, for example, the mental or physical mistreatment of women by men . . . The stronger the inference of risk of harm the lesser the likelihood of tolerance."[24]

---

20 (1992), 70 C.C.C. (3d) 129 (S.C.C.).
21 The court referred to a dissenting judgment in *R. v. Dominion News and Gift*, [1963] 2 C.C.C. 103 (Man. C.A.), which was relied on by the Supreme Court in hearing the appeal of that decision at [1964] 3 C.C.C. 1 (S.C.C.).
22 (1985), 18 C.C.C. (3d) 193 (S.C.C.).
23 *Butler, supra* note 20 at 149.
24 Ibid. at 150.

In applying this standard to the three categories of pornography, the Court stated that sex with violence will almost always be undue exploitation. Sex that is degrading and dehumanizing may be undue exploitation if risk of harm is substantial. The third category, sex without violence or degradation, is generally tolerated in our society unless it employs children.

Only if the material is found to unduly exploit sex is the internal necessities test applied.

The portrayal of sex then must be examined in context to determine the dominant theme of the work as a whole—that is, is undue exploitation of sex the main object of the work, or is this portrayal of sex essential to a wider artistic, literary, or other similar purpose? Community standards are still important. The question is whether the sexually explicit material, when viewed in the context of the whole work, would be tolerated by the community as a whole.

Summary

The *Butler* decision marks a distinct shift in the definition of obscenity. The basis of deciding whether material offends community standards is whether the material is seen as causing harm to society, not whether it offends present standards of community morality.[25]

In *R. v. Smith*,[26] the accused was charged and convicted of making obscene material, possessing obscene material for distribution, and distributing obscene material through internet websites. Six of the offences related to audiovisual depictions of women and the seventh related to stories. The audiovisual material did not include depictions of any sexual acts, but did include depictions of nude women pierced by arrows and knives. The court stated:

> In determining whether material depicts explicit sex, the trier of fact must consider the circumstances and context of the material. Even where no sexual act is depicted, material may still depict explicit sex. The trier of fact will determine whether a reasonable person who viewed the material would determine, in all the circumstances, that the material was explicitly sexual in nature. The part of the body depicted; the nature of the depiction; the context of the depiction; the accompanying dialogue, words, or gestures; and all other surrounding circumstances will be relevant to this determination.[27]

The court continued:

> In most cases, it will be unnecessary to define "explicit sex" because whether a depiction portrays "explicit sex" will be apparent from a consideration of the contextual factors. Thus, . . . in considering whether a dominant characteristic of the material is the undue exploitation of sex and violence, the jury should be instructed to first determine whether the material portrays explicit sex, or explicit sex and violence, a determination to be made after considering the surrounding circumstances, including the nature of the violence inflicted. The jury may be instructed that explicit sex captures portrayals at the far end of the spectrum, displayed in a graphic and unambiguous way. If they determine that the material depicts explicit sex and violence, they would then be asked to determine whether that portrayal was unduly exploitative on the application of all the factors involved in the community standards test, bearing in mind the direction in Butler that the portrayal of explicit sex with violence will almost always constitute the undue exploitation of sex.[28]

---

25 *See* R. Jochelson, "After Labaye: The Harm Test of Obscenity, the New Judicial Vacuum, and the Relevance of Familiar Voices" (2009) 46 Alta. L. Rev. 741–767, for a discussion of whether the law on obscenity has been affected by the decision of the Supreme Court of Canada in *R. v. Labaye*, which is discussed on pages 187–188.

26 (2005), 198 C.C.C. (3d) 499 (Ont. C.A.); leave to appeal refused (2005), 352 N.R. 197n (S.C.C.). Note that this case provides a good review of the case law, including *Sharpe* and *Jorgenson*.

27 Ibid. at 513.

28 Ibid. at 514.

c. Defence of Public Good

A defence to charges under s. 163 is the defence of the public good:

(3) No person shall be convicted of an offence under this section if the public good was served by the acts that are alleged to constitute the offence and if the acts alleged did not extend beyond what served the public good.

There are two parts to this defence: that the public good was served, and that the acts (e.g., publishing or selling obscene books) did not go beyond what served the public good. Material that otherwise would be obscene will not be considered obscene if this defence is established.

Something serves the public good if it is necessary or advantageous to objects of general interest, such as religion, science, literature, or art. In *Delorme v. R.*,[29] the accused, who ran a bookstore, was charged with selling an obscene book. The book was about a woman who was subjected to many cruel and violent sexual acts. Experts testified that the book had value as a psychological study and would be useful to students of literature or psychology. The book had a plain cover that would not attract attention. One expert testified that the book was difficult to read and not within everyone's grasp. The court held that, although the book may have been of benefit to certain students, since it was available in a public bookstore it could not be said that the public good was being served. The defence failed, and the accused was convicted.

d. Obscenity and the Charter

Butler dealt with the argument that s. 163 violates the Charter. First, with reference to s. 1 of the Charter, it was argued that the definition of obscenity in s. 163 is too vague to be "a limit prescribed by law" and so imprecise that it is not "a reasonable limit prescribed by law." The Court disagreed, stating that the section plus court decisions—including the one the Court was now making—provide an intelligent and enforceable test.

Next, the Court looked at whether s. 163 violates the Charter guarantee to freedom of expression. The Court said that it does but that it is a reasonable limitation under s. 1 of the Charter. Using the test set out in *R. v. Oakes*[30] for determining whether a law that violates the Charter is a reasonable limitation, the Court held that the object of the legislation is not to enforce moral standards, which would not be a valid objective. Rather, it is to prevent harm to society. The Court quoted the *Report on Pornography* (the MacGuigan Report), which stated:

> The clear and unquestionable danger of this type of material is that it reinforces unhealthy tendencies in Canadian society. [I]t reinforces male–female stereotypes, makes degradation, humiliation, victimization and violence in human relationships appear normal and acceptable. A society which holds that egalitarianism, non-violence, consensualism and mutuality are basic to any human interaction, whether sexual or not, is clearly justified in controlling and prohibiting any medium . . . which violates these principles."[31]

However, is banning obscene materials a pressing and substantial objective? The Court said "yes"; the harm caused by the proliferation of materials that seriously offend our fundamental values is a substantial concern that justifies the restriction of freedom of expression.

The Court also found that s. 163's definition of obscenity meets the proportionality test. Even though it may be impossible to prove that pornography directly harms society, it is reasonable

---

29 (1973), 15 C.C.C. (2d) 350; 21 C.R.N.S. 305 (Que. C.A.).
30 (1986), 24 C.C.C. (3d) 321 (S.C.C.). See *Oakes* test in Chapter 2 at 26.
31 *Butler, supra* note 20 at 157, quoting the *Report on Pornography* by the Standing Committee on Justice and Legal Affairs (the MacGuigan Report, 1978).

to assume that exposure to it affects people's beliefs and attitudes. There is a sufficient rational link between the criminal sanction and the objective, and the law minimally impairs the right to freedom of expression. The section does not prohibit all sexually explicit erotica, but only that material which creates a risk of harm to society.

LO4   2. Child Pornography

163.1 (1) In this section, "child pornography" means

(a) **a photographic, film, video or other visual representation, whether or not it was made by electronic or mechanical means,**

(i) **that shows a person who is or is depicted as being under the age of eighteen years and is engaged in or is depicted as engaged in explicit sexual activity, or**

(ii) **the dominant characteristic of which is the depiction, for a sexual purpose, of a sexual organ or the anal region of a person under the age of eighteen years; or**

(b) **any written material or visual representation, or audio recording that advocates or counsels sexual activity with a person under the age of eighteen years that would be an offence under this Act.**

In *R. v. I.(J.E.)*,[32] the accused was charged with possession of child pornography, as defined by s. 163.1(1). The accused videotaped four teenage friends of his daughter, as well as an adult woman, in various stages of undress in the bathroom of his home without their knowledge. He had a board at the base of a linen closet that could be removed while standing in the stairwell, permitting a direct view of the bathroom. The four girls were approximately 16 years old at the time.

In convicting the accused, the trial judge found that the dominant characteristic of the videotapes was for a sexual purpose. The accused appealed to the British Columbia Court of Appeal. In dismissing the appeal and upholding the conviction, the court stated:

> In this case, it is not determinative that the images depict only nude teenage girls and do not display overt sexual acts. Photographs of nude children may well constitute child pornography depending on their context. Part of the relevant context of these images is the surreptitious taking of the images, which resulted in the "unguarded depiction of the sexual organs and nudity of the subject". These images were not taken innocently. They constitute a serious violation of the privacy and dignity of these four young women. As the trial judge noted, the images resulted in the "sexual embarrassment" of the subjects.

> There is no suggestion that the images were taken accidentally, or for a medical, scientific, educational, artistic or other lawful purpose. I do not accept the appellant's suggestion that the purpose of these videos was to annoy the subjects of the video. The videos show a clear interest in the nakedness of the teenage girls, and of the adult woman. Given the content and context of the videotapes, the only reasonable and objective conclusion is that the dominant characteristic of these videotapes was for a sexual purpose.[33]

---

32   (2005), 204 C.C.C. (3d) 137 (B.C.C.A.).
33   Ibid. at 143–144.

In *R. v. Beattie*,[34] the Ontario Court of Appeal found that material that describes sex with children as enjoyable, normal, and beneficial, and the children as willing, may send the implicit message that sex with children can and should be pursued. If so, it is within the meaning of advocating or counselling sexual activity with children under s. 163.1(b). In this case, the accused was in possession of a binder that contained stories that graphically described, but did not expressly advocate, sexual activities between adults and children under the age of 14.

Under s. 163.1(2), it is an offence to print, publish, or possess for the purpose of publishing child pornography. Under s. 163.1(3), it is an offence to import, distribute, sell, or possess for purposes of distribution or sale child pornography. In *R. v. Pecchiarich*,[35] the accused was convicted of distributing child pornography by modem on computer bulletin boards. The uploaded files were stories about children having sex with adults, animals, and other children. The accused also created graphic images of children having sex.

Section 163.1 also creates the offence of possessing child pornography in subsection (4) and the separate offence of accessing child pornography in subsection (4.1). In *R. v. Morelli*,[36] the Supreme Court of Canada dealt with the distinction between these offences. A computer technician, while repairing Morelli's computer in Morelli's house, noticed several links to child pornography. After obtaining a warrant to search the computer, the police found pornographic images of children on the computer and the accused was charged with, and convicted of, possession of child pornography. The Court quashed the conviction, finding that there was no evidence of possession. The Court stated that possession of an illegal image in a computer requires possession of the underlying data file, not its mere visual depiction. Simply viewing images online constitutes the separate crime of accessing child pornography.

Essential elements of possession are knowledge and control. "Personal possession" requires that the accused knows that he or she has physical custody of the object, and knows what the object is. Both types of knowledge must co-exist with an act of control. "Constructive possession" exists where the accused does not have physical custody of the object but (1) has knowledge of the character of the object, (2) knowingly puts or keeps the object in a particular place, whether or not that place belongs to the accused, and (3) intends to have the object in the particular place for his or her use or benefit or that of another person. The image file—the digital information encoding the image—can be possessed even if the image is not visible. If the image is displayed on a person's computer monitor, the underlying information might be outside that person's possession. It could be located on a server that is thousands of kilometres away, over which that person has no control. The Court also addressed how possession applies to files in an internet cache (copies of files automatically stored on the hard drive by a web browser). The automatic caching of a file to a hard drive does not, without more, constitute possession. Although the cached file may be in a place over which the computer user has control, it is necessary to satisfy the *mens rea* requirements of possession. It must be shown that the file was knowingly stored and retained through the cache.

a. Defences

Section 163.1(5) allows the defence of mistake of age only if all reasonable steps were taken to ascertain the age of the young person and to ensure, where the person was 18 years of age or older, that the representation did not depict the person as being under 18.

---

34   (2005), 201 C.C.C. (3d) 533.
35   (1995), 22 O.R. (3d) 748 (Ont. Prov. Ct.); reported in *The Lawyers Weekly*, September 29, 1995.
36   [2010] 1 S.C.R. 253 (S.C.C.). See Chapter 5 for a discussion of this case in relation to search.

Section 163.1(6) sets out another defence by providing that no person shall be convicted of an offence under s. 163.1 if the alleged act

(a) **has a legitimate purpose related to the administration of justice or to science, medicine, education or art; and**

(b) **does not pose an undue risk of harm to persons under the age of eighteen years.**

The Supreme Court of Canada considered this defence in *R. v. Katigbak*.[37] The accused was charged with possessing 628 images and 30 video clips of child pornography, which he had collected over a seven-year period. He claimed that he possessed the child pornography for the purpose of creating an art exhibition that would present the issue of child exploitation from the perspective of the child. He was acquitted at trial. On appeal, the Supreme Court found that the trial judge erred in her interpretation of the phrase "legitimate purpose" in s. 163.1(6) by inquiring solely into the accused's *subjective* purpose for possessing the material. The Court ordered a new trial. Regarding s. 163.1(a), the Court stated that the question is whether a reasonable person would conclude that (1) there is an objective connection between the accused's actions and his or her purpose, and (2) there is an *objective* relationship between his or her purpose and one of the protected activities (administration of justice, science, medicine, education, or art). The Court noted that the relationship between Katigbak's purpose of creating an art exhibition and the protected activity of "art" was not in issue. However, the connection between the repeated collection and storing of child pornography over a seven-year span and Katigbak's stated purpose of creating an art exhibition was highly contentious at trial. A new trial was required to address the objective component of the legitimate purpose part of the defence.

Regarding the second part of the defence, the Court stated, "The words 'undue risk of harm' set out in s. 163.1(6)(b) should be interpreted to mean a significant risk of objectively ascertainable harm as required by the law of obscenity, rather than the former 'moral views of the community' approach. Relying on the moral views of the community would be as unworkable for child pornography offences as it is for obscenity charges. Reasonable people may hold sharply divergent views about the level of risk to young persons that should be tolerated as a result of artistic expression, or scientific research. Instead, the courts must ask whether the harm is objectively ascertainable and whether the level of the harm poses a significant risk to children. It goes without saying that the harm may be either physical, psychological, or both."[38]

An earlier version of s. 163.1(6) referred to the defence of "artistic merit," rather than the current "legitimate purpose related to . . . art." Artistic merit was an issue in a highly publicized case involving an artist named Eli Langer.[39] His paintings were seized from an exhibit at a Toronto art gallery, and he and the gallery owner were charged under this section. The paintings represented children having sex with adults. The charges were finally dismissed on the grounds that the works had artistic merit. On the issue of community standards, the judge found that the work did not pose a risk of harm to children. The judge found that the intent and effect of the work was not to condone child sexual abuse but to lament the reality of it.

In considering artistic merit in the context of possession of child pornography, the court in *Langer* found that it must include consideration of contemporary standards of community

---

37   2011 SCC 48.
38   Ibid. at para. 67.
39   *Ontario (Attorney General) v. Langer* (1995), 97 C.C.C. (3d) 290 (Ont. C.A.); leave to appeal refused (1995), 100 C.C.C. (3d) vi (S.C.C.).

tolerance. The test for the defence of artistic merit is objective. The defence of artistic merit was discussed in *R. v. Sharpe*,[40] and the Supreme Court of Canada concluded "that artistic merit should be interpreted as including any expression that may reasonably be viewed as art. Any objectively established artistic value, however small, suffices to support the defence."[41] However, the Court did not agree with the court in *Langer* that a community standard should be incorporated into the defence because Parliament clearly intended that some pornographic material and possibly harmful material would escape prosecution on the basis of section 163.1(6); otherwise, Parliament would not have included the section.

In *R. v. Smith*, the court stated that "it would have been open to the trial judge to say that, if the jury found the materials to be close to the line, in recognition of the importance of artistic freedom of expression, tolerance is to be preferred."[42]

b. Child Pornography and the Charter

In *Sharpe*, the accused was acquitted at trial and his acquittal was upheld by the British Columbia Court of Appeal; and section 163.1(4) was struck down as being unconstitutional. The Supreme Court of Canada found that, while subsections 1(a), 1(b) and (4) violated s. 2 of the Charter, the violation was justified under s. 1. The Court stated that "prohibiting the possession of child pornography restricts the rights protected by s. 2(b) and the s. 7 liberty guarantee. While the prurient nature of most of the materials defined as 'child pornography' may attenuate its constitutional worth, it does not negate it, since the guarantee of free expression extends to even offensive speech."[43]

Society's interest in protecting children from the evils associated with child pornography must be balanced with the freedom of expression. The Court decided that the appropriate remedy was to read in an exclusion of the application of section 163.1 in certain situations. Persons who take pictures of themselves engaged in lawful sexual activity, or self-created expressive material, such as a teenager's diary, are examples of situations where section 163.1 would not apply. The Court upheld the defence of artistic merit stating that "the various statutory defences (i.e., artistic merit; educational, scientific, or medical purpose; and public good) must be interpreted liberally to protect freedom of expression, as well as possession for socially redeeming purposes.[44] The Court allowed the Crown's appeal, upheld the constitutionality of section 163.1 and sent *Sharpe* back for trial.

3. Online Luring of a Child

Section 172.1 makes it an offence to use a computer system to communicate with a child for the purpose of facilitating the commission of various sexual offences with respect to the child. The designated sexual offences vary by the age of the child:

(a) under age 18—sexual exploitation, incest, a child pornography offence, procuring (s. 212), or sexual assault;

(b) under age 16—sexual interference, invitation to sexual touching, bestiality (s.160(3)), exposure of genitals (s. 173(2)), or abduction (s. 280); and

(c) under age 14—abduction (s. 281).

---

40 (2001), 150 C.C.C. (3d) 321 (S.C.C.).
41 Ibid. at 355–356.
42 *Smith, supra* note 26 at 515.
43 *Sharpe, supra* note 40 at 34.
44 Ibid. at 378.

The offence is committed if the child was actually under the specified age or if the accused believed the child was under that age. If a person was represented to the accused as under the specified age, it will be presumed that the accused believed that the person was under that age. This presumption can be rebutted by evidence to the contrary. It is not a defence that the accused believed that the child was over the specified age, unless the accused made a reasonable effort to determine the age of the child.

In *R. v. Legare*,[45] a 32-year-old male and a 12-year-old female had a conversation in an online chat room. He identified himself as a 17-year-old male and she identified herself as a 13-year-old female. Both indicated a desire to engage in explicit sexual activity with each other. After she provided her telephone number, he called immediately and told her, in coarse and explicit language, that he "would love" to perform oral sex on her. He was charged under s. 172.1(1)(c) with communicating with a person who was under the age of 14 years, for the purpose of facilitating the commission of an offence under s. 151 (sexual interference) or 152 (invitation to sexual touching).[46] The trial judge acquitted him because the accused did not specifically request that he and the girl meet, nor did he intend to lure her to a real meeting. The trial judge ruled that an intent to lure a child to a meeting was required to constitute "facilitating" under s. 172.1(1)(c). On appeal, the Supreme Court of Canada set aside the acquittal, ordered a new trial, and addressed several aspects of s. 172.1:

1. *Essential elements.* There are three essential elements of the offence: (1) an intentional communication by computer (2) with a person whom the accused knows or believes to be under 14 years old (3) for the specific purpose of facilitating the commission of a specified secondary offence with respect to the underage person.

2. *Subjective intention.* The focus of s. 172.1 is on the accused's intention at the time of the communication by computer and that intention must be determined subjectively. The accused must have engaged in the communication with the specific intent of facilitating the commission of one of the secondary offences.

3. *Facilitating.* "Facilitating," in the context of s. 172.1, "includes helping to bring about and making easier or more probable the commission of the secondary offence—for example, by 'luring' or 'grooming' young persons to commit or participate in the prohibited conduct; by reducing their inhibitions; or by prurient discourse that exploits a young person's curiosity, immaturity or precocious sexuality."[47]

4. *Secondary offence.* The offender does not need to meet or intend to meet the victim with a view to committing any of the secondary offences. It is also not necessary that the acts of the accused be capable of facilitating the commission of the secondary offence.

The court also stated that the offence under s. 172.1 is a preparatory crime that captures otherwise legal conduct meant to culminate in the commission of a completed crime. It criminalizes conduct that precedes the commission of the specified secondary sexual offences and even precedes an attempt to commit them.

Courts have also dealt with the claim that the accused believed that the child was an adult. In *R. v. Alicandro*,[48] the accused entered a computer chat room and struck up a conversation with a police officer who was posing as a 13-year-old girl. The accused said that he was nude and asked

45   (2009), 249 C.C.C. (3d) 129 (S.C.C.)
46   At the time of the offence, s. 172.1 included these offences in paragraph (c).
47   *Legare, supra* note 45 at para. 28.
48   (2009), 246 C.C.C. (3d) 1 (Ont. C.A.).

the "girl" if she would "like to see." The "girl" expressed concern about her mother being around. After the accused repeated his offer, the "girl" said, "But I'm only 13." He then focused his webcam on his genitals and sent to the "girl" a video of himself masturbating. He was charged under s. 172.1 and convicted. He claimed that he believed that the "girl" was at least 18. He stated that he had reviewed the electronic profile of the "girl," which indicated that she was 18. He understood that people could not enter the chat room if they were under 18. He also said that everyone lies about their age in chat rooms. The Ontario Court of Appeal, however, found that his claimed belief that the "girl" was 18 was not a defence because he had not made a reasonable effort to determine the age of the person he was dealing with.

In a similar computer chat room case, *R. v. Levigne*,[49] the Alberta Court of Appeal stated that an honest, but mistaken, belief as to the person's age is not enough to rebut the presumption that the accused believed that the person was under the specified age in s. 172.1. Objectively reasonable steps to determine the age of the person are required. In this case, the accused was communicating with a police officer who represented himself online as a 13-year-old boy. The accused's belief that he was communicating with an adult was based on assumptions and beliefs that did not constitute objectively reasonable steps. He relied on indicators of adulthood such as a false chat room profile, the person's slow typing speed, and the fact that some adults will falsely claim online that they are children. He also assumed, based on his own experience, that a chat room moderator would screen for and exclude underage participants.

C. DISORDERLY CONDUCT

1. Indecent Acts

> **173. (1) Every one who wilfully does an indecent act**
>
> **(a) in a public place in the presence of one or more persons, or**
>
> **(b) in any place, with intent thereby to insult or offend any person,**
> **is guilty of an offence punishable on summary conviction.**

The essential elements of this offence are the following:

a. Indecency

As mentioned earlier, indecency is not defined in the Code. Generally, it refers to a violation of community standards of decency or good taste. A common example of an indecent act is when a person exposes his or her "private parts" (which is indecent exposure). But simply being nude in public, such as lying nude on a public beach, is not an indecent act, although the person could be charged under s. 174. Some courts have held that an indecent act must have an element of "moral turpitude." This is why, for example, a person who for a joke ran naked through a football stadium was acquitted of a charge under this section.[50]

b. Wilfulness

The term "wilfully" has the same meaning as in most other sections of the Code: to do an act purposely and with a criminal intention.

49 (2009), 248 C.C.C. (3d) 337 (Alta. C.A.).
50 *R. v. Springer* (1975), 24 C.C.C. (2d) 56 (Sask. Dist. Ct.).

c. Place of the Act

The act may occur in a public place. Courts have interpreted "public place" broadly as meaning a place where the public is able to view the indecent act. This position is consistent with the purpose of the section, which is not to prohibit "indecent acts" but to prohibit indecent acts that might be upsetting to the public that is exposed to them. In *R. v. Buhay*,[51] a man, while standing in the doorway of his home, exposed his genitals to two 13-year-old boys who were outside on the street between three and seven metres away. The accused was convicted. In contrast, in *R. v. Sloane*,[52] a prostitute performed an indecent act on a man in a car that was parked in an empty parking lot in a dark area. The act was seen by an officer who had been following the car and who walked up to the car to look through the windows. The appeal court found that the indecent act had not taken place in public.

In *R. v. Clark*,[53] the court held that a living room is not a public place. The accused masturbated near his uncovered living room window. His neighbours saw him and called police. The accused was arrested and charged under sections 173(1)(a) and 173(1)(b). The trial judged acquitted him on the s. 173(1)(b) charge but convicted him under 173(1)(a), finding that the accused had converted his living room into a public place. On appeal to the Supreme Court of Canada, the Court held that the accused's living room was not a public place stating:

> The living room of his private home was not a place "to which the public [had] access as of right or by invitation, express or implied." . . . I do not believe it contemplates the ability of those who are neither entitled nor invited to enter a place to see or hear from the outside, through uncovered windows or open doors, what is transpiring within. . . . (T)the trial judge thus erred in concluding that the appellant's living room had been "converted" by him into a public place simply because he could be seen through his living room window and, though he did not know this, was being watched by Mr. and Mrs. S. from the privacy of their own bedroom 90 to 150 feet away.[54]

d. The Presence of One or More Persons

Court decisions agree that where there is more than one participant in the act, no one participant counts as being the person in the presence of whom the act is performed. In other words, there must be a third, non-participating person before whom the indecent act is performed.[55]

Similarly, a police officer was not considered a "person" in *R. v. Hastings*.[56] The court held that urinating on a public street at night, when there is no exposure to any person other than a police officer, is not an offence.

In *R. v. Follett*,[57] the accused performed an indecent act in a public washroom with another man. The act was captured on a surveillance video. The court held that the act was not performed in the presence of others. The videotape could not substitute for a person.

If the indecent act is done with the specific intent to insult or offend any person, under s. 173(1)(b) it makes no difference where the act occurs. In other words, the indecent act may occur in any place, public or private; but it must be shown that the accused did the act in order to insult or offend someone.

---

51   (1986), 30 C.C.C. (3d) 30 (Man. C.A.).
52   (1994), 89 C.C.C. (3d) 97 (Ont. C.A.); leave to appeal to the Supreme Court of Canada refused 91 C.C.C. (3d) vi.
53   (2005), 193 C.C.C. (3d) 289 at 293 (Ont. C.A.).
54   Ibid.
55   See, for example, *Sloane, supra* note 52.
56   (1947), 90 C.C.C. 150 (N.B.C.A.).
57   (1994), 98 C.C.C. (3d) 493 (Nfld. C.A.); leave to appeal to S.C.C. refused 101 C.C.C. (3d) vi.

2. Causing a Disturbance

175. (1) Every one who

(a) not being in a dwelling-house, causes a disturbance in or near a public place,

(i) by fighting, screaming, shouting, swearing, singing or using insulting or obscene language,

(ii) by being drunk, or

(iii) by impeding or molesting other persons, . . .

is guilty of an offence punishable on summary conviction.

The essential elements of this offence are these: the accused was not in a dwelling-house; he or she caused a disturbance; the disturbance occurred in a public place or near a public place; and the disturbance was caused by conduct such as fighting or screaming, or by the person being drunk, or impeding or molesting other persons.

a. Dwelling-house

Dwelling-house is defined in s. 2 as

the whole or any part of a building or structure that is kept or occupied as a permanent or temporary residence, and includes

(a) a building within the curtilage of a dwelling-house that is connected to it by a doorway or by a covered and enclosed passageway, and

(b) a unit that is designed to be mobile and to be used as a permanent or temporary residence and that is being used as such a residence.

In *R. v. Jones*,[58] an issue was whether the administrative office of a university was a dwelling-house. Students at Simon Fraser University conducted a "sit-in" at the university. They occupied the administrative office and prevented officials and administrators from entering the office. They were charged under s. 175(1)(a)(iii) with causing a disturbance by impeding other persons. The lawyer for the students argued that the sit-in occurred in a dwelling-house within the meaning of the definition in s. 2 and that, therefore, no offence was committed. The lawyer argued that, for legal purposes such as being sued, the "residence" of a university is its administrative office. The court agreed that for certain legal purposes, but not for the purpose of s. 175, the administrative office is the residence of the university. The lawyer also argued that because the students brought and used sleeping bags and food, they used the premises as their temporary residence within the meaning of the definition in s. 2. The court disagreed, stating that trespassers cannot turn university property into a dwelling-house by wrongfully occupying it.

In *R. v. Campbell*,[59] the accused was charged with causing a disturbance in a public place by using insulting or obscene language. He was in the hallway and TV room of a hospital when the incident occurred. The trial court dismissed the charge on the grounds that the TV room and hallway were dwelling places. An appeal court disagreed, holding that although the rooms of the patients were probably dwelling places, a TV room and hallway where the public could come and go were not dwelling places.

---

58   (1970), 1 C.C.C. (2d) 232 (B.C.C.A.).
59   (1980), 22 C.R. (3d) 219 (Alta. Q.B.).

b. Disturbance

The meaning of "disturbance" was discussed by the Supreme Court of Canada in *R. v. Lohnes*.[60] The accused was charged with causing a disturbance because he had, on two occasions, while standing on his verandah, shouted obscenities to his neighbour, with whom he had a long-running dispute. The neighbour filed a complaint, and the accused was convicted at trial. On appeal to the Supreme Court of Canada, the issue was whether the prohibited act (shouting obscenities) had caused a disturbance. The Court noted that the meaning of "disturbance" can range from something innocuous, such as a jarring colour, to incidents of violence or apprehension for physical safety. The Court said that its task was to decide where to draw the line for a disturbance that creates criminal liability. In doing so, the Court had to consider two conflicting values: the individual right to sing, shout, or otherwise express oneself; and the right of the community to peace and tranquility. In looking at previous decisions, the Court noted that "emotional upset" had not been sufficient cause for an act to be considered a "disturbance" for criminal liability. For example, in *R. v. C.D.*,[61] where the accused shouted obscenities and rammed his car into the complainant's car, reducing the latter's wife to tears, the appeal court overturned a conviction for causing a disturbance because the emotional upset experienced by the complainant and his wife was not enough to constitute a disturbance. Similarly, in *R. v. Wolgram*,[62] shouting obscenities in a barroom was not a disturbance, because no one appeared to be disturbed and there was no interference with the ordinary use of a public place. On the other hand, in *R. v. Swinimer*,[63] the accused's fighting, shouting, and obscene language in front of his residence interfered with the usual activities of his neighbours; for example, one neighbour had to return to her children's bedroom to calm them down. In *R. v. Chikoski*,[64] shouting obscenities at an officer caused 200 nearby workers to stop work to watch the dispute.

The Court, in *Lohnes*, concluded that the conduct must cause a disturbance that creates an interference with the ordinary and customary use by the public of the place in question. There must be more than mere mental or emotional annoyance or disruption. "By addressing 'disturbance' in a public context, Parliament signaled that its objective was not the protection of individuals from emotional upset, but protection of the public from disorder calculated to interfere with the public's normal activities."[65] There was no evidence of a disturbance in the use of the premises in question, and no evidence that the conduct of the complainant or anyone else in the area was affected or disturbed by the conduct of the accused. The Court allowed the appeal and quashed the convictions.

L05 D. SOLICITING AND PROCURING FOR PROSTITUTION

Prostitution, which is engaging in sexual activity for payment, is not an offence. The Code controls prostitution in three other ways. First, to solicit in public is an offence; second, to engage in "pimping"—that is, in procuring a person to be a prostitute—is an offence; third, there are several offences related to keeping a common bawdy-house (house of prostitution).

---

60 (1992), 69 C.C.C. (3d) 289 (S.C.C.).
61 (1973), 13 C.C.C. (2d) 206 (N.B.C.A.).
62 (1976), 29 C.C.C. (2d) 536 (B.C.S.C.).
63 (1978), 40 C.C.C. (2d) 432 (N.S.C.A.).
64 (1973), 14 C.C.C. (2d) 38 (Ont. Prov. Ct.).
65 *Lohnes, supra* note 58 at 297.

Section 197 states that "prostitute means a person of either sex who engages in prostitution." Until this definition was added, there had been conflicting decisions on whether a man could be a prostitute. Note also that the pronoun "he" in these offences, and in all parts of the Code, refers to male and female persons (Interpretation Act, R.S.C. 1985, c. I-21).

1. Procuring for Prostitution

Section 212 sets out the offences involving procuring:

212. (1) Every one who

    (a) procures, attempts to procure or solicits a person to have illicit sexual intercourse with another person, whether in or out of Canada,

    (b) inveigles or entices a person who is not a prostitute to a common bawdy-house . . . for the purpose of . . . prostitution,

    (c) knowingly conceals a person in a common bawdy-house . . .

    (d) procures or attempts to procure a person to become, whether in or out of Canada, a prostitute, . . .

    (g) procures a person to enter or leave Canada, for the purpose of prostitution, . . .

    (h) for the purposes of gain, exercises control, direction or influence over the movements of a person in such manner as to show that he is aiding, abetting or compelling that person to engage in or carry on prostitution with any person or generally,

    (i) applies or administers to a person or causes that person to take any drug, intoxicating liquor, matter or thing with intent to stupefy or overpower that person in order thereby to enable any person to have illicit sexual intercourse with that person, or

    (j) lives wholly or in part on the avails of prostitution of another person, . . .

a. Prostitution

"Prostitution" is not defined in the Code, but it has been given a wide meaning by the courts. In *R . v. Lantay*,[66] the Ontario Court of Appeal held that prostitution is not limited to sexual intercourse: It also includes a woman offering herself for money as a participant in physical acts of indecency for the sexual gratification of men. This case involved masturbation performed on customers of a massage parlour. The court held that this conduct amounted to prostitution. The Supreme Court of Canada has stated that there is little dispute as to the basic definition of prostitution: "that being the exchange of sexual services of one person in return for payment by another."[67]

b. Prostitution under the Age of 18

The offences in s. 212(1) are indictable, and the maximum penalty is a ten-year prison term. However, this section contains more severe penalties for cases in which the prostitute is under the age of 18. If the accused is convicted under s. 212(1)(j) of living on the avails of a prostitute

66   [1966] 3 C.C.C. 270 (Ont. C.A.).
67   Ref re Criminal Code ss. 193 and 195.1(1)(c) (1990), 56 C.C.C. (3d) 65 (S.C.C.).

who is under 18, the maximum penalty increases to fourteen years imprisonment and the minimum is two years. In addition, a minimum penalty of five years will be imposed if the person not only lives on the avails of a prostitute who is under 18 but also

(i) for the purposes of profit aids, abets, counsels or compels the person under that age to engage in prostitution, and

(ii) uses, threatens to use or attempts to use violence, intimidation or coercion in relation to the person under that age. (s. 212(2.1))

Under s. 212(4), it is an offence to obtain or communicate for the purpose of obtaining, for consideration, the sexual services of a person under 18. The maximum penalty is five years' imprisonment; the minimum is six months. "Consideration" means money or something else of value.

c. Illicit Sexual Intercourse

The Supreme Court of Canada said, in *Deutsch v. the Queen*,[68] that the term "illicit sexual intercourse" in s. 212(1)(a) means sexual intercourse that is not authorized or sanctioned by lawful marriage. The accused was interviewing a prospective employee and told her that if she took the job she might be required to have sexual intercourse with clients. She was also told that she could make a lot of money doing this. The Court held that the accused could be convicted of the offence of procuring if the Crown could prove that the employer intended to induce or persuade the woman to seek employment that would require her to have intercourse with clients, and that during the interview the employer did, in fact, offer her a large financial reward for having intercourse with clients.

LO6 ### d. Living on the Avails of Prostitution

In *R. v. Celebrity Enterprises Ltd.*,[69] the British Columbia Court of Appeal considered s. 212(1)(j), which refers to living on the avails of prostitution. The court held that the Crown must prove that the accused received some of the proceeds of the prostitute's earnings, or that those proceeds somehow supported the accused's living. The accused were operators of a nightclub that was frequented by prostitutes. Their convictions for living on the avails of prostitution were overturned because indirect benefits, such as admission fees to the club, could not be considered "avails of prostitution."

In *R. v. Patterson*,[70] the court found that the accused could be found guilty of living on the avails of prostitution without having received any money directly. Patterson and his two accomplices, Briscoe and Roberts, forced J.G., a teenaged female, to work as a prostitute. The three worked together. They controlled her movements and they took her money. Patterson argued that he should not have been found guilty of living on the avails of prostitution because there was no evidence that the appellant had received any of J.G.'s earnings. In dismissing his appeal, the court stated:

> The verdict . . . is fully supported by the evidence that the three accused, acting in concert but with the appellant as leader, controlled the complainant's movements and forced her to act as a prostitute for their financial benefit. On the evidence, it was open to the jury to find the appellant guilty of living on the avails of prostitution as a party to the offence. While

68 (1986), 27 C.C.C. (3d) 385 (S.C.C.).
69 (1978), 41 C.C.C. (3d) 540 (B.C.C.A).
70 (2003), 174 C.C.C. (3d) 193.

under the appellant's control, J.G. gave Briscoe $200 earned for her first act of prostitution and $1,000 the next day when her regular customer paid her for oral sex and intercourse. Alternatively, the jury was entitled to find the appellant guilty of the offence when Roberts received money from the complainant on the basis that they had acted in concert.[71]

Section 212(3) creates a mandatory presumption that a person is living on the avails of prostitution when the person is living with or is habitually in the company of a prostitute:

(3) Evidence that a person lives with or is habitually in the company of a prostitute or lives in a common bawdy-house, is in the absence of evidence to the contrary, proof that the person lives on the avails of prostitution . . .

This section was challenged in *R. v. Downey*[72] as a violation of the presumption of innocence under the Charter. The Supreme Court of Canada agreed that the section is an infringement but held that it is justifiable under s. 1 of the Charter.[73] The objective of the legislation—to deal with the "social evil" of pimping—is sufficiently important to override the presumption of innocence. The section also meets the proportionality test. There is a rational connection between the fact and the presumption—that is, it is reasonable to presume that persons who have close connections to prostitutes are living on the avails of prostitution. This presumption recognizes the well-documented reluctance of prostitutes to testify against their pimps. As well, all an accused must do to rebut the presumption is raise a reasonable doubt. The Court noted that women who are prostitutes are often abused and exploited by their pimps. This presumption is an attempt to protect them by eliminating the necessity of having them testify.

A decision of the Ontario Court of Appeal[74] has held that a charge of "living on the avails" means that the accused "was living parasitically on the earnings of the prostitute for his own advantage." So, where the accused and the prostitute are in a legitimate and normal living arrangement as spouses or roommates, and share living expenses, the accused cannot be said to be "living on the avails."

In *R. v. Barrow,*[75] the accused, who ran an escort agency, argued that she did not have a parasitic relationship with the escorts because her relationship with the escorts was supportive rather than exploitative. She provided services that allowed the women to remain off the streets in relative safety. The escorts were not forced to take a particular job, nor to perform any sexual acts. She provided advice and, in some cases, friendship. The Ontario Court of Appeal rejected her argument and concluded that the element of parasitism was found in the fact that she was in the business of rendering services to the escorts because they were prostitutes. Her occupation was parasitic in that it would not have existed if the escorts were not prostitutes. The fact that on some occasions the escorts did not provide sexual services simply meant that the accused did not live wholly on the avails of prostitution.

In *Bedford v. Canada (Attorney General),*[76] the Ontario Court of Appeal held that the prohibition on living on the avails of prostitution is unconstitutional. The court found that the prohibition was overly broad and grossly disproportionate to the extent that it criminalized non-exploitative commercial relationships between prostitutes and other people. The court stated that the objective of the prohibition is to prevent the exploitation of prostitutes by

---

71   Ibid. at 206.
72   (1992), 72 C.C.C. (3d) 1 (S.C.C.).
73   The Court used the test set out in *R. v. Oakes*; see Chapter 2, page 26.
74   *R. v. Grilo* (1991), 64 C.C.C. (3d) 53 (Ont. C.A.). See also *R. v. Bramwell* (1993), 86 C.C.C. (3d) (B.C.C.A.).
75   (2001), 155 C.C.C. (3d) 362 (Ont. C.A.); leave to appeal to S.C.C. refused 160 C.C.C. (3d) vi.
76   (2012) O.J. No. 1296 (Ont. C.A.); this case has been appealed to the Supreme Court of Canada. This case also dealt with the constitutionality of s. 210 (bawdy-houses) and s. 213(1)(c) (communicating for the purpose of prostitution), discussed on page 186.

pimps; however, it applies generally to people who provide goods or services to prostitutes, such as managers, drivers, and security personnel. The court "read-in" words of limitation to s. 212(1)(j) so that the prohibition applied only to those who lived on the avails of prostitution in circumstances of exploitation.

2. Soliciting

Section 213 creates the offences concerning the public solicitation of sex:

> **213. (1) Every person who in a public place or in any place open to public view**
>
> **(a) stops or attempts to stop any motor vehicle,**
>
> **(b) impedes the free flow of pedestrian or vehicular traffic or ingress to or egress from premises adjacent to that place, or**
>
> **(c) stops or attempts to stop any person or in any manner communicates or attempts to communicate with any person for the purpose of engaging in prostitution or of obtaining the sexual services of a prostitute is guilty of an offence punishable on summary conviction.**

This section makes it an offence for both the prostitute and the person seeking the services of a prostitute to communicate in public. This section of the Code has been the subject of several challenges under the Charter as a violation of fundamental justice under s. 7 and freedom of expression under s. 2(b). The Supreme Court of Canada considered three cases that were being appealed on this issue at the same time.[77] All of the judges held that s. 213(c) violates the guarantee of freedom of expression. A majority of the judges went on to hold that this section is a reasonable limitation under s. 1 of the Charter. The objective of the law, the Court held, is to prevent the nuisance caused by the public purchase of sex. The Court considered the street congestion, noise, and oral harassment of non-participants in urban environments as part of the social nuisance caused by this conduct. A majority of the judges also agreed that the offence does not violate a principle of fundamental justice under s. 7. A minority disagreed, stating that where communication is a protected right (i.e., freedom of expression) and prostitution itself is legal, the possibility of imprisonment for this offence is too drastic a response. In other words, a person can be imprisoned (i.e., denied liberty under s. 7) without the principle of fundamental justice being followed; the penalty must be in proportion to the offence.

In *Bedford*,[78] the Ontario Court of Appeal held that the prohibition on communicating for the purpose of prostitution does not violate the principles of fundamental justice. The court disagreed with the lower court's view that the impact of the prohibition is grossly disproportionate to the legislative objective (the social nuisance associated with street prostitution) because it deprives street prostitutes of the opportunity to screen customers, which enhances their safety.

L07 E. DISORDERLY HOUSE AND COMMON BAWDY-HOUSE

1. Disorderly House

"Disorderly house" is a general term that refers to a common bawdy-house, a common gaming house, or a common betting house. It is an offence to "keep" a disorderly house, to be "found in" a disorderly house, or to "knowingly permit" a place to be used as a disorderly house.

---

77   Ref re Criminal Code, *supra* note 67.
78   *Bedford, supra* note 76a.

The term "keeper" is defined in s. 197:

"keeper" includes a person who

(a) **is an owner or occupier of a place,**

(b) **assists or acts on behalf of an owner or occupier of a place,**

(c) **appears to be, or to assist or act on behalf of an owner or occupier of a place,**

(d) **has the care or management of a place, or**

(e) **uses a place permanently or temporarily, with or without the consent of the owner or occupier.**

The Supreme Court of Canada has held that a person cannot be convicted of keeping a disorderly house simply because he or she falls within the above description. In general, to be a keeper, a person must participate in the wrongful use of the disorderly house.[79]

If a person is "found in" a disorderly house, then it is up to that person to show some evidence that he or she had a lawful excuse for being there; for example, a furnace repairer would have a lawful excuse if present in the house to repair the furnace.

If the owner or someone else having charge or control of a place is charged with "knowingly permitting" the place to be used as a disorderly house, then that person will be guilty only if he or she had knowledge of how the place was being used. A landlord who does not know that one of his or her apartments is being used for illegal betting could not be criminally liable.

This section of the chapter deals with common bawdy-house. Common gaming house and common betting house are discussed in the online supplemental material for this book.

2. Common Bawdy-house

A common bawdy-house is defined in s. 197(1) as a place that is kept or occupied or resorted to by one or more persons for the purpose of prostitution or acts of indecency. It is an offence to be an inmate or to be found in, without lawful excuse, a common bawdy-house. It is also an offence for an owner of a place or someone otherwise having control of a place to knowingly permit the place to be used as a common bawdy-house (s. 210(1)).

The Supreme Court, in *R. v. Labaye*,[80] set out the two requirements that must be met to establish indecent criminal acts under this section. In this case, the accused was charged with keeping a common bawdy-house contrary to s. 210(1). He owned a club that permitted couples and others to meet each other for group sex. In order to enter the club, a person had to be a member. They were interviewed to ensure that they were aware of the nature of the activities that went on in the club, and they were required to pay an annual membership fee. A locked apartment (the accused's apartment) on the third floor of the club was made available for persons wishing to engage in group sexual activities. This area could be accessed using a keypad, and members were supplied with the code. This was the only place where group sex took place. Mattresses were scattered about the floor of the apartment, and there people engaged in acts of cunnilingus, masturbation, fellatio, and penetration. Undercover police officers, who joined the club as members, visited the club over a period of time. They observed various group sexual activities, including instances of a single woman engaged in sex with several men, while other men watched and masturbated.

79 *R. v. Kerim*, [1963] 1 C.C.C. 233 (S.C.C.).
80 (2005), 203 C.C.C. (3d) 170 (S.C.C.).

At trial, the judge found that the third floor of the bar was a public place because it was readily accessed by the members, and that the acts were indecent because they were "degrading and dehumanizing, desensitized sexuality, exploited women, and predisposed people to act in an anti-social manner."[81] The accused was convicted. On appeal to the Supreme Court of Canada, the Court stated:

> *Indecent criminal conduct will be established where the Crown proves beyond a reasonable doubt the following two requirements:*
>
> 1. *That, by its nature, the conduct at issue causes harm or presents a significant risk of harm to individuals or society in a way that undermines or threatens to undermine a value reflected in and thus formally endorsed through the Constitution or similar fundamental laws by, for example:*
>
>   (a) *confronting members of the public with conduct that significantly interferes with their autonomy and liberty; or*
>
>   (b) *predisposing others to anti-social behaviour; or*
>
>   (c) *physically or psychologically harming persons involved in the conduct, and*
>
> 2. *That the harm or risk of harm is of a degree that is incompatible with the proper functioning of society.*
>
> *As the above makes clear, the categories of harm capable of satisfying the first branch of the inquiry are not closed, nor is any one of the listed categories in itself an integral part of the definition of harm. For example, predisposition to anti-social behaviour, while central to this Court's analysis in Butler, is but one illustration of the type of harm that undermines or threatens to undermine one of society's formally recognized values.*
>
> *This test, applied objectively and on the basis of evidence in successive cases as they arise, is directed to articulating legal standards that enhance the ability of persons engaged in or facilitating sexual activities to ascertain the boundary between non-criminal conduct and criminal conduct. In this way, the basic requirements of the criminal law of fair notice to potential offenders and clear enforcement standards to police will, it is hoped, be satisfied.[82]*

In quashing the conviction, the Court found that entry to the club and participation in the activities was voluntary. No one was forced to do anything or watch anything. No one was paid for sex. While men considerably outnumbered women on the occasions when the police visited, there was no suggestion that any of the women were there involuntarily, or that they did not willingly engage in the acts of group sex.[83] In addition, the sexual acts at issue were conducted behind closed doors and accessed only by members in possession of the proper numerical code. A number of steps were taken to ensure that members of the public who might find the conduct inappropriate did not see the activities; pre-membership interviews were conducted to screen out persons not sharing the same interests, and to advise others; and a doorman controlled access to the principal door.[84]

In a similar case, *R. v. Kouri*,[85] the accused was convicted of keeping a common bawdy-house under s. 210(1). He operated a nightclub where the doorman would ask each couple as

---

81   Ibid. at 171.
82   Ibid. at 189.
83   Ibid. at 175.
84   Ibid. at 190.
85   (2005), 203 C.C.C. (3d) 217; aff'g (2005), 191 C.C.C. (3d) 42 (S.C.C.).

they entered if they were "liberated." If they answered "yes," they were charged a $6.00 fee and allowed to enter. Every half hour, a black, translucent curtain closed around the dance floor while slow music played for 8 to 12 minutes. At these times, up to seventy people, comprising almost eighty percent of the clientele would be on the dance floor engaging in group sex activities. These included sexual caresses, masturbation, fellatio, and penetration. While the curtain served to separate the dance floor from the rest of the premises, it did not prevent observation of the sexual activities from the seating area of the club.

The Quebec Court of Appeal overturned the conviction. The Supreme Court of Canada dismissed the Crown's appeal, stating:

> *The main issue at trial was whether the respondent had the requisite* mens rea, *or criminal intent, to be found guilty of keeping a bawdy-house. . . . Like the majority of the Court of Appeal, I am satisfied that the controls at the door, put in context, were sufficiently clear and comprehensive. Only couples were admitted. The club's policy required the doorman to ask each couple whether they were "liberated." The exterior of the building displayed large posters of partially undressed dancers. All this provided ample indication that sexually explicit activity was to be expected inside.*[86]

To be convicted of keeping a common bawdy-house, as well as participating in the illegal activity, the accused must have some degree of control over the care and management of the premises. In *R. v. Corbeil*,[87] the accused was a masseuse at a massage parlour that offered masturbation to its clients. She would keep half the fee and turn the other half over to the owners of the parlour. Also, it was up to the masseuses to keep a record of the clients. The Supreme Court of Canada held that, although she occupied a space and used it, she did not exercise the requisite care and control necessary for the offence.

One isolated act of prostitution is not enough to make a place a bawdy-house. There must be frequent resort to, or habitual use of, the place for purposes of prostitution or indecent acts. In *Paterson v. R.*,[88] two women went with three plain-clothes police officers to a suburban home for the purpose of prostitution. On their arrival, the two women went to another part of the house. They later returned wearing nothing but their underwear. At this point, the officers disclosed their identity and charged the two women with keeping a common bawdy-house. The Supreme Court of Canada held that to be convicted of "keeping," a person must frequently or habitually use the premises for the purposes of prostitution. The Court found the women not guilty because there was no evidence that the home had been used for prostitution on any other occasion.

A similar decision was reached in *R. v. Evans, Lee and Woodhouse*,[89] which involved a house that was being used for a stag party. Three women had sexual intercourse with a number of men at the party and were paid for their services. The house had never been used before for prostitution. The issue was whether the large number of acts of intercourse that occurred in one evening were enough to convict the women and two male occupants of keeping a common bawdy-house. The court held that they were not guilty because the use of the house on one evening did not amount to frequent or habitual use of the premises for prostitution. In *R. v. Tardif*,[90] as well, the Quebec Court of Appeal held that where there was evidence that on one day five men attended a massage parlour and were offered sexual services, this was not sufficient to establish frequent or habitual use.

---

86   Ibid. at 224.
87   (1991), 64 C.C.C. (3d) 272 (S.C.C.).
88   (1968), 2 C.C.C. 247 (S.C.C.).
89   (1973), 11 C.C.C. (2d) 130 (Ont. C.A.).
90   (1995), 97 C.C.C. (3d) 381 (Que. C.A.).

The Ontario Court of Appeal has held that any defined space—even a parking lot—can be a bawdy-house if acts of prostitution take place there. However, persons cannot be convicted of keeping a common bawdy-house where they were present in a parking lot on a number of occasions but exercised no control over the lot and had no interest in the lot as owners, tenants, or licensees.[91]

The Supreme Court of Canada has upheld the validity of the offences of keeping, being found in, and being an inmate of a common bawdy-house as not being violations of freedom of expression or liberty.[92]

In *Bedford v. Canada (Attorney General)*,[93] the Ontario Court of Appeal held that the bawdy-house prohibition is unconstitutional. The court found that it is overly broad because it captures conduct that is unlikely to lead to the problems Parliament intended to combat (neighbourhood disruption or disorder and risks to public health and safety). In particular, the prohibition makes it illegal for a single prostitute to operate discreetly by herself in her own premises. The court also found that the impact of the prohibition is grossly disproportionate to the legislative objective because the safest way to sell sex is for a prostitute to work indoors in a location under her control. The court suspended its declaration of the invalidity of the bawdy-house provisions for 12 months to give Parliament an opportunity to change the provisions so that they will be compliant with the Charter.

---

91 *R. v. Pierce* (1982), 66 C.C.C. (2d) 388 (Ont. C.A.).
92 Ref re Criminal Code, *supra* note 67.
93 *Bedford, supra* note 76a.

Questions for Review and Discussion

1. List the offences concerning sexual activity and children. Indicate the age the victim must be for each offence to occur.

2. Give an example of a person in a position of authority or trust under s. 153. Make a list of the factors you think put a person in a position of authority or trust, or in a position of dependency.

3. **a.** When is consent not a defence to offences involving sexual conduct and children?
   b. What are the exceptions to situations where consent is not a defence?
   c. Why do these exceptions exist?

4. **a.** What has become the most important test for determining whether material is obscene?
   b. Explain the nature of the test.

5. Explain the elements of the offence involving child pornography.

6. What is the test for deciding whether a theatrical performance is immoral, indecent, or obscene?

7. **a.** What are the elements of the offence of causing a disturbance?
   b. How has the Supreme Court of Canada defined the term "disturbance" for this offence?

8. L. was charged with sexual touching under s. 151 of the Code. The complainant was under 14 at the time of the incident, so even though she consented, her consent was not a defence unless the exception in s. 150.1(2) applied. The accused was over 12 and under 16 years of age and less than two years older than the complainant. The

only issue for the court was whether the accused was in a position of authority or trust toward the complainant. Six years earlier, at the age of 10, the accused had been placed in the home of the complainant as a foster child. Sexual activity began between the two about seven months after the accused came to the home. The complainant testified that she said nothing to her parents because the accused was stronger, and because she did not know what the accused would do and did not think her mother would believe her. The sexual activity progressed, and they eventually had intercourse. The final incident that led to the charge occurred when the complainant was 12 and she realized that she might become pregnant. She told the accused that they must stop, but he would not accept this. They were finally discovered when she confided to her best friend, who then told her mother.

The trial judge found that the accused was in a position of trust and that, therefore, the defence of consent was not available to him. He was convicted. The accused has appealed his conviction. Make a decision in this case. Was the accused in a position of trust? See *R. v. L.(D.B.)* (1995), 25 O.R. (3d) 649 (Ont. C.A.).

9. **a.** Cameron was the manager of an art gallery. She was charged with exposing to public view seven obscene drawings in her gallery. She collected the drawings from other galleries and from the artists themselves. She arranged for the display of the drawings in her gallery. She argued that she did not know the drawings were obscene. Should Cameron be convicted? See *R. v. Cameron*, [1966] 4 C.C.C. 273 (Ont. C.A.); aff'd (1967), 2 C.C.C. (2d) 195 (S.C.C.).

b. Britnell, the operator of a bookstore, was charged with selling obscene books. The accused carried a stock of nearly 250,000 books in his store. The ordering of the copies of obscene

books was done by a clerk, not the accused. The accused stated that he was unaware of the presence of the books in his store. Should Britnell be convicted? See *R. v. Britnell* (1912), 20 C.C.C. 85 (Ont. C.A.).

c. Are your decisions in the above two cases the same or different? Explain.

10. Do you agree or disagree with the Supreme Court decision in *Butler* (see page 171)? Do you believe that the types of pornography identified by the Supreme Court of Canada as being harmful to society are harmful? Do you agree that s. 163 is a reasonable limitation to freedom of expression? Discuss your position.

11. Daniels is charged under s. 163.1(2) with possessing child pornography. He paid a subscription fee entitling him to access to a computer "bulletin board" from which he could download files, which included pornographic material. The bulletin board was controlled by a systems operator. To download files containing child pornography, Daniels had to make a special request to the systems operator. There was no doubt that Daniels knew exactly what he was ordering because the contents were described in graphic detail. He began downloading child pornography to his computer but he stopped the downloading process before it was completed by using a "skip file" function on his computer. None of the pornographic images was found on his computer hard drive. Should Daniels be convicted? See *R. v. Daniels* (2004), 191 C.C.C. (3d) 393 (Nfld. & Lab. C.A.).

12. Explain the ways that the Criminal Code controls prostitution.

13. Name three offences that can be committed in relation to disorderly houses.

14. How has the Supreme Court of Canada defined the term "indecency"?

15. What conduct is required for prostitution?

16. **a.** Discuss the decision of the Supreme Court of Canada in upholding s. 213(c). Do you agree or disagree with the decision?
    b. Some people have suggested prostitution should be legalized and "red light" districts established. Discuss the pros and cons of these ideas.

17. At 1:00 a.m., a police officer was proceeding in an unmarked vehicle when he observed Kimberly, whom he believed to be a prostitute, hitchhiking. He testified that it was his practice to stop and see if he could make an arrest if he saw someone on the street he recognized as a prostitute. He stated that he saw her hitchhiking, looking at the passing vehicles, but he did not see anybody else stop. The officer said he "drove up and asked her how much, and she said $40 for a blow job, so I arrested her for prostitution." Kimberly was charged under s. 213(1)(c) on the basis that she attempted to stop a person for the purpose of engaging in prostitution. Should she be convicted? See *R. v. Lane* (2000), 33 C.R. (5th) 107.

18. The accused was the keeper of Madame de Sade's House of Erotica, a house which offered women (mistresses) for hire for the purposes of sado-masochistic activities involving "domination," "bondage," and "erotica sessions." She argued that the sado-masochistic activities were not about sex, but about pain and humiliation. She testified that the rule for all of the rooms in the house was that sex was forbidden; that is, no intercourse, no oral sex, and no masturbation by a mistress. Should she be convicted under s. 210(1) of keeping a common bawdy-house? See *R. v. Bedford* (2000), 143 C.C.C. (3d) 311 (Ont. C.A.); leave to appeal to S.C.C. refused 147 C.C.C. (3d) vi.

19. The accused operated the Pussy Cat Club where, in exchange for money, a woman would dance nude for the customer in a private room. The customer was permitted to be nude and would usually masturbate. Customers were warned before they entered about what activities took place. No physical contact was allowed between the customer and the dancer. The accused were charged with keeping a common bawdy-house. Should they be convicted? See *R. v. Tremblay* (1993), 84 C.C.C. (3d) 97 (S.C.C.).

20. Elena, age 20, came to Canada from Romania to work as a stripper. Canadian immigration officials gave her a visa and a work permit. Saftu, an agent in Toronto, made the necessary arrangements for her. Her understanding was that in addition to stripping at clubs booked by Saftu, she could make extra money by "table dancing." Saftu paid her airfare to Toronto, which she was expected to repay at a rate of $300 or $400 per week. He also paid for the hotel where she stayed for the first week she was in Toronto, which she was also expected to repay. She was also required to pay Saftu $110 per week as an agency fee. Saftu booked her into a club that had a separate VIP lounge, where strippers performed "private dances." Saftu explained to her that she could make more money doing private dances. Private dances involved physical contact with the customers and cost twice as much as table dancing. Women providing a private dance were expected to be nude after the first song. What occurred after the first song was for individual dancers to decide; however, private dances generally involved the nude dancers moving around, and touching, rubbing, and lying or sitting on the customers. There was considerable pressure on Elena to do private dances. Saftu was charged with three offences under s. 212(1)(g), (h), and (j). Should he be convicted? See *R. v. Saftu*, [2001] O.J. No. 3046 (O.C.J.).

CHAPTER 8

Murder, Manslaughter, and Infanticide
PART VIII OF THE CODE

Key points explained in this chapter are

LO1 the rules of causation that apply to homicide;

LO2 the difference between culpable and non-culpable homicide;

LO3 when a culpable homicide is murder;

LO4 the classification of murder for sentencing;

LO5 the offence of attempted murder;

LO6 when a culpable homicide is manslaughter;

LO7 when murder may be reduced to manslaughter; and

LO8 how infanticide can be an offence and also a partial defence to murder.

This chapter defines homicide, distinguishes non-culpable from culpable homicide, and examines the elements of the three types of culpable homicide.

A. HOMICIDE

Homicide is the causing of death of a human being. Not all homicides are crimes, however—only those which are culpable. Section 222 defines homicide and sets out the three types of culpable homicide: murder, manslaughter, and infanticide:

> **222. (1) A person commits homicide when, directly or indirectly, by any means, he causes the death of a human being.**
>
> **(2) Homicide is culpable or not culpable.**
>
> **(3) Homicide that is not culpable is not an offence.**
>
> **(4) Culpable homicide is murder or manslaughter, or infanticide.**

1. Meaning of "Human Being"

Since homicide is the causing of the death of a human being, it is important to know when, under criminal law, a human being comes into existence. Section 223 states:

223. (1) A child becomes a human being within the meaning of this Act when it has completely proceeded, in a living state, from the body of its mother whether or not

(a) it has breathed,

(b) it has an independent circulation, or

(c) the navel string is severed.

Thus, in the context of criminal law, a fetus (i.e., an unborn child) is not a human being for the purpose of determining whether a homicide has occurred.[1]

Section 223 then goes on to state:

(2) A person commits homicide when he causes injury to a child before or during its birth as a result of which the child dies after becoming a human being.

In other words, under this section it is homicide if injury is caused to a fetus that results in its death after being born. If the fetus dies before being born, then the death is not homicide. In *R. v. Prince*,[2] the accused attacked a woman who was obviously pregnant. The child was born premature and died 19 minutes after birth because of the injuries suffered by the mother. The court held that the accused was responsible for the child's death and convicted him of manslaughter.

Under s. 238, it is an offence, although not culpable homicide, to cause the death of a child in the act of birth before it becomes a human being, unless it is necessary to save the life of the mother.

2. Causation

The *actus reus* of all homicide cases is causing the death of a human being. Recall that Chapter 3 dealt with the concept of causation. The Supreme Court of Canada in *R. v. Smithers*[3] held that the proper test for causation is that the death must be caused by an act that is at least a contributing cause outside the *de minimis* (trivial) range or as rephrased in *R. v. Nette*,[4] a significant contributing cause. This means that even if there are concurrent causes of death, the accused may still be responsible if the accused's act was a significant contributing cause. Similarly, where there is an intervening act, the question is whether the act of the accused continued to be a significant contributing cause or whether the intervening act broke the chain of causation.

In addition to case law that deals with causation, the Code contains several sections that deal with specific homicide situations where questions of causation may arise. These sections deal with intervening causes or where the conduct in question may be considered too remote for liability. These sections override any case law, and a court will rely on the case law only where a factual situation falls outside of these sections.[5]

a. Section 224

224. Where a person, by an act or omission, does any thing that results in the death of a human being, he causes the death of that human being notwithstanding that death from that cause might have been prevented by resorting to proper means.

---

1   See, e.g., *R. v. Sullivan* (1991), 63 C.C.C. (3d) 97 (S.C.C.).
2   (1988), 44 C.C.C. (3d) 510 (Man. C.A.).
3   [1978] 1 S.C.R. 506; also discussed in Chapter 3 at page 38.
4   (2001), 158 C.C.C. (3d) 486 at 522 (S.C.C.); see also a discussion of this case in Chapter 3 at page 39.
5   Ibid. para. 48.

R. v. Tower [6] is one of the few cases that refer to this section. The accused was in an argument with the victim, a neighbour. He hit the victim across the back with a pair of long-handled pruning shears. The police and paramedics arrived, but the victim refused medical treatment. The next day, his roommates tried to get him to go to the hospital, but he refused. A day later, the victim was arrested by the police for an altercation with his roommates. They noticed he was in pain, but he again refused medical treatment. He died overnight in custody. It was discovered that he had a ruptured spleen that led to internal bleeding and caused his death. The accused argued that the actions of the police in not getting medical treatment for the victim and the victim's refusal to get medical treatment were intervening causes. The court rejected this argument, noting that the police did not have the authority to force the victim to have treatment and that the victim refused all attempts to provide him with medical treatment. The court stated that s. 224 reflects the common law rule that failure to seek medical care is not an intervening act that breaks the chain of causation. Tower's conviction for manslaughter was upheld by the court of appeal.

b. Section 225

A similar situation is addressed by s. 225:

> **225. Where a person causes to a human being a bodily injury that is of itself of a dangerous nature and from which death results, he causes the death of that human being notwithstanding that the immediate cause of death is proper or improper treatment that is applied in good faith.**

In *R. v. Kitching*,[7] the accused appealed his conviction for manslaughter. The victim, who was intoxicated and asleep at a bar, was removed by two employees. He was unconscious when they carried him out of the bar and dropped him, face down on the pavement. He suffered severe head injuries and was brain-dead when doctors disconnected the devices maintaining his heart and other organs after removing his kidneys for a transplant. The accused argued that the cause of death was the medical treatment. The court noted that it is not necessary that the accused be the sole or effective cause of death. There may be two or more independent operative causes of death. Although the immediate cause of death was the medical operation, a jury could still find the accused to be responsible for the death. On appeal, his conviction was upheld.

c. Section 226

> **226. Where a person causes to a human being a bodily injury that results in death, he causes the death of that human being notwithstanding that the effect of the bodily injury is only to accelerate his death from a disease or disorder arising from some other cause.**

This section is very similar to the rule in *Smithers*[8] that an accused takes the victim with whatever disabilities the victim has. Thus, when a person injures another in a way that, by itself, would not cause the death, if the injury accelerates the death from other causes, then the person has still committed homicide.

---

6   (2008), 54 C.R. (6th) 338 (N.S.C.A.)
7   (1976), 32 C.C.C. (2d) 159 (Man.C.A.).
8   *Smithers, supra* note 3.

3. Culpable and Non-culpable Homicide

a. Non-culpable Homicide

There are two types of **non-culpable homicide**: justifiable and excusable. Homicide is justifiable if it is authorized or ordered by the law. Examples of justifiable homicide include a soldier killing an enemy during wartime, the execution of a person sentenced to death, and a police officer shooting a person in the course of duty. In these situations, the law may either require the killing, as when a death penalty is imposed, or permit the killing, as when a police officer finds it necessary to kill someone. (Note that Canadian law no longer allows the death penalty.)

Excusable homicide may occur where there was self-defence, or defence of others, or defence of property. These excuses were discussed in Chapter 4.

Homicide may also be excusable where it is accidental. For example, where a person is doing a lawful act and unintentionally and without negligence kills another person, the death is considered accidental and no criminal liability will be attached. However, as is discussed later, where a person is doing an unlawful act and accidentally causes a death, the homicide may be culpable.

b. Culpable Homicide

Culpable homicide refers to homicide that is "morally blameworthy." It is causing death that is not justified or excusable. Culpable homicide consists of three offences: murder, manslaughter, and infanticide. Murder is the most serious type of culpable homicide. Murder requires a specific intent to cause either a person's death or bodily harm knowing it is likely to cause death. Manslaughter, on the other hand, is a general intent crime that is often charged when the accused has recklessly caused a death. For example, Alfred is angry with his child Billy and beats the child severely. Billy dies from the beating. If it is clear that Alfred did not specifically intend to cause Billy's death but only had the general intention to do the act of beating, and was reckless about the consequences of the beating, he will probably be charged with manslaughter and not with murder.

Infanticide is a rarely used offence that only applies to certain situations involving newborn children.

Before deciding whether a death involves murder, manslaughter, or infanticide, one must first decide whether the homicide is culpable. Section 222(5) lists the methods by which culpable homicide can be committed:

> **222. (5) A person commits culpable homicide when he causes the death of a human being,**
>
> > **(a) by means of an unlawful act,**
> >
> > **(b) by criminal negligence,**
> >
> > **(c) by causing that human being, by threats or fear of violence or by deception, to do anything that causes his death, or**
> >
> > **(d) by wilfully frightening that human being, in the case of a child or sick person.**

By Means of an Unlawful Act (s. 222(a))

There are many types of unlawful acts, ranging from those which involve serious personal injury to those which are prohibited for the purpose of regulating some activity. An unlawful act can be created by federal or provincial legislation. When considering whether an act is "unlawful" for the purposes of s. 222, the courts do not treat all unlawful acts the same.[9] The unlawful act cannot be an absolute liability offence and must be dangerous; that is, an act that is likely to injure another. An objective standard is used to determine if the unlawful act is dangerous: Would a reasonable person realize that the act would subject a person to a risk of harm that is not trivial or transitory?[10]

By Criminal Negligence (s. 222(b))

A person who has caused a death by criminal negligence can be charged either with manslaughter by criminal negligence (s. 222(5)(b)) or with criminal negligence causing death (s. 220). These are identical offences, both using the definition of criminal negligence in s. 219. Chapter 9 fully examines the offence of causing death by criminal negligence.

By Threats of Fear or Violence (s. 222(c)); Frightening a Child or Sick Person (s. 222(d))

Another way of committing culpable homicide is by causing a person to do something, through threats, fear of violence, or deception, that results in his or her death.[11] It is also culpable homicide to cause a person's death, where the person is a child or sick person, by wilfully frightening him or her.

Sections 222(c) and (d) should be read with s. 228, which provides that a person does not commit culpable homicide by influence on the mind alone or by any disease or disorder resulting from influence on the mind alone except if the death is caused to a child or sick person by wilfully frightening the child or sick person. These sections are rarely used today; subsequently, there is little reported case law.

Once it is established that the homicide is culpable, the next step is to determine whether the homicide is murder, manslaughter, or infanticide.

03 B. MURDER

Culpable homicide is murder where certain additional factors are present besides the culpable causing of death. Murder is classified as first-degree or second-degree murder. In general, first-degree murder is more serious and has a greater penalty.

Section 229 sets out the circumstances where a culpable homicide is murder:

1. Section 229(a)

229. Culpable homicide is murder

    (a) where the person who causes the death of a human being

        (i) means to cause his death, or

        (ii) means to cause him bodily harm that he knows is likely to cause his death, and is reckless whether death ensues or not

Murder under s. 229(a)(i) is the simplest form of the offence. All that must be shown is that the accused, by a voluntary act, caused a person's death, and that the accused intended to cause that person's death. Since it may be impossible to produce evidence that shows a person actually

---

9   *R. v. Larkin* (1942), 29 Cr. App.R. 18 at 23. See also *R. v. Paice* (2005), 195 C.C.C. (3d) 97 (S.C.C.), discussed in Chapter 4. In *Paice*, the accused was charged with the unlawful act manslaughter after the victim died from injuries inflicted by the accused during a fist fight.
10 *R. v. Creighton* (1993), 83 C.C.C. (3d) 346 (S.C.C.).
11 See, e.g., *R. v. Graves* (1913), 21 C.C.C. 44 (S.C.C.).

had the mental intention to cause another person's death, courts have long taken the position that it may be assumed that a person intends the natural consequences of his or her acts. As one judge stated, "If a man is aware that certain consequences will probably follow the act which the person contemplates doing and yet deliberately proceeds to do that act, the person must be taken to have intended those consequences to follow even though he may have hoped they would not."[12] So, if Hannah puts a bomb in Carl's car, knowing that Carl will be driving the car soon, and the bomb goes off, killing Carl, a jury can assume that Hannah intended to kill Carl.

Murder under s. 229(a)(ii) differs from murder under s. 229(a)(i) in that the specific intent necessary is not to cause death, but to cause bodily harm that the accused knows is likely to cause death. There must be, (a) subjective intent to cause bodily harm and (b) subjective knowledge that the bodily harm is of such a nature that it is likely to result in death.[13] The Supreme Court has noted that the requirement of recklessness is almost an afterthought because a person is obviously reckless who intentionally causes grievous bodily harm that the person knows is likely to cause death. The court also noted that the *mens rea* for murder under s. 212(a)(ii) is only slightly relaxed from that required for murder under s. 212 (a)(i).[14]

Intoxication can sometimes be raised as defence to reduce a murder charge to manslaughter because a person who is intoxicated cannot foresee the consequences of his or her actions. In *R. v. Seymour,*[15] the accused was convicted of second-degree murder in the stabbing death of his wife. He had been drinking heavily throughout the course of the evening and early morning hours prior to the stabbing. Expert witnesses estimated that, when he returned home to the apartment he shared with his wife and five children, his blood alcohol was approximately two and a half times the legal driving limit. He awakened the children and told them to pack because they were moving back to their former home in another town. When the victim arrived home, approximately an hour later, an argument ensued. The accused went to the kitchen, got a knife, and stabbed or slashed the victim six times, including three times in the side of her neck. The accused then stabbed himself in the neck. One of the children pulled the knife out of her father's neck.

On appeal to the Supreme Court of Canada, the Court stated, "One of the effects of severe intoxication is an inability to foresee the consequences of one's actions, much less intend them."[16] The Court ordered a new trial, saying that it would be up to a jury to consider whether intoxication affected his ability to have the required foresight.

2. Section 229(b)

229. Culpable homicide is murder . . .

> **(b) where a person, meaning to cause death to a human being or meaning to cause him bodily harm that he knows is likely to cause his death, and being reckless whether death ensues or not, by accident or mistake causes death to another human being, notwithstanding that he does not mean to cause death or bodily harm to that human being**

This paragraph provides that where a person's conduct would fall under s. 229(a) but, by accident or mistake, the wrong person dies, the person has still committed murder, even

---

12 *R. v. Krafchenko* (1914), 22 C.C.C. 277 (Man.K.B.) at 297.
13 *R. v. Nygaard* (1989), 51 C.C.C. (3d) 417 (S.C.C.).
14 *R. v. Cooper* (1993), 78 C.C.C. 3d 289 (S.C.C.).
15 (1996), 106 C.C.C. (3d) 520 (S.C.C.).
16 Ibid. at 520. See also *R. v. MacKinlay* (1986), 28 C.C.C. (3d) 306 (Ont. C.A.) at 322. and *R. v. Dickson* (2006), 213 C.C.C. (3d) 474 (B.C.C.A.).

though he or she had no intent to harm the person who died. In *R. v. Droste*,[17] the accused planned to murder his wife by staging a car accident. Instead, his wife was only injured, while his two children, who were in the back seat, died. The court held that the accused was properly convicted of murdering his children. The intent he had to kill his wife was "transferred" to the victims of his act.

In *R. v. Fontaine*,[18] the accused was convicted of first-degree murder, after he deliberately drove his car, containing three passengers, into a semi-trailer parked in an oncoming lane, in a failed suicide attempt. One of his passengers died and the other two were injured. The question on appeal was whether a person who intends to kill himself and instead kills another can be said to have the necessary intent for murder. In overturning the conviction, the Manitoba Court of Appeal held that intent is not transferred if an accused attempts to kill himself but mistakenly kills someone else. The court stated that principles of criminal law allow punishment of the morally blameworthy and that first-degree murder (murder that is planned and deliberate) is the most stigmatizing offence known to law, whereas suicide is normally seen as the act of a person who is ill and in need of treatment, which is why attempted suicide is no longer a crime under the Criminal Code. The court stated:

> [to] equate the mens rea for suicide with murder would offend all three principles enumerated by the Supreme Court of Canada [in Creighton]. It is not consistent with the stigma and available penalties, and it is not proportionate to the moral blameworthiness of the offender. I conclude that the words of the provision in s. 229(b) of the Criminal Code are reasonably capable of more than one meaning. Given that ambiguity, the statutory interpretation rule of strictly construing penal legislation in favour of the accused would result in a conclusion that s. 229(b) refers to the killing of another and not the killing of oneself.[19]

3. Section 229(c)

229. Culpable homicide is murder . . .

   (c) **where a person, for an unlawful object, does anything that he knows or ought to know is likely to cause death, and thereby causes death to a human being, notwithstanding that he desires to effect his object without causing death or bodily harm to any human being.**

This subsection makes homicide murder where a person, for an unlawful object, does something that he or she knows or ought to know is dangerous to life and that causes the death of a human being. The use of the words "ought to know" in s. 229(c) means that an *objective* test is used to determine whether the accused is responsible for the death. Unlike s. 229(a)(ii), which uses a *subjective* test (i.e., "Did the accused actually know that the harm was likely to cause death?"), this section asks, "Would a reasonable person have known that the thing being done was dangerous to life?"[20] In *R. v. Martineau*,[21] the Court said that all offences of murder require a subjective intent. Therefore, the part of s. 229(c) that sets out an objective standard is unconstitutional and not enforceable.

It is essential that the accused acted for an unlawful object other than the injury that causes the death. In other words, the act that caused the death must have been done to further or achieve

17   (1979), 49 C.C.C. (2d) 52 (Ont. C.A.); [1984] 1 S.C.R. 208.
18   (2002), 168 C.C.C. (3d) 263 (Man. C.A).
19   Ibid. at 276–277.
20   The issue of subjective and objective intent is discussed in detail in the next section, Section 230 and the Constructive Murder Rule.
21   (1990), 58 C.C.C. (3d) 353 (S.C.C.).

an unlawful object, that is, purpose. The Supreme Court of Canada has said that the unlawful object in this section must be a serious crime that is an indictable offence requiring *mens rea*.[22]

Section 229(c) was applied in *R. v. Meiler*,[23] in which the accused was convicted of second-degree murder and attempted murder. The accused and his wife, Dianne, were separated. After the separation, Meiler suspected that his wife had been dating a man named Nick Biuk, whom the accused had known as a casual friend for three years. Bothered by the prospect that his wife was seeing another man, he made inquiries and was eventually satisfied that she was not involved with Biuk. His wife later told him she was involved with a man named Dan Roach, whom she had known many years before, and that the relationship was casual. The accused believed that the relationship was more serious than his wife let on, and became convinced that his wife was continually lying to him about her relationship with Roach. On the day of the shooting, the accused, who had weekend custody of his two children, arranged to drop them off at his brother-in-law's house. While there, he saw his wife and asked her to stop seeing Roach. She said she could not do that. At trial, his brother-in-law testified that the accused then stated, "I guess I know what I am going to do. I am going to kill Dan [Roach] and Dianne."[24] As he was leaving his brother-in-law's house, he saw Biuk and Roach arrive and go into the house. Meiler drove home and returned with a shotgun. On arriving at the house, he accidentally crashed into the back of his wife's car, which was parked in the driveway. He exited his car, cocked the gun, which was loaded, and put his finger on the trigger. At this point, there was conflicting evidence as to what happened next. The accused testified that he was tackled by the brother-in-law and accidentally pulled the trigger, fatally shooting Biuk, who was standing nearby.

In the instruction to the jury, the trial judge said that Meiler would be guilty of murder under section 229(c) if the jury found that he (1) for an unlawful object (killing Roach or his wife) (2) did anything (carrying a loaded, cocked gun with his finger on the trigger) (3) that he knew was likely to cause the death of a human being and (4) caused the death of a human being (Biuk)—whether or not the gun was accidentally discharged.[25]

The Ontario Court of Appeal approved of the jury directions and confirmed Meiler's conviction. The court pointed out that the case law made it clear that section 229(c) may apply to circumstances in which there had been an unintentional killing. The court stated that section 229(c) does not require an accused to foresee the precise situation or all of the events that result in death. The court found that it was sufficient foresight that the acts done for the unlawful object were likely to cause death, and those acts were sufficiently linked to the death to have caused death within the meaning of the section. The ordinary meaning of the section required nothing more.[26]

It should be noted that some legal scholars feel that the *Meiler* case resurrects a type of constructive murder that the Supreme Court found unconstitutional (see below for the discussion on constructive murder) "in that it requires an act in pursuit of an unlawful object and recklessness as to causing death instead of an intent to cause bodily harm and recklessness as to causing death."[27]

---

22   *R. v. Vasil* (1981), 58 C.C.C. (2d) 97 (S.C.C.).
23   (1999), 136 C.C.C. (3d) 11 (Ont. C.A.).
24   Ibid. at 16.
25   Ibid. at 22.
26   Ibid. at 26.
27   D. Stuart, *Canadian Criminal Law*, 4th ed. (Toronto: Carswell, 2001), at page 199. See also R. J. Delisle, "Unlawful Object Murder is Alive and Well" (1995), 25 C.R. (5th) 179.

4. Section 230 and the Constructive Murder Rule

Section 230, which is still in the Criminal Code, has, through a series of Supreme Court decisions, been found to be unconstitutional and, therefore, unenforceable. Under this section, culpable homicide is murder where a person causes a person's death whether or not the person knew death was likely and whether or not he or she intended to cause death. This section only applied where the death was caused while one of the offences listed in the section was being attempted or committed. The offences listed in s. 230 include serious crimes, such as assaulting a peace officer, sexual assault, kidnapping, robbery, and breaking and entering.

The effect of s. 230 was that a person could be found guilty of murder even though the person caused the death accidentally. This type of offence is referred to as "constructive murder" because actual intent to cause death is not required. Even though the section is no longer in effect, it is worth looking at the legal reasoning used by the Supreme Court of Canada in finding the section invalid because the Court used general principles applicable to other offences in the Code.

The consequence of applying s. 230 was highlighted in *R. v. Rowe*,[28] in which the accused was found guilty of murder when his gun accidentally went off during a robbery. The bullets went through a door, killing a person who was hiding behind it. The Supreme Court of Canada upheld the validity of the constructive murder law. Rowe was executed, since at the time (1951), Canada still had the death penalty. With the enactment of the Charter, the Court was given the opportunity to re-examine this law.

The first cases under the Charter to challenge the law were *R. v. Vaillancourt*,[29] and *R. v. Laviolette*.[30] The section challenged was s. 230(d). (This section was repealed in 1991.)

> **230. Culpable homicide is murder where a person causes the death of a human being while committing or attempting to commit [listed offences] whether or not the person means to cause death to any human being and whether or not he knows that death is likely to be caused to any human being, if . . .**
>
> **(d) he uses a weapon or has it upon his person**
>
>> **(i) during or at the time he commits or attempts to commit the offence, or**
>>
>> **(ii) during or at the time of his flight after committing or attempting to commit the offence, and death ensues as a consequence.**

Section 230(d) provided the widest circumstances in which culpable homicide could be murder. A person who accidentally caused a death could be convicted of murder if the other elements of the offence were present. In effect, murder under s. 230(d) was an absolute liability offence.

In *Vaillancourt*, the accused was charged with murder after his accomplice in a robbery shot and killed a bystander. Vaillancourt was charged with murder because of s. 21(2), which made him a party to the offence. He testified that he and the accomplice had planned to use knives for the robbery. When the accomplice showed up with a gun, Vaillancourt asked him to take out the bullets before the robbery. In fact, three bullets were found in the accomplice's glove by the police at the scene of the crime. *Laviolette* also involved the combined operation of s. 21(2) and s. 230(d). The accused took part in a break and enter. The owner was beaten to death by one of the accused's accomplices.

28   (1951), 100 C.C.C. 97, 12 C.R. 148 (S.C.C.).
29   (1987), 39 C.C.C. (3d) 118 (S.C.C.).
30   (1987), 38 C.C.C. (3d) 476 (S.C.C.).

The Supreme Court of Canada held in both of these cases that s. 230(d) violated the Charter's guarantees of fundamental justice and the presumption of innocence. The Court found the violation of fundamental justice on two grounds. First, for a serious offence, the *mens rea* must reflect the nature of the particular crime. For example, theft requires proof of a mental element of dishonesty. The Court said that murder is distinguished from manslaughter by the type of *mens rea* required (i.e., intention instead of recklessness). However, murder under s. 230(d) does not require any type of intention. Second, the *mens rea* required for an offence must reflect the stigma and sentence attached to the crime. Convicting a person of the serious crime of murder, the penalty for which is life imprisonment, when the person did not subjectively or objectively intend to cause death, offends the Charter. For these two reasons alone, the section is unenforceable.

The Court went on to consider whether the section violates the presumption of innocence. This presumption requires that all elements of an offence be proved against an accused before a finding of guilty is made. When an accused can be found guilty of murder without proof of even objective foreseeability, the presumption of innocence is violated. Furthermore, s. 1 of the Charter cannot save this section.

Since it was not necessary for the decision, the Court did not rule on whether objective foreseeability was sufficient for murder. However, the judgment did strongly suggest that subjective foreseeability was required.

A few years later, the Court was again asked to consider the requirement of *mens rea* for murder. In question this time was s. 230(a):

(a) he means to cause bodily harm for the purpose of

(i) facilitating the commission of the offence, or

(ii) facilitating his flight after committing or attempting to commit the offence, and death ensues from the bodily harm . . .

The Court issued concurrent judgments in five cases.[31] In brief, the Court held that the offence of murder requires subjective foreseeability. The decisions repeated the statements in *Vaillancourt* and *Laviolette*—that it is a principle of fundamental justice that the punishment for an offence must be in proportion to the seriousness of the offence. Murder is the most serious peacetime crime; therefore, the charge of murder must be reserved for those who either intend to cause death or intend to cause bodily harm that they know will likely cause death.

Strictly speaking, the decision of the Court only concerned s. 230(a). However, given the strong statement from the Court that murder requires subjective intent, it appeared that the entire section was invalid. This was confirmed a year later, when the Court was asked to consider s. 230(c), under which murder is committed if a person

(c) . . . wilfully stops, by any means, the breath of a human being for a purpose mentioned in paragraph (a), and the death ensues therefrom.

In *R. v. Sit*,[32] the accused was charged with murder under this section for causing death to a victim during an attempted kidnapping. The Court confirmed its previous decisions and held that murder requires subjective foreseeability.

31 *Martineau, supra* note 21; *R. v. Luxton* (1990), 58 C.C.C. (3d) 449 (S.C.C.); *R. v. Rodney* (1990), 58 C.C.C. (3d) 408 (S.C.C.); *R. v. Arkell* (1990), 59 C.C.C. (3d) 65 (S.C.C.); *R. v. Logan and Johnson* (1990), 58 C.C.C. (3d) 391 (S.C.C.).
32 (1991) 66 C.C.C. (3d) 449 (S.C.C.).

LO4

5. Classification of Murder for Sentencing

In 1976, legislation was enacted by Parliament to abolish capital punishment (the death penalty). Before this legislation was brought into effect, murder was punishable either by death or by life imprisonment. Generally, at the time the law was repealed, the only murder cases punishable by death were those in which a police officer, prison guard, or other similar person was killed in the course of duty.

Murder is now classified under s. 231 as either first-degree or second-degree murder.

Murder is first-degree if it is planned and deliberate killing (s. 231(2)), and irrespective of whether it is planned and deliberate where

- the victim is a police officer, prison guard, or person working in a prison or other similar person acting in the course of duty;
- a person causes a person's death while committing or attempting to commit the following offences: s. 76(l) (hijacking aircraft), s. 271 (sexual assault), s. 272 (sexual assault with a weapon), s. 273 (aggravated sexual assault), s. 279 (kidnapping and forcible confinement), and s. 279.1 (hostage taking);
- a person commits criminal harassment (s. 264) that is intended to cause the person murdered to fear for his or her safety or the safety of anyone known to the person murdered;
- a person commits any indictable offence where the act or omission constitutes terrorist activity;
- a person commits an offence under s. 81 (using explosives) for the purpose or benefit of assisting a criminal association; or
- a person commits an offence under s. 423.1 (intimidation of participant in the justice system).

All murder that is not first-degree is second-degree.

a. Meaning of "Planned and Deliberate"

Section 231 does not create a substantive offence; its purpose is to determine the punishment for a person who has committed murder. Therefore, before it can be considered whether the death was "planned and deliberate," the Crown must prove beyond a reasonable doubt that the accused is guilty of murder.[33]

Having proved the murder, the Crown must then prove that the murder was both planned and deliberate. The terms "planned" and "deliberate" mean different things. It is possible for a murder to be planned but not deliberate. For example, a man might make plans over a period of days to kill his wife but at the moment of the actual killing be acting impulsively and not deliberately. "Planned" refers to a calculated scheme or design that has been carefully thought out. The term "deliberate" as used in the Code means more than intentional; it is closer in meaning to "considered, not impulsive."[34] One judge has stated that "deliberation proceeds from the will enlightened by an intelligence which has had time to reflect upon the nature and the quality of the incriminating act."[35] In considering whether a murder was planned and deliberate, the jury is concerned with the accused's "mental processes." It should consider the accused's actions, conduct, statements, and capacity to plan and deliberate.[36]

In distinguishing between "wilfulness" and "deliberation," the court in *R. v. K.(M.M.)* stated that "wilfulness does not . . . equate with deliberation. Wilfulness in this context goes to the

---

33   *R. v. Mitchell* (1965), 1 C.C.C. 155 (S.C.C.) and *Droste, supra* note 17.
34   *More v. R.* (1963), 3 C.C.C. 289 (S.C.C.).
35   *Pilon v. R.* (1966), 2 C.C.C. 53 (Que. C.A.).
36   *Mitchell, supra* note 33.

intention to commit murder, rather than to where there was deliberation and a weighing of the consequences of murder."[37]

The Supreme Court of Canada established in *R. v. Nygaard*[38] that it is not necessary for the planning and deliberation to be for causing death. It is possible for "planned and deliberate" to apply to a murder under s. 229(a)(ii). In other words, a person can plan and deliberately cause such harm that he or she knows is likely to cause death. Also, a murder under s. 229(b), where, by accident or mistake the wrong person dies, can be planned and deliberate.[39]

In *R. v. Wallen*,[40] the Supreme Court of Canada considered the effect of intoxication on the ability to plan and deliberate. The accused was charged with murdering his wife from whom he was separated. He believed that his wife was having an affair with her employer. On the day of the killing, the accused had taken tranquillizers and consumed a large amount of alcohol. He went to his wife's office armed with two guns. He shot his wife and then fired several shots at her employer. Wallen was convicted of first-degree murder. On appeal, the issue was whether the trial judge had given proper instructions to the jury on the different effects of intoxication on the intent to kill and on the intent needed for planning and deliberation. The Supreme Court of Canada stated that the trial judge must tell the jury that a lesser degree of intoxication is needed to negate the intent for planning and deliberation than to negate the intent for committing the murder. A person may be intoxicated but still have the intent to kill, even while the intoxication may prevent that person from being able to plan and deliberate. Since first-degree murder is the most serious offence in the Code in terms of penalty, it is important that the jury be clearly instructed on the difference between intent for planning and deliberation and intent to cause death. In this case, the trial judge differentiated the two intents but may have misled the jury regarding the different levels of intoxication required to negate the two intents. The Court allowed the appeal and ordered a new trial.

b. Punishment for First- and Second-degree Murder

There are special sections of the Code that deal with the penalties for murder. Under s. 235, both first- and second-degree murder are punishable by a minimum of life imprisonment. The difference between the two offences with regard to punishment concerns eligibility for parole. Under s. 745, a person convicted of first-degree murder cannot be paroled until he or she has served 25 years of the sentence. A person who has been convicted of second-degree murder may be eligible for parole after serving at least 10 years, but no more than 25 years. The trial judge usually sets the number of years to be served before parole eligibility. However, if the person convicted of second-degree murder has a previous conviction for murder, the period to be served before parole eligibility is 25 years.

Until December 2011, when the law was amended, a person imprisoned for first- or second-degree murder could apply for early parole after serving at least 15 years. This was called the "faint hope clause." An application was made to a judge and jury under s. 745.6. They looked at such factors as the character of the applicant, the conduct of the applicant while serving the sentence, the nature of the offence, and any other factors that the judge believed were relevant. After hearing the evidence, the jury could order that a lesser number of years of imprisonment without eligibility for parole be served, or that the person's ineligibility for parole be terminated. If the jury made the order, the applicant still had to apply for parole to the parole board who could

---

37 (2006), 213 C.C.C. (3d) 538 (Alta. C.A.) at 541.
38 *Nygaard, supra* note 13.
39 *Droste (No. 2), supra* note 17.
40 (1990), 54 C.C.C. (3d) 383 (S.C.C.).

turn down the application. The faint hope clause is still available to persons convicted of murder who were already serving sentences or who were awaiting sentencing before the law repealing the faint hope clause came into effect.

A person who is given a life sentence and then released on parole is not totally free: The person will remain on parole for the rest of his or her life. This involves, among other things, reporting to parole officers as required.

6. Attempted Murder

239. (1) Every person who attempts by any means to commit murder is guilty of an indictable offence . . .

Attempted crimes were discussed in Chapter 3. Recall that s. 24(1) creates the offence of attempting to commit an offence. Murder is the sole offence where there is a specific offence for an attempt. The purpose of s. 239 is to create a higher maximum penalty than for other attempts. Section 463(a) provides that, unless otherwise provided by law, the maximum term of imprisonment for an attempted offence for which the offence is punishable by life imprisonment is 14 years' imprisonment. With s. 239, the maximum penalty for attempted murder is life imprisonment. As with other attempted crimes, the *mens rea* for attempted murder is the same as that required for the completed offence of murder.

An attempted murder charge may be used where there is a failure to establish causation because of an intervening act. In *R. v. Sarrazin*,[41] the victim had suffered life-threatening injuries from a shooting. He was operated on and released from the hospital. It was expected that he would make a full recovery. Five days later, he died from a blood clot. An autopsy revealed that he had ingested cocaine 30 to 45 minutes before his death. Pathologists were unable to state with certainty whether the death was caused by the shooting injury or the cocaine. The Supreme Court held that the trial judge erred in not leaving to the jury the possibility of finding him guilty of attempted murder, if the jury found that the prosecutor failed to prove beyond a reasonable doubt that a significant cause of death was the shooting. The Court stated, "The Crown must establish beyond a reasonable doubt that the shooting significantly contributed to Noël's death . . . If the evidence of the Crown pathologist left the members of the jury with a doubt on that account, then at most the respondents could be convicted of an attempt to murder— an attempt foiled by the skill of the surgeon, Dr. Freeman. If that view were taken by the jury (and of course we do not know what its members thought), the appropriate verdict (attempted murder) was not one of the options given to them."

The issue of whether the doctrine of transferred intent applies when there is an attempted murder was considered in *R. v. Gordon*.[42] The accused fired several shots from a distance at a drug dealer who had just previously assaulted him. The dealer was outside a crowded café. The shots missed the dealer but hit several bystanders, severely injuring them. Gordon was charged with attempted murder of not only the drug dealer but also the bystanders, as well as aggravated assault. He was found guilty of all charges. He appealed his convictions of attempted murder of the bystanders, arguing that the doctrine of transferred intent does not apply to the crime of attempted murder. The court of appeal agreed that the common law doctrine of transferred intent does not apply where the offence is attempted murder. The court identified several problems that would arise if a person could be charged for the attempted murder of a person whom he did not intend to harm. For example, the court

41   [2011] 3 S.C.R. 505.
42   (2009), 241 C.C.C. (3d) 388 (Ont. C.A.).

pointed out that an attempt does not require a harm or result for the *actus reus*. Thus, Gordon, who had the *mens rea* of intending to kill the dealer, can be convicted of attempted murder even though the dealer was not harmed. If attempted murder was extended to bystanders, it would raise the difficult issue of how to decide which unharmed bystanders should be considered too remote for a charge of attempted murder; for example, should those who only heard the gunshot be included? Although noting that if a bystander died, Gordon could be convicted of murder under s. 229(b), the court set aside the convictions for attempted murder of the bystanders and substituted convictions for aggravated assault.

7. Accessory after the Fact

When the offence is murder, there is also the specific offence of being an accessory after the fact:

> **240. Every one who is an accessory after the fact to murder is guilty of an indictable offence and liable to imprisonment for life.**

This section, like the attempted murder section, creates a separate offence for the purpose of setting a higher penalty than that provided for under s. 463 for being an accessory for other offences.

L06 C. MANSLAUGHTER

The common law defined murder as unlawful killing with malice aforethought, and manslaughter as unlawful killing without malice aforethought. Today, manslaughter is still defined in relation to murder:

> **234. Culpable homicide that is not murder or infanticide is manslaughter.**

The effect of this section is that once a homicide is found to be culpable, the next step is determining whether it is murder or infanticide; if the culpable homicide is neither, then the homicide is manslaughter. As discussed below, manslaughter requires a less blameworthy degree of fault and is not as serious an offence as murder. Manslaughter cases can result from a wide variety of situations, from facts just short of murder to facts that involve criminal negligence. Although the maximum penalty is life imprisonment, lesser penalties are often given. It is not uncommon, where a person has been charged with murder, for a jury to be instructed that it may bring in a verdict of guilty of manslaughter where it finds that the killing has been unlawful but that the Crown has failed to prove beyond a reasonable doubt the additional element needed for murder. Similarly, when an accused appeals his or her conviction for murder, the appeal court may substitute a verdict of guilty of manslaughter.

1. By an Unlawful Act or Criminal Negligence (s. 222(5)(a))

Manslaughter can arise where the death is caused by means of an unlawful act or by criminal negligence.

The *actus reus* of unlawful act manslaughter is causing a death by means of an unlawful act. The unlawful act must be objectively dangerous. In addition, in *R. v. Gossett,*[43] the Supreme Court of Canada held that the proper test to be applied is that the behaviour was a marked departure from the standard of care of a reasonably prudent person.

---

43   (1993), 83 C.C.C. (3d) 494 (S.C.C.).

The *mens rea* requirement for unlawful act manslaughter has been the subject of several Supreme Court of Canada decisions. These cases were discussed in Chapter 3. After the Supreme Court decisions, which held that murder requires subjective intent, some legal scholars believed that the Court might come out with a decision requiring all true criminal offences to have subjective intent. This has not happened. In fact, as it was pointed out in Chapter 3, it appears that only a few offences are required under the Constitution to have subjective *mens rea*. The key cases that settled this issue involved unlawful act manslaughter.

In *R. v. Creighton*,[44] the accused was a drug user who injected a woman with cocaine. She died from a drug overdose. The Supreme Court held that Creighton had committed manslaughter, in that he had committed an unlawful act that was dangerous and that a reasonable person would have known subjected the victim to a risk of harm that was not trivial or transitory. The Court rejected the argument that the standard should be foreseeability of death, and upheld the lower standard of foreseeability of harm.

The Court stated the test for finding unlawful act manslaughter. First, there must be an unlawful act (which is sometimes called the "predicate offence"). The unlawful act must be dangerous and cause the death. In committing the unlawful act, the conduct of the accused must be a marked departure from the conduct of a reasonable person. Second, the accused must have the *mens rea* required for the unlawful act (in this case, injecting the cocaine). Third, the unlawful act must be a federal or provincial offence and cannot be an absolute liability offence. Fourth, the *mens rea* for causing the death is objective foreseeability of bodily harm that is neither trivial nor transitory in nature.

R. v. T.(K.)[45] demonstrates that the act must be not only dangerous but also unlawful. A 13-year-old boy, T., threw a shovel at a moving car, hitting a teenage passenger in the head and causing his death. The incident occurred after a group of friends spent the night stealing cars and joyriding. T., while standing on a boulevard, threw the shovel at the car three or four times, as the driver of the car deliberately drove past him. On the last throw, the shovel hit the deceased, who was then hanging halfway out of one of the car windows. T. was convicted of unlawful act manslaughter. The Manitoba Court of Appeal overturned the conviction, finding that the trial judge made a legal error when she convicted T. on the basis that his actions were dangerous. The trial judge did not identify the predicate offence (the unlawful act) and find that the essential elements of the offence were proved beyond a reasonable doubt. The court said that finding an action to be dangerous does not prove, in and of itself, the essential elements of the unlawful act. It was essential that the Crown identify the unlawful act being relied upon, and that the judge determine whether the Crown had proved the *actus reus* and *mens rea* of that offence beyond a reasonable doubt. The judge would then have had to address whether the Crown had proved beyond a reasonable doubt that there was objective foreseeability of bodily harm for the offence of manslaughter.

In many situations, a charge of manslaughter can be based either on an unlawful act or on criminal negligence. In *R. v. Mack*,[46] three men, including the deceased and the accused, were sitting in a mobile home. Each of the men had taken heroin that evening. While still feeling the effects of the drug, the accused found a gun in the bedroom and took it to the kitchen table to examine it. Although he claimed that he did not remember pointing the gun at anyone, at some point in the evening he fired three shots, striking the deceased twice and the other man once. The court held that a jury could find the accused guilty of manslaughter if it

---

44   *Creighton, supra* note 10.
45   (2005), 199 C.C.C. (3d) 551; leave to appeal to S.C.C. quashed 205 C.C.C. (3d) vi.
46   (1975), 22 C.C.C. (2d) 257; 29 C.R.N.S. 270 (Alta. C.A.).

believed beyond a reasonable doubt either that the accused committed the unlawful act of pointing the gun at the deceased, or that the accused was criminally negligent in the manner in which he handled the gun.

LO7 2. Murder Reduced to Manslaughter

A person who has been charged with murder may be convicted of manslaughter instead by successfully raising either intoxication or provocation as a defence.

a. Intoxication

The defence of intoxication is explained in Chapter 4. *R. v. Seymour*,[47] discussed earlier in this chapter, showed how murder can be reduced to manslaughter when the accused is intoxicated. The accused's intoxication prevented him from being able to foresee the consequences of his actions and thus he was unable to form the intent to cause harm. In sum, where the Crown proves that the accused unlawfully caused a death but cannot prove that the accused had the specific intent for the offence of murder, the accused can be convicted of the lesser included offence of manslaughter. Also as discussed above, intoxication can be used as a partial defence where the Crown is attempting to prove that the murder was planned and deliberate.

b. Provocation

The defence of provocation can also be partial defence that can reduce the offence of murder to manslaughter:

232. (1) Culpable homicide that otherwise would be murder may be reduced to manslaughter if the person who committed it did so in the heat of passion caused by sudden provocation.

(2) A wrongful act or insult that is of such a nature as to be sufficient to deprive an ordinary person of the power of self-control is provocation for the purposes of this section if the accused acted on it on the sudden and before there was time for his passion to cool.

(3) For the purposes of this section, the questions

    (a) whether a particular wrongful act or insult amounted to provocation, and

    (b) whether the accused was deprived of the power of self-control by the provocation that he alleges he received,

are questions of fact, but no one shall be deemed to have given provocation to another by doing anything that he had a legal right to do, or by doing anything that the accused incited him to do in order to provide the accused with an excuse for causing death or bodily harm to any human being.

To summarize, provocation, as defined in s. 232, consists of these elements:

- a wrongful act or insult
- sufficient to deprive an ordinary person of the power of self-control
- which actually provoked the offender
- who acted in response to it, on the sudden, before there was time for his or her passion to cool.

---

47 *Seymour, supra* note 15.

These four elements are used to form two tests, one objective and the other subjective, for determining whether provocation can be raised as a defence. Both tests, (1) whether an act or insult would deprive an ordinary person of self-control and (2) whether the accused acted on the sudden, before his or her passion had time to cool, are issues of fact, which means that these are questions for the jury. However, it is a question of law, that is, a question for the judge, if there is any evidence on which to base the defence. In *R. v. Tran*,[48] the Supreme Court said that the judge can decide whether there is an "air of reality" to the defence, that is, whether there is foundation of evidence for the defence. The court went on to state, "In a jury trial, the judge is the gatekeeper and judge of the law and must therefore put the defence to the jury only where there is evidence upon which a 'reasonable jury acting judicially' could find that the defence succeeds."[49]

Notice that s. 232 states that it is not provocation if a person (the victim) does anything that he or she has a legal right to do. Courts have narrowly defined "legal right" in this section as "a right which is sanctioned by law (e.g. self-defence or a sheriff serving a warrant) and not something which a person may do without incurring legal liability."[50] In *R. v. Thibert*, discussed further below, it was argued that the victim had a legal right to insult the accused; therefore, the insult was not provocation. The Supreme Court rejected this argument, stating, "The words or acts put forward as provocation need not be words or acts which are specifically prohibited by the law."[51] The Court quoted with approval a statement from a decision of the Ontario Court of Appeal: "The absence of a remedy against doing or saying something or the absence of a specific legal prohibition in that regard does not mean or imply that there is a legal right to so act."[52]

The section also provides that an accused cannot rely on "self-induced" provocation as a defence; that is, where the accused does something to incite the victim to do something so the accused can use the defence of provocation. This section appears to prevent "bogus" claims of provocation.[53]

The First Test: Wrongful Act or Insult

The first test is whether the wrongful act or insult was of a nature sufficient to deprive an ordinary person of self-control. This is the objective test. The ordinary person is much like the reasonable person. However, the Supreme Court has pointed out that the reasonable person is used to set a standard for legal behaviour (i.e., the reasonable person does not commit culpable homicide). The objective standard of the ordinary person is to allow compassion in the law "to weigh in the balance those very human frailties which sometimes lead people to act irrationally and impulsively against the need to protect society by discouraging acts of homicidal violence."[54]

One issue for the courts has been what, if any, personal characteristics of the accused to ascribe to the "ordinary person." Obviously, if too many characteristics are ascribed, the standard is no longer objective. On this issue, the Supreme Court in *Thibert*, stated:

> The 'ordinary person' must be of the same age, and sex, and share with the accused such other factors as would give the act or insult in question a special significance and have experienced the same series of acts or insults as those experienced by the accused. [In other words]. . . the wrongful act or insult must be one which could, in light of the past history of the relationship

48 [2010] 3 S.C.R. 350.
49 Ibid. at para. 41.
50 *R. v. Thibert* (1996), 104 C.C.C. (3d) 1 (S.C.C.).
51 Ibid. at para. 29.
52 Ibid. at para. 29; see also *R. v. Galway*, [1972] 2 O.R. 630 (C.A.) at p. 649.
53 See Don Stuart, *Canadian Criminal Law*, 4th ed. (Toronto: Carswell, 2001) at 536–537.
54 *Thibert, supra* note 50 at para. 4.

between the accused and the deceased, deprive an ordinary person, of the same age, and sex, and sharing with the accused such other factors as would give the act or insult in question a special significance, of the power of self-control.[55]

In *Thibert*, the wife of the accused had told him two months previously that she was having an affair and subsequently moved out. On the day of the killing, the accused met his wife in the parking lot of her workplace to attempt to convince her to move back. The victim, with whom she was having the affair, came out of the building and started to lead her back inside. The accused then got a gun out of the car. He testified that he meant to use the gun as a "bluff" to get his wife to talk to him privately. The victim, while laughing and grinning, then started walking towards the accused holding the woman by the shoulders and moving her back and forth in front of him, taunting the accused with, "Go ahead and shoot me, big fellow." The court considered that, given the history between the victim and the accused, a jury could find the actions of the deceased to be taunting and insulting. The court stated, "It might be found that, under the same circumstances, an ordinary person who was a married man, faced with the break-up of his marriage, would have been provoked by the actions of the deceased so as to cause him to lose his power of self-control. There was some evidence, therefore, that would satisfy the objective element of the test."[56]

In a more recent decision, *R. v. Tran*, the Supreme Court has made clear that the ordinary person standard reflects contemporary norms and values, such as the commitment to equality in the Charter of Rights. The Court stated:

For example, it would be appropriate to ascribe to the ordinary person relevant racial characteristics if the accused were the recipient of a racial slur, but it would not be appropriate to ascribe to the ordinary person the characteristic of being homophobic if the accused were the recipient of a homosexual advance. Similarly, there can be no place in this objective standard for antiquated beliefs such as "adultery is the highest invasion of property" . . . *nor indeed for any form of killing based on such inappropriate conceptualizations of "honour."*[57]

In *Tran*, the accused and his wife had been separated for several months when he unexpectedly and uninvited entered her locked apartment. Unknown to her, he had kept a key to the apartment they had both formerly occupied. He found his wife and her boyfriend in bed. After the initial confrontation, where he kicked and scratched both victims, he went to the kitchen and returned with a knife and attacked the boyfriend, stabbing him 17 times, killing him. He was charged with five offences including second-degree murder. On appeal to the Supreme Court of Canada, the issue was whether the defence of provocation could be raised against the charge of second-degree murder. The Supreme Court upheld the conviction for murder, holding that there was not even enough evidence of provocation for the defence to go to the jury. The Court stated, "The discovery of his estranged wife's involvement with another man is not an 'insult' within the meaning of s. 232 of the Criminal Code. The accused's view of his estranged wife's sexual involvement with another man after the couple had separated—found at trial to be the insult—cannot in law be sufficient to excuse a loss of control in the form of a homicidal rage and constitute an excuse for the ordinary person of whatever personal circumstances or background."[58]

---

55   *Thibert, supra* note 50 at paras. 18–19.
56   *Thibert, supra* note 50 at para. 24.
57   *Tran, supra* note 48 at para. 34. The court in *Tran*, in discussing outdated and unacceptable norms, referred to *R. v. Mawgridge*, a 1707 English court decision, where the judge set out four categories of provocation, one of which envisaged a husband catching a man in the act of adultery with his wife. The basis of the provocation, the judge wrote, was that "jealousy is the rage of a man, and adultery is the highest invasion of property."
58   *Tran, supra* note 48 at para. 7.

The Second Test: Upon the Sudden

An accused who meets the first test for provocation must still satisfy the second test. This second test—the subjective test—is that the accused must have acted upon the sudden and before his or her passion had time to cool. The court in *Tran* explained that the reason that the act must be "on the sudden" is to distinguish a response taken in vengeance from one that was provoked. In other words, the accused must have reacted almost instantaneously after the insult. For example, where the accused had been insulted, but had waited four or five minutes before shooting the victim, the defence of provocation was not available.[59] In *R. v. Young*,[60] an argument between the accused and his girlfriend was interrupted when they left their apartment. He went to his mother's house, and she went with a girlfriend to her apartment. They all met back at the apartment when the accused came back for his medicine and the victim and her friend came back for a bottle of juice. The accused, the victim, and her friend then left the apartment again. They were on the stairs outside the apartment when he stabbed her to death. The court noted that the accused had been hearing that the relationship was over for more than four hours, with only one interruption—when everyone left the apartment the first time. The shock value of anything she might have said would have worn off by then. The court concluded that there was no evidence to suggest that the accused had acted in the heat of passion or on the sudden. Similarly, in *Tran*, the court found that Tran knew that his wife was involved with another man so he could not argue that he was unprepared for what he found when he entered the apartment uninvited and unexpected.

.08 D. INFANTICIDE

1. The Offence of Infanticide

> **233. A female person commits infanticide when by a wilful act or omission she causes the death of her newly-born child, if at the time of the act or omission she is not fully recovered from the effects of giving birth to the child and by reason thereof or of the effect of lactation consequent on the birth of the child her mind is then disturbed . . .**

Section 2 of the Code defines "newly-born child" as a person under the age of one year. The elements of the offence that the Crown must prove are these:

- The accused must be a woman who caused the death of her child.
- The child must have been under the age of one year.
- The death must have been caused by a wilful act or omission of the accused.
- At the time of the wilful act or omission, the accused must not have fully recovered from the effect of giving birth to the child or of lactation.
- By reason of the birth or lactation, the accused's balance of mind must have been disturbed.

As mentioned earlier, this offence is rarely charged. It was first introduced into the law of Canada in 1948. It is based on the reasoning that a woman may be mentally disturbed from the effects of giving birth or of lactation and thus be less responsible for her actions. In this situation, the law mitigates the severity of punishment for what would otherwise be murder or manslaughter, the maximum punishment being five years' imprisonment (s. 237). The Ontario Court of Appeal examined the *mens rea* and *actus reus* elements of the offence in *R. v. L.B.*[61]

---

59 *R. v. Olbey* (1979), 50 C.C.C. (2d) 257 (S.C.C.).
60 (1993), 78 C.C.C. (3d) 538 (N.S.C.A.).
61 [2011] O.J. No. 891.

One issue in the case was whether the *mens rea* requirement for infanticide was the same as that for murder (an intentional killing) or that required for unlawful act manslaughter. The court held that the *mens rea* for infanticide is the same as that required for unlawful act manslaughter, noting that neither the seriousness of the offence nor the stigma attached to it require a higher *mens rea*. The Crown must prove the *mens rea* associated with the unlawful act that caused the child's death and objective foreseeability of the risk of bodily harm to the child. The court also stated that it is the *actus reus* of the offence that distinguishes it from murder or manslaughter. When the charge is infanticide, to prove the *actus reus*, the Crown must prove not only the wilful act or omission that caused the death but also that the mother of the newly-born child was mentally disturbed because of giving birth or lactation.

One of the elements of the offence that the Crown may have difficulty proving is that the accused was suffering from a mental disturbance when she caused the death of her child. Section 663 deals with this issue by providing, where all of the elements of the offence are proven except that the balance of her mind was disturbed because of giving birth or lactation, that she can still be convicted unless evidence establishes that the act or omission was not wilful. The purpose of s. 663 is to avoid the problems that arise where the Crown is able to prove all the elements of the offence except those concerning the woman's mental state, or where the accused raises as her defence that she was fully recovered and that her mind was not disturbed. The result in either case would be that she would be entitled to be acquitted of infanticide and could not be charged later with murder or manslaughter, since an accused cannot be tried twice for the same homicide.

2. Infanticide as a Partial Defence to Murder

Where the accused is charged with murder, the Ontario Court of Appeal has held that infanticide can be used as a partial defence leading to a conviction of infanticide. In *R. v. L.B.*,[62] mentioned above, the mother who admitted committing infanticide was charged with two counts of first-degree murder for the deaths of her children: one died at 6 weeks of age and the other died four years later when he was 10 weeks old. Both infants were smothered in their cribs. Both deaths were attributed at the time of their deaths to SIDS (sudden infant death syndrome). The deaths were revealed as murders by the mother to her physician years later after she had been admitted to a psychiatric facility. The trial court found that there was evidence to prove the charges of first-degree murder but there was also evidence to indicate that the mother's mind was sufficiently disturbed to satisfy the requirements for infanticide. The trial court allowed infanticide to be used as a defence and convicted her of two counts of infanticide. On appeal, the issue was whether infanticide can be a defence. The Ontario Court of Appeal upheld the trial court's decision, stating that infanticide is both a stand-alone offence and where the charge is murder, a partial defence. The court explained that infanticide is the least "blameworthy" type of homicide compared to murder or manslaughter, as evidenced by the differences in penalty. Yet the operation of s. 662, which allows the court to convict for a lesser included offence (in this case, infanticide), only applies where the more serious offence is not proved. The result is that if the Crown proves the essential elements of murder, the mother must be convicted of murder even if the homicide fits within the meaning of infanticide. To determine whether this was the intent of Parliament in creating the offence, the court referred back to the original statute that created the offence of infanticide and found that the original wording allowed both for the offence of infanticide and the defence of infanticide, and that, although the section was reworded in 1954, there was no evidence that Parliament

---

62 Ibid.

meant to omit infanticide as a partial defence to murder. The court also noted that it has been the "accepted wisdom" in Canada that infanticide is both an offence and partial defence, and a critical analysis of the offence supports the long-held assumption.

Questions for Review and Discussion

1. Explain the legal meaning of the term "human being." Is it homicide to cause the death of a child before he or she is born? What if the child does not die until after birth?

2. What rules have developed through case law for determining causation in a homicide case?

3. Explain the special rules of causation in sections 224–226.

4. What is the difference between culpable and non-culpable homicide? Make up some examples of justified and excusable homicide.

5. Briefly define the types of culpable homicide under s. 222.

6. Would the following acts be unlawful under s. 222(5)? What other information do you need?
   a. Failure of a person to file his income tax return by the deadline
   b. Failure of a person to provide necessaries of life for his children
   c. Failure of a person to have his dog vaccinated for rabies
   d. Driving through a stop sign

7. Answer these questions about the offences of murder under s. 229:
   a. Which subsection deals with "transferred intent," and what does this phrase mean?
   b. Which subsection sets out the simplest form of murder?
   c. Which subsection uses an "objective test," and what does this mean?
   d. What has happened to the subsection that allows objective intent?

8. Why has the Supreme Court ruled constructive murder under s. 230 unconstitutional and unenforceable? Do you agree?

9. Discuss the differences between first-degree and second-degree murder.

10. How have courts interpreted the words "planned and deliberate" as used in the Code?

11. a. How did the common law distinguish manslaughter from murder?
   b. How is manslaughter defined today?
   c. How does manslaughter most often arise?

12. Under what circumstances can a charge of murder be reduced to manslaughter?

13. What are the elements of the offence of infanticide? When would infanticide be used as a defence? Is it a complete defence? Explain.

14. Some legal scholars have criticized the narrow definition of "legal right," used in the defence of provocation, particularly in cases involving domestic violence. Should a spouse be able to use the defence of provocation when a spouse rudely ends a relationship? Does the defence deny women equal protection of the law? See Kent Roach, *Criminal Law*, 4th ed. (Toronto: Irwin Law Inc., 2009) at 358 and 359.

15. L was convicted of murdering D, a taxi driver. He appealed the judge's decision to not allow the defence of provocation to go to the jury. On the night of the death, L had been out drinking. In the early morning, he ended up in a cab. He found a knife in the back seat and used it to force the cab driver to stop the cab and get in the trunk. After driving around for awhile, he pulled over and opened the trunk "to give the driver some air." The cab driver had found a hammer in the trunk and tried to hit L with it. L grabbed the hammer and started beating the driver with it, eventually killing him. What grounds do you think the judge used to deny L the defence of provocation? Write a decision stating your own opinion. See *R. v. Louison* (1975), C.C.C. (2d) 266 (Sask. C.A.).

16. Brown had been drinking in a tavern for most of the evening with Schmidt. At closing time, he agreed to drive Schmidt home. However, he first drove to an empty field for the ostensible purpose of drinking some beer. While there, Brown savagely beat Schmidt, inflicting many minor injuries and several facial wounds, not mortal in themselves. Schmidt was abandoned in the field, where he died after some extended but uncertain time. The doctor who performed the autopsy stated that, in his opinion, the deceased died from loss of blood through the facial wounds, but that the injuries would not have caused death if they had received attention. He said that he did not think death was caused by pneumonia resulting from exposure to the cold night air, but he could not exclude that possibility.

a. Has Brown caused Schmidt's death? Does it make any difference whether the death resulted from loss of blood or pneumonia?

b. Does the fact that Brown had been drinking all evening give him any special defence? Explain. See *R. v. Popoff* (1959), 125 C.C.C.116 (B.C.C.A.).

17. Bertrand and Annie were deeply in love. Annie's young daughter would not accept Bertrand, and Annie grew despondent about her relationship with Bertrand. She began to discuss committing suicide. Bertrand could not accept the thought of going on without Annie, so he planned to die with her. Annie lay on top of Bertrand. He held a gun in such a way that a single bullet would go through both of them. The shot was fatal to Annie and seriously wounded Bertrand. He was charged with murder. What argument would you make on his behalf? See *R. v. Gagnon* (1993), 84 C.C.C. (3d) 143 (Que. C.A.).

18. N. was charged with second-degree murder in the stabbing death of his wife. After N. and his wife immigrated to Canada, his wife started smoking, drinking alcohol, and being disrespectful to N. She did not follow other norms of their culture. She became pregnant and, after the birth of their child, she left the home and moved into an apartment. On the night she was killed, the accused visited her at her apartment and they argued about the victim's lifestyle. The accused testified that the victim said that she would continue to live her life as she pleased, and that there was nothing he could do about it. The victim attempted to push the accused out the door. N. stabbed her in the heart and throat, killing her. N. raised the defence of provocation. Should the defence succeed? Why or why not? See *R. v. Nahar* (2004), 181 C.C.C. (3d) 449 (B.C.C.A.).

19. Shanks was angry that his cat had been attacked by another neighbourhood cat. He went to the house of the owner of the cat, Mrs. Spurrell, and angrily confronted her. She apologized. The accused continued to argue and to swear. Mr. Spurrell heard the confrontation and came to the door; he and the accused argued, the accused threatening to kill him and his cat. The accused then moved toward the road and challenged Mr. Spurrell to fight. Mr. Spurrell's daughter came to the door and told Shanks that her father was ill and had just had a stroke and asked him not to fight with him. She moved to the road where Shanks was standing. Mr. Spurrell's daughter put her arm on Shanks' chest to keep him from fighting her father. Shanks then picked Spurrell up by the waist, threw him over his shoulder and onto the ground, and pulled his shirt over his head. The daughter's husband then broke up the fight. Mr. Spurrell was taken into the house

where he lay down. Later that night when his breathing became irregular, his family called an ambulance. He was dead on arrival to the hospital. The medical evidence was that he had suffered a stroke. What can Shanks be charged with? What would the prosecution have to prove? See *R. v. Shanks*, [1994] O.J. No. 4491.

20. It is no longer an offence for a person to attempt to commit suicide; but aiding, abetting, or counselling a person to commit suicide is an offence under s. 241. Sue Rodriguez, who was terminally ill with ALS (amyotrophic lateral sclerosis), challenged this section under s. 7 of the Charter as a violation of her liberty and security of her person. The Supreme Court, in a 5 to 4 decision, held that the section does not violate s. 7 of the Charter. In 2012, the issue was revisited when Gloria Taylor, who suffers from ALS, argued, along with other plaintiffs, before the B.C. Supreme Court, that s. 241 of the Criminal Code is a violation of her Charter rights. The court agreed and held that the law is an unjustifiable violation of her right under s. 15 of the Charter to equality before the law and her right to life under s. 7 of the Charter. The court suspended its decision for one year to allow time for Parliament to consider new legislation. However, it also allowed an exemption for Gloria Taylor that allows her to proceed with a physician-assisted death under specified conditions. It is expected that the federal government will appeal the decision and that it will eventually be heard by the Supreme Court of Canada.

How do you think the B.C. court was able to reach a decision different from that of the Supreme Court in *Rodriguez*? Research the Sue Rodriguez and Gloria Taylor cases to compare the decisions. Do you think attitudes in Canada have changed since the *Rodriguez* case?

Three U.S. states and several European countries allow physician-assisted suicide. Research the law in these jurisdictions. What kinds of regulations or conditions do other countries use to protect vulnerable people?

Debate whether physician-assisted suicide should be legal in Canada. See *Rodriguez v. British Columbia (Attorney General)*, [1993] 3 S.C.R. 519 and *Carter v. Canada (Attorney General)*, [2012] B.C.J. No. 1196 (B.C.S.C.).

21. The accused was involved in a car collision and charged with impaired driving causing death. The victim had severe injuries including broken ribs and injury to his lungs. He was unable to breathe on his own so a breathing tube was inserted. After six days, the tube was taken out so a bronchoscope could be inserted to examine the injury to his lungs. The throat of the victim swelled after the breathing tube was taken out, as a result of the tube being in his throat for six days. Doctors were unable to perform a successful tracheotomy, and the victim died. Should the accused be liable for the death of the victim? What sections of the Code are relevant? See *R. v. McCallum* (1990), 24 M.V.R. 94 (Ont. C.A.).

22. The accused was charged with manslaughter. He and the deceased had argued one evening at a school meeting. The accused struck the deceased twice. At that point, both were pushed outside the building. The body of the deceased was found some hours later. Medical evidence indicated that the deceased was a man in poor physical condition; his heart was abnormally small, and he suffered from Bright's disease. He had also been indulging freely in alcoholic beverages. The doctor who testified at the trial said that the blows struck by the accused were one cause of death, others being the man's bad health and drinking. What argument would the defence make? What argument would the prosecution make? Which argument would succeed? See *R. v. Nicholson* (1926), 47 C.C.C. 113 (N.S.S.C.).

CHAPTER 9

Criminal Negligence and Legal Duties
PART VIII OF THE CODE

Key points explained in this chapter are

LO1 the difference between civil negligence and criminal negligence, particularly the *mens rea* requirement for criminal negligence;

LO2 the elements of the offences of criminal negligence; and

LO3 offences which place on a person a duty to act.

The term "penal negligence" refers to all offences that are negligence-based; that is, those offences that use an objective test for *mens rea*. This chapter examines two of those offences: criminal negligence causing bodily harm and criminal negligence causing death. This chapter also examines some of the various offences that place a duty on a person to act; that is, they create an offence for a failure to act.

A. CRIMINAL NEGLIGENCE

219. (1) Every one is criminally negligent who

(a) in doing anything, or

(b) in omitting to do anything that it is his duty to do, shows wanton or reckless disregard for the lives or safety of other persons.

(2) For the purpose of this section, "duty" means a duty imposed by law.

Section 219 defines criminal negligence. Notice that it does not refer to a specific type of conduct. Any act that shows wanton or reckless disregard for the lives or safety of other persons may be a criminally negligent act. Similarly, any omission, or failure to act, where there is a legal duty to act, may be criminally negligent if the omission shows wanton or reckless disregard for the lives and safety of others. The terms "reckless" and "wanton" are not defined. It has been suggested that these terms were added to the offence in 1955 to distinguish criminal negligence from civil negligence; that is, to indicate the more serious nature of criminal negligence.[1]

---

1   D. Stuart, *Canadian Criminal Law*, 4th ed. (Toronto: Carswell, 2001) at 251.

"Duty" is defined as a duty imposed by law. Duties include not only those specified in the Code or other statutes but also those imposed by the common law. For example, under the common law, a person carrying a dangerous weapon, such as a rifle, is under a duty to take proper precautions. An example of a duty imposed by the Code is found in s. 263(1), which states that a person who makes an opening in ice that is open to or frequented by the public is under a duty to guard that opening in a manner adequate to prevent accidents.

1. Criminal Negligence Distinguished from Civil Negligence

Chapter 3 discussed the offences of penal negligence—those offences which require only an objective test for *mens rea*. Recall that the civil law imposes on all persons a duty to act in a manner that does not cause harm to other persons or their property. A person who breaches a duty to take reasonable care, and as a result causes harm unintentionally but carelessly, may be found negligent by a civil court and ordered to make compensation to the injured person.[2] A person is civilly negligent who fails to meet the standards of a reasonable person. This is an objective standard or test.

Criminal negligence, like other offences of penal negligence, involves a greater degree of misconduct than civil negligence. All human beings occasionally fail to meet the standard of the reasonable person. When a failure results in a loss to another person, usually the wrongdoer is not punished but is required to compensate the victim for the loss. However, at some point the conduct is such a departure from what society expects that the wrongdoer becomes guilty not only of civil negligence but also of a criminal offence, and liable to punishment.

2. Determining the *Mens Rea* for the Offences of Criminal Negligence

Although it is now settled that the *mens rea* for criminal negligence is objective, it has taken several Supreme Court cases to establish this. In 1960, the Supreme Court of Canada, in *O'Grady v. Sparling*,[3] stated that the test for criminal negligence is subjective—that it must be proved that the accused adverted to (actually realized) the risk. In spite of the principle of *stare decisis*, lower courts had difficulty following this decision. Most lower court decisions after *O'Grady* found it difficult to follow this test and used a test of gross negligence (conduct that is a marked departure from that of a reasonable person) for a finding of criminal negligence.

In *R. v. Tutton* and *R. v. Waite*, the Supreme Court of Canada again reviewed the *mens rea* required for criminal negligence. Unfortunately, the Court was unable to agree on the test for criminal negligence. The first decision released was *Tutton*.[4] The accused were the parents of a child who had died. The parents belonged to a religious group that believed in faith healing. Their son was diagnosed as having diabetes. The mother received instruction on how to treat the child's condition. However, both parents believed that the child would be cured through faith. At one point, the parents stopped administering the insulin the child needed. The child became ill, and they were warned of the importance of continuing the insulin injections. They again stopped giving him the insulin, and he died three days later. The parents were charged with causing the boy's death by criminal negligence in that they had failed in their duty to provide necessary medical treatment. The evidence was that they were loving and responsible parents. Their defence was that they honestly believed that their son had been cured by divine intervention. The Ontario Court of Appeal stated that a subjective test must be used to

---

2   See Chapter 2, page 13, for a discussion of some of the differences between criminal and civil law.
3   (1960), 128 C.C.C. (3d) 1 (S.C.C.).
4   (1989), 48 C.C.C. (3d) 129 (S.C.C.).

determine whether the parents had been reckless and wanton. The appeal to the Supreme Court was heard by six justices. Two justices stated that an objective standard should be used: There must be conduct which reveals a marked and significant departure from the standard of a reasonably prudent person in the circumstances. One justice agreed that an objective standard should be used but added that, when applying an objective norm, "a generous allowance" must be made for factors that are particular to the accused, such as youth, mental development, and education. The other three justices stated that a subjective test should be used, and reaffirmed the test set out in *O'Grady*.

The decision of the two justices who were in favour of the objective test stated:

Our concept of criminal culpability relies primarily upon a consideration of the mental state which accompanies or initiates the wrongful act, and the attribution of criminal liability without proof of such blameworthy mental state raises serious concerns. Nonetheless, negligence has become accepted as a factor which may lead to criminal liability and strong arguments can be made in its favour. Section 202 [now 219] affords an example of its adoption. . . . Negligence connotes the opposite of thought-directed action. In other words, its existence precludes the element of positive intent to achieve a given result . . . What is punished . . . is not a state of mind but the consequences of mindless action. This is apparent . . . from the words of the section which make criminal, conduct which shows wanton and reckless disregard . . .[5]

The two justices added that, in applying this standard to the facts of this case, it would be up to the jury to decide whether the parents' belief was reasonable and honest. They would have to consider the whole background of the case, including the experience of the parents with the child's illness: that they had seen the effect of the withdrawal of insulin on one occasion, that they had been informed of the necessity of the insulin, and that the mother had received some formal instruction in providing care for the child. As well, they would have to consider whether the belief in a miraculous cure, although honest, was reasonable.

All six justices agreed that the case had to be tried again because the judges' instructions to the jury were wrong. The six judges also agreed that, regardless of whether the test for the *mens rea* was objective or subjective, it would be the same whether the conduct was an act or omission.

In *Waite*,[6] which was released at the same time as *Tutton*, the same judges took the same positions. Waite was found not guilty at trial of four counts of causing death by criminal negligence and one count of causing bodily harm by criminal negligence. After drinking several cans of beer, the accused and two friends got in his car and followed a hayride made up of several tractors pulling wagons. The accused passed the hayride, turned his car around, and drove back toward the wagons. There was evidence that he said to his companions, "Let's see how close we can get," or "Let's play chicken." He then drove down the left side of the road, without his headlights on. When he was within fifty metres of the wagons, he swerved to the right to go around the wagons and struck five people who were running alongside the wagons. Four died and one was injured. The trial judge instructed the jury that they needed to use a subjective standard to find Waite guilty of criminal negligence—that is, to find that he deliberately assumed the risk of his conduct. He was found not guilty of criminal negligence but guilty of dangerous driving. On appeal, the Ontario Court of Appeal disagreed with the trial judge's directions and stated that an objective standard should be used and that the *mens rea* can be objectively determined from the accused's conduct. A new trial

5   Ibid. at 139.
6   (1989), 38 C.C.C. (3d) 1 (S.C.C.).

was ordered. The Supreme Court of Canada agreed with the court of appeal that a new trial was necessary because of errors in the judge's directions to the jury, but took the same inconclusive positions on whether an objective or a subjective standard should be used.

There are usually a total of nine Supreme Court justices. At the time these cases were heard, two were ill and one had resigned. The decisions in *Creighton* and the companion cases made it clear that for criminal offences, an objective standard is permissible under the Charter. In *Creighton*,[7] which involved unlawful act manslaughter, Justice McLachlin, who wrote the majority's decision, did not make a ruling on the *mens rea* requirement for criminal negligence because it was not necessary to decide the case. However, the justice did comment that the *actus reus* for manslaughter by criminal negligence requires a marked and substantial departure from the standards of a reasonable person and that the *mens rea* is the objective standard of a reasonable person.

It is now clear that the Supreme Court has adopted Justice McLachlin's statement on the elements of criminal negligence. For example, in *R. v. J.F.*,[8] the accused was charged with manslaughter by criminal negligence and manslaughter by unlawful act for failing to provide necessaries of life in the death of his foster child. The child had been beaten and abused by his wife and had died. His wife was convicted of manslaughter. He was charged on the basis that, although he had not participated in the abuse, he had done nothing to prevent it. He was convicted of manslaughter by criminal negligence but acquitted of manslaughter by failing to provide necessaries. His appeal reached the Supreme Court on the issue of whether the verdicts in his case were inconsistent. He argued that it was inconsistent to be acquitted of the less serious charge of failing to provide necessaries of life but to be convicted of the more serious charge of causing death by criminal negligence. The court agreed on the basis that the facts underlying both offences were the same and the test for criminal negligence, which is a marked and substantial departure test, is higher than the marked departure test required for failing to provide necessaries.

Even though the marked and substantial departure test has become the standard for criminal negligence, there will still be some dispute as to how strictly the objective standard should be applied. Recall that another issue in *Creighton* was whether personal factors such as age, education, and psychological condition should be considered in applying the reasonable person standard.[9] The Supreme Court split 5 to 4 on this issue, with the slim majority holding that personal characteristics short of incapacity to understand the risk should not be considered. Some legal scholars believe that this standard is too rigid and predict that lower courts will have trouble enforcing it.[10]

R. v. Ubhi,[11] a court of appeal case decided after *Creighton*, considered the *mens rea* for criminal negligence and the place of personal characteristics. The accused was the driver of a dump truck loaded with hot asphalt. While Ubhi was driving down a steep incline, the brakes on the truck failed. The truck hit a recreational vehicle and killed two persons. It was discovered that the truck's brakes were faulty and had not been adjusted for quite some time. The trial court held that the standard to be used in a case of criminal negligence is objective and that the driver's conduct in not maintaining the brakes amounted to a marked and substantial departure from the standard of a reasonable person. The accused was convicted. On appeal, new evidence was produced which indicated that the driver had the mental age

7 (1993), 83 C.C.C. (3d) 346 (S.C.C.); see also discussion of this case in Chapters 3 and 8.
8 (2008), 236 C.C.C. (3d) 421 (S.C.C.).
9 See Chapter 8.
10 See *Stuart, supra* note 1 at 260.
11 (1994), 27 C.R. (4th) 332 (B.C.C.A.); leave to appeal to S.C.C. refused, 31 C.R. (4th) 405.

of a six- or seven-year-old child. The British Columbia Court of Appeal used an objective standard and, relying on *Creighton*, held that personal characteristics are irrelevant except as they affect capacity to understand the risk. Here, the fresh evidence of the accused's mental deficiency did go to the issue of capacity. Had it been admitted, it could have altered the result of the trial, in that a jury might have concluded that the accused lacked the capacity to understand the necessity of ensuring that the brakes of the truck were maintained in proper working order. The court ordered a new trial.

The decision in *Ubhi* can be compared to the decision in *R. v. Canhoto*.[12] A grandmother believed she could communicate directly with angels and spirits as well as detect evil spirits in people. She also believed that she could expel those spirits through prayer and by forcing persons to drink water until they vomited. The grandmother believed that her two-year-old granddaughter, Kira, was possessed by evil spirits, and she decided to expel the evil spirits from her. She took Kira into the kitchen and began to pray and force water down her throat. Kira resisted, and a neighbour who was visiting held her legs. Kira eventually fell silent and was placed onto the kitchen floor, where she died. The mother, who was also present, was charged with manslaughter on the basis of criminally negligent conduct contributing to the death of her daughter. She was convicted and appealed. The appeal was dismissed and the conviction upheld. The court found that the mother appreciated the risk to her child despite her religious beliefs. Relying on *Creighton*,[13] the court found that it was not a case of incapacity, but a case of subjugating awareness of risk to religious beliefs.

Although *Creighton* held that personal characteristics short of incapacity to understand the risk should not be considered, the state of mind or the circumstances of the accused are to be considered. In *R. v. Beatty*,[14] the Supreme Court of Canada explained that the marked departure test for penal negligence includes considering the state of mind of the accused and whether it raises a reasonable doubt about a marked departure:

> [T]he trier of fact should be satisfied on the basis of all the evidence, including evidence about the accused's actual state of mind, if any, that the conduct amounted to a marked departure from the standard of care that a reasonable person would observe in the accused's circumstances. Moreover, if an explanation is offered by the accused, then in order to convict, the trier of fact must be satisfied that a reasonable person in similar circumstances ought to have been aware of the risk and of the danger involved in conduct manifested by the accused.[15]

The test for penal negligence in *Beatty* is sometimes referred to as the "modified objective test" because it takes account of the state of mind or circumstances of the accused in determining what a reasonable person would do. In other words, the issue is whether a reasonable person in the circumstances of the accused would have been aware of the risks arising from the conduct of the accused.

As discussed in Chapter 3, *Beatty* was applied in *R. v. Martin*.[16] Martin was acquitted of dangerous driving caused by his inability to properly shift gears in a standard transmission car. Although he had experienced some stalling of the car, he had no experience with losing control of the car due to spinning wheels as he tried to shift gears on wet pavement. The court found that a reasonable driver in Martin's circumstances would not have recognized a risk of losing control of the car in a manner that would be dangerous to others.

---

12   (1999), 140 C.C.C. (3d) 321 (Ont. C.A.)
13   *Creighton, supra* note 7.
14   [2008] 1 S.C.J. No. 5.
15   Ibid. at para. 8.
16   (2012), B.C.C.A. 194.

LO2   3. The Offences of Criminal Negligence

There are two offences of criminal negligence: criminal negligence causing death, and criminal negligence causing bodily harm. Both are indictable. Criminal negligence causing death is punishable by up to life imprisonment; criminal negligence causing bodily harm is punishable by up to ten years' imprisonment. Recall from Chapter 8 that culpable homicide under s. 222(5)(b) includes criminal negligence; therefore, manslaughter by criminal negligence is an offence that is identical to criminal negligence causing death.

Although many cases of criminal negligence involve the use of cars, any act can give rise to a charge of criminal negligence. The following are a few examples:

In *R. v. Petzoldt*,[17] the accused was an unemployed animal trainer and performer. He owned two chimpanzees, which he kept in the basement of his house. The female chimp was 150 centimetres tall and weighed 91 kilograms. While he was walking the chimp on a busy street, she reached out and grabbed an eight-year-old girl and bit her on the head and shoulder. The animal had demonstrated its aggressive and dangerous character several times before. The animal trainer was found guilty of criminal negligence causing bodily harm. The judge said that since the accused knew the animal was dangerous, in taking it for a walk on a main street he showed wanton and reckless disregard for the safety of others.

In *R. v. Popen*,[18] the accused's wife was convicted of physically abusing their 19-month-old daughter, causing her death. There was no evidence that the accused had abused the child, but he was aware of his wife's actions. The Ontario Court of Appeal held that a parent has a legal duty under the common law to protect his or her child from abuse by the other parent. Therefore, Popen could be properly charged with criminal negligence causing death.

R. v. Rogers[19] involved criminal negligence caused by breach of a duty imposed by s. 198, which states that a person who undertakes to provide medical or surgical treatment is under a duty to have and use reasonable knowledge, skill, and care. Rogers was an unlicensed physician. At the time of the events leading to the charge, he was registered as a naturopathic physician. The practice of naturopathy is defined as the art of healing by natural methods or therapies. Rogers prescribed a low-calorie, low-protein diet for a young child who was suffering from a skin disease. After following the diet for about eight weeks, the child's condition became so severe that he was hospitalized. The day after he entered the hospital, he died. The testimony of medical doctors indicated that the child died from gross malnutrition. The appeal court upheld Rogers' conviction for criminal negligence causing death, stating that in judging whether the conduct is wanton or reckless, the court must look at the standards of reasonable people, not the standards of the accused.

In *R. v. Gagnon*,[20] the accused, with three others, was riding in a car travelling at between 95 and 110 kilometres an hour. After the four drank several bottles of beer, the accused threw the empty bottles out on the roadside. One bottle smashed against a rock, and its fragments hit and seriously injured a woman sitting nearby. The court considered that the road was heavily travelled at that time of year and that it was well known that many travellers used the wayside to go walking or to sit and rest. The accused, the court found, had thrown the bottles at random with no concern for the consequences of his act. The accused was found guilty of criminal negligence causing bodily harm.

---

17   (1973), 11 C.C.C. (2d) 320 (Ont. Co. Ct.).
18   (1981), 60 C.C.C. (2d) 232 (Ont. C.A.).
19   (1968), 4 C.C.C. 278 (B.C.C.A.); leave to appeal refused [1968] S.C.R. ix.
20   (1956), 115 C.C.C. 82 (Que. Ct. of Sessions of the Peace).

In *R. v. Morrisey*,[21] the accused was drinking with a friend and the friend's father at a hunting camp. The accused also started taking prescription drugs. At one point in the evening, the accused drove the father home. When he returned to the camp, he found his friend asleep on the upper bunk. He decided to wake his friend. With a loaded gun in his hand, he jumped on the lower bunk, slipped, and fell, causing the gun to discharge and killing the friend. There was no evidence that the accused intended to kill his friend. He pleaded guilty to criminal negligence causing death and unlawfully pointing a firearm. He appealed his sentence. The Supreme Court of Canada dismissed his appeal stating that this was a particularly grave offence.

L03 B. DUTIES TENDING TO PRESERVATION OF LIFE

Certain sections of the Code impose specific duties to act. This chapter discusses only some of the Code sections which impose a duty to act.[22] Most criminal offences require active misconduct; in contrast, these sections make it possible for a person to be found guilty of not doing something. As discussed earlier, a breach of one of these duties may be the basis for a charge of criminal negligence causing bodily harm or death, if the failure to act shows wanton or reckless disregard for the lives and safety of others. The charge can also be brought under the section imposing the duty.

1. Duty of Persons to Provide Necessaries

215. (1) Every one is under a legal duty

(a) **as a parent, foster parent, guardian or head of a family, to provide necessaries of life for a child under the age of sixteen years;**

(b) **to provide necessaries of life to their spouse or common-law partner; and**

(c) **to provide necessaries of life to a person under his charge if that person**

    (i) **is unable, by reason of detention, age, illness, mental disorder or other cause, to withdraw himself from that charge, and**

    (ii) **is unable to provide himself with necessaries of life.**

(2) Every one commits an offence who, being under a legal duty within the meaning of subsection (1), fails without lawful excuse, the proof of which lies on him, to perform that duty, if

(a) **with respect to a duty imposed by paragraph (1)(a) or (b),**

    (i) **the person to whom the duty is owed is in destitute or necessitous circumstances, or**

    (ii) **the failure to perform the duty endangers the life of the person to whom the duty is owed, or causes or is likely to cause the health of that person to be endangered permanently; or**

(b) **with respect to a duty imposed by paragraph (1)(c), the failure to perform the duty endangers the life of the person to whom the duty is owed or causes or is likely to cause the health of that person to be injured permanently.**

---

21   (2000), 148 C.C.C. (3d) 1 (S.C.C.).
22   Examples of other duties include s. 129(b), failing to assist a police officer after being given reasonable notice; s. 68, failing to disperse after a reading of the riot act; and s. 252, failing to stop, give name and address, or offer assistance after a motor or water vessel accident.

This section places on parents, spouses, and persons in charge of other persons the duty to provide the necessaries of life for their children, spouses, or charges. Notice that for an offence to have been committed, it is not enough that there has been a failure to provide without lawful excuse. Under paragraph (1)(a) or (b), the person to whom the duty is owed must also, because of the failure to provide, either be in destitute or necessitous circumstances, or that person's health or life must be endangered. So, a wife who fails to support her husband cannot be convicted of this offence if her husband has sufficient means of his own. If, however, the person to whom the duty is owed falls under paragraph (1)(c), the offence is only committed if his or her health or life is endangered.

Section 215(4)(b) further provides that evidence that a person has in any way recognized a child as being his or her child, is, in the absence of any evidence to the contrary, proof that the child is the person's child. For example, when a man supports a child who is not biologically his, this would be evidence that he has recognized the child as his own. Unless evidence is presented that provides another explanation for his actions, the child will be presumed to be his.

The definition of "guardian" is very broad. It would cover a situation where, for example, David has left his child in the care of Jenny. Jenny then has, in fact, the custody and control of the child.

Where a person has another person under his or her charge, the duty to provide is imposed only if the person under charge is unable, for a reason listed in s. 215(l)(c)(i), to withdraw from the charge and if the person under charge is unable to provide for himself or herself. *R. v. Peterson*[23] considered a person's duty to provide to a person under charge. The accused, Dennis Peterson, appealed his conviction for failing to provide necessaries of life to his father, thereby endangering his father's life. The accused lived with his 84-year-old father, Arnold Peterson, in a three-storey house. The house had been divided into three apartments. The father lived on the first floor and in the basement, the son lived on the second floor, and a grandson lived on the third floor. All of the units were separated by locked doors. The police had contact with the father and the son over several months as they had received calls about Arnold, who had needed help getting home. One time, he collapsed and, when the police arrived, seemed confused about where he was and where he lived. The police told the son about agencies that might help him handle his father, including a church across the street from the house that had a "meals on wheels" program; but he failed to contact them. Finally, the police received a call about an elderly man sitting on a porch with a dead dog. An officer found Arnold in filthy clothes. There was a strong odour coming from him. He had lost weight and had to hold up his pants with his hands. He appeared hungry and told the officer he had last eaten a few days ago. Arnold's apartment did not have a working kitchen, and there was a broken toilet in the bathroom. The kitchen was full of dead cockroaches, and the basement floor was covered with dog feces. The officer did not believe that he was able to care for himself and apprehended him under the Ontario Mental Health Act and took him to a hospital. He was subsequently admitted to a nursing home.

It was determined that Arnold was in the early stages of Alzheimer's disease and needed supervision such that he would be personally checked every half hour. He was able to feed himself, but he needed supervision and would probably forget to eat if he were not reminded. He needed help bathing and supervision for dressing appropriately for the weather. The examining doctor's opinion was that his living situation at the house was unsafe and very non-hygienic, and that Arnold would not be able to take care of himself in such an environment.

---

23 (2005), 201 C.C.C. (3d) 220 (Ont. C.A.).

At the trial, it was noted that Dennis and his sister had power of attorney for taking care of Arnold's finances and personal care. Dennis never contacted his sister to tell her that their father was deteriorating.

The appeal court first considered the nature of the duty under s. 215(1)(c), stating, "The duty arises when one person is under the other's charge, is unable to withdraw from that charge, and is unable to provide himself or herself with necessaries of life." The court noted that the phrase "necessaries of life" includes not only food, shelter, care, and medical attention necessary to sustain life, but also appears to include protection of the person from harm. The failure to provide necessaries includes not only a failure to do a discrete act but also a failure to act in an ongoing relationship over a period of time. The word "charge" connotes, among other things, the duty or responsibility of taking care of a person or thing. The fact that a parent does not understand that he cannot take care of himself or that he is in an unsafe environment is not a defence for an accused.

The court concluded, "The offence is made out by conduct showing a marked departure from the conduct of a reasonably prudent person having the charge of another in circumstances where it is objectively foreseeable that failure to provide necessaries of life would risk danger to life or permanent endangerment of the health of the person under the charge and includes an assessment of whether the person in charge could have acted other than as he or she did."

The court agreed with the findings of the trial court: (1) Arnold was dependent on his son; (2) Dennis was aware of his father's dependency; (3) Dennis controlled Arnold's living conditions and kept him in an unsafe living environment; (4) Dennis had control over Arnold's personal care—he had the power of attorney and publicly he was seen by neighbours as taking care of his father; (5) Dennis chose not to make decisions that would have provided Arnold with the necessaries he needed—he did not follow up on the officer's suggestions to contact community services; and (6) due to age and illness, Arnold was unable to withdraw himself from the appellant's charge.

The court of appeal dismissed Dennis' appeal.

a. Necessaries of Life

"Necessaries" in this section of the Code are those things necessary for the preservation of life. This includes food, shelter, clothing, medical treatment, and, as found in *Peterson*, protection of the person from harm. However, this is probably not a complete list, since what is considered a necessary will depend on the particular circumstances of the case.[24]

b. Lawful Excuse

The failure to provide necessaries must be without "lawful excuse." The Code has not clearly defined lawful excuse. However, courts have stated that inability to provide because of lack of money (for example, the parents are unable to find employment) is a lawful excuse.[25] Also, the person must be aware that the necessaries are required before he or she can be found guilty of failing to provide them.[26] Also, when the spouse or child has adequate means of his or her own, the accused has a lawful excuse, since the spouse or child is not in destitute or necessitous circumstances.

---

24 See, for example, *R. v. Sidney* (1912), 20 C.C.C. 376 (Sask. C.A.).
25 See, for example, *R. v. Bunting* (1926), 45 C.C.C. 135 (Ont. C.A.).
26 *R. v. Steele* (1952), 102 C.C.C. 273 (Ont. C.A.).

c. Destitute and Necessitous Circumstances

The fact that a spouse or child is on welfare or receiving charity from friends or relatives does not mean that he or she is not in destitute or necessitous circumstances. As one judge aptly pointed out, families receive relief because they are in destitute or necessitous circumstances. They do not cease to be in such circumstances because they have received relief to keep them from famishing or suffering.[27]

Furthermore, s. 215(4)(d) states that the fact that a spouse or child is receiving or has received necessaries from a person who is not under a legal duty to provide them cannot be used as a defence by an accused. For example, if a wife has been deserted by her husband and is forced to live with her parents because she has no means of her own, her husband cannot defend himself on the grounds that she is not destitute or in necessitous circumstances, even if the parents support her at a very high standard of living.

d. Danger to Life or Health

The offence may be committed where the failure to provide necessaries either endangers the life of the person to whom the duty is owed, or causes or is likely to cause the health of that person to be permanently endangered. Whether a person's life has been endangered, or health permanently endangered, depends on the particular facts of each case.

The Supreme Court of Canada considered a charge under this section in *R. v. Naglik*.[28] Naglik and her husband were convicted of aggravated assault and failure to provide necessaries to their 11-week-old son. One of the issues on the appeal was whether s. 215 imposes an objective or a subjective standard for the mental element of the offence. This decision was one of the companion cases that came out with the Supreme Court's decision in *Creighton*,[29] discussed above and in Chapters 3 and 9. It was held that this is an offence of "penal negligence" and that it requires the objective standard of a marked departure from the standard of a reasonable parent. The question was, in brief, whether a reasonable parent would have foreseen the risk of harm to the child. The Court also restated that the personal characteristics of the accused, except for those characteristics that deprive him or her of the capacity to appreciate the risk, should not affect the objective standard.

In *R. v. J.R.B.*,[30] the victim was less than one month old and had suffered fractures in both her arms. The victim's mother was convicted for her failure to seek prompt medical attention for her daughter. In upholding the conviction, the court discussed the meaning of s. 215(2)(a)(ii):

> The essence of endangering is putting at risk of harm. Applying this meaning to section 215(2)(a)(ii) leads to the conclusion that the legislative intention is to create an offence when the failure of a parent to provide the necessaries of life for her child is likely to put the child at risk of permanent harm to her health.

> This is, in fact, the only rational interpretation of section 215(2)(a)(ii). . . . Parliament intended that conviction would follow, not only if the parent's failure to provide necessaries would "likely cause permanent injury to the child's health," but if the failure would likely put the child at risk of permanent harm to her health. . . . Ms. J.R.B. failed to obtain prompt medical

27 *R. v. Wilson* (1933), 60 C.C.C. 309 (Alta. C.A.).
28 (1993), 83 C.C.C. (3d) 526 (S.C.C.). The Supreme Court set aside her conviction on other grounds of appeal and ordered a new trial.
29 *Creighton, supra* note 7.
30 (2004), 187 C.C.C. (3d) 176 (N.L.C.A.).

attention for her baby. It was objectively foreseeable in the circumstances that this failure was likely to put the infant at risk of permanent harm to her health. Ms. J.R.B.'s conduct was a marked departure from the standard of a reasonably prudent parent in the circumstances.[31]

2. Duties of Persons Undertaking Dangerous Acts

a. Where Medical or Surgical Treatment Is Administered

216. Every one who undertakes to administer surgical or medical treatment to another person or to do any other lawful act that may endanger the life of another person is, except in cases of necessity, under a legal duty to have and to use reasonable knowledge, skill and care in so doing.

This section does not create an offence but merely defines the duty that persons who administer medical or surgical treatment are under. Section 216 would most often be used in conjunction with the offence of criminal negligence. Thus, a person who breaches a duty or does any legal act that endangers the life of someone else has not committed an offence under s. 216 unless the breach of the duty is criminally negligent. Notice the exception: No duty is imposed "in cases of necessity." Presumably, this would apply in an emergency situation to protect those who attempted to give aid but failed to have or use reasonable knowledge, skill, or care.

R. v. Thornton[32] is an example of a case where an offence other than criminal negligence was the charge. The accused was charged with committing a common nuisance under s. 180:

180. (1) Every one who commits a common nuisance and thereby

    (a) endangers the lives, safety or health of the public, or

    (b) causes physical injury to any person, is guilty of an indictable offence . . .

(2) For the purposes of this section, every one commits a common nuisance who does an unlawful act or fails to discharge a legal duty and thereby

    (a) endangers the lives, safety or health of the public . . .

The accused had tested positive twice for the HIV virus, which he knew could lead to AIDS. He also knew that the virus was transmitted through blood. He then proceeded to donate blood to the Red Cross, knowing also that the Red Cross would not knowingly accept donations of blood from persons who had tested positive for the HIV virus. The screening process caught his blood, and he was charged with committing a common nuisance. His defence was that it is not an offence to donate contaminated blood. On appeal, the Supreme Court of Canada held that s. 216 imposed a duty of care on him when he donated blood to the Red Cross. He failed his duty of care under s. 216 by not disclosing to the Red Cross that his blood contained HIV antibodies, therefore committing a common nuisance that endangered the lives, safety, and health of the public.

b. Where Omission Is Dangerous to Life

217. Every one who undertakes to do an act is under a legal duty to do it if an omission to do the act is or may be dangerous to life.

---

31   Ibid. at 183–184
32   (1993), 82 C.C.C. (3d) 530 (S.C.C.). See also *R. v. Williams* (2001), 158 C.C.C. (3d) 523 (Nfld. C.A.).

This section provides that where a person begins to do an act, he or she is under a legal duty to complete it if the omission of the act is or may be dangerous to life. For example, if Alex sees Ivan drowning, he is under no legal obligation to save Ivan. But if Alex throws Ivan a rope and, before Ivan can grab it, pulls it back in, Alex has breached a legal duty to act. Alex undertook to act, and Ivan's life was endangered by the omission. Like s. 216, this section does not create an offence, but could be used as the grounds for a charge of criminal negligence.

> **217.1 Everyone who undertakes, or has the authority, to direct how another person does work or performs a task is under a legal duty to take reasonable steps to prevent bodily harm to that person or to any other person, arising from that work or task.**

This section clarifies that where a person directs another person to do work or a task, the person is under a legal duty to take reasonable steps to prevent bodily harm to that person or to any other person.

3. Child Abandonment

> **218. Everyone who unlawfully abandons or exposes a child who is under the age of ten years, so that its life is or is likely to be endangered or its health is or is likely to be permanently injured,**
>
> > **(a) is guilty of an indictable offence and liable to imprisonment for a term not exceeding five years; or**
> >
> > **(b) is guilty of an offence punishable on summary conviction and liable to imprisonment for a term not exceeding eighteen months.**
>
> **214. In this Part, "abandon" or "expose" includes**
>
> > **(a) a wilful omission to take charge of a child by a person who is under a legal duty to do so, and**
> >
> > **(b) dealing with a child in a manner that is likely to leave that child exposed to risk without protection . . .**

Section 218 makes it an offence to abandon a child under the age of 10. Notice that under s. 214, which defines the terms "abandon" and "expose," the offence can be committed either by a failure to act (i.e., a "wilful omission") or by positive misconduct (i.e., dealing with the child in a manner that exposes the child to risk). "Abandon" has also been defined by the courts as "leaving children to their fate."[33]

In *R. v. Motuz and Motuz*,[34] the parents left their two children, aged four and five, alone and locked in a farmhouse while they went out drinking. The farmhouse was about 1.2 kilometres from the nearest neighbour. After the parents had been gone for three hours, the house caught fire and burned down. Both children died. In finding the parents guilty, the judge described the parents' conduct as a total abandonment of parental responsibility.

A similar case of child abandonment is *R. v. Holzer*.[35] The mother of a 15-month-old boy left the child in an unlocked pickup truck in the unheated parking lot of a shopping mall in March. The temperature in the lot was –14°C. She had meant to drop off a bill payment but

---

33 *Re Drummond Infants Adoption* (1968), 1 D.L.R. (3d) 309 (B.C. Sup. Ct. Chambers).
34 (1965), 2 C.C.C. 162 (Man. C.A.).
35 (1988), 63 C.R. (3d) 301 (Alta. Q.B.).

ended up playing bingo. The child was found by a security guard. The court found the mother guilty of child abandonment. The child had no protection from the risk of abduction and only limited protection from freezing.

Questions for Review and Discussion

1. What kinds of acts can lead to liability for criminal negligence?

2. What essential elements must be present before an omission to act can be criminally negligent?

3. What are the main differences between civil negligence and criminal negligence?

4. Do you agree with the courts that the proper test for the *actus reus* of criminal negligence is the objective test of a marked and substantial departure from the standards of a reasonable person? Discuss.

5. List the offences of criminal negligence.

6. Describe the following:
   a. The persons who are under a duty to provide necessaries
   b. The persons to whom the duty is owed
   c. The circumstances in which a breach of duty is an offence

7. What are "necessaries of life"?

8. In what circumstances may a person who is under a duty to provide necessaries of life have a lawful excuse for not providing them?

9. Why does the law in "cases of necessity" where medical or surgical treatment is administered not impose a duty to have and use reasonable knowledge, skill, and care?

10. Does the law always impose a duty to act if the failure to act will endanger a person's life? If not, in what circumstances does a person have a duty to act? Do you agree with the present law? Explain.

11. Do you think the offence of child abandonment should only apply to children under ten? Explain.

12. LeMay and Sullivan were midwives who helped women who wished to have their babies at home. They had no formal medical training. They attended at the birth of a child of J.V. at her request. The child was partially born but LeMay and Sullivan were unable to complete the delivery. The woman was taken to the hospital by ambulance, where the delivery was completed using "a basic delivery technique." However, the child was dead. LeMay and Sullivan were charged with criminal negligence causing death. What do you think were the issues in this case? How would you resolve them? (Note: You may need to refer to some of the sections covered in Chapter 8.) See *R. v. Sullivan* (1991), 63 C.C.C. (3d) 97 (S.C.C.).

13. Mr. and Mrs. Simon and their seven children lived in a two-room house on a farm in Saskatchewan. For the past two months, Mrs. Simon's 20-year-old brother, Rodney, had been living with them. Because of the limited space, Mrs. Simon did not want her brother staying in the house. She had complained about this to Mr. Simon on several occasions. One night after Mr. Simon and Rodney had returned from work, Mr. and Mrs. Simon argued about whether Rodney should continue living with them. Mrs. Simon finally said there wasn't room for everyone and that she was leaving. She then put on a jacket and hat. She had, however, nothing on her feet except house slippers and stockings and was otherwise thinly clad. Before she left, she told her ten-year-old son, Jimmy, to put on his coat and come with her. A few minutes after Mrs. Simon and Jimmy left,

Rodney asked Mr. Simon if they should go after them. The temperature that night was –40°C. Mr. Simon said no, that they had probably gone to a neighbour's for the night. The neighbour lived one-and-a-half miles to the south. The next day, Rodney went to the neighbour's to see if Mrs. Simon and Jimmy were there. On the way, he found their bodies frozen stiff. Apparently they had taken a wrong turn and lost their way.

With what offence or offences, if any, could Mr. Simon or Rodney be charged? What would the Crown have to show? What other information would be relevant? See *R. v. Sidney* (1912), 20 C.C.C. 376 (Sask. C.A.).

14. L. drove his van with two passengers, D. and G., to a friend's house. He left both passengers at the friend's house and drove off. At the end of the block, he turned around and drove back to the house. He saw D. standing in the road. He stopped his van about five feet in front of D., who was smiling and laughing, and who then jumped on the hood. L. drove the van for a few seconds down the road. He stopped when he realized "what was going on was wrong." At this point, D. slid to the ground. He was unconscious and bleeding from the head. L. ran to get help. D. later died. L. was charged with criminal negligence causing death. What does the Crown need to prove in this case? Make a decision acquitting or convicting the accused. See *R. v. L.(J)* (2006), 204 C.C.C. (3d) 324 (Ont. C.A.).

15. The accused was living with her elderly aunt. The aunt became ill with gangrene and was confined to bed. Only the accused was aware of the aunt's condition. The accused did not provide or attempt to obtain any medical assistance for her aunt. She also did not provide food for her, although she accepted food that was brought to the house by tradespeople. The aunt died from the gangrene and the accused was charged with manslaughter. Should she be convicted? See *R. v. Instan*, [1893] 1 Q.B. 450; 17 Cox's C.C. 602.

CHAPTER 10

Offences Involving Motor Vehicles
PART VIII OF THE CODE

Key points explained in this chapter are

LO1 the *actus reus* and *mens rea* of the offence of dangerous driving,

LO2 when a driver's failure to stop a vehicle constitutes a criminal offence,

LO3 motor vehicle offences that involve the consumption of alcohol or drugs,

LO4 the authority of police to test a driver for alcohol or drugs,

LO5 the rights of a driver regarding random police "spot checks" and breathalyzer testing, and

LO6 the difference between drinking and driving offences under the Criminal Code and offences under provincial highway traffic legislation.

We do not usually think of car drivers as potential criminals, yet the careless use of motor vehicles is a major cause of death and injury today. Society has had to resort to the criminal law to prevent and control the dangerous use of automobiles.

The Criminal Code contains a number of offences relating to the operation of motor vehicles. Some of these are similar to provincial highway traffic offences; for example, the Code includes an offence for failing to stop at the scene of an accident. Most provincial highway traffic statutes contain similar offences. The provinces create traffic offences as part of their authority to regulate the use of roads and highways. To control the flow of traffic, for example, the provinces set speed limits and make rules regarding turns. Where the use of motor vehicles creates a risk of injury or death, the federal government uses its authority to make criminal law. Remember that however similar a provincial offence may seem to a federal one, the Code offence is more serious, and a crime.

"Motor vehicle" is defined in s. 2 of the Code as a vehicle, other than railway equipment, "that is drawn, propelled or driven by any means other than muscular power." This definition would cover, besides cars, such vehicles as farm tractors, snowmobiles, and motorcycles. For some offences, other methods of transportation (e.g., boats, aircraft, railway equipment) are specifically included.

A. CRIMINAL NEGLIGENCE AND MOTOR VEHICLE OFFENCES

A person who causes death or injury by criminally negligent driving will ordinarily be charged with either the offence of criminal negligence causing death or the offence of criminal negligence causing bodily harm. The one exception to this is where the criminally negligent driving occurred while "street racing." When it is being judged whether driving is criminally negligent, the same questions arise as in any other case of criminal negligence. Recall from Chapter 9 that the Supreme Court of Canada has determined that the marked and substantial departure test has become the standard for criminal negligence.[1]

01 B. DANGEROUS OPERATION OF A MOTOR VEHICLE

> **249. (1) Every one commits an offence who operates**
>
> (a) **a motor vehicle in a manner that is dangerous to the public, having regard to all the circumstances, including the nature, condition and use of the place at which the motor vehicle is being operated and the amount of traffic that at the time is or might reasonably be expected to be at that place**

The key element of this offence is driving that is dangerous to the public. There need not be actual danger to the public, but only driving that was dangerous to anyone who might reasonably have been expected to be in the vicinity of the dangerous driving.[2] Furthermore, any passengers in the car that is being dangerously driven and the officer in the police cruiser stopping the car are part of the public.[3]

This offence also applies to operators of boats and other water vehicles, and to operators of railway equipment, as well as to motor vehicle operators (s. 249(1)(b)–(d)). The offence is a hybrid offence. If the offence causes bodily harm or causes death, the offence is an indictable offence with longer maximum sentences (s. 249(3) and (4)).

In addition, a person convicted of an offence under s. 249 will be given a mandatory order prohibiting the offender from driving for a set period of time, depending on whether it is a first or subsequent offence. For example, for a first offence, an offender will be prohibited from operating a motor vehicle for a period of not more than three years plus any period of imprisonment, and not less than one year.

1. The *Mens Rea* of Dangerous Driving

The Supreme Court of Canada, in *R. v. Hundal*,[4] considered the *mens rea* requirement for the offence of dangerous driving. The accident occurred during the afternoon in heavy traffic on a wet street in downtown Vancouver. The accused was driving an overloaded dump truck when he ran a red light. His truck hit a car, killing the driver. The issue on appeal was whether the offence of dangerous driving is based on objective or subjective *mens rea*. The Court held that the offence requires a modified objective test. It noted that since driving is a licensed activity, it can be assumed that all drivers are mentally and physically capable of driving and are aware of the rules of the road. Furthermore, licensed drivers choose to drive, and therefore place themselves in a responsible position to other people who use the

---

1   See Chapter 9, page 217 for discussion.
2   *R. v. Mueller* (1975), 29 C.C.C. (2d) 243 (Ont. C.A.).
3   *R. v. Edlund* (1990), 23 M.V.R. (2d) 31 (Alta. C.A.).
4   (1993), 79 C.C.C. (3d) 97 (S.C.C.).

roads. The Court concluded, "As a result, it is unnecessary for a court to establish that the particular accused intended or was aware of the consequences of his or her driving . . . As a general rule, a consideration of personal factors, so essential in determining subjective intent, is simply not necessary in light of the fixed standards that must be met by licensed drivers."[5] The Court also noted that driving is an automatic and routine activity; it is almost impossible to determine the state of mind of a driver at any particular moment. "It would be a denial of common sense for a driver whose conduct was objectively dangerous, to be acquitted on the ground that he was not thinking of his manner of driving at the time of the accident."[6] The question to be asked is whether the accused's conduct was a marked departure from the conduct of a reasonable person. Normally the mental element will be inferred from the conduct. Thus, it can be assumed that a reasonable person would be aware of the risks arising from the dangerous driving. To avoid criminal liability, a person who is accused of dangerous driving is entitled to offer an explanation, such as the sudden onset of an illness. In sum, the *mens rea* should be assessed objectively, but in the context of all the surrounding circumstances.

Applying its reasoning to the facts of this case, the Court considered that the trial judge carefully examined the circumstances of the accident: the busy downtown traffic, the weather conditions, the condition of the accused's vehicle, and so on. The Court found that the accused's manner of driving represented a gross (marked) departure from the standard of a reasonable prudent driver, and that the accused offered no excuse for his conduct. The accused's appeal was dismissed.

In *R. v. Beatty*,[7] the Supreme Court of Canada confirmed its decision in *Hundal*[8] that the test for dangerous driving is whether the conduct of the accused was a marked departure from the conduct of a reasonable person. The court went on to explain the distinction between civil negligence and penal negligence:[9]

> A mere departure from the standard expected of a reasonably prudent person will meet the threshold for civil negligence, but will not suffice to ground liability for penal negligence. The distinction between a mere departure and a marked departure from the norm is a question of degree. . . .[T]he trier of fact should be satisfied on the basis of all the evidence, including evidence about the accused's actual state of mind, if any, that the conduct amounted to a marked departure from the standard of care that a reasonable person would observe in the accused's circumstances. Moreover, if an explanation is offered by the accused, then in order to convict, the trier of fact must be satisfied that a reasonable person in similar circumstances ought to have been aware of the risk and of the danger involved in conduct manifested by the accused.

2. The *Actus Reus* of Dangerous Driving

In the *Beatty* case, the Supreme Court of Canada also addressed the test for the *actus reus* of the offence of dangerous driving. The prosecution must prove beyond a reasonable doubt that, viewed objectively, the accused was driving in a manner that was "dangerous to the public, having regard to all the circumstances, including the nature, condition and use of the place at which the motor vehicle is being operated and amount of traffic that at the time is or might reasonably be expected to be at that place." The Court stated that it is

---

5   Ibid. at 105.
6   Ibid.
7   [2008] 1 S.C.J. No. 5.
8   *Hundal, supra* note 4.
9   For further discussion of the distinction between civil negligence and penal negligence, see Chapter 2 at page 13.

the manner in which the motor vehicle was operated that is at issue, not the consequences of the driving. If the consequence of the driving is death, it may make the offence more serious under s. 294(4), but it has no bearing on the question of whether the offence of dangerous driving has been made out.

Beatty was charged with three counts of dangerous driving. His pick-up truck, for no apparent reason, suddenly crossed the solid centre line on the highway and collided with an oncoming vehicle, killing all three occupants. The issue was whether this act of negligence was sufficient to constitute dangerous driving causing death under s. 249(4). Regarding the *actus reus* of the offence, the court found that, viewed objectively, Beatty's failure to keep his truck in its own lane was highly dangerous to other persons lawfully using the highway on their side of the highway. Regarding the *mens rea*, the court found that there was no evidence of improper driving before the truck crossed the centre line and that the few seconds of negligent driving was the only evidence about Beatty's manner of driving. The court concluded that Beatty's momentary lapse of attention was not sufficient to support a finding of a marked departure from the standard of care of a prudent driver.

R. v. Jiang[10] is another case that dealt with the *actus reus* of dangerous driving. The accused fell asleep and missed a bend in the road. The car went over the curb, continued across the sidewalk and through a parking lot, striking two children, injuring one and killing the other. The accused was charged with one count of dangerous driving causing bodily harm and one count of dangerous driving causing death. Evidence by an expert in the diagnosis and treatment of sleep and anxiety disorders suggested that the accused was suffering from undiagnosed chronic insomnia at the time of the accident. The expert testified that the accused responded well to treatment and that the accused was not aware of the sleep disorder before the accident. The trial judge acquitted the accused on both charges on the basis that her conduct in the few seconds before she fell asleep did not satisfy the test for dangerous driving. The court stated:

> a sleeping driver is not driving of his or her own volition and acts committed while in that automatic state of mind cannot form the actus reus of dangerous driving. That is not to say that a sleeping driver can never be convicted of dangerous driving. The actus reus of the offence may consist not of driving while in a state of sleep, but of embarking on driving or in continuing to drive in the face of a real risk of falling asleep.[11]

3. Street Racing

Section 249.4 creates the offence of dangerous driving while street racing. It requires dangerous driving as defined in s. 249 (1)(a), and street racing, which is defined in s. 2 as operating a motor vehicle in a race with at least one other motor vehicle on a street, road, highway, or other public place. It is a hybrid offence; if bodily harm or death is caused, it is an indictable offence and more severe sentences can be imposed. In addition to the offence of dangerous driving while street racing, the Code includes the offences of causing bodily harm by criminal negligence while street racing (s. 249.3) and causing death by criminal negligence while street racing (s. 249.2).

---

10   (2007), 220 C.C.C (3d) 55 (B.C.C.A.).
11   Ibid. at 62.

4. The Charter and Dangerous Driving

In the *Hundal* case, discussed above, the accused argued that because a prison sentence can be imposed for dangerous driving, a conviction requires proof beyond a reasonable doubt of a subjective mental element of an intention to drive dangerously. The Supreme Court of Canada agreed that s. 7 of the Charter prohibits imprisonment in the absence of proof of *mens rea*; however, *mens rea* for a particular offence may be subjective or objective. Regarding dangerous driving, the *mens rea* requirement of s. 7 of the Charter can be satisfied by proof of negligence. The conduct is measured on the basis of an objective standard without establishing the subjective mental state of the accused.

L02 C. FAILING TO STOP WHEN INVOLVED IN AN ACCIDENT

252. (1) Every person commits an offence who has care, charge or control of a vehicle, vessel or aircraft that is involved in an accident with

(a) another person,

(b) a vehicle, vessel or aircraft, or

(c) in the case of a vehicle, cattle in the charge of another person,

and with intent to escape civil or criminal liability fails to stop the vehicle, vessel or, where possible, the aircraft, give his or her name and address and, where any person has been injured or appears to require assistance, offer assistance.

This offence is an indictable offence. Longer maximum sentences can be imposed if the person committed the offence knowing that another person involved in the accident (a) suffered bodily harm or (b) is dead, and if the accused was reckless as to whether death resulted and death of the person did result (s. 252(1.2) and (1.3)).

The elements of this offence are (a) having the care, charge, or control of a vehicle that (b) is involved in an accident with a person, another vehicle, or cattle, and (c) failing to stop, to give assistance or name and address (d) with the intent of escaping civil or criminal liability. Note that this offence creates three legal duties: the driver must stop, give assistance, and give his or her name and address.

1. Care, Charge, or Control

To commit this offence a person must have care, charge, or control of the vehicle. Ordinarily, this person is the driver. However, when the owner of the car is a passenger, he or she could have care, charge, or control. For example, in *R. v. Slessor*,[12] one of the judges hearing the case on appeal stated that a passenger could have care, charge, or control where, for example, the car was being driven by a chauffeur or by an employee of the passenger. However, where a person allows another person to drive his or her car, in a social or business situation, it will usually be the driver who has the care, charge, or control of the vehicle.

---

12 [1970] 2 C.C.C. 247 (Ont. C.A.).

2. Involved in an Accident

It is immaterial whether damage actually occurs as a result of the accident. The accused's vehicle need not have actually collided with another car or person. A driver who caused an accident, or helped to cause it, and witnessed the accident occurring, would be "involved" in the accident. For example, a person who changed lanes abruptly in such a way that a car travelling behind braked suddenly, went out of control, hit the curb, and rolled off the highway, has been involved in the accident. However, a person who did not see the accident and was unaware that it had occurred, even though causing it, would not be involved in the accident.

R. v. McColl[13] dealt with the meaning of being involved in an accident with "another person" (s. 252 (1)(a)). McColl and three others left a house party in a truck to buy more beer. McColl, the driver, and the three passengers were in the front seat. While driving the wrong way on a divided street, the truck swerved and struck a tree. All four suffered head injuries. The three passengers made their way to a convenience store where a staff person called for transportation to a hospital. McColl offered no assistance and was seen by one of the passengers walking across the street and was not seen again. McColl, who had suffered a concussion, claimed that he did not remember leaving the truck and awoke at his mother-in-law's house the next morning. McColl was charged under s. 252. The Alberta Court of Appeal stated that there are two possible interpretations of s. 252(1)(a): that it does not apply to single vehicle accidents or that it includes any incidents causing injury or damage, including single vehicle accidents. After reviewing the legislative history of the provision, the court concluded that Parliament's original intention when it was enacted in 1910 was to make it an offence for a driver to leave an accident scene, including a single vehicle accident scene, without offering assistance to an injured person. Despite wording changes over the years that can be interpreted as meaning that s. 252(1)(a) is limited to accidents in which the vehicle collides with "another person," the court found that Parliament's original intention had not changed. McColl was convicted.

3. Failure to Render Assistance

Giving assistance does not mean applying first aid. It means taking the necessary steps to ensure that medical assistance or first aid help reaches the scene of the accident as quickly as possible.

4. Failure to Stop with Intent to Escape Criminal or Civil Liability

Courts have held that the intent required for this element of the offence is intent to escape liability arising from the accident and not from another cause. So, if a person fails to stop to avoid liability for unpaid parking tickets, the intent for the offence has not been proved.[14]

The offence creates a mandatory presumption, which is set out in s. 252(2):

(2) In proceedings under subsection (1), evidence that an accused failed to stop his vehicle, vessel or, where possible, his aircraft, as the case may be, offer assistance where any person has been injured or appears to require assistance and give his name and address is, in the absence of evidence to the contrary, proof of an intent to escape civil and criminal liability.

---

13   (2008), 235 C.C.C. (3d) 319 (Alta. C.A.).
14   *R. v. Hofer* (1982), 2 C.C.C. (3d) 236 (Sask. C.A.).

In other words, once it has been demonstrated that the accused was involved in an accident, he or she is required to give an explanation for not stopping. This section was applied in *R. v. Gosselin*.[15] The accused was the driver of a car that hit two pedestrians who were walking on the shoulder of the road. He drove a brief distance past the accident and then stopped his car and walked back. There was conflicting evidence regarding whether he offered any assistance. By the time he arrived at the scene, another car had stopped and some of the occupants had already gone to a farmhouse for help. The accused then went back to his car and drove 2.1 kilometres to a restaurant, where he called the police to report the accident. The police told him that an ambulance and police car were already on the scene. The accused did not give his name to the police or state that he was the driver. He called the police back 22 minutes later and gave his name and stated that he was the driver of the vehicle. The police told him to remain at the restaurant until they arrived, and he did. His statement to the police was that he left the accident to get help. At his trial, he was convicted of failing to remain. The trial judge relied on s. 252(2) to convict him. On appeal, the Ontario Court of Appeal held that the judge made an error in applying this section. There was "evidence to the contrary" that the accused did not leave the scene to escape liability. Where a judge does not either reject this evidence or disbelieve it, the presumption in this section cannot be applied and the Crown must prove beyond a reasonable doubt that the accused left the scene to escape liability. The trial judge, although he doubted the accused's evidence, did not reject it. In fact, the court of appeal stated that the two phone calls to the police and the fact that the accused stayed at the restaurant were evidence to the contrary that would be difficult to reject (the phone calls were recorded). Once it is established that the Crown cannot rely on s. 252(2), the judge must consider all the evidence to determine whether the Crown has proved beyond a reasonable doubt that the accused left the scene of the accident with the intent to escape liability. The trial judge did not do this, so the case was sent back for a new trial.

This type of clause is open to challenge under the Charter for offending the presumption of innocence. The court of appeal in *Gosselin* considered this issue as well. It concluded that although the clause does offend the presumption of innocence, it is a reasonable limitation under s. 1 of the Charter. The court used the test set out by the Supreme Court of Canada in *R. v. Oakes*.[16] It held that the objective of the law, which is to curb injuries to persons and damage to property, is sufficiently important to override the Charter right; and that the duties imposed by the section are reasonable and not out of proportion to the objective of the law. The Court of Appeal in Nova Scotia has also upheld this section as being a justifiable infringement of the Charter.[17]

LO3 D. IMPAIRED OPERATION AND HAVING OVER 80 MG OF ALCOHOL IN 100 ML OF BLOOD

1. The Offences

The two main offences involving driving while using alcohol or drugs are driving while impaired and driving with more than 80 mg of alcohol in 100 mL of blood ("driving over 80"). They are set out in s. 253. For the offence of impaired driving, the impairment can be caused by drugs or by alcohol.

---

15 (1988), 45 C.C.C. (3d) 568 (Ont. C.A.).
16 See Chapter 2, page 26, for a discussion of the test in *Oakes*.
17 *R. v. T.(S.D.)* (1985), 18 C.C.C. (3d) 125 (N.S.C.A.).

253. (1) Every one commits an offence who operates a motor vehicle[18] **. . . or has the care or control of a motor vehicle . . . whether it is in motion or not,**

   (a) **while the person's ability to operate the vehicle . . . is impaired by alcohol or a drug; or**

   (b) **having consumed alcohol in such a quantity that the concentration in the person's blood exceeds eighty milligrams of alcohol in one hundred millilitres of blood.**

(2) For greater certainty, the reference to impairment by alcohol or a drug in paragraph (1)(a) includes impairment by a combination of alcohol and a drug.

There are two ways these offences can be committed: A person can be actually operating (i.e., driving) a vehicle, or a person can have care or control of the vehicle. In other words, a person does not have to be operating a vehicle to have care and control of it, and the vehicle need not be in motion. This means, for example, that if the police see an obviously impaired person enter the driver's side of a car and put the key in the ignition, they can charge that person with having care and control, even before the vehicle is set in motion.

2. Elements of the Offences

In a 2012 case, R. v. Boudreault[19], the Supreme Court of Canada set out the essential elements of "care or control": (1) an intentional course of conduct associated with a motor vehicle; (2) by a person whose ability to drive is impaired, or whose blood alcohol level exceeds the legal limit; (3) in circumstances that create a realistic risk of danger to persons or property. Boudreault was intoxicated and unfit to drive when it was time for him to return home after a night of drinking. At his request, a taxi was called for him, for which he had to wait outside. The weather was cold, –15C and windy. He got into his truck, started the engine, turned on the heat and fell asleep. When the taxi arrived, the driver called the police. Boudreault was arrested and charged under s. 253(1)(a) and (b). He was acquitted on both counts at trial but the Quebec Court of Appeal set aside the acquittals and entered convictions. The court of appeal found that there was a risk that Boudreault might have set the truck in motion since his blood alcohol level was more than three times the legal limit and could have greatly affected his judgment had he awakened. The Supreme Court of Canada reinstated the acquittals.

The key legal issue in the case was whether a risk of danger is an essential element of the offence of care or control under s. 253. The Supreme Court held that such a risk is an essential element and that the risk of danger must be realistic and not just theoretically possible. It is not necessary that the risk be probable, or even serious or substantial. The Court noted that an accused will normally be convicted if the accused is found intoxicated behind the wheel of a motor vehicle with nothing to stop the accused from setting the vehicle in motion either intentionally or accidentally. The Court stated:

> *Absent evidence to the contrary, a present ability to drive while impaired, or with an excessive blood alcohol ratio, creates an inherent risk of danger. In practice, to avoid conviction, the accused will therefore face a tactical necessity of adducing evidence tending to prove that the inherent risk is not a realistic risk in the particular circumstances of the case.*[20]

---

18   Section 253(1) also applies to the operation and care or control of a boat, aircraft, or railway equipment.
19   2012 SCC 56
20   Ibid at para 13

In this case, the trial judge concluded, based on the facts, that Boudreault would not have set the vehicle in motion and that there was no realistic risk of danger. The trial judge found that Boudreault, despite his intoxication, knew what he was doing and took the necessary precautions. Based on his experience, Boudreault was aware of the gravity of driving while impaired. The judge found that Boudreault took care to arrange an alternate plan for getting home safely and that the evidence established that his plan would have prevented him from driving.

3. The Presumption of Having Care or Control

When a person is found in the driver's seat, s. 258(1)(a) creates the following presumption:

> (a) **where it is proved that the accused occupied the seat or position ordinarily occupied by [the driver of] a motor vehicle . . . the accused shall be deemed to have had the care or control of the vehicle . . . unless the accused establishes that the accused did not occupy that seat or position for the purpose of setting [the vehicle] in motion . . .**

Thus, if a person is in the driver's seat of a car, it will be presumed that the person had the care or control of the car unless the person can show that he or she did not intend to put it in motion. Until *R. v. Ford*,[21] discussed below, some courts had held that this presumption meant that an accused could avoid a conviction by showing that he or she did not intend to set the car in motion. For example, in *R. v. McPhee*,[22] the accused, a taxi driver, realized that he was impaired. He attempted to call his supervisor to request that someone take his taxi off the road. The line was busy, so he went to his cab and turned on the ignition so that he could use the car radio to call the dispatcher, who could relay the message to his supervisor. Before anyone arrived, he was found by the police asleep in the car. He was acquitted of having care and control while impaired because he did not enter the vehicle for the purpose of setting it in motion.

This interpretation of the presumption was changed by the Supreme Court of Canada in *Ford*.[23] The accused had been attending a party on a cold winter night. During the evening, he started the car to warm the engine so that it would start when he was ready to go home. He did not intend to drive home, however; he had arranged for someone else to drive, since he knew he was impaired. The police found him behind the wheel with the motor running. The Court affirmed the decision of the court of appeal, which held that intent to drive the vehicle is not necessary for the offence. The Court stated that care and control can be shown where the accused does anything involving use of the car where the car could be unintentionally set in motion, "creating the danger that the section is designed to prevent." If the accused rebuts the presumption by showing that he or she did not enter the vehicle for the purpose of putting it in motion, it is still open to the Crown to prove that the accused had care or control by proving that the accused performed an act or series of acts that might put the vehicle in motion.

21   (1982), 65 C.C.C. (2d) 392 (S.C.C.).
22   (1976), 25 C.C.C. (2d) 412 (Ont. C.A.).
23   *Ford, supra* note 25.

In the *Boudreault* case,[24] discussed above, the Supreme Court of Canada noted that the presumption means, at a minimum, that an accused who was intoxicated and in the driver's seat of a motor vehicle, cannot, *for that reason alone*, be convicted under s. 253, if the accused satisfies the court that he or she did not have the intention to set the vehicle in motion. In other words, proof of voluntary intoxication and being behind the wheel of the vehicle do not by themselves alone necessarily establish "care or control". The Court found that something more is required and, as discussed above, the Court concluded that the "something more" is a realistic risk of danger.

In *R. v. Diotte*,[25] the New Brunswick Court of Appeal held that an overt act is not necessary to establish care and control. The police found the accused sleeping in his car, which was parked sideways on a street so that it completely blocked one lane of the road. The engine was not running and the lights were off, but the keys were in the ignition. The accused failed a breath test and was charged with having care and control while having over 80 mg of alcohol in 100 mL of blood. The trial judge acquitted the accused because the Crown failed to prove that the accused performed an overt action that involved him with the car in a way that created a danger to the public. The court of appeal rejected this position, stating that the position of the car on the roadway created a hazard to the public and that the accused had the immediate capacity and means of operating the vehicle.

4. The Charter and Section 258

The presumption under s. 258 has been challenged under the Charter as a violation of the presumption of innocence. The Supreme Court of Canada has held that even though the presumption violates the right to be presumed innocent, the provision is a reasonable limitation under s. 1 of the Charter. The court held that the objective of protecting the public from drunk drivers is "sufficiently important to warrant overriding a constitutionally protected right."[26]

5. The Meaning of "Impaired"

In general, an accused is impaired within the meaning of s. 253 if, as a result of consuming alcohol or drugs, he or she is no longer in complete control of the motor vehicle. The proof of impairment can be based on a number of factors, including actual driving behaviour, a breathalyzer test, and the appearance and behaviour (e.g., slurred speech, smell of alcohol on the breath) of the accused when examined by the police.

In *R. v. McKenzie*, the court made the following statement about proof of impairment:

There appears to be no single test or observation of impairment of control of faculties, standing alone, which is sufficiently conclusive. There should be consideration of a combination of several tests and observations such as general conduct, smell of the breath, character of the speech, manner of walking, turning sharply, sitting down and rising, picking up objects, reaction of the pupils of the eyes, character of the breathing.[27]

24 Supra, note 19.
25 (1991) 64 C.C.C. (3d) 209 (N.B.C.A.).
26 *R. v. Whyte* (1988), 42 C.C.C. (3d) 97 (S.C.C.).
27 (1955), 111 C.C.C. 317 (Alta. Dis. Ct.) at 319.

In *R. v. Stellato*,[28] the Ontario Court of Appeal held that any degree of impairment, from slight to great, is sufficient for the offence. This decision, which was later approved by the Supreme Court of Canada, rejected the need for proof of driving that was a marked departure from the driving of a reasonable person for the offence of impaired driving.

In *R. v. Graat*,[29] the Supreme Court of Canada affirmed a decision of the Ontario Court of Appeal which held that non-expert opinion is admissible evidence in determining whether a person is impaired. Medical expertise is not necessary to identify whether a person is impaired, since most people can express an opinion on impairment from their own experience.

As mentioned, impairment can be from alcohol or drugs. One court has said that the term "drug" should be given a broad meaning to include any substance that, if consumed, will bring about impairment.[30] Also, it has been held that it is not necessary to prove whether the impairment is from alcohol or drugs.[31]

6. Voluntariness

The question of voluntariness often arises when the accused claims that he or she was unaware of the effects of the drug or alcohol; for example, a person may claim that he or she unwittingly became impaired after taking a prescription drug. In general, a person who can establish that he or she was not aware, and should not have reasonably been aware, that the medication would cause impairment, will avoid conviction for impairment. On the other hand, a mistaken belief as to how much one can drink before becoming impaired will not be a defence. Nor will overestimating the time it will take for medication to take effect.[32]

Whether an accused's impairment was voluntary or involuntary was discussed in *R. v. McLeod*.[33] The accused was charged with impaired driving. He testified that he had two drinks of whisky; then, intending to take two "222" pills, he mistakenly took two pills prescribed for his diabetes. A doctor testified that the diabetes medication could cause symptoms of impairment, and that the accused would be unaware of such symptoms. The court held that, through no act of his own will, the accused became incapable of appreciating that he was, or might become, impaired. In such circumstances, the accused could not be convicted of impaired driving.

In *R. v. Honish*,[34] the accused was charged with impaired driving causing bodily harm. At the time of the accident, he was depressed about problems with his marriage. He had several drinks and then, intending to commit suicide, took a large quantity of pills. He testified that he then lay down on his bed. The next thing he remembered was waking up in the hospital. He had, within an hour of taking the pills, driven his car and collided with another car. At his trial, he argued that his intoxication was involuntary. He appealed his conviction to the Alberta Court of Appeal. The court dismissed his appeal, holding that his intoxication was voluntary in the sense that he voluntarily consumed the drugs and alcohol, and also in the sense that he knew that the combination would have an impairing effect. The fact that he was depressed and may have felt compelled to commit suicide did not prevent his acts from being voluntary.

---

28 (1993), 78 C.C.C. (3d) 380 (Ont. C.A.); appeal dismissed 90 C.C.C. (3d) 160n (S.C.C.).
29 (1982), 2 C.C.C. (3d) 365 (S.C.C.).
30 *R. v. Marionchuk* (1978), 42 C.C.C. (2d) 573 (Sask. C.A.).
31 *R. v. MacAuley* (1975), 25 C.C.C. (2d) 1 (N.B.C.A.).
32 *R. v. Penner* (1974), 16 C.C.C. (2d) 334 (Man. C.A.); *R. v. Murray* (1985), 22 C.C.C. (3d) 502 (Ont. C.A.).
33 (1972), 6 C.C.C. (2d) 81 (Sask. D.C.).
34 (1991), 68 C.C.C. (3d) 329 (Alta. C.A.); aff'd (1993), 78 C.C.C. (3d) 96 (S.C.C.).

LO4 ## 7. Authority to Test for Alcohol or Drugs

In addition to a roadside screening test for alcohol, a peace officer can demand tests of physical coordination to test for alcohol or drugs. The authority for giving these tests is set out as follows:

> **254. (2) If a peace officer has reasonable grounds to suspect that a person has alcohol or a drug in their body and that the person has, within the last three hours, operated a motor vehicle . . . or had the care or control of a motor vehicle . . . whether it was in motion or not, the peace officer, may by demand, require the person to comply with paragraph (a), in the case of a drug, or with either or both paragraphs (a) or (b) in the case of alcohol:**
>
> > **(a) to perform forthwith physical coordination tests prescribed by regulation to enable the peace officer to determine whether a demand may be made under subsection (3) or (3.1) and, if necessary, to accompany the peace officer for that purpose; and**
> >
> > **(b) to provide forthwith a sample of breath that, in the peace officer's opinion, will enable a proper analysis to be made by means of an approved screening device and, if necessary, to accompany the peace officer for that purpose.**

Notice that an officer can demand that a person take a screening or physical coordination test based on "reasonable grounds to suspect" that the person has alcohol or drugs in his or her body. Reasonable grounds to suspect are grounds that would lead an ordinary, prudent, and cautious person to have a strong and honest suspicion. This is a lower standard than a demand for a breathalyzer test or a test of bodily fluids for drugs or alcohol, which requires "reasonable grounds to believe." The results of the initial testing may provide the officer with the grounds for demanding the breathalyzer test in the case of alcohol, while the results of the physical coordination test may allow for a demand of further drug testing at the station by an officer who is trained as a drug recognition expert (D.R.E.).

a. The Meaning of "Forthwith"

The demand under s. 254(2) must be made "forthwith." Several cases have concerned the meaning of the term "forthwith." In *R. v. Grant*,[35] an officer pulled over the accused driver because he suspected him of driving while disqualified. While talking to him, he smelled alcohol on his breath. The officer then made a breathalyzer demand. However, the officer did not have the equipment in his car and had to call another officer to deliver it to him. The equipment did not arrive until half an hour later. The Supreme Court of Canada held that the term "forthwith" suggests that the test should be given immediately. In this case, the demand was not authorized by s. 254 because it was not a demand to provide a sample "forthwith" but a demand for the accused to give a breath sample when the equipment arrived, half an hour later. Therefore, the accused could not be found guilty of the offence of refusing to comply with a demand made under s. 254. Subsequent provincial court of appeal cases have held that generally, the officer should be equipped with the device; but where, for example, there is a five-minute lapse while the equipment is being obtained, the officer can make a valid demand

---

35 (1991), 67 C.C.C. (3d) 268 (S.C.C.).

for the breath sample.[36] The Newfoundland Court of Appeal has stated that whether the time lapse is reasonable depends on the circumstances. In general, a delay of half an hour or more is not acceptable; if the delay was under half an hour, the court must look at the circumstances in deciding if such delay was valid.[37]

The validity of a delay was considered in *R. v. Pierman*,[38] a decision of the Ontario Court of Appeal. The officer in this case waited 15 minutes before administering the test, as recommended by the manufacturer of the device. Otherwise, if the accused had had a drink within the previous 15 minutes, the machine might have registered a "false fail" because of the residual alcohol in his mouth. Since the accused was observed leaving a tavern and admitted to having a couple of beers, the court considered that it was reasonable to assume that he had consumed alcohol within the last 15 minutes. The court said that the police could take a flexible approach to administering the test "forthwith." Usually the test must be administered immediately; but where the officer is of the opinion that the test will be contaminated because of mouth alcohol, the officer may wait 15 minutes.

This issue was considered again by the Supreme Court of Canada in *R. v. Bernshaw*.[39] The accused had been stopped by a police officer because of his erratic driving. The officer observed that the accused's eyes were red and that his breath smelled of alcohol. He asked the accused if he had been drinking and the accused replied, "Yes." Based on this information, the officer demanded a breath sample. The officer did not inquire as to when the accused had last had a drink, nor did he wait 15 minutes to administer the test. The accused failed the screening test, and the officer demanded a breathalyzer test. On appeal, the accused argued that the officer did not have reasonable grounds for demanding the breathalyzer test because the officer did not know when the accused had last consumed alcohol, and therefore did not know if the screening test was accurate. The Court considered the decision in *Pierman* and decided to adopt the "flexible approach." The Court stated that in general, the screening test should be administered immediately. However, an officer who has a factual basis for believing that an immediate test will provide an inaccurate reading can wait up to 15 minutes before administering the test. There was no evidence to indicate when the accused had his last drink; therefore, the officer was acting properly when he asked for the breath sample immediately and when he used the "fail" on the screening test as the basis for demanding a breathalyzer test. A related issue was whether the police are obligated, before taking a sample, either to wait 15 minutes or to find out when the driver had last consumed alcohol. The Court held that the police are not required to ask the driver when he or she last consumed alcohol. The suspect may volunteer such information, or the officer may inquire, but there is no obligation for one to ask or for the other to answer such a question. If the officer has no grounds for believing that the screening test results will be unreliable, h.e or she can demand a sample and use those results as the basis for demanding a breathalyzer test.

Another case that discussed the meaning of "forthwith" was *R. v. George*, where the court stated, "Based on *Grant*,[40] it is understood that to be 'forthwith,' the demand must be that the detainee provide the sample after 'a brief period of detention, if not "immediately.""[41]

36   See, for example, *R. v. Misai* (1993), 79 C.C.C. (3d) 339 (Ont. C.A.); *R. v. Higgins* (1994), 88 C.C.C. (3d) 232 (Man. C.A.).
37   *R. v. Payne* (1994), 91 C.C.C. (3d) 144 (Nfld. C.A.).
38   (1994), 92 C.C.C. (3d) 160 (Ont. C.A.); aff'd (1996), 103 C.C.C. (3d) 382.
39   (1995), 95 C.C.C. (3d) 193 (S.C.C.).
40   *Grant*, *supra* note 40.
41   *R. v. George* (2004), 187 C.C.C. (3d) 289 (Ont. C.A.) at 295; see also *R. v. Danychuk* (2004), 183 C.C.C. (3d) 337 (Ont. C.A.) at 342.

The Ontario Court of Appeal has held that the demand does not need to be in any particular form as long as it is made clear to the driver that the sample must be given forthwith. The court stated in *R. v. Torsey*:

> We agree with the summary conviction appeal judge that the missing word "forthwith" did not render the demand invalid. The demand need not be in any particular form, provided it is made clear to the driver that he or she is required to give a sample of his or her breath "forthwith." This can be accomplished through words or conduct, including the tenor [of the officer's] discussion with the accused.[42]

b. Testing for Alcohol or Drugs

Testing for Alcohol

Under s. 254(3), the officer may demand that the person take a breathalyzer test, if the officer has reasonable grounds to believe that the person has consumed alcohol within the last three hours and is committing or has committed an offence under s. 253 (impaired driving). If the officer has reasonable grounds to believe that the person is incapable of taking a breathalyzer test or that taking the test would be impracticable, the officer may demand a blood sample.

The development of machines capable of measuring blood–alcohol levels has greatly simplified the task of controlling driving that is impaired by alcohol. The offence of driving with more than 80 mg of alcohol in 100 mL of blood does not require any proof of bad driving, or any other evidence of impairment.

There are two types of tests in use today. The first involves a screening device that is usually administered on the spot when the driver is stopped. This practice is sometimes called "roadside testing," although the test is not necessarily administered on the roadside. Anyone operating a boat, aircraft, or railway equipment may be required to take the test. A person who "fails" this test will be asked to take a breathalyzer test at the police station. The result of the second test shows the exact amount of alcohol in the person's blood, and is the basis upon which the charge is laid.

An "approved screening device" is an instrument that can evaluate a person's blood–alcohol level immediately. Approved devices are listed in the Code in s. 254. The technology is constantly changing; most commonly, however, a person breathes into the device, which then flashes a red, yellow, or green light. A red flash indicates that the driver's blood–alcohol level is over the 80 mg limit. If the device signals red, the driver is taken to the police station for a breathalyzer test, which is more precise.

Since the breathalyzer test is usually taken at the police station, there will be some delay between the time of the alleged offence (driving over 80) and the testing. The previous Section 258(1)(c)(ii) provided that, where the test is taken within two hours of the alleged offence, there is a presumption that the results of the breathalyzer test indicate the level of alcohol at the time the offence was committed unless "evidence to the contrary" is raised. This allowed the defence to rebut the presumption by introducing evidence that the accused's blood–alcohol level was different at the time of the offence and at the time of the testing. An example of this defence being used successfully was the case of *R. v. St. Pierre*.[43] The accused was stopped by the police because of her erratic driving. She failed a screening test and was taken to the station for a breathalyzer test. The machine was in use, so she had to wait about an hour. During that hour, she made several trips to the washroom, where she consumed two small bottles of vodka. After taking the breathalyzer test, which showed that she had 180 mg

42   (2007), 217 C.C.C. (3d) 571 (Ont. C.A.) at 574; leave to appeal to S.C.C. refused June 28, 2007.
43   (1995), 96 C.C.C. (3d) 385 (S.C.C.).

of alcohol in 100 mL of blood, she told the officers that she was an alcoholic and that she had drunk the vodka in the washroom. She gave the empty bottles to the officer. At her trial, her counsel argued that evidence that she had consumed alcohol at the station was "evidence to the contrary." The trial judge agreed, and she was acquitted. The court of appeal disagreed and entered a conviction. The case finally reached the Supreme Court on the issue of whether "evidence to the contrary" means evidence that an accused person's blood–alcohol level was lower at the time of the offence or just evidence that it was different. The Court held that the plain meaning of the term is that evidence to the contrary is evidence that an accused person's blood–alcohol was different at the two points of time: the time of the alleged offence and the time of the testing. (However, evidence of the normal biological processes of absorption and elimination of alcohol is not evidence to the contrary. It can be assumed that Parliament knew that blood–alcohol levels change constantly, but enacted the presumption anyway.) In *St. Pierre*, there was evidence to the contrary that the accused's blood–alcohol was different. Thus, the presumption was rebutted. However, this did not mean that the breathalyzer certificate showing the test results could not be used. An accused can still be convicted if, on the basis of all the evidence, the judge is satisfied beyond a reasonable doubt that the offence was committed. In this case, however, there was no other evidence establishing the accused's blood–alcohol level; therefore, the Court restored her acquittal.

The amended s. 258(1)(c) eliminates this defence. This section states that evidence of the results of the analysis is conclusive proof that the concentration of alcohol in the accused's blood is as determined by the testing unless there is evidence tending to show (a) that the approved instrument was malfunctioning, or was operated improperly, (b) that the malfunction or improper operation resulted in the determination that the concentration of alcohol in the accused's blood exceeded 80 mg of alcohol in 100 mL of blood, and (c) that the concentration of blood would not have exceeded 80 if the instrument were not malfunctioning or operated improperly.

Testing for Drugs

Section 254 contains detailed provisions for testing for impairment by drugs. In summary, if the suspect "fails" the physical coordination test (Standardized Field Sobriety Test), giving the officer reasonable grounds to believe the suspect is impaired by drugs and/or alcohol, the officer may by demand require the person to submit to an evaluation by a D.R.E. officer to determine whether there are reasonable grounds to believe that the person is impaired. If, on completion of the evaluation, the D.R.E. officer has reasonable grounds to believe that the person is impaired, the officer can demand that the person provide a sample of bodily fluid or a blood sample to determine if the person has drugs in his or her body. Samples of blood may be taken only by or under the direction of a qualified medical practitioner who is satisfied that taking the samples would not endanger the person's life or health.

The Standardized Field Sobriety Test may include an eye test called the Horizontal Gaze Nystagmus test in which the officer looks at the suspect's eyes as they track an object from side to side. The officer checks to see at what point the eyes jerk or bounce involuntarily. An intoxicated person's eye will jerk before the eye looks at a 45 degree angle. Another test is the walk-and-turn test, in which the officer directs the suspect to walk in a straight line, pivot, and walk back while keeping his or her arms down and counting the steps out loud. The officer watches how well the suspect follows directions and balances. A similar balance test is the one-legged stand test in which the officer directs the suspect to raise a foot slightly off the ground, hold still, count from 1 to 30, and look down at the foot.

L05   ## c. Random Stopping and the Charter

Most provinces today have legislation that allows for random stopping of vehicles, or "spot checks." When a driver is stopped, the police usually ask to see the person's driver's licence, car registration, and proof of insurance. At the time the car is stopped, the police are able to observe the driver for signs of impairment to determine whether there are grounds to demand a breath sample. There have been several Charter challenges concerning random stops. One issue has been whether a person is detained when stopped. Under the Charter, a person who is detained has a right to consult counsel and must be informed of that right. The Supreme Court of Canada has held that a person is detained during a random spot check or when stopped and required to give a breath sample. However, it is a reasonable limitation on the right to counsel to limit this right to situations where the more serious breathalyzer test is used.[44]

The Supreme Court has also held that allowing the police to give roadside sobriety tests or to ask drivers about their alcohol consumption without giving the right to consult counsel is a reasonable limitation.[45]

Similarly, random spot checks have been challenged as an arbitrary detention that infringes the Charter. Again, the Supreme Court has said that random spot checks are a reasonable limitation on the right not to be arbitrarily detained. The objective of controlling the social evil of drunk driving is of sufficient importance that the infringement is justified.[46] The Supreme Court has also held that requiring a driver to show a driver's licence, car registration, and proof of insurance does not violate a person's right to be free from unreasonable search and seizure. The Court has held that such a demand does not constitute a search within s. 8 of the Charter because it is not an intrusion on a reasonable expectation of privacy. There is no intrusion where a person is required to produce a licence, permit, or other documentation that indicates that the person has complied with the law that is a condition for exercising the right.[47]

In *R. v. Orbanski*, the Supreme Court stated:

> the challenge in this area of law enforcement is increased by the fact the activity in question (use of a vehicle on a highway) is ongoing and the drinking driver who has exceeded permissible limits presents a continuing danger on the highway. The aim is to screen drivers at the road stop, not at the scene of an accident.[48]

d. The Right to Counsel and the Breathalyzer Test

Once a demand for a breathalyzer test or a drug test has been made, the police must inform the suspect of the right to counsel. Chapter 5 discussed the right to counsel generally in any case where there is a detention or arrest. In brief, the right to counsel includes the right to be informed about whatever legal services are available. In most provinces, these include free, 24-hour, preliminary legal advice from a "duty counsel," as well as Legal Aid for those who meet the financial criteria. The officer, as part of the duty to inform, must also tell the detained person how to contact the available legal services (e.g., by providing a toll-free telephone number, or the phone numbers of lawyers acting as duty counsels).

---

44   *R. v. Thomsen* (1988), 40 C.C.C. (3d) 411 (S.C.C.), and *R. v. Therens* (1985), 18 C.C.C. (3d) 481 (S.C.C.).
45   *R. v. Orbanski* (2005), 196 C.C.C. (3d) 481 (S.C.C.).
46   *R. v. Hufsky* (1988), 40 C.C.C. (3d) 398 (S.C.C.); *R. v. Ladouceur* (1990), 56 C.C.C. (3d) 22.
47   Ibid.
48   *Orbanski, supra* note 50 at 49.

These rules regarding the right to counsel have a special significance in "over 80" cases. When a detained person expresses a desire to speak to a lawyer, the police cannot administer the test until the person has had a reasonable opportunity to do so. In *R. v. Prosper*,[49] a Nova Scotia case, the accused was pulled over after he was observed driving in an erratic manner on a Saturday afternoon in Halifax. He was told that he had a right to call any lawyer he wished, and that he could apply for Legal Aid. When he got to the station, he told the police that he would take the test but that he wanted to speak to a lawyer first. He was unable to contact any lawyer on the Legal Aid list. Nova Scotia did not have a free duty counsel system in place at this time, and Legal Aid lawyers were not taking calls outside of business hours. Eventually, the accused agreed to take the test. His sample was over 80, and he was charged with the offence. He was acquitted at his trial because the breathalyzer certificate that gave the results of the test was not allowed as evidence. The trial court judge ruled that his right to counsel had been violated.

On appeal to the Supreme Court of Canada, two of the issues were these: Are governments required by the Constitution to ensure that there is free and immediate legal advice available on request? And in the circumstances, were the accused's rights violated? The Supreme Court held that there is no obligation to provide free preliminary legal advice upon detention. However, the majority of the justices held that once a person has asserted his or her desire to speak with a lawyer, the police must "hold off" further questioning or eliciting of incriminating evidence until the accused has had a reasonable opportunity to do so. The justices stated that the police must hold off even if this means that the breathalyzer test cannot be given within the two-hour period so that the presumption in s. 258(1)(c)(ii) is lost. Although there might be some situations of urgency where the police do not have to hold off, losing an evidentiary presumption is not one of them. The Court stated, "While this alternative [holding off] may not be ideal from the Crown's perspective . . . this is a trade-off that governments which persist in refusing to implement a "Brydges duty counsel" system [free preliminary advice] will have to endure and accept."[50]

The Court added that the meaning of "reasonable opportunity" will depend on the surrounding circumstances, such as availability of duty counsel.

Future cases will have to set more detailed guidelines as to what is reasonable in the circumstances, and what are situations of urgency where police do not have to hold off.

E. REFUSAL TO COMPLY WITH A DEMAND

It is an offence under s. 254(5) to refuse, without a reasonable excuse, to comply with a request for any of the tests discussed above.

1. Reasonable Excuse for Failure to Comply

In *R. v. Nadeau*,[51] the judge concluded that a "reasonable excuse" must relate to some circumstance that renders compliance with the demand either extremely difficult or likely to involve a substantial risk to the health of the person on whom the demand has been made. In *R. v. Cordeiro*,[52] the court found that the accused had a lawful excuse because of "extreme difficulty." The accused's dentures were so poorly fitted that when he tried to give a breath sample, they came loose, making it impossible for him to exhale enough for a proper reading. In

49   (1994), 92 C.C.C. (3d) 353 (S.C.C.).
50   Ibid. at 374.
51   (1974), 19 C.C.C. (2d) 199 (N.B.C.A.).
52   Reported in *The Lawyers Weekly*, February 19, 1988.

R. v. Phinney,[53] the Nova Scotia Court of Appeal held that there is not an all-inclusive definition of reasonable excuse. In this case, the court held that the accused had an honest belief based on reasonable grounds that the machine was not functioning properly. This was a reasonable excuse for refusing the test. In *R. v. Iron*,[54] the accused would have been driven over 150 kilometres and left with no place to stay or way to get home for the sake of a breathalyzer test. The court held that he had a reasonable excuse for refusing.

Of course, as the cases above indicate, a person also has a right to refuse to take a test if the demand is not made within s. 254—for example, if the demand is not made "forthwith."

In *R. v. Swietorzechi*,[55] the accused was convicted of the offence of failing to comply with a demand to provide a breath sample. The demand was made to the accused when he appeared at the police station. He argued that he had not driven the car to the station and, therefore, was not obligated to take the test. The court held that this element of the offence (i.e., the driving) must exist in fact before the officer can make the demand; it is not enough that the officer has a reasonable suspicion that the accused operated or had care and control of a motor vehicle. In this case, the officer did not know that the accused had driven to the station; therefore, the accused was justified in refusing to take the test.

2. Unacceptable Excuses

The following excuses for refusing the test were judged not reasonable: The accused had a sincere belief that the results would not be accurate because the accused had consumed alcohol after driving,[56] the accused was on medication,[57] the accused was not being permitted to smoke,[58] and the accused would suffer a financial loss if he left his truck and its cargo, which was likely to spoil.[59]

.06 F. PENALTIES FOR IMPAIRED DRIVING AND DRIVING-OVER-80 OFFENCES

The penalties for impaired driving and driving-over-80 offences are fines and terms of imprisonment (s. 255), court-ordered driving prohibitions (s. 259), and penalties for summary conviction offences generally (s. 787). Offences under sections 253 (impaired or over 80) and 254 (refusing to take physical sobriety or breath test or provide a blood sample) are hybrid offences. There are minimum penalties for these offences, whether they are treated as summary conviction or as indictable. The highest maximum penalties are reserved for impaired driving or driving-over-80 that causes death (life imprisonment and ten year driving prohibition) or bodily harm (ten year imprisonment and ten year driving prohibition).

Provincial laws that regulate the highways also include penalties for persons convicted under the Criminal Code of the offences of impaired driving, testing over the legal limit for blood–alcohol level, or refusing to be tested.[60] For example, Ontario's *Highway Traffic Act* sets out the following penalties that can be imposed for those convicted of these offences: (1) roadside suspension; (2) administrative monetary penalty; (3) alcohol education program;

53   (1979), 49 C.C.C. (2d) 81 (N.S.C.A.).
54   (1977), 35 C.C.C. (2d) 279 (Sask. Q.B.).
55   (1995), 97 C.C.C. (3d) 285 (Ont. C.A.).
56   *R. v. Dunn* (1980), 8 M.V.R. 198 (B.C.C.A.).
57   *R. v. Frohwerk* (1979), 48 C.C.C. (2d) 214 (Man. C.A.).
58   *R. v. Leduc* (1987), 56 C.R. (3d) 270 (Que. C.A.); reversed [1989] 1 S.C.R. 1586 on other grounds.
59   *R. v. Gidney* (1987), 7 M.V.R. (2d) 90 (N.S.C.A.).
60   For a list of provincial and territorial statutes, see question 15 at the end of the chapter.

(4) alcohol treatment program; (5) installation of a breathalyzer ignition device to prevent the vehicle from starting if the driver's blood–alcohol level exceeds a certain amount; (6) vehicle impoundment; (7) minimum jail sentence for second, third, and subsequent offences; (8) fine; and (9) licence suspension.

Provincial statutes also contain provisions for penalties related to drinking and driving behaviour that is not an offence under the Criminal Code. For example, Ontario's *Highway Traffic Act* includes penalties for testing at a blood–alcohol level from .05 to .08: (1) roadside suspension, (2) administrative monetary penalty, (3) alcohol education program, (4) alcohol treatment program, and (4) ignition interlock condition.

Questions for Review and Discussion

1. Explain the differences between the federal and provincial powers to create driving offences.

2. What are the elements of the offence of dangerous driving?

3. Annette is involved in an accident as a driver of a motor vehicle. What are Annette's legal responsibilities under the Criminal Code?

4. What is the difference between the offence of impaired driving and the offence of driving with 80 mg of alcohol in 100 mL of blood?

5. How have the courts defined "care or control" as used in s. 253?

6. The accused was charged with having care and control of a motor vehicle while impaired. He was found by the police sleeping in his truck, which was located on private property, roughly three metres from the road. His head was by the passenger side door and his lower body, which extended under the steering wheel, was encased in a sleeping bag. The key was in the ignition, and the stereo was playing loudly. The engine and lights were not on. His evidence was that a friend drove him to a party in the accused's truck. The accused was tired and went to sleep in the truck while waiting for his friend to drive him home. He testified that he had no intention of driving home. It was conceded that he was impaired at the time he was found by the police. The issue for the court was whether he had care and control.

Should the accused be convicted? Discuss the arguments for and against. See *R. v. Toews* (1985), 21 C.C.C. (3d) 24 (S.C.C.).

7. The accused was charged with dangerous driving. The evidence was that he had had very little sleep over a five-day period. He had worked three days on an afternoon shift and then spent two days helping his father move to a new residence. At the end of the fifth day, he had one or two beers and then got in his car to drive to a restaurant for something to eat. On a busy four-lane highway, he fell asleep at the wheel and collided with a car going the opposite way. He testified that he knew he was exhausted but felt that he was driving normally. Should he be convicted? See *R. v. Mason* (1990), 60 C.C.C. (3d) 338 (B.C.C.A.).

8. The accused was a passenger in his own car when the driver hit a pedestrian. The driver stopped about 33 metres from the accident, started to reverse, then got confused and drove about 200 metres. The accused then took over driving, went another 33 metres, turned around, and went back to the accident. The accused was charged with failure to remain. Should he be convicted? See *R. v. Shea* (1982), 17 M.V.R. 40 (Nfld. C.A.).

9. John knew that he was very intoxicated when he left the bar and headed toward his car. He saw Mary, a total stranger, walking down the street. He stopped her and asked her to drive him home. She protested that she didn't have a licence and didn't know how to drive. He finally persuaded her to drive the car. After driving a short distance, she hit another car.

    Can John be charged with a driving offence? Discuss. See *R. v. Keen* (1994), 10 M.V.R. (3d) 320 (Alta. C.A.).

10. Leanne was the driver in a high-speed police chase. The police car pursuing her car failed to yield at an intersection and collided with a vehicle going the other way. As a result of the accident, Leanne was charged with impaired driving causing bodily harm. What is the main issue in this case, and how would you resolve it?

11. S. was found driving a riding lawnmower on a paved road after leaving the scene of an accident. He was given a breathalyzer test and his readings ranged from .151 to .260. What charges can be laid against him? What does the Crown need to prove? See *R. v. Smith*, [1999] O.J. No. 5238.

12. On a clear day, MacGillivray drove his motorboat at a high speed toward an area where he knew that there could be swimmers. He drove the boat through a group of seven boys who were swimming and the boat struck and fatally injured one of them. He did not see the swimmers. He was charged under s. 249(4). Should he be convicted? See *R. v. MacGillivray* (1995), 97 C.C.C. (3d) 13 (S.C.C.).

13. Shepherd was charged with impaired driving and "driving over 80." A police officer saw Shepherd's vehicle fail to stop at a stop sign and then travel at 20 to 25 kilometres per hour over the speed limit. The officer activated his police cruiser's siren and lights in an effort to get the vehicle to pull over. The vehicle accelerated and changed lanes multiple times over approximately a three-kilometre distance before finally pulling over. Shepherd explained that he had not stopped because he thought the police car was an ambulance. The officer noted that Shepherd looked lethargic and fatigued and had red eyes. He could smell alcohol on his breath. He also noted that his movements and speech were slow and deliberate. On the basis of these observations, the officer formed the opinion that Shepherd was intoxicated. The officer made a breathalyzer demand. Although the trial judge accepted the officer's evidence that he subjectively believed that Shepherd's ability to drive was impaired by alcohol, he concluded that this belief was not objectively reasonable. The trial judge relied heavily on the accused's explanation that he thought the police car was an ambulance. The trial judge noted that this was "just as valid an explanation" for Shepherd's erratic driving as the suggestion that he was impaired by alcohol. He acquitted Shepherd of the charges. Was the trial judge correct? See *R. v. Shepherd* (2009), 245 C.C.C. (3d) 137 (S.C.C.).

14. At a roadside police check-stop near a town's 125th anniversary celebrations, Forsythe failed a screening test. The police made a demand for a breath sample pursuant to s. 254(3). After making the demand and before leaving for the police station to take the breath sample, the police called a tow truck to impound the vehicle. The police knew that it would take about 30 minutes for the tow truck to arrive, so they waited at the scene with Forsythe until the tow truck arrived before leaving for the station, which was about 3 minutes away. At the station, two breath samples indicated that the level of alcohol in Forsythe's blood exceeded the statutory limit. The defence argued that the breathalyzer evidence should be excluded because the police did

not comply with s. 254(3), which requires that the police take an accused's breath sample "as soon as practicable." Do you agree that the breath samples were not taken as soon as practicable? If they were not taken as soon as practicable, does that mean that the breathalyzer evidence should be excluded? See *R. v. Forsythe* (2009), 250 C.C.C. (3d) 90 (Man. C.A.).

15. What are the penalties in your province or territory for (a) being convicted under the Criminal Code of the offences of impaired driving, testing over the legal limit for blood–alcohol level (.08), or refusing to be tested, and (b) drinking and driving behaviour that is not an offence under the *Criminal Code*? These are the provincial and territorial statutes: British Columbia *Motor Vehicle Act*, Alberta *Traffic Safety Act*,

Saskatchewan *Highway Traffic Act*, Manitoba *Highway Traffic Act*, Ontario *Highway Traffic Act*, Quebec *Highway Safety Code*, New Brunswick *Motor Vehicle Act*, Nova Scotia *Motor Vehicle Act*, Newfoundland and Labrador *Highway Traffic Act*, Prince Edward Island *Highway Traffic Act*, Northwest Territories *Motor Vehicle Act*, Yukon *Motor Vehicles Act*, and Nunavut *Motor Vehicle Act*.

16. If a police officer arrests a person at the roadside on an impaired driving charge, is the officer required to tell the person that, if he or she chooses to consult counsel, that consultation will occur at the police station and not at the roadside? See *R. v. Devries* (2009), 244 C.C.C. (3d) 354 (Ont. C.A.).

CHAPTER 11

Assaults and Related Offences against the Person

PART VIII OF THE CODE

Key points explained in this chapter are

LO1 the legal requirements to establish any assault offence;

LO2 the limits on use of force by police and others in authority;

LO3 the specific assault offences, such as assault causing bodily harm and aggravated sexual assault;

LO4 the meaning of "sexual" in sexual assault offences;

LO5 whether consent of the victim may be a defence to an assault charge; and

LO6 offences related to assault, including "stalking," kidnapping, abduction, and hate crime.

This chapter covers offences involving actual or threatened violence against persons. Part VIII of the Code also contains offences against a person's reputation, such as libel, as well as offences against marriage, such as bigamy and the unlawful solemnization of marriage.

A. UTTERING THREATS

264.1 (1) Every one commits an offence who, in any manner, knowingly utters, conveys or causes any person to receive a threat

(a) **to cause death or bodily harm to any person;**

(b) **to burn, destroy or damage real or personal property; or**

(c) **to kill, poison or injure an animal or bird that is the property of any person.**

1. Elements of the Offence

The *actus reus* of this offence is the uttering (i.e., speaking or writing) of words that are a threat of death or serious bodily harm. In *Clemente v. The Queen*,[1] the Supreme Court of Canada addressed how to determine whether the speaking or writing of words is a threat. It also explained the *mens rea* of the offence. The accused, Clemente, who was on welfare, was

---

1   (1994), 91 C.C.C. (3d) 1 (S.C.C.).

told that his case was being transferred back to his former social worker, J.M. He became very upset and said that he would blow up her office and strangle her if she became his social worker again. A few days later, he told his current social worker that there would be a dead body in J.M.'s office if his case was transferred. He repeated the threat the next day in a telephone conversation. He was charged and convicted of uttering threats. He appealed his conviction to the court of appeal, which upheld the conviction. He then appealed to the Supreme Court of Canada, which held that to determine whether words are a threat, courts must look at whether a reasonable person would have considered that the words were uttered as a threat. The courts must review the words objectively in light of the circumstances in which they were uttered, the manner in which they were spoken, and the person to whom they were addressed. So, for example, words spoken in jest or in such a manner that they could not be taken seriously could not lead a reasonable person to conclude that they conveyed a threat. Regarding *mens rea*, the Court stated that the *mens rea* for this offence requires that the accused uttered the words with the intent that they would intimidate or be taken seriously. Finally, the Supreme Court held that it is not necessary to find that the words were spoken with the intent of being conveyed to the potential victim. Applying this reasoning to the facts of the case, the Court found that the offence was committed, and dismissed the appeal.

No other action beyond the threat is necessary for this offence. It is the meaning of the words that is important. In *R. v. Leblanc*,[2] the Supreme Court of Canada established that it does not matter whether the person making the threat intends to carry it out; rather, the criminal sanction is aimed at the fear that the issuer of the threat instills in the victim.

The Quebec Court of Appeal has held that the threat does not need to be made to a specific person; it can be made to members of an identifiable group. In *R. v. Remy*,[3] after two black men were killed by the police in Montreal, the accused threatened to kill the next police officer who killed a black person in similar circumstances. The court held that the offence was committed even though the identity of the victim was unknown when the threat was made. The court noted that the officer's identity would become known when the conditions of the threat (i.e., the killing of a black person in similar circumstances) were met.

The meaning of "serious bodily harm" was examined by the Supreme Court of Canada in *R. v. McCraw*.[4] The accused had been seen at the practices of the Ottawa Roughriders cheerleaders. He phoned some of the cheerleaders and, using an assumed name, asked them to pose for photographs. At the same time, he wrote to three of the cheerleaders. In the letters, he described the sexual acts that he intended to perform on them. He concluded the letters with a threat that he would have intercourse with them even if he had to rape them. The case reached the Supreme Court on the issue of whether the threat to rape the women was a threat to cause serious bodily harm under s. 264.1. To answer this question, the Court looked at three underlying questions: What is serious bodily harm? Can psychological harm cause serious bodily harm? And can a threat to rape be a threat to cause serious bodily harm? After considering the definition of "bodily harm" in s. 2 of the Code[5] and the dictionary meaning of "serious," the Court defined serious bodily harm as being "any hurt or injury that interferes in a grave or substantial way with the physical integrity or well-being of the complainant . . ." As to the second question, the Court found that serious bodily harm includes psychological harm so long as the psychological harm substantially interferes with the health or well-being of the

2   (1989), 50 C.C.C. (3d) 192n (S.C.C.).
3   (1993), 82 C.C.C. (3d) 176 (Que. C. A.).
4   (1991), 66 C.C.C. (3d) 517 (S.C.C.).
5   Section 2 defines bodily harm as "any hurt or injury to a person that interferes with the health or comfort of the person and that is more than merely transient or trifling in nature."

complainant. To answer the third question, the Court said that it must first look at the threat to rape generally. The Court noted that violence is inherent in the act of rape: "[To] argue that a woman who has been forced to have sexual intercourse has not necessarily suffered grave and serious violence is to ignore the perspective of women . . ."[6] The Court added that rape is the ultimate violation of personal privacy and causes devastating psychological consequences that may last a lifetime. Therefore, no other conclusion can be drawn but that rape can cause serious bodily harm. So also can the threat to rape.

In determining whether the particular words in this case were a threat to cause serious bodily harm, the Court stated that it must look objectively at the context of all the words used, at the person to whom the words were directed, and at the circumstances in which the words were uttered. To any reasonable person, the threat to rape would mean the threat of sexual penetration without consent, achieved by means of violence or threatened violence. Here, the threat was made to young women, and it included graphic descriptions of various sexual acts that the accused would perform on them. The clear inference was that the three women would be forced to submit to sexual penetration without consent by the use of violence. The complainants testified that they had to carry out their activities knowing that they were being stalked, and that this resulted in restrictions on their movements and actions. The Court concluded that the threat was a threat to cause serious bodily harm. The accused's appeal of his conviction was dismissed.

⏺01 B. ASSAULT

1. Defined

265. (1) A person commits an assault when

(a) without the consent of another person, he applies force intentionally to that other person, directly or indirectly;

(b) he attempts or threatens, by an act or a gesture, to apply force to another person, if he has, or causes that other person to believe on reasonable grounds that he has, present ability to effect his purpose; or

(c) while openly wearing or carrying a weapon or an imitation thereof, he accosts or impedes another person or begs.

(2) This section applies to all forms of assault, including sexual assault, sexual assault with a weapon, threats to a third party or causing bodily harm and aggravated sexual assault.

Notice that the section defines three different sets of circumstances in which an assault may occur. The section does not set out three separate offences but rather describes three ways that the offence of assault may be committed. The accused in *R. v. MacKay*[7] was charged with aggravated assault, contrary to s. 268(2), after striking a bicyclist with his motorcycle and causing very serious injuries to the victim. The accused was acquitted at trial. The Court of Appeal of New Brunswick allowed the Crown's appeal and ordered a new trial limited to assault as defined in s. 265(1)(b). Both the Crown and the accused appealed this decision. In dismissing the appeal, the Supreme Court of Canada stated, "In our view, the court of appeal was correct in

---

6   *McCraw, supra* note 4 at 526.
7   (2005), 203 C.C.C. (3d) 289 (S.C.C.).

granting the Crown's appeal on the basis of reversible error in respect of the definition of assault. However, it erred in restricting the scope of the new trial. Sections 265(1)(a) and 265(1)(b) do not create separate offences but simply define two ways of committing the same offence."[8]

Under subsection (1)(a), force must be actually used, and lack of valid consent is an essential element. Where the use of force is only threatened or attempted, subs. (1)(b) requires that the person who was threatening or attempting the assault was able to carry out the assault, or caused the victim to believe on reasonable grounds that he or she was able to carry out the assault. Subsection (1)(c) defines a specific situation in which it may be implied that the use of force is being threatened. Note that subs. (2) provides that the definitions in this section apply to all forms of assault, including sexual assault.

2. Assault: Section 265(1)(a)

a. Elements

The *actus reus* of assault under s. 265(1)(a) consists of (a) the physical act of applying force to another person, and doing so (b) in a circumstance to which the other person did not consent. The *mens rea* of assault consists of the intention to apply force to the other person, indicated by the word "intentionally."

R. v. Vandergraaf[9] is an example of a case that turned on whether the accused had the necessary *mens rea* to be convicted of assault. The accused tried to throw a small glass bottle on the ice at a hockey game. His aim was off, and he hit a person who was standing in the front row at ice level. The accused was charged with assault but acquitted on appeal because there was no evidence that he intended to apply force to the victim.

The amount of force required as part of the *actus reus* of assault was addressed in *R. v. Burden*.[10] The British Columbia Court of Appeal held that an assault can be committed even when no degree of strength or power is exerted. In this case, the victim was sitting on a bus when the accused sat next to her. The accused stared at the victim for a short time, and then put his hand on her thigh for between five and ten seconds. There were two other people on the bus at the time. In convicting the accused, the court quoted with approval the following passage from an eighteenth-century English authority:

> *Battery [assault] seems to be, when an injury whatsoever, be it ever so small, is actually done to a person of a man in an angry or revengeful, or rude, or insolent manner . . . For the law can not draw the line between different degrees of violence and therefore totally prohibits the first and lowest stage of it, every man's person being sacred . . .*[11]

b. Consent

As noted above, part of the *actus reus* of assault under s. 265(1)(a) is lack of consent. Any touching of a person may be an assault if it is done without that person's consent. What in one situation might be a gesture of love and affection, in another situation might be a criminal assault.

Before a person can give consent to an act, he or she must understand the nature of that act and actively consent to it. The law draws a distinction between mere submission and positive consent. As one court stated, "Consent means an active will in the mind of the [victim] to permit the doing of the act complained of; and that knowledge of what is to be done, or of the

---

8   Ibid. at 291.
9   (1994), 93 C.C.C. (3d) 286 (Man. C.A.).
10   (1981), 64 C.C.C. (2d) 68 (B.C.C.A.).
11   Ibid. at 70.

nature of the act that is being done, is essential to a consent to the act."[12] So, for example, to obtain valid consent, doctors must inform patients of procedures they intend to perform. Some persons, such as the mentally disabled and young children, are incapable of giving consent. Thus, before a child receives medical treatment, unless emergency conditions exist, a doctor will obtain the consent of the child's parents or guardian.

A case concerning the validity of consent is *R. v. Ssenyonga*.[13] The accused, knowing that he had AIDS, had unprotected sex with several women, who subsequently contracted the HIV virus. He was charged with three counts of aggravated sexual assault. He was acquitted at his trial, the judge holding that the victims consented to the application of force involved in sexual intercourse, and that the presence of the virus was irrelevant. The victims were not misled as to the nature of the act of intercourse.

But in a later case, *R. v. Cuerrier*,[14] the Supreme Court held that an accused has obtained consent by fraud, which may vitiate consent to sexual intercourse with him, if he knows he is HIV positive, fails to disclose that fact, and sexual contact with him poses a significant risk of serious bodily harm. An accused who obtains consent in these circumstances may be found guilty of contravening s. 265. The Court, disagreeing with the court in *Ssenyonga*, found that fraud was not limited to the nature and quality of the act. The Court stated that "it is no longer necessary when examining whether consent in assault or sexual assault cases was vitiated by fraud to consider whether the fraud related to the nature and quality of the act." The Court continued, "The deadly consequences that non-disclosure of the risk of HIV infection can have on an unknowing victim make it imperative that as a policy the broader view of fraud vitiating consent . . . should be adopted. . . . "[15]

In *R. v. Mabior*, the Supreme Court reviewed its decision in *Cuerrier* and concluded that "the *Cuerrier* requirement of a 'significant risk of serious bodily harm' entails a realistic possibility of transmission of HIV. This applies to all cases where fraud vitiating consent to sexual relations is alleged on the basis of the non-disclosure of HIV-positive status."[16] In *Mabior*, the Court found that there is not a realistic possibility of transmission of HIV if the accused, at the time of sexual relations, had a low viral load and condom protection was used. Therefore, in these circumstances, it is not necessary for the accused to disclose his HIV status.

For consent to be valid, it must be freely given. Section 265(3) lists some of the situations where there is no consent because it is not given voluntarily:

(3) For the purposes of this section, no consent is obtained where the complainant submits or does not resist by reason of

    (a) the application of force to the complainant or to a person other than the complainant,

    (b) threats or fear of the application of force to the complainant or to a person other than the complainant,

    (c) fraud, or

    (d) the exercise of authority.

---

12   *R. v. Lock* (1872), 12 Cox C.C. 244 at page 245.
13   (1993), 81 C.C.C. (3d) 257 (Ont. Ct. Gen. Div.).
14   (1998), 127 C.C.C. (3d) 1 at 45 (S.C.C.). See also *R. v. Williams* (2003), 176 C.C.C. (3d) 449 (S.C.C.).
15   *Cuerrier*, ibid. at 47.
16   *R. v. Mabior*, 2012 SCC 47.

The court in *R. v. Quashie* stated that "in order for bodily harm to vitiate consent, they [the jury] had to find both that the appellant had intended to inflict bodily harm on the complainant and that the appellant had caused her bodily harm."[17]

In *R. v. Saint-Laurent*,[18] the Quebec Court of Appeal held that exercise of authority is not limited to situations where there is a right to give orders and enforce obedience. It also refers to situations where there is an imbalance of power, such as between psychiatrist and patient.

c. The Limited Scope of Consent

Certain sports, such as hockey, involve physical contact. Courts have held that the players give implied consent to the use of force in these games. However, the force used may exceed that to which the consent was given. One judge has said that "there is a question of degree involved, and no athlete should be presumed to accept malicious, unprovoked or overly violent attack."[19] An example of a case where the force used was held to exceed the consent given is *R. v. Cey*,[20] where a fight broke out during a hockey game. One of the players involved in the fight walked over to a player who was standing off to the side and hit him in an unprotected part of the head. The victim suffered a serious eye injury, and the attacker was found guilty of assault. A different result was arrived at in *R. v. Leclerc*,[21] which also involved an incident during a hockey game. The accused was pursuing the complainant down the ice, and they collided as the accused hit the complainant in the back with his stick. The complainant's head hit the boards. A penalty was called against the accused for a deliberate attempt to injure. It was later determined that the complainant had suffered a dislocation of a portion of his spine and was permanently paralyzed from the neck down. The trial judge accepted evidence that, even though this game took place within a non-contact hockey league, in practice all players expected and accepted the contacts inherent in the game. He also accepted evidence that the accused had lost his balance and shoved the complainant in the back to push him off in order to avoid more violent contact. The accused was acquitted at his trial, and the Crown appealed. The court of appeal stated that to determine whether consent to conduct can be implied, the court should look at such factors as the setting of the game, the nature of the league, the age of the players, the conditions under which the game is played, the extent of the force used, the degree of risk or injury, and the probability of serious harm. However, the court continued, deliberate infliction of injury will generally be outside the immunity provided by implied consent. In this case, the trial court judge found that the push or shove was part of an "instinctive reflex action." While the no-contact rule was relevant in determining the scope of the implied consent, the trial judge also found that the rule was often breached. Having regard to the facts as found by the trial judge, the appeal court dismissed the appeal of the acquittal.

Another type of case where consent is limited is where two people agree to fight. Until 1991, the law was not clear on whether the fact that the parties consented to fight could be a defence where one person was injured. Some courts had allowed the defence of consent even when one person suffered bodily harm;[22] other courts had followed the English common law, which says that a person cannot give valid consent to physical force used in anger or where

17 (2005), 198 C.C.C. (3d) 337 (Ont. C.A.) at 354.
18 (1993), 90 C.C.C. (3d) 291 (Que. C.A.); leave to appeal refused 175 N.R. 240n.
19 *R. v. Maki* (1970), 1 C.C.C. (2d) 333 (Ont. Prov. Ct.).
20 (1989), 48 C.C.C. (3d) 480 (Sask. C.A.).
21 (1991), 67 C.C.C. (3d) 563 (Ont. C.A.).
22 *R. v. Bergner* (1987), 36 C.C.C. (3d) 25 (Alta. C.A.).

it is likely to cause or does cause bodily harm. For example, in *R. v. Squire*,[23] the court said, "Where two persons engage in a fight in anger by mutual consent, the blows struck by each constitute an assault on the other unless justifiable in self defence."

The case that finally settled the law was *R. v. Jobidon*,[24] a decision of the Supreme Court of Canada. Jobidon and a man named Haggart were drinking in a bar. Haggart walked over to Jobidon and punched him in the face because he believed that a week earlier Jobidon had punched a friend of his. They started fighting. It appeared that Haggart was winning the fight, but the owner of the bar broke up the fight and told Jobidon to leave. Jobidon waited outside the bar; when Haggart came out, they exchanged mutual invitations to fight. Jobidon rushed at Haggart, and hit him in the head, knocking him unconscious and onto the hood of a car. He struck Haggart several more times in the head. Haggart was taken to the hospital. He never regained consciousness and died the next day. Jobidon was charged with manslaughter (causing death by an unlawful act assault). The trial judge found Jobidon not guilty. He found that the two had consented to fight, that it was a fight in anger, and that physical injury was intended. However, the judge also found that Jobidon did not intentionally exceed the consent that Haggart gave, and that he struck the final blows in the reasonable but mistaken apprehension that Haggart was still capable of returning to the fight. The decision of the trial judge was appealed. The appeal court granted the appeal and entered a guilty verdict. The court held that the common law limitations on the defence of consent should apply to the offence of assault:

> The so-called consents to fight are often more apparent than real and are obtained in an atmosphere where reason, good sense and even sobriety are absent. In a case such as the one at hand it seems scarcely necessary to mention that often the results are very serious. To interpret the Criminal Code otherwise would continue to legitimize . . . uncivilized brawling.[25]

The Supreme Court of Canada dismissed the accused's appeal. The Court held that the common law rules that determine when consent is not legally effective still apply in Canada. Section 8 of the Code preserves common law rules that are not inconsistent with the Code or other federal legislation.[26] Therefore, a person cannot give valid consent to physical force used in anger or where it is likely to cause or does cause bodily harm. This common law rule is based on public policy that it is not in the public interest to allow adults to hurt each other without a good reason. Thus, the rule does not apply to sporting activities, where the force used is within the customary rules of the game, to medical treatment or surgery, or even to stuntmen, who agree in advance to perform risky or daredevil activities. The judgment also created an exception where consent can be a defence, for what the Court described as "schoolyard scuffles where boys and girls immaturely seek to resolve differences through fighting." However, the Court left open the possibility of a charge of assault in situations where boys or girls under the age of 18 truly intend to harm one another and cause more than trivial bodily harm.

Since the decision in *Jobidon*, the situation of schoolyard fights has been before the courts. In *R. v. W.(G.)*,[27] two 16-year-old boys were involved in a consensual fist fight. The students attended the same high school. They knew of each other, but had not met. Two days before

23   (1975), 26 C.C.C. (2d) 219 (Ont. C.A.) at 230.
24   (1988), 45 C.C.C. (3d) 176 (Ont. C.A.); appeal dismissed (1991), 66 C.C.C. (3d) 454 (S.C.C.).
25   *R. v. Jobidon* (1988), ibid. at 184.
26   Section 8(3) of the Code states, "Every rule and principle of the common law that renders any circumstance a justification or excuse for an act or a defence to a charge continues in force and applies in respect of proceedings for an offence . . . except in so far as they are altered by or are inconsistent with this Act . . . " See Chapter 4 for discussion.
27   (1994), 90 C.C.C. (3d) 139 (Ont. C.A.).

the fight, someone told the accused that the victim wanted to fight him. On the day of the fight, the accused received another message that the victim wanted to fight him. They met in the smoking area outside the school. They exchanged words, then pushes, and finally blows. The accused hit the victim three times in the face. The fight ended when the victim's nose began bleeding heavily. The victim received serious injuries: His nose was broken and he lost his vision in one eye for several hours. The accused was not hurt. His defence of consent was rejected at trial, and a conviction was entered. He appealed to the Ontario Court of Appeal. The court found that the "co-existence of an intention to cause serious harm, the use of force clearly capable of causing that result and the actual occasioning of bodily harm made this fight much more serious than an ordinary schoolyard scuffle." The court concluded that the case clearly involved the type of situation described in *Jobidon*, where consent should not be a defence. The accused's appeal was dismissed.

A later decision of the Ontario Court of Appeal reached the opposite conclusion. In *R. v. S.M.*,[28] two 16-year-old girls argued in a restaurant and eventually came to blows outside the restaurant. The accused hit the complainant in the face, causing a cut on her nose that did not require stitches. The accused was found guilty of assault, the trial judge holding that consent was not available as a defence. On appeal, the court distinguished this case from R. v. W.(G.). The court considered the intent of the accused, the nature of the assault, and the harm caused. The court found that neither girl intended to hurt the other, and that the injuries were far less serious than in *R. v. W.(G.)*. Therefore, this case fell within the exception of the ordinary "schoolyard scuffle" as set out in *Jobidon*. The court allowed the appeal and entered an acquittal.

In summary, consent of the victim is not a defence to an assault charge if the accused intended and caused serious bodily harm to the victim. If an accused caused serious bodily harm in the course of a rough contact sport, such as hockey, but did not intend to cause serious bodily harm, consent can be a defence. Similarly, if a consensual fight between youths (e.g., a schoolyard scuffle) results in serious bodily harm to one of the participants, consent can be a defence if the accused did not intend to cause serious bodily harm.

3. Assault: Section 265(1)(b)

Actual physical contact is not required for an assault. Subsection (1)(b) defines an attempted or threatened use of force as an assault. The *actus reus* of this offence requires that the accused (a) attempted or threatened to apply force to another person and (b) had the ability to apply the force or (c) caused the other person to believe on reasonable grounds that the accused had the ability to apply the force. This last part of the *actus reus* essentially means that a reasonable person in the position of the other person would believe that the accused could actually apply the attempted or threatened use of force. The *mens rea* of the offence requires that the accused intended or meant to make the attempt or the threat to apply force to the other person.

An example of this type of assault is found in *R. v. Judge*.[29] The accused, accompanied by other men, approached the victim, who was inside a locked car; and, while using words and gestures which indicated that he had a weapon, he threatened to "burn" the victim. A court of appeal upheld the accused's conviction. Similarly, pointing a gun at a person without a lawful excuse such as self-defence would be an assault.[30] Even where the accused does not intend to carry out the threat, if the victim reasonably believes that the accused has the ability to carry out the threat, the offence will have been committed. This point is illustrated by a

---

28 (1996), 97 C.C.C. (3d) 281 (Ont. C.A.).
29 (1957), 118 C.C.C. 410 (Ont. C.A.).
30 *Kwaku Mensah v. R.* (1946), 2 C.R. 113.

New Brunswick case, *R. v. Horncastle*,[31] where an argument between a husband and wife led to the husband taking up a gun and threatening to shoot his wife. It was argued that the husband was not guilty of assault because he did not intend to actually shoot his wife. The court of appeal disagreed, and entered a verdict of guilty of assault. The court ruled that the making of the threat, coupled with the ability to carry it out, constituted the offence of assault.

The courts have held that words alone, no matter how threatening, do not constitute an assault. In *R. v. Byrne*,[32] the accused was charged with robbery, which in one form is assault with the intent to steal. The accused had walked up to the box office of a movie theatre and said to the cashier, "I've got a gun. Give me all your money or I'll shoot." Although he had a coat draped over his arm, no gun was visible. Then, while the cashier was gathering the money, the accused fled. The court held that the accused had not committed an assault, since there were no acts or gestures accompanying his verbal threats; therefore, he could not be found guilty of robbery as charged.

L02 ## 4. The Permissible Use of Force

Previous chapters have discussed how, in certain circumstances, the law allows persons to apply physical force to other persons. For example, a peace officer, or a person assisting a peace officer, can use as much force as is reasonably necessary to make an arrest.[33] Similarly, a person can use a reasonable amount of force in self-defence, or to defend his or her family or property.[34] Section 43 creates another situation where force may be used:

> **43. Every schoolteacher, parent or person standing in the place of a parent is justified in using force by way of correction toward a pupil or child, as the case may be, who is under his care, if the force does not exceed what is reasonable under the circumstances.**

This section allows a parent, or a person standing in the place of a parent, such as a teacher,[35] to use a reasonable amount of force for the correction of a child. In all the situations where the use of force is allowed, once the amount of force exceeds what is reasonable and necessary in the circumstances, an assault is committed.

The Supreme Court of Canada, in *Ogg-Moss v. The Queen*,[36] said that s. 43 only allows force to be used for correction (i.e., for the education of the child) and is not a general authorization for the use of force. So where the child is mentally disabled and will not remember the "correction" within minutes of it being applied, this section cannot be used to justify the force.

In *Canadian Foundation for Children, Youth and the Law v. Canada (Attorney General)*,[37] the Supreme Court of Canada explained the meaning of force that is "reasonable under the circumstances":

> *Generally, s. 43 exempts from criminal sanction only minor corrective force of a transitory and trifling nature. On the basis of current expert consensus, it does not apply to corporal punishment of children under two or teenagers. Degrading, inhuman or harmful conduct is not protected. Discipline by the use of objects or blows or slaps to the head is unreason-*

---

31 (1972), 8 C.C.C. (2d) 253 (N.B.C.A.).
32 [1968] 3 C.C.C. 179 (B.C.C.A.).
33 See Chapter 5.
34 See Chapter 4.
35 As a matter of policy, many school boards no longer allow teachers to use corporal punishment. See *Canadian Foundation for Children, Youth and the Law v. Canada (Attorney General)* (2000), 146 C.C.C. (3d) 362 (Ont. S.C.J.), aff'd (2004) 180 C.C.C. (3d) 353 (S.C.C), which held that s. 43 does not violate ss. 7, 12, or 15 of the Charter.
36 (1984), 14 C.C.C. (3d) 116 (S.C.C.).
37 *Canadian Foundation for Children, Youth and the Law, supra* note 35.

able. Teachers may reasonably apply force to remove a child from a classroom or secure compliance with instructions, but not merely as corporal punishment. Coupled with the requirement that the conduct be corrective, which rules out conduct stemming from the caregiver's frustration, loss of temper or abusive personality, a consistent picture emerges of the area covered by s. 43. It is wrong for law enforcement officers or judges to apply their own subjective views of what is "reasonable under the circumstances"; the test is objective. The question must be considered in context and in light of all the circumstances of the case. The gravity of the precipitating event is not relevant.

In *R. v. Peterson*,[38] the accused and his wife and two children, aged five and two, were visiting Canada from the United States. The family was at a restaurant when the father and children went to the car to get a birthday present for the mother. The five-year-old girl began fighting with her brother and pushed him out of the car. When he tried to get back into the car, she slammed the door, catching his fingers in the door. After tending to his son, the father took the girl out of the car, placed her across the trunk, and spanked her on her bare bottom. A witness called the police, and the father was charged with assault. He used s. 43 as a defence. The trial judge found that this spanking was for corrective purposes. The father, although angry, was not out of control. When the girl was examined at a hospital shortly after the incident, it was found that the spanking had left no marks. The parents testified as to when they used this form of discipline for their children. The judge found that their discipline routines were reasonable and designed to properly correct and educate their children. In deciding whether the correction exceeded what was reasonable, the judge considered the nature of the offence calling for correction, the age and character of the child, the likely (and actual) effect of the punishment on the child, the degree of gravity of the punishment, the circumstances in which it was inflicted, and the injuries (if any) inflicted. Applying these criteria, the court found that the force used by the accused in spanking his daughter did not exceed what was reasonable in the circumstances.

In *R. v. Graham*,[39] a teacher who spanked a student and was charged with assault relied on s. 43. The child was eight or nine years old at the time of the incident and was known to be a disruptive student. The accused was the school principal and the child's homeroom teacher. During math class, the child refused to do her work and was bothering other students. The accused finally lifted her up and struck her on the bottom with an open hand.

Among the factors the court considered were these:

- the way the physical punishment was inflicted,
- the part of the body where force was applied,
- whether the force was reasonable and not excessive,
- the conduct of the child and the nature of the offence,
- whether the child was capable of appreciating correction,
- the age and character of the child, and
- whether the punishment was arbitrary or capricious or carried out in anger.

The court also bore in mind that ensuring respect for authority is part of the duty of the teacher as an educator. In this case, the child was spanked for very undisciplined behaviour. She was bright and capable of understanding the correction. The force was reasonable and not excessive. A red mark remained on her buttocks for some 24 hours. There was no

---

38 (1995), 98 C.C.C. (3d) 253; 39 C.R. (4th) 329 (Ont. Ct. of J. (Prov. Div.)).
39 (1995), 39 C.R. (4th) 339 (N.B.Q.B.).

evidence that the teacher acted in anger. The accused had taught for 24 years. By all accounts, he was a good teacher and was well-liked and respected. Interestingly, the court held that two policy documents on discipline from the school district were not admissible as evidence of community standards of tolerance with respect to the physical punishment of students. The court held that such documents are not applicable to a criminal trial where s. 43 is concerned: The policy of a school board cannot affect criminal law. The accused was acquitted at his trial, and the Crown's appeal was dismissed.

C. THE OFFENCES OF ASSAULT

Once it is established that an assault as defined in s. 265 has taken place, the person who has committed the assault will be charged under one of the other Code sections that define the several different offences of assault. The offence actually charged will depend on the nature and seriousness of the assault and on the surrounding circumstances; for example, it is a more serious offence to commit an assault with a weapon than without one.

1. Assault under Section 266

Section 266 makes it a hybrid offence to commit an assault. Assault under s. 266 is the least serious type of assault. It may be used when the assault consists only of threats or attempts, or when the victim has not suffered any bodily harm. It was formerly called "common assault" and is sometimes today referred to as "Level 1" assault, or simple assault.

2. Assault with a Weapon and Assault Causing Bodily Harm

Section 267 states that every one commits an offence who, in committing an assault,

    (a) carries, uses or threatens to use a weapon or an imitation thereof, or

    (b) causes bodily harm to the complainant.

Bodily harm is defined in s. 2 of the Code as "any hurt or injury to a person that interferes with the health or comfort of the person and that is more than merely transient or trifling in nature."

The application of this definition of bodily harm was discussed in *R. v. Dixon*,[40] a decision of the Court of Appeal of the Yukon Territory. The victim had been assaulted by the accused. Her injuries included small bruises on her face and shoulder and a laceration to the back of her head. She testified that she was "all better" within the month. The trial judge held that her injuries did not amount to bodily harm; there was no evidence that the injuries affected her health or comfort, and the injuries, which lasted no longer than a month, were trifling and transient. The court of appeal disagreed and ordered that a conviction of assault causing bodily harm be entered against the accused. The court of appeal held that "transient and trifling in nature" refers to a very short period of time, and to injury of a very minor degree. While the decision did not state exactly what a transient period of time is, one judge stated that it is simply insupportable to describe as transient an injury that lasts a month. Also, the court noted, it was clear that from the time of the injury until the time treatment was completed, the victim had been deprived of a sense of comfort. The court stated that in this case, the trial judge's decision demonstrated an absence of any reasonable regard for the ordinary meaning of the words.

---

40 (1988), 42 C.C.C. (3d) 318 (B.C.C.A.).

The British Columbia Court of Appeal, in *R. v. Brooks*,[41] held that for the offence of assault causing bodily harm, it is not required that the accused be able to foresee that bodily harm would result. In this case, the victim and his family were returning from a vacation in their motorhome at around midnight. The accused was driving his jeep on the same road. The jeep was behind the motorhome, and the accused passed it. For some reason, the accused became enraged at the way the motorhome was being driven, and forced it to the side of the road. The accused walked over to the motorhome, reached through the window, and pulled the victim from the vehicle. Both were immediately hit by a passing car, and the victim was seriously injured. In this situation, it was irrelevant that the accused did not foresee the harm that resulted.

This ruling was followed in *R. v. Swenson*,[42] where a bouncer in a bar threw a patron out after he became involved in a fight. The victim landed on his head and suffered serious injuries. The court held that the *mens rea* for the offence is the intent to apply force—it is not necessary that the bodily harm be foreseeable. However, the Supreme Court of Canada held in another case[43] that for the offence of aggravated assault, the *mens rea* is foreseeability of harm. Thus, it is possible that the Supreme Court may hold that this offence also requires objective foreseeability of harm.

Section 2 defines "weapon":

"weapon" means any thing used, designed to be used or intended for use

> **(a) in causing death or injury to any person, or**
>
> **(b) for the purpose of threatening or intimidating any person; and, without restricting the generality of the foregoing, includes a firearm.**

In *R. v. McLeod*,[44] the court held that a weapon does not need to be an inanimate object. A dog can be a weapon. The accused had ordered her dog to attack the victim, which it did. The court of appeal entered a conviction against the accused for assault with a weapon.

3. Aggravated Assault

268. (1) Every one commits an aggravated assault who wounds, maims, disfigures or endangers the life of the complainant.

Aggravated assault is an indictable offence with a longer maximum sentence (14 years' imprisonment) than assault under s. 265 or s. 266.

Courts have held that "maiming" means disabling a person so that he or she is less capable of self-defence. "Maims" include injuries such as a broken leg and damaged eyesight. "Wounding" involves breaking the skin (which includes perforating an eardrum), while "disfiguring" seems to mean harming a person so that he or she is less physically attractive.[45]

In *R. v. Godin*,[46] the Supreme Court of Canada held that an intent to wound, maim, disfigure, or endanger life is not necessary for this offence. The *mens rea* is objective foresight of bodily harm.

---

41 (1988), 41 C.C.C. (3d) 157 (B.C.C.A.).
42 (1994), 91 C.C.C. (3d) 541 (Sask. C.A.).
43 *R. v. Godin* (1994), 89 C.C.C. (3d) 574 (S.C.C.).
44 (1993), 84 C.C.C. (3d) 336 (Y.T.C.A.).
45 See, for example, *R. v. Schultz* (1962), 133 C.C.C. (Alta. C.A.) on maiming; and *R. v. Littletent* (1985), 17 C.C.C. (3d) 520 (Alta. C.A.), where a perforated eardrum was considered a wounding.
46 *Godin, supra* note 43.

In *R. v. Williams*,[47] the accused and the victim had a sexual relationship. About five months after the beginning of the relationship, the accused learned that he had tested HIV positive. He continued to have unprotected sexual intercourse with the victim without disclosing to her that he was HIV positive. The victim later learned that she was HIV positive. The accused admitted that he infected the victim with HIV. It was possible, however, that he infected the victim before learning of his HIV positive status. The Supreme Court of Canada found that the accused could not be convicted of aggravated assault, but he had been properly convicted of attempted aggravated assault. The Court stated that the *mens rea* for aggravated assault is the *mens rea* for assault plus objective foresight of the risk of bodily harm. There was no doubt that the mental element of aggravated assault was proven beyond a reasonable doubt. However, regarding the *actus reus*, the Crown was unable to prove beyond a reasonable doubt that the accused, after learning of his HIV status, endangered the life of the victim, because she was possibly already infected. Prior to learning his HIV status, there was an endangerment but no intent; after learning of his HIV status, there was intent but a reasonable doubt about the existence of any endangerment.

4. Assaulting a Peace Officer

270. (1) Every one commits an offence who

(a) **assaults a public officer or peace officer engaged in the execution of his duty or a person acting in aid of such an officer;**

(b) **assaults a person with intent to resist or prevent the lawful arrest or detention of himself or another person; or**

(c) **assaults a person**

(i) **who is engaged in the lawful execution of a process against lands or goods or in making a lawful distress or seizure, or**

(ii) **with intent to rescue anything taken under lawful process, distress or seizure.**

The offences listed under s. 270 have the common element of an assault of a person who is engaged in an act of law enforcement, such as a police officer making an arrest, or a person seizing property under lawful process (e.g., a court order). A question that often arises under this section is whether the person assaulted was acting within his or her scope of authority at the time of the assault. For example, a person who assaults a police officer who is making an illegal arrest cannot be charged under s. 270, although another type of assault may be charged. An interesting case that illustrates this point is *Corrier v. R.*[48] The police were investigating the theft of two wheels from a car. After searching the accused's trunk and finding nothing, the accused was told his car was being seized "to check it out." Apparently, the police wanted to take the car to the station to examine its wheels. On being told that his car was being seized, the accused rolled up his window, catching the police officer's arm between the glass and the car frame, and drove off. After the officer succeeded in freeing his arm, the accused attempted to run him over. The court found that the police officer, by attempting to seize the car over the owner's objections and without arresting him, had exceeded the powers given to him. The accused, therefore, could not be convicted of assaulting an officer in the execution of duty.

---

47   (2003), 176 C.C.C. (3d) 449 (S.C.C.).
48   (1972), 7 C.C.C. (2d) 461 (N.B.C.A.). For a discussion of consent in HIV assault cases, see pages 255–256.

However, the court substituted a conviction of common assault (this is now assault under s. 266), since the accused had used more force than necessary to resist the seizure of his car.

The extent of the police officer's authority is not always easy to determine. The Supreme Court of Canada considered this issue in *R. v. Stenning.*[49] The case involved police constables who were investigating a disturbance outside a building. Seeing a suspicious movement inside, they entered the building through an open window. They found two men in the building who refused to identify themselves. One of the men struck one of the constables in the face. It turned out that this man was the son of the owner of the building; he was not involved in the outside disturbance. The Court found the accused guilty of assaulting an officer in the execution of duty. The Court stated:

> *Assuming that Wilkinson [the constable] did technically trespass on the premises, the fact remains that he was there to investigate an occurrence which had happened earlier in the evening, which involved the firing of a rifle. He was charged under s. 47 of the Police Act, R.S.O. 1960, c.298, with the duty of preserving the peace, preventing robberies and other crimes, and apprehending offenders. He was in the course of making an investigation, in carrying out that duty, when he was assaulted by the respondent.*[50]

Both *Stenning* and *R. v. Tunbridge*,[51] which had the opposite result, demonstrate how difficult it is to decide whether police are engaged in the execution of their duty.[52] In *Tunbridge*, the police were called to investigate a domestic quarrel. The husband appeared to be intoxicated, and the wife said she wished to take the children and leave the home. While the wife was dressing one child, the father took the other child onto his lap. When the wife was ready to leave, the man refused to let the child go. The police scuffled with the accused in an attempt to take the child from him. The man was charged with assault under s. 246(2) (now s. 270). The Court directed that the accused be acquitted, stating, "In the absence of reasonable apprehension of injury to the child or of some breach of the peace I think the constables exceeded their duty when they purported to decide that the child should be taken from the father and then proceeded with their attempt physically to take it."[53]

R. v. Plummer,[54] discussed in Chapter 6 (see page 158), is another case in which the accused was charged with assaulting a police officer and was acquitted, in part because the officer was not in the execution of his duty when he attempted to arrest the accused.

L04 D. SEXUAL ASSAULT

In 1983, the offences of rape and indecent assault were repealed and replaced by the new offences of sexual assault. With the changes in the law, the victim can be either a man or a woman, and the attacker can be of the same sex as the victim. A spouse can be charged with sexual assault. The old offence of rape was in Part V of the Code, with the offences involving public morals and disorderly conduct. The new offences have been placed with other offences against the person. This emphasizes that they involve violence to another person.

49 (1970), 3 C.C.C. 145 (S.C.C.). See also *R. v. Landry* (1986), 25 C.C.C. (3d) 1 (S.C.C.), in which the Court upheld an assault conviction where the police entered an apartment without a warrant to make an arrest. The accused resisted and was charged under what is now s. 270. The Court held that the police officer was in the execution of his duty when he had reasonable grounds for believing that the person he was seeking was within the premises.
50 *Stenning*, ibid. at 148.
51 (1971), 3 C.C.C. (2d) 303 (B.C.C.A.).
52 See a discussion of the meaning of "execution of duty" in Chapter 6 (page 157).
53 *Tunbridge, supra* note 51 at 305.
54 (2006), 214 C.C.C. (3d) 84 at 102 (Ont. C.A.).

1. The Offences of Sexual Assault

There are three sexual assault offences:

- sexual assault (s. 271);
- sexual assault (a) with a weapon, (b) threatening to cause bodily harm to a person other than the complainant, or (c) causing bodily harm to the complainant (s. 272); and
- aggravated sexual assault (s. 273).

The wording of these offences corresponds with the wording of the offences of assault, discussed above: assault (s. 266); assault with a weapon or assault causing bodily harm (s. 267); and aggravated assault (s. 268). As with other assaults, the type of sexual assault that is charged will depend on the circumstances surrounding the offence and the nature of the sexual assault.

The definition of assault in s. 265 applies to sexual assault offences. In general, as discussed above, assault involves the intentional or threatened application of force or touching without consent. The *actus reus* of sexual assault offences necessarily includes a sexual touching without consent. Depending on the specific offence charged under s. 272 or s. 273, other elements of the *actus reus* will be required, such as a weapon or bodily harm or wounding or endangering the life of the complainant. These additional *actus reus* elements are discussed below. The *mens rea* of sexual assault offences is the intention to touch in a manner that is sexual where the accused knows or is wilfully blind or reckless to the fact that the accused is not consenting. It is not required that the accused did the touching for the purpose of sexual gratification.

Key issues in sexual assault cases include these: Was the touching "sexual"? Did the complainant consent to the sexual touching? If the complainant did not consent, did the accused have an honest but mistaken belief that the complainant consented? If so, should the accused be able to rely on the mistake as a defence? These issues are discussed below.

2. The Meaning of "Sexual"

The Code does not define the term "sexual," leaving this task to the courts. The Supreme Court of Canada considered this issue in *R. v. Chase*.[55] The accused, a neighbour, entered the home of the victim, a 15-year-old girl. Her brother was the only other person in the house. The accused seized the girl by the shoulders and grabbed her breasts. He was unable to touch her anywhere else because she fought back. The accused left the house when the victim's brother called another neighbour. The trial court convicted the accused of sexual assault. The court of appeal overturned the conviction and substituted a conviction for assault on the grounds that "sexual" requires involvement of the genitalia. The Supreme Court of Canada disagreed and overturned the court of appeal's decision. The Court said that sexual assault does not depend solely on contact with any specific part of the human anatomy; rather, it is an assault of a sexual nature that violates the sexual integrity of the victim. The test for deciding whether the conduct has the required sexual nature is objective. The question asked is this: "Viewed in the light of all the circumstances, is the sexual nature or carnal context of the assault visible to a reasonable observer?"[56] Relevant factors are the nature of the conduct, the situation in which it occurred, the words and gestures accompanying the act, and all other surrounding circumstances, including threats, which may or may not be accompanied by the use of force. The objective test of "sexual" set out in *Chase* was confirmed by the Supreme Court of Canada in *R. v. Lutoslawski*.[57]

---

55   (1987), 37 C.C.C. (3d) 97 (S.C.C.).
56   Ibid. at 103.
57   [2010] 3 S.C.R. 60 (S.C.C.).

In *R. v. V.(K.B.)*,[58] the Ontario Court of Appeal applied the decision in *Chase* to confirm a conviction of sexual assault against a man who grabbed his three-year-old son's genitals as a punishment for grabbing his own genitals. The decision stated that "a sexual assault does not require sexuality and indeed may not even involve sexuality. It is an act of power, aggression and control. In general sexual gratification if present is at best a footnote."[59]

In *R. v. Kindellan*,[60] the accused was a male stripper. As part of his act, he pulled a female patron to the stage, handcuffed her, and pulled her hands back and forth between his legs. He had performed this part of his act on more than 50 occasions with no complaint. However, this time the woman complained and the accused was charged with sexual assault. The trial judge convicted him, and the conviction was upheld on appeal. It was not relevant that the act was not done for sexual gratification but as part of a performance. The victim had suffered an affront to her sexual dignity.

3. The Meaning of "Consent"

The principles concerning consent that apply to sexual assault are the same as those for any assault. The consent to a sexual touching must be freely given, with knowledge of the nature of the act being consented to. One sexual assault case[61] applied the rule in *R. v. Jobidon*,[62] that a person cannot consent to having serious bodily harm inflicted on himself or herself. The accused had tied the complainant's arms and legs to a bed, beat her repeatedly with a belt, and inserted an object into her rectum. He was charged with sexual assault causing bodily harm. He claimed that she consented to this treatment. She said that she had not consented. The trial judge refused to let the defence of consent go to the jury on the grounds that consent was not a defence. The accused was convicted, and appealed. The court of appeal dismissed his appeal. It stated that, regardless of whether one accepted his or her version of the events, it was clear that he applied force to her that, viewed objectively, would cause serious bodily harm, and that the decision in *Jobidon* therefore applied.

The provisions of s. 265(3) regarding consent also apply to sexual assault. Therefore, consent is not valid if it is the result of any of the following: the application, or threat of application, of force; fraud; or the exercise of authority. In 1992, Parliament enacted what became known as the "no means no" law, which added a definition of consent and a list of circumstances where there is no consent. The preamble to the Act states that the purpose of the legislation is to protect the constitutional rights of women and children. Part of the legislation is now s. 273.1 of the Criminal Code:

273.1 (1) Subject to subsection (2) and subsection 265(3), "consent" means, for the purposes of sections 271, 272 and 273, the voluntary agreement of the complainant to engage in the sexual activity in question.

(2) No consent is obtained, for the purposes of sections 271, 272 and 273, where

(a) the agreement is expressed by the words or conduct of a person other than the complainant;

(b) the complainant is incapable of consenting to the activity;

---

58   (1992), 71 C.C.C. 65 (Ont. C.A.); aff'd (1993), 82 C.C.C. (3d) 382 (S.C.C.).
59   Ibid. at 70.
60   [1988] B.C.W.L.D. 3041 (B.C. Co. Ct.).
61   *R. v. Welch* (1995), 101 C.C.C. (3d) 216; 25 O.R. (3d) 665 (Ont. C.A.). See also *R. v. Robinson* (2001), 153 C.C.C. (3d) 398 (Ont. C.A.).
62   *Jobidon, supra* note 24.

(c) **the accused induces the complainant to engage in the activity by abusing a position of trust, power or authority;**

(d) **the complainant expresses, by words or conduct, a lack of agreement to engage in the activity; or**

(e) **the complainant, having consented to engage in sexual activity, expresses, by words or conduct, a lack of agreement to continue to engage in the activity.**

(3) Nothing in subsection (2) shall be construed as limiting the circumstances in which no consent is obtained.

Paragraph (a) applies to situations where, for example, pimps are involved. It makes it clear that only the people involved can consent to sexual activity. Paragraph (b) could apply to situations where the victim is intoxicated or mentally disabled. Paragraph (c) applies to situations such as between doctors and patients, employers and employees, and teachers and students. It does not mean that there cannot be sexual activity between people in such relationships, but only that there is no consent where there is an abuse of the position of trust, power, or authority. Under paragraph (e), a complainant can withdraw consent to continue in sexual activity.

Note that subsection (3) states that these are not the only situations where there is no consent. In *R. v. M.(L.M)*,[63] the Supreme Court of Canada held that in a sexual assault case, it is not necessary that the victim offer some minimal word or gesture of objection for there to be no consent, and that lack of resistance cannot be equated with consent. The victim was a 16-year-old girl. The accused was her stepfather. The victim was in bed when she and her younger sister began to argue. She called to her mother and stepfather for help. He came into her room and touched her genitals, while the younger sister was hiding under the bed. The next night, a similar incident occurred. On both occasions, the victim pretended to be asleep. She explained her behaviour by saying that she was afraid of her stepfather. Several days later, she told her social worker what had happened. The court of appeal dismissed the accused's conviction, holding that lack of resistance must be equated with consent. A dissenting judge disagreed, stating:

> *every consent involves a submission or lack of resistance, but it does not follow that every submission or lack of resistance means consent. The lack of maturity and vulnerability of the complainant and the extent to which the accused must be taken to be aware of these traits are all elements which must be considered.*[64]

The Supreme Court of Canada, in a very brief judgment, supported the dissenting judge and restored the conviction.

In *R. v. Stender*,[65] the accused was charged with two counts of sexual assault. Following the end of a two-year relationship with his girlfriend, M.O., the accused threatened to disseminate nude photographs of M.O. to her friends and acquaintances unless she had sex with him. The photographs depicted M.O. in various sexual acts with the accused. Thereafter, M.O. engaged in sexual intercourse with the accused. The Ontario Court of Appeal found that the accused's conduct in threatening to disseminate the nude photographs of M.O. if she did not engage in sex with him constituted extortion as defined in s. 346(1) of the Code. His threats to expose the photographs were coupled with demands for sexual favours. By his threats, he induced M.O. to accede to his demands for sex, thus interfering with her freedom of choice and coercing her into doing

63 (1992), 78 C.C.C. (3d) 318 (N.S.C.A.); appeal allowed (1994), 89 C.C.C. (3d) 96 (S.C.C.).
64 *R. v. M.(L.M.)* (1992), ibid. at page 327.
65 (2004), 188 C.C.C. (3d) 514 (Ont. C.A.); appeal to S.C.C. dismissed (2005), 201 C.C.C. (3d) 319 (S.C.C.).

something that she would otherwise have chosen not to do. The court concluded that consent to sexual intercourse within the meaning of s. 273.1(1) of the Code was not given by M.O. It followed, therefore, that the *actus reus* and the *mens rea* of sexual assault were established.

In *R. v. J.A.*,[66] the Supreme Court of Canada addressed the issue of whether a person can perform sexual acts on an unconscious person if the person consented to those acts in advance of being rendered unconscious. J.A. choked his long-time partner K.D. until she was unconscious. K.D. estimated that she was unconscious for less than three minutes. She consented to the choking and understood that she might lose consciousness. She stated that she and J.A. had experimented with "erotic asphyxiation" and that she had lost consciousness before. When K.D. regained consciousness, she was on her knees with her hands tied behind her back and J.A. was inserting a dildo into her anus. She had consented to the insertion of a dildo in this way on a previous occasion. After J.A. removed the dildo, he and K.D had consensual vaginal intercourse. At trial, J.A. was convicted of sexual assault. The Ontario Court of Appeal overturned the conviction. The court held that individuals could consent in advance to sexual activity that occurs while they are unconscious.

On appeal to the Supreme Court of Canada, the Crown argued that a person who consents in advance of unconsciousness does not have an operating mind and is, therefore, incapable of consenting while unconscious. The Crown argued that to allow consent in advance of unconsciousness would condone non-consensual sex and sexual exploitation. The defence argued that a person may engage in sexual activity with an unconscious person if he does not exceed the bounds of what the unconscious person consented to and expected. The defence argued that if the court decided otherwise, the court would be criminalizing benign and essentially consensual sexual activity. The Supreme Court of Canada restored the conviction. The Court stated that consent for sexual assault requires the complainant to provide actual active consent throughout every phase of the sexual activity. It is not possible for an unconscious person to satisfy this requirement, even if she expresses her consent in advance. After reviewing s. 273.1(2)(d) and (e) as well as s. 273.2(b) and case law, the Court concluded that "Parliament viewed consent as requiring a 'capable' or operating mind, able to evaluate each and every sexual act committed. To hold otherwise runs counter to Parliament's clear intent that a person has the right to consent to particular acts and to revoke her consent at any time."[67]

In *R. v. Hutchinson*,[68] the accused was charged with aggravated sexual assault on the basis that he endangered the life of C by poking holes in the condoms they used during sexual intercourse. They had an intimate relationship for about nine months. After she broke up with him, he told her that he had poked holes in all of the condoms that she kept by her bed because he had wanted to have a baby with her. She became pregnant and decided to have an abortion. She testified that she would not have consented to sexual intercourse with him if she had been aware of the condition of the condoms. The trial court acquitted him, and the Crown appealed. The Nova Scotia Court of Appeal held that s. 273.1(1) requires the trier of fact to consider whether C voluntarily agreed to unprotected sex with the accused. The court found that the sabotaging of the condoms fundamentally altered the nature of the sexual activity in question. Therefore, her consent could be found not to be reasonably informed and freely exercised. Applying the test in *R. v. Cuerrier* (see page 255), the court also concluded that even if C were found to have consented, there was evidence upon which a trier of fact could find that the consent was vitiated by fraud. The court ordered a new trial.

---

66   [2011] S.C.J. 28.
67   See also *R. v. Ashlee* (2006), 212 C.C.C. (3d) 477 (Alta. C.A.); leave to appeal refused (2006), 213 C.C.C. (3d) vi (S.C.C.).
68   (2010), 251 C.C.C. (3d) 51 (N.S.C.A.).

L05   # 4. Honest Mistake of Consent

The defence of mistaken belief in consent may be an issue in any assault case; however, the defence arises most often in cases of sexual assault. Mistaken belief in consent is a mistake-of-fact defence that is a denial of the *mens rea* of the offence. It requires that an accused believed that the complainant affirmatively communicated by words or conduct her agreement to engage in sexual activity with the accused.[69] The defence does not impose any burden of proof on an accused, and may arise on any evidence, including evidence introduced by the Crown. It is not a defence to argue that the complainant did not resist or was silent, as this ambiguous behaviour does not constitute a defence that the complainant consented.

A number of Supreme Court of Canada cases have looked closely at the use of this defence in sexual assault cases. In *Pappajohn v. The Queen*,[70] the Court held that an honest but mistaken belief that the victim consented is a defence, even if the belief is not based on reasonable grounds. However, reasonableness is a factor in deciding whether the belief was honest. The defence requires that there be some supporting evidence beyond the mere assertion of belief in consent. The Court referred to this supporting evidence as giving an "air of reality" to the defence. In *Pappajohn*, the victim was a real estate agent who was showing a house to the accused. Once they were in the house, he attacked her. He was charged with rape (this case took place before the offence of rape was repealed). He claimed that she had consented. She claimed that she had not, and there was evidence that she had attempted to fight back. Despite his claim of honest mistake, the accused was convicted because the court found that there was insufficient evidence to place the defence of honest mistake before the jury. The court found that the evidence of the accused "speaks of actual consent, even cooperation, and leaves little if any room for the suggestion that she may not have been consenting but he thought she was."

After the decision in *Pappajohn*, the following was added to the Code:

265. (4) Where an accused alleges that he believed that the complainant consented to the conduct that is the subject-matter of the charge, a judge, if satisfied that there is sufficient evidence and that if believed by the jury, the evidence would constitute a defence, shall instruct the jury, when reviewing all the evidence relating to the determination of the honesty of the accused's belief, to consider the presence or absence of reasonable grounds for that belief.

This section supports the decision in *Pappajohn* and restates the common law developed by the courts. First, it confirms the common law rule that a judge can only put a defence before a jury if there is sufficient evidence on which the accused could be acquitted if the evidence is believed by a reasonable jury. Second, it states that when there is evidence of mistaken belief in consent, the jury should consider the reasonableness of the belief in deciding if the belief was an honest mistake. However, the jury is not required to find that the belief was reasonable for the defence to succeed.

The constitutionality of s. 265(4) was challenged in *R. v. Osolin*.[71] The accused argued that requiring a judge to allow the jury to consider defences only if there is "sufficient evidence" violates the presumption of innocence and denies the right to a trial by jury (one of the duties of the jury being to decide the facts of the case). The Supreme Court of Canada held that the section does not violate the presumption of innocence. The section is consistent with the rule of evidence,

69   *R. v. Ewanchuk* (1999), 131 C.C.C. (3d) 481 (S.C.C.) at 499–500.
70   (1980), 52 C.C.C. (2d) 481 (S.C.C.).
71   (1993), 86 C.C.C. (3d) 481 (S.C.C.).

applicable to all defences, that a judge cannot put a defence before a jury unless there is some evidence that, if believed by a jury, would lead to an acquittal. The section, which only restates the "air of reality" test, does not violate the right to a jury trial, because it is a question of law whether there is enough evidence for a defence to be considered by a jury. The Court continued:

> One of the reasons that the jury has been able to function so very well is that the trial judges have been able to direct the mind of the jurors to the essential elements of the offence and to those defences which are applicable . . . Speculative defences that are unfounded should not be presented to the jury. To do so would be wrong, confusing and unnecessarily lengthen jury trials.[72]

In *Osolin*, the victim was dragged naked from her friend's home to a car. She was driven to another place, where she was tied to a bed and subjected to sexual intercourse. A medical examiner shortly afterwards found that her condition was consistent with being sexually assaulted. The accused said that she had consented; the victim said that she had not. The Supreme Court held that the judge was correct in not allowing the defence to go to the jury. The mere assertion of consent is not enough; there must be some other evidence that supports mistaken belief.

The Supreme Court also considered the defence in *R. v. Park*.[73] The victim had met the accused in a parking lot, where he helped her move her car from an icy spot. She gave him her phone number. About a week later, they went out on a date, where some sexual activity short of intercourse took place. Two weeks later, the accused called the victim at 6 a.m. after driving all night from Winnipeg. He asked if he could stop by. She agreed. A few minutes later, she met him at her door in her bathrobe and greeted him with a kiss on the cheek. At this point, their stories diverged. He claimed that she willingly participated in sexual activity, but that there was no intercourse. She claimed that he forced her to have intercourse and that she actively resisted. After the incident, he left and she went to her counsellor. A hospital examination indicated that her condition was consistent with consensual or non-consensual intercourse. The trial judge refused to allow the defence of honest but mistaken belief in consent. The accused was convicted. The court of appeal held that the trial judge should have allowed the defence because there were factors that gave the defence an "air of reality"—for example, the telephone conversation at 6 a.m., her greeting him in a bathrobe, the kiss, and their prior sexual relationship. The Supreme Court of Canada disagreed. All of these factors were indications that she might consent to sex but not that she did consent. Here, there was no evidence that would give an "air of reality" to the defence of mistaken belief.

The Court reaffirmed its decision in *Osolin* and clarified the "air of reality" test by stating that it is not the trial judge's job to weigh the evidence or to decide whether the evidence is believable—this is the jury's job. However, it is the trial judge's job to determine whether there is any evidence that could support the accused's assertion of consent. This supporting evidence might be independent "real evidence" but does not need to be. The evidence may come from the detailed testimony of the accused or of the complainant. The totality of the evidence for the accused must reasonably and realistically be capable of supporting the defence. The Court concluded:

> To summarize, when the complainant and the accused give similar versions of the facts and the only material contradiction is in their interpretation of what happened, then the defence of honest but mistaken belief in consent should generally be put to the jury, except in cases where the accused's conduct demonstrates recklessness or wilful blindness to the absence

---

72   Ibid. at 529.
73   (1995), 99 C.C.C. (3d) 1 (S.C.C.).

of consent. On the other hand judges have generally refused to put the defence of honest but mistaken belief in consent to the juries when the accused clearly bases his defence on voluntary consent, and he also testifies that the complainant was an active, eager partner, whereas the complainant testifies that she vigorously resisted. In such cases, the question is generally simply one of credibility, of consent or no consent.[74]

Osolin and *Park* demonstrate how the Supreme Court has limited the defence of mistaken belief in consent by requiring that it have at least an air of reality. In 1992, Parliament went further by enacting s. 273.2 as part of the "no means no" law. The defence cannot be used if (a) the belief resulted from the accused's intoxication, recklessness or wilful blindness; or (b) the accused did not take reasonable steps to determine whether the complainant was consenting.

273.2. It is not a defence to a charge under section 271, 272 or 273 that the accused believed that the complainant consented to the activity that forms the subject-matter of the charge, where

> **(a) the accused's belief arose from the accused's**
>
> > **(i) self-induced intoxication, or**
> >
> > **(ii) recklessness or wilful blindness; or**
>
> **(b) the accused did not take reasonable steps, in the circumstances known to the accused at the time, to ascertain that the complainant was consenting.**

In *R. v. Darrach*,[75] the Ontario Court of Appeal addressed the issue of whether s. 273.2(b) is unconstitutional because by requiring the accused to take "reasonable steps" it introduces an objective component into the *mens rea* of sexual assaults:

> *the offence of sexual assault carries with it a sufficient social stigma as to require a subjective fault requirement on the part of the accused person. . . .notwithstanding section 273.2(b), the offence is still largely one based on subjective fault—at least to a level that would satisfy constitutional requirements. . . . No doubt, the provision can be regarded as introducing an objective component into the mental element of the offences but it is one which, in itself, is a modified one. It is personalized according to the subjective awareness of the accused at the time. The accused is to take "reasonable steps" in the circumstances known to the accused at the time, to ascertain that the complainant is consenting. . . . the accused it not under an obligation to determine all relevant circumstances—the issue is what he actually knew, not what he ought to have known. . . . The provision does not require that a mistaken belief in consent must be reasonable in order to exculpate. The provision merely requires that a person about to engage in sexual activity take "reasonable steps. . .to ascertain that the complainant was consenting.*[76]

The *Pappajohn* case must now be read in light of the "reasonable steps" requirement in s. 273.2. Citing the dissenting reasons of the judge in *R. v. Esau*,[77] the Ontario Court of Appeal in *Darrach*,[78] stated, "A person is not entitled to take ambiguity as the equivalent of consent. If a person, acting honestly, and without wilful blindness, perceives his companion's conduct as

---

74 Ibid. at 17.
75 (1998), 122 C.C.C. (3d) 225 (Ont. C.A.), aff'd (2000) 148 C.C.C. 97 (S.C.C.). See also *R. v. Darrach* (1994), 17 O.R. (3d) 481 (Prov. Div.) for a discussion of the question as to whether or not Darrach, properly attentive to the issue of consent (i.e., not wilfully blind), could have, in light of the ambiguity, honestly concluded that the complainant had the capacity and was consenting to the sexual activity.
76 *Darrach* (1998), ibid. at 252.
77 (1997), 116 C.C.C. (3d) 289 (S.C.C.) at page 314.
78 *Darrach* (1998), *supra* note 75 at 253.

ambiguous or unclear, his duty is to abstain or obtain clarification on the issue of consent." This appears to be the rule at common law. In this situation, to use the words of the court in *R. v. Morgan*,[79] "it is only fair to the woman and not in the least unfair to the man that he should be under a duty to take reasonable care to ascertain that she is consenting to the intercourse and be at risk of prosecution if he fails to take such care." As Glanville Williams, put it, "the defendant is guilty if he realized the woman might not be consenting and took no steps to find out."[80]

The Supreme Court of Canada stated in *R. v. Daigle* that "the appellant could not rely on the defence of honest but mistaken belief since he had not taken reasonable steps to ascertain that the victim was consenting."[81]

In *R. v. Malcolm*,[82] the complainant and her husband hosted a New Years' Eve party, attended by the accused, who was a good friend of the complainant's husband. At some point, the complainant's husband left the party. After the complainant went to bed, the accused entered the complainant's bedroom while she slept and got into bed with her and engaged in sexual activity. When the complainant turned to face the accused, she reacted to his presence, ordered him out of the house and called police. The complainant testified that she thought the accused was her husband. The accused was charged with sexual assault and was acquitted at trial. On appeal, the Manitoba Court of Appeal set aside the acquittal and ordered a new trial. The court held that

> *once the air of reality test is met, the issue is whether the accused is aware of circumstances which would lead a reasonable man to inquire further into the issue of consent. If the circumstances known to the accused are such that a reasonable man would not or might not take further steps to ascertain consent, then the accused will not be required to take any further steps either.*[83]

Considering all of the case law reviewed above, it appears that s. 273.2(b) must be considered in situations where there is an air of reality to the accused's assertion of honest belief in consent, and the accused is neither wilfully blind nor reckless in that belief, but circumstances exist which call into question the reasonableness of the accused's actions.

Section 273.2(b) requires the court to apply a quasi-objective test to the situation. First, the circumstances known to the accused must be ascertained. Then the issue is this: If a reasonable man was aware of the same circumstances, would he take further steps before proceeding with the sexual activity? If the answer is "yes," and the accused has not taken further steps, then the accused is not entitled to the defence of honest belief in consent. If the answer is "no," or even "maybe," then the accused would not be required to take further steps and the defence will apply.

The Supreme Court of Canada confirmed in *Ewanchuk*[84] that there is no defence of "implied" consent to sexual assault. The accused argued that, in the face of a conclusion by the trier of fact that the complainant did not consent, the complainant's conduct may still raise a reasonable doubt as to consent. The Court emphasized that the trier of fact can come to only two conclusions as to consent: Either the complainant consented, or she did not.

The principle of wilful blindness was discussed by the Supreme Court of Canada in *Sansregret v. The Queen*.[85] The accused was charged with rape on the grounds that the

79   [1976] A.C. 182 (H.L.) at 203.
80   Glanville Williams, *Textbook of Criminal Law* (London: Stevens & Sons, 1978), at 101.
81   (1998), 127 C.C.C. (3d) 129 (S.C.C.) at 130.
82   (2000), 147 C.C.C. (3d) 34 (Man. C.A.) at 43-44; leave to appeal to S.C.C. refused (2001), 150 C.C.C. (3d) vi (S.C.C.).
83   Ibid.
84   *Ewanchuk, supra* note 69.
85   (1985), 18 C.C.C. (3d) 223 (S.C.C.).

victim's consent had been extorted by threats or fear of bodily harm. The accused and the victim had been living together, but the latter had broken off the relationship because of the former's violence toward her. A few days later, the accused broke into the victim's home at 4:30 a.m. armed with a file-like weapon. To calm him down, the victim told him there was a chance of reconciliation and consented to having intercourse with him. After he left her home, she called the police and claimed to have been raped. The police investigated, but no charges were laid. However, the accused's probation officer had become involved; and there was evidence that he had asked her not to press charges. Three weeks later, the accused again broke into her house. She seized the phone to call the police but he ripped the phone out of the jack. He was armed with a butcher knife. He was furious and violent. The victim testified that she was in fear of her life and sanity. She again pretended that there was hope of recon-ciliation and consented to have intercourse with him. In the morning, she drove the accused to the location he requested. She then went to her mother's home and called the police.

At his trial, the accused was found guilty of breaking and entering and unlawful confinement but not guilty of rape, even though the trial judge found that there was no real consent. The judge stated that the accused "saw what he wanted to see, heard what he wanted to hear, believed what he wanted to believe." However, the judge acquitted him of the rape charge because of his honest belief in her consent. The Supreme Court of Canada disagreed and held that the defence of mistake of fact was not available to the accused because of his "wilful blindness." The Court defined wilful blindness as follows: "[W]ilful blindness arises where a person who has become aware of the need for some inquiry [in this case, whether the victim was giving true consent] declines to make the inquiry because he does not wish to know the truth. He would prefer to remain ignorant."[86] The Court concluded that because of the earlier episode and the rape complaint, for the accused to proceed with intercourse constituted "self-deception to the point of wilful blindness."

5. Age of Complainant

As discussed in Chapter 7, s. 150.1 provides that there are certain sexual offences involving children where consent is no defence. With regard to sexual assault offences under sections 271, 272, or 273, s. 150.1 provides that consent is no defence where the complainant is under the age of 16. However, s. 150.1(2) and s. 150.1(2.1) create exceptions to this rule where the complainant and the accused are relatively close in age and the charge is under s. 271, which is the least serious form of sexual assault. These subsections provide that consent can be a defence where the accused and complainant are not in a relationship of trust or authority, dependency, or exploitation, and where either of two sets of circumstances exists:

(a)   the complainant is between the ages of 12 and 14 and the accused is less than two years older than the complainant (s. 150.1(2)); or

(b)   the complainant is between the ages of 14 and 16 and the accused is less than five years older than the complainant and the accused is married to the complainant (s. 150.1(2.1)).

Where the complainant's age is relevant to whether consent is valid, the accused may want to raise the defence of mistake of fact as to the complainant's age. The defence requires that the accused took all reasonable steps to ascertain the age of the complainant (s. 150.1(4) and (6)).

---

86   Ibid. at 235.

Both the general rule under s. 150.1(1) regarding consent not being a defence if the complainant is under 16, and the rules under s. 150.1(4) and (6) regarding mistake as to age, are open to challenge under the Charter as violating a principle of fundamental justice (s. 7), and as denying equality under the law (s. 15).

6. Sexual Assault with a Weapon or Causing Bodily Harm

Sexual assault under s. 272 is more serious than s. 271 assault. It involves either a weapon, or actual or threatened bodily harm, or more than one assailant:

> **272. (1) Every person commits an offence who, in committing a sexual assault,**
>
> **(a) carries, uses or threatens to use a weapon or an imitation of a weapon;**
>
> **(b) threatens to cause bodily harm to a person other than the complainant;**
>
> **(c) causes bodily harm to the complainant; or**
>
> **(d) is a party to the offence with any other person**

In *R. v. Lamy*,[87] the accused, in the course of committing a sexual assault, penetrated the victim's vagina with a 24-inch bamboo dildo that was in the shape of a baseball bat. The Supreme Court of Canada found that the dildo was a weapon within the definition of weapon in s. 2, which provides that a weapon means any thing used, designed to be used, or intended for use in causing death or injury to any person. It is not necessary that the thing be designed to injure or intended to injure. The Court also found that if an object is used in inflicting physical or psychological injury in the commission of a sexual assault, it is not necessary that the injury amount to bodily harm to trigger the application of s. 272(1)(a).

7. Aggravated Sexual Assault

The most serious offence of sexual assault is aggravated sexual assault, which involves serious bodily harm to the complainant:

> **273. (1) Every one commits an aggravated sexual assault who, in committing a sexual assault, wounds, maims, disfigures or endangers the life of the complainant.**

The offence is indictable with a maximum sentence of life imprisonment. If a firearm was used, there is also a mandatory minimum sentence of four years.

The meaning of "wounding," "maiming," and "disfiguring" are discussed earlier in this chapter under "Aggravated Assault" (s. 268). (See page 262.)

L06 E. OTHER OFFENCES AGAINST THE PERSON

1. Criminal Harassment

> **264. (1) No person shall, without lawful authority and knowing that another person is harassed or recklessly as to whether the other person is harassed, engage in conduct referred to in subsection (2) that causes the other person reasonably, in all the circumstances, to fear for their safety or the safety of anyone known to them.**

---

87 (2002), 162 C.C.C. (3d) 353 (S.C.C.).

(2) The conduct mentioned in subsection (1) consists of

    (a) repeatedly following from place to place the other person or anyone known to them;

    (b) repeatedly communicating with, either directly or indirectly, the other person or anyone known to them;

    (c) besetting or watching the dwelling-house, or place where the other person, or anyone known to them, resides, works, carries on business or happens to be; or

    (d) engaging in threatening conduct directed at the other person or any member of their family.

The *mens rea* for this offence is to knowingly or recklessly harass a person by engaging in the conduct stated in s. 264(2), thereby causing a person to fear for his or her safety or another person's safety.

This is sometimes called the anti-stalking law. It is particularly aimed at protecting women who are being harassed by men, such as ex-husbands or ex-boyfriends. The section has been challenged as violating s. 7 of the Charter for being too vague and for violating the right to freedom of expression under s. 2 of the Charter.[88] The Alberta Court of Queen's Bench[89] found that, although there are terms that need to be defined by the courts, such as "fear for their safety," "repeatedly follow," and so on, they are terms capable of being given a "settled meaning" by the courts. Therefore, the section is not overly vague. As to the issue of freedom of expression, the court stated that the behaviour defined in s. 264 is only prohibited when it causes the other person to be harassed or to reasonably fear for his or her safety. This type of conduct is an act of violence that can cause psychological harm and so is not protected under the Charter's freedom of expression provisions. The application by the accused to have the section struck down was dismissed and was upheld on appeal.

The court stated in *Sillipp*[90] that a jury should be instructed to find the accused guilty of criminal harassment if they believed beyond a reasonable doubt that

- the accused engaged in the conduct set out in section 264(2)(a), (b), (c), or (d) of the Criminal Code;
- the complainant was harassed;
- the accused knew or was reckless or wilfully blind as to whether the complainant was harassed;
- the conduct caused the complainant to fear for her safety or the safety of anyone known to her; and
- the complainant's fear, in all the circumstances, was reasonable.[91]

The court in *R. v. Hawkins*[92] found that a single incident is sufficient for a conviction under s. 264(1). Repeated conduct is not required. Hawkins, who was upset that his driver's licence had been suspended by a government office, telephoned a government employee and informed her that he was told by his psychologists that he was 85% likely to kill government employees within the next year and that he had a 100% chance of getting away with it. The court concluded that

---

88   See Chapter 1 at page 8 regarding vague laws violating the principles of fundamental justice under the Charter.
89   *R. v. Sillipp* (1997), 120 C.C.C. (3d) 384 (Alta. C.A.); leave to appeal to S.C.C. refused (1998), 142 C.C.C. (3d) 195n.
90   Ibid.
91   Ibid. at 393.
92   (2006), 215 C.C.C. (3d) 419 (B.C.C.A.).

in this single incident Hawkins had engaged in threatening conduct within the meaning s. 264(2)(d). The fact that he added that he did not believe his psychologists and wished to pursue lawful means to regain his driver's licence, did not change the threatening nature of his conduct.

In *R. v. K.(K.)*,[93] a female jogger was passed on a residential street by K. who was running with a "loping, almost gorilla-like" gait. It was dark and the street lights were on. After running ahead of her, he disappeared from view and shortly thereafter came out from behind some bushes, stood in the middle of the street and faced her with his arms outstretched. Feeling threatened, she stopped and ran away in the opposite direction. K. ran after her and was catching up with her when she ran to a house and rang the doorbell. As she waited for someone to come to the door, K stood at the end of the driveway and stared at her. K was convicted of criminal harassment. On appeal to the Ontario Court of Appeal, K. argued (a) that his actions did not amount to threatening conduct under s. 264 and (b) that the trial court erred in finding that the complainant was harassed when this single incident was not linked to past conduct nor did it carry with it the threat of future contact. The court dismissed the appeal. Although the trial judge had stated that, because K. did not speak to the complainant, it was not possible to discern what he was about to do when he blocked her way and chased her, the court found that his conduct alone was sufficient to establish threatening conduct within the meaning of s. 264(2)(d). The court also found that although K.'s conduct occurred over a relatively short time period and there was no prior contact with the complainant, the conduct was highly threatening and persistent.

2. Unlawfully Causing Bodily Harm

Section 269 states that it is an offence to cause bodily harm to any person. This offence covers any unlawful act that causes bodily harm.

In *R. v. DeSousa*,[94] the offence was analysed by the Supreme Court of Canada. The accused had been at a party on New Year's Eve. The victim was standing about 2.5 metres from a group of men when a fight broke out. The men started throwing bottles. One crashed on the wall near the victim. A glass fragment struck her arm, seriously gashing it. The accused was charged with unlawfully causing bodily harm. He challenged the validity of the offence under the Charter. He argued that the unlawful act could include absolute liability offences, which would offend s. 7 of the Charter by allowing criminal liability where there is no moral fault. He also questioned whether the offence requires an intentional causing of bodily harm as part of the *mens rea* of the offence. The Supreme Court of Canada held that it would offend s. 7 of the Charter to base criminal liability on an absolute liability offence. However, the unlawful act in s. 269 can be interpreted as referring to provincial or federal offences only, and as excluding absolute liability offences. This is consistent with general rules of criminal law interpretation. Furthermore, in light of previous court decisions, the meaning of "unlawful" in the context of s. 269 is that the unlawful act must be at least objectively dangerous—that is, a reasonable person would realize that the unlawful act would create a risk of bodily harm. The bodily harm must be more than merely trivial or transitory in nature and, the Court stated, will usually involve an act of violence done deliberately to another person. On the second issue, the Court held that there was no requirement that the accused intend to cause bodily harm. Unlawfully causing bodily harm is one of the offences that does not require subjective intent.[95] Section 269 requires only objective foresight of bodily harm. The Court found that s. 269 is not unconstitutional and sent the case back for trial.

93 2009 ONCA 100.
94 (1992), 76 C.C.C. (3d) 124 (S.C.C.).
95 See Chapter 3, page 48, "*Mens Rea* and the Charter," for a discussion of offences that do not require subjective intent.

3. Kidnapping

279. (1) Every person commits an offence who kidnaps a person with intent

   (a) to cause the person to be confined or imprisoned against the person's will;

   (b) to cause the person to be unlawfully sent or transported out of Canada against the person's will; or

   (c) to hold him for ransom or to service against the person's will.

Subsections (1.1), (1.2), and (1.3) set out detailed sentencing provisions, including mandatory minimum sentences if a firearm was used in the kidnapping. The maximum sentence for kidnapping is life imprisonment.

Subsection (2) states that a person commits an offence who,

without lawful authority, confines, imprisons or forcibly seizes another person.

This section creates the offences of kidnapping, forcible seizure, confinement, and imprisonment. Kidnapping is the most serious offence and requires specific intent to carry out one of the purposes in subsections (1)(a) to (c).

The term "kidnapping" is not defined in the Code. It has, however, long been an offence at common law, being considered a form of aggravated false imprisonment. Some help in defining the term is given by the English case of *R. v. Reid*.[96] A husband had been charged with kidnapping his wife. In finding that a man can be convicted of the offence even though the victim is his wife, the court accepted a definition of kidnapping that referred to the stealing, carrying away, or secreting of a person against that person's will. The offence, the court stated, is complete when the victim is seized and carried away. The kidnapping must be done against the person's will.

In *R. v. Brown*,[97] the Ontario Court of Appeal considered this question: If A willingly goes with B because of the false statements made by B, has A been taken against his or her will? The accused picked up a 10-year-old girl by falsely telling her that her father had asked him to drive her to school. Instead, the accused drove the girl out of the city to an isolated spot. When he approached her, she attempted to get out of the car. The accused then choked her until she was unconscious. Believing her to be dead, he put her body in the car trunk and drove to a garbage dump, where he covered the body with garbage. After the accused drove away, the girl escaped to a farmhouse. The accused argued that since the child went with him willingly, he could not be convicted of kidnapping. The court rejected this argument, stating that the kidnapping occurred as soon as the accused's false statements induced the victim to enter the car. The victim did not act willingly when her actions were induced by false statements. Furthermore, the accused's actions of choking her, placing her in the trunk, and driving her to a garbage dump were "clearly within the kidnapping section." The accused was convicted of kidnapping.[98]

The offences under s. 279 contain a reverse onus clause:

(3) In proceedings under this section, the fact that the person in relation to whom the offence is alleged to have been committed did not resist is not a defence unless the accused proves that the failure to resist was not caused by threats, duress, force or exhibition of force.

96 (1972), 2 All E.R. 1350 (C.A.).
97 (1972), 8 C.C.C. (2d) 13 (Ont. C.A.).
98 In *R. v. Oakley* (1977), 36 C.C.C. (2d) 436, the Alberta Court of Appeal followed the *Brown* decision. See also *R. v. T.S.M.*, [2002] B.C.J. No. 1683 (B.C.P.C.).

The Ontario Court of Appeal, in *R. v. Gough*,[99] held that this clause is an unconstitutional infringement of the Charter and not valid. The accused had known the victim for about five years. At one point, they were engaged to be married. The victim had broken off the engagement, however, because of the accused's violence toward her. After breaking the engagement, she went into hiding. She had been hiding for several weeks when she left the house to run errands. She told her friend that if she did not come back or was seen in the presence of the accused, the police should be called. While on her errands, she did encounter the accused and went with him to a restaurant. Over her protests, he insisted on driving her home. They first went to a dental clinic, where she paid a bill. He went into the clinic with her. They then went to a doughnut shop to continue their conversation. He again insisted on driving her home. Once they were in the car, he said they were going for gas and then for a ride. She testified that when she said she did not want to go for a ride, an angry, blank look came over his face. She thought he was going to hit her, so she remained silent. They then drove for several days to the city where the victim's parents lived. They visited with her parents and spent the night. The next morning, the police arrived. The accused was arrested and charged with kidnapping.

At the trial, the judge instructed the jury that to use the defence of consent, the accused was required to prove that the victim's failure to resist was not caused by threats, duress, force, or exhibition of force. The accused was convicted. On appeal, he argued that s. 279(3) violates the Charter. The Ontario Court of Appeal, using the *Oakes* test set out by the Supreme Court of Canada,[100] held that the clause does violate the Charter and is not a justifiable limitation. It gave these reasons:

- The clause requires the accused to prove the state of mind of the victim (i.e., that the victim failed to resist because she consented and not because of threats). Proving the victim's state of mind is an unreasonably heavy burden to put on the accused.
- The proved fact does not rationally tend to prove the presumed fact. In other words, the proved fact that the victim did not resist does not tend to prove that the victim's failure to resist was caused by fear of threats.

The court set aside the accused's conviction and ordered a new trial. A decision of the Alberta Court of Queen's Bench[101] also found the subsection unconstitutional. It will be up to the Supreme Court of Canada to finally decide the constitutionality of s. 279(3).

4. Unlawful Confinement

Kidnapping requires moving the victim from one place to another; unlawful confinement or imprisonment involves physically restraining a person from moving from place to place. In *R. v. Gratton*,[102] the accused was charged with unlawfully confining a woman to whom he had been engaged. The victim testified that she was home alone with her two children when at about 1:30 a.m., she heard a banging on her window. It was the accused. He then went to the back door and pounded on it. She agreed to let him in because she thought he would break the door down. She then asked the accused what he wanted. He rushed out to the porch and returned with a loaded shotgun. He then brought out her two children from their bedroom with the gun pointed at them. He pulled the telephone from the wall. They then talked for a long time. At one point, he became very angry and punched a hole through a wall. The police

---

99   (1985), 18 C.C.C. (3d) 453 (Ont. C.A.).
100 *R. v. Oakes* (1986), 24 C.C.C. (3d) 321 (S.C.C.); see Chapter 2, pages 26–27, for a discussion of the *Oakes* test.
101 *R. v. Grift* (1986), 28 C.C.C. (3d) 120 (Alta. Q.B.). See also *R. v. Pete* (1998), 131 C.C.C. (3d) 233 (B.C.C.A.).
102 (1985), 18 C.C.C. (3d) 462 (Ont. C.A.); leave to appeal to S.C.C. refused, [1985] 1 S.C.R. viii.

came to the door at about 5:45 a.m. They found the victim hysterical, shaking, and trembling. She did not answer their questions, but said, "I can't. He's going to kill me." They found the gun and shells, which he had hidden when the police came to the door. The court held that there was ample evidence for a jury to find that the victim had been unlawfully confined. The confinement did not need to be for the whole period of time the accused was in the house, but only for a "significant period of time." His using the gun, pulling the telephone out of its connection, and displaying the gun in front of the children were all acts that must have had the effect of threatening her and overcoming her resistance.

5. Abduction

There are three basic differences between an abduction offence and kidnapping: (1) A mental element or intent is required; (2) the victim of abduction is always a young person (under 14 or under 16, depending on the offence); and (3) kidnapping requires a taking of the victim against the victim's will, whereas abduction is possible in some situations even though the victim consents.

a. Abduction by a Person without Lawful Authority

In general, sections 280 and 281 address abduction of a child by a person who is not a parent of the child, while sections 282 and 283, discussed below, involve abduction by a parent of the child.

Child under 16

> **280. (1) Every one who, without lawful authority, takes or causes to be taken an unmarried person under the age of sixteen years out of the possession of and against the will of the parent or guardian of that person or of any other person who has the lawful care or charge of that person is guilty of an indictable offence . . .**

Abduction under s. 280 refers to the abductor as one who, without lawful authority, takes an unmarried child under the age of 16 against the will of the parent or guardian of the child. The section primarily concerns abduction by a non-parent. However, the wording of the section appears to also allow a parent who takes a child without lawful authority to be charged with abduction (e.g., a parent who, by court order, has no custody or access rights to the child).

Before amendments to the Code in 1983, this offence applied only to female victims, when the taking was for the purpose of marriage or illicit sexual intercourse. The current offence does not require any specific intent but only that the unmarried child is taken against the will of the parent or the guardian.

Section 286 provides that the consent of the young person is no defence. So, for example, in *R. v. Langevin*,[103] the accused was found guilty of abducting two 14-year-old girls, even though the court said that the girls had taken a very active, if not leading, part in the occurrence.

Section 285 does provide a defence, however:

> **285. No one shall be found guilty of an offence under sections 280 to 283 if the court is satisfied that the taking, enticing away, concealing, detaining, receiving or harbouring of any young person was necessary to protect the young person from danger of imminent harm . . .**

---

103 (1962), 133 C.C.C. 257 (Ont. C.A.).

This defence is one of necessity. It requires some evidence that, from the accused's perspective, using the modified objective standard, (a) there was a danger of imminent harm to the young person and (b) there were no reasonable legal alternatives to taking the young person. In addition, the harm to the young person by taking him or her was proportional to the potential harm to the young person that was being avoided.[104]

The defence was raised in *R. v. Adams*.[105] Adams and a man named Dodge began living together with Dodge's young daughter, Sabrina. Adams claimed that their relationship deteriorated because of Dodge's drinking and violence. She thought of leaving, but did not want to leave Sabrina, to whom she had become very attached. Adams' mother, her friends, and Adams' sister concocted a plan to take Adams and Sabrina to a women's shelter when Dodge was not home. The plan was carried out. While at the women's shelter, Adams and Sabrina were interviewed by a Children's Aid Society worker, who concluded that Sabrina had not been physically abused. Adams and Sabrina left the shelter to stay with Adams' aunt because Adams knew that the Children's Aid worker planned to apprehend Sabrina. A few days later, she applied for interim custody of Sabrina; shortly after that, she surrendered to the police. Sabrina was returned to her father, and Adams and her mother and friends were charged with abduction. They were convicted. Their main ground of appeal was that the judge had not instructed the jury properly on the defence of honest but mistaken belief that Sabrina was in danger of imminent harm. The appeal court ruled that to use the defence, the belief must be honest, though it need not be reasonable. However, the reasonableness of the defence should be considered in deciding whether the belief was honest. In addition, the defence was not made out unless the taking of Sabrina was necessary in an objective sense based on the facts as the accused honestly believed them to be. The taking must be a response to the perceived danger of imminent harm. In this case, the instructions of the judge adequately directed the jury. Therefore, the appeal was dismissed.

An element of the offence is that the accused must have taken the person out of the possession of his or her parents. Thus, if a person leaves home and later goes with the accused, the accused cannot be found guilty of abduction. Of course, if the accused aided the young person in leaving home by giving transportation or other encouragement, the fact that he or she did not physically "take" the young person will not save the accused. *R. v. Cox*[106] considered whether a girl was taken against the will of her parent when the parent allowed the girl to be taken based on the accused's fraudulent statements. The accused told the girl's mother that he needed a babysitter for his three children. The mother allowed her 15-year-old daughter to go with the accused in his car. When the accused did not turn at the street where he said his house was located, the girl became alarmed and escaped from the car. At his trial, it was found that the accused had used a false name and address and had lied about his employment situation. The court of appeal held that a consent obtained by fraud or trick is not consent; thus, before a person can be said to do an act willingly, he or she must be consciously consenting to the act.

Child under 14

281. (1) Every one who, not being the parent, guardian or person having the lawful care or charge of a person under the age of fourteen years, unlawfully takes, entices away, conceals, detains, receives or harbours that person with intent to deprive a parent or guardian, or any other person who has the lawful care or charge of that person, of the possession of that person is guilty of an indictable offence...

---

104 *R. v. VandenElsen* (2003), 177 C.C.C. (3d) 332.
105 (1993), 79 C.C.C. (3d) 193 (Ont. C.A.).
106 (1969), 4 C.C.C. 321 (Ont. C.A.).

Notice that this offence of abduction is committed even if the accused only "harbours" or "receives" the child. For example, if a 12-year-old runs away from home and is allowed to stay in the home of a person, that person may be convicted of the offence if the necessary intent is proven. It will not matter that the person did not entice or encourage the child to leave home. It is a necessary element of the offence that the detention is for the purpose of depriving a parent or guardian of possession. The Supreme Court of Canada considered the *mens rea* for this offence in *R. v. Chartrand*.[107] The accused, a 43-year-old man, was hitting golf balls in a schoolyard in Ottawa. An 8-year-old boy, Tyler, and his friends were also in the yard. They asked if they could catch the balls with their gloves. After doing this for a while, some of the boys left to get refreshments. Tyler stayed. The accused began photographing him. When Tyler's friends returned, they found the accused taking pictures of Tyler at the edge of the school-yard in a wooded area. They began to interfere with the picture taking. Eventually, the accused suggested to Tyler that they go somewhere else. Tyler agreed to go in the accused's car, even though his friends told him not to go. The friends returned home and told one of their mothers that Tyler had gone off with a man in a red car. She called Tyler's father. Tyler's father, the boys, and a police officer began to look for him. They found him between 30 and 90 minutes later, at a beach, where the accused was photographing him.

The accused was charged with abduction. The trial judge directed an acquittal on the grounds that there was no evidence on which a jury could conclude that the accused intended to deprive the parents of possession of Tyler. On appeal, the Supreme Court of Canada considered the meaning of "unlawfully" and the required *mens rea*. The Court held that the offence does not require an additional unlawful act. "Unlawfully" as it is used in this offence merely means without lawful justification, authority, or excuse. The Court distinguished this offence from unlawfully causing bodily harm, for which an unlawful act (the predicate offence) is required.

To determine the *mens rea* for the offence, the Court first looked at the meaning of "deprive a parent . . . of the possession . . ." The Court explained that possession is not limited to circumstances in which the parent or guardian is actually in physical possession of the child. The concept of possession relates to the ability of the parent to exercise his or her right of control over the child. Therefore, a child playing with a group of other children is still in the possession of his or her parent. The deprivation of possession may only be for a short time and need not be an attempt at permanent removal. In this case, Tyler was in the possession of his parents at the time of the incident.

Regarding the meaning of "with intent to," it is enough that the taker knows or foresees that his or her actions would be certain or substantially certain to result in the parents being deprived of the ability to exercise control over their child.

The Court concluded that there was sufficient evidence on which a jury could convict and sent the case back for trial.

The defence that abduction was necessary to protect the young person from harm (s. 285, above) applies to this offence. Section 284 sets out another defence:

> **284. No one shall be found guilty of an offence under sections 281 to 283 if he establishes that the taking, enticing away, concealing, detaining, receiving or harbouring of any young person was done with the consent of the parent, guardian or other person having the lawful possession, care or charge of that young person.**

---

107 (1994), 91 C.C.C. (3d) 396 (S.C.C.).

b. Abduction by a Parent

Sections 282 and 283 address abductions by parents. They were enacted because s. 281 proved to be inadequate to deal with the problem of parents abducting their own children. In *R. v. Kosawan*,[108] a court in Manitoba held that in the absence of a custody order restricting parental rights, each parent has an equal right to custody; therefore, it is not an unlawful act for one parent to take the children. This situation encouraged parents who did not yet have a formal custody order to take the children from the other parent, especially since the parent who has actual possession of the child has a strategic advantage when seeking a custody order.

Contrary to Custody Order

Section 282 provides that a person commits an offence who,

> **being the parent, guardian or person having the lawful care or charge of a person under the age of fourteen years, takes, entices away, conceals, detains, receives, or harbours that person, in contravention of the custody provisions of a custody order in relation to that person made by a court anywhere in Canada, with intent to deprive a parent or guardian or any other person who has the lawful care or charge of that person, of the possession of that person.**

Abduction under s. 282 requires that the parent, guardian, or other person having lawful care or charge of a child under 14 take the child in contravention of a custody order with intent to deprive the other parent of possession.

The defences under sections 284 and 285 are available to the accused. Another defence—that the accused was mistaken about the existence of a custody order—was allowed in *R. v. Ilczysyn*,[109] a decision of the Ontario Court of Appeal. The accused had lived with a man named West in a common law relationship from August 1982 to March 1985. They had a child in September 1984. In March 1985, the accused was sent to a reformatory for an 18-month sentence. While she was in the reformatory, West obtained a custody order giving him exclusive custody of the child. The accused did not object. When she was paroled in August 1985, she resumed living with West. In January or February of 1986, she called her lawyer to find out if the custody order was still valid. Her understanding was that, as long as she had resumed cohabiting with West, the order was no longer valid. She lived with West and the child until April, when they had a "falling out." In May, she picked the child up from the babysitter and went to another city. About five weeks later, she was apprehended and charged with abduction. She was acquitted on the grounds either that the custody order became invalid when she began living with West, or that it would be against public policy to enforce it. The court of appeal disagreed and held that West had legal custody of the child. However, the accused had made a mistake about the validity of the order and could use the defence of mistake of law. The rule that mistake of law is not a defence did not apply in this case because the mistake concerned the civil law. The court dismissed the Crown's appeal from her acquittal.

In *R. v. Hammerbeck*,[110] the court of appeal held that the defence of mistake regarding the validity of the order can be used even if the mistake is not reasonable. In other words, a subjective test is used: Did the accused have an honest, even though unreasonable, belief that the order was invalid?

108 [1980] 6 W.W.R. 674 (Man. Cty. Ct.).
109 (1988), 45 C.C.C. (3d) 91 (Ont. C.A.).
110 (1991), 68 C.C.C. (3d) 161 (B.C.C.A.).

Subsection (2) was added to s. 282 to deal with situations where the defence of honest mistake is raised. It provides that, where an accused successfully raises the defence of mistake and is found not guilty because there is a reasonable doubt as to whether the accused knew there was a valid custody order, the accused can be convicted under s. 283, where it is irrelevant whether a custody order exists.

Regardless of Custody Order

Abduction under s. 283 is identical to abduction under s. 282 except that s. 283 applies whether or not there is a custody order. An example of the application of this section is *R. v. Cook*,[111] a decision of the Nova Scotia Court of Appeal. The parents, who were living in Ontario, decided to separate. The mother left their five-year-old child with the father and moved to Nova Scotia. While the child was visiting with her mother, the mother applied for custody in Nova Scotia. On the date of the hearing, the father arrived from Ontario and took the child, without the mother's consent, back to Toronto. He was charged with abduction under what is now s. 283. The father's argument was that he was only doing what he was legally entitled to do. Their agreement when they separated was that he would have custody of the child. He felt that the custody application by the mother should have been made in Ontario. The court of appeal did not accept his argument, stating that the purpose of the offence is to "force parents to seek the assistance of the courts before taking possession of a child without the consent of the other parent." It was clear that the accused's intention was to deprive the mother of possession. The court of appeal confirmed his conviction.

In *R. v. Dawson*,[112] another decision of the Nova Scotia Court of Appeal, the elements of the offence were considered and upheld by the Supreme Court of Canada. The accused, who was the father of the child, had a common law relationship with the mother. When they separated, the father took custody of their child. No formal custody order was made. After a few years, the mother decided to apply for custody. She obtained an order that the child not be removed from the province during the time that the custody issue was being settled. Disregarding the order, the father took the child to the United States, where he was apprehended two years later and charged with abduction. He argued that he had not taken the child from the mother's possession, since at all times the child had been legally in his possession. The court agreed with his argument, and he was acquitted. On appeal, the court held that the trial judge was in error. The section is aimed at protecting both the parent's possession of the child and right to possession. Under Nova Scotia law, both parents have an equal right to custody until such time as a custody order is made. Although the mother did not have actual possession, she had a statutory and common law right to possession. The essential element of the offence is the intention of the accused to deprive the other parent of possession or the right to possession. The critical issue in this case was whether the accused had the intent to deprive the mother of her right to possession.

Notice that to bring a charge under this section, the consent of the Attorney General or counsel instructed by the Attorney General is necessary. This requirement indicates that the circumstances are to be carefully considered before a charge is laid.

---

111 (1984), 12 C.C.C. (3d) 471 (N.S.C.A.).
112 (1995), 100 C.C.C. (3d) 123 (N.S.C.A.); application for leave to appeal to S.C.C. dismissed (1996), 111 C.C.C. (3d) 1 (S.C.C.).

6. Inciting Hatred

A person commits an offence under s. 319, if the person,

(1) by communicating statements in any public place, incites hatred against any identifiable group where such incitement is likely to lead to a breach of the peace; or

(2) by communicating statements, other than in private conversation, wilfully promotes hatred against any identifiable group.

(3) No person shall be convicted of an offence under subsection (2)

    (a) if he establishes that the statements communicated were true;

    (b) if, in good faith, he expressed or attempted to establish by argument an opinion upon a religious subject or an opinion based on a belief in a religious text;

    (c) if the statements were relevant to any subject of public interest, the discussion of which was for the public benefit, and if on reasonable grounds he believed them to be true; or

    (d) if, in good faith, he intended to point out, for the purpose of removal, matters producing or tending to produce feelings of hatred towards an identifiable group in Canada.

The Attorney General must give consent before proceedings for these offences can be started. "Communicating" includes use of the telephone, broadcasting, or any other audible or visible means. An "identifiable group" is defined in s. 318 as "any section of the public distinguished by colour, race, religion or ethnic origin."

The Supreme Court of Canada has held that s. 319(2) contains a stringent *mens rea* requirement that necessitates either intent to promote hatred or knowledge of the substantial certainty that hatred would be promoted.[113] The court also found that the meaning of "hatred" is restricted to "the most severe and deeply-felt form of opprobrium."

These offences have rarely been used; however, two cases, which were finally heard by the Supreme Court of Canada, are of interest because they considered the application of freedom of expression under the Charter. The cases were *R. v. Keegstra*,[114] and *R. v. Andrews and Smith*.[115] Keegstra was a high school history teacher in Alberta who was charged with an offence under s. 319(2). For years he had taught that the Holocaust (the killing of six million Jews during World War II) had never happened and that the story had been started by an international Jewish conspiracy. The charges were laid after a parent discovered what was being taught and complained to the authorities. Andrews and Smith were members of a Toronto-based political party that supported white supremacy. They were charged under s. 319(2) for publishing a neo-Nazi magazine that claimed, among other things, that non-white and non-Aryan groups were inferior and responsible for violent crime in Canada.

In both cases, the accused argued that the offences for which they were charged violated their freedom of expression as protected under the Charter. They also argued that s. 319(3)(a) creates an unjustifiable reverse onus clause, in that an accused cannot be convicted if he or

---

113 *R. v. Keegstra* (1990), 61 C.C.C. (3d) 1 (S.C.C.).
114 Ibid.
115 (1990), 61 C.C.C. (3d) 490 (S.C.C.).

she can establish (prove on a balance of probabilities) that the statements are true. Thus, a jury could convict an accused if it had even a doubt about the truth of the statements. In other words, the Crown did not have to establish an element of the offence—that statements were not true—beyond a reasonable doubt.

The Alberta Court of Appeal, in *Keegstra*, held that the section was unconstitutional; the court acquitted Keegstra. The Ontario Court of Appeal, in *Andrews and Smith*, reached the opposite conclusion and held that the offence does not violate the Charter. The Supreme Court of Canada released concurrent judgments in the two cases. In a four-to-three split, the majority upheld the validity of the offence. The Court agreed with the Alberta court that the offence violates the right to freedom of expression and that s. 319(3)(a) creates a reverse onus clause. However, it also found that both are justifiable limitations. After discussing the importance of freedom of expression in a democratic society, the Court stated:

> *The suppression of hate propaganda undeniably muzzles the participation of a few individuals in the democratic process, and hence detracts somewhat from free expression values, but the degree of this limitation is not substantial . . . expression can work to undermine our commitment to democracy where employed to propagate ideas anathematic to democratic values. Hate propaganda works in just such a way, arguing as it does for a society in which . . . individuals are denied respect and dignity because of racial or religious characteristics. This brand of expressive activity is wholly inimical to the democratic aspirations of the free expression guarantee.*[116]

F. RECOGNIZANCES TO KEEP THE PEACE

Under s. 810, if a person fears on reasonable grounds that another person will cause personal injury to him or her or to his or her spouse or child or will damage his or her property, he or she may lay an information before a justice. The justice will require the parties to appear before the court. If satisfied that the person has reasonable grounds for the fear, the court may

> **(a) order that the defendant enter into a recognizance, with or without sureties, to keep the peace and be of good behaviour for any period that does not exceed twelve months, and comply with such other reasonable conditions prescribed in the recognizance . . . as the court considers desirable for securing the good conduct of the defendant**

If the defendant fails or refuses to enter into the recognizance, the court may commit the defendant to prison for a term not greater than 12 months.

This section gives courts the authority to exercise what is sometimes called "preventative justice." By entering a recognizance, which is often referred to as a "peace bond," the defendant agrees to keep the peace and to comply with any other conditions prescribed by the court.

The court must consider before making an order, whether the recognizance should include as a condition a prohibition from possessing a firearm or other weapon (see s. 810(3.1)), or a prohibition from being within a certain distance of a place where the person on whose behalf the information has been laid regularly is, or a prohibition from communicating with that person (see s. 810(3.2)).

---

116 *Keegstra, supra* note 113 at 50.

A surety is a person who is willing to be responsible for ensuring that the defendant keeps the peace. Sometimes, a sum of money must be given to the court by the defendant or the surety as additional encouragement for the defendant to keep the peace. The money is forfeited if the defendant does not honour the recognizance. It is not necessary that an assault or any other offence be committed before a justice uses the powers given by this section; however, those powers can only be exercised upon "reasonable grounds" that a breach of the peace will occur in the future.[117]

In addition to the authority under this section, the justice has a general authority derived from the common law to maintain order and preserve the peace by ordering persons whom he or she thinks may breach the peace to enter a recognizance.[118] The difference between the common law authority and that given under s. 810 was explained by the British Columbia Supreme Court in *R. v. White*:[119]

> *Under s. 717 [now s. 810] of the Code a defendant cannot be bound over unless the magistrate is satisfied that the informant has reasonable grounds for his fears, whereas the prerequisite to the exercise of the common law jurisdiction is that the magistrate (on facts established to his or her satisfaction) has probable grounds to suspect or be apprehensive that there may be a breach of the peace.*[120]

In other words, under s. 810, it is the informant who must have reasonable grounds for fearing future injury, while under the common law, it is the justice who must have reasonable grounds for those fears. So, for example, a justice could require a person to enter a recognizance even though no other person had complained. This was, in fact, what the magistrate in *White* had attempted to do. He could not decide whether the informant or the defendant was telling the truth, and so ordered them both to enter recognizances. However, the British Columbia Supreme Court found that the magistrate did not have reasonable grounds to exercise his common law authority, since his decision was based on speculation and conjecture as to what the actual facts of the case were.

---

117 See, for example, *R. v. White* (1969), 1 C.C.C. 19 (B.C.S.C.).
118 See, for example, *MacKenzie v. Martin* (1954), 108 C.C.C. 305 (S.C.C.), where it was established that the authority exists in Ontario.
119 *White, supra* note 117.
120 Ibid. at 29.

Questions for Review and Discussion

1. What test is used to determine whether words are a threat under s. 264.1?

2. Briefly describe the three sets of circumstances under which an assault may occur.

3. What was the decision of the Supreme Court of Canada in *Jobidon*? Do you agree with the result?

4. Why does the law make an attempted or threatened use of force an offence?

5. Has the offence of assault been committed where the alleged assailant threatens a person with a weapon but does not actually intend to apply force to the victim? What question do you need to ask to answer this?

6. Can threatening words alone constitute the offence of assault? Explain.

7. Discuss the circumstances in which the use of force may be lawful.

8. Why is there more than one offence of assault? What are the different offences?

9. How does the Code define "bodily harm"?

10. Distinguish the following terms: wounding, maiming, and disfiguring.

11. What are the elements of the offence of sexual assault?

12. What meaning has been given to the term "sexual"?

13. What is the law regarding an honest mistake of consent?

14. What are some of the limits on using the defence of honest mistake in a sexual assault case?

15. What kinds of behaviour do you think would be harassment under s. 264? Make up some examples.

16. How is the offence of unlawfully causing bodily harm different from assault?

17. What is the main difference between kidnapping and the offences of forcible seizure, confinement, and imprisonment?

18. Can a parent ever be found guilty of abducting his or her own child? Explain.

19. Do you agree with the Supreme Court of Canada decision in *Keegstra*? Discuss the pros and cons of the decision.

20. What is a recognizance? What is a surety?

21. What is the main difference between the court's common law authority to order persons to enter recognizances and the authority given by the Code?

22. Is it necessary that an offence be committed before a judge can order a person to enter a recognizance? Explain.

23. Bob and Tony are two high school students. One afternoon they were playing basketball in the gym when Bob ran into Tony, knocking him to the floor. Tony got up angrily and punched Bob in the mouth. At that point, they began fighting violently until some other students were able to separate them. What charges, if any, could be laid, and against whom? Explain.

24. Paula was involved in a bitterly contested divorce. During one acrimonious court hearing, she burst out, "I am leaving that man and that woman [referring to his girlfriend] better stay out of my way—otherwise they're dead." She was charged with uttering a threat. Should she be convicted? Explain. See *R. v. Payne-Binder* (1991), 7 C.R. (4th) 308 (Yukon Terr. C.A.).

25. The town of Marlboro closed off a downtown street one summer to create a mall. The area became a hangout for teenagers, who sometimes became quite rowdy. One evening, Constable Jones observed two young persons, a man and woman, kissing and wrestling in the middle of the sidewalk. Constable Jones told them to get up and stop acting like idiots. A third person, a young woman named Molly, then yelled an obscenity at him. Jones arrested Molly and attempted to take her to his police cruiser. By this time, a crowd had developed, which made it difficult for Jones to escort Molly to the cruiser. While all this was happening, Sandra stepped forward and slapped Jones in the face. She was promptly arrested. Sandra was charged with assaulting a peace officer engaged in the execution of his duty. Jones gave evidence at Sandra's trial that he had not arrested Molly for yelling at him; rather, his authority had been flouted and he wanted to have her arrested "to prevent further trouble." Should the court find Sandra guilty of the charge? If not, what other offence could she be charged with? Explain. See *R. v. Allen* (1971), 4 C.C.C. (2d) 194 (Ont. C.A.).

26. Sam, age 19, had been dating Barbara, age 15. Barbara's parents did not like Sam and thought he was a bad influence on their daughter. The previous Wednesday they had forbidden Barbara to see him any longer. On Friday night, Barbara packed a suitcase and slipped out of the house. She went to Sam's apartment and told him she had run away from home. He let her in, and she spent Friday and Saturday night at his apartment. On Sunday night, her parents found out where Sam lived. They went to Sam's place and forced her to go home with them. Can Sam be charged with abduction? What difference would it make if Sam had picked her up on Friday night and driven her to his apartment? What if Sam had called her and encouraged her to leave home and live with him?

27. Burns, a male police officer, and a woman knew one another but had had almost no contact for three years. While the woman was walking down the main street of town, Burns was walking behind her. He "wolf-whistled" at her and said "nice butt" or "nice ass" and then, after she walked faster to get away from him, he called out, "Are those pants painted on?" Burns was charged with harassment under s. 264. Should he be convicted? See *R. v. Burns* 2008 ONCA 6.

28. Carl and his former wife are the parents of a 5-year-old boy. The custody order provides that the mother, who lives in Prince Edward Island, has custody of the boy and Carl has access rights, which include periods of time in which the boy would be with him in Arizona. While bathing the boy in Arizona, Carl noticed a severe rash on the child's penis and generally in his genital area. The boy was examined by a pediatrician, who referred the boy to Arizona child protective services, which began an investigation into possible sexual abuse. On the day before the boy was scheduled to be returned to PEI, Carl advised the mother that he would not be returned because the sexual abuse investigation had been initiated but not completed. The mother obtained a court order requiring Carl to return the boy immediately. Carl waited until the investigation, which found no evidence of sexual abuse, was completed before he returned the boy to PEI. Carl was convicted under s. 282(1) and appealed. Should the conviction be overturned? See *R. v. Muirhead* (2008), 230 C.C.C. (3d) 236 (P.E.I.C.A.).

29. David Ahenakew, a leader in the Federation of Saskatchewan Indian Nations, gave a speech to a conference concerning a proposed policy of the federal government to require aboriginal persons who were seeking medical care to sign a consent form. The purpose of the conference was to publicize the government's proposal and encourage opposition to it. In the course of his speech, Ahenakew stated that the Second World War was created by the Jews. After the speech, while being interviewed by a newspaper reporter, Ahenakew stated that, prior to the Second World War, the Jews owned nearly all of Germany and that was why Hitler "fried six million of them." When the reporter asked how the Holocaust could be justified, Ahenakew said "You know, how . . . do you get rid of a . . . disease like that that's gonna take over, that's gonna dominate . . . ?" He also stated that Hitler "cleaned up a hell of a lot of things, didn't he? You'd be dominated by, you'd be owned by the Jews right now the world over." Ahenakew concluded the interview by saying, "Anyway, . . . to hell with the Jews. I can't stand them and that's it." Ahenakew was charged under s. 319(2) with promoting hatred. Should he be convicted? See *R. v. Ahenakew* 2009 SKPC 10; 2008 ONCA 6.

CHAPTER 12

Theft, Robbery, and Extortion

PART IX OF THE CODE

Key points explained in this chapter are

LO1 the basic legal requirements of the offence of theft;

LO2 theft offences and offences resembling theft, including identity theft, "joyriding," credit card offences, and unauthorized use of computer facilities;

LO3 what forms of deceit constitute fraud;

LO4 the difference between robbery and theft; and

LO5 when threatening a person can be considered extortion.

The offences covered in Part IX of the Code concern violations of a person's property rights. A property right includes a right of possession or ownership of a place or a "thing." Owning a car or home and renting an apartment are examples of property rights. Common offences against property rights include theft and "breaking and entering." Except for the offences of robbery and extortion, these crimes do not involve personal violence. This chapter deals with theft, fraud, robbery, and extortion. Chapter 13 deals with other property offences: break and enter, possession offences, mischief, and arson.

LO1 A. THEFT

Briefly, theft is the act of a person who dishonestly takes property belonging to another with the intention of depriving the owner of it either permanently or temporarily. Section 322(1) of the Code defines the offence of theft:

> **322. (1) Every one commits theft who fraudulently and without colour of right takes, or fraudulently and without colour of right converts to his use or to the use of another person, anything, whether animate or inanimate, with intent,**
>
> (a) **to deprive, temporarily or absolutely, the owner of it, or a person who has a special property or interest in it, of the thing or of his property or interest in it;**
>
> (b) **to pledge it or deposit it as security;**
>
> (c) **to part with it under a condition with respect to its return that the person who parts with it may be unable to perform; or**

(d) **to deal with it in such a manner that it cannot be restored in the condition in which it was at the time it was taken or converted.**

(2) **A person commits theft when, with intent to steal anything, he moves it or causes it to move or to be moved, or begins to cause it to become movable.**

The *actus reus* of theft is the taking or converting of anything. It also includes moving or beginning to cause it to become moveable, if it is done with the intent to steal. The *mens rea* of theft is that the taking or converting was done fraudulently and without colour of right. It also requires that the accused had the intent to deprive the owner of the property temporarily or permanently. The *mens rea* may also include the intent to do other specific actions with the property: depositing it as security, parting with it in circumstances that make it doubtful that it will be returned, or dealing with it in a way that makes it impossible to restore it to its condition at the time it was taken.

Section 334 sets out the penalties for the various offences of theft. It distinguishes between theft over $5000 and theft of $5000 or less.

1. "Converting" Property

A person has converted property to his or her use when the person has legally obtained the property but fails to return it. So, for example, a person who borrows library books and does not return them, and who has the intent of depriving the owner (the library) of them, has committed theft. The taking or converting can be absolute or temporary. In this way, an illegal borrowing can be theft.

The victim of the theft does not need to be the owner of the property. For example, a person who has rented property has a special interest in it. One case has even held that a neighbour taking care of a dwelling-house in the owner's absence has a special property interest in the house.[1]

The Supreme Court of Canada considered theft by conversion in *R. v. Milne.*[2] The accused was the owner of a company that provided goods and services to the Hudson's Bay Company. The Bay paid the accused with a cheque, which the accused deposited in his account. By error, the Bay sent a second cheque. Milne, realizing the error, deposited the cheque and withdrew the money from the account. The trial court convicted Milne of theft by conversion. The judge concluded that the actions of depositing the cheque, knowing that it was sent in error, and then withdrawing the money, constituted a theft by conversion.

The court of appeal disagreed, holding that there was not a theft because, under property law, the ownership of the money passed to Milne, even though the Bay had a right to recover the money in a civil court action. The Supreme Court of Canada restored the conviction, stating that where a person mistakenly transfers property to a recipient, and the recipient knows of the mistake, ownership of the property does not pass for the purpose of the criminal law if the law of property creates a right of recovery. A recipient who then converts the property to his or her own use fraudulently and without colour of right, and with the intent to deprive the transferor of the property, is guilty of theft.

Milne was applied in *R. v. Smith.*[3] The accused had purchased a quantity of coffee beans. The terms of the sale were a 20 percent down payment on delivery, with the balance to be paid in three days. The accused wrote a cheque for the down payment, knowing that there

1   *R. v. Rodrique* (1987), 61 C.R. (3d) 381 (Que. C.A.).
2   (1992), 70 C.C.C. (3d) 481 (S.C.C.).
3   (1992), 77 C.C.C. (3d) 182 (Ont. C.A.); aff'd (1993), 84 C.C.C. (3d) 160 (S.C.C.).

were insufficient funds to cover it. He then resold the coffee beans. The cheque for the down payment was never replaced, and the balance was never paid. The Ontario Court of Appeal upheld his conviction. The court stated that the *mens rea* for this offence is satisfied if the accused knows that the transferor has mistakenly transferred the property and the accused keeps the property. The transfer was induced by the accused's fraud. Since the victim had a right under civil law to recover the beans, the offence was made out. The court commented that the term "mistake" has a broad meaning. It does not matter whether the mistake was made unilaterally by the transferor or was induced by the recipient's fraud, as in this case. The Supreme Court of Canada affirmed the decision.[4]

2. Taking or Converting "Anything"

In most situations, it is clear what "anything" means. However, the Supreme Court of Canada had to consider whether the offence of theft had taken place in an unusual situation. In *R. v. Stewart*,[5] the accused was hired by union organizers to obtain a list of the names and addresses of about 600 employees of a hotel. The union was trying to organize the hotel's employees. Stewart approached a security guard and offered him money to obtain the information. The security guard went to the police instead. The police taped a conversation between the guard and Stewart, and eventually charged him with counselling theft. The case was appealed to the Supreme Court of Canada on the issue of whether confidential information was included within the term "anything" in s. 322. There was no written list or other tangible thing involved. The confidential information was to be copied or memorized. The Court held that confidential information is not property: "[T]o be the object of theft, 'anything' must be property in the sense that to be stolen it has to belong in some way to someone. For instance, no conviction for theft would arise out of a taking or converting of the air that we breathe, because air is not property."[6]

The Court also mentioned that it is in society's interest that there be a free flow of information. In addition, the Court noted that if information were considered property, a person who memorized confidential information, knowing that it was stolen, could be charged with having possession of stolen property for every day that he or she had not forgotten it. Finally, the Court stated that confidential information should perhaps be protected somehow under the Criminal Code. However, it is up to Parliament to enact appropriate legislation; it is not up to the courts to expand the offence of theft.

3. Fraudulently and without Colour of Right

a. Fraudulently

Some courts have held that fraudulent conduct requires a dishonest or immoral intent. In *Cooper v. R.*,[7] the accused was charged with the theft of an aircraft. The accused went to the grounds of the flying school where he had begun taking flying lessons. Using a canoe, he went out to the aircraft, which was moored at a buoy. Without permission, he got in and started the plane, intending to bring it alongside a dock. He missed the dock once and was making a second attempt when he was stopped. The evidence indicated that the accused intended only to show the plane to some friends. The court found the accused innocent of the charge of theft.

---

4   Ibid.
5   (1988), 41 C.C.C. (3d) 481 (S.C.C.).
6   Ibid. at page 489.
7   (1946), 2 C.R. 408 (N.S.C.A.).

It was held that he had not taken the aircraft fraudulently. Even though the accused had taken the plane within the meaning of s. 322 (he had deprived the owner of it temporarily), he had done so only to show it to his friends; thus, he did not take it with a criminal, or dishonest, intent.

In *Handfield v. R.*,[8] accused brothers were charged with theft of an election poster. Their defence was lack of criminal intent. They had passed a residence on which was standing an election poster inviting the electorate to vote for the Progressive Conservatives. The accused removed the poster and placed it on the lawn of a person whom they knew to be a Liberal supporter. One of the accused said that he took the poster to "play a trick" and that he never meant to steal it. The court held that the accused did not take the election poster fraudulently. The court concluded that, although the accused should possibly be given a penalty, they should not be subjected to conviction as common thieves and to a criminal record for the future.

In *R. v. Kerr*,[9] the accused was celebrating a victory in a dog competition. For some reason, the accused and two companions went to the airport, where a cleaner saw them. All three were staggering and acting in a foolish manner. The accused was carrying one of the ashtrays belonging to the airport. The cleaner saw the ashtray being carried out by the accused. The ashtray was of a floor type and nearly a metre in height. The behaviour of the men made the cleaner think that they were carrying away the ashtray as a prank, and he thought it would be left outside the airport door. Later, two police officers visited the accused's home and saw the ashtray resting on the lawn in front of the house. The accused said that he did not mean to take the ashtray, and that he had intended to return it but the police arrived before he was able to do so. The court decided that the accused did not commit the offence of theft, stating that "the accused's stupid and foolish actions clearly showed the absence of any criminal intent."

Court decisions have not been consistent, so the "prank" defence does not always succeed. In *Bogner v. The Queen*,[10] the accused had taken a rocking chair off the porch of a hotel. The hotel owner's wife chased the accused. She saw a police car and informed the police of what had happened. The accused were later arrested for theft. At trial, they testified that the taking of the chair was a joke and that they meant to return it later. Their conviction was upheld on appeal. The court stated that the offence was complete when the chair was taken without any justification. The owner had been deprived of it; it was not necessary to prove a general dishonest state of mind.

In *R. v. Dalzell*,[11] the court considered the meaning of "fraudulently" where there was no prank. The accused, who was earning a master's degree in social work, was working with a group of young offenders. The youths told her that they shoplifted frequently and were almost never caught; and that when they were caught, they were let go without the police being called. To encourage shopkeepers to support a program she was developing, the accused formulated a plan to prove to them that their anti-shoplifting strategies were not working. She stole several items from some stores in a mall. She had planned to make a list of the items and then return them to the store managers to make a point about how easy it was to steal from them. However, a security guard observed her taking the items and arrested her for theft. She was acquitted because the trial judge found that she did not have a fraudulent intent. The appeal court agreed with the trial judge as to the meaning of "fraudulently": "Fraudulently in section 283 means a dishonest state of mind, leading to a dishonest intention to 'appropriate' the property taken." The court concluded that there was evidence on which the trial judge could base a decision that there was no fraudulent intent.

---

8   (1953), 17 C.R. 343 (Que. C.A.).
9   (1965), 4 C.C.C. 37 (Man. C.A.).
10   (1975), 33 C.R.N.S. 349 (Que. C.A.).
11   (1983), 6 C.C.C. (3d) 112 (N.S.C.A.).

b. Without Colour of Right

The term "colour of right" with regard to theft refers to a situation where a person asserts a possessory right—that is, a claim of ownership or lawful possession—to the thing that was allegedly stolen. In other words, if a person puts forth what he or she believes to be an honest claim of ownership, that person, even though mistaken, will have a colour of right to the "thing" and cannot be found guilty of the offence of theft.

In *R. v. Wudrick*,[12] the accused, who was a railway employee, believing certain watermelons in a car on the railway tracks had been abandoned, took two. In fact, the melons had not been a "colour of right"—in other words, a possessory claim to the watermelons. The court concluded that the accused's belief—that the melons were waste and that there was nothing wrong in taking them—was an honest belief. The accused was acquitted.

In *R. v. Howson*,[13] the complainant parked his car on a private parking lot without the permission of the owner. Howson, at the request of the superintendent of the lot, towed the complainant's car to his premises, where it remained until the complainant found it there. The complainant demanded the return of his car; Howson refused to release it until he was paid a towing and storage charge. The complainant eventually paid the amount demanded, under protest. He then recovered his car, and Howson was charged with theft.

Howson, in fact, could not legally keep the complainant's car; however, Howson stated that he took the car believing that he had a possessory claim to it until such time as he was paid a towing and storage charge. In other words, he claimed an honest belief that he had a "colour of right" to the car. The court accepted this argument, and he was acquitted.

4. Doctrine of Recent Possession

The courts have developed through case law the doctrine of recent possession. It states that where it is proved that the accused has possession of recently stolen property, and no explanation is given for that possession, the trier of fact (jury, or judge if no jury) may but not must draw an inference that the accused is guilty of theft or offences incidental to theft (e.g., break and enter, or possession of stolen property), even if there is no other evidence of guilt.

The Supreme Court of Canada affirmed the existence of this doctrine in *R. v. Kowlyk*.[14] There had been three break and enters in the Winnipeg area over a short period of time. The police arrested the accused's brother and brought him to the house that he shared with the accused. When they arrived, the brother yelled to the accused, "The police are here!" The accused ran upstairs and started to go out the window, but stopped when he saw the police outside. The police searched the house and found items from the three break and enters in the accused's locked bedroom, in the same containers as when stolen. The accused was charged with break and enter. The Supreme Court of Canada upheld the accused's conviction, stating that when the presumption applies, the accused may be found guilty even though there is no other evidence of guilt.

The presumption does not apply, however, when the accused offers an explanation that might reasonably be true, even if the trier of fact is not satisfied of its truth. In such cases, the Crown must prove all the elements of the offence beyond a reasonable doubt to gain a conviction. For example, Allen is charged with possession of stolen property, a television set. The TV does not look new, and Allen tells the court that he bought it from a friend who said

12   (1959), 123 C.C.C. 109 (Sask. C.A.).
13   (1966), 3 C.C.C. 348 (Ont. C.A.).
14   (1988), 43 C.C.C. (3d) 1 (S.C.C.).

she did not need it any longer. If Allen's explanation might be true, to obtain a conviction the Crown will have to prove beyond a reasonable doubt every element of the offence of possession of property obtained by crime.

In *R. v. Killam*,[15] the British Columbia Court of Appeal had to consider whether goods were "recently" stolen. The accused was found in possession of a shipment of stolen pearls worth between $250,000 and $1,000,000. The pearls had been stolen eight-and-a-half months earlier. One of the judges stated that the question of whether goods have been recently stolen is answered by looking at all the circumstances, such as the nature of the item stolen, how rare it is, the ease with which it can be passed from hand to hand, and the ease of its identification. Thus, clothing, household appliances, and jewellery might have a short period to be considered recently stolen, while extraordinary, unique, large, or unusual goods might have a longer period. The volume of the goods might also have a bearing. The shipment of pearls weighed about 270 kilograms—enough to supply the Canadian market for several years. The judge concluded in the circumstances of this case that possession of the pearls was of recently stolen property.

L02 B. THEFT OFFENCES AND OFFENCES SIMILAR TO THEFT

The Criminal Code contains a number of specific theft offences. Some of these are described in the following paragraphs.

1. Identity Theft and Identity Fraud

a. Identity Theft

It is well recognized that identity theft is a growing problem in Canada. It has been estimated that identity theft may cost Canadian consumers, banks and credit card firms, stores, and other businesses more than $2 billion annually.[16]

In 2010, Parliament created new offences involving the misuse of a person's identity information:

- obtaining and possessing identity information with the intent to use the information deceptively, dishonestly, or fraudulently in the commission of a crime (s. 402.2(1)); and
- trafficking in identity information, an offence that targets those who transfer or sell information to another person with knowledge of, or recklessness as to, the possible criminal use of the information (s. 402.2(2)).

Section 402.1 defines "identity information" as any information, including biological or physiological information, of a type that is commonly used alone or in combination with other information to identify or purport to identify an individual. The information includes, among other things, a fingerprint, name, address, date of birth, signature, user name, credit or debit card number, Social Insurance Number, driver's licence number, or password.

402.2 (1) Everyone commits an offence who knowingly obtains or possesses another person's identity information in circumstances giving rise to a reasonable inference that the information is intended to be used to commit an indictable offence that includes fraud, deceit or falsehood as an element of the offence.

---

15   (1973), 12 C.C.C. (2d) 114 (B.C.C.A.); cited with approval in *Saieva v. The Queen* (1982), 68 C.C.C. (2d) 97 (S.C.C.).
16   See the Department of Justice (at **justice.gc.ca**) backgrounder on *Identity Theft*, January 2010.

(2) Everyone commits an offence who transmits, makes available, distributes, sells or offers for sale another person's identity information, or has it in their possession for any of those purposes, knowing that or being reckless as to whether the information will be used to commit an indictable offence that includes fraud, deceit or falsehood as an element of the offence.

Parliament also created a third new offence of unlawfully possessing or trafficking in government-issued identity documents that contain information of another person:

56.1 (1) Every person commits an offence who, without lawful excuse, procures to be made, possesses, transfers, sells or offers for sale an identity document that relates or purports to relate, in whole or in part, to another person.

"Identity document" refers to an identity document issued by the federal government, a provincial government, or a foreign government. Section 56.1(3) lists several examples, including a Social Insurance Number, driver's licence, health insurance card, birth certificate, passport, or employee identity card.

Prior to the creation of these three offences, it was not an offence to collect personal information for the purpose of assuming someone else's identity. These offences focus on the preliminary steps of collecting, possessing, and trafficking in identity information for the purpose of eventual use in existing crimes such as personation, fraud, or misuse of debit card or credit card data. Identity theft is different from identity fraud, which refers to the subsequent deceptive use of the identity information of another person in connection with various crimes. Identity theft takes place in advance of, and in preparation for, identity fraud.[17]

b. Identity Fraud

A person who passes himself or herself off as another for a criminal purpose has committed the offence of identity fraud under s. 403:

403. (1) Every one commits an offence who fraudulently personates another person, living or dead,

> **(a) with intent to gain advantage for themselves or another person,**
>
> **(b) with intent to obtain any property or an interest in any property,**
>
> **(c) with intent to cause disadvantage to the person being personated or another person, or**
>
> **(d) with intent to avoid arrest or prosecution or to obstruct, pervert or defeat the course of justice.**

"Personating" a person includes pretending to be the person or using the person's identity information as if it pertains to the person using it (s. 403(2)).

The intent required for this offence—to gain an advantage or cause a disadvantage—has been given a broad meaning. For example, in *Rozon v. The Queen*,[18] the accused, on being asked to identify himself, handed to the police officers a medical insurance card belonging to another person. He did so to avoid being arrested on a warrant issued against him. The accused was convicted of personation because he deliberately and in bad faith sought to gain the "advantage" of avoiding arrest.

---

17   Ibid.
18   (1975), 28 C.R.N.S. 232 (Que. C.A.).

In a similar case, *R. v. Dozois*,[19] the accused, whose driver's licence was suspended, was convicted of personation when he used his passenger's licence after being stopped by police for a traffic violation.

In *R. v. Hetsberger*,[20] the accused agreed to help N. enter the United States under a false name. He purchased a plane ticket in another person's name and gave it to her. The court convicted the accused of aiding N. to fraudulently impersonate another person. The court noted that the advantage obtained need not be an economic one. In this case, gaining illegal entry into the United States qualified as an advantage.

2. "Joyriding"

It is possible to "take" a motor vehicle or boat without the consent of its owner and not be committing the offence of theft. This offence is loosely referred to as "joyriding."

> **335. (1) Subject to subsection (1.1) every one who, without the consent of the owner, takes a motor vehicle or vessel with intent to drive, use, navigate or operate it or cause it to be driven, used, navigated or operated or is an occupant of a motor vehicle knowing that it was taken without the consent of the owner, is guilty of an offence punishable on summary conviction.**

> **(1.1) Subsection (1) does not apply to an occupant of a motor vehicle or vessel who, on becoming aware that it was taken without the consent of the owner, attempted to leave the motor vehicle or vessel, to the extent that it was feasible to do so, or actually left the motor vehicle or vessel.**

Notice that joyriding is a summary conviction offence. Since most cars are worth more than $5000, this offence allows a young person who takes a car for a joyride, intending to return it, to be charged with a less serious offence rather than the more serious offence of "theft over $5000." The Supreme Court of Canada has held that joyriding is not an included offence in theft, but that in certain fact situations, either offence could be charged, and that it is up to the Crown to decide which offence to charge.[21]

In *R. v. Wilkins*,[22] the accused, for the purpose of playing a joke, took a police officer's motorcycle while the officer was standing on the sidewalk making out a ticket. He intended to drive it only a short distance. He was charged with theft of the motorcycle under s. 283 (now s. 322). The court held that the accused should have been charged under s. 295 (now s. 335) and that he was not guilty of theft. In its judgment, the court stated:

> *[T]he facts could not possibly justify a conviction of theft. The accused did not intend to steal the vehicle, that is, to convert the property to his own use, but only to drive it as contemplated by s. 295 (s. 335). His intention was merely to play a joke on the policeman . . . the intention to perpetrate this joke, stupid though it was, is incompatible with the evil intent which is inherent in the crime of theft.*[23]

19   (1974), R.L. 285 (Que. C.A.).
20   (1980), 51 C.C.C. (2d) 257 (Ont. C.A.).
21   *LaFrance v. The Queen* (1973), 13 C.C.C. (2d) 289 (S.C.C.).
22   (1964), 44 C.R. 375 (Ont. C.A.); [1965] 2 C.C.C. 189.
23   *Wilkins* (1964), ibid. at 380, cited to C.R.

3. Credit Card Offences

Section 342(1) deals with the theft or forgery of a credit card. It provides that a person commits an offence who

(a) **steals a credit card,**

(b) **forges or falsifies a credit card,**

(c) **possesses, uses or traffics in a credit card or a forged or falsified credit card, knowing it was obtained, made or altered**

   (i) **by the commission in Canada of an offence, or**

   (ii) **by an act or omission anywhere that, if it had occurred in Canada, would have constituted an offence, or**

(d) **uses a credit card that he knows has been revoked or cancelled.**

This section also deals with the use of credit card data, including personal authentication information such as a personal identification number (PIN) or password. Subsection (3) makes it an offence to, fraudulently and without colour of right, possess, use, traffic in, or permit another person to use credit card data that would enable a person to use a credit card or to obtain services that are provided by the issuer of the credit card.

Court decisions have held that where a person innocently finds a credit card but then intends to use it or does use it, that credit card has been "obtained by the commission of an offence." The reasoning is that once the person has the intent to use the credit card, his or her possession of it becomes a theft by conversion.[24]

In *R. v. Mayer*,[25] the accused was convicted on 55 counts of using a forged credit card, contrary to s. 342(1)(c). Mayer participated in a large debit card skimming, counterfeiting, and fraud ring that looted card owners and banks of more than $1 million. The ring operated by having employees at six businesses swipe customers' bank cards, using a "skimmer" device, which captured and stored the electronic data and the PIN entered by the customer. The data stored in the skimmer was later downloaded on a computer and uploaded onto a blank card. The PIN was then matched to each new card, allowing the use of the forged card at an ATM or at a merchant's terminal.

Section 342.01 deals with offences related to devices that are used for copying credit card data or for forging or falsifying credit cards. It is an offence for a person, without lawful justification or excuse, to make, repair, buy, sell, export, import, or possess such a device if they know that the device has been used or is intended to be used for such purposes. (This section was added to the Code after the decision in the *Mayer* case, above.) In *R. v. Beauchamp*,[26] the accused operated a business, Canadian Barcode, in which they sold devices and supplies intended to be used to commit credit card fraud. One of the devices was designed to fit over the card reader slot of an ATM and to record and store credit and debit card information of each card as it passed through the device and into the ATM. The device was able to store the financial data contained on the magnetic stripes on the backs of 150–200 cards. The financial data captured by the device was then transferred from the device onto forged credit cards. The accused were convicted under s. 342.01(1)(b) of selling a device that they knew was

24   See, for example, *R. v. Zurowski* (1983), 5 C.C.C. (3d) 285 (Alta. C.A.); and *R. v. Elias* (1986), 33 C.C.C. (3d) 476 (Que. C.A.), aff'd 46 C.C.C. (3d) 447 (S.C.C.).
25   [2006] A.J. No. 324.
26   [2010] O.J. No. 1435.

intended for use in the forging of credit cards. At sentencing, an aggravating factor considered by the court was that one of the accused was aware that the proceeds of the credit card fraud had been used to fund terrorist activities, and yet he continued selling the devices.

4. Computer Offences

a. Unauthorized Use of a Computer

342.1 (1) Every one who, fraudulently and without colour of right,

(a) **obtains, directly or indirectly, any computer service,**

(b) **by means of an electro-magnetic, acoustic, mechanical or other device, intercepts or causes to be intercepted, directly or indirectly, any function of a computer system,**

(c) **uses or causes to be used, directly or indirectly, a computer system with intent to commit an offence under paragraph (a) or (b) or an offence under section 430 in relation to data or a computer system, or**

(d) **uses, possesses, traffics in or permits another person to have access to a computer password that would enable a person to commit an offence under paragraph (a), (b) or (c)**

is guilty of an indictable offence and is liable to imprisonment for a term not exceeding ten years, or is guilty of an offence punishable on summary conviction.

There are three ways an offence under this section can occur: by obtaining, intercepting, or using a computer service fraudulently and without colour of right. "Computer service" includes data processing and the storage or retrieval of data (s. 342.1(2)).

In *R. v. Forsythe*,[27] hard copy printouts of criminal records and other police information were found in the offices of an investigation agency operated by Forsythe. The printouts came from a computer system of the RCMP and the Edmonton Police Service. One of Forsythe's employees, Wagner, who had formerly worked at the Edmonton Police Service, initiated the obtaining of the printouts by contacting Curtis, an employee of the Edmonton Police Service. Forsythe knew what Wagner was doing, and that the printouts of police information were in his company's files. He also billed clients for the information. The issue for the court was whether Forsythe should be ordered to stand trial for fraudulently and without colour of right obtaining, directly or indirectly, a computer service, contrary to s. 342.1(a). The court found that there was not sufficient evidence to order Forsythe to stand trial. The court noted that "to obtain something is to gain or attain possession of it. It is an active verb as opposed to the passive action of only having or possessing." Finding computer printouts in Forsythe's office was not evidence of active or fraudulent obtaining by Forsythe. The court concluded that Parliament did not intend to make criminals of all those who come into possession of such printouts. Parliament's aim was to catch only those who actively obtained them in a fraudulent manner. In this case, if fraud were proven, the actions of Wagner and Curtis would fit the crime described in 342.1(1)(a).

---

27 [1992] A.J. No. 1182.

b. Possession of a Device to Obtain Computer Service

342.2(1) Every person who, without lawful justification or excuse, makes, possesses, sells, offers for sale or distributes any instrument or device or any component thereof, the design of which renders it primarily useful for committing an offence under section 342.1, under circumstances that give rise to a reasonable interference that the instrument, device or component has been used or is or was intended to be used to commit an offence contrary to that section,

> **(a) is guilty of an indictable offence . . .**

This section makes it an offence to make, possess, sell, offer for sale, or distribute any instrument, device, or component whose design makes it primarily useful for committing an offence under s. 342.1 The Crown must prove that the accused had the device under circumstances that give rise to a reasonable inference that the device has been used or was intended to be used to commit an offence of unauthorized use of a computer under s. 342.1. This section is similar to s. 342.01, discussed above, which makes it an offence to make or sell a device used for copying credit card data.

In *R. v. Coman*,[28] the accused was involved in a sophisticated debit card skimming, counterfeiting, and bank fraud scheme. Three of the charges related to the scheme were under sections 342.01, 342(3) and 342(1)(c), discussed above. However, another charge was laid under s. 342.2 in relation to a video camera that Coman concealed in a customized housing attached to an ATM. The camera was positioned over the PIN pad so as to record the PIN entered by the customer. He was charged and convicted under s. 342.2 of possessing an instrument or device (the camera), primarily useful for committing an offence under s. 342.1, under circumstances that make it reasonable to infer that it has been used, or is intended to be used, to commit an offence under that section. The offence under s. 342.1 in this case was fraudulently, by means of an electromagnetic device, cause to be intercepted, directly or indirectly, a function of the Royal Bank of Canada automated teller computer system, contrary to section 342.1(1)(b).

L03   C. FRAUD

Under s. 380(1), fraud is committed by a person who

> **by deceit, falsehood or other fraudulent means, whether or not it is a false pretence within the meaning of this Act, defrauds the public or any person, whether ascertained or not, of any property, money or valuable security.**

The term "false pretence" used in this section is defined in s. 361 as a representation by words or other means about facts that the accused knows to be untrue and that is made with dishonest intent to make someone do something. The offence of fraud includes false pretences but also other forms of deceit. At one time, a government commission recommended repealing the offences of false pretences and having one offence of fraud.[29]

The Supreme Court of Canada, in *R. v. Theroux*,[30] considered the *actus reus* and *mens rea* of the offence of fraud. The accused was a businessman involved in residential construction. The company he directed was building two residential projects. The buyers were told that

---

28   [2004] A.J. No. 383.
29   Law Reform Commission of Canada, Working Paper 19, *Criminal Law, Theft and Fraud* (1977).
30   (1993), 79 C.C.C. (3d) 449 (S.C.C.).

their deposits were insured by the Fédération de Construction du Québec. In fact, the deposits were not insured. The company failed, and most of the buyers lost their deposits. Theroux, as the director of the company, was held responsible for the misrepresentations that the deposits were guaranteed. At his trial, he was convicted of fraud after it was found that the representations were made for the purpose of obtaining the depositors' signatures and deposits. His defence—that he honestly believed that the projects would be built—was rejected. The court of appeal upheld the conviction, holding that all that was required was a dishonest act that had the consequence that someone was deprived of something.

The case was appealed to the Supreme Court of Canada on the issue of whether the accused's honest belief that the housing projects would be completed and that no one would be hurt was a defence. In other words, for the required *mens rea* to exist, must the accused subjectively believe that his or her act is dishonest? To answer this question, the Court first looked at the *actus reus* for fraud. The Court examined its previous decision in *R. v. Olan*,[31] in which the *actus reus* of the offence was analysed extensively. The Court summed up its findings in *Olan*:

- The *actus reus* has two elements: deprivation and dishonesty.
- The dishonest act is established by proof of an act of deceit, falsehood, or other fraudulent means.
- The element of deprivation is established by proof of detriment, prejudice, or risk of prejudice to the economic interests of the victim caused by the dishonest act. Actual economic loss is not essential; placing the interest at risk is enough.

What constitutes a lie or deceitful act is judged on objective grounds: Did the accused represent a situation as of a certain character when it was not? Other fraudulent means are also determined by an objective test: Would a reasonable person consider the dealings dishonest?

The Court noted that *Olan* was an important decision in that it broadened the offence of fraud by finding that deceit and actual economic loss are not necessary for the offence. Any dishonest act and an economic risk of deprivation are enough to establish the *actus reus*.

The Court then considered the *mens rea* of fraud and concluded that it requires the subjective awareness that one is undertaking a prohibited act that could deprive another person of property or put that property at risk. It is no defence that the accused hoped that the deprivation would not take place or believed that there was nothing wrong with what he or she was doing. Recklessness may also be sufficient for the *mens rea* where the accused has knowledge that the prohibited consequences are likely and commits acts being reckless as to whether those consequences will occur.

The Court held that the accused in *Theroux* had committed the *actus reus* of the offence by committing deliberate falsehoods that resulted in deprivation for the depositors, who did not get the insurance protection they believed they were getting, and who placed their money at risk. The *mens rea* was established because the accused knew that he was depriving the depositors of something they thought they had.

In a case released at the same time, *R. v. Zlatic*,[32] the Supreme Court of Canada again considered the elements of the offence. The accused operated a wholesale clothing company. He had obtained clothing on credit from his suppliers. Instead of paying off his creditors as he sold the clothing, he gambled the money away, eventually going bankrupt. He was charged with fraud. The Court held that the *actus reus*, or prohibited act, in this case was

---

31 (1978), 41 C.C.C. (2d) 145 (S.C.C.).
32 (1993), 79 C.C.C. (3d) 466 (S.C.C.).

using the money for gambling rather than for paying off creditors. The Court applied the test of the reasonable person and concluded that the accused's use of the money in which his creditors had an interest was wrongful in that most reasonable people would have found his actions dishonest. This was not just unwise business practice but a wrongful use of money for a purpose that had nothing to do with the business. The *mens rea* consisted of the accused's knowledge that the gambling could place the victims' interest in the money at risk. It was no defence that he believed that he would win and be able to pay off his creditors.

Fraud can take many forms. The following three cases are examples of some of the ways that fraud can been committed:

- *R. v. Kirkwood*.[33] The accused was the owner of a video store and had been making illegal copies of videotapes and selling or renting them. The trial judge dismissed the charges of fraud against the accused because there was no relationship between the accused and the "victim" of the crime, the holder of the copyright. The trial court said that for the offence of fraud, the accused must cause the victim to act to his or her detriment. The court of appeal disagreed with this narrow interpretation, stating that where fraud is based on deceit or falsehoods, it may be that a relationship between the victim and the accused must exist. However, where the charge is based on "other fraudulent means," it does not matter that the victim was unaware of the accused. Deprivation is satisfied by injury to the economic interests of the victim. In this case, intent to injure the economic interests of the victim could be inferred from the accused's willingness to deal in the copied tapes.

- *R. v. Gaetz*.[34] The accused was charged with defrauding the bank of a sum of money. The accused operated a car dealership. He borrowed money from the bank to purchase cars for lease. He was to make payments to the bank during the period of the lease, but to repay the bank in full when the leases were terminated. The leases terminated earlier than expected. The accused was experiencing financial difficulty, so instead of paying the bank in full he continued to make payments as if the cars were still being leased. The Supreme Court of Canada upheld the decision of the Nova Scotia Court of Appeal that the deceit of continuing the payments led to an extension of credit by the bank. The accused's appeal against his conviction was dismissed.

- *R. v. Wendel and Ballan*.[35] The victim was a 76-year-old woman who had signed a contract for $7000 worth of renovations to her home. Evidence was that the value of the renovations would reasonably be $800 to $1300. After obtaining her signature on the contract, the accused took the victim to her bank and attempted to have her withdraw $6000. He told suspicious bank employees that he was her grandson. The bank employees refused to release the money and called police. Here, the fraud was not deceit or misrepresentation but "other fraudulent means." The court applied the test of whether ordinary people would find that the actions of the accused were dishonest, and found the accused guilty.

Other fraud offences concern illegal business practices that tend to cheat the public, including the following:

- manipulating the price of stocks or shares or anything else offered for sale to the public (s. 380(2));
- using the mail to send letters concerning schemes designed to deceive or defraud the public (s. 381);

---

33   (1983), 5 C.C.C. (3d) 393 (Ont. C.A.).
34   (1993), 84 C.C.C. (3d) 351 (S.C.C.); affirming (1992), 77 C.C.C. (3d) 445 (N.S.C.A.).
35   (1992), 78 C.C.C. (3d) 279 (Man. C.A.).

- manipulating the stock market by creating a misleading or false appearance of active public trading (s. 382);
- any fraudulent behaviour relating to the sale or mortgaging of property (ss. 385 and 386); and
- making a false statement about a company to induce persons to become shareholders, or to deceive shareholders, or to induce anyone to put up security or advance money for a company (s. 400).

L04 D. ROBBERY

343. Every one commits robbery who

(a) steals, and for the purpose of extorting whatever is stolen or to prevent or overcome resistance to the stealing, uses violence or threats of violence to a person or property;

(b) steals from any person and, at the time he steals or immediately before or immediately thereafter, wounds, beats, strikes or uses any personal violence to that person;

(c) assaults any person with intent to steal from him; or

(d) steals from any person while armed with an offensive weapon or imitation thereof.

Section 2 of the Code provides that "steal" means "to commit theft." In general, the difference between theft and robbery is that robbery involves actual violence, or the possibility of violence, to another person. Both theft and assault may be lesser included offences for robbery. Recall from Chapter 3 that a lesser included offence is one that has some but not all of the elements of the major offence.

1. Robbery under Section 343(a)

Section 343(a) sets out the basic definition of the offence of robbery: theft accompanied by actual violence or by threats of violence. The violence need not be severe, nor need it cause an injury to the victim. Generally, any form of physical interference, from a push to a punch, will amount to "violence" for the purposes of s. 343. Similarly, a threat of any form of violence will generally be within the meaning of s. 343.[36] To "extort" means to compel or to force.

The violence or threat of violence need not be directed at the person being robbed. If the accused struck an innocent bystander at the scene of the theft, he would be guilty of robbery if the striking was for one of the specified purposes.

In *R. v. Newell*,[37] the court of appeal for Newfoundland and Labrador surveyed Canadian case law on the issue of when the threat or violence must occur. The court concluded that the violence or threat of violence has to be before or contemporaneous with the theft. So, for example, a person who shoplifts an item from a store and who is then confronted in the parking lot by a security guard has not committed robbery under this section even if a tussle takes place.

---

36 See, for example, *R. v. Lecky* (2001), 157 C.C.C. (3d) 351 (Ont. C.A.), where the court stated, "Once a threat was proved, there was no additional requirement of some minimum level of violence in order to establish robbery as defined in s. 343(a)."
37 (2007), 217 C.C.C. (3d) 483 (Nfld. & Lab. S.C.).

The Ontario Court of Appeal, in *R. v. Sayers and McCoy*,[38] held that robbery under this section does not require that the accused be armed; the threat of violence is enough. In *Sayers and McCoy*, the accused entered a bank. While one of the accused stood at the door and watched for police, the other jumped on the counter and yelled at the cashiers, "This is a robbery in progress . . . Give me the money . . . I'm not going to hurt anyone." He went up to two tellers and grabbed the cash from their drawers. He then came to the third cashier and tried to open her cash drawer, but found it was locked. He screamed at her, "Unlock the drawer! This is a robbery!" The bank employees testified that they were concerned and afraid. Neither of the accused was armed. After taking the money, the men fled on foot and were apprehended by the police. The appeal court held that the words and gestures of the accused "could only have the effect of causing reasonable apprehension of physical harm unless the tellers complied with the demand." The court held that the conduct of the accused fell within the definition of robbery under s. 343(a). It set aside their acquittals and entered convictions for robbery.

The courts considered the meaning of "threat of violence" in *R. v. Pelletier*.[39] This case had facts similar to *Sayers and McCoy*. The accused was in a bank when he jumped over the counter so that he was standing next to the tellers. He told the manager to get out of his office. The tellers stepped back from their drawers, believing that a holdup was in progress. The accused did not say anything else during the incident. He took the money out of the drawers and threw one drawer on the floor in anger when it would not open. He was not wearing a mask and was not armed with a weapon. However, witnesses noted that he acted brusquely and did not hesitate to throw the drawer on the floor when he could not open it. He was convicted and appealed on the grounds that his actions and the words that preceded the theft did not constitute threats of violence to the victims. The Crown argued that at the very least there was an implied threat of violence in his behaviour. The court, citing the Supreme Court of Canada in *R. v. McCraw*,[40] defined "threat" as a tool of intimidation designed to instill fear. In the context of this case, "a threat of violence is characterized by conduct which reflects an intent to have recourse to violence to carry out the theft or prevent resistance to the theft." The court noted that a threat may be expressed or implicit and may be made by words, writings, or actions. The determination as to whether a threat was made, the court said, requires an objective test: Would a reasonable person have felt frightened? It is the threat that is assessed, not the strength of the nerves of the person being frightened. The court agreed with the trial judge that the intimidating actions of the accused were directed toward people who are always susceptible to being victims of this type of crime. His conduct left no doubt as to his intentions should there be resistance. His appeal was dismissed.

2. Robbery under Section 343(b)

Under s. 343(b), assault is a lesser included offence for robbery. In other words, the offence of robbery includes the elements of the offence of assault. Unlike robbery under s. 343(a), the violence must be to the person being robbed. The Ontario Court of Appeal, in *R. v. Oakley*,[41] held that the words "uses any personal violence" are coloured by the preceding words, "wounds, beats or strikes"; therefore, for robbery under this subsection, there must be more than a "technical assault"—that is, something more than a touching without consent. The accused was a passenger in his sister-in-law's car when he began hallucinating. He thought his sister-in-law was the devil and that she was taking him to the hospital to be killed. He put

---

38 (1983), 8 C.C.C. (3d) 572 (Ont .C.A.).
39 (1992), 71 C.C.C. (3d) 438 (Que. C.A.).
40 (1991), 66 C.C.C. (3d) 517 (S.C.C.). See discussion of *McCraw* in Chapter 11, page 252.
41 (1986), 24 C.C.C. (3d) 351 (Ont. C.A.).

the car into park while it was moving, causing it to come to an abrupt stop. He then demanded that she give him the keys. When she refused, he took the keys from her and ordered her out of the car. Then he drove off. The court held that no robbery had occurred here under s. 343(b) because there was an assault only in the technical sense.

3. Robbery under Section 343(c)

Section 343(c) provides that if the victim was assaulted with the intent to steal, the offence of robbery has been committed whether a theft took place or not. For example, if Carlos knocks Usman to the ground with the intent to grab Usman's wallet and then a witness' screams cause Carlos to flee before he can get Usman's wallet, the offence of robbery has still been committed.

4. Robbery under Section 343(d)

Section 343(d) provides that robbery is committed if a person steals while he or she is armed with an offensive weapon or with an imitation of an offensive weapon. Section 2 of the Code provides that the definition of "weapon" applies to "offensive weapon." "Weapon" is defined in s. 2 as

any thing used, designed to be used or intended for use

(a) in causing death or injury any person, or

(b) for the purpose of threatening or intimidating any person and, without restricting the generality of the foregoing, includes a firearm.

Almost any object can be an offensive weapon. The person must be armed with something, however. In *R. v. Sloan*,[42] the accused was charged with attempted robbery under s. 343(d). The accused, whose head and upper body were partially covered with a bedsheet, had come to a hotel in the middle of the night and ordered the night clerk to open the office where the money was kept. The clerk refused. He was prodded backwards in the chest by something protruding from under the sheet. He said to the accused, "Don't push me. I've got a couple of cracked ribs." The accused then said, "If you don't open that door, you'll be in worse shape." The clerk turned, and in so doing hit the protruding object and discovered it was a finger, not a gun barrel. At that point. the accused fled.

The court held that the accused did not have an "offensive weapon or an imitation thereof." Part of the judgment states:

> In this case, all that is shown is that the accused . . . simulated the conduct of a man armed with a weapon. He acted a part or played out a pantomime to give the impression that he had a weapon. While the conduct might have justified a conviction under ss. (a) (theft with threat of violence) or (c) (theft with assault) of s. 302 [now s. 343] of the Code, . . . it does not meet the requirements of s. 302(d). To arm oneself with a weapon means to equip oneself, to acquire, to become possessed of some instrument which is either a weapon or an imitation of a weapon. I am not of the opinion that in these circumstances a man can be armed with his own finger and I am satisfied that the word "imitation" as used in s. 302(d) refers to an imitation of the weapon and cannot be stretched to include a simulation of conduct or actions.[43]

---

42   (1974), 19 C.C.C. (2d) 190 (B.C.C.A.).
43   Ibid. at 198.

L05 # E. EXTORTION

> **346. (1) Every one commits extortion who, without reasonable justification or excuse and with intent to obtain anything, by threats, accusations, menaces or violence induces or attempts to induce any person, whether or not he is the person threatened, accused or menaced or to whom violence is shown, to do anything or cause anything to be done . . .**
>
> **(2) A threat to institute civil proceedings is not a threat for the purposes of this section.**

Extortion is essentially equivalent to the word "blackmail." An extortion occurs when one person threatens another with some consequence, so that the person is forced to commit an act, or to omit doing something that he or she otherwise would have done.

In *R. v. Natarelli and Volpe*,[44] the accused were convicted of extortion for threatening the life of the victim if he did not deliver to them a large sum of money. The Supreme Court of Canada stated that there were three elements to the offence of extortion: The accused used threats, the accused did so with the intention of obtaining something by the use of threats, and either the use of the threats or the making of the demand for the thing sought to be obtained was without reasonable excuse or justification.

With respect to the last requirement, the Court said that once the threats to cause death or bodily harm with intent to obtain the money were proved, the accused were guilty of extortion even though they honestly believed that they had a right to the money. In other words, Amar cannot threaten William with death or harm in an attempt to force William to do something, even if Amar honestly believes he has a reasonable justification for making the threat. An example of a justified threat is the threat of a creditor to a debtor to turn over an account to a collection agency if payment of the debt is not made. However, if the creditor threatens the person with violence if payment is not made, even though the creditor is owed the money, there will be no reasonable justification for making such a threat.

In *R. v. Noel*,[45] the accused threatened the mother of a man who owed him money. The money was never paid. At trial, the judge found the accused guilty of attempted extortion. On appeal, the court held that it was not necessary to transfer funds to make out the offence. The offence was committed when the threat was made. The court entered a conviction for extortion instead of attempted extortion.

The court in *R. v. Alexander* stated that "[s]ection 346(1) is broadly worded to criminalize threats of any kind made in an attempt to induce any person to do anything, if those threats are made with the intention of obtaining anything. The section is aimed at those who would use coercion to overcome the free will of others for the purpose of extracting some gain."[46]

1. Threat or Menace

It is an essential element of the offence of extortion that there is a threat, accusation, menace, or violence. In *R. v. Rousseau*,[47] the Supreme Court of Canada found that the offence had not occurred because none of these elements was present. The accused was a lawyer who had been representing two men charged with theft. The men were employees of a security

---

44   (1967), 1 C.R.N.S. 302 (S.C.C.).
45   (2001), 156 C.C.C. (3d) 169 (N.B.C.A.) at 173.
46   (2005), 206 C.C.C. (3d) 233 (Ont. C.A.) at 251; leave to appeal refused (2006), 206 C.C.C. (3d) 233n (S.C.C.).
47   (1985), 21 C.C.C. (3d) 1 (S.C.C.).

company that was under contract to protect the premises from which the goods had been stolen. The accused approached the lawyer for the security company and offered to get the charges dropped in exchange for some money. The accused had already worked out a deal with the police to have some of the charges dropped. Although the accused was guilty of obstructing justice, he was not guilty of extortion.

The threat or menace involved need not amount to a threat to harm or murder the victim. A threat, for example, to damage the victim's property is sufficient for the purposes of s. 346.

In *R. v. Barros*,[48] the accused was a former police officer who was working as a private investigator. He was hired by the lawyer for Qureshi who had been charged with various drug offences. Barros discovered the identity of a police informant who had provided information leading to the drug charges. He set up a meeting with police officers to explain that if the charges were not dropped, Barros would be forced to report the informer's identity to Qureshi's lawyer and whatever the lawyer did with that information would be up to him. Barros pointed out to the police officers that his police experience was that in these circumstances, the charges would be stayed. He also noted that Qureshi's lawyer had used such information in the past to obtain a stay of charges. One of the officers testified that he understood Mr. Barros to be asking him to drop the charges against Qureshi if he didn't want the identity of the informer to be revealed. Barros was charged with extortion. The Supreme Court of Canada held that the trial judge erred in concluding that the indirect suggestions and veiled references by Barros were not capable of satisfying the threat element of extortion. The Court stated that a veiled reference may constitute a threat if it is sufficient, in light of all the circumstances, to convey to the victim the consequences which he or she fears or would prefer to avoid. The question was what would a reasonable person in the position of the police officer understand Barros to be communicating to him? The officer understood that a refusal to drop the charges would put at risk disclosure of his source, and at least the potential of retaliation. The Court ordered a new trial.

2. "Anything"

The Supreme Court of Canada stated in *R. v. Davis* that "anything" is not limited to something proprietary or a pecuniary interest, and that "anything" should be given a "wide, unrestricted applicaton."[49] In this case, the accused had taken nude and semi-nude photographs of several women on the pretext of helping them obtain modelling jobs. He then threatened to send the photos to their parents or to pornographic magazines if they did not have sex with him. The Supreme Court upheld his convictions for extorting "sexual favours."

---

48   2011 SCC 51; [2011] 3 S.C.R. 368. Another aspect of this case—a charge of obstruction of justice—is discussed in Chapter 6.
49   (1999), 139 C.C.C. (3d) 193 (S.C.C.) at 214.

Questions for Review and Discussion

1. Is a property right the same as ownership? Explain.

2. If a person "takes" an MP3 player on Friday, without the owner's consent, and returns it undamaged on the following Monday, has that person committed the offence of theft? Explain.

3. What is theft by "conversion"?

4. What does "colour of right" mean?

5. Is it possible to steal confidential information? Explain.

6. Explain the "doctrine of recent possession."

7. Explain the elements of the offence of joyriding. Why is this offence treated differently from theft?

8. How is the offence of theft related to the offence of robbery?

9. What are the elements of the offence of extortion?

10. What constitutes a threat for the purposes of extortion?

11. Jocelyn grabs at Noreen's purse. Noreen holds tight. Without actually touching her, Jocelyn "wrenches" the purse out of Noreen's hands. Noreen stumbles but does not fall. Is Jocelyn guilty of robbery? Discuss.

12. Johnson opened a bank account and was accidentally given the account number of another person who had not yet used the account. The person then made several deposits in the account. When Johnson discovered the account balance, he immediately withdrew the money. Can he be charged with theft? Explain. See *R. v. Johnson* (1978), 42 C.C.C. (2d) 249 (Man. C.A.).

13. Mr. Miller was having difficulty with his cable TV reception. By hooking up a device he built, he was able to get clearer reception. However, he also started receiving a pay TV station for which he was not paying. Has he committed an offence? Discuss.

14. Alvin and Bernice are husband and wife. Before the marriage, Alvin collected valuable coins. After the marriage, Alvin stopped collecting, but he did keep all of the coins he had collected before the marriage. Bernice took the coins one day, without letting her husband know, and sold them for $500. She spent the money on herself. Alvin did not discover that the coins were missing until a month later. His wife pretended that she didn't know what had happened to them. Can Bernice be convicted of theft if it is established that she took the coins?

15. D. made a deal with Z. to buy Z.'s van, which was equipped with a steam cleaning unit. In exchange for the van, he gave Z. cash and a trailer. After the transaction, he discovered that the van had a lien against it, and the steam cleaning unit was not functioning—it needed major repairs. He tried several times to contact Z. without success. In his mind, the deal was "dead." He finally went to Z.'s home and took the trailer, which he then sold to another person. Z. contacted the police, and D. was charged with theft. Make a decision in this case. Did D. take the trailer without colour of right? See *R. v. Dorosh* (2004), 183 C.C.C. (3d) 224 (Sask. C.A.).

16. B. was charged with robbery. He appealed his conviction on the grounds that the charge should have been theft, as there was no threat of violence. B. entered a bank. He had the hood of his jacket on his head and was wearing sunglasses. He had his hand in his pocket. He passed

the teller a note and by gestures and sounds indicated he wanted the large bills. The teller froze and did not react. B. grabbed the drawer and threw it down when he could not open it. He reached across the till, grabbed some bills, and fled. Make a decision in this case. Should the accused be charged with theft or robbery? See *R. v. Bourassa* (2004), 189 C.C.C. (3d) 438 (N.S.C.A.).

17. M.M. borrowed $7000 from H.A.'s wife to finance a lawsuit against P.G. M.M. later settled her action against P.G. and received a monetary settlement. She did not tell H.A.'s wife that the action had been settled. H.A.'s wife found out about the settlement and attempted to contact M.M. to discuss the status of the loan. When M.M. did not reply, H.A. wrote to her demanding repayment and threatening a lawsuit. Finally, H.A. prepared a letter addressed to M.M.'s employer, whom H.A. knew. The letter read in part: "I would like to make you aware of highly questionable ethical and moral conduct on behalf of one of your employees—[M.M.] There are too many good people looking for work in our present times without having such people of low character represent you and your products." H.A. sent a copy of the letter to M.M. at her place of employment along with a note asking M.M. if she had "any advice, direction or suggestions" before H.A. sent the letter to M.M.'s employer. H.A. was charged with extortion. Should he be convicted? See *R. v. H.A.* (2005) 206 C.C.C. (3d) 233 (Ont. C.A.).

18. Wolsey was a pharmacist whose business consisted primarily of filling prescriptions for methadone for drug addicts. Under the Pharmacare program of the Ministry of Health of British Columbia, there were two ways a pharmacist could claim payment for dispensing methadone. If the methadone was prescribed for general pain management, the narcotic compound ("NC") code was to be used. If the methadone was prescribed to assist patients to avoid the use of illicit drugs, then the methadone for maintenance ("MM") code was to be used. Initially, the same amount was paid to pharmacists regardless of whether the methadone was dispensed for pain management or for methadone maintenance. Later, the ministry changed its claims payment policy and put a financial cap on the amount of money it would pay per month for methadone maintenance. After the change in the policy, Wolsey used the NC code instead of the MM code in making claims for methadone dispensed for methadone maintenance. The loss to the Pharmacare program resulting from the wrongful use of the NC code was in excess of $533,000. Wolsey was charged under s. 380 with fraud. In his analysis of the *actus reus* of defrauding the public or any person of any money "by deceit, falsehood, or other fraudulent means," the trial judge found that there was a reasonable doubt about whether Wolsey knew that the NC code was to be used exclusively for pain management claims. The judge acquitted Wolsey. Was the judge correct? See *R. v. Wolsey* (2008), 233 C.C.C. (3d) 205 (B.C.C.A.).

CHAPTER 13

Break and Enter, Possession Offences, Mischief, and Arson

PART IX OF THE CODE

Key points explained in this chapter are

LO1 when going into a place constitutes the offence of breaking and entering;

LO2 the legal meaning of possession for the purposes of possession offences;

LO3 the wide range of acts that may constitute the offence of mischief; and

LO4 the legal meaning of arson, and the distinctions among the various arson offences in the Criminal Code.

This chapter concerns other property offences in Part IX of the Code. They involve entering property, including a dwelling-house; possession of property for the purpose of committing an offence or possession of property obtained by crime; damaging property or interfering with the lawful enjoyment of property; or burning property.

A. BREAK AND ENTER

Section 348 states that a person commits an offence who

(a) **breaks and enters a place with intent to commit an indictable offence therein,**

(b) **breaks and enters a place and commits an indictable offence therein, or**

(c) **breaks out of a place after**

(i) **committing an indictable offence therein, or**

(ii) **entering the place with intent to commit an indictable offence therein.**

The offence is a hybrid offence unless it is committed in relation to a dwelling-house, in which case it is an indictable offence with a maximum sentence of life imprisonment.

"Dwelling-house" is defined in s. 2 as

the whole or any part of a building or structure that is kept or occupied as a permanent or temporary residence, and includes

(a) **a building within the curtilage of a dwelling-house that is connected to it by a doorway or by a covered and enclosed passage-way, and**

(b) a unit that is designed to be mobile and to be used as a permanent or temporary residence and that is being used as such a residence.

Apartments and hotel rooms are considered dwelling-houses. Even a tent that people intend to sleep in has been considered a dwelling-house. The term "curtilage" refers to buildings close by a dwelling-house that are used for domestic activities—for example, garages and sheds.

1. The Presumptions and the Charter

Chapter 2 discussed reverse onus clauses, mandatory presumptions, and the Charter. It explained that many of these clauses are being struck down as violations of the presumption of innocence. Although there are many presumptions and reverse onus clauses in other parts of the Code, they are especially common in the offences involving break and enter. These clauses are all open to challenge under the Charter. Existing case law will be mentioned in the following discussion. Some of these decisions are from provincial courts of appeal. It will be up to the Supreme Court of Canada to decide whether any particular clause is invalid for infringing the Charter.

2. Elements of Break and Enter

There are three offences in this section: break and enter with intent to commit an indictable offence; break and enter and committing an indictable offence; and breaking out of a place after intending to commit or committing an indictable offence.

a. Break

321. . . .

"break" means

(a) to break any part, internal or external, or

(b) to open any thing that is used or intended to be used to close or to cover an internal or external opening.

Breaking can involve jimmying a door or window, picking a lock, or breaking a window. However, breaking also includes a number of ways of entering a place that would not normally be associated with the term. Opening a door with a stolen or "found" key, lifting a latch, raising an already open window, and simply opening an unlocked door are all examples of breaking for the purposes of the offence of breaking and entering.

In *R. v. Jewell*,[1] the accused was charged with breaking and entering into a house, which had been unoccupied for some time and was in dilapidated condition. He was able to enter the house through the open screen door and inner door. The accused admitted that he entered the house for the purpose of stealing something. The court concluded that because the accused entered through an already open door, it could not be said that he "broke into" the building.

However, in *R. v. Bargiamis*,[2] it was held that further opening an already ajar door does constitute breaking. In *Bargiamis*, the door was open about two centimetres, and the accused pushed it open to allow himself space to enter. The difference between these two cases seems to be that in *Bargiamis*, some minimal force was used to gain entry, while in *Jewell*, no force was needed to enter the building.

---

1   (1975), 22 C.C.C. (2d) 252 (Ont. C.A.).
2   (1970), 4 C.C.C. 258 (Ont. C.A.).

b. Enter

350. (a)   **a person enters as soon as any part of his body or any part of an instrument that he uses is within any thing that is being entered; and**

(b)   **a person shall be deemed to have broken and entered if**

(i)   **he obtained entrance by a threat or artifice or by collusion with a person within, or**

(ii)   **he entered without lawful justification or excuse, the proof of which lies on him, by a permanent or temporary opening.**

An entrance is made as soon as any part of the body of the accused, or any part of the instrument used by him, is within any part of the place being entered. For example, if the police catch Deborah with a hand inside a window that she opened, she has entered the place for the purposes of s. 348.

In *R. v. Marshall*,[3] the accused was charged with breaking and entering. A police officer on patrol noticed a window on the premises pushed in about 30 centimetres. The window consisted of six glass panels, five of which were broken. One police officer searching in the vicinity of the broken window found the accused lying on his back on the ground, concealed in a trench less than two metres from the building. His hand was cut and his left boot was off. The accused later testified that he had been leaning against the building when he broke the window.

It was acknowledged by the accused, that there had been a "breaking." The court held that there had been an "entering" as well. The accused had put only his hand through the window in the process of breaking it, but that was enough to constitute an entering. It was, therefore, established that the accused had broken and entered the building. However, it was not proved that he had done so with the intent to commit an indictable offence, and he was acquitted.

Section 350(b)(ii) provides that when a person gains entry by threats or with "inside help," he has still broken and entered. The section also states that a person is presumed to have broken and entered a building if he or she entered through a "permanent or temporary opening." Open doors and windows are not permanent or temporary openings. In *R. v. Sutherland*,[4] the accused entered through a garage that consisted of three walls and an opening at one end for the entrance of a car. He entered for the purpose of stealing gasoline, and was charged with breaking and entering. The court held that the opening in the garage was really not an "opening" but was, in fact, an "entrance." An opening in s. 350 refers to a hole in a wall or door, or to an opening where a door or window has not yet been placed. Areas where people usually enter buildings are not openings.

Section 350(b)(ii) also contains a reverse onus clause. The phrase, "the proof of which lies on him," means that it is up to the accused to show that the entrance was made with lawful justification. This element has been challenged as a violation of the presumption of innocence. In *R. v. Singh*,[5] the Alberta Court of Appeal stated that the effect of this section is that once it is proved that the accused entered, he or she will be deemed to have broken in unless the accused proves on a balance of probabilities that he or she entered with a lawful justification or excuse. The court held that this provision is not justifiable, since an accused could be convicted of break and enter where a reasonable doubt existed as to whether he or she

---

3   (1970), 1 C.C.C. (2d) 505 (B.C.C.A.).
4   (1967), 2 C.C.C. 84; 50 C.R. 197 (B.C.C.A.).
5   (1987), 41 C.C.C. (3d) 278 (Alta. C.A.).

entered unlawfully. However, rather than strike down the entire section as unconstitutional, the court held that it could be applied without the phrase "the proof of which lies on him." In other words, the Crown must prove that the accused entered without lawful justification.

An example of lawful justification being applied is found in *R. v. Farbridge*.[6] The accused entered a department store during business hours with the intent to hide in the store until it was closed and then steal clothing. The Alberta Court of Appeal held that he had not broken and entered under s. 350(b) because he had entered with lawful justification—that is, with the lawful justification that any person has to enter a store during business hours.

c. Place

Section 348(3) provides that "place" means

(a) a dwelling-house;

(b) a building or structure or any part thereof, other than a dwelling-house;

(c) a railway vehicle, a vessel, an aircraft or a trailer; or

(d) a pen or enclosure in which fur-bearing animals are kept in captivity for breeding or commercial purposes.

d. Intent to Commit an Indictable Offence

Once it is established that the accused broke in or out of a place, it must be shown that he or she committed an indictable offence, or that he or she entered with the intent to commit an indictable offence.

The most common indictable offence relating to a break-in is theft. However, any other indictable offence—assault, for example—can be the object of a break-in under a breaking and entering charge.

In *Macleod v. R.*,[7] the accused was ordered out of his host's home, where he had been drinking. He later returned and broke into the home to retrieve a bottle of liquor that he had brought to the home earlier. The accused was acquitted on a charge of breaking and entering because he did not break and enter with the intent to commit an indictable offence.

For the same reason, a person who breaks into a cottage only to seek shelter from a storm has not committed an offence under s. 348, because there is no intent to commit an indictable offence.

3. Presumption of Intent

Section 348(2) provides that evidence that an accused

(a) broke and entered a place or attempted to break and enter a place is, in the absence of evidence to the contrary, proof that he broke and entered the place or attempted to do so, as the case may be, with intent to commit an indictable offence therein; or

(b) broke out of a place is, in the absence of any evidence to the contrary, proof that he broke out after

(i) committing an indictable offence therein, or

(ii) entering with intent to commit an indictable offence therein.

6   (1984), 15 C.C.C. (3d) 521 (Alta. C.A.).
7   (1968), 2 C.C.C. 365 (P.E.I.S.C.).

This subsection creates a presumption that requires evidence that the accused did not break into or out of the place for the purpose of committing an indictable offence. Although this evidence would usually come from the accused, it is possible that the evidence could come from the Crown. If evidence to the contrary is presented, the Crown must prove every element of the offence beyond a reasonable doubt.

The application of this presumption and the meaning of the phrase "evidence to the contrary" were considered by the Supreme Court of Canada in *R. v. Proudlock*.[8] The accused had been drinking at a party in an apartment above a restaurant. He had been living in the apartment with the son of the owner of the restaurant. At some point in the evening, he broke into the restaurant by breaking a window and climbing through. He encountered the restaurant's janitor, who asked him what he was doing. The accused replied that he had been given the key by the owner's son and was looking for some soup. He then left by the back door. When asked by the police why he had broken into the restaurant, he said he did not know but that he had no intention of stealing anything. At trial, the judge said he did not believe that the accused did not intend to steal anything, but his testimony was evidence to the contrary; therefore, the Crown had to prove the offence beyond a reasonable doubt. On appeal, the Supreme Court disagreed with the trial judge, holding that evidence that is disbelieved is not evidence to the contrary. To rebut the presumption, the evidence must be believable and raise a reasonable doubt. The Court ordered that a conviction be entered.

The decision in *Proudlock* was made before the Charter was enacted, so the Supreme Court did not deal with the issue of whether the section violates the Charter. However, the British Columbia Court of Appeal, in *R. v. Slavens*,[9] found that this section does violate the Charter. The accused was found in a locked parking area of an apartment building by the apartment manager. When confronted, he ran out of the area, where the police were waiting. He was charged with breaking out with intent. The appeal court said that the presumption violates the presumption of innocence under the Charter:

> *In order to avoid a conviction, the accused . . . has the burden cast upon him to rebut the presumption by ensuring that there is evidence to the contrary before the court . . . And the evidence to the contrary must be sufficient to raise a reasonable doubt that the accused committed an indictable offence . . . or that he entered in the first instance with the intent of committing an indictable offence.*[10]

However, the court held that the presumption is saved by s. 1 of the Charter. The court relied on evidence that personal property crimes had reached epidemic proportions, and that the presumption only gives the Crown an "evidentiary assist." Therefore, the presumption is a reasonable and justifiable limit under s. 1 of the Charter.

4. Home Invasion

Section 348.1 does not create an offence of home invasion. It makes home invasion an aggravating circumstance of certain offences, which can result in a more severe sentence for a person who is convicted of one of the specified offences.

348.1 If a person is convicted of an offence under section 98 or 98.1, subsection 279(2) or section 343, 346 or 348 in relation to a dwelling-house, the court imposing the sentence on the person shall consider as an aggravating

8   (1978), 43 C.C.C. (2d) 321 (S.C.C.).
9   (1991), 64 C.C.C. (3d) 29 (B.C.C.A.).
10 Ibid. at 34.

circumstance the fact that the dwelling-house was occupied at the time of the commission of the offence and that the person, in committing the offence,

    (a) **knew that or was reckless as to whether the dwelling-house was occupied; and**

    (b) **used violence or threats of violence to a person or property.**

The specified offences are these: breaking and entering to steal a firearm (s. 98), robbery to steal a firearm (s. 98.1), unlawful confinement (s. 279(2)), robbery (s. 343), extortion (s. 346), and break and enter (s. 348). In *R. v. C.(D.J.)*,[11] the Saskatchewan Court of Appeal identified the essential elements of a home invasion: occupancy of a dwelling-house at the time one of the offences is committed, knowledge or recklessness as to whether the dwelling-house was occupied, and actual or threatened violence to persons or property. In rejecting the Crown's argument that a mandatory starting point for a sentence for home invasion is seven years, the court stated that "each case involving a home invasion within the meaning of s. 348.1 must be decided on its own facts having regard to aggravating factors such as (i) the motive for unlawfully entering the dwelling-house; (ii) the degree of violence inflicted on the victim; (iii) the nature of the accompanying listed offences; and (iv) other factors relevant to the listed offences."

5. Being Unlawfully in a Dwelling-House

349. (1) Every one who without lawful excuse, the proof of which lies on him, enters or is in a dwelling-house with intent to commit an indictable offence therein is guilty of an indictable offence . . .

(2) . . . evidence that an accused, without lawful excuse, entered or was in a dwelling-house is, in the absence of any evidence to the contrary, proof that he entered or was in the dwelling-house with intent to commit an indictable offence therein.

Notice that the place entered must be a dwelling-house. Also, for the purpose of s. 349, "enters" has the same meaning as it does under s. 348 and as defined under s. 350.

To commit an offence under s. 349, a person does not have to break in. For example, a person who walked through an open door into a dwelling-house could not be found guilty of breaking and entering (s. 348), but could be found guilty of unlawfully being in a dwelling-house. Also, the person does not need to enter for the purpose of committing an indictable offence; the person can form that intent once in the dwelling-house.

This offence has two elements that have been attacked as violations of the Charter right to be presumed innocent. First, subsection (1) sets out a reverse onus clause, requiring the accused to prove that the entry was not unlawful. Second, subsection (2) sets out a mandatory presumption that evidence that the entry was unlawful is, "in the absence of evidence to the contrary," evidence that the accused entered or was in the dwelling-house for the purpose of committing an indictable offence. These elements of the offence were considered by the Ontario Court of Appeal in *R. v. Nagy*.[12] The accused entered M.'s house through an unlocked door at about 3 p.m. M. was sleeping upstairs when he was awakened by someone downstairs saying "hello." M. asked the accused, who by this time was on the third stair leading upstairs, what he wanted. The accused said something about being stuck and needing a tow. There

---

11 (2009), 245 C.C.C. (3d) 258 (Sask. C.A.).
12 (1988), 45 C.C.C. (3d) 350 (Ont. C.A.).

was some evidence that he turned his back to M. and took off rubber gloves. The accused then called to a person in a car that was running in the driveway. The accused's son then entered the house and asked M. if he owned a dog, and said that there was an injured dog on the road. At that point, M.'s son walked in and the accused and his son left. M.'s son followed them and could find neither a stuck car nor an injured dog.

The trial judge convicted the accused of being unlawfully in the house. He rejected the accused's explanation as impossible to believe and held that there was no evidence to the contrary for explaining the accused's presence in the house. The court of appeal stated that the "without lawful excuse" requirement in subsection (1) is an element of the offence and that the accused must prove on a balance of probabilities that he or she had a lawful excuse for being in the dwelling-house. The court did not consider whether the subsection offended the Charter, because it was not necessary; the Crown had proved that the accused's entry was unlawful without relying on the reverse onus clause. With regard to subsection (2), the court found that it contains a mandatory presumption that requires the trier of fact to convict in the absence of evidence to the contrary. This subsection infringes on the presumption of innocence for two reasons: first, because it is not a necessary inference that a person who enters a dwelling-house without a lawful excuse is doing so with intent to commit an indictable offence; and second, because the subsection may require a person to testify or give evidence to avoid a conviction where the Crown has not proved every element of the offence beyond a reasonable doubt. This violates the accused person's right to remain silent, which is an underlying principle of the presumption of innocence. The court found, however, that the objective of protecting people and property from the crimes of break and enter is sufficiently pressing to justify an infringement of the Charter. Therefore, the court held that the subsection is a justifiable limitation under s. 1. The accused's appeal from conviction was dismissed.

.02 B. OFFENCES INVOLVING POSSESSION

The next two offences to be discussed—possession of break-in instruments, and possession of property obtained through the commission of an indictable offence—share the element of possession as the *actus reus* of the offence.

1. Possession

> **4. (3) For the purposes of this Act,**
>
> (a) **a person has anything in possession when he has it in his personal possession or knowingly**
>
>   (i) **has it in the actual possession or custody of another person, or**
>
>   (ii) **has it in any place, whether or not that place belongs to or is occupied by him, for the use or benefit of himself or of another person; and**
>
> (b) **where one of two or more persons, with the knowledge and consent of the rest, has anything in his custody or possession, it shall be deemed to be in the custody and possession of each and all of them.**

There are two types of possession: actual possession under s. 4(3)(a), and constructive possession under s. 4 (3)(a)(i) and (ii) and under s. 4.3(b).

All forms of possession require the knowledge of what the "thing" is and a measure or right of control over the thing.

a. Knowledge

This requirement of knowledge for possession was first set out by the Supreme Court of Canada in *R. v. Beaver*.[13] The accused was charged with possession of a narcotic and with trafficking in a narcotic. The evidence was that he sold a package of morphine to an undercover police officer. His defence was that he honestly believed that the package contained only powdered milk sugar. The Court held that his honest belief that the package contained milk sugar was a defence to the charge of possession. The Court quoted with approval a statement made in a British Columbia Court of Appeal decision, *R. v. Hess*:

> To constitute possession within the meaning of the criminal law it is my judgment that whereas here there is a manual handling of the thing it must be co-existent with knowledge of what that thing is, and both these elements must be co-existent with some act of control (outside of public duty).[14]

b. Control

Control over the thing does not necessarily mean actual physical control. Control refers to exercising authority over the thing. For example, a person can have control by allowing another person to keep the thing. Also, the control does not need to be absolute; a "measure" of control is sufficient.

c. Constructive Possession and Control

Constructive possession means that the person does not have actual possession of the thing. The case that decided that control was necessary for constructive possession is *R. v. Terrence*.[15] The accused was charged with being in possession of a stolen automobile in which he was a passenger. The evidence was that he was watching television one night when a friend, Hayes, arrived and asked if anyone wanted to go for a ride. The accused said "sure" and went with Hayes. The car that Hayes was driving was stolen and was eventually stopped by the police. The accused was charged with and convicted of possession. He appealed his conviction, arguing that a measure of control is necessary for the charge, regardless of whether the accused knew that the vehicle was stolen. The Supreme Court of Canada agreed with the court of appeal and held that a measure of control is necessary for constructive possession. The conviction was overturned.

d. Consent and Possession

For joint possession under s. 4.3(b), consent is required. Consent is really a form of control. If a person can consent or withhold consent to the possession, that person is exercising control over the thing. This type of control was demonstrated in *Re Chambers v. The Queen*.[16] The accused was charged with possession of narcotics for the purpose of trafficking. She was living with her boyfriend, who she knew was importing drugs. When their house was searched, drugs were found in her closet in the bedroom they shared. The case reached the Ontario Court of Appeal on the issue of whether she could properly be charged with possession. The court held that the required element of control was found in the fact that she could either give consent or withhold consent to the drugs being stored in her closet. The court sent the case back for trial.

---

13 (1957), 118 C.C.C. 129 (S.C.C.).
14 Ibid. at 140.
15 (1983), 4 C.C.C. (3d) 193 (S.C.C.).
16 (1985), 20 C.C.C. (3d) 440 (Ont. C.A.).

2. Possession of Breaking-in Instruments

Under section 351, a person commits an offence who

> **without lawful excuse, the proof of which lies on them, has in their possession any instrument suitable for the purpose of breaking into any place, motor vehicle, vault or safe under circumstances that give rise to a reasonable inference that the instrument has been used or is or was intended to be used for any such purpose.**

In *Mongeau v. R.*,[17] the accused was arrested along with L. The accused was driving L.'s car when he was stopped by the police and asked for his driver's licence and car registration.

The arresting officer testified that he had no particular suspicion of either of the parties, and that he was merely making a routine spot check. He asked the accused to open the trunk of the car, and the accused did so. The officer observed a packsack and asked what it contained. The accused said that he thought the packsack contained tools, which it did. As the two of them were examining the trunk, the second police officer, who had remained in the police car, watched L., who had stayed in his automobile, open the door and deposit another bag underneath the car. When this was examined, it was found to contain dynamite, caps, and fuse. Both men were then arrested and charged under s. 351.

The accused argued that he did not have possession of the tools and dynamite and had only guessed that the bag in the trunk contained "ordinary tools" because he could see a wooden handle sticking out of the bag. He further explained that he was driving the car, which was L.'s, because L. had an injured foot.

The court acquitted the accused on the charge of possession for these reasons:

- While the accused was in control of the automobile in which the articles were found, his control was merely due to the fact that he was sitting in the driver's seat at the time the police stopped the automobile to check it. The checking of the car was merely routine; the police officer testified that he had no suspicion of either of the parties.
- The mere fact that the accused was driving the car at the time on behalf of the owner, who was also present in the car, did not establish that he had control over, or even knowledge of, the tools or dynamite.
- The explanation offered by the accused was a reasonable one in the circumstances, and he was entitled to the benefit of any doubt that might arise in respect thereof.

a. Instruments Suitable for Breaking In

The term "instrument" is not defined in the Code. In *R. v. Hayes*,[18] the accused was found in possession of certain documents. These documents consisted of elaborate plans or sketches of two villages in Ontario showing the exact location of two banks, and a minute and detailed description of the interior of one of those banks. The documents also contained recipes for making explosives, information about bulletproof vests, and descriptions of other instruments. The sole question in the case was whether the documents, or plans, found in the possession of the accused fell within the category of "instruments for house-breaking, vault-breaking or safe-breaking" (as break-in instruments were previously defined). The court concluded that a "breaking" instrument necessarily implies an object, or article, or tool that may be used to break something in the sense of the meaning of "break" as it is defined by s. 321. Objects such as a

---

17   (1957), 25 C.R. 195 (Que. C.A.).
18   [1958] 29 C.R. 235 (Ont. C.A.).

crowbar, a jack, a screwdriver, and even a bent coat hanger, can all be described as "breaking" instruments. Having thus defined "instrument," the court decided that the documents in the possession of the accused could not be classified as "house, vault or safe-breaking" instruments.

Another case that considered whether articles found in the possession of the accused were break-in instruments is *R. v. Benischek*.[19] In the trunk of a motor vehicle owned by the accused, the police seized a briefcase. In the briefcase, the police found bottles containing nitric and sulphuric acid, bicarbonate of soda, a measuring bottle and cup, rubber gloves, and a plastic spatula. The evidence established that the chemicals and implements were all necessary for making nitroglycerine, a powerful explosive used for safe-breaking. Glycerine, an essential ingredient for making the explosive, was not found in the possession of the accused. However, glycerine has several legitimate uses and is readily available at any drugstore. The court concluded:

> Having in mind that the only purpose that could be served by using all the objects found was to make nitroglycerine they are in my opinion substantial things having physical characteristics enabling them to be used to facilitate a breaking and constitute therefore an instrument for safe-breaking.[20]

b. Reasonable Inference

Once it is shown that a person possessed instruments that could be used for "breaking into any place, motor vehicle, vault or safe," it must then be demonstrated that a reasonable inference can be drawn from the circumstances that the instruments were used or were intended to be used to break into a place, motor vehicle, safe, or vault.

In *R. v. Kozak and Moore*,[21] the accused were found with screwdrivers, a pair of pliers, a metal expandable tool, a wrench, two pallet knives, and two pairs of gloves. The question was whether these "otherwise innocent instruments" were to be used for an intended break-in. The accused were observed using binoculars to study the rear door of an apartment building. One of the accused was found in possession of a card on which was written the licence plate number of the car owned by the occupant of the apartment. The court held that such circumstances were capable of giving rise to a reasonable inference that the instruments in possession of the accused were to be used to break into the apartment they were studying.

A case that reached the opposite conclusion is *R. v. Sullivan and Godbolt*.[22] The accused were found in possession of possible safe-breaking instruments: a set of pole-climbers, a three-pound hammer, two pieces of soap, steel punches, pieces of wire, a pair of pliers, and a quantity of rubber tape. The court believed the evidence of the accused that all of these items could be, and were intended to be, used for a legitimate contracting business.

The Supreme Court of Canada has considered whether this offence contains a reverse onus clause in the phrase "every one who without lawful excuse, the proof of which lies on him." In *R. v. Holmes*,[23] the accused was charged with possession of break-in instruments when he was found with a pair of Vise-Grips and a pair of pliers. Before entering a plea to the charge, the accused applied to have the indictment quashed on the grounds that the section offended the Charter. The Supreme Court agreed with the decision of the Ontario Court of Appeal, which held that this offence does not contain a reverse onus provision. The Crown

19 (1963), 3 C.C.C. 286 (Ont. C.A.).
20 Ibid. at 288.
21 (1975), 20 C.C.C. (2d) 175 (Ont. C.A.).
22 (1946), 85 C.C.C. 349 (B.C.C.A.).
23 (1985), 41 C.C.C. (3d) 497 (S.C.C.).

must prove all three elements of the offence beyond a reasonable doubt: (1) that the accused had possession (2) of break-in instruments (3) under circumstances that gave rise to a reasonable inference that the instruments had been or were intended to be used for the purpose of a break-in. Once these three elements are proved, the onus shifts to the accused to raise a defence; that is, to present evidence that raises a reasonable doubt. The words of the questioned phrase are superfluous; the accused has the same defences available that would be available even if those words were not contained in the offence. The Supreme Court dismissed the accused's appeal and sent the case back for trial.

3. Possession of Property Obtained by Crime

a. Elements of the Offence

Section 354 provides that it is an offence for a person knowingly to have in his or her possession any "thing" (either in whole or in part) that was obtained, directly or indirectly, by the commission of an indictable offence. It is also an offence under s. 354 for a person to have in his or her possession the proceeds of a transaction involving a thing obtained by a crime. Section 354 is often used for possession of stolen property.

Section 354(1) states:

354. (1) Every one commits an offence who has in his possession any property or thing or any proceeds of any property or thing knowing that all or part of the property or thing or of the proceeds was obtained by or derived directly or indirectly from

> **(a) the commission in Canada of an offence punishable by indictment; or**

> **(b) an act or omission anywhere that, if it had occurred in Canada, would have constituted an offence punishable by indictment.**

Paragraph (b) applies to situations where the thing is obtained by a criminal act outside Canada. As long as the act is one that would be an indictable offence if performed in Canada, it will be an offence to have possession of the property or thing.

The elements of an offence under s. 354 are that the accused (1) has a thing in his or her possession and (2) knows that the thing was obtained by the commission of an indictable offence in Canada or by an act committed outside of Canada that would have been an indictable crime within Canada.

b. Possession

The definition of possession in s. 4(3) was discussed above. Section 358 further provides that for the purposes of s. 354 (and s. 342 regarding theft, and s. 356(1)(b) regarding theft from mail), the offence of "having in possession" is complete when a person has, alone or together with someone else, possession or control over the "thing," or when that person aids in concealing or disposing of it. So, for example, a person who helps someone sell stolen property is considered to have possession.

In *R. v. Kinna*,[24] one of the issues considered was whether the accused had possession of a stolen typewriter. According to the evidence, the accused and W. were in the accused's room in downtown Vancouver. After some time, W. went across to his own room and brought back a typewriter. W. then said it would have to be sold, as they needed money. He spoke of the typewriter in terms indicating that it had been stolen. W. entered a store to sell

---

24   (1951), 98 C.C.C. 378 (B.C.C.A.). See also *R. v. Bertucci* (2002), 169 C.C.C. (3d) 453 at 459 (Ont. C.A.).

the typewriter while the accused remained outside. A police officer saw the accused there and questioned him. The accused told the officer a false story. W. was arrested in the store. The accused was not arrested until the next day.

The court held that the accused did not have possession of the typewriter. Mere knowledge that a thing is stolen is insufficient, and a person cannot be said to consent to possession by another (and thereby be in possession) unless that person has some control over the thing. The court concluded that the accused did not have a measure of control over the typewriter.

Some cases have held that physical possession, knowledge, and control may not always be sufficient for criminal liability. For example, in *R. v. York*,[25] the Court of Appeal of British Columbia held that possession is an offence requiring a dishonest intent and requires proof of blameworthy conduct. The accused and a business partner rented a warehouse to use in a business they were starting. The partner called the accused one morning and said that there was furniture and lumber at the warehouse and asked the accused if he knew where the goods had come from. The accused said "no" and met the partner at the warehouse, where they found a trailer containing furniture as well as furniture in the warehouse. After speaking to the manager of the warehouse, the accused formed the belief that the contents were probably stolen. He testified that at that point he "panicked." He did not want to be caught with the goods. He shut and locked the door of the warehouse and then moved the trailer to another location. He testified that although he didn't know what to do with the property he did want to return it to the owners. He thought of calling the police, but was afraid they wouldn't believe him. He was arrested while moving the trailer. He was acquitted at his trial of theft, but convicted of possession. The trial judge found that he had knowledge, possession, and control. The court of appeal dismissed his conviction. Although he had knowledge and control, he did not have a dishonest intent to deal with the stolen goods, which is an element of possession. The court stated:

> I think the law can be summarized as follows. Personal possession is established where an accused person exercises physical control over a prohibited object with full knowledge of its character, however brief the physical contact may be, and where there is some evidence to show the accused person took custody of the object willingly with intent to deal with it in some prohibited manner.[26]

c. Knowledge

Section 354 requires proof that an accused has knowledge the property was obtained from the commission of an indictable offence. The court in *R. v. Vinokurov*[27] stated that where a statute requires actual knowledge, wilful blindness is enough because it is the equivalent of knowledge. However, recklessness is not sufficient: "wilful blindness is imputed knowledge while recklessness is something less than that."[28]

An example of a case of "turning a blind eye" is *R. v. Marabella*.[29] The accused, a scrap and salvage dealer, was charged with having possession of stolen copper. The police seized, in a salvage yard, over a ton of new copper that had been stolen a few nights earlier from a manufacturing company. The accused had delivered the copper to the salvage yard owner after purchasing it from B. The main issue was whether the accused should have known that the copper was stolen, considering the circumstances in which B. had sold it to him.

25 (2005), 193 C.C.C. (3d) 331 (B.C.C.A.).
26 Ibid. at 7.
27 (2001), 156 C.C.C. (3d) 300 (Alta. C.A.).
28 Ibid. at 305.
29 (1957), 177 C.C.C. 78 (Ont. C.A.).

The court considered these facts: B. was not connected with a business that sold copper. The copper was purchased at a private residence, where copper is not normally found. The accused did not usually deal in new copper, yet this copper was not scrap material. From its size, shape, and appearance, the accused must have known that it was new and unused. There was also the matter of the price paid. The price paid by the accused, according to his own statement, was 25 cents per pound (55 cents per kilogram). This was little more than one-half of the amount normally paid for scrap copper. Even in view of all of the unusual and suspicious circumstances described above, the accused never questioned B. as to the source of the copper.

The court concluded that, in such circumstances, the accused was guilty of having possession of stolen property. To avoid obtaining knowledge that would have been dangerous to him—namely, that the copper was stolen—he had deliberately refrained from asking for further information. A person who consciously omits to ask questions because he or she wishes to remain in ignorance is deemed to have "guilty knowledge."

d. Possession of a Stolen Motor Vehicle

Section 354(2) deals with situations where a motor vehicle is the thing in possession. If a person has in his or her possession a motor vehicle with an identification number that has been tampered with, the vehicle is presumed to have been stolen, or obtained by another crime.

> **354. (2) In proceedings in respect of an offence under subsection (1), evidence that a person has in his possession a motor vehicle the vehicle identification number of which has been wholly or partially removed or obliterated or a part of a motor vehicle being a part bearing a vehicle identification number that has been wholly or partially removed or obliterated is, in the absence of any evidence to the contrary, proof that the motor vehicle or part, as the case may be, was obtained, and that such person had the motor vehicle or part, as the case may be, in his possession knowing that it was obtained,**
>
> > **(a) by the commission in Canada of an offence punishable by indictment; or**
> >
> > **(b) by an act or omission anywhere that, if it had occurred in Canada, would have constituted an offence punishable by indictment.**
>
> **(3) For the purposes of subsection (2), "vehicle identification number" means any number or other mark placed on a motor vehicle for the purpose of distinguishing the motor vehicle from other similar motor vehicles.**

Section 354(2) contains two presumptions: (1) that a vehicle that has had its identification number removed partially or wholly has been obtained through the commission of an indictable offence, and (2) that the person who has possession of the vehicle has knowledge that the vehicle was obtained through the commission of an indictable offence. To rebut these presumptions, the accused need only raise a reasonable doubt. However, if the accused does not do so, the jury (or judge, if no jury) must conclude that the presumed facts are true. Both of these presumptions have been challenged as violations of the Charter presumption of innocence. In *Re Boyle and the Queen*,[30] the Ontario Court of Appeal considered the constitutionality of these presumptions. The court held that the first presumption is constitutionally valid; the fact that the vehicle identification number has been obliterated is cogent evidence that at some time the vehicle was stolen or otherwise obtained through the commission of a crime. The court held, however, that the

---

30 (1983), 5 C.C.C. (3d) 193 (Ont. C.A.).

second presumption is invalid. Guilty knowledge is an element of the offence. It is not reasonable to expect that people other than car dealers would even be aware of the location of vehicle identification numbers. The presumption is not limited to recently stolen vehicles. So, upon proof that a person has possession of a vehicle that has its identification number obliterated, that person may be found guilty of possession, even though there is no evidence that the person knew the vehicle was stolen. This is not a reasonable limitation on the presumption of innocence; rather, it is arbitrary. However, the offence can still operate with this presumption severed. In other words, the Crown has the burden of proving guilty knowledge like any other element of the offence.

C. LAUNDERING PROCEEDS OF CRIME

Laundering the proceeds of crime, often referred to as "money laundering," appears to be an increasing problem in Canada and internationally. It is estimated that the amount of money laundered in Canada per year is between $5 and $15 billion.[31] Laundering is often associated with the illegal drug trade; for example, a person sells illegal drugs and uses the money to buy legal goods to sell through a legitimate business.

Under s. 462.31, a person commits an offence who "uses, transfers the possession of, sends or delivers to any person or place, transports, transmits, alters, (or) disposes of . . . any property or any proceeds of property . . ."[32] with intent to conceal or convert it, knowing that all or part of the property was obtained as a result of the commission of a designated offence. "Designated offence" is defined in s. 462.3 of the Code, and includes indictable offences under any Act of Parliament. It also includes acts or omissions that occur outside of Canada that would be indictable if committed in Canada.

In *R. v. Daoust*,[33] the Supreme Court of Canada held that "transfer of possession" applies to the person who has control of the property, and not the person who is receiving it or buying it. In this case, police had set up a sting operation where they were selling apparently stolen goods to a second-hand shop. The accused shop owner and the manager were charged with laundering the proceeds of crime. The accused's convictions were overturned on appeal. The Supreme Court dismissed the Crown's appeal stating that the *actus reus* of the offence had not been made out. The activities criminalized by s. 462.31 all concern the same person—the person who originally has the object in his or her possession and seeks to dispose of it.

In *R. v. Battista*,[34] Peloso and Battista were charged with conspiracy to launder the proceeds of crime. Peloso was also charged with laundering the proceeds of crime. Peloso worked as a teacher and also operated a construction company. Over a 13-month period, Peloso deposited $975,323 from Battista into four separate bank accounts. During this period, Peloso had an income of $50,364. Peloso then transferred the funds back to Battista as certified cheques or he made payments toward the purchase of properties registered in the names of members of Battista's family. Peloso claimed that he did not know that the funds were the proceeds of crime and that he borrowed the money from Battista to repay gambling debts. The court found that Peloso's testimony was not credible. The court found that Peloso was wilfully blind to the fact that the money was obtained from crime. He suspected the funds were proceeds of crime but did not inquire because he did not want to know the truth. Peloso and Battista were convicted.

---

31 "Money Laundering in Canada," *Juristat*, Canadian Centre for Justice Statistics, 2011.
32 The Supreme Court in *R. v. Daoust* (2004), 180 C.C.C. (3d) 449 (S.C.C.), held that the words in the English version "or otherwise deals with" are of no effect because they do not appear in the French translation of the Criminal Code. Therefore the only way to commit this offence is by doing one of the specifically listed acts.
33 (2004), 180 C.C.C. (3d) 449 (S.C.C.).
34 [2010] O.J. No. 4217 (Ont. C.J.).

L03 D. MISCHIEF

430. (1) Every one commits mischief who wilfully

    (a) destroys or damages property;

    (b) renders property dangerous, useless, inoperative or ineffective;

    (c) obstructs, interrupts or interferes with the lawful use, enjoyment or operation of property; or

    (d) obstructs, interrupts or interferes with any person in the lawful use, enjoyment or operation of property.

(1.1) Every one commits mischief who wilfully

    (a) destroys or alters data;

    (b) renders data meaningless, useless or ineffective;

    (c) obstructs, interrupts or interferes with the lawful use of data; or

    (d) obstructs, interrupts or interferes with any person in the lawful use of data or denies access to data to any person who is entitled to access thereto.

The term "property" refers to both real property and personal property. In brief, real property consists of immovable things—land and things attached to the land (e.g., a house or garage). Personal property consists of movable things, such as automobiles and furniture. "Data" is defined in s. 342.1 as

> **representations of information or of concepts that are being prepared or have been prepared in a form suitable for use in a computer system.**

There are many ways of committing the offence of mischief. For example, mischief in regard to a car (which is personal property) includes damaging the car by breaking its radio antenna, or rendering the car dangerous by tampering with its brake system, or obstructing the use of the car by blocking a public highway.

Mischief in regard to a building (which is real property) includes damaging the building by breaking its windows, or rendering the building dangerous by weakening a step in a stairway, or obstructing the use of the building by barricading the entrance so that no one can get in. Placing graffiti on a building can also be the basis of a mischief charge.

An example of mischief in relation to data under s. 430(1.1) is altering a computer disk so that the data stored on it cannot be accessed by the owners. Similarly, computer hackers can be charged with mischief if the hacking results in destroying or altering data on the computer.

Mischief charges often are laid in situations in which large crowds have formed and are out of control. For example, after the final game of the 2011 Stanley Cup playoffs in Vancouver, numerous mischief charges were laid against rioters apparently upset about the outcome of the game. Many of the charges were in relation to the breaking of store windows and the burning of a car.

At the 2010 international summit of the leaders of G20 countries in Toronto, over 1100 people were held by police in the largest mass arrest in Canadian history. Although the protests related to the G20 summit were mainly peaceful and most of those arrested were released without charge, 317 people were charged. Many of the charges were mischief charges. A specific incident involved a well-known anti-globalization organizer who was convicted of counselling mischief for encouraging people to tear down the security fence during the summit.

Reported G20 cases of mischief involve the accused persons pleading guilty to causing various kinds of property damage during the protests. In *R. v. Henry*,[35] the accused, who was part of the "Black Bloc" group, smashed large windows of a Starbucks coffee shop and a Bell Mobility store, resulting in significant repair costs and loss of business and wages paid to staff for missed shifts. In *R. v. Cote*,[36] the accused admitted wilfully damaging two police cars, one with a wooden stick, the other by kicking in the window. In *R. v. Muzin*,[37] the accused threw two pieces of granite through one or more large windows of the Toronto Police Headquarters. In *R. v. Coon*,[38] the accused threw a table through the window of a store and a wooden sign through the glass door of another store, resulting in various costs to the stores, totalling more than $33,000.

A trivial interference with property will not be considered mischief. In *R. v. Chapman*,[39] the accused was charged with wilfully interfering with the lawful use of property. The accused, who was 18 years old, and two younger companions were walking along a street late at night when they saw a small car parked in the street. As a prank, they pushed the car between 3 and 10 metres down the street and left the scene. They did not try to start the car, which was not damaged in any way. The only inconvenience to the owner of the car was that he had to walk a short extra distance the next morning. The court found the accused not guilty. There was no significant interference with the use of the car, nor was there an intention to interfere with the lawful use of the car. Similarly, in *R. v. Quickfall*,[40] the accused was charged under s. 430(1)(a) for damaging property by placing a poster on a lamppost. The court of appeal found that his actions did not impair the use or value of the property; therefore, the offence was not committed.

1. Lawful Use and Enjoyment of Property

Court decisions have not been consistent on the meaning of interfering with the lawful use and enjoyment of property as used in s. 430(1)(c) and (d). In *R. v. Drapeau*,[41] the accused was charged with mischief under s. 430(1)(d). The complainants were his neighbours, with whom he had been embroiled in a series of disagreements, misunderstandings, provocations, and reprisals. The evidence at the trial was that over a period of four summers, the accused had stared at his neighbours and made objectionable noises when they were in their backyard. The court held that the actions of the accused, while they may have been bizarre and objectionable, did not constitute an interference with the complainants' enjoyment of their property. One of the judges stated that enjoyment of property refers to the act of, or entitlement to, possession of the property. The actions of the accused did not interfere with the enjoyment of property in this sense. One dissenting judge stated that enjoyment of property should not be given such a restricted meaning but should include the satisfaction a person derives from his or her property.

The court of appeal, in *R. v. Nicol*,[42] agreed with the dissenting judge in *Drapeau*. In this case, the accused shouted obscenities at her neighbours when they were in their backyard. There were numerous complaints about her abusive behaviour that resulted in two charges of mischief under s. 430(1)(d). Her conviction was upheld on appeal.[43]

35   (2011), 278 C.C.C. (3d) 344 (Ont. C.J.).
36   (2011) ONCJ 778 (Ont. C.J.).
37   2012 ONCJ 83 (Ont. C.J.).
38   2012 ONCJ 72 (Ont.C.J.).
39   [1969] 3 C.C.C. 358 (B.C. Co. Ct.).
40   (1993), 78 C.C.C. (3d) 563 (Que. C.A.).
41   (1995), 96 C.C.C. (3d) 554 (Que. C.A.).
42   (2002), 170 C.C.C. (3d) 59 (Man. C.A.).
43   See also *R. v. Maddeaux* (1997), 115 C.C.C. (3d) 122 (Ont. C.A.); leave to appeal to S.C.C. refused 118 C.C.C. (3d) vi. The court applied broader meaning to "enjoyment of property." The accused was convicted of mischief for interfering with a neighbouring tenant's enjoyment of property by making loud noises.

In *R. v. W.(T.)*,[44] a teenager, W, held a very noisy party while his parents were away. The party went into the early morning hours of the next day. Noise was caused by a band in attendance at that party and the noise of party-goers who were also apparently consuming alcohol. A neighbour, who was trying to sleep, made unsuccessful attempts to persuade W to keep the noise down, as did the RCMP. W was charged with mischief under s. 430 (1)(c). The trial judge acquitted W on the basis that "enjoyment" of property under s. 430(1)(c) did not include a right to sleep uninterrupted by excessive noisy parties from adjacent properties. On appeal, the B.C. Supreme Court set aside the acquittal and entered a conviction. The court concluded that Parliament intended to make it an offence to wilfully disturb a person's pleasurable enjoyment of property, including by excessive noise that prevents the enjoyment of sleep.

2. "Wilfully"

The important issue in many mischief cases is whether the damaging, rendering dangerous, or obstructing was done wilfully. "Wilfully" usually means intentionally. As one judge has put it, "Wilfully means not merely to commit an act voluntarily but to commit it purposely with an evil intention, or in other words it means to do so deliberately, intentionally, and corruptly and without any justifiable excuse."[45]

So if a student breaks a window in his school building, it must be shown that the student broke the window deliberately and with a criminal (i.e., evil) intent. The student would not be guilty of mischief if the window was broken accidentally, or with a justifiable excuse such as to escape from a fire.

Section 429(1) extends the meaning of "wilfully," when it is mentioned in Part XI of the Code, to include recklessness:

> **429. (1) Every one who causes the occurrence of an event by doing an act or by omitting to do an act that is his duty to do, knowing that the act or omission will probably cause the occurrence of the event and being reckless whether the event occurs or not, shall be deemed, for the purposes of this Part, wilfully to have caused the occurrence of the event.**

In other words, a person may not intend to damage property, but if that person does some act and knows that the damage will probably occur and takes an unjustifiable risk that the damage will not occur, then that person will be considered to have wilfully or intentionally caused the damage if it occurs.

In *R. v. Wendel*,[46] the accused was charged with breaking and entering with the intent to commit mischief. Early in the evening, the accused with other youths had obtained some beer, which they drank while sitting under a bridge. They then went to an apartment building and found a vacant apartment with a slightly open door. They went in and drank more beer. Later, the caretaker of the building came to the apartment and could not get in because the door had been locked from the inside. There was no question that the youths had broken and entered the apartment. The only question was whether they had intended to wilfully obstruct or interfere with the lawful use of the apartment. The court held that even under the extended meaning of "wilfully" in s. 429(1), the accused was not guilty. He and the others entered the apartment for the purpose of drinking beer, not for the purpose of obstructing or interfering with the use of the property.

44 (1993), 21 W.C.B. (2d) 194 (B.C.S.C.).
45 *R. v. Duggan* (1906), 12 C.C.C. 147 (Man. C.A.).
46 [1967] 2 C.C.C. 23 (B.C.C.A.).

The extended meaning of "wilfully" (i.e., to include recklessness) was applied in *R. v. Gotto*.[47] The accused and a group of others were driving down a highway when they came upon an unattended car. They decided to vandalize it. The accused set fire to a road map that he found in the car, in order to have light so that he could see under the front seat. He left the map near the car when he and the others left. The car caught fire and was destroyed. The accused argued that he was not guilty because he had not wilfully set fire to the car. However, the court disagreed and held that his conduct fell within the meaning of "wilfully" as defined under s. 429(1). He knew that damage to the car would probably result if he did not take precautions to remove the burning map. He made no attempt to remove it and was reckless about whether or not the damage would occur.

3. Labour Disputes

Mischief charges may result during a labour dispute such as a strike. An example of such a case is *R. v. Mammolita*,[48] a decision of the Ontario Court of Appeal. There was a legal strike of employees at a factory in Thunder Bay. Several months after the employer had obtained an injunction limiting pickets to 10 people, 75 to 100 people formed a picket line and stopped the management and office personnel from entering the building. The police were called and were able to form a wedge to allow the management to pass through. Police photographs were taken of the strikers, and eventually 33 people were charged with mischief for wilfully obstructing or interfering with the lawful use and operation of the property of the company. The accused were acquitted at their trial on the grounds that their mere presence and passive acquiescence at the time did not make them liable for the offence. The court of appeal disagreed and ordered a new trial, stating that

> a person may be guilty as a principal of committing mischief . . . if he forms part of a group which constitutes a human barricade or other obstruction. The fact that he stands shoulder to shoulder with other persons even though he neither says anything nor does anything further may be an act which constitutes an obstruction . . . However, criminal liability only results if the act is done wilfully . . . It may not be very difficult to infer that a person standing shoulder to shoulder with other persons in a group so as to block a roadway knows that his act will probably cause the obstruction and is reckless if he does not attempt to extricate himself from the group.[49]

The right to strike and picket is protected under s. 430(6) and (7):

430. (6) No person commits mischief within the meaning of this section by reason only that

> (a) **he stops work as a result of the failure of his employer and himself to agree on any matter relating to his employment;**

> (b) **he stops work as a result of the failure of his employer and a bargaining agent acting on his behalf to agree on any matter relating to his employment; or**

> (c) **he stops work as a result of his taking part in a combination of workmen or employees for their own reasonable protection as workmen or employees.**

47 [1974] 3 W.W.R. 454 (Sask. Dist. Ct.).
48 (1983), 9 C.C.C. (3d) 85 (Ont. C.A.).
49 Ibid. at 89.

(7) No person commits mischief within the meaning of this section by reason only that he attends at or near or approaches a dwelling-house or place for the purpose only of obtaining or communicating information.

Thus, in *R. v. Dooling*,[50] where the accused were participating in a lawful strike and picketing their employer, the accused were acquitted of mischief. The court held that for there to be an offence under this section, there must be some physical act that has the effect of obstructing, interrupting, or interfering with the use of the property. The fact that people were persuaded not to do business with the employer was an inevitable consequence of the labour dispute.

L04 E. ARSON

Arson is the intentional or reckless causing of damage by fire or explosion to property. The definitions of "property" and "wilfully" (s. 429(1)), discussed above in relation to mischief, also apply to arson. Most arson offences involve the burning of property. In *R. v. Jorgenson*,[51] the meaning of "burning" was explained:

> There must be actual combustion, although it is not necessary for the material to blaze openly, so long as it comes to a red heat. Charring, that is, the carbonization of the material by combustion, is evidence of burning, but blackening of the material not accompanied by any degree of consumption is not[,] nor is mere scorching . . . So long as there is burning in that sense, the extent and duration of the fire is immaterial, and the damage may be insignificant.[52]

In *Jorgenson*, the accused was charged with setting fire to a building. The only evidence of burning on the building consisted of three blister marks on a small area of paint on a metal door. The court held that the blistering did not amount to burning because there had been no consumption of material.

There are several offences involving arson. The most serious arson offence is arson causing danger to human life (s. 433). Where there is no danger to human life, a person who sets fire can be charged with arson causing damage to property. If the damage is to the property of others, the person can be charged under s. 434. If the damage is to the person's own property and the fire seriously threatens the health, safety, or property of another person, the person who set the fire may be charged under s. 434.1.

In *R. v. D.(S.D.)*,[53] the accused was charged with two counts of arson under s. 433 and s. 434. She and a friend decided to steal a bag of potato chips from a convenience store. She went to the rack of chips in the store and, with a lighter, burned a hole in the corner of one of the bags. Her plan was to let the air escape so the bag could be collapsed and hidden under her coat. She left the rack for a few moments when she thought the clerk was looking at her suspiciously. When she returned the bag was on fire and melting on to the other bags on the rack. She tore it off the rack and stamped out the fire. Believing that the fire was out, she and her friend left the store. A fire resulted causing $110,000 worth of damage. The court of appeal held that the trial court properly found her not guilty of arson. There was no evidence of a specific intent to burn the store, and no proof that she knew that burning the chip bag would have a probable consequence of burning the building. In other words, there was no proof of intention or recklessness required for the offence of arson. Instead the court substituted a conviction for the lesser included offence of mischief.

---

50 (1994), 94 C.C.C. (3d) 525 (Nfld. S.C.).
51 (1954), 111 C.C.C. 30 (B.C.C.A.).
52 Ibid. at 43.
53 (2002), 164 C.C.C. (3d) 1 (Nfld. & Lab. C.A.).

The offence of fraudulently burning property is contained in s. 435:

435. (1) Every person who, with intent to defraud any other person, causes damage by fire or explosion to property, whether or not that person owns, in whole or in part, the property, is guilty of an indictable offence . . .

(2) Where a person is charged with an offence under subsection (1), the fact that the person was the holder of or was named as beneficiary under a policy of fire insurance relating to the property in respect of which the offence is alleged to have been committed is a fact from which intent to defraud may be inferred by the court.

This offence applies to situations where, for example, a person burns down a building he or she owns to collect the insurance money. In *R. v. R.N.D.*,[54] a young offender was charged with attempting to defraud the provincial insurance company and with fraudulently burning property. The evidence was that he had been approached by the owner of a car worth approximately $11,000 and asked to get rid of it in exchange for a case of beer and $20. He drove the car to a field and set fire to it. Later, the owner filed an insurance claim that the car had been stolen. The accused was convicted of both offences. His appeal of the conviction for defrauding the insurance company was allowed, since he was unaware that the car was insured against damage by fire. The court dismissed his appeal of the conviction for arson, however. The offence required that the accused wilfully and for a fraudulent purpose set fire to the vehicle. The test for fraudulent purpose is the community's standards for dishonesty. The court held that it was open to the trial judge to infer that the accused knew that the car had a substantial market value and that it was being destroyed for a fraudulent purpose.

The offence of arson by criminal negligence is contained in s. 436:

436. (1) Every person who owns, in whole or in part, or controls property is guilty of an indictable offence . . . where, as a result of a marked departure from the standard of care that a reasonably prudent person would use to prevent or control the spread of fires or to prevent explosions, that person is a cause of fire or explosion in that property that causes bodily harm to another person or damage to property.

(2) Where a person is charged with an offence under subsection (1), the fact that the person has failed to comply with any law respecting the prevention or control of fires or explosions in the property is a fact from which a marked departure from the standard of care referred to in that subsection may be inferred by the court.

In *R. v. Harricharan*,[55] the accused woke up one morning in his home, which was located in a rural area, to a loud bang. He discovered that the garage attached to his house was on fire. He ran to find the card with the emergency number written on it. He couldn't find it. Then he ran upstairs, packed a suitcase of clothes, threw them through the window, and jumped out. Then he got a ladder to climb back into the house to get more items out of the house. This time he collected more personal papers and clothing. When the smoke entered the bedroom, he climbed out. By this time, he was so exhausted that he went to the barn and collapsed. A neighbour driving to work saw the fire and called the fire department. By the time the fire department arrived, only the brick walls were left of the house. Harricharan was

54   (1994), 89 C.C.C. (3d) 449 (B.C.C.A.).
55   (1995), 98 C.C.C. (3d) 145 (Ont. C.A.).

charged with arson by negligence. It was argued that, in trying to save his personal belongings instead of going for help, he had behaved in a way that was a marked departure from the standard of care of a reasonable person. He was convicted at trial, and appealed. The appeal court allowed his appeal and entered an acquittal on the grounds that there was no causal connection proved between the accused's failure to get help and the spread of the fire.

F. LEGAL JUSTIFICATION AND COLOUR OF RIGHT

Section 429(2) provides a defence to any charge of mischief, arson, and cruelty to animals.

(2) No person shall be convicted of an offence under sections 430 to 446 where he proves that he acted with legal justification or excuse and with colour of right.

A person acts with legal justification or excuse when his or her actions are permitted by law. This legal permission for acts that would otherwise be unlawful can be based on either common law or statutory law. There are, for example, provincial statutes that allow the killing of a dog that is found injuring or killing cattle.

Recall that in general, "colour of right" means an honest belief in facts that, if they actually existed, would provide a legal justification or excuse for the actions of the accused.[56] The belief can be based on a mistake of fact or a mistake of law. If the accused acted with colour of right, the accused is not guilty because he or she was acting without the *mens rea* required to commit the offence. However, simply having an honest belief is not enough to raise a defence under s. 429(2); there must be reasonable grounds for the belief.[57] The accused must prove beyond a reasonable doubt that he or she had the honest belief; however, it is not necessary to prove that the right actually existed.[58]

In the following three cases, colour of right was a defence to a charge of wilfully damaging property.

In *R. v. Pimmett*,[59] the accused was charged with wilfully damaging a telephone pole that was located on his land. Many years earlier, a telephone line to a summer hotel had been erected across his property. The telephone company had never acquired a right to use the land for this purpose. Without deciding whether the accused actually had the right to remove the pole, the court held that the accused was not guilty because he reasonably believed that he had the right to remove the pole, which he considered to be a nuisance.

In *R. v. Adamson*,[60] the accused was charged with wilfully damaging another's land by crossing the land with a load of hay. The accused believed that she had a right to cross the land because the municipality had passed a resolution authorizing her to do so. While the municipality had the authority to open temporary roads across private property, a resolution of the municipal council did not have the effect of opening the road. In short, the resolution was merely a preliminary step before the municipality's decision became law. The court held that the accused had a colour of right for crossing the land because the municipality had the right to open temporary roads and the accused had an honest belief, based on reasonable grounds, that the resolution had that effect.

In *R. v. Johnson*,[61] the accused was charged with wilfully damaging the fence of Mott. There was some confusion as to whether the accused had a right-of-way over Mott's land.

---

56   See defence of "mistake of fact" and "mistake of law" in Chapter 4.
57   *R. v. Ninos and Walker*, [1964] 1 C.C.C. 326 (N.S.C.A.).
58   *R. v. Lilly* (1983), 5 C.C.C. (3d) 1 (S.C.C.). See also *R. v. Dorosh* (2004), 183 C.C.C. (3d) 224 (Sask. C. A.) at 231.
59   (1931), 56 C.C.C. 363 (Ont. C.A.).
60   (1916), 25 C.C.C. 440 (Sask. C.A.).
61   (1904), 8 C.C.C. 123 (Ont. C.A.).

The court held that the accused had reasonable grounds for honestly believing that he did have a right-of-way. Therefore, he had a colour of right for taking down part of a fence that was blocking his use of the right-of-way. In other words, the accused may not have had a legal right or justification for damaging part of the fence. However, he had an honest belief, based on reasonable grounds, that he had such a right. Therefore, he was not guilty of the offence of wilfully damaging Mott's fence.

Notice that s. 429(2) says that the accused must prove "that he acted with legal justification or excuse and with colour of right." This appears to state that both legal justification or excuse and colour of right must be proved in order for the accused to have a defence. However, the courts have interpreted "and" to mean "or." Thus, the accused may prove either legal justification or colour of right as a defence to a charge of mischief, arson, or cruelty to animals.

In general, a person who owns something may legally damage or destroy it. However, s. 429(3) clarifies this right:

(3) Where it is an offence to destroy or to damage anything,

> **(a) the fact that a person has a partial interest in what is destroyed or damaged does not prevent him from being guilty of the offence if he caused the destruction or damage; and**

> **(b) the fact that a person has a total interest in what is destroyed or damaged does not prevent him from being guilty of the offence if he caused the destruction or damage with intent to defraud.**

In *R. v. Surette*,[62] the accused damaged a car that was registered in his wife's name. He was charged with mischief for damaging her property. His defence was colour of right. He had purchased the car from lottery winnings but had put it in her name because he had some outstanding bills. He never intended the car to be a gift to her. The accused and his wife were separated at the time. She testified that her husband had paid for the car and maintained it. The appeal court upheld his acquittal. The fact that a car is registered in a person's name does not mean that person is the owner. Here, the accused had reasonable grounds for believing that he had total interest in the vehicle. A person can damage his or her own property as long as there is no intent to defraud.

---

62 (1993), 82 C.C.C. (3d) 36 (N.S.C.A.).

Questions for Review and Discussion

1. Define for the purposes of "breaking and entering" the following words: (a) "break," (b) "enter," and (c) "place."

2. How have courts dealt with the presumption of intent under s. 348(2)?

3. What is the difference between the offence of "breaking and entering" and being unlawfully in a dwelling-house?

4. How does the criminal law define the term "possession"?

5. What are break-in instruments?

6. What are the elements of the offence of possession of property obtained by crime?

7. Does a person have to know for certain that an object is stolen before being convicted of possession of stolen property? Explain.

8. Make up an example of a situation that would lead to a charge of laundering proceeds of crime.

9. The accused was charged with possession of drugs. She allowed her daughter to use her car, and had also lent her car to the daughter of a friend. When it was returned, she found a bag in the trunk containing marijuana. She testified that when she found the drugs, she slammed the trunk closed. Then in a panic, she drove around the city seeking her friends to ask for advice, as she feared her daughter's involvement. She was in an accident when the drugs were discovered. Should she be found guilty? Make a decision. See *R. v. Christie* (1978), 41 C.C.C. (2d) 282 (N.B.S.C.A.D.).

10. Make up several examples of conduct that would be covered by the offence of mischief.

11. What is the meaning of "property" in relation to mischief and arson?

12. What is the meaning of "wilfully" in relation to mischief and arson?

13. In an arson case, which of the following would be sufficient evidence of burning? (a) Blackening of the material, (b) scorching of the material, (c) charring of the material, (d) flames on the material, and/or (e) blistering of the material?

14. List the offences of arson. Which is the most serious? Why do you think this offence is the most serious?

15. Explain the difference between legal justification and colour of right.

16. Aran is in a music band. The group often practises in his basement late at night. His neighbour, Frank, can hear the music, and it prevents him from sleeping. Frank has called the police. Can Aran be charged with mischief? Explain. See *R. v. Phonix* (1991), 64 C.C.C. (3d) 252 (B.C. Prov. Ct.).

17. Al was the president of a union. He led a demonstration in the lobby of the building where the Ministry of Labour and a number of commercial offices were located. Al instructed the demonstrators that since the police would not let them go up to the ministry offices, no one should be allowed to go upstairs. The demonstrators then linked arms and blocked access to the elevators. Office workers testified that they were stopped from reaching the elevators. What offence has Al committed? Explain. See *R. v. Biggin* (1980), 55 C.C.C. (2d) 408 (Ont. C.A.).

18. T. was building a house on a lot overlooking the ocean. His neighbour, C., had a willow tree in his backyard, which had branches overhanging T.'s lot. T. told his neighbour that he planned to prune the overhanging branches, as he was legally entitled to do. While C. was away on vacation, T. hired an arbourist who cut down the willow tree and some cedars in C.'s yard. The arbourist stated that he was told that C. had agreed to having the trees removed. With what offence can T. be charged? What else do you need to know to make a case against T.? See *R. v. Toma* (2000), 147 C.C.C. (3d) 252 (B.C.C.A.).

APPENDICES

Controlled Drugs and Substances Act
(S.C. 1996, c. 19)

The Controlled Drugs and Substances Act (CDSA) creates a scheme for the regulation of dangerous drugs, their precursors (substances used to produce the drugs), and other substances. The CDSA replaced the Narcotic Control Act (NCA) and Parts III and IV of the Food and Drugs Act (FDA). Part III of the FDA concerned controlled substances, such as amphetamines, while Part IV concerned restricted drugs such LSD. The CDSA came into force in May 1997.

Although the CDSA is the main piece of legislation controlling illegal drugs, the Criminal Code does have one specific section aimed at illicit drug use. Under s. 462.2 of the Criminal Code, it is an offence to knowingly import or export, manufacture, promote, or sell instruments or literature for illicit drug use. These are summary conviction offences punishable for a first offence by a fine not exceeding $100,000 and/or a term of imprisonment not exceeding six months. For a subsequent offence, the penalty is a fine not to exceed $300,000 and/or imprisonment for a term not exceeding one year.

A controlled substance is defined as a substance contained in Schedules I–V of the CDSA. The CDSA has included the term "analogue," which is defined as a substance that, in relation to a controlled substance, has a substantially similar chemical structure.

The schedules in the CDSA list the following substances:

- Schedule I includes the most dangerous drugs and narcotics, such as amphetamines, cocaine, and heroin;
- Schedule II includes cannabis, its preparations, derivatives, and similar synthetic preparations;
- Schedule III lists drugs and narcotics such as LSD and mescaline;
- Schedule IV includes drugs such as barbiturates and their derivatives;
- Schedule V contains substances that were not previously included in the FDA; and
- Schedule VI lists precursors.

A. THE OFFENCES

The CDSA sets out the following offences with respect to controlled substances:

- possession,
- double doctoring,

- trafficking,
- possession for the purpose of trafficking,
- importing and exporting, and
- production of a substance.

1. Possession

Section 4(1) sets out the offence of possession:

> **4. (1) Except as authorized under the regulations, no person shall possess a substance included in Schedule I, II, or III.**

Under s. 2 of the CDSA, "possession" means possession as defined in s. 4(3) of the Criminal Code. Court decisions on the meaning of possession were discussed in Chapter 13. Recall that there are two types of possession: actual and constructive. Both forms of possession require knowledge of what the thing is and some right of control over it. Constructive possession means that the person does not have actual possession of the thing but still exercises control over it. Where joint possession is an issue, knowledge and consent, which is a form of control, must exist.[1]

Under s. 4 of the CDSA, except for certain cannabis offences, possession is a hybrid offence. If it is treated as a summary conviction offence, the maximum punishment is a fine of $1000 and/or imprisonment for a term of six months. If the offence is treated as indictable, the penalty ranges from 3 to 7 years' imprisonment, depending on the schedule in which the substance is listed.

For Schedule II cannabis offences, possession of smaller amounts is treated as a summary conviction offence. These amounts (1 g for cannabis resin and 30 g for cannabis) are set out in Schedule VIII. The maximum punishment for this possession offence is a $1000 fine and/or 6 months' imprisonment.

2. Double Doctoring

Where a person is seeking to obtain from a practitioner a controlled substance or a prescription for a controlled substance listed in Schedules I–IV, it is a hybrid offence under s. 4(2) for the person to fail to disclose to the practitioner the particulars relating to the acquisition of any prescription or controlled substance obtained in the previous 30 days. "Practitioner" is defined in s. 2 of the Act as "a person who is registered and entitled under the laws of a province to practise in that province the profession of medicine, dentistry or veterinary medicine and includes any other person or class of persons prescribed (by the regulations) as a practitioner."

If the offence is treated as a summary conviction offence, it is punishable on a first offence by a fine not exceeding $1000 and/or 6 months' imprisonment. If the offence is treated as indictable, the maximum punishment ranges from 18 months to 7 years' imprisonment, depending on the schedule in which the substance is listed.

---

1   For a discussion of constructive and joint possession, see *R. v. Pham* (2005), 203 C.C.C. (3d) 326 (Ont. C.A.); affd [2006] 1 S.C.R. 940.

3. Trafficking and Having Possession for the Purpose of Trafficking

Section 5 of the CDSA makes it an offence to traffic in any substance included in Schedules I–IV or any substance represented to be such a substance. It also makes it an offence to be in possession of such substances for the purpose of trafficking.

"Traffic" is defined in s. 2 of the Act:

"traffic" means, in respect of a substance included in any of Schedules I to IV,

    (a) to sell, administer, give, transfer, transport, send or deliver the substance,

    (b) to sell an authorization to obtain the substance, or

    (c) to offer to do anything mentioned in paragraph (a) or (b),

otherwise than under the authority of the regulations.

Notice that there are many ways to traffic in a controlled substance including giving a drug to a person. However, conveying, or carrying, or moving a narcotic from one place to another for one's own use does not constitute trafficking.

The accused does not have to actually handle the drugs to commit the offence of trafficking. He or she need only exercise control over them. For example, in *R. v. MacFadden*,[2] the accused phoned a delivery service and asked that a parcel be delivered to a garage operator. The parcel contained cannabis. The accused was aware of this fact but the garage operator was not. The accused was arrested before he could retrieve the parcel after it had been delivered to the garage. The accused argued that his actions did not amount to trafficking. The court disagreed and concluded that the accused did traffic the cannabis because he exercised control over it.

In *R. v. Rowbotham*,[3] the accused was charged, along with others, with a conspiracy to traffic in a narcotic. The accused had met with an undercover police officer and agreed to supply him with a quantity of marijuana. However, the accused insisted that the drug be delivered and payment made in Texas. At his trial, the accused was acquitted on the grounds that it was not proved that trafficking was an offence in Texas. This was necessary to establish the conspiracy charge in Canada under the Criminal Code, s. 465(3):

Every one who, while in Canada, conspires with any one to [commit an indictable offence] in a place outside of Canada that is an offence under the laws of that place shall be deemed to have conspired to do that thing in Canada.

The Ontario Court of Appeal ordered a new trial, affirmed by the Supreme Court of Canada, on the grounds that it was not necessary to prove that trafficking was an offence in Texas. There was ample evidence that the accused had committed the offence of trafficking in Canada. He had offered to sell drugs to a police agent, and under the definition of trafficking, this act constituted the offence. It did not matter that the drugs had not been delivered, nor payment made.

Where the charge is possession for the purposes of trafficking, the Crown must prove possession plus an intent to distribute the drug. For example, in *R. v. Young*,[4] the accused was living in Vancouver; his friend, G., lived in Sechelt. The accused and G., contributing

2   (1972), 16 C.R.N.S. 251 (N.B.S.C. App. Div.).
3   (1992), 85 C.C.C. (3d) 575 (S.C.C.); aff'g (1992) 76 C.C.C. (3d) 542 (Ont. C.A.).
4   (1971), 2 C.C.C. (2d) 560 (B.C.C.A.).

the money in equal portions, arranged to buy one kilo of marijuana in Vancouver and for the accused to transport the drugs to Sechelt. The accused was arrested and charged with possession for the purpose of trafficking while he was delivering the marijuana. The accused contended that he had purchased the marijuana on behalf of himself and G. for their personal use, and that therefore it could not be said that he was trafficking when he transported the drug to his friend's house. The court, however, stated that the fact that the accused was transporting the marijuana not only for himself, but also for another, and the fact that it might be used by others, sufficed to support a conviction of trafficking. The facts demonstrated that there was something more extensive than mere conveying, or carrying, or moving of the marijuana incidental to personal use.

In *R. v. Rousseau*,[5] the accused, a physician, was charged with trafficking after he sold prescriptions for narcotics. He was acquitted at his trial on the basis that his acts were not trafficking. The court of appeal held that the intention of Parliament was to prohibit all forms of conduct that result in the circulation of a narcotic. The accused's actions fell under either the term "administer" or the term "sell." The court allowed the Crown's appeal and entered a conviction.

Trafficking is punishable either on summary conviction or by indictment. If the offence involves a Schedule I or II substance, the offence is indictable and the maximum punishment is imprisonment for life. However, there is an exception for Schedule II substances (e.g., cannabis) where the amount does not exceed that listed in Schedule VII (3 kg for cannabis and cannabis resin). The maximum penalty is imprisonment of 5 years less a day. Offences involving Schedule III substances (e.g., LSD), if treated as indictable, are punishable by up to 10 years' imprisonment; if treated as summary conviction offences, the punishment may not exceed 18 months' imprisonment. For Schedule IV substance offences, if treated as indictable, the penalty is imprisonment for up to 3 years; as a summary conviction offence, the punishment may not exceed one year's imprisonment.

In 2012, the CDSA was amended to add mandatory minimum prison sentences to Schedule I and II offences. Where a trafficking offence is indictable and subject to life imprisonment, there is a minimum sentence of 1 or 2 years' imprisonment, depending on the circumstances surrounding the case; for example, committing an offence on or near school grounds is considered more serous and is, therefore, punishable by a minimum of 2 years' imprisonment.

4. Importing and Exporting

Section 6 makes it an offence to import or export any scheduled substance to or from Canada. Importing is not defined in the CDSA. It has been said that the term should be given its ordinary and natural meaning, that is, "(t)o import into Canada means to bring goods from anywhere outside Canada to anywhere inside Canada."[6]

The penalty depends on the schedule in which the substance is found. If the substance is in Schedule I or II, the offence is indictable and the maximum punishment is life imprisonment. For a Schedule III or VI substance, the offence is hybrid. If treated as indictable, the maximum punishment is imprisonment not exceeding 10 years. For a Schedule IV or V substance, the offence is hybrid and, if treated as indictable, the punishment may not exceed 3 years' imprisonment.

5   (1991), 70 C.C.C. (3d) 445 (Que. C.A.); leave to appeal refused (1992), 70 C.C.C. (3d) vi (S.C.C.).
6   *R. v. Bell* (1983), C.C.C. (3d) 97 (S.C.C.).

If the offence is treated as a summary conviction offence, the maximum punishment for Schedule III or VI substances is imprisonment not exceeding 18 months; for Schedule IV or V substances, imprisonment not exceeding one year.

Until 1987, there was a minimum penalty of 7 years' imprisonment for anyone convicted of importing or exporting narcotics. This offence could be committed regardless of the amount of the drug brought into the country, even if it was brought in for personal use only. In 1987, the Supreme Court of Canada held that the minimum penalty was "cruel and unusual punishment" under the Charter and of no force or effect.[7]

The 2012 amendments re-introduced minimum penalties for importing or exporting schedule I or II drugs. Depending on the circumstances (e.g., the amount of drugs involved or whether the drugs were imported for trafficking), the penalty is a minimum of 1 or 2 years imprisonment.

5. Production of a Substance

Section 7 of the CDSA makes it an offence to produce a substance included in Schedules I–IV. The penalty for production of a substance, like the other offences, depends on the schedule in which the substance is found. The production of a Schedule I or II substance is an indictable offence and the maximum punishment is life imprisonment, unless the substance is cannabis. If the substance is cannabis, the maximum punishment is imprisonment not exceeding 14 years. The production of a Schedule III or IV substance is a hybrid offence. If an offence is treated as indictable and it involves a Schedule III substance, the maximum punishment is imprisonment not exceeding 10 years; if it involves a Schedule IV substance, the maximum is imprisonment not exceeding 3 years. If the offence is treated as a summary conviction offence and it involves a Schedule III substance, the maximum punishment is imprisonment not exceeding 18 months; if it involves a Schedule IV substance, the maximum is imprisonment not exceeding one year.

The 2012 amendments add mandatory minimum terms of imprisonment for producing substances in Schedules I to IV. The minimum terms range from 18 months to 3 years, depending on the schedule involved. Cannabis is treated separately. The penalty depends on the number of plants produced; from 6 months for more than 5 plants but less than 201 plants, to 3 years for more than 500 plants.

Section 7.1, added in 2011, makes it an indictable offence, punishable by up to ten years less a day imprisonment, to produce, sell, or import anything knowing that it will be used to produce certain substances listed in Schedules I and III (e.g., methyldesorphine).[7a]

In *R. v. Arnold*,[8] the British Columbia Court of Appeal stated that cultivation starts when the seeds are planted and continues until the plants are harvested. A person who has begun to cultivate does not cease to cultivate during times when the crop is left alone to mature in the environment created by the person. The Ontario Court of Appeal has held that the drying and curing of marijuana plants does not constitute cultivating.[9]

---

7   *R. v. Smith* (1987), 34 C.C.C. (3d) 97 (S.C.C.).
7a   See item 18 of Schedule I and subitem 1(9) of Schedule III.
8   (1990), 74 C.R. (3d) 394 (B.C.C.A.).
9   *R. v. Gauvreau* (1982), 65 C.C.C. (2d) 316 (Ont. C.A.).

B. REGULATIONS AND EXEMPTIONS UNDER SECTIONS 55 AND 56

Section 55 sets out the authority of the Governor in Council to make regulations under the Act for carrying out the purposes and provisions of the Act, including regulation for medical, scientific, and industrial applications and distribution of controlled substances and their precursors.

Section 56 of the CDSA allows for the federal Minister of Health to exempt any person or class of persons or any controlled substance or precursor from the application of any of the provisions of the Act or the regulations "if in the opinion of the Minister, the exemption is necessary for a medical or scientific purpose or is otherwise in the public interest." A case which examined the use of this section is *Canada (Attorney General) v. PHS Community Services Society*.[10] As described by the Supreme Court, in the 1980s, illegal drug use and associated diseases such as HIV/AIDS and hepatitis C reached crisis levels in Vancouver's downtown east side. After several years of research, planning, and intergovernmental cooperation, a plan was devised to deal with the complex needs of the drug users. Part of this plan included a strictly regulated and supervised safe injection site, Insite, where users would receive clean needles and could inject their drugs (which they had to provide) under medical supervision. They could also receive counselling, health care information, referrals to other services, and access to an on-site detox centre. Insite was given its first exemption under s. 56 in 2003. It was renewed in 2006 and 2007. By all accounts, it was successful in saving and improving lives, without increasing drug use and crime in the surrounding neighbourhood. Insite was supported by local police and the city and provincial governments. In 2008, the Minister of Health decided to deny further extension of the exemption. Various interested parties began legal proceedings to keep Insite open. After winning both cases at the provincial level, Insite was granted a judicial exemption that allowed it to remain open while the case was being appealed.

The case finally reached the Supreme Court of Canada, which released its decision in 2011. There were several issues raised on appeal. On the issue of whether the CDSA was constitutionally valid legislation, the Court found that the CDSA was valid federal legislation in that its purpose was the protection of public health and safety. Although valid legislation, the Court agreed with the claimants that s. 4 of the Act engaged the Charter rights of the claimants to life and liberty because it exposed them to the possibility of incarceration for possession of drugs. The Court explained, however, that although s. 4 limited their rights under s. 7, it had to be interpreted within the total context of the Act.

The Court explained that the scheme of the CDSA had two purposes: (1) the protection of public health and (2) the maintenance of public safety. Public safety is achieved through prohibition of possession and trafficking in controlled substances while the public health purpose is achieved through the prohibitions and by regulations which allow exemptions for the use of listed substances for medical and scientific purposes. Sections 55 and 56 act as "safety valves" to prevent the CDSA from applying where "such application would be arbitrary, overbroad or grossly disproportionate in its effects." The Court said, "Indeed, if one were to set out to draft a law that combats drug abuse while respecting Charter rights, one might well adopt just this type of scheme—a prohibition combined with the power to grant exemptions."[10a] Therefore, the Court found that the CDSA did not violate the s. 7 rights of the claimants.

10 2011 SCC 44
10a Ibid. at para. 114.

The next issue was whether the Minister in denying the exemption had violated the rights of the claimants. The Court made the point that the Charter applies to decisions of the Minister. His discretion is not absolute.[11] Since it was already found that the rights of the staff and clients were engaged under s. 7 of the Charter, the question was whether the Minister's decision was a denial of fundamental justice. The Court first considered whether the decision was arbitrary. The Court found that evidence indicated that exempting Insite furthered the CDSA objectives of supporting public safety and health, and that there had been no negative effects caused by Insite. The Court noted that the criminal law had done little to reduce drug use in the Vancouver neighbourhood. In sum, denying the exemption was not necessary to achieve government objectives and was inconsistent with the government's interest. Therefore the decision was arbitrary. The Court also found that in this case, the effect of denying the service of Insite to the population it serves is grossly disproportionate to any benefit Canada might derive from presenting a uniform stance on the possession of narcotics. The Court further stated that the decision of the Minister undermined the very purpose of the CDSA—protection of health and public safety. In conclusion, the Court held that the Minister's decision was a denial of fundamental justice.

The Court ordered the Minister to grant an exemption to Insite under s. 56. For future decisions, the Court suggested that in striking the proper balance between public health and public safety goals, the Minister should generally grant an exemption where, as here, the evidence is that the facility will decrease death and disease without a negative impact on public safety. The Minister must consider whether denying an exemption would cause deprivations of life and security of the person that are not in accordance with the principles of fundamental justice. Factors to consider include "the impact of such a facility on crime rates, the local conditions indicating a need for such a supervised injection site, the regulatory structure in place to support the facility, the resources available to support its maintenance, and expressions of community support or opposition."[12]

C. THE CHARTER AND THE USE OF MARIJUANA

In the last several years, there have been several court cases questioning whether the criminalization of marijuana use violates the Charter, or is even a proper subject of criminal law. The first cases to raise these issues revolved around the medical use of marijuana by seriously ill persons who found that the substance helped to relieve some of their symptoms. In *R. v. Parker*,[13] the accused used marijuana medicinally because he suffered from a very severe form of epilepsy. Surgery had failed to control his seizures, and he found that smoking marijuana substantially reduced them. The Ontario Court of Appeal found that the prohibition on the possession of marijuana violated s. 7 of the Charter because no provision had been made for a person who required marijuana for medical purposes. The court found that s. 56 of the CDSA, which allows for an exemption by the Minister, was no answer to the deprivation of someone's rights for this reason: "Section 56 fails to answer Parker's case because it puts an unfettered discretion in the hands of the Minister to determine what is in the best interests of Parker and other persons like him and leaves it to the Minister to avoid a violation of the patient's security of person."[14] The Court found that the violation in this case could not be

---

11   Ibid at para.117.
12   Ibid at para.153.
13   (2000), 146 C.C.C. (3d) 193 (Ont. C.A.).
14   Ibid. at 216.

saved by s. 1 of the Charter. The court struck down the provision on the possession of marijuana in s. 4, but suspended the declaration of invalidity for 12 months to allow Parliament
to fill the void.

Just before the 12-month period ended, the federal government enacted regulations
for the medicinal use of marijuana—the Marijuana Medical Access Regulations (MMAR)
S.O.R./2001-227. These regulations allowed seriously ill persons to legally possess and cultivate marijuana. The person could also designate someone to grow marijuana for them, if
the person was approved and given a production license. The production person could not
accept remuneration, and could not combine his or her crops with anyone else's. These
regulations were challenged in *R. v. Hitzig*.[15] The Ontario Court of Appeal agreed that the
regulations violate s. 7 of the Charter in two ways. First, requiring some applicants to obtain
the support of two medical specialists, and other applicants only one, was an arbitrary bar-
rier that served no purpose. Second, the restrictions on designated producers (e.g., not
being allowed to be remunerated, only being allowed to grow for one person, and not being
allowed to combine crops) prevented the formation of compassion clubs and other more
efficient means of supplying permit holders. The court's solution was to declare invalid only
the specific regulations that violated s. 7 (i.e., the regulation requiring two medical specialists to support the application, and the restrictions on producers). This decision allowed the
remainder of the regulations for providing medicinal marijuana to stand. The Supreme Court
of Canada refused to hear an appeal of this decision.

The next challenge of the marijuana laws came in the cases of *R. v. Malmo-Levine*;
R. v. Caine,[16] where the Supreme Court of Canada heard the appeals of two similar cases and
issued one judgment. In *Malmo-Levine*, the accused was charged with possession of marijuana. He argued, first, that Parliament does not have the authority under s. 91 of the Constitution
Act, 1982 (this is the section that gives the federal government the authority to enact criminal
law) to criminalize simple possession of marijuana. He argued, second, that even if Parliament
does have authority, it has been exercised in a manner that is contrary to the Charter.

The Supreme Court noted that controversy over the criminalization of marijuana has
"raged" for over 30 years, starting with the LeDain report in 1972. The Court reviewed reports
and research on the effects of marijuana, and concluded that its use raises issues of public
health and safety and that there is a reasoned apprehension of harm to vulnerable people,
even if on some points "the jury is still out." Parliament, therefore, can use the criminal law
to control the use of marijuana. On the second issue, concerning the Charter, the accused
argued that the law infringes his liberty under s. 7.

The Court stated that a criminal law that is arbitrary or irrational will infringe on the principles of fundamental justice under s. 7. However, in this case, given the state interest in the
avoidance of harm to others, the prohibition is neither irrational nor arbitrary. The appellants
also argued that the fact that a person could be imprisoned for simple possession violated
the Charter. The Court responded that the mere availability of imprisonment was not the
important factor but how the penalty was applied. In fact, most first offenders were given
conditional discharges. Therefore the penalty was not "grossly disproportionate" and did
not violate the s. 12 prohibition against cruel and unusual punishment. Finally, the accused
argued that the law offended s. 15 of the Charter, which states that "every individual is equal
before and under the law and has the right to the equal protection and equal benefit of the
law without discrimination and, in particular, without discrimination based on race, national

15   (2003), 177 C.C.C. (3d) 449 (Ont. C.A.); leave to appeal refused 182 C.C.C. (3d) 449 (S.C.C.).
16   (2003), 179 CCC (3d) 417 (S.C.C.).

or ethnic origin, colour, religion, sex, or mental or physical disability."[17] The Court responded that using marijuana is a personal lifestyle choice, not a personal characteristic that can be related to those in s. 15. The Court dismissed the appeals of the accused.

D. SEARCHES AND SEIZURES UNDER THE CONTROLLED DRUGS AND SUBSTANCES ACT

Sections 11–13 set out the powers of search and seizure in the CDSA, which are similar to the powers set out under the Criminal Code.

1. Without a Warrant

Where it would be impracticable to obtain a warrant due to "exigent circumstances," s. 11(7) of the CDSA gives a police officer the same powers of search and seizure that exist if a warrant had been obtained (see discussion below).

Exigent circumstances generally exist where there is an imminent danger of loss, removal, destruction, or disappearance of the evidence if the search or seizure is delayed. So, for example, vehicles, boats, and aircraft may, in certain circumstances, be searched without a warrant, because they move away. However, there must be reasonable grounds for believing that drugs are present. Mere suspicion is not enough.

In *R. v. McCormack*,[18] the accused was charged with possession of cocaine for the purposes of trafficking, as well as possession of cocaine and possession of a restricted weapon. When the police arrived at McCormack's apartment, they entered to ensure that no one was present and then they waited outside for the warrant to arrive. The reason for the initial warrantless search was that they believed that McCormack's girlfriend had witnessed his arrest and they were afraid that she might have access to his residence and destroy the evidence.

The court held that exigent circumstances can exist where a third party observed the arrest of the accused and the third party had access to the accused's residence and had the ability to destroy evidence. In this case, the court found that the police had ample information upon which to obtain a search warrant, and that the first condition of section 11(7) was satisfied. Given the concern of the police that the woman they believed to be McCormack's girlfriend witnessed his arrest, exigent circumstances existed.[19]

2. With a Warrant

Section 11 of the Act reads:

> **11. (1) A justice who, on an *ex parte* application is satisfied by information on oath that there are reasonable grounds to believe that**
>
> > **(a) a controlled substance or precursor in respect of which this Act has been contravened,**
> >
> > **(b) any thing in which a controlled substance . . . referred to in paragraph (a) is contained or concealed,**
> >
> > **(c) offence-related property, or**

---

17 See the Charter of Rights and Freedoms, s. 15(1).
18 (2000), 143 C.C.C. (3d) 260 (B.C.C.A.); leave to appeal to S.C.C. refused 147 C.C.C. (3d) vi.
19 Ibid. at 261–262.

(d) any thing that will afford evidence in respect of an offence under this Act . . .,

is in a place, may, at any time, issue a warrant authorizing a peace officer, at any time, to search the place for any such controlled substance, precursor, property or thing and to seize it.

Section 11(2) of the CDSA authorizes the use of telewarrants as set out in s. 487.1 of the Criminal Code.

Section 11(5) allows the police to search any person who is found in the place at the time of the search. The officer, before searching a person, must have reasonable grounds to believe that the person searched has on their person drugs, a precursor, property, or something set out in the warrant.

Section 11(6) allows a peace officer to seize property not listed in the warrant, including anything the police officer believes on reasonable grounds is offence-related property or evidence of an offence under the Act.

Unlike a warrant under s. 487 of the Criminal Code, which can only be executed by day unless the justice is satisfied that there are reasonable grounds for it to be executed by night, a warrant under the CDSA can be used at any time of the day or night without the need for a special endorsement to that effect.

Section 12 of the CDSA allows police, for the purpose of exercising any powers described in s. 11 to enlist any assistance the police deem necessary, and allows them "to use as much force as is necessary in the circumstances."

Cases decided under the Narcotic Control Act (NCA) are still useful in interpreting this section. In *R. v. Gimson*,[20] the Ontario Court of Appeal held that s. 14 of the NCA allowed police to make unannounced entries and to break open any door if necessary to gain entry. The decision said that the provisions of the NCA recognize that police need special powers when dealing with drug offences. Here, the police had reliable information that a place was being used to sell cocaine and that the door would be barred. Therefore, the police were justified in forcing entry without announcing themselves. However, the Charter still applies; and when the police use force, they must be able to justify its use. Similarly, in *R. v. Genest*,[21] the Supreme Court of Canada recognized that police may need to use force, but added this: "The greater the departure from the common law and the Charter, the heavier the onus on the police to show why they thought it necessary to use force in the process of an arrest or a search." For example, the police may need to act quickly to preserve evidence, or there may be a real threat that violence will occur. These powers have been continued in the CDSA.

The case of *R. v. Lau*,[22] a decision of the B.C. Court of Appeal, considered the use of force under the current legislation. The police had a warrant to search a house rented by Lau. The police did not announce themselves or knock. They entered the house by using a battering ram to knock the door down. Inside, they found a two-stage marijuana grow operation with 252 plants. The police explained that the use of a battering ram to enter was police policy whenever a drug offence was involved. The court stated that the Act makes it clear that the police may use force and enter without announcing themselves when executing a warrant only where "exigent circumstances" exist. In this case, there were no exigent circumstances. The Court set aside the accused's conviction for producing marijuana.

20   (1991), 60 C.C.C. (3d) 552 (S.C.C.); aff'g (1990), 54 C.C.C. (3d) 232 (Ont. C.A.).
21   (1989), 45 C.C.C. (3d) 385 (S.C.C.).
22   (2003), 175 C.C.C. (3d) 273 (B.C.C.A.). See also *R. v. Saunders* (2004), 181 C.C.C. (3d) 268 (Nfld. C.A.) at 275; aff'd 189 C.C.C. (3d) 436 (S.C.C.), for the general principles for a warrant. See also *R. v. Tessling* (2004), 189 C.C.C. (3d) 129 (S.C.C.) in Chapter 5.

APPENDIX B

Youth Criminal Justice Act
(S.C. 2002, c. 1)

For over 100 years, Canada has had special legislation to deal with young people who commit criminal offences. A basic principle underlying this legislation has been that young people should be treated differently from adults in the criminal justice system.

In 1984, the Young Offenders Act (YOA) came into force. This legislation replaced the Juvenile Delinquents Act (JDA) and resulted in major changes in how young offenders were handled.

The philosophy of the JDA was that young people who broke the law should be treated as "misguided" and in need of care and protection. It looked at juvenile delinquency as a social welfare problem. So, for example, young people were not charged with specific offences but with "juvenile delinquency," which included not only criminal offences but also provincial offences and offences that were offences only for children (status offences), such as truancy, "unmanageability," and "sexual immorality and similar forms of vice." Thus, the JDA handled a wide range of youths, from those who committed true criminal offences to those with problems more related to child protection. Since the JDA was seen as intended to help and not punish young people, rights and liberties of young people were not emphasized. For example, court hearings often took place without legal representation for the young person.

In contrast to the JDA, the YOA set up a more legalistic system, one that acknowledged that the legislation is criminal law. It also attempted to blend and balance competing principles of criminal law and child welfare. It dealt only with youths who were charged with criminal offences. The YOA also raised the age for criminal responsibility from 7 to 12 and covered young people up to and including the age of 17. It emphasized protection of society, recognized that young offenders should be held accountable, and introduced legal rights for youth. The YOA also retained much of a welfare approach by emphasizing the needs of youth and by including principles that permitted sentences that were disproportionate to the seriousness of the offence in order to address the welfare or treatment needs of youths. Maximum sentences for young offenders were much less than maximum sentences for adults.

The YOA, for many years, was widely criticized in the media, in public opinion surveys, and by politicians as too lenient on young offenders. Much of this criticism was based on misperceptions about youth crime, the legislation, and the operation of the youth justice system. However, statistics support the views of other critics that, under the YOA, too many young people were being charged and incarcerated. In addition, despite alternative measure programs being available, courts were being overused for minor offences committed by youths.

In response to these and other issues, the government introduced legislation to repeal the YOA and replace it with the Youth Criminal Justice Act (YCJA). The YCJA came into force April 1, 2003. The following discussion includes amendments that came into force in 2012.

A. PREAMBLE AND DECLARATION OF PRINCIPLE

The YCJA contains a preamble and a declaration of principles to clarify the purpose, principles, and objectives of the youth justice system. While the preamble is not legally enforceable, it contains significant statements from Parliament on how the legislation should be interpreted, including the following:

- Society has a responsibility to address the developmental challenges and needs of young persons.
- Communities and families should work in partnership with others to prevent youth crime by addressing its underlying causes, responding to the needs of young persons and providing guidance and support.
- Accurate information about youth crime, the youth justice system, and effective measures should be publicly available.
- Young persons have rights and freedoms, including those set out in the United Nations Convention on the Rights of the Child.
- The youth justice system should take account of the interests of victims and ensure accountability through meaningful consequences and rehabilitation and reintegration.
- The youth justice system should reserve its most serious interventions for the most serious crimes and reduce the overreliance on incarceration.

The Declaration of Principle (s. 3) sets out key principles and provides guidance on the priority that should be given to the key principles in the YCJA:

- The youth justice system is intended to protect the public by (i) holding young persons accountable through measures that are proportionate to the seriousness of the offence and the degree of responsibility of the young person, (ii) promoting the rehabilitation and reintegration of young persons, and (iii) supporting crime prevention by referring young persons to programs or agencies in the community to address the circumstances underlying their offending behaviour.
- The youth justice system must be separate from that of adults and must be based on the principle of diminished moral blameworthiness or culpability.
- The youth justice system must reflect the fact that young persons lack the maturity of adults. The youth system is different from the adult system in many respects, including these: measures of accountability are consistent with young persons' reduced level of maturity, procedural protections are enhanced, rehabilitation and reintegration are given special emphasis, and the importance of timely intervention is recognized.
- Young persons are to be held accountable through interventions that are fair and in proportion to the seriousness of the offence.
- Within the limits of fair and proportionate accountability, interventions should reinforce respect for societal values; encourage the repair of harm done; be meaningful to the young person; respect gender, ethnic, cultural, and linguistic differences; and respond to the needs of Aboriginal young persons and of young persons with special requirements.

- Youth justice proceedings require special guarantees to protect the rights of young people; courtesy, compassion, and respect for victims; the opportunity for victims to be informed and to participate; and that parents be informed and encouraged to participate in addressing the young person's offending behaviour.

B. JURISDICTION

Young persons who are 12 to 17 years of age are subject to the YCJA. At age 18, a person becomes an adult for criminal law purposes. The relevant time for determining a young person's age is when the offence was alleged to have been committed. If the young person becomes an adult during the trial, the case still continues in youth court as if the person were still a young person. Children under 12 who break the criminal law are handled under provincial legislation, usually child welfare laws.

The YCJA applies only to young people who are charged with criminal offences. Young people who break provincial laws are dealt with under provincial legislation.

C. EXTRAJUDICIAL MEASURES

The YCJA encourages a reduction in the use of the youth court and an increase in the use of non-court measures for minor offences. The Act refers to these measures as extrajudicial measures. They are based on the idea that it is often harmful for a young person to go through the formal criminal justice system. In addition, extrajudicial measures can be a faster and more effective means of holding a young person accountable for a minor offence.

In addition to the general principles in the Declaration of Principles, s. 4 of the YCJA sets out specific principles to guide the use of extrajudicial measures, including the following:

- extrajudicial measures should be used in all cases where they would be adequate to hold the young person accountable;
- extrajudicial measures are presumed to be adequate to hold first-time, non-violent offenders accountable; and
- extrajudicial measures may be used if the young person has previously been dealt with by extrajudicial measures or has previously been found guilty of an offence.

Section 5 sets out the objectives of extrajudicial measures, including these:

- repairing the harm caused to the victim and the community;
- providing an opportunity for victims to participate in decisions;
- ensuring that the measures are proportionate to the seriousness of the offence; and
- encouraging the involvement of families, victims, and other members of the community.

The types of extrajudicial measures include taking no further action; verbal warnings and cautions from police; Crown cautions; and informal police diversion, such as referrals to community programs or agencies that may help the young person not to commit offences. The referrals may be to a wide range of community services, including recreational services or counselling. Another type of extrajudicial measure is an extrajudicial sanction, which is discussed below.

The YCJA requires police to consider using extrajudicial measures before turning to the court process and laying charges.

D. EXTRAJUDICIAL SANCTIONS

Extrajudicial sanctions (s. 10) are a more formal type of extrajudicial measure. They may be pre-charge or post-charge. Often, they involve the young person making restitution to the victim or performing community service. If the young person carries out the extrajudicial sanction, he or she will not be prosecuted in youth court. If the young person fails to carry out the extrajudicial sanction, the case may proceed through the court process. Although the Act does not require the establishment of extrajudicial sanctions programs,[1] these programs exist in every province and territory.

Extrajudicial sanctions may be used only if the young person admits responsibility for the offending behaviour and consents to the sanction. The admission of responsibility is not a guilty plea. Before consenting to the sanction, the young person must be given an opportunity to consult with a lawyer. The Attorney General of the province must determine that there is sufficient evidence to proceed with the prosecution of the offence. The sanction must also be part of a program designated by the Attorney General.

E. PRE-TRIAL PROCEDURES AND RIGHTS

Young people have the same rights as adults when detained or arrested—for example, the right to remain silent, the right to know the reasons for the detention, and the right to a lawyer. They also have additional rights in recognition of their immaturity. For example, there are special rules regarding the admission of statements made by young persons to the police and others who are persons in authority (see discussion below).

1. Fingerprinting and Photographing

The Identification of Criminals Act applies to young persons who commit offences that would, if committed by an adult, subject the adult to the Act. This Act applies to persons who are charged with committing indictable offences and allows for such persons to be fingerprinted and photographed.

2. Right to Counsel

The right to counsel is treated very specifically and seriously by the YCJA at all stages, from the first detention through to any hearing to review the sentence or level of custody. A step-by-step process for encouraging young people to be represented is set out in s. 25. It states that the youth has a right to personally retain and instruct counsel. This means that the lawyer must take instructions from the youth and not, for example, from the young person's parents. The police must not only inform the youth of the right to counsel but also give the youth the opportunity to consult counsel. A young person who appears in court without a lawyer will be advised of his or her right to a lawyer and will be given reasonable opportunity to obtain

---

1   *R. v. S.(S.)* (1990), 57 C.C.C. (3d) 115 (S.C.C.)

a lawyer. Where the young person wishes to obtain a lawyer but is unable to do so, the court must refer the young person to the province's legal assistance plan. If the province does not have a plan, or if the youth is not eligible for legal assistance, the court must direct the Attorney General of the province to appoint a counsel to represent the youth. Where a youth chooses to proceed without a lawyer, on the request of the young person the court can appoint a suitable adult to assist the young person.

In sum, any young person who wishes to have a lawyer is entitled to one even if he or she is not eligible under the province's legal assistance plan.

3. Statements Made to Person in Authority

Section 146 of the Act states that no oral or written statement made by the youth to the police or to any other person in authority (e.g., in some circumstances, a teacher or principal of a school) at the time the youth is arrested or detained, or in circumstances where the peace officer or other person has reasonable grounds for believing that the young person has committed an offence, is admissible against the young person unless certain conditions are met:

- the statement was voluntary;
- the person in authority clearly explained that (a) the youth is under no obligation make a statement, (b) a statement by the youth may be used as evidence in court, (c) the youth has a right to consult a lawyer and a parent, and (d) a statement by the youth must be made in the presence of the youth's lawyer and parent, unless the youth desires otherwise;
- the youth, before giving a statement was given a reasonable opportunity to consult with the lawyer and the parent; and
- the youth was given a reasonable opportunity to make the statement in the presence of the lawyer and parent.

The exception to the above is given in s. 146(3), which provides that these requirements do not apply where a young person gives a spontaneous statement to a peace officer or other person in authority before the officer or other person can comply with the requirements.

If the young person waives the rights under s. 146, the waiver must be in writing or videotaped, or audiotaped; where it is in writing, it must contain a statement signed by the young person that the young person has been apprised of the rights being waived.

The YCJA provides under s. 146(6) that a judge may admit into evidence a statement when a failure by the police or other person in authority to comply with the requirements regarding a clear explanation is a technical irregularity, and the judge determines that admitting the statement would not bring into disrepute the principle in the YCJA that young persons are entitled to greater procedural protections than adults to ensure that they are treated fairly and that their rights are protected. There are no reported cases of a judge finding that a noncompliance with the requirements was merely a technical irregularity.

4. Pre-trial Detention and Release

Young people have basically the same rights as adults to be released while awaiting trial. Where young people are detained, the general rule under s. 30(3) is that they are to be held separate and apart from adults unless this is not possible because of the youth's safety or the safety of others, or because there is no youth facility within reasonable distance. However, a young person who is 18 at the time of the detention will be detained with adults, unless the young person applies to the court to be detained in a facility for youth and the youth court is satisfied that, having regard to the best interests of the youth and to the safety of others, the youth should be detained in a facility for young persons.

Section 29 of the YCJA contains pre-trial detention rules that are different from the Criminal Code rules that apply to adults.

A court may detain a youth only if the following criteria are met:

(a) the youth has been charged with a serious offence (an offence for which an adult would be liable to imprisonment for 5 years or more) or the youth has a history of either outstanding charges or findings of guilt;

(b) one of the following grounds exists:

   (i) there is a substantial likelihood that, if released, the youth will not appear in court;

   (ii) detention is necessary for public protection, having regard to the circumstances, including whether there is a substantial likelihood that the young person will, if released, commit a serious offence; or

   (iii) if the youth has been charged with a serious offence and neither (i) nor (ii) applies (i.e., detention is not needed to ensure that the youth appears in court or to protect the public), but there are exceptional circumstances that justify detention as necessary to maintain confidence in the administration of justice; and

(c) releasing the youth with conditions (e.g., a curfew) would not be sufficient to address the court's concern about releasing the youth (i.e., appearing in court, public protection, or maintaining confidence in the administration of justice).

In addition, the Act provides that

- pre-trial detention is not to be used as a substitute for child protection, or mental health or other social measures; and
- if a young person would otherwise be detained, the judge is required to inquire as to whether a responsible adult is available who would be willing to take care of the young person as an alternative to pre-trial detention.

5. Notice to Parents

Parents have a right to be given notice as soon as possible that their child has been detained pending court appearance under s. 26. The notice, either oral or written, must give the place of detention and the reason for the arrest.

The parent must receive written notice where the young person is issued a summons or appearance notice, or is released on a promise to appear, or has entered a recognizance. Where the whereabouts of the parents are unknown or it appears that no parent is available, notice can be given to an adult relative who is known to the young person and seems likely to assist the young person. If no such adult relative is available, notice can be given to any adult known to the young person who seems likely to assist the young person.

If the parent does not voluntarily attend the court hearing, the court can order the parent to appear.

F. THE TRIAL

The trial of a young person in youth court follows the procedures used for trying summary conviction offences. The Crown has the burden of proving the case beyond a reasonable doubt, and the youth can raise whatever defences apply. Witnesses are examined and cross-examined. The youth will be found guilty or not guilty. The trials are generally open to the public. However, s. 132 allows the judge to exclude the public if

    (a) any evidence or information presented to the court would be injurious or seriously prejudicial to the young person on trial, to a child or young person who is a witness, or to a child or young person who is a victim of the offence; or

    (b) it would be in the interest of public morals, the maintenance of order, or the proper administration of justice to exclude any or all members of the public from the court room.

G. YOUTH SENTENCING

1. Purpose and Principles

Under the YCJA, all trials are held in youth court. If there is a finding of guilt, then the sentence is determined. A young person could receive either a youth sentence or, in very exceptional circumstances, an adult sentence, depending on the charge and the circumstances surrounding the offence. (Adult sentences for young persons are discussed below.)

Section 38 of the YCJA includes a specific purpose for sentencing, as well as a set of principles to guide judges in deciding on a fair and proportionate sentence for a youth. The purpose of a sentence, under the YCJA, is to hold a youth accountable through just sanctions that ensure meaningful consequences for them and to promote their rehabilitation and reintegration into society, thereby contributing to the long-term protection of the public.

Some of the specific sentencing principles include these:

- the sentence that a youth receives cannot be more severe than the sentence an adult would receive for the same offence,
- the sentence must be similar to other youth sentences in similar cases, and
- the sentence must be proportionate to the offence and degree of responsibility of the young person.

In addition, within the limits of proportionality, the sentence

- must be the least restrictive alternative,
- must be the one that is most likely to rehabilitate and reintegrate the young person back into society,
- may include the objectives of denunciation and specific deterrence, and
- must promote in the young person a sense of responsibility and acknowledgement of the harm done by the offence.

In general, the YCJA does not allow a custody sentence unless the young person commits a violent offence or the young person is a serious repeat offender. The Act defines "violent offence" as an offence in the commission of which a young person causes, attempts to cause, or threatens to cause bodily harm, or endangers the life or safety of a person by creating a substantial likelihood of bodily harm.

The specific restrictions in s. 39(1) on the use of custody as a sentence are these: a young person cannot be sentenced to custody unless he or she (a) has committed a violent offence; (b) has failed to comply with non-custodial sentences; (c) has committed a serious indictable offence and has a history that indicates a pattern of findings of guilt or extrajudicial sanctions; or (d) in exceptional cases, has committed an indictable offence and the aggravating circumstances of the offence are such that to impose a sentence other than custody would not be consistent with the purpose and principles of sentencing.

In the exceptional cases under (d), the judge must give reasons why the case is an exceptional case. Before making any custody order, the court must also consider all reasonable alternatives to custody and must determine that there is no reasonable alternative that would be capable of holding the young person accountable in accordance with the purpose and principles of sentencing under the Act.

2. Youth Sentences

The possible sentences are set out in s. 42. They include the following:

- a reprimand, which is a stern warning from the judge that is used in minor cases;
- an absolute discharge, which means that although the young person has been found guilty, a conviction is not entered (the young person can then truthfully state—e.g., on a job application—that he or she has never been convicted of a crime);
- a conditional discharge, which has the same effect as an absolute discharge except that the youth must satisfy certain conditions (e.g., attending school, reporting to and being supervised by the provincial director) before the discharge becomes absolute;
- a fine not exceeding $1000;
- an order for the young person to make financial compensation to the victim;
- an order for the young person to make restitution of property to the victim;
- a community service order;
- probation for a period not exceeding 2 years;
- an attendance order, which requires the young person to attend a program at specified times and on conditions set by the judge;
- a deferred custody and supervision order, which allows a young person who would otherwise be sentenced to custody to serve the sentence in the community under conditions (if the young person violates the conditions, he/she can be sent back to custody);
- an intensive support and supervision order, which is similar to a probation order but provides closer monitoring, supervision, and support of the young person; and
- a custody and supervision order, which requires the young person to be sent to custody for a certain period of time, which is followed by a period of supervision in the community.

The community supervision portion of a custody and supervision order is not parole. The judge, when imposing the sentence, clearly states in open court the amount of time to be served in custody and the amount of time to be served in the community. In general, two-thirds of the sentence will be served in custody and one-third will be served in the community. For example, if a youth is sentenced to 9 months, the judge will state that the youth must serve 6 months in custody and 3 months in the community. The YCJA requires that a plan for reintegrating the young person back into the community be prepared for each youth in custody to assist the youth when he or she is released.

The maximum length of a youth sentence for most offences is 2 years. For most offences for which an adult would be liable to life imprisonment, the maximum youth sentence is 3 years. In addition, the YCJA also sets out longer sentences that may be used only with young persons convicted of murder. The youth sentence for a young person found guilty of first-degree murder is 10 years, with a maximum of 6 years in custody, the remainder to be served under conditional supervision. For second-degree murder, the sentence is 7 years, with 4 years in custody and the remainder under supervision.

The YCJA also permits an intensive rehabilitative custody and supervision order. It is a special treatment sentence for serious violent offenders. The court can make this order if a young person has been found guilty of (a) a serious violent offence (murder, attempted murder, manslaughter, aggravated sexual assault) or (b) an offence in which the young person caused or attempted to cause serious bodily harm and for which an adult could be imprisoned for more than 2 years, if the young person had previously been found guilty at least twice of such an offence. A court can make this order only if the young person is suffering from a mental or psychological disorder, or emotional disturbance. As well, an individualized treatment plan must be developed for the young person; an appropriate program must be available; and the young person must be suitable for admission to the program.

H. ADULT SENTENCES

The YCJA gives the youth court the power to impose adult sentences on youths in certain exceptional cases. Any youth 14 years of age or older who is convicted of an offence punishable by more than 2 years in jail, could receive an adult sentence if the Crown is successful in its application to the court for an adult sentence.

The test for an adult sentence, in s. 72, states that a court can impose an adult sentence only if (a) the prosecution rebuts the presumption that the young person has diminished moral blameworthiness or culpability and (b) a youth sentence would not be of sufficient length to hold the young person accountable. If the prosecution cannot satisfy the court that the young person, at the time of the offence, had the moral blameworthiness of an adult, rather than the diminished moral blameworthiness of a young person, the court must impose a youth sentence. Similarly, if the prosecution cannot show that a youth sentence would not be long enough to hold the young person accountable, a youth sentence must be imposed.

If a young person is 14 years of age or older and is charged with a serious violent offence, the prosecutor must consider applying to the court for an adult sentence. If the prosecutor decides not to apply for an adult sentence, the prosecutor must inform the court. A province may decide to change the age from 14 to 15 or 16.

A young person under age 18 who receives an adult sentence must be placed in a youth facility. While under the age of 18, the young person may not be transferred to an adult correctional facility.

I. PUBLICATION OF A YOUTH'S IDENTITY

The general rule under the YCJA is that the identity of a youth who has been involved in the youth justice system should be protected. The policy reason underlying this rule is that publishing the name of a youth would interfere with the youth's rehabilitation and, in the long run, potentially increase the risk to public safety. The YCJA does, however, provide for certain exceptions. The YCJA permits the publication of information that identifies a youth if the youth receives an adult sentence. It also allows publication of the identity of a youth who has received a youth sentence for a violent offence if

- the court takes account of the Act's purpose and principles, including the principle that in comparison to adults, youths are presumed to have diminished moral blameworthiness for offences that they commit, and that measures ordered by the court must promote the youth's rehabilitation;
- there is a significant risk that the youth will commit another violent offence; and
- publishing the identity of the youth is necessary to protect the public from risk.

Publication of identifying information is also permitted, on application to a youth court by a peace officer, when a youth is at large and is considered by the court to be dangerous.

J. TERMINATION OF SENTENCE AND THE USE OF RECORDS

The philosophy of the YCJA is that a person should not be unnecessarily burdened with a "record" of having been a young offender. At the same time, the YCJA recognizes the importance of maintaining records for investigating crime and of having a person's record if that person is again before the courts. The Act tries to balance these two interests.

There are two sections dealing with young persons and their records after the sentence is completed.

1. Termination of Sentence

Section 82 provides that, for many purposes, once the young person has completed the sentence or been given an absolute discharge, he or she will be deemed not to have been found guilty of or convicted of an offence. For example, once a young person completes the terms of probation, he or she is deemed not to have been convicted of any offence. This means that on job application forms, for example, the young person can state that he or she has not been convicted of an offence. The YCJA provides for certain exceptions where the youth has become involved again in alleged or actual criminal activity. A court may consider the finding of guilt in making a decision regarding (a) pre-trial detention or sentencing or (b) an application for an adult sentence. Also, a parole board may consider the finding of guilt in deciding on conditional release of an offender or an application for a record suspension (formerly referred to as a pardon).

If the young person has no further dealings with the criminal justice system, the findings of guilt will be treated as if they do not exist.

2. The Use of Records

Sections 114 to 116 set out the various organizations that can keep records of offences. Records may be kept by the police force responsible for investigating the offence and by the court that deals with the case. Also, certain government agencies and organizations may keep records. Where a young person is charged with an indictable offence, the records concerning the young person can be sent to the central repository maintained by the RCMP.

Section 119 deals with who can have access to these records. In general, disclosure of records is only allowed in certain circumstances—for example, if the youth is again before the courts for a youth or adult sentence, or is reasonably suspected of committing an offence. The records can be disclosed to the young person, to the young person's parents or counsel, to the Attorney General or the Attorney General's agent, to the court, or to any peace officer investigating an offence that the young offender is reasonably suspected of having committed.

Section 128 sets out the rules for non-disclosure and the destruction of records. In brief, the section provides that after certain crime-free qualifying times, records kept under sections 114 to 116 may not be available for inspection. For example, records cannot be inspected after 3 years from the time a young offender was found guilty of a summary conviction offence.

Legal Rights under the Canadian Charter of Rights and Freedoms
(Constitution Act, 1982, Part I)

These are the rights and freedoms in the Canadian Charter of Rights and Freedoms that are most relevant to the criminal law.

7. Everyone has the right to life, liberty and security of the person and the right not to be deprived thereof except in accordance with the principles of fundamental justice.

8. Everyone has the right to be secure against unreasonable search or seizure.

9. Everyone has the right not to be arbitrarily detained or imprisoned.

10. Everyone has the right on arrest or detention

    (a) to be informed promptly of the reasons therefor;

    (b) to retain and instruct counsel without delay and to be informed of that right; and

    (c) to have the validity of the detention determined by way of *habeus corpus* and to be released if the detention is not lawful.

11. Any person charged with an offence has the right

    (a) to be informed without unreasonable delay of the specific offence;

    (b) to be tried within a reasonable time;

    (c) not to be compelled to be a witness in proceedings against that person in respect of the offence;

    (d) to be presumed innocent until proven guilty according to law in a fair and public hearing by an independent and impartial tribunal;

    (e) not to be denied reasonable bail without just cause;

    (f) except in the case of an offence under military law tried before a military tribunal, to the benefit of trial by jury where the maximum punishment for the offence is imprisonment for five years or a more severe punishment;

(g) not to be found guilty on account of any act or omission unless, at the time of the act or omission, it constituted an offence under Canadian or international law or was criminal according to the general principles of law recognized by the community of nations;

(h) if finally acquitted of the offence, not to be tried for it again and, if finally found guilty and punished for the offence, not to be tried or punished for it again; and

(i) if found guilty of the offence and if the punishment for the offence has been varied between the time of commission and the time of sentencing, to the benefit of the lesser punishment.

12. Everyone has the right not to be subjected to any cruel and unusual treatment or punishment.

13. A witness who testifies in any proceedings has the right not to have any incriminating evidence so given used to incriminate that witness in any other proceedings, except in a prosecution for perjury or for the giving of contradictory evidence.

14. A party or witness in any proceedings who does not understand or speak the language in which the proceedings are conducted or who is deaf has the right to the assistance of an interpreter.

ABSOLUTE LIABILITY OFFENCE An offence in which the Crown only has to prove the *actus reus* of the offence to gain a conviction. There is no defence of due diligence.

ACCESSORY AFTER THE FACT A person who receives, assists, or offers comfort to a party to an offence for the purpose of enabling that person to escape.

ACQUITTAL A finding that the accused is not guilty of the offence with which he or she was charged.

ACQUITTED An accused who is found not guilty of the offence will be acquitted of the charge by the court.

ACTUS REUS The physical element of a crime. Latin for "guilty action."

AIDING OR ABETTING Helping or encouraging a person to commit an offence.

ALIBI A defence that says the accused was somewhere else when the crime took place.

ARBITRARY DETENTION A detention that is not based on any criteria; that is, it is random. Section 9 of the Charter guarantees the right not to be arbitrarily detained.

ARRAIGNMENT The stage in a trial when the charge is read to the accused, who then enters a plea of guilty or not guilty.

ARREST Detaining a person for the purpose of bringing the accused before the court.

ARREST WARRANT Issued by a justice of the peace to give the police the authority to detain a person in order to bring that person before the court.

ATTEMPT Trying to commit but not completing an offence. An offence under s. 24 of the Code: requires intent to commit the offence, some act or omission toward completing the crime, and non-completion.

ATTORNEY GENERAL The member of the provincial or federal Cabinet who is responsible for the administration of justice.

BALANCE OF PROBABILITIES The burden of proof in civil cases. The burden is met if it can be said that it is more likely than not that the defendant has committed the wrong. See *defendant*.

BEYOND A REASONABLE DOUBT The burden of proof on the prosecution in a criminal trial. The accused's guilt must be proved beyond a reasonable doubt. See *reasonable doubt*.

BREACH OF THE PEACE A situation that involves a threat of violence, such as when a group of people are loitering and threatening to become violent.

CANADIAN CHARTER OF RIGHTS AND FREEDOMS Part I of the Constitution Act, 1982, which sets out individual rights and freedoms.

CASE LAW The body of law that consists of the decisions of judges. See *common law*.

CIVIL LAW Another term for private law. Also refers to the legal system used in many European countries and Quebec.

CIVIL WRONG A private wrong that gives the victim a right to sue for compensation in a civil court.

CLAIM OF RIGHT An honest belief in the right to possess property. A person who is in possession of property under a claim of right is protected from criminal liability for defending the possession.

COLOUR OF RIGHT Where the accused honestly but mistakenly believes in a state of facts that if they existed would give the accused a legal justification or excuse for his or her actions.

COMMON LAW The body of laws developed by judges following the rule of precedent when making decisions in cases. See case *law*.

CONSPIRACY An agreement by two or more persons to do an unlawful act.

COUNSEL   A term used to refer to a lawyer (e.g., defence counsel).

COUNSELLING AN OFFENCE   Advising, recommending, procuring, soliciting, or inciting the commission of an offence.

CRIMINAL CODE   A federal law that is the main source of criminal law in Canada. It sets out offences, penalties, and rules of procedure.

CRIMINAL OFFENCE   The term "criminal offence" includes summary conviction offences, as well as those that are indictable; it does not include provincial offences.

CRIMINAL PROCEDURE   The rules that must be followed when enforcing the criminal law; e.g., the rules for making a valid arrest or the steps to be followed in a trial.

CROWN ATTORNEY   The lawyer who represents the government in prosecuting criminal cases. Sometimes the lawyer is referred to as Crown Counsel.

CULPABLE HOMICIDE   Homicide that is "morally blameworthy"; causing death that is not justified or excusable.

DEFENDANT   In a criminal case, the person charged with a crime. In a civil case, the person being sued.

DETENTION   A person is detained when he or she submits or acquiesces to the deprivation of liberty when he or she believes there is no choice to do otherwise.

DISSENTING OPINION   In an appeal that has been heard by more than one judge, the minority opinion.

DUAL PROCEDURE OFFENCE   An offence that can be tried by summary conviction procedure or by indictment. Decisions on how to try these offences are made by the Crown attorney. Also known as *hybrid offence*.

DUE DELIGENCE   A defence used for strict liability offences. It has two parts: The accused will be found not guilty upon proving on a balance of probabilities that he or she (a) acted as a reasonable person in the circumstances, or (b) had an honest but mistaken belief in facts that, if they had been true, would have rendered the act innocent.

DUTY COUNSEL   A lawyer "on duty," who is paid by Legal Aid to assist persons who have been arrested or detained.

FUNDAMENTAL JUSTICE (PRINCIPLE OF)   A principle found in the basic tenets of the legal system. In deciding that a principle is a principle of fundamental justice, a court must determine that it is (1) a legal principle; (2) fundamental to the way in which the legal system ought fairly to operate; and (3) precise enough to provide a manageable standard against which to measure deprivations of life, liberty, or security of the person (s. 7 of the Charter). Sections 8–14 of the Charter are specific examples of principles of fundamental justice; e.g., the right to be secure against arbitrary search and seizure (s. 8).

GENERAL INTENT OFFENCE   An offence that requires an intent to achieve the immediate result. See *specific intent offence*.

(THE) HOLDING IN A CASE   The court's decision in a case. The majority opinion in a case where more than one judge hears a case and more than one opinion is given.

HYBRID OFFENCE   An offence that can be tried by summary conviction procedure or by indictment. The decision on how to try the offence is made by the Crown attorney. Also known as *dual procedure offence*.

INDICTABLE OFFENCE   The most serious crimes, which are tried by indictment.

INTRA VIRES   Refers to a law that is within the authority of the government to pass. The opposite of *ultra vires*.

JUSTIFICATION   Where a person's conduct, which would otherwise be criminal, is allowed by law.

LESSER INCLUDED OFFENCE   An offence that has some but not all of the elements of the major offence; e.g., theft is a lesser included offence to robbery.

MANDATORY PRESUMPTION   An element of an offence where a fact is presumed to exist until the accused disproves it. Mandatory presumptions are subject to attack under the Charter as violations of the presumption of innocence.

MARKED DEPARTURE (CONDUCT THAT IS A)   A basis for criminal liability where the accused's conduct is a "marked departure" from the conduct of a reasonable person.

MENS REA   The mental element of a crime. Latin for "guilty mind."

MISTAKE OF FACT   An error as to some circumstance that results in a person committing a crime.

MISTAKE OF LAW   An error as to the legal status of a circumstance or fact.

NON-CULPABLE HOMICIDE   Homicide that is justifiable or excusable under the law; e.g., a soldier killing an enemy soldier in wartime or a police officer killing a person in the course of duty.

NOTWITHSTANDING/OVERRIDE CLAUSE   Refers to s. 33 of the Charter, which allows the federal or a provincial government to enact a law that violates certain sections of the Charter in certain circumstances.

OBJECTIVE FORESEEABILITY (OR FORESIGHT)   A description of a mental state where a reasonable person would have foreseen the consequences of the conduct.

OBJECTIVE STANDARD (OR TEST)   Refers to the conduct of a reasonable person.

OFFICIALLY INDUCED ERROR   A defence to a charge of committing certain offences that the accused broke the law because he or she was misled by an official in charge of enforcing the law.

OVERRIDE CLAUSE   See *notwithstanding/override clause*.

PARTIES TO AN OFFENCE   The people who can be charged with a particular offence.

PENAL NEGLIGENCE   A type of *mens rea* which is based on an objective standard; requires that the Crown establish (a) the *actus reus*—that the conduct was either a marked departure from that of a reasonable person or a dangerous and unlawful act, and (b) the *mens rea*—that a reasonable person would have foreseen the risk of harm.

PERSONAL PROPERTY   Tangible property that is not real property. See *real property*.

PLAINTIFF   The person in a civil trial claiming to be injured. The person bringing the lawsuit.

PRECEDENT (RULE OF)   A precedent is a rule to be followed in similar cases. The rule of precedent states that when making a decision a judge must follow the decisions of (i.e., apply the same rule of law as) higher court judges in cases with the same or similar fact situations. A judge must also attempt to follow decisions of same-level courts.

PRELIMINARY INQUIRY   A pre-trial hearing for certain indictable offences; it can weed out weak cases and lets the accused see the Crown's case. Also called a preliminary hearing.

PRESUMPTION OF INNOCENCE   The right to be presumed innocent until proven guilty in a fair and public hearing by an impartial tribunal. This right is guaranteed by the Charter. It means that the burden of proving the charge is on the prosecution.

PRINCIPAL   The party to an offence who actually commits the *actus reus* and has the *mens rea* for the offence. Also known as the perpetrator.

PROSECUTOR   The person, usually a Crown attorney, who presents the case against the defendant.

REAL PROPERTY   Land and everything attached to it, e.g., houses and trees. See *personal property*.

REASONABLE DOUBT   Real doubt that an honest juror has after considering all the circumstances of the case, doubt that results in the juror being unable to say, "I am morally certain of the accused's guilt." See *beyond a reasonable doubt*.

REASONABLE GROUNDS   In general, grounds that would lead an ordinary, prudent, and cautious person to have a strong and honest belief about the situation at issue.

REASONABLE LIMITATION (OR REASONABLE LIMITS) A term used in s. 1 of the Charter. Refers to a law that violates a Charter right but is upheld because it is a justifiable limitation in a free and democratic society.

RECKLESSNESS A type of mental element that may be required for a crime. Where a person does not intend a certain consequence but knows that the consequence is possible and chooses to run the risk that the consequence will not occur.

RECOGNIZANCE An agreement or promise made by an accused to pay a certain amount of money to the court for failing to appear on a particular court date.

REVERSE ONUS CLAUSE An element of an offence that shifts part of the burden of proof to the accused in a criminal trial. Reverse onus clauses are subject to attack under the Charter for offending the presumption of innocence.

RIGHT TO REMAIN SILENT A principle of fundamental justice. A right of an accused person, guaranteed by the Charter and flowing from the presumption of innocence, to say nothing pre-trial or at the trial. The right is consistent with the burden of proof being on the prosecution to prove the case against the accused.

SPECIFIC INTENT OFFENCE An offence that requires an additional intent beyond the intent to achieve the immediate result. An intent to further an illegal goal. See *general intent offence*.

STARE DECISIS Latin for "to stand by." Refers to the rule that judges must follow the decisions used in earlier cases when the facts are the same or similar. See *precedent, rule of*.

STATUTE LAW Laws made by our provincial and federal legislatures.

STRICT LIABILITY OFFENCE An offence for which the Crown only has to prove the *actus reus*. The accused will be convicted unless he or she can establish that he or she acted with due diligence.

SUBJECTIVE FORESEEABILITY (or foresight) A description of a mental state where the accused actually foresaw the consequences of his or her conduct.

SUMMARY CONVICTION OFFENCE The least serious criminal offence, which is tried by summary conviction procedure.

SUMMONS Issued by a justice of the peace and delivered to the named person, ordering that person to appear in court on a certain day at a certain time.

SUPREMACY OF PARLIAMENT Refers to the rule that within its areas of authority, Parliament is the supreme law maker. Applies to any law-making body.

SURETY A person who signs a recognizance with an accused and thereby agrees to be responsible for ensuring that the accused appears for his or her court date.

TRIER OF FACT In a trial with a judge and jury, the jury is the trier of fact; i.e., the jury must decide what happened in the case. Where there is no jury, the judge is trier of fact. See *trier of law*.

TRIER OF LAW In a trial, the judge is the trier of law; i.e., he or she must decide what law applies to the case. See *trier of fact*.

TORT A civil wrong; sometimes an intentional act or omission, but more often based on negligence or careless conduct.

TORT LAW The law regarding civil wrongs. A tort is a wrong which gives a person the right to sue for compensation. See *civil wrong*.

ULTRA VIRES Refers to actions that are beyond the authority of a government; e.g., when a government passes a law in an area over which it does not have authority. Latin for "beyond the powers."

WILFUL BLINDNESS A type of *mens rea* where the accused is aware of the need to make an inquiry but chooses not to, i.e., to remain ignorant.

VOID FOR VAGUENESS Refers to a law that violates the s. 7 of the Charter (right to fundamental justice) because it does not give people fair notice of what conduct is prohibited.

INDEX